**Reader Series
in Library and Information Science**

READER IN

LIBRARY ADMINISTRATION

edited by

Paul Wasserman
and
Mary Lee Bundy

NCR MICROCARD® EDITIONS
901 TWENTY-SIXTH STREET, N.W., WASHINGTON, D. C. 20037, 202/333-6393
INDUSTRIAL PRODUCTS DIVISION, THE NATIONAL CASH REGISTER COMPANY

1968

Z
678
W37

Copyright © 1968 by The National Cash Register Company, Dayton, Ohio, United States of America. All Rights Reserved. Printed in the U.S.A. Published by Microcard Editions, 901 26th St. N.W., Washington, D.C. 20037, a part of the Industrial Products Division, The National Cash Register Company.

Library of Congress Catalog Card Number 68-28324

Foreword

Unlike many other academic disciplines, librarianship has not yet begun to exploit the contributions of the several disciplines toward the study of its own issues. Yet the literature abounds with material germane to its concerns. Too frequently the task of identifying, correlating, and bringing together material from innumerable sources is burdensome, time consuming or simply impossible. For a field whose stock in trade is organizing knowledge, it is clear that the job of synthesizing the most essential contributions from the elusive sources in which they are contained is overdue. This then is the rationale for the series, *Readers in Library and Information Science.*

The *Readers in Library and Information Science* will include books concerned with various broad aspects of the field's interests. Each volume will be prepared by a recognized student of the topic covered, and the content will embrace material from the many different sources from the traditional literature of librarianship as well as from outside the field in which the most salient contributions have appeared. The objectives of the series will be to bring together in convenient form the key elements required for a current and comprehensive view of the subject matter. In this way it is hoped that the core of knowledge, essential as the intellectual basis for study and understanding, will be drawn into focus and thereby contribute to the furtherance of professional education and professional practice in the field.

Paul Wasserman
Series Editor

Contents
An Overview

Part I   **INTRODUCTION TO THE STUDY OF ADMINISTRATION**   1

Part II   **UNDERSTANDING ORGANIZATIONAL BEHAVIOR**   41
Introduction to Bureaucracy   43
The Decision-Making Approach   63
Organizational Dynamics   95

Part III   **THE SEARCH FOR RATIONALITY**   123
Formulation of Objectives   125
Controlling and Reappraising   147
Assessment of Results   167

Part IV   **MANAGEMENT OF RESOURCES**   179
Authority   181
Personnel   209
Finance and Budgetary Control   227
Communication   239

Part V   **THE STRUGGLE FOR EXISTENCE**   255
Introduction to the Political Process   257
Libraries in Politics   281

Part VI   **KEY ISSUES**   323
Leadership   325
Innovation   349
Professionalism   377

Contents

I-INTRODUCTION TO THE STUDY OF ADMINISTRATION

The Proverbs of Administration-Herbert A. Simon   3
Notes on a General Theory of Administration-Edward H. Litchfield   16
Development of Administration in Library Service-Paul Wasserman   29

II-UNDERSTANDING ORGANIZATIONAL BEHAVIOR

Introduction to Bureaucracy

Bureaucracy in Modern Society-Peter M. Blau   44
Bureaucratic Structure and Personality-Robert K. Merton   56

The Decision-Making Approach

A Bibliographical Essay on Decision Making-William J. Gore and Fred S. Silander   64
Fact and Value in Decision-Making-Herbert A. Simon   78
Decision Making in Libraries-Mary Lee Bundy   86

Organizational Dynamics

Hierarchy, Specialization, and Organizational Conflict-Victor A. Thompson   96
Conflict in Libraries-Mary Lee Bundy   114

III-THE SEARCH FOR RATIONALITY

Formulation of Objectives

The Objectives of a Business-Peter F. Drucker   126
The Administration of Libraries-John Walton   139
Methodology for the Formulation of Objectives in Public Libraries-Paul Wasserman   141

Controlling and Reappraising

Some Social Processes for Control-Robert A. Dahl and Charles E. Lindblom   148

Assessment of Results

Measuring Municipal Activities: Public Libraries-Clarence E. Ridley and Herbert A. Simon   168
Measuring Performance in a Special Library-Paul Wasserman   174

IV-MANAGEMENT OF RESOURCES

Authority

The Theory of Authority-Chester I. Barnard   182
Authority Structure and Organizational Effectiveness-Amitai Etzioni   193
A Purchase of Mechanical Dictation Equipment-Kenneth R. Shaffer   206

Personnel

The Human Side of Enterprise-Douglas M. McGregor   210
Handling the Problem Staff Member-Alfred L. Brophy and George M. Gazda   217

Finance and Budgetary Controls

The Study of Budgeting-Frederick C. Mosher   228

Communication

Barriers and Gateways to Communication-Carl R. Rogers and F. J. Roethlisberger   240
Aspects of Upward Communications in a Public Library-Millicent D. Abell   248

V-THE STRUGGLE FOR EXISTENCE

Introduction to the Political Process

The Public Library as a Pressure Group-Phillip A. Monypenny   258
The Political Function-Edward C. Banfield and James Q. Wilson   265
Power and Community Structure-Peter H. Rossi   274

Libraries in Politics

The Library's Political Potential-Oliver Garceau   282
The Role of Interest Groups in the Formation of a Library-Ruth Aronson   299
Book Selection and Censorship: The Encounter-Marjorie Fiske   306
The University of Massachusetts Case-Library Journal   318

VI-KEY ISSUES

Leadership

The Administrator-Robert M. Hutchins   326
The Business Executive: The Psychodynamics of a Social Role-William E. Henry   335
Leadership in Administration-Philip Selznick   341

Innovation

Innovational and Authoritarian Personalities-Everett E. Hagen   350
Bureaucracy and Innovation-Victor A. Thompson   359
Automation as Innovation-Mary Lee Bundy   369

Professionalism

Professionalism Reconsidered-Mary Lee Bundy and Paul Wasserman   378
Libraries and Labor Unions-Library Journal   394

Introduction

This is a book with a mission. Its purpose is to influence the teaching of administration in library schools and to redirect the concern of the library administrator to those issues most central to his requirements. The collection of readings brought together here is designed to accomplish this purpose by drawing together important insights from relevant behavioral disciplines and from librarianship. It is designed to be read and discussed both within and outside formal courses in library administration.

The volume proceeds from the premise that basic understanding of organizational issues enhances the capacity to perform as an administrator. This work seeks to increase the reader's sophistication about the true nature of what transpires in organizations. While the content here is essentially theoretical and conceptual, its ends are pragmatic. A basic assumption throughout is that organizational affairs in libraries are more like than different from other organizational forms. Those elements common to the administrative process, particularly as seen in the large and complex organization, receive most attention. And it is the behavioral dimensions which are considered most fully. The volume also draws into focus the key professional issues which will influence the future of libraries as organizations—particularly as they relate to change and professionalism. As partisans of innovation, the editors see professionalism and disposition toward change as equally essential ingredients in the fostering of progress.

The orientation of this volume is therefore different from that of a typical textbook in library administration. It attempts to provide insight into precisely what happens within organizations as well as in their environments which have an influence upon them. It does not include prescriptions or descriptions. Instead, it orients the reader toward an understanding of organizational dynamics with libraries as the case in point. The book focuses upon administrative processes rather than upon techniques. It is concerned more with why and what rather than with how and what should. It cannot be too much emphasized that the intent of the present work is not to provide solutions or formulae. Rather it is to present the modern library as a complex organization and to identify the issues which make the role of the administrator an exceedingly difficult one.

The essential difficulty in preparing a volume such as the present one has been the need to delimit from a very large number of potential entries those deemed to be most relevant. A balance was sought between those fundamental contributions of the supportive disciplines—sociology, psychology, political science and administration—and that generated in and of librarianship. Whenever contributions which bridged from the basic disciplines into librarianship were available, they have been included. If the balance is weighted more heavily on the side of the supportive disciplines, it is because the library literature has not yet reached a level to challenge the more fundamental insights contained in materials from other disciplines.

The volume is divided by broad topic and then further subdivided. Each section is preceded by a statement which introduces the general theme. Individual selections are prefaced by brief comments on the issues treated in the article. Sketches following each piece offer biographical details about the authors. In cases where an author's work appears more than once, this sketch appears following the first selection. Many of the selections did not fit neatly into the framework of the volume and could as easily have been placed in one section as another. The content of the volume must then be viewed in its entirety for there are common themes which crisscross between and among the arbitrarily constructed sections.

A volume of this kind can be used in a number of ways: in place of a textbook and as an accompaniment to class lectures, as a supplementary course reading, and as a basis for individual study with or without a discussion sequence. It may also be studied to advantage by practicing administrators not engaged in formal study. The inspiration for this volume came from actual teaching experience which demonstrated the need to collect the most significant writings in one source and thereby avoid costly effort on both sides of the circulation desk of the library. If the work is successful, it will influence its reader to go beyond the confines of this volume and on to the fuller writings of the authors from whom only selections have been drawn.

It is the express intent of the present work to clarify the issues fundamental to genuine understanding of modern library organizations and their administration. In this way, it is hoped that the sophistication of the present and the next generation of library administrators may be enhanced. For if the true role and responsibilities, as well as the alternatives and strategies of the creative administrator are widely understood, perhaps the field of librarianship will be more adroitly navigated toward its sought for goals.

In the preparation of this work the editors were invaluably assisted by Mrs. Gayle Araghi and Mrs. Gilda Nimer who served as their research aides. Mrs. Effie Knight and the office staff of the School of Library and Information Services at the University of Maryland contributed in numerous ways to the volume's preparation. The editors are also indebted to the publishers and to the authors whose contributions are acknowledged throughout the book.

College Park, Maryland
March 15, 1968

Paul Wasserman
Mary Lee Bundy

I

INTRODUCTION TO THE STUDY OF ADMINISTRATION

This entire volume is given over to a concern with administration, to its procedures, to its philosophy, and to its responsibilities. To set the stage for the contributions which follow, the editors might have drawn together essays which would have detailed the evolution of managerial theory from the early efforts of the scientific management school of Frederick Taylor and his followers down to the work of the modern management scientists. Instead, because the central thrust of this work is behavioral, it was in order to so orient the reader that the choices were made.

Not always have librarians accepted the view that administration in general, and library administration in particular, constitutes a legitimate field of intellectual pursuit. Perhaps these readings will help to influence wider acceptance of the viability of such study. For in a time when the responsibilities of the administrative role grow ever more complex, insulation from the concepts and insights which in combination explain the realities of the organizational world, is a luxury which the library field can ill afford—either among its managerial class or among those who ply the professional craft. The nature of management is here viewed as the object of scholarly inquiry. Out of the sophistication which it engenders may come not only improved understanding, but the requisite strategies which lead ultimately to progress, innovation and enhanced professionalism.

The Proverbs of Administration

by Herbert A. Simon

This classic piece survives and offers valid lessons for the student of administration more than twenty years after it first appeared. In traditional teaching, following the classical school, a number of principles were derived as guidelines for effective practice. Simon masterfully identifies the inherent contradictions of these propositions. He counsels against too rigid acceptance of the notions of task specialization, hierarchical lines of authority, limited span of administrative control, and the ordering of work by purpose, process, clientele or place. Through logical and detached illustration, each principle is seen to suffer from superficiality, unreality and oversimplification. Simon's plea for a more rigorous approach to a theoretical base for the study of administration through empirical research, has been a decisive element in the direction of scholarship in administration during the period following the appearance in print of this seminal contribution.

A fact about proverbs that greatly enhances their quotability is that they almost always occur in mutually contradictory pairs. "Look before you leap!"—but "He who hesitates is lost."

This is both a great convenience and a serious defect—depending on the use to which one wishes to put the proverbs in question. If it is a matter of rationalizing behavior that has already taken place or justifying action that has already been decided upon, proverbs are ideal. Since one is never at a loss to find one that will prove his point—or the precisely contradictory point, for that matter—they are a great help in persuasion, political debate, and all forms of rhetoric.

But when one seeks to use proverbs as the basis of a scientific theory, the situation is less happy. It is not that the propositions expressed by the proverbs are insufficient; it is rather that they prove too much. A scientific theory should tell what is true but also what is false. If Newton had announced to the world that particles of matter exert either an attraction or a repulsion on each other, he would not have added much to scientific knowledge. His contribution consisted in showing that an attraction was exercised and in announcing the precise law governing its operation.

Most of the propositions that make up the body of administrative theory today share, unfortunately, this defect of proverbs. For almost every principle one can find an equally plausible and acceptable contradictory principle. Although the two principles of the pair will lead to exactly opposite organizational recommendations, there is nothing in the theory to indicate which is the proper one to apply.[1]

It is the purpose of this paper to substantiate this sweeping criticism of administrative theory, and to present some suggestions—perhaps less concrete than they should be—as to how the existing dilemma can be solved.

SOME ACCEPTED ADMINISTRATIVE PRINCIPLES

Among the more common "principles" that occur in the literature of administration are these:

1. Administrative efficiency is increased by a specialization of the task among the group.

2. Administrative efficiency is increased by arranging the members of the group in a determinate hierarchy of authority.

3. Administrative efficiency is increased by limiting the span of control at any point in the hierarchy to a small number.

4. Administrative efficiency is increased by grouping the workers, for purposes of control, according to (*a*) purpose, (*b*) process, (*c*) clientele, or (*d*) place. (This is really an elaboration of the first principle but deserves separate discussion.)

Since these principles appear relatively simple and clear, it would seem that their application to concrete problems of administrative organization would be unambiguous and that their validity would be easily submitted to empirical test. Such,

---

SOURCE: Reprinted from Herbert A. Simon, "The Proverbs of Administration," *Public Administration Review*, 6 (Winter, 1946), pp. 53-67, by permission of the American Society for Public Administration and the author.

however, seems not to be the case. To show why it is not, each of the four principles just listed will be considered in turn.

Specialization. Administrative efficiency is supposed to increase with an increase in specialization. But is this intended to mean that *any* increase in specialization will increase efficiency? If so, which of the following alternatives is the correct application of the principle in a particular case?

1. A plan of nursing should be put into effect by which nurses will be assigned to districts and do all nursing within that district, including school examinations, visits to homes or school children, and tuberculosis nursing.
2. A functional plan of nursing should be put into effect by which different nurses will be assigned to school examinations, visits to homes of school children, and tuberculosis nursing. The present method of generalized nursing by districts impedes the development of specialized skills in the three very diverse programs.

Both of these administrative arrangements satisfy the requirement of specialization—the first provides specialization by place; the second, specialization by function. The principle of specialization is of no help at all in choosing between the two alternatives.

It appears that the simplicity of the principle of specialization is a deceptive simplicity—a simplicity which conceals fundamental ambiguities. For "specialization" is not a condition of efficient administration; it is an inevitable characteristic of all group effort, however efficient or inefficient that effort may be. Specialization merely means that different persons are doing different things—and since it is physically impossible for two persons to be doing the same thing in the same place at the same time, two persons are always doing different things.

The real problem of administration, then, is not to "specialize," but to specialize in that particular manner and along those particular lines which will lead to administrative efficiency. But, in thus rephrasing this "principle" of administration, there has been brought clearly into the open its fundamental ambiguity: "Administrative efficiency is increased by a specialization of the task among the group in the direction which will lead to greater efficiency."

Further discussion of the choice between competing bases of specialization will be undertaken after two other principles of administration have been examined.

Unity of Command. Administrative efficiency is supposed to be enhanced by arranging the members of the organization in a determinate hierarchy of authority in order to preserve "unity of command."

Analysis of this "principle" requires a clear understanding of what is meant by the term "authority." A subordinate may be said to accept authority whenever he permits his behavior to be guided by a decision reached by another, irrespective of his own judgment as to the merits of that decision.

In one sense the principle of unity of command, like the principle of specialization, cannot be violated; for it is physically impossible for a man to obey two contradictory commands—that is what is meant by "contradictory commands." Presumably, if unity of command is a principle of administration, it must assert something more than this physical impossibility. Perhaps it asserts this: that it is undesirable to place a member of an organization in a position where he receives orders from more than one superior. This is evidently the meaning that Gulick attaches to the principle when he says,

> The significance of this principle in the process of co-ordination and organization must not be lost sight of. In building a structure of co-ordination, it is often tempting to set up more than one boss for a man who is doing work which has more than one relationship. Even as great a philosopher of management as Taylor fell into this error in setting up separate foremen to deal with machinery, with materials, with speed, etc., each with the power of giving orders directly to the individual workman. The rigid adherence to the principle of unity of command may have its absurdities; these are, however, unimportant in comparison with the certainty of confusion, inefficiency and irresponsibility which arise from the violation of the principle.[2]

Certainly the principle of unity of command, thus interpreted, cannot be criticized for any lack of clarity or any ambiguity. The definition of authority given above should provide a clear test whether, in any concrete situation, the principle is observed. The real fault that must be found with this principle is that it is incompatible with the principle of specialization. One of the most important uses to which authority is put in organization is to bring about specialization in the work of making decisions, so that each decision is made at a point in the organization where it can be made most expertly. As a result, the use of authority permits a greater degree of expertness to be achieved in decision-making than would be possible if each operative employee had himself to make all the decisions upon which his activity is predicated. The individual fireman does not decide whether to use a two-inch hose or a fire extinguisher; that is decided for him by his officers, and the decision is communicated to him in the form of a command.

However, if unity of command, in Gulick's sense, is observed, the decisions of a person at any point in the administrative hierarchy are subject to influence through only one channel of authority; and if his decisions are of a kind that require expertise in more than one field of knowledge, then advisory and informational services must be relied upon to supply those premises which lie in a field not recognized by the mode of specialization in the organization. For example, if an accountant in a school department is subordinate to an educator, and if unity of command is observed, then the finance department cannot issue direct orders to him regarding the technical, accounting aspects of his work. Similarly, the director of motor vehicles in the public works department will be unable to issue direct orders on care of motor equipment to the fire-truck driver.[3]

Gulick, in the statement quoted above, clearly indicates the difficulties to be faced if unity of command is not observed. A certain amount of irresponsibility and confusion are almost certain to ensue. But perhaps this is not too great a price to pay for the increased expertise that can be applied to decisions. What is needed to decide the issue is a principle of administration that would enable one to weigh the relative advantages of the two courses of action. But neither the principle of unity of command nor the principle of specialization is helpful in adjudicating the controversy. They merely contradict each other without indicating any procedure for resolving the contradiction.

If this were merely an academic controversy—if it were generally agreed and had been generally demonstrated that unity of command must be preserved in all cases, even with a loss in expertise—one could assert that in case of conflict between the two principles, unity of command should prevail. But the issue is far from clear, and experts can be ranged on both sides of the controversy. On the side of unity of command there may be cited the dictums of Gulick and others.[4] On the side of specialization there are Taylor's theory of functional supervision, Macmahon and Millett's idea of "dual supervision," and the practice of technical supervision in military organization.[5]

It may be, as Gulick asserts, that the notion of Taylor and these others is an "error." If so, the evidence that it is an error has never been marshalled or published—apart from loose heuristic arguments like that quoted above. One is left with a choice between equally eminent theorists of administration and without any evidential basis for making that choice.

What evidence there is of actual administrative practice would seem to indicate that the need for specialization is to a very large degree given priority over the need for unity of command. As a matter of fact, it does not go too far to say that unity of command, in Gulick's sense, never has existed in any administrative organization. If a line officer accepts the regulations of an accounting department with regard to the procedure for making requisitions, can it be said that, in this sphere, he is not subject to the authority of the accounting department? In any actual administrative situation authority is zoned, and to maintain that this zoning does not contradict the principle of unity of command requires a very different definition of authority from that used here. This subjection of the line officer to the accounting department is no different, in principle, from Taylor's recommendation that in the matter of work programming a workman be subject to one foreman, in the matter of machine operation to another.

The principle of unity of command is perhaps more defensible if narrowed down to the following: In case two authoritative commands conflict, there should be a single determinate person whom the subordinate is expected to obey; and the sanctions of authority should be applied against the subordinate only to enforce his obedience to that one person.

If the principle of unity of command is more defensible when stated in this limited form, it also solves fewer problems. In the first place, it no longer requires, except for settling conflicts of authority, a single hierarchy of authority. Consequently, it leaves unsettled the very important question of how authority should be zoned in a particular organization (i.e., the modes of specialization) and through what channels it should be exercised. Finally, even this narrower concept of unity of command conflicts with the principle of specialization, for whenever disagreement does occur and the organization members revert to the formal lines of authority, then only those types of specialization which are represented in the hierarchy of authority can impress themselves on decision. If the training officer of a city exercises only functional supervision over the police training officer, then in case of disagreement with the police chief, specialized knowledge of police problems will determine the outcome while specialized knowledge of training problems will be subordinated or ignored. That this actually occurs is shown by the frustration so commonly expressed by functional supervisors at their lack of authority to apply sanctions.

Span of Control. Administrative efficiency is supposed to be enhanced by limiting the number of subordinates who report directly to any one administrator to a small number—say six. This notion that the "span of control" should be narrow is confidently asserted as a third incontrovertible principle of administration. The usual commonsense arguments for restricting the span of control are familiar and need not be repeated here. What is not so generally recognized is that a contradictory proverb of administration can be stated which, though it is not so familiar as the principle of span of control, can be supported by arguments of equal plausibility. The proverb in question is the following: Administrative efficiency is enhanced by keeping at a minimum the number of organizational levels through which a matter must pass before it is acted upon.

This latter proverb is one of the fundamental criteria that guide administrative analysts in procedures simplification work. Yet in many situations the results to which this principle leads are in direct contradiction to the requirements of the principle of span of control, the principle of unity of command, and the principle of specialization. The present discussion is concerned with the first of these conflicts. To illustrate the difficulty, two alternative proposals for the organization of a small health department will be presented—one based on the restriction of span of control, the other on the limitation of number of organization levels:

1. The present organization of the department places an administrative overload on the health officer by reason of the fact that all eleven employees of the department report directly to him and the further fact that some of the staff lack adequate technical training. Consequently, venereal disease clinic treatments and other details require an undue amount of the health officer's personal attention.

It has previously been recommended that the proposed medical officer be placed in charge of the venereal disease and chest clinics and all child hygiene work. It is further recommended that one of the inspectors be designated chief inspector and placed in charge of all the department's inspectional activities and that one of the nurses be designated as head nurse. This will relieve the health commissioner of considerable detail and will leave him greater freedom to plan and supervise the health program as a whole, to conduct health education, and to coordinate the work of the department with that of other community agencies. If the department were thus organized, the effectiveness of all employees could be substantially increased.

2. The present organization of the department leads to inefficiency and excessive red tape by reason of the fact that an unnecessary supervisory level intervenes between the health officer and the operative employees, and that those four of the twelve employees who are best trained technically are engaged largely in "overhead" administrative duties. Consequently, unnecessary delays occur in securing the approval of the health officer on matters requiring his attention, and too many matters require review and re-review.

The medical officer should be left in charge of the venereal disease and chest clinics and child hygiene work. It is recommended, however, that the position of chief inspector and head nurse be abolished and that the employees now filling these positions perform regular inspectional and nursing duties. The details of work scheduling now handled by these two employees can be taken care of more economically by the secretary to the health officer, and, since broader matters of policy have, in any event, always required the personal attention of the health officer, the abolition of these two positions will eliminate a wholly unnecessary step in review, will allow an expansion of inspectional and nursing services, and will permit at least a beginning to be made in the recommended program of health education. The number of persons reporting directly to the health officer will be increased to nine, but since there are few matters requiring the coordination of these employees, other than the work schedules and policy questions referred to above, this change will not materially increase his work load.

The dilemma is this: in a large organization with complex interrelations between members, a restricted span of control inevitably produces excessive red tape, for each contact between organization members must be carried upward until a common superior is found. If the organization is at all large, this will involve carrying all such matters upward through several levels of officials for decision and then downward again in the form of orders and instructions—a cumbersome and time-consuming process.

The alternative is to increase the number of persons who are under the command of each officer, so that the pyramid will come more rapidly to a peak, with fewer intervening levels. But this, too, leads to difficulty, for if an officer is required to supervise too many employees, his control over them is weakened.

If it is granted, then, that both the increase and the decrease in span of control has some undesirable consequences, what is the optimum point? Proponents of a restricted span of control have suggested three, five, even eleven, as suitable numbers, but nowhere have they explained the reasoning which led them to the particular number they selected. The principle as stated casts no light on this very crucial question. One is reminded of current arguments about the proper size of the national debt.

Organization by Purpose, Process, Clientele, Place. Administrative efficiency is supposed to be increased by grouping workers according to (*a*) purpose, (*b*) process, (*c*) clientele, or (*d*) place. But from the discussion of specialization it is clear that this principle is internally inconsistent; for purpose, process, clientele, and place are competing bases of organization, and at any given point of division the advantages of three must be sacrificed to secure the advantages of the fourth. If the major departments of a city, for example, are organized on the basis of major purpose, then it follows that all the physicians, all the lawyers, all the engineers, all the statisticians will not be located in a single department exclusively composed of members of their profession but will be distributed among the various city departments needing their services. The advantages of organization by process will thereby be partly lost.

Some of these advantages can be regained by organizing on the basis of process *within* the major departments. Thus there may be an engineering bureau within the public works department, or the board of education may have a school health service as a major division of its work. Similarly, within smaller units there may be division by area or by clientele: e.g., a fire department will have separate companies located throughout the city, while a welfare department may have intake and case work agencies in various locations. Again, however, these major types of specialization cannot be simultaneously achieved, for at any point in the organization it must be decided whether specialization at the next level will be accomplished by distinction of major purpose, major process, clientele, or area.

The conflict may be illustrated by showing how the principle of specialization according to purpose would lead to a different result from specialization according to clientele in the organization of a health department.

1. Public health administration consists of the following activities for the prevention of disease and the maintenance of healthful conditions: (1) vital statistics; (2) child hygiene—prenatal, maternity, postnatal, infant, preschool, and school health programs; (3) communicable disease control; (4) inspection of milk, foods, and drugs; (5) sanitary inspection; (6) laboratory service; (7) health education.

One of the handicaps under which the health department labors is the fact that the department has no control over school health, that being an activity of the county board of education, and there is little or no coordination between that highly important part of the community health program and the balance of the program which is conducted by the city-county health unit. It is recommended that the city and county open negotiations with the board of education for the transfer of all school health work and the appropriation therefor to the joint health unit. . . .

2. To the modern school department is entrusted the care of children during almost the entire period that they are absent from the parental home. It has three principal responsibilities toward them: (1) to provide for their education in useful skills and knowledge and in character; (2) to provide them with wholesome play activities outside school hours; (3) to care for their health and to assure the attainment of minimum standards of nutrition.

One of the handicaps under which the school board labors is the fact that, except for school lunches, the board has no control over child health and nutrition, and there is little or no coordination between that highly important part of the child development program and the balance of the program which is conducted by the board of education. It is recommended that the city and county open negotiations for the transfer of all health work for children of school age to the board of education.

Here again is posed the dilemma of choosing between alternative, equally plausible, administrative principles. But this is not the only difficulty in the present case, for a closer study of the situation shows there are fundamental ambiguities in the meanings of the key terms—"purpose," "process," "clientele," and "place."

"Purpose" may be roughly defined as the objective or end for which an activity is carried on; "process" as a means for accomplishing a purpose. Processes, then, are carried on in order to achieve purposes. But purposes themselves may generally be arranged in some sort of hierarchy. A typist moves her fingers in order to type; types in order to reproduce a letter; reproduces a letter in order that an inquiry may be answered. Writing a letter is then the purpose for which the typing is performed; while writing a letter is also the process whereby the purpose of replying to an inquiry is achieved. It follows that the same activity may be described as purpose or as process.

This ambiguity is easily illustrated for the case of an administrative organization. A health department conceived as a unit whose task it is to care for the health of the community is a purpose organization; the same department conceived as a unit which makes use of the medical arts to carry on its work is a process organization. In the same way, an education department may be viewed as a purpose (to educate) organization, or a clientele (children) organization; the forest service as a purpose (forest conservation), process (forest management), clientele (lumbermen and cattlemen utilizing public forests), or area (publicly owned forest lands) organization. When concrete illustrations of this sort are selected, the lines of demarcation between these categories become very hazy and unclear indeed.

"Organization by major purpose," says Gulick, "... serves to bring together in a single large department all of those who are at work endeavoring to render a particular service."[6] But what is a particular service? Is fire protection a single purpose, or is it merely a part of the purpose of public safety?—or is it a combination of purposes including fire prevention and fire fighting? It must be concluded that there is no such thing as a purpose, or a unifunctional (single-purpose) organization. What is to be considered a single function depends entirely on language and techniques.[7] If the English language has a comprehensive term which covers both of two subpurposes it is natural to think of the two together as a single purpose. If such a term is lacking, the two subpurposes become purposes in their own right. On the other hand, a single activity may contribute to several objectives, but since they are technically (procedurally) inseparable, the activity is considered a single function or purpose.

The fact, mentioned previously, that purposes form a hierarchy, each subpurpose contributing to some more final and comprehensive end, helps to make clear the relation between purpose and process. "Organization by major process," says Gulick, "... tends to bring together in a single department all of those who are at work making use of a given special skill or technology, or are members of a given profession."[8] Consider a simple skill of this kind—typing. Typing is a skill which brings about a means-end coordination of muscular movements, but at a very low level in the means-end hierarchy. The content of the typewritten letter is indifferent to the skill that produces it. The skill consists merely in the ability to hit the letter "*t*" quickly whenever the letter "*t*" is required by the content and to hit the letter "*a*" whenever the letter "*a*" is required by the content.

There is, then, no essential difference between a "purpose" and a "process," but only a distinction of degree. A "process" is an activity whose immediate purpose is at a low level in the hierarchy of means and ends, while a "purpose" is a collection of activities whose orienting value or aim is at a high level in the means-end hierarchy.

Next consider "clientele" and "place" as bases of organization. These categories are really not separate from purpose, but a part of it. A complete statement of the purpose of a fire department would have to include the area served by it: "to reduce fire losses on property in the city of X." Objectives of an administrative organization are phrased in terms of a service to be provided and an area for which it is provided. Usually, the term "purpose" is meant to refer only to the first element, but the second is just as legitimately an aspect of purpose. Area of service, of course, may be a specified clientele quite as well as a geographical area. In the case of an agency which works on "shifts," time will be a third dimension of purpose—to provide a given service in a given area (or to a given clientele) during a given time period.

With this clarification of terminology, the next task is to reconsider the problem of specializing the work of an organization. It is no longer legitimate to speak of a "purpose" organization, a "process" organization, a "clientele" organization, or an "area" organization. The same unit might fall into any one of these four categories, depending on the nature of the larger organizational unit of which it was a part. A unit providing public health and medical services for school-age children in Multnomah County might be considered (1) an "area" organization if it were part of a unit providing the same service for the state of Oregon; (2) a "clientele" organization if it were part of a unit providing similar services for children of all ages; (3) a "purpose" or a "process" organization (it would be impossible to say which) if it were part of an education department.

It is incorrect to say that Bureau A is a process bureau; the correct statement is that Bureau A is a process bureau *within* Department X.[9] This latter statement would mean that Bureau A incorporates all the processes of a certain kind in Department X, without reference to any special subpurposes, subareas, or subclientele of Department X. Now it is conceivable that a particular unit might incorporate all processes of a certain kind but that these processes might relate to only certain particular subpurposes of the department purpose. In this case, which corresponds to the health unit in an education department mentioned above, the unit would be specialized by both purpose and process. The health unit would be the only one in the education department using the medical art (process) and concerned with health (subpurpose).

Even when the problem is solved of proper usage for the terms "purpose," "process," "clientele," and "area," the principles of administration give no guide as to which of these four competing bases of specialization is applicable in any particular situation. The British Machinery of Government Committee had no doubts about the matter. It considered purpose and clientele as the two possible bases of organization and put its faith entirely in the former. Others have had equal assurance in choosing between purpose and process. The reasoning which leads to these unequivocal conclusions leaves something to be desired. The Machinery of Government Committee gives this sole argument for its choice:

> Now the inevitable outcome of this method of organization [by clientele] is a tendency to Lilliputian administration. It is impossible that the specialized service which each Department has to render to the community can be of as high a standard when its work is at the same time limited to a particular class of persons and extended to every variety of provision for them, as when the Department concentrates itself on the provision of the particular service only by whomsoever required, and looks beyond the interest of comparatively small classes.[10]

The faults in this analysis are obvious. First, there is no attempt to determine how *a* service is to be recognized. Second, there is a bald assumption, absolutely without proof, that a child health unit, for example, in a department of child welfare could not offer services of "as high a standard" as the same unit if it were located in a department of health. Just how the shifting of the unit from one department to another would improve or damage the quality of its work is not explained. Third, no basis is set forth for adjudicating the competing claims of purpose and process—the two are merged in the ambiguous term "service." It is not necessary here to decide whether the committee was right or wrong in its recommendation; the important point is that the recommendation represented a choice, without any apparent logical or empirical grounds, between contradictory principles of administration.

Even more remarkable illustrations of illogic can be found in most discussions of purpose *vs.* process. They would be too ridiculous to cite if they were not commonly used in serious political and administrative debate.

> For instance, where should agricultural education come: in the Ministry of Education, or of Agriculture? That depends on whether we want to see the best farming taught, though possibly by old methods, or a possibly out-of-date style of farming, taught in the most modern and compelling manner. The question answers itself.[11]

But does the question really answer itself? Suppose a bureau of agricultural education were set up, headed, for example, by a man who had had extensive experience in agricultural research or as administrator of an agricultural school, and staffed by men of similarly appropriate background. What reason is there to believe that if attached to a Ministry of Education they would teach old-fashioned farming by new-fashioned methods, while if attached to a Ministry of Agriculture they would teach new-fashioned farming by old-fashioned methods? The administrative problem of such a bureau would be to teach new-fashioned farming by new-fashioned methods, and it is a little difficult to see how the departmental location of the unit would affect this result. "The question answers itself" only if one has a rather mystical faith in the potency of bureau-shuffling as a means for redirecting the activities of an agency.

These contradictions and competitions have received increasing attention from students of administration during the past few years. For example, Gulick, Wallace, and Benson have stated certain advantages and disadvantages of the several modes of specialization, and have considered the conditions under which one or the other mode might best be adopted.[12] All this analysis has been at a theoretical level—in the sense that data have not been employed to demonstrate the superior effectiveness claimed for the different modes. But though theoretical, the analysis has lacked a theory. Since no comprehensive framework has been constructed within which the discussion could take place, the analysis has tended either to the logical one-sidedness which characterizes the examples quoted above or to inconclusiveness.

The Impasse of Administrative Theory. The four "principles of administration" that were set forth at the beginning of this paper have now been subjected to critical analysis. None of the four survived in very good shape, for in each case there was found, instead of an unequivocal principle, a set of two or more mutually incompatible principles apparently equally applicable to the administrative situation.

Moreover, the reader will see that the very same objections can be urged against the customary discussions of "centralization" *vs.* "decentralization," which usually conclude, in effect, that "on the one hand, centralization of decision-making functions is desirable; on the other hand, there are definite advantages in decentralization."

Can anything be salvaged which will be useful in the construction of an administrative theory? As a matter of fact, almost everything can be salvaged. The difficulty has arisen from treating as "principles of administration" what are really only criteria for describing and diagnosing administrative situations. Closet space is certainly an important item in the design of a successful house; yet a house designed entirely with a view to securing a maximum of closet space—all other considerations being forgotten—would be considered, to say the least, somewhat unbalanced. Similarly, unity of command, specialization by purpose, decentralization are all items to be considered in the design of an efficient administrative organization. No single one of these items is of sufficient importance to suffice as a guiding principle for the administrative analyst. In the design of administrative organizations, as in their operation, over-all efficiency must be the guiding criterion. Mutually incompatible advantages must be balanced against each other, just as an architect weighs the advantages of additional closet space against the advantages of a larger living room.

This position, if it is a valid one, constitutes an indictment of much current writing about administrative matters. As the examples cited in this chapter amply demonstrate, much administrative analysis proceeds by selecting a single criterion and applying it to an administrative situation to reach a recommendation; while the fact that equally valid, but contradictory, criteria exist which could be applied with equal reason, but with a different result, is conveniently ignored. A valid approach to the study of administration requires that *all* the relevant diagnostic criteria be identified; that each administrative situation be analyzed in terms of the entire set of criteria; and that research be instituted to determine how weights can be assigned to the several criteria when they are, as they usually will be, mutually incompatible.

AN APPROACH TO ADMINISTRATIVE THEORY

This program needs to be considered step by step. First, what is included in the description of administrative situations for purposes of such an analysis? Second, how can weights be assigned to the various criteria to give them their proper place in the total picture?

The Description of Administrative Situations. Before a science can develop principles, it must possess concepts. Before a law of gravitation could be formulated, it was necessary to have the notions of "acceleration" and "weight." The first task of administrative theory is to develop a set of concepts that will permit the description, in terms relevant to the theory, of administrative situations. These concepts, to be scientifically useful, must be operational; that is, their meanings must correspond to empirically observable facts or situations. The definition of "authority" given earlier in this paper is an example of an operational definition.

What is a scientifically relevant description of an organization? It is a description that, so far as possible, designates for each person in the organization what decisions that person makes and the influences to which he is subject in making each of these decisions. Current descriptions of administrative organizations fall far short of this standard. For the most part, they confine themselves to the allocation of *functions* and the formal structure of *authority*. They give little attention to the other types of organizational influence or to the system of communication.[13]

What does it mean, for example, to say: "The department is made up of three bureaus. The first has the function of _____, the second the function of _____, and the third the function of _____?" What can be learned from such a description about the workability of the organizational arrangement? Very little, indeed. For from the description there is obtained no idea of the degree to which decisions are centralized at the bureau level or at the departmental level. No notion is given as to the extent to which the (presumably unlimited) authority of the department over the bureau is actually exercised or by what mechanisms. There is no indication of the extent to which systems of communication assist the coordination of the three bureaus or, for that matter, to what extent coordination is required by the nature of their work. There is no description of the kinds of training the members of the bureau have undergone or of the extent to which this training permits decentralization at the bureau level. In sum, a description of administrative organizations in terms almost exclusively of functions and lines of authority is completely inadequate for purposes of administrative analysis.

Consider the term "centralization." How is it determined whether the operations of a particular organization are "centralized" or "decentralized?" Does the fact that field offices exist prove anything about decentralization? Might not the same decentralization take place in the bureaus of a centrally located office? A realistic analysis of centralization must include a study of the allocation of decisions in the organization and the methods of influence that are employed by the higher levels to affect the decisions at the lower levels. Such an analysis would reveal a much more complex picture of the decision-making process than any enumeration of the geographical locations of organizational units at the different levels.

Administrative description suffers currently from superficiality, oversimplification, lack of realism. It has confined itself too closely to the mechanism of authority and has failed to bring within its orbit the other, equally important, modes of influence on organizational behavior. It has refused to undertake the tiresome task of studying the actual allocation of decision-making functions. It has been satisfied to speak of "authority," "centralization," "span of control," "function," without seeking operational definitions of these terms. Until administrative description reaches a higher level of sophistication, there is little reason to hope that rapid progress will be made toward the identification and verification of valid administrative principles.

Does this mean that a purely formal description of an administrative organization is impossible—that a relevant description must include an account of the content of the organization's decisions? This is a question that is almost impossible to answer in the present state of knowledge of administrative theory. One thing seems certain: content plays a greater role in the application of administrative principles than is allowed for in the formal administrative theory of the present time. This is a fact that is beginning to be recognized in the literature of administration. If one examines the chain of publications extending from Mooney and Reilley, through Gulick and the President's Committee controversy, to Schuyler Wallace and Benson, he sees a steady shift of emphasis from the "principles of administration" themselves to a study of the *conditions* under which competing principles are respectively applicable. Recent publications seldom say that "organization should be by purpose," but rather that "under such and such conditions purpose organization is desirable." It is to these conditions which underlie the application of the proverbs of administration that administrative theory and analysis must turn in their search for really valid principles to replace the proverbs.

The Diagnosis of Administrative Situations.
Before any positive suggestions can be made, it is necessary to digress a bit and to consider more closely the exact nature of the propositions of administrative theory. The theory of administration is concerned with how an organization should be constructed and operated in order to accomplish its work efficiently. A fundamental principle of administration, which follows almost immediately from the rational character of "good" administration, is that among several alternatives involving the same expenditure that one should always be selected which leads to the greatest accomplishment of administrative objectives; and among several alternatives that lead to the same accomplishment that one should be selected which involves the least expenditure. Since this "principle of efficiency" is characteristic of any activity that attempts rationally to maximize the attainment of certain ends with the use of scarce means, it is as characteristic of economic theory as it is of administrative theory. The "administrative man" takes his place alongside the classical "economic man."[14]

Actually, the "principle" of efficiency should be considered a definition rather than a principle: it is a definition of what is meant by "good" or "correct" administrative behavior. It does not tell *how* accomplishments are to be maximized, but merely states that this maximization is the aim of administrative activity, and that administrative theory must disclose under what conditions the maximization takes place.

Now what are the factors that determine the level of efficiency which is achieved by an administrative organization? It is not possible to make an exhaustive list of these, but the principal categories can be enumerated. Perhaps the simplest method of approach is to consider the single member of the administrative organization and ask what the limits are to the quantity and quality of his output. These limits include (*a*) limits on his ability to perform and (*b*) limits on his ability to make correct decisions. To the extent that these limits are removed, the administrative organization approaches its goal of high efficiency. Two persons, given the same skills, the same objectives and values, the same knowledge and information, can rationally decide only upon the same course of action. Hence, administrative theory must be interested in the factors that will determine with what skills, values, and knowledge the organization member undertakes his work. These are the "limits" to rationality with which the principles of administration must deal.

On one side, the individual is limited by those skills, habits, and reflexes which are no longer in the realm of the conscious. His performance, for example, may be limited by his manual dexterity or his reaction time or his strength. His decision-making processes may be limited by the speed of his mental processes, his skill in elementary arithmetic, and so forth. In this area, the principles of administration must be concerned with the physiology of the human body and with the laws of skill-training and of habit. This is the field that has been most successfully cultivated by the followers of Taylor and in which has been developed time-and-motion study and the therblig.

On a second side, the individual is limited by his values and those conceptions of purpose which influence him in making his decisions. If his loyalty to the organization is high, his decisions may evidence sincere acceptance of the objectives set for the organization; if that loyalty is lacking, personal motives may interfere with his administrative efficiency. If his loyalties are attached to the bureau by which he is employed, he may sometimes make decisions that are inimical to the larger unit of which the bureau is a part. In this area the principles of administration must be concerned with the determinants of loyalty and morale, with leadership and initiative, and with the influences that determine where the individual's organizational loyalties will be attached.

On a third side, the individual is limited by the extent of his knowledge of things relevant to his job. This applies both to the basic knowledge required in decision-making—a bridge designer must know the fundamentals of mechanics—and to the information that is required to make his decisions appropriate to the given situation. In this area, administrative theory is concerned with such fundamental questions as these: What are the limits on the mass of knowledge that human minds can accumulate and apply? How rapidly can knowledge be assimilated? How is specialization in the administrative organization to be related to the specializations of knowledge that are prevalent in the community's occupational structure? How is the system of communication to channel knowledge and information to the appropriate decision-points? What types of knowledge can, and what types cannot, be easily transmitted? How is the need for intercommunication of information affected by the modes of specialization in the organization? This is perhaps the *terra incognita* of administrative theory, and undoubtedly its careful exploration will cast great light on the proper application of the proverbs of administration.

Perhaps this triangle of limits does not completely bound the area of rationality, and other sides need to be added to the figure. In any case, this enumeration will serve to indicate the kinds of considerations that must go into the construction of valid and noncontradictory principles of administration.

An important fact to be kept in mind is that the limits of rationality are variable limits. Most important of all, consciousness of the limits may in itself alter them. Suppose it were discovered in a particular organization, for example, that organizational loyalties attached to small units had frequently led to a harmful degree of intra-organizational competition. Then, a program which trained members of the organization to be conscious of their loyalties, and to subordinate loyalties to the smaller group to those of the large, might lead to a very considerable alteration of the limits in that organization.[15]

A related point is that the term "rational behavior," as employed here, refers to rationality when that behavior is evaluated in terms of the objectives of the larger organization; for, as just pointed out, the difference in direction of the individual's aims from those of the larger organization is just one of those elements of nonrationality with which the theory must deal.

A final observation is that, since administrative theory is concerned with the nonrational limits of the rational, it follows that the larger the area in which rationality has been achieved the less important is the exact form of the administrative organization. For example, the function of plan preparation, or design, if it results in a written plan that can be communicated interpersonally without difficulty, can be located almost anywhere in the organization without affecting results. All that is needed is a procedure whereby the plan can be given authoritative status, and this can be provided in a number of ways. A discussion, then, of the proper location for a planning or designing unit is apt to be highly inconclusive and is apt to hinge on the personalities in the organization and their relative enthusiasm, or lack of it, toward the planning function rather than upon any abstract principles of good administration.[16]

On the other hand, when factors of communication or faiths or loyalty are crucial to the making of a decision, the location of the decision in the organization is of great importance. The method of allocating decisions in the army, for instance, automatically provides (at least in the period prior to the actual battle) that each decision will be made where the knowledge is available for coordinating it with other decisions.

Assigning Weights to the Criteria. A first step, then, in the overhauling of the proverbs of administration is to develop a vocabulary, along the lines just suggested, for the description of administrative organization. A second step, which has also been outlined, is to study the limits of rationality in order to develop a complete and comprehensive enumeration of the criteria that must be weighed in evaluating an administrative organization. The current proverbs represent only a fragmentary and unsystematized portion of these criteria.

When these two tasks have been carried out, it remains to assign weights to the criteria. Since the criteria, or "proverbs," are often mutually competitive or contradictory, it is not sufficient merely to identify them. Merely to know, for example, that a specified change in organization will reduce the span of control is not enough to justify the change. This gain must be balanced against the possible resulting loss of contact between the higher and lower ranks of the hierarchy.

Hence, administrative theory must also be concerned with the question of the weights that are to be applied to these criteria—to the problems of their relative importance in any concrete situation. This question is not one that can be solved in a vacuum. Arm-chair philosophizing about administration—of which the present paper is an example— has gone about as far as it can profitably go in this particular direction. What is needed now is empirical research and experimentation to determine the relative desirability of alternative administrative arrangements.

The methodological framework for this research is already at hand in the principle of efficiency. If an administrative organization whose activities are susceptible to objective evaluation be subjected to study, then the actual change in accomplishment that results from modifying administrative arrangements in these organizations can be observed and analyzed.

There are two indispensable conditions to successful research along these lines. First, it is necessary that the objectives of the administrative organization under study be defined in concrete terms so that results, expressed in terms of these objectives, can be accurately measured. Second, it is necessary that sufficient experimental control be exercised to make possible the isolation of the particular effect under study from other disturbing factors that might be operating on the organization at the same time.

These two conditions have seldom been even partially fulfilled in so-called "administrative experiments." The mere fact that a legislature passes a law creating an administrative agency, that the agency operates for five years, that the agency is finally abolished, and that a historical study is then made of the agency's operations is not sufficient to make of that agency's history an "administrative experiment." Modern American legislation is full of such "experiments" which furnish orators in neighboring states with abundant ammunition when similar issues arise in their bailiwicks, but which provide the scientific investigator with little or nothing in the way of objective evidence, one way or the other.

In the literature of administration, there are only a handful of research studies that satisfy these fundamental conditions of methodology—and these are, for the most part, on the periphery of the problem of organization. There are, first of all, the studies of the Taylor group which sought to determine the technological conditions of efficiency. Perhaps none of these is a better example of the painstaking methods of science than Taylor's own studies of the cutting of metals.[17]

Studies dealing with the human and social aspects of administration are even rarer than the technological studies. Among the more important are the whole series of studies on fatigue, starting in Great Britain during World War I and culminating in the Westinghouse experiments.[18]

In the field of public administration, almost the sole example of such experimentation is the series of studies that have been conducted in the public welfare field to determine the proper case loads for social workers.[19]

Because, apart from these scattered examples, studies of administrative agencies have been carried out without benefit of control or of objective measurements of results, they have had to depend for their recommendations and conclusions upon *a priori* reasoning proceeding from "principles of administration." The reasons have already been stated why the "principles" derived in this way cannot be more than "proverbs."

Perhaps the program outlined here will appear an ambitious or even a quixotic one. There should certainly be no illusions, in undertaking it, as to the length and deviousness of the path. It is hard to see, however, what alternative remains open. Certainly neither the practitioner of administration nor the theoretician can be satisfied with the poor analytic tools that the proverbs provide him. Nor is there any reason to believe that a less drastic reconversion than that outlined here will rebuild those tools to usefulness.

It may be objected that administration cannot aspire to be a "science;" that by the nature of its subject it cannot be more than an "art."

Whether true or false, this objection is irrelevant to the present discussion. The question of how "exact" the principles of administration can be made is one that only experience can answer. But as to whether they should be logical or illogical there can be no debate. Even an "art" cannot be founded on proverbs.

FOOTNOTES

[1] Lest it be thought that this deficiency is peculiar to the science—or "art"—of administration, it should be pointed out that the same trouble is shared by most Freudian psychological theories, as well as by some sociological theories.

[2] Luther Gulick, "Notes on the Theory of Organization," in Luther Gulick and L. Urwick (eds.), *Papers on the Science of Administration* (Institute of Public Administration, Columbia University, 1937), p. 9.

[3] This point is discussed in Herbert A. Simon, "Decision-Making and Administrative Organization," 4 *Public Administration Review* 20-21 (Winter, 1944).

[4] Gulick, "Notes on the Theory of Organization," p. 9; L. D. White, *Introduction to the Study of Public Administration* (Macmillan Co., 1939), p. 45.

[5] Frederick W. Taylor, *Shop Management* (Harper & Bros., 1911), p. 99; Macmahon, Millett, and Ogden, *The Administration of Federal Work Relief* (Public Administration Service, 1941), pp. 265-68; and L. Urwick, who describes British army practice in "Organization as a Technical Problem," Gulick and Urwick (eds.), *op. cit.*, pp. 67-69.

[6] *Op. cit.*, p. 21.

[7] If this is correct, then any attempt to prove that certain activities belong in a single department because they relate to a single purpose is doomed to fail. See, for example, John M. Gaus and Leon Wolcott, *Public Administration and the U. S. Department of Agriculture* (Public Administration Service, 1940).

[8] *Op. cit.*, p. 23.

[9] This distinction is implicit in most of Gulick's analysis of specialization. However, since he cites as examples single departments within a city, and since he usually speaks of "grouping activities" rather than "dividing work," the relative character of these categories is not always apparent in this discussion (*op. cit.*, pp. 15-30).

[10] *Report of the Machinery of Government Committee* (H. M. Stationery Office, 1918).

[11] Sir Charles Harris, "Decentralization," 3 *Journal of Public Administration* 117-33 (April, 1925).

[12] Gulick, "Notes on the Theory of Organization," pp. 21-30; Schuyler Wallace, *Federal Departmentalization* (Columbia University Press, 1941); George C. S. Benson, "International Administrative Organization," 1 *Public Administration Review* 473-86 (Autumn, 1941).

[13] The monograph by Macmahon, Millett, and Ogden, *op. cit.*, perhaps approaches nearer than any other published administrative study to the sophistication required in administrative description. See, for example, the discussion on pp. 233-36 of headquarters-field relationships.

[14] For an elaboration of the principle of efficiency and its place in administrative theory see Clarence E. Ridley and Herbert A. Simon, *Measuring Municipal Activities* (International City Managers' Association, 2nd ed., 1943), particularly Chapter I and the preface to the second edition.

[15] For an example of the use of such training, see Herbert A. Simon and William Divine, "Controlling Human Factors in an Administrative Experiment," 1 *Public Administration Review* 487-92 (Autumn, 1941).

[16] See, for instance, Robert A. Walker, *The Planning Function in Urban Government* (University of Chicago Press, 1941), pp. 166-75. Walker makes out a strong case for attaching the planning agency to the chief executive. But he rests his entire case on the rather slender reed that "as long as the planning agency is outside the governmental structure . . . planning will tend to encounter resistance from public officials as an invasion of their responsibility and jurisdiction." This "resistance" is precisely the type of non-rational loyalty which has been referred to previously, and which is certainly a variable.

[17] F. W. Taylor, *On the Art of Cutting Metals* (American Society of Mechanical Engineers, 1907).

[18] Great Britain, Ministry of Munitions, Health of Munitions Workers Committee, *Final Report* (H. M. Stationery Office, 1918); F. J. Roethlisberger and William J. Dickson, *Management and the Worker* (Harvard University Press, 1939).

[19] Ellery F. Reed, *An Experiment in Reducing the Cost of Relief* (American Public Welfare Administration, 1937); Rebecca Staman, "What Is the Most Economical Case Load in Public Relief Administration?" 4 *Social Work Technique* 117-21 (May-June, 1938); Chicago Relief Administration, *Adequate Staff Brings Economy* (American Public Welfare Association, 1939); Constance Hastings and Saya S. Schwartz, *Size of Visitor's Caseload as a Factor in Efficient Administration of Public Assistance* (Philadelphia County Board of Assistance, 1939); Simon et al., *Determining Work Loads for Professional Staff in a Public Welfare Agency* (Bureau of Public Administration, University of California, 1941).

ABOUT THE AUTHOR—Herbert A. Simon's work was first significantly influenced by Charles E. Merriam whom he followed in the introduction of psychological and sociological insights and methods to the study of political science. Simon's classic volume, influenced by the work of Chester Barnard, is *Administrative Behavior*, first issued in 1947. In this book he advanced theoretical ideas which have come to influence the use of empirical methods in the study of administration. Throughout his career Herbert

Simon has been in the forefront in applying new techniques to the study of organizations. As one analyst has suggested, Simon capitalizes upon his "ability to break down the barriers of disciplines, to use the tools current in one discipline to attack problems in another . . . or to juxtapose two ways of looking at the same event."[1] He was also among the very first to demonstrate the utility of mathematics and computer science as analytical tools of the social sciences.

Herbert Simon completed his undergraduate and graduate work at the University of Chicago receiving his doctorate in 1943. He served as staff member of the International City Managers' Association and as director of Administrative Measurement Studies at the University of California, Berkeley. From 1942 to 1949 he was a faculty member of the Illinois Institute of Technology. Since 1949 he has been with Carnegie Institute of Technology where he is now Professor of Computer Science and Psychology in the Graduate School of Industrial Administration. He has been Chairman of the Board of Directors of the Social Science Research Council and consultant to many governmental agencies and corporations. He is the author of a large number of monographs, articles and study reports in a very wide range of behavioral disciplines.

---

[1] J. S. Coleman, Review of *Models of Man* in *American Journal of Sociology*, 63 (May, 1958), p. 674.

Notes on a General Theory of Administration

by Edward H. Litchfield

The article which follows introduced a unique new publication designed as an interdisciplinary medium for those scholars of administration interested in furthering its theoretical base. The journal was Administrative Science Quarterly. *Since that time it has come to occupy a strategic place in the annals of organization theory. The primary contribution of Litchfield's piece was to identify the parameters, and the underlying hypotheses and propositions of a theory derived as the basis for analysis of the process of administration in organizations of every type.*

Litchfield saw the lack of an adequate theory as hindrance both to the integration of knowledge developed in allied fields and to the orientation of thought about administration to a larger concept of social action. After laying the ground work by detailing the need for a preliminary working model, the author specifies a series of propositions as a tentative explanation of the basic elements which form the processes of administration. The work remains a significant challenge paper designed to serve as the basis for testing the constructs in the empirical world.

With the introduction of this *Quarterly* it is perhaps appropriate to review the state of our thinking about administration. In addition I hope that this essay will add several propositions which may bring us a little closer to a working theory of the nature of the administrative process. I do not believe we have such a theory today.

We would probably all agree that the years since World War II have seen an unprecedented increase in our knowledge of selected aspects of administration. There has been an acceleration of empirical investigation in the corporation, the government department, the hospital, the air wing, and other institutional settings. Likewise, there has been a tremendous growth in group dynamics and human relations research. Perhaps most important, the decade has seen either the introduction, or the first major unfolding, of operations research, game theory, cybernetics, and communication theory. Statistical theory and analysis and tremendous technological development in machine operation have provided new tools and new dimensions for decision-making activities. Spurred by the postwar growth of the behavioral sciences and assisted by a growing body of learning theory, both research worker and practitioner have given considerable attention to the individual's behavior in his role as an administrator.

These are contributions of far-reaching consequence, for they have not only added factual data which help in our understanding of administration, but they have also provided a conceptual depth which is urgently needed by a technically disposed profession supported by largely institutionally oriented academic disciplines. When fully absorbed and accepted in our thinking, the new materials will greatly assist administration's effort to achieve scientific stature. But beyond the substantive value of these individual contributions lie two further considerations of import both for practicing and academic members of the administrative profession.

First, it will be noted that most of the new thought has come from the fields of mathematics, engineering, anthropology, sociology, or some one of the emerging behavioral sciences. Relatively little has been contributed by academic students of administration per se, by practicing members of the profession, or by the disciplines of economics and political science. Members of cultures in which law is the dominant discipline in administration will observe that none of the new thinking has come from the legal profession. Second, it is equally apparent that these additions to our knowledge have been concerned with selected parts of administration and not with the whole. Indeed, for the most part, their contribution to administration was incidental to another purpose.

SOURCE: Reprinted from Edward H. Litchfield, "Notes on a General Theory of Administration," *Administrative Science Quarterly*, 1 (June, 1956), pp. 3-29, by permission of the publisher and the author.

Thus, game theory enriches our view of policy formulation, knowledge of the dynamics of group relations provides new insights for the exercise of authority, and learning theory offers new perspective for decision making, but none of these is concerned with the larger problem of the total administrative process.

The last decade saw another development of parallel significance for the field of administration. As other disciplines were illuminating selected portions of the administrative process, Talcott Parsons and others were elaborating at least the beginnings of a comprehensive theory of social action which might provide an over-all framework within which to develop a more specific theory of administration.[1] If Parsonian thought has not entirely satisfied administration's specialized needs, it must at least provoke us into the construction of a more acceptable framework.

Thus, it seems to me that we find ourselves at a critical juncture in our development. Associated disciplines are helping us to learn a great deal about portions of the subject of administration, while others are adumbrating concepts of the totality of action of which administration is a part. Flanked thus by singularly seminal movements, the question becomes, "What have we been doing to further our understanding of administration as a whole?" For, until we know the process and its setting, we can neither effectively integrate new materials others give us nor orient our process in a larger concept of social action.

The answer to this question is not particularly encouraging. During the decade, public administration, after a half-century's diversion by Frank J. Goodnow, has readmitted policy formulation to its concept of administrative functions. This is helpful even if in their zeal some may have swung into the position of that school of academic business administration which is unable to discern anything but policy in administration. Business administration has made a considerable effort to digest such new knowledges as grew from operations research, from statistical theory in decision making, and from the several other subjects already discussed. Hospital administrators are coming to understand that administration in the context of the hospital is neither exclusively housekeeping on the one hand nor deciding substantive medical issues on the other. Military administration probably has been the most self-conscious and thorough in re-examining both its theory and practice. To its self-appraisal we owe a large part of the more fundamental work whose results have now begun to spill over into other applied fields. If much of theoretical or methodological importance has occurred in educational administration, it has escaped our attention.

These have been significant developments. I do not minimize them. On the other hand, they have not told us much about the whole administrative process, its essential characteristics, its relationship to its environment, the way in which it becomes behavior, or its function in modern society. They are of a lesser order of magnitude than either the generic thought of Parsons or the more specific insights which others have given us of selected aspects of administration. Throughout the decade Herbert Simon's work was the only constant exception to this general disregard of the whole process and its behavioral implications.[2] Despite his real contributions, and occasional important additions from Alexander Leighton and others outside the profession of administration, we closed the ten-year period with little more by way of a comprehensive theory of administration than we had been given by Chester Barnard almost twenty years before.

CRITICISM OF EXISTING THOUGHT AND THEORY

If we are lacking in comprehensive theory, we do at least have some thought which we may examine. It is scattered from field to field, seldom internally consistent and often unarticulated. Viewed in aggregate, it has a number of inadequacies which hamper the growth of administration as a science. Let us begin with the simplest and most generally recognized. Our confusion of terminology makes it difficult to speak accurately to one another within any one field, let alone across fields and across cultures. Administration has an elevated meaning in some societies and a clerical connotation in others. "Management" and "administration" are thought of as interchangeable in much of the business world in this country but as quite distinct in much of public administration and in the military services.[3] Constitutional lawyers have distinguished between "administration" and "execution." "Decision making" and "policy formulation" may be used by one as synonymous and by another as discrete subjects. "Coordination" may either include, or specifically exclude, "control," and it may be either a process or a state of being. "Organization" is now a pattern for the distribution of authority, and again it becomes a total set of behavioral and value relationships. The consequence is that we are unable to speak precisely excepting in our own immediate circles where we have developed ephemeral professional dialects.

The second and, from my point of view, the most serious indictment which must be made of present thought is that it has failed to achieve a level of generalization enabling it to systematize and explain administrative phenomena which occur in related fields. Indeed, so far are we from broad generalizations about administration that we appear to maintain that there is not a generic administrative process but only a series of isolated types of administration. We seem to be saying that there is business administration and hospital administration and public administration; that there is military administration, hotel administration, and school administration. But there is no administration. We buttress this conclusion and make a general theory more difficult of attainment by developing separate schools in these fields in our universities. We organize ourselves into separate professional societies, and we have developed separate bodies of literature which speak to one another infrequently.

Let us examine this splintering in the context of a specific situation. The reader is visited by a medical friend who has just accepted his first administrative post as superintendent of a large hospital. His board is composed in part of businessmen who "want the institution run on a businesslike basis." Being municipally owned, the hospital must function in accordance with civil service regulations, central budget controls, and a variety of other public administration concepts and practices. The new superintendent is soon deluged with invitations to become a member of several specialized hospital administration societies and is urged to subscribe to specialized hospital administration literature. Hearing reference to "good management" and "sound administrative practice" on all sides, he turns to the reader, who is an administration expert, and asks for some reading material which will help him to understand what his severally oriented colleagues are talking about. What shall the reader tell him—that there is no such thing as administration, there is only business administration and public administration and hospital administration? Almost certainly each of us would support the view that the three had much in common and that he would find that eventually he could deal with all three in many of the same terms. But what shall we suggest that he read which will clearly describe this common ground in administration? Where will he find a statement of the content and the character of the administrative process? We will almost certainly be forced to give him materials in all three fields, along with some of the technical writings in specialized management fields such as finance and personnel, and then expect him to do his own synthesizing. If he is not satisfied, we will introduce him to Barnard, and if he still feels we haven't given him sufficient guidance, we will conclude with our ultimate bromide, "There is much of this that a man just has to learn for himself."

Actually our practice is years ahead of our thought. There is abundant evidence to demonstrate our unexpressed conviction that there is much that is common in administration. Here are a few illustrations of the point. The emerging concepts of human relations, communications, or operations research are as applicable to a hospital as they are to a bank. The constant movement of executive personnel from business to government, from the military forces into large business, from both government and business into education, is emphatic testimony supporting our conviction that knowledges and skills are transferable from field to field because of an essential universality in the administrative process itself. Again, it is a commonplace to observe that management consulting firms find their knowledges and skills applicable in the department store, on the one hand, and in the government bureau or the university, on the other. We are thus faced with the curious dichotomy of a practice which acknowledges common ground among applied fields of administration and of a body of thought which makes no effort to delineate areas of common interest. As theorists we have not yet established generalized concepts which keep pace with the facts of contemporary administration.

Third, if current thought fails to generalize the constants or universals in administration, it may also be criticized for its failure to accord a broad role to the variables in the administrative process. Thus, while we are prepared to insist that there are many applied types of administration, we seem to be saying that within any one field the process is relatively fixed. The often violent attack upon the "principles in administration" school of thought was a reaction against the view that in any single field administration must be regarded as a constant pattern of functions and activities. It is true that we have been influenced by social science research sufficiently to accommodate "the informal organization" and that under pressure of "good public relations" we have adapted administrative performance to some of the demands of the communities in which we find ourselves. It is also true that, in our unwillingness to seek broad generalizations about administration in all fields, we have admitted modifications in administration by insisting that the specialized situation of competition, or politics, or military necessity, and so on, made administration different in each of our fields. This admission is important in modifying our rigidity of thought in this particular connection even though we have found it stultifying in our attempts to develop conceptual generalization. In spite of all of these modifications in the type of absolutist administrative thought which reached its peak in the highly legalistic nineteenth-century public bureaucracies and in classical military management, we have not yet crossed an essential divide. That circumstances modify administrative activity we concede, but we must go further and affirm our view that administration is not only constant and universal in some respects but is also a variable in an equation of action; that one of its fundamental characteristics is its relationship to the other variables in that equation. Beyond this we must articulate those other variables so that we may understand their interrelationship. We must maintain that ultimate understanding of the administrative process comes only with an appreciation of the place of that process in a larger system of administrative action.

Fourth, I think it not unfair to say that our present thinking has a fractured quality about it. Communication theory may be good, budgetary concepts may be entirely sound, and it may be that we have a reasonably clear concept of how policies are formulated. These and the other parts of administration have concerned us more than the whole. We often regard these parts as discrete subjects. At best we regard them as sequential. POSDCORB,[4] like much earlier and later thought, was principally deficient in that it viewed administration more as a list of activities than as an organized arrangement of interdependent parts. I am not suggesting that we should know less about the constituent elements in the process. I am insisting that in addition to knowing the parts we must understand the attributes and characteristics of administration as a totality.

Finally, many of us have felt for a long time that such theory as we do have is set forth in terms which lend themselves neither to empirical verification nor to critical theoretical analysis. We urgently need our thought set forth in straightforward propositions which we may then establish, modify, or destroy as research or more careful analysis may dictate.[5] There is little prospect that the study of administration will ever approach scientific stature unless we are able to so articulate our thought.

NEED FOR A WORKING THEORY

This is not intended as an idle exercise in criticism. There are urgent reasons for the early development of at least a working theory of administration. Three are particularly compelling.

First, it is virtually impossible to codify our existing knowledge without some conceptual framework within which to do so. Theory is important for this purpose in any field of investigation, but it is crucially significant in an applied field which must ultimately draw together knowledges now scattered through all of the social and behavioral sciences and through the many applied areas of business, public, military, hospital, and educational administration. As a framework for the organization of materials, a working theory is equally needed by the management consultant, the teacher, the professionally conscious administrator, and the research worker.

Second, a comprehensive theory is needed as a guide to research. However tentative that theory may be, it should help to discern gaps in both existing knowledge and ongoing research and thus to further the design of other research efforts. It would also provide working hypotheses as guides to individual research efforts and as vehicles for the subsequent incorporation of research efforts into organized bodies of thought.

Finally, a tenable theory of administration could become an extremely useful guide to administrative behavior. The analytical and intellectually self-conscious practitioner will readily recognize the importance of a broad theoretical framework which he may use as a measure of his personal performance and which may provide a behavioral check list in his day-to-day undertakings. Educators who do not subscribe to the "either you are born with it or you aren't" school will also find it of primary importance in shaping curricula and in guiding potential administrators.

However urgent a general theory of administration may be, it is unlikely that it can be set forth in the near future. In the first place, there appear to be few among us whose current range of thought would meet the criticisms set forth here. Second, our knowledge is still extremely fragmentary. Thus, while we have been learning about small group dynamics, as David Truman has pointed out,[6] we still know very little about the dynamics of the large institutions in which administration comes to full bloom. We have a new understanding of the functions of choice in decision making, but we know very little about the psychological mechanisms involved in its exercise. We have given little if any systematic attention to the impact of a total culture upon administrative values, practices, and behavior. Cross-cultural data are even fewer. Even Kurt Lewin's "elements of construction" are difficult to evolve in the absence of definitions which have achieved even minimal acceptance.[7]

Certainly this essay does not pretend to present a general theory of administration. It will attempt to set forth a series of working hypotheses or propositions which may provide at least the beginnings of a framework for a general theory of administrative action. They will serve their purpose best if they are used as targets for future effort. That they will provoke criticism one would expect. That they may prompt more constructive thought is what I earnestly hope. They are by no means complete, they are often less specific than they should be, and they are frequently less precise than I would wish. But whatever their imperfections, I suggest the following propositions.

FIRST MAJOR PROPOSITION: *The administrative process is a cycle of action which includes the following specific activities:*

A. Decision making
B. Programming
C. Communicating
D. Controlling
E. Reappraising

This pattern of actions is found in various forms in all phases of administration. It occurs in policy areas; it is essential to personnel, finance, and other types of resources management; and it is to be found in the executive function as well. The specific activities and the cycle as a whole provide the mechanism by means of which all of the separate functions of administration are carried on. It is at once a large cycle which constitutes the administrative process as a totality and a series of small cycles which provide the means for the performance of specific functions and subfunctions and even for individual technical activities.

In an idealized form it occurs as a logical sequence in which there is a progression from the making of a decision to the interpretation of the decision in the form of specific programs, to the communication of that programmed decision, to the establishment of controls for the realization of the decision, and finally to a reappraisal of the decision as programmed, communicated, and controlled. In fact, however, the cycle often occurs in abbreviated form. Thus the practicalities of programming a decision may lead to immediate reappraisal, eliminating the steps of communication and control. Again, total group participation in decision making may eliminate much of communication. If individual steps are abbreviated or even eliminated, the cycle is nonetheless complete. In fact, the steps probably are there, even though in quite attenuated form.

Many such cycles are in action in the administrative process at any one time. One elaborate cycle may be proceeding at board of directors' level regarding fundamental objectives, while smaller and still sequential cycles may be going forward in finance and sales, and at the same time very immediate, specific, and perhaps abbreviated cyclical actions occur in the office or in the mind of a district sales manager concerned with a particular problem devoid of any policy, methodological, financial, or human relations significance. There is thus a series of wheels within wheels, tangent now at one point, now at another. The totality is administrative action, and the wheels are similar not in size but in the articulate and inarticulate uniformity of their components.

The grouping of these activities is made cyclical by the presence of the activity of reappraisal, for this brings the sequence back to substantially the point at which it began. Yet while it completes a full cycle the sequence does not necessarily lead again to identical action. If the original decision is precisely reaffirmed, the sequence of the five activities is no more than a revolution around a constant axis. However, if the original decision is modified in the light of evidence presented in the reappraisal, the axis may move and the circle take on a cycloidal form. With the passage of time and subsequent revolutions in the cycle, an extensive cycloidal pattern may develop.

Minor Proposition: *Decision making may be rational, deliberative, discretionary, purposive, or it may be irrational, habitual, obligatory, random, or any combination thereof. In its rational, deliberative, discretionary, and purposive form, it is performed by means of the following subactivities*:

    a. Definition of the issue
    b. Analysis of the existing situation
    c. Calculation and delineation of alternatives

d. Deliberation
e. Choice[8]

The sequence of activity from definition of issue to choice is again idealized. It presumes rationality and the existence of discretion. It contemplates the opportunity for deliberation, the possibility of calculating alternatives, and the existence of knowledge with which to estimate the situation. It is seldom that all of these factors are in fact present. Yet only if we view the pattern in its idealized form are we able to understand the nature of the parts as they occur individually or in combination.

Definition of the issue is the isolation both of problems (in the sense that a problem is a difficulty) and also of opportunities in which no difficulty is present. Thus it has both a corrective and creative aspect. A problem may require diagnosis, whereas an opportunity may be defined by research. In any event the function of issue definition is the clarification and description of the question at hand. Efficiency in subsequent steps in the cycle is obviously dependent upon the precision with which this first activity is undertaken.

Situation analysis involves a systematic effort to present facts regarding the existing situation where they may be known and estimates regarding that situation when facts are impossible to obtain. This must include a factual statement of prevalent values when those are part of the situation and relevant to subsequent choice. Many techniques assist the administrator in the performance of this activity. They include accounting, opinion surveys, market analyses, field testing of products, operations research, intelligence reports, and countless other similar analytical tools.

Alternative calculation involves two major steps: first, a systematic isolation and description of known alternative courses of action; and, second, a statement of the consequences of the alternatives where the latter are known. Where they are unknown, they must be estimated. These estimates will often themselves take the form of alternatives. In any event, this distinctive activity is concerned with known facts, assumed facts, and factual statement of values. Here we are assisted by such methods and techniques as economic forecasting, market projections, linear programming, and game theory.[9]

Deliberation is the next step. In it one is concerned with reviewing the issue in the light of what is known in the existing situation and with regard to the alternative courses of action which appear to be available. It involves an assessment of values, an appraisal of probabilities where chance alone is involved, and strategy where knowledge is imperfect. Deliberation approaches rationality as the values become explicit, as probabilities are analyzed, and as risk calculation can be reduced to a mathematical operation.

Having defined the issues, assembled and stated the facts regarding the existing situation, calculated and delineated the alternative courses of action with their known and estimated consequences, and reviewed all in terms of an explicit statement of ordered values, one is then prepared to choose. Choice under these circumstances is influenced by several considerations: first, free will or discretion and, second, the presence of rationality. Thus, a "wise choice" is apt to be one which the administrator had the discretion to make, had the rationality to base upon the known and estimated data at hand, and had the critical faculty to appraise in terms of the relative significance of those data.

In making choices, the administrator must understand that there is not always one right answer. Truth is frequently plural, and therefore the objective in the exercise of choice is rationality and not a pursuit of a nonexistent absolute. Failure to recognize both the plurality and relativity of correctness in decision making may lead to a time-losing indecision and a precarious mental health for those who must choose.

Actually few decisions are made by means of this full sequence of actions. The issue may be so patent as to make definition unnecessary. Often little effort is made to ascertain or estimate facts. Built-in biases frequently result in only the most superficial calculation of alternatives, and deliberation may be short-circuited by unspecified values or an unwillingness or inability to think in strategic terms. The elimination of certain of the steps may mean poor decisions, or again it may mean that specialized circumstances make one or more steps self-evident or unnecessary.

We must also recognize the extent to which decision making is influenced by limitations upon rationality. Simon has developed this at some length.[10] The administrator must not only allow for his own irrationality, he must also calculate the actions of others as being both rational and irrational. Thus, our decisions may be partly rational and partly irrational. To the extent that they are rational they must anticipate opponents' decisions which are also both irrational as well as rational. The character of calculated irrationality may be analyzed both by probability theory and by strategic calculation.

We may say much the same thing about the purposive-involuntary variable in decision making. Again, discretion in the selection of values and actual choice is circumscribed by community and professional standards and by prior decisions which may be part of tradition or which are passed down through the organization from higher levels. Likewise, factors of time modify deliberation and the opportunity both to analyze an existing situation fully and to calculate possible alternatives. Yet with all of its variables and modifiers, the progression from definition to choice is constant. Only the internal relationships among steps will vary.

Minor Proposition: *Decisions become guides to action after they have been interpreted in the form of specific programs.*

Decisions must be interpreted by specific programs which provide the direction for detailed operation. These might be called plans, were "planning" not a confused term which is sometimes used with reference to an "outline of alternatives," and in this sense is a part of decision making. Again, the term is used as synonymous with "programming" as the latter term is used here. One may therefore more accurately speak of planning alternatives (in the decision-making process) and of program planning as an activity designed to implement decisions. Program planning rests on a wide range of specific methods and techniques. These include capital budgets, operating budgets, manning tables, organization charts, tables of equipment, and a variety of similar means of translating a decision into specific programs for the allocation of money, manpower, authority, physical resources, and so on. The completeness of the program is a determining consideration in the effectiveness of the original decision.

Minor Proposition: *The effectiveness of a programmed decision will vary with the extent to which it is communicated to those of whom action is required.*

Communication follows the programming of decisions in cases in which those who must act have not participated in the original decision. Communication is a method by which an individual or group transmits stimuli which modify the behavior of another individual or group. While it is an activity employed in administration, it is obviously broader than the administrative process, for there is communication among individuals who have no administrative relationship to one another. We may therefore say that we are concerned here with the use of the method of communication for the restricted purposes of the administrative process.

Carl Hovland has focused our attention upon three aspects of communication: the stimuli (which he calls "cues"), the responses to the stimuli, and finally the laws and principles relating these two classes of events.[11] This threefold focus has applicability to communication as a method of administration. Let us examine each. We already give considerable attention to the stimuli in our analyses of the role of staff meetings, policy manuals, training sessions, annual reports, house organs, and similar communication media. We are learning to pay an increasing amount of attention to responses as a result of our increasing concern with employee motivations and morale. But most important is the relation of stimuli to response. Communication as a deliberate and purposive act of administration must determine whether it seeks a response which sets off patterns of behavior already well established or whether it seeks a response which is basically new. At this point administrative science must look to learning theory for assistance.

Communication in administration involves three primary responsibilities. First, the administrator must establish the channels, the methods, and the opportunities for communicating with all of those above, below, and around him whose actions he would influence. Second, he must establish channels and provide the opportunity for others to communicate with him. Third, he must assure the existence of channels of communication among all those in the organization who must influence one another if the organization is to achieve its total objectives. Each of these is a deliberate action which he must take. In two instances it is his responsibility to provide structure on the one hand and to utilize it on the other.

Minor Proposition: *Action required by a programmed and communicated decision is more nearly assured if standards of performance are established and enforced.*

Standard setting and enforcement may be more generally known as "control." Communication was concerned with stimuli which would call up desired responses, and control is concerned with a definition of the desired response and the methods of assuring its occurrence. In other words, control is an action which provides norms which will serve as a guide to the actors and against which to measure their actions. Both standard setting and enforcement are carried on by means of elaborate techniques of control. They may be techniques designed to control basic programs and operations, such as a budget, an organization chart, or a functional statement. Or they may be processive tools such as job standardization, wage and salary schedules, purchasing specifications, or cost and quality controls. All play essentially the same role in the action cycle.

A notable characteristic of control action is its tendency to become an end in itself. Thus we have the familiar phenomenon of the controller who seems more concerned with his accounting mechanisms than with the management purpose which they presumably exist to further. This often results from the fact that there is an internal element of completeness within the control activity. Having set a standard, reviewed performance in terms of the standard, and then enforced the standard, the person performing the action has, in a sense, completed a full and satisfying cycle. Standard enforcement in fact becomes standard realization and, hence, achievement. It is the only action in the cycle outside of decision making which has this organic unity about it which encourages its use as end rather than means.

While the subactions of control are standard setting and enforcement, the primary working methods are determined by the properties of the thing which is controlled. Thus control of people is achieved by means of a skillful manipulation of various types of rewards and punishments designed to appeal to the several motives of the groups and individuals concerned. Control of money comes with skillful manipulation of that resource in terms of its own laws of behavior.

Minor Proposition: *Decisions are based on facts, assumptions, and values which are subject to change. To retain their validity, decisions must therefore be reviewed and revised as rapidly as change occurs.*

A decision which has been programmed, communicated, and controlled has validity only for the limited period in which the facts, assumptions, and values upon which it was based have retained their original character. Only for such a period can the first four steps in the action cycle be regarded as static. In fact, not only are the facts, assumptions, and values in a state of constant flux, but the fact of decision in itself often brings substantial alteration in the total pattern of circumstance on the basis of which the decision was made. Hence a fully articulated decision—that is, one which has been made, programmed, communicated, and controlled—in itself brings about sufficient change to necessitate its own reconsideration. This is the activity of reappraisal.

Reappraisal is necessitated not only by change but by the possible imperfection of the original decision which time and circumstance may make apparent. New insights may be gained which improve the administrator's understanding of a more nearly correct decision, even though the facts themselves have not been altered. Here we return to a recognition of the plurality of truth as noted in our discussion of the decision-making activity. Thus we reappraise decisions because of our acceptance of the concepts of "contingent universe" and "organic incompleteness" which are implicit in cybernetic thought.[12]

Reappraisal may be accomplished in several ways. In its simplest form it is no more than a review of the original issue in terms of new data, new assumptions, new strategies, and new values which have bearing on the decision but which arise from extraneous sources. Thus, new information about Soviet military production may require the reappraisal of a foreign policy decision which had been based upon different fact assumptions. This may be referred to as a "feed-in" activity. Quite different is the process of "feedback," which is the essence of cybernetic theory. Here we contemplate the reappraisal of an original decision upon the basis of facts and values which have been generated by and as a result of the original decision. Reappraisal therefore provides for self-generated change and growth.

Whether the reappraisal be "feed-in," "feedback," or a combination, its function is the same. It is needed to complete the action cycle in order to make it dynamic rather than static. This is the action which induces change and growth. It must be specifically provided for in the action pattern if growth is to be accepted as both constant and necessary. Only through reappraisal can administration adjust to the constancy of evolution; otherwise the administrator is apt to pursue a concept of the permanent and absolute. This is a vehicle for incorporating into administration an understanding of stability through change rather than through an artificial staticity.

SECOND MAJOR PROPOSITION: *The administrative process functions in the areas of:*

    A. Policy B. Resources C. Execution

A "policy" is a definition of those objectives which guide the actions of a whole enterprise or a significant portion thereof. It is thus distinguished from the general term "decision," which may guide actions without reference to such objectives. The "resources" of administration are four: people, money, authority, and materials. "Execution" is a function of integration and synthesis which is intended to achieve a dynamic and total organism. All functional areas are requisite to the process. Execution divorced from policy is aimless. Similarly, the policy function tends to become remote and sterile unless associated with resources and execution.

Minor Proposition: *Action in each functional area is accomplished by means of the action cycle previously described.*

The policy function is conventionally referred to as "policy making" or "policy formulation." In fact it is far more. Policies are not only made, they are also programmed, communicated, controlled, and reappraised. It is only in this total sweep of the action cycle that the policy function has full meaning and is satisfactorily distinguished from the activity of decision making.

The action cycle is also the vehicle for the accomplishment of the resources function. In determining the need for money or people, the administrator defines his problem, estimates his situation, calculates his alternatives, makes a choice, and thus in fact makes a decision. In allocating personnel by manning tables, authority by functional statements or charts, or money by budgets, he is in fact programming his decision. Direction of personnel is communication. Organization charts and manuals, budgets and inventories, are forms of control of money, authority, and materials. The final step of reappraisal is provided for in budget analysis and revision and in a whole series of other resource function techniques.

The action cycle is repeated in the executive function. Setting the policies and resources in motion, synthesizing their conflicting values and tendencies, and integrating the resulting management are achieved by a constant series of cyclical movements from decision to reappraisal to new decision and further reappraisal. Maintaining them in dynamic equilibrium is realized in the same way.

Minor Proposition: *Each function seeks a value which when realized is its contribution to the administrative process.*

Policy seeks purposive direction for the enterprise. The resource function seeks economy both in the sense of productivity and of frugality. Execution seeks and is evaluated by the degree to which it achieves a state of dynamic coordination.

These are the contributions of the three functional areas. Together they constitute an organism whose direction is purposive and whose resources are productively and frugally employed.

Minor Proposition: *Each function has distinctive characteristics which govern the application of the cycle to it.*

We have observed that policies involve questions of value and fact. Values are plural and facts are contingent. As a consequence the action cycle employed in the policy function is modified. The four resources have different characteristics. People are moved by varying combinations of rewards and punishments. Money is moved by factors of scarcity. Authority has properties which influence the way in which it may be allocated and exercised. The executive function achieves synthesis and maintains a dynamic organism by observing the laws of equilibrium and decay whether they be drawn from modern group dynamics or are as remote as Henri Bergson's "law of twofold frenzy."[13] In each case, the cycle is constant, but it is performed in the context of a function which responds to its specialized properties.

Minor Proposition: *The functional areas of administration are integrally related to one another.*

We have already observed that each of the functions is requisite to the total process. It is equally true that the areas are integrally related to one another. Obviously policy is the major determinant of the character of the resource and executive functions, but it is also true that resources are important determinants of policy and that execution may be either the realization or destruction of policy. Administrative behavior must be calculated to recognize that a new policy has immediate implications for authority, finance, and personnel. One follows the other automatically. No one can be isolated from the other, for they are in fact a continuum of reciprocating parts.

THIRD MAJOR PROPOSITION: *The administrative process is carried on in the context of a larger action system, the dimensions of which are:*[14]

    A. The administrative process
    B. The individual performing the administrative process
    C. The total enterprise within which the individual performs the process
    D. The ecology within which the individual and the enterprise function.

Each of these dimensions has both constant properties and variables. We have examined the constants of the administrative process and must now note its variables. Likewise, we must observe the way in which these dimensions are related. In fact, the process which we have examined in the abstract becomes a real thing only in the hands of the persons performing it and in the context of specific total organizations and, in particular, total environments. These three dimensions affect the administrative process by altering its variables. It in turn alters each of them in its impact upon their variables. We thus have a concept of a system containing four dimensions, each of which has a structure comprising a number of variables which interact upon one another.

Furthermore, the other dimensions have no constant impact on the administrative process. At one point the impact of the individual administrator may be decisive and at another time relatively inconsequential. Thus in a highly articulated bureaucracy, the variations among administrators will affect the way in which the process is performed to lesser extent than in a new organization which has been less rigidly structured. In other words, there are not only variables within each dimension but there is variation in the relative roles among the dimensions in this total action system.

There are significant parallels between this proposition and the broad aspects of Parsons' theory of action.[15] He postulates three systems of action —personality, social, and culture. He further maintains that these are "reciprocally interrelated" and suggests the existence of "roles" within systems. His personality system corresponds to the dimension of the individual as an administrator. His cultural system is quite similar to the concept of the total ecological setting. Our administrative process and the total enterprise dimensions probably assume the status of "roles" in his social system. Our thinking finds further parallels in his article in this issue of the *Administrative Science Quarterly*.

Minor Proposition: *While constant in basic structure, the administrative process will vary in important aspects, depending upon the personality of the person performing it.*

The cycle of administrative action and the functions of the administrative process are constants regardless of who performs them. The manner in which the actions are taken and the functions are accomplished, however, will vary with the characteristics of the individual. These variations in manner are as important as the constancy in structure. The self-contained administrator may deliberate alone, while the new and uncertain executive may take elaborate counsel. Deliberation is present in both cases, but the methods of its exercise are importantly different. Or, in estimating the existing situation, a Wilson may collect his own facts, whereas an Eisenhower will assemble information by means of an elaborate staff organization. Different individual administrators have radically different effects upon the whole organization. Authority as a resource may be delegated to many by a generalist, or to a few by a specialist. As a consequence the authority structure will be flat in one case and pyramided in the other. The consequences of these varying ways in which two types of personalities allocate authority are far reaching, but the resource function has nevertheless been satisfied.

Bureaucracy seeks to minimize the impact of these variables among personalities through the use of standardizing practices which will offset personality differences. For example, a military staff study requires concurrence among all units in the organization which may be affected by the proposal which the staff study contains. This assures a widespread participation in decision making and thus offsets the variation between officer X, who may realize the importance of participation, and officer Y, whose tendencies are to proceed unilaterally.

Minor Proposition: *While constant in basic structure, the administrative process will vary in important respects, depending upon the character of the total enterprise within which it is performed.*

The way in which the administrative process is performed will vary with the character of the organization. One-man decision making in a academic atmosphere is less likely than in a family-owned manufacturing organization, yet there is decision making in both cases. Reappraisal may be infrequent in a conservative British textile firm but constant in a young and aggressive corporation like General Dynamics.

The administrator communicates in a different way in an organization with a well-developed, informal structure than he does in an enterprise which has a high turnover rate and which is composed of persons whose backgrounds and associations are quite diverse. Yet the communication activity is there; only the ways of its exercise and the degree of its effectiveness will change. The impersonality of social relations which increases as an organization grows in size and complexity presents problems in communication unknown in simpler organizations. Standard setting (control) is one thing in an organization without internal social cohesion and quite another in Hawthorne's Bank Wiring room.[16]

In one sense the administration profession has overemphasized the impact of the total enterprise upon the administrative process. Here I am referring to the insistence that the fields of business, government, hospital, or the military administration are all discrete subjects. Yet the true meaning of difference escapes us unless we first isolate the constant properties or universal characteristics of administration. Our point here is that the study of difference occasioned by enterprise variations is necessary, but only following a prior understanding of the constants in this process.

Minor Proposition: *While constant in basic structure, the administrative process will vary in important respects depending upon the environment in which the individual and total enterprise function.*

The administrative process will also vary with the physical, cultural, and technological environment within which it is performed. Communication is obviously influenced by a changing technology which eliminates much of the significance of distance. It is similarly influenced by conversational practice resulting from social systems of rank and class. Effectiveness of the control activity may depend upon the financial and psychological resources which the community provides as alternatives to acceptance of a distasteful standard of working norms. Indonesian understanding of "the good neighbor" raises problems in limiting supervisory spans which are missing in societies where efficiency means more and neighborliness less. Controls which may be imposed and forced in one atmosphere may be vitiated by the existence of community or professional standards or values which preclude the individual's accepting the control provided by administration. Part of the theory of the Nürnberg trials is closely related to this.

Minor Proposition: *The types of relationships existing among the three dimensions other than the administrative have an effect upon the administrative process.*

My colleague, James Thompson, has suggested that "there appear to be four major types of relationships which an enterprise may have with organized elements of environment."[17] He notes competition, bargaining, cooptation, and coalition as the primary types of relationships between the dimension of the whole enterprise and the dimension of the environment. He then points out that these relationships between two dimensions have important bearing on the decision-making activity, for they alter the way in which it is carried on and vary the number of the participants therein. Thus the relationships between two dimensions have caused variation in the third, the administrative process. It would appear probable that we may generalize beyond this and say that there are definable relationships among each of the three non-administrative dimensions and that the variations among those relationships will have consequent bearing upon the administrative process itself.

In this major proposition we have thus been concerned with three different considerations. In the first place, we have noted the way in which variations in any one of the three dimensions directly affect the administrative process. Second, we have noted the way in which variations in the total combination of the three will affect the administrative process. Finally, it has been pointed out that varying relationships between any two (other than the administrative process dimension) will have corresponding variable effects upon the process per se.

FOURTH MAJOR PROPOSITION: *Administration is the performance of the administrative process by an individual or a group in the context of an enterprise functioning in its environment.*

The administrative process is a series of interdependent steps which may be isolated and described in the abstract. Administration, on the other hand, is the performance of the process in the specific contexts of enterprise and environment. As such it is primarily behavior, though in other times and cultures it may have been thought of as largely law.

We have already observed that the parts of the action cycle are reciprocally influential, that the functions performed by the administrative process are integrally related to one another. They suggest an interdependence which is increased once the interdimensional influences have been introduced.

This complex of interrelationships probably constitutes a whole, though it is not yet clear whether this entity can be referred to as a "system" with all of the "organic" implications of that term as it is used in the life sciences.[18] There would, however, appear to be a totality in administration (not in the administrative process) which is significant.

Minor Proposition: *Administration as a totality has definable attributes. They are:*

    a. *It seeks to perpetuate itself.* As a definable complex, administration has many of the characteristics of other total organizations. Like them, its first attribute is its tendency to perpetuate itself.

    b. *It seeks to preserve its internal well-being.* It is sufficiently self-conscious to attempt to protect itself against disruption from within or destruction from without. It is therefore concerned with its own internal workings and the morale and welfare of its participants.

    c. *It seeks to preserve itself vis-à-vis others.* Each individual behavior pattern composing a complete administrative process maintains a competitive relationship with other behavior patterns constituting other processes.

    d. *It seeks growth.* Like all other organisms, it is aware of the fact that it cannot stand still for long but must go either forward or backward. In its dynamic phases, therefore, it normally seeks to grow. Much of the impetus for mergers, for "empire building," and for entrepreneurial effort in general is made not only on behalf of the corporation, or the bureau, or the institution, but also on behalf of a separate and identifiable administration.

Minor Proposition: *The attributes of the totality of administration have significant effects upon administrative behavior.*

These attributes of totality are really properties of organic compulsion and as such are compulsive as far as behavior is concerned. Thus, the successful administrator seeks internal cohesion among the members of the administrative group. He seeks to keep his group intact. He presses for individual identification with the total process. He stresses competition as a means of preserving his "administration's" relationship to others. In short, he performs in such a way as to attempt to perpetuate the process, maintain its internal well-being, preserve its position among competitors, and, indeed, to help it grow.

FIFTH MAJOR PROPOSITION: *Administration and the administrative process occur in substantially the same generalized form in industrial, commercial, civil, educational, military, and hospital organizations.*

The concept of the universality of administration and of the administrative process has been implicit in much which has been set forth above. It must now be made explicit as a separate proposition. This is particularly important both for the classification of existing knowledge and as a hypothesis for subsequent investigation.

The cyclical development of administrative action, beginning with decision making and moving through reappraisal, occurs in all types of organizations. Similarly, each of them is served by administration through the accomplishment of the same basic functions in the areas of policy, resources, and execution. Again, the process is no less organic in a hospital than it is in a manufacturing establishment. Finally, the process is but a portion of a larger action system, whether that system occurs in the Department of the Interior or in General Motors. The process becomes a whole as administration when performed by an individual within an enterprise functioning in its own ecological setting.

In every case, there is a constancy in fundamental properties. The differences which exist from one field of application to another are differences which result from the factors suggested in our discussion of the four dimensions constituting action. These are the fundamental differences; the variations in institutional application are derivative. When thus analyzed, however, these more fundamental differences are seen to be but variations in the way in which a constant process is performed or accomplished. They do not argue against a basic universality.

CONCLUSION

These propositions are far from complete, are seldom as precise as they should be, and doubtlessly are but partially correct. Whatever their inadequacies, my intention has been to frame the propositions in such a way as to meet the criticisms of existing administrative thought which were made earlier in this paper. Specifically, I have sought generalizations broad enough to encompass phenomena in several applied fields. The propositions have been calculated to view the whole administrative process and the whole of administration rather than any one or less-than-whole combination of its parts. I have attempted to relate the process and administration to larger concepts of action systems. Finally, the propositions themselves have been stated in terms which it is hoped will make it possible to test them both empirically and in subsequent analysis. At best they are notes looking in the direction of broad theory.

FOOTNOTES

[1] Talcott Parsons and Edward A. Shils, eds., *Toward a General Theory of Action* (Cambridge, Mass., 1951).

[2] Herbert A. Simon, *Administrative Behavior* (New York, 1947). Other articles by Simon include: Staff and Management Controls, *Annals of the American Academy of Political and Social Sciences*, vol. 292 (March 1954), and A Comparison of Organization Theories, *Review of Economic Studies*, vol. 20(1), no. 51 (1952-1953).

[3] During the thirties the term "administrative management" was introduced. It meant everything and nothing. After years of usage in public administration it found its way into business and educational organizations by way of consulting firms working in all of these fields.

[4] Luther Gulick and L. Urwick, eds., *Papers on the Science of Administration* (New York, 1937).

[5] Such propositions are well illustrated in Alexander H. Leighton's volume, *The Governing of Men* (Princeton, N.J., 1945).

[6] David B. Truman, "The Impact on Political Science of the Revolution in the Behavioral Sciences," in *Research Frontiers in Politics and Government* (Washington, D.C., 1955).

[7] Kurt Lewin, *Field Theory in Social Science* (New York, 1951).

[8] For a parallel analysis, see Peter Drucker, *The Practice of Management* (New York, 1954), ch. xxviii.

[9] For game theory, see J. von Neumann and Oskar Morgenstern, *Theory of Games and Economic Behavior* (Princeton, N. J., 1944); Martin Shubik, *Readings in Game Theory and Political Theory* (Garden City, N. Y., 1954); J. D. Williams, *The Compleat Strategyst* (New York, 1954); and J. C. C. McKinsey, *Introduction to the Theory of Games* (New York, 1952). Linear programming is well set out in A. Charnes, W. W. Cooper, and A. Henderson, *An Introduction to Linear Programming* (New York, 1953).

[10] Simon, *Administrative Behavior*, ch. iv.

[11] Carl Hovland, "Psychology of the Communication Process," in Wilbur Schramm, ed., *Communications in Modern Society* (Urbana, Ill., 1948), p. 59.

[12] See Norbert Wiener, *The Human Use of Human Beings* (Boston, Mass., 1950).

[13] Henri Bergson, *The Two Sources of Morality and Religion* (Garden City, N. Y., 1954).

[14] Here the term "dimension" refers to a category of variables.

[15] Parsons and Shils, *op. cit.*

[16] F. J. Roethlisberger and William J. Dickson, *Management and the Worker* (Cambridge, Mass., 1939).

[17] "Administrative Process Working Papers" (unpublished Cornell manuscript, Dec. 31, 1955).

[18] See Walter B. Cannon, *The Wisdom of the Body* (New York, 1932); Joseph Needham, *Order and Life* (New Haven, Conn., 1936); and Sir Charles Sherrington, *Man on His Nature* (Garden City, N. Y., 1953).

ABOUT THE AUTHOR—Edward H. Litchfield demonstrated the application of the universality of the administrative process through his own successive management of organizations engaged in corporate, academic, governmental, and military affairs. He was most often in the public eye during his controversial tenure as Chancellor of the University of Pittsburgh. In 1955 he went to Pittsburgh with a mandate to make it "one of the world's foremost universities." His efforts were bold, rapid, and frequently very costly. They resulted in a highly enthusiastic student body, a faculty divided between those strongly pro, tending to be the newer elements on the Pittsburgh scene, and those anti. The financial problems of the institution proved ultimately to be insurmountable but the reforms which Litchfield initiated including a reduction in the number of students-to-faculty ratio, marked improvements in faculty salaries and a significantly increased proportion of faculty members having advanced degrees and reputations of stature, made a decisive impact upon the quality of the institution. Litchfield was Chairman of the Board of SCM Corporation until his death in March, 1968.

In his earlier career Edward Litchfield served as deputy director of the Michigan Civil Service Commission and as lecturer at the University of Michigan. His federal service, from 1946 to 1949 took him to Moscow, Germany and London as American representative. He returned to the academic world as professor of administration and later Dean of the Graduate School of Public Administration at Cornell (1950-1955) while also serving as President of the Governmental Affairs Institute, and from 1956 board chairman. He held important posts in the corporate world, serving as a board member of a number of prominent national corporations, and he was awarded a number of honorary degrees. He was also executive director of the American Political Science Association. Litchfield's doctorate in political science was received from Michigan in 1940. Among his more important publications were *Voting Behavior* (1940), and *Governing Post War Germany* (1953).

Development of Administration in Library Service

by Paul Wasserman

The following piece took stock of the state of administration in librarianship a decade ago. Its inclusion here forces a brief reassessment of progress during the intervening period. While the library survey may be even more pervasive now than then, this practice has yet to afford significant insight into issues applicable generally to situations outside the framework of the institution studied. The teaching of administration in library education appears to be very little advanced beyond the elemental level of a decade ago; the administrative process is still misunderstood, unknown or ignored. A continuing proliferation of courses on administration of special types of library provides ample testimony to this unchanged situation. The literature of library administration remains basically uninfluenced by transfer of insights developed in more advanced disciplines studying administration. It is only in the technical sphere where important progress has been made. This has begun to influence a pronounced variation in educational preparation for librarianship both within the framework of the traditional setting as well as in centers developing outside the field. This factor aside, the focus upon administration as a field of serious study in librarianship remains underdeveloped. Developments viewed as promising in 1956 have yet to advance along the optimistic lines then identified. There is still hope that with the increased availability of research support, progress will be made. But the weight of evidence of the last ten years provides the field with little cause for self-congratulation. In important measure, the present volume is designed to be another attempt to improve sophistication about management and managerial issues within librarianship.

This article attempts to assess the point to which management of libraries has progressed, to draw parallels with related fields, and to point out avenues which appear most promising for furthering development of management theory and practice in the library field. One distinct limitation of present-day thinking about management or administration is that there has not yet been developed a standard or universally accepted terminology covering managerial activity. To avoid confusion over semantics, the terms administration and management will be used interchangeably; what is meant here is that group of executive functions commonly associated with the management or administration of any organizational enterprise.

In 1900, libraries were small compared to their modern counterparts, librarianship was fundamentally a custodial function, and the techniques of management were relatively simple. Public library clienteles were small and highly literate, and consequent demands upon librarians were modest.

College libraries were designed primarily to serve the faculty and only incidentally the students, and the duties of the librarian were frequently absorbed by any available professor. As libraries grew in size, methods were devised locally to organize and preserve the collections, and these techniques were passed on to apprentices or other library workers through individual or class instruction. Early in the century the principal attributes necessary for the library administrator were scholarly attainment and local library experience.

If there are serious questions about the magnitude to which management functions in large public and research libraries have grown in the last half century, Tables I and II, which detail the growth of selected public and university libraries respectively, should help to dispel them. Enormous advances have been made in the scale of financial appropriations, in the size of library book stocks, and in the number of employees needed to render these collections useful. One inevitable by-

---

SOURCE: Reprinted from Paul Wasserman, "Development of Administration in Library Service: Current Status and Future Prospects," *College and Research Libraries*, 19 (July, 1958), pp. 283–294, by permission of the Association of College and Research Libraries.

TABLE I
Statistics of Public Libraries

LIBRARY	OPERATING EXPENDITURES 1900[1]	OPERATING EXPENDITURES 1955[2]	NUMBER OF BOOKS 1900[1]	NUMBER OF BOOKS 1955[2]	ALL STAFF 1921[4]	ALL STAFF 1956[5]
BOSTON	$302,457	$3,222,637	772,432	2,085,660		740
CLEVELAND	72,943	4,270,787	165,868	2,819,142	529	896
CHICAGO	272,790	4,777,672	258,498	2,294,369	453	1,204
MINNEAPOLIS	61,295	1,651,351	114,000	960,040	168	354
ST. LOUIS	78,225	1,453,043	135,000	1,066,339	230	340

TABLE II
Statistics of University Libraries

LIBRARY	OPERATING EXPENDITURES 1900[1]	OPERATING EXPENDITURES 1955[3]	NUMBER OF BOOKS 1900[1]	NUMBER OF BOOKS 1955[3]	ALL STAFF 1920–21[6]	ALL STAFF 1955[3]
COLUMBIA		$1,288,145	295,000	2,116,641	62	312
CHICAGO		718,066	329,778	1.911.111	93	121
ILLINOIS	$ 1,495	1,443,114	42,314	2,888,557	51	245
CALIFORNIA (BERKELEY)	12,940	2,015,520	79,417	2,063,082	28	309
HARVARD	78,820	2,034,163	560,000	5,955,766	65[4]	376
YALE	34,500	1,061,116	285,000	4,280,473	43	233

[1] U. S. Education Bureau, *Report,* I (1900), 923–1165.
[2] U. S. Office of Education, *Circular No. 471,* "Statistics of Public Libraries in Cities With Population of 100,000 or More: Fiscal Year 1955."
[3] *CRL,* XVII (1956), 58–65.
[4] American Library Association, *Bulletin,* XVI (1922), 426–451.
[5] Enoch Pratt Free Library, *Salary Statistics for Large Public Libraries,* 1956.
[6] Princeton University Library, *College and University Library Statistics,* 1919/20 *to* 1943/44. 1947.

product of such a growth pattern has been the development of the host of administrative problems which are a function of large and complex organizations. A crucial question is the degree of understanding of the major issues of organizational management among library administrators and how well this understanding and the skills and insights which grow out of it have kept pace with the rapidly increasing size of library operations.

REVIEW OF THE LITERATURE

In a survey made for the ACRL College Libraries Section in December, 1949, sixty-three libraries from twenty-nine states replied to a questionnaire which listed areas considered most to require research investigation in the college library field. Administration ranked first in frequency of response and greatly outranked all other issues.[1] Yet, while there is almost universal agreement that one of the critical needs is better understanding of management, there has been a paucity of serious analyses of this question. Careful scrutiny of library literature over the last thirty years reveals few significant contributions. Brief review of some of these may aid in understanding the present level of thinking.

In 1930, Donald Coney suggested some applications of scientific management to libraries.[2] This early effort classified library functions in management terms and discussed proposed methods for improving objectives in large research libraries, production problems, the functionalization of work, the standardization of methods, and efficiency in the use of personnel. However, twenty-two years later, in an article on management advances, the same author concludes by saying, "There is a regrettable lack of firsthand acquaintance with management literature, and of orientation in the management field, on the part of library administrators and those who write on library management. Much of librarians' writing on this subject is more descriptive than analytical, and often, more naive than sophisticated. There is a real lack of bridging literature, that is, articles that relate the concepts and practices of professional management literature to library situations. There is probably a need for some means of directing librarians to those parts of management writing that have applicability to library work."[3]

In what is probably the most advanced treatment yet attempted, Paul Howard delineates key elements of administrative theory and applies these principles to library situations in an effort to develop a theoretical framework for management functions as applied to libraries.[4] Howard describes and illustrates library applications of the following functions of administration: directing, ordering, supervising, controlling, organizing, evaluating, and representing. Two of his conclusions are noteworthy: "A knowledge of the true functions of library management should enable the library profession to select candidates for managerial positions much more accurately than is possible at the present time" and "It should be possible to work from this [framework], or similar basis, toward the formulation of a comprehensive and definitive theory of library management."[5] Since 1940, no major advances in the theory of library administration have been made beyond the introductory propositions advanced by Howard.

In sharp contrast with other professions, no book or monograph has yet been written which attempts to evolve and apply a theoretical framework as a tool for achieving a better understanding of library administration. A few books have appeared; several are even distinctive and definitive works, which treat the organization and problems of particular types of libraries—public, college, university, or special. The characteristics which all these volumes share is the great degree of concern with descriptive detail and not theory, the concentration upon the distinctive institutional problems and the operating features of the type of library treated, the great emphasis upon method and technique, and the unconcern with principles which may be common in the administration of any large library effort, regardless of type.

It would be unfair, of course, to exclude from all mention the important work which was done from the mid-1930's into the 1940's at the University of Chicago where a concerted effort was made to link the study of library administration to that of public administration. This work culminated in significant volumes such as Carleton Joeckel's *Government of the American Public Library* (1935) and Arnold Miles and Lowell Martin's *Public Administration and the Library* (1941), and in the academic preparation of some of the leading administrative practitioners which the library field has developed. The fundamental orientation of this movement, however, was institutional, and the theoretical bases were never fully developed. Cognizance must also be given to the specialized materials which have been developed to aid the library administrator in approaching the technical problems of administration with sharper and more effective tools. Perhaps the most important effort of this type was Emma Baldwin and William Marcus's *Library Costs and Budgets; A Study of Cost Accounting in Public Libraries* (1941).

The large mass of material published in the professional journals of librarianship dealing with management issues can best be characterized as a type of latter-day folklore. There is a plethora of how-we-do-it articles which describe particular techniques employed by individual libraries, with the presumption that methods which work (or seem to work) one place are sound operating principles to guide action elsewhere. The literature is deficient in contributions which attempt to theorize and very little can be generalized when the preponderance of published offerings are accounts of noncumulative, isolated experiences. Virtually no writing has attempted to distill from a study of administrative practices in a number of institutions a set of hypotheses which might provide a framework for understanding common situations in different settings.

The promise which Carleton Joeckel held out for advancement of administration in 1938, "[Library administration] is new in the sense that the close and scientific study of library administration as a subject worthy of consideration in itself is only in its beginnings,"[6] has not been fulfilled.

CURRENT ORIENTATIONS TO ADMINISTRATION

One relatively widespread phenomenon which suggests that library management in many institutions is being subjected to increased scrutiny, is the library survey. This device (broadly analogous to the use of management consulting firms in industry and government), attempts to focus detached professional thinking upon the administrative issues facing the library under surveillance. In a perceptive, but perhaps too-gentle critique, Ralph Shaw characterizes the historical evolution of the library survey through three phases: The first period controlled by "macromanagement" experts, broad guaged administrative generalists;

the second phase given over to the "micromanagement" specialists, expert in the technical library functions; and the present stage, in which a first-rate survey team is directed by a broadly oriented management generalist, aided by a crew of specialists who function as staff assistants to the survey director.[7] Even if we accept Shaw's judgment, while incidence of the use of the library survey appears to be increasing, there is no indication that this device is adding appreciably to the total understanding of library administration. That is not to say that individual surveys may not be extremely valuable to the institutions under investigation. Such studies frequently do provide the means for obtaining keen diagnosis of problems and equally penetrating proposals for the solution of problems. Unfortunately, however, each survey situation is an isolated entity, detached and disassociated from other comparable operations. A large number of library surveys have been published, a corps of survey experts has been developed, but out of this phenomenon has come no new understanding or insights, no distillation of administrative principles, no accretions to the knowledge of the controllable or uncontrollable variables of the administrative process in the library organization. There has not been one significant comparative analysis of administrative issues growing out of these efforts.

Another characteristic of present day thinking about library administration is the prevalence of sharply different points of view and attitudes toward what are the most effective means for advancing understanding and practice of management in libraries. One position is enunciated most clearly by the documentalist school. This group, identified largely with Dean Jesse H. Shera and the Western Reserve School of Library Science Center for Documentation and Communication Research, energetically attempts to apply to librarianship the skills and techniques of the basic and applied sciences. For this group, the most crucial issues facing library administration are the technical problems, and primary concern is centered upon the development of effective devices for the retrieval of information.

At another pole is the faction whose position is most clearly articulated by Lawrence Clark Powell who suggests that "To administer libraries calls for gifts of the mind and the spirit" and, almost as an afterthought, "as well as theoretical knowledge of management and a knack for gimmicks and gadgets."[8] In describing a proposed program in library education, his primary concern is with a "rededication to the simple facts of library life."[9] This, in essence, is the position of the humanist who sees the library administrator as scholar and bookman, with management only a minor function which he performs as an aside, and, presumably, intuitively.

TRAINING FOR LIBRARY ADMINISTRATION

The most penetrating discussion of educational preparation for administration in libraries was contributed by Martin in 1945.[10] He characterizes courses in administration offered in library schools as susceptible of three different levels of presentation. The first type treats material under the general rubric of administration which is not covered elsewhere in the curriculum—book charging systems, order routines, statistical records, preparation and care of materials, etc. The second kind considers the "elements of management"—those topics or problems with which a library administrator deals on a day-to-day basis. This type of presentation is exemplified by a concern with such issues as buildings and equipment. Martin then advocates that such courses be advanced to a third level and centered around what he terms the "administrative process." While he, unfortunately, presents little amplification of the details and content of such a course, the implications are that the material considered would be of a theoretical as well as applied nature. Martin's first level is not administration at all. His second level covers actual operational functions and their control, rather than administration. It is only his proposed third level which would seriously concern itself with a different order of performance—the functions of the executive in management— as contrasted with the functions of library operations.

Interestingly enough, while Martin's analysis was published a dozen years ago, since which time professional education has swung almost exclusively from the undergraduate to the graduate level and in the process undergone a decided reorientation of values and emphases, a review of present-day courses reveals only a few instances of major modifications in the content of the formal courses in administration toward an administrative process orientation.

The remarks which follow are based upon written communications with every ALA accredited library school and an analysis of the syllabi, outlines, and reading lists used by these programs in their courses in administration. Out of a total of thirty-six inquiries, replies were received from twenty-five schools. Of this number, only eighteen had made available their materials in time to be considered in this study. Several schools were not willing to provide details of their courses; others indicated that the administration courses were being revised and that new materials were not yet available. However, every school of major national reputation did comply in full or in part, and is, therefore, represented in the conclusions drawn. Admittedly, it is difficult to assess the level of instruction exactly and fairly, based solely upon examination of outlines and reading lists without the complementary insights gained from personal interviews with the instructors. Systematic analysis of the materials at hand leads to the following conclusions.

Only three of the eighteen schools responding approach the teaching of administration from the standpoint of an "administrative process." In each of these three instances, there are clear indications that a conscious attempt is being made to study library administration as a substantive area and to distinguish administration from a preoccupation with the techniques and methods of the production and service functions of libraries.

Seven schools are apparently treating administration in exactly the same way which Martin characterized as the first level of instruction and continue to offer courses covering materials and subjects which are not considered elsewhere in the curriculum. The other eight schools provide courses which appear to fit the description of Martin's second category, in which administration is equated with concern for physical plant, legal foundation, financial control, etc.

Certain other attributes of courses in library administration are worth noting here. In nearly every program there are specialized courses in the administration of distinctive types of libraries. Either these faculties believe the process of administration varies in different types of libraries, or these are not courses in administration, but treatments of the problems or functions of public, college, university, or special libraries.

Reading lists in administration courses draw most heavily from the library literature. While there is occasional reference to, or assignment in, the broader management literature of business administration, public administration, or administrative behavior, this is uncommon. If the thesis advanced earlier that library literature is poor in substantive contributions toward understanding of administration is correct, the student suffers from an inappropriate intellectual diet.

One almost universal characteristic of the course or courses in administration (based upon a review of the catalogs of the schools) is their elective feature. A survey of the work of practicing librarians would doubtless reveal that many exercise control over, and responsibility for, the work of others. The degree of responsibility would vary widely, between one extreme of supervision of one or two clerical assistants to that of the highest management post in a large organization. An understanding of administration would appear to be equally relevant as part of the professional equipment of every librarian, including specialists in research, reference, and cataloging, who, while not directly concerned with administrative performance, need to understand the theory and framework of administration if only to appreciate their roles in the total organization in which they function, and their own relationship to it.

The central theme of this paper is not education for librarianship. But in its concern with key issues of present-day library administration, some general judgments must be made about the caliber, extent, and effectiveness of academic preparation. Library administration, as it is practiced, and even more particularly, as it is taught, is not a model of intellectual refinement. It does not have a clearly defined, well-organized body of subject knowledge. Its subject knowledge has no simple, or even complex, theoretical basis or structure. Its literature is a motley of descriptive treatment of operating methods used in individual, varied settings. The content of most of the courses appears to describe practices and to make general recommendations for what are presumed to be successful techniques. Where it might, and perhaps should, improve itself by borrowing heavily from many diverse disciplines such as business, law, economics, political science, and education, it does not, or does not very often.

Underlying the issue of education for administration is the question of who is best equipped to teach the courses. Powell makes the point in discussing this issue that "Librarianship today is suffering from ... [being] taught by teachers who have never been successful librarians, or even librarians at all."[11] According to this standard, only those who have administered are qualified to teach administration. A perfunctory review of the backgrounds of those who actually offer the courses, in *Who's Who in Library Service*, suggests that the overwhelming majority are drawn from the ranks of the practitioners, present and past.

There is a serious question of how useful this has been. While this group may, in fact, have administered or be administering libraries with notable success, they have up to this point contributed little to furthering the development and understanding of the subject of library administration. One alternative would be to turn the instructional reins over to a research-oriented group. The rationale is best expressed in the following passage taken from another field.[12] "The practitioner, both by equipment and by temperament, is geared to action, and the scientist to explanation. The practitioner's action is not random, or irrational however. It is based on a kind of wisdom and experience which can best be described as clinical acumen. Clinical acumen is not something mystical. It is compounded of partly conscious, partly unconscious, knowledge and facts which form the basis for a rational judgment. One procedure for developing a more scientific base for welfare practice, I believe, will be the identification and explication of the elements that enter into clinical acumen." Further and more specifically, "the formulation of practitioner knowledge into testable proposition calls for a kind of competence and interest not possessed by most practitioners. It calls for the kind of analytical, generalizing ability and interests possessed by scientists whose major concern is with analysis and generalization."

If this point of view were to be generalized and applied to librarianship, it would not suggest necessarily that every administrator by virtue of this exposure was incapable of conceptualizing his experience, or that a research-oriented person necessarily could. It would suggest, however, that there is a propensity for this to be the case. If then the practitioner is considered to be less well equipped to distill from experience the actual principles which guide him because of a fundamental action-focus, and if the social scientist is basically concerned with introducing order and relationships to what appear otherwise to be unconnected phenomena, and if research may aid in providing meaningful generalization, the case for the non-administrator or scholar-teacher, is strengthened.

PUBLIC ADMINISTRATION

Assuming administration to be common to all large-scale organizations and assuming that the problems, issues and approaches which develop in one type of institutional environment may have relevance for other settings, a comparative review may prove of interest. Library administration parallels public administration in a number of ways, and, in a very real sense, library administration is only an extension of public administration. There have been, traditionally, two major avenues by which to study public administration. The first is the so-called "organization" or "program" approach, in which administration is viewed from the point of view of a specific type of functioning unit—police, prison, fire, municipal government, etc. This approach, which considers the usual group of administrative problems—planning, personnel, budget, etc.—is concerned with administration as a process, but primarily it focuses upon the specific tasks and functions of particular agencies or types of agencies. This approach is supported by the theory that administration cannot be studied meaningfully apart from the specific program to be administered, that an administrator administers something, and that this something is highly important to the manner of administration. Translated into library terms, this same point of view is presumably reflected in the widespread prevalence in library schools of distinct courses in public, college, university and special library administration.

The second major approach rests on the concept of administration as management. According to this notion, there are certain managerial processes which run through the whole of administration, whatever the program. Among these are planning, programming, organizing, directing, coordinating, reporting, and appraising, and each of these processes is sufficiently alike from program to program to justify special study of the process itself.

Those who speak authoritatively for public administration today, generally accept the concept of management as a process running through all organizations, while recognizing, of course, that management does not take place in a vacuum. While the curricula of individual universities offering programs in public administration offer concentrations in specialized program areas such as police administration and city management, "it is clear that the universities have accepted the concept of public administration as a process in setting up their educational programs for the public service, for the emphasis is on management rather than program."[13]

In spite of disclaimers within the profession to the contrary, and certainly to a degree which is nowhere near being paralleled in the field of library administration, public administration is the focus of considerable research attention. As a matter of fact, research has progressed to the point where public administration is now widely conceived of as an "interaction" discipline, drawing many of its key contributions from other behavioral sciences. The great value of such a cross-disciplinary approach is that while researchers in other fields may focus upon the same problems, their perspectives and conceptual tools are considerably different. This tendency has given rise to some new and stimulating approaches to administrative problems, and to a wider exploration of new methods, techniques, and research frameworks. Some of the insights currently being used in studying public administration as an applied area are being drawn from a number of what would formerly have been considered novel sources, including the following fields:

Politics—Research attention is being directed more and more to the question of political behavior as a tool for understanding administrative issues. What was once a public administration taboo (on the theory that administration and politics were dichotomous issues), is now generally viewed as a crucial element of the administrative process. While the amount of reciprocal contribution from politics to public administration, and vice versa, has been very limited, indications are that this may not continue to be the case.

History—In cognizance of the generally accepted difficulty of applying the scientific methods of controlled experiment to a dynamic social field, increasing research attention is being brought to bear on the record of the past. Perhaps the greatest lesson to be learned here is the means of coping with the type of administrative issue which is recurrent.

Cultural Anthropology—Particular attention is being directed to understanding cultures and issues of underdeveloped areas, and the lessons learned from these cross-cultural studies are providing useful insights for assessing administrative problems of more complex societies. This discipline has proved crucial in advancing the study of comparative administration, a topic which relates to perhaps the single fastest growing program area in the public administration field.

Sociology—Many of the issues which form the basis of inquiry into human organizations such as status, class, and power, are proving equally useful in furthering understanding of administration. The literature of bureaucracy has enriched the study of public administration immeasurably and provided many meaningful insights.

Social Psychology—Closely tied to sociology and social anthropology, this discipline has provided administration with the valuable concept of the informal group, studies of leadership, role playing, and the entire area of tests and measurement.

Economics—There has been considerable exchange between economics and public administration and even a tendency to converge. The managerial economics theory of the firm has its parallel in the public corporation, and the firm as a system of power and the public agency as an equilibrating economic force, tend to cross and to provide each other with corresponding insights.

Business Administration—Scientific management has grown up out of the field of business administration and been adapted to the public sphere. The insights into human behavior gained from the Elton Mayo Hawthorne experiments on social conditions in the plant, and the Harvard Business School case study method, have each been translated into public administration terms.

Obviously, administration in the public field faces many internal, technical problems. However, the insights being gained through other social sciences are causing a review and re-evaluation of many old questions. Many writers have spoken of the revolution in the social sciences, that is, the mushrooming of widespread study in all the areas of social interest. New fields are being born such as cybernetics, econometrics, and sociometry. Cross disciplinary advances are being made to formulate new methods of attacking administrative problems—leadership studies, small group theory, communication theory, game, and role theory. If public administration, which has a genetic and even organizational relation only to political science, is reviewing its own position in these new terms, what then should be the implications for library service, which is the genetic offspring of all the social disciplines? And if the following criticisms can be legitimately levelled at the general program of research activity in the field of public administration, what could not be said of library administration?[14]

(1) There has not been enough research performed; the stimulus for research effort has been insufficient; and research output is falling behind the needs.

(2) There has been insufficient planning, direction, and channeling of research efforts; areas of crucial concern have been neglected.

(3) There has been insufficient communication within the field with the result that few know what others are doing; and the outlets for research products are inadequate.

(4) There is inadequate communication between this field and related fields of the social sciences in either direction; there is inadequate collaboration, cooperation, and interaction among them.

EDUCATIONAL ADMINISTRATION

The field of contemporary education is characterized by a vital concern with the questions of administrative leadership. Undoubtedly, the single most conspicuous achievement has been the evolution of the Cooperative Program in Educational Administration. Developing from a concern with the underlying issues of educational leadership, three major associations in the education field, in conjunction with the W. K. Kellogg Foundation, planned to study the question and sponsored five regional conferences during 1949-50. Out of these sessions was born the Cooperative Program in Educational Administration, financed by grants from the Kellogg Foundation totalling several million dollars, and designating at first five, and later three, more educational institutions, where the program was to be carried out. The grants were specifically earmarked for "action-research" programs in the field of educational leadership. Each individual study center evolved a series of objectives which were used to direct the specific lines which the inquiry was to take at that university.

A development of interest is the general revision of the program reported in 1955 at one of the regional centers, the Midwest Administration Center, at the University of Chicago.[15] The major lines along which research was to be directed here were: (1) the formulation of a general theory of administration to guide both practice and research, (2) the classification of administrative functions, roles, and effects through experimentation and research, (3) rigorous application of present knowledge and of accumulating theory and research to the selection and preparation of persons for administrative roles, (4) continuous re-education of those engaged in administration through more effective use of a combination of conferences, discussion groups, publications, audio-visual presentation and consultative service, and (5) improvement of the situation through which education is provided. A key element in this program involves the preparation of a field staff comprised of younger educational administrators with interest in theory and research who are to be trained on an interdisciplinary basis over a period of one to three years as part of their orientation to the program. Some of the resources which Chicago planned to use in this program included the departments and professional schools of anthropology, political science, sociology, industrial relations, business, law and social service.

Perhaps the most perceptive summary of advances in thinking about administration in the field of education is provided by John Walton who suggests that "the mounting interest in the theoretical aspects of educational administration indicates a dissatisfaction with the traditional study of the subject and a desire to formulate a rubric of administrative doctrine, if not a scientific theory."[16] Even more interesting are Walton's observations about the three possible channels along which the theory of educational administration may develop, observations which may, incidentally, be equally relevant for library administration.

The first avenue would arise from the assumption that the administrative function cannot be abstracted from the other functions of the educational enterprise and that the educational administrator is principally a scholar rather than administrator. The second possible type of theory to emerge would be to abstract administration from the other functions of an institution so that it might become a science. This would require the identification and classification of the elements of administration and the formulation and testing of precise causal relations. Such a theory would provide for specialists in administration, rather than education, who might presumably be interchangeable from one institution to another—school, hospital, library, etc. The third theory is only a reflection of what the author suggests most often unwittingly happens. Because education is a complex, unwielding, heterogeneous, social institution, the primary requisite of an administrator is the facility to see relationships. Such an administrator would need to know how to run an organization but also would have much to say about its purposes. Specialists provide the administrator with facts and technical data, but decision-making about all aspects of education—purposes as well as procedures—would be left to the administrator. This presupposes the availability of an administrator who is endowed with the capacity to attack not only administrative issues but substantive educational questions as well. Obviously, the third alternative would provide the most satisfactory solution; unfortunately, there are no hints about where to find or how to develop such a class of administrators.

Not only is there active concern with administration at the lower levels of education, but college and university administration is the focus of considerable attention as well. Evidence of this concern is expressed by one university president who writes, "The duties are so complex that it is surprising that this vocational field has not been accepted generally as a discrete art or science requiring special educational training. Higher education has instructional programs preparing people for everything but its own operation" and, "It is high time that administration in higher education was recognized for what it is, a vitally necessary function, one of the most difficult of all areas of administrative activity, and an undertaking to be consciously prepared for."[17]

One noteworthy development in recognition of this need has been the program evolved at the Harvard Business School. Aided by a Carnegie Foundation grant and sponsored by the Association of American Colleges, in 1955 the Institute for College and University Administrators was begun. This has been an attempt to adapt the same techniques used in the short training programs for business executives which the Harvard Business School provides, to the training of college officials. The value of the program has been characterized by the Carnegie Corporation as follows: "the Corporation undertook what appeared at the time to be a rather speculative venture, but one that proved to be eminently successful."[18]

CURRENT DEVELOPMENTS

The degree of concentration of thinking and activity in the two fields reviewed suggests clearly that in comparison, the theoretical and practical study of administration in the library field is lagging considerably. However, the picture is not completely black. Several recent developments are particularly noteworthy.

The most dramatic event has been the establishment by the Ford Foundation of the Council on Library Resources. Well financed and ably directed, this agency is charged with the responsibility for stimulating developments which will improve the methods and mechanisms for the effective operation and management of large research libraries. A reasonable assumption would be that as a result of this program inroads may be made into areas which relate to the central issues of library administration.

Another important development has been the award by the Carnegie Corporation to the School of Library Service of Western Reserve University where Dean Shera is directing a study to "undertake a thorough examination of education for librarians, and, on the basis of this research, develop a model curriculum at Western Reserve." Presumably, in this study attention may, in some measure, be directed to the issue of educational preparation for library administration.

The recent organizational revision of the American Library Association giving rise to the new Library Administration Division is another hopeful factor. The central focus of this group will almost certainly be those theoretical and practical issues facing all of library administration, regardless of type. Undoubtedly, this body will aid in creating a better climate of understanding, and may also prove to be influential in stimulating study, research, and writing on management issues.

Finally, there is the proposal advanced by Keyes Metcalf in his final Harvard report, for providing special training for administration.[19] Metcalf indicates that one of the pressing problems of American librarianship is the shortage of leaders qualified for the major administrative posts in the large research libraries of the country, and suggests a limited program of fellowships for students who hold advanced degrees in subject fields and the basic professional degree in librarianship who have demonstrated aptitude in administrative library positions. His projected program of instruction calls for a carefully directed plan of internship in the Harvard University Library, formal training in substantive areas making use of the following professional schools at Harvard—Graduate School of Business, Graduate School of Education, and Graduate School of Public Administration—and advanced study in one of the departments of the Graduate School of Arts and Sciences. The outline calls for two and one-half years of academic study (one-half year of which would be in bibliography and library administration) and another academic year of internship in conjunction with the usual language examinations and dissertation leading to the Ph.D. In a somewhat modified form the program would lead to an M.A. Such a course would provide the student with advanced scholarly work while at the same time exposing him to the problems faced by the practicing administrator. While this plan is particularly earmarked for research library administrators, it conceivably could have implications for administration of other types of libraries. The program for library administrators under Metcalf at the Graduate School of Library Service at

Rutgers University represents a step in the training of potential leaders. It is different, of course, from the proposal of Metcalf for Harvard.

SUGGESTED AVENUES FOR ADVANCING LIBRARY ADMINISTRATION

The material presented up to this point has been based upon empirical observation flavored by the author's personal reactions to the facts. So much for the diagnosis. What of the prognosis? As is probably true of most of the deep-seated problems facing all the professions, the real answers are not yet known and may only be learned after considerable research effort of a fundamental order. The crucial issue, really, is where, how, and by whom this research in administration in librarianship is to be done. As has been indicated, seldom is the practitioner equipped to distill theory and principles from practice. Library administration must profit from the same insights and techniques which are being brought to bear upon other fields of administrative activity. In effect, this means that the barriers must be lowered and the host of social and behavioral sciences invited, even urged, to bring their conceptual tools to bear upon the problems of library administration.

An excellent precedent has been set. In the Public Library Inquiry a team of trained social scientists (including librarians), pooled their skills, insights, and ideas and studied the major issues facing the public library. The sum total was an essential and perceptive assessment of American public library service at mid-century. A number of philanthropic foundations have over the years evidenced a sympathetic interest in the problems of librarianship. It should not be unduly optimistic to anticipate a well-conceived research design in library administration using the talents of a range of behavioral and technical administrative disciplines. While it is abundantly clear that the answers to all the questions may not be expected to spring from one large-scale undertaking, it is equally clear that a forceful first-wave assault could be made by this means.

If, as has been suggested, programs in other fields have been fertilized by advances in the social sciences while library administration has remained insulated and isolated, perhaps an expedient for training in administration would result from exposing library students to such courses in other professional schools. This device would capitalize on the close geographical and intellectual proximity to other professional schools which library schools enjoy. Perhaps an even more effective device would be to cross over into other disciplines and to bring their instructional personnel into the library school where they might offer the course or courses in administration. One important advantage would be to provide such instructors with a direct and conscious focus upon the library as the central institution of administrative concern. As a matter of fact, in such diverse fields as business, public administration, education, social service, law and medicine, personnel trained in such behavioral disciplines as sociology, anthropology, and psychology are being added to professional school faculties in increasing numbers. The use of these specialists introduces new orientations in teaching and provides a new stimulus to the study of administrative and organizational problems in these fields. It also makes possible the blending of behavioral concepts and techniques in planning for, and research in, these applied fields. Might the library field not profit by this type of exposure?

If there continues to be little or no basic research conducted in library schools, professional training programs will continue to be primarily technical or vocational. Exactly this criticism has often been lodged at the schools of business administration. The case could undoubtedly be made with equal vigor against library education. Unless there is more fundamental study and the subsequent understanding of basic issues which grows out of research study, there will continue to be little more to feed into the library curriculum than the limited contributions contained in the periodical literature.

If administration of libraries is to profit from developments in parallel fields, a need exists for comparative studies drawing contrasts and comparisons between library administration and administration of other institutions. A model of this type is Paul Allen's recent study of educational and business administration.[20] Allen's observations point up corollary ideas for library administration: (1) There is a basic, universal process of administration applicable in the fields of educational and business administration regardless of the type of enterprise to be administered, (2) the principles or integrants of the process of administration may be defined and delimited, (3) these integrants are consistent and tenable regardless of the area of administration, and (4) the obvious dissimilarities in educational and business administration are a result of structural or situational expediency and not a difference in the process of administration per se. Allen suggests further that training in both business and education places primary emphasis on technical subject matter and little or none on administration, and points to the need for further comparative studies where administration is of concern.

A host of comparative questions suggest themselves—how do the skills and characteristics of library administrators compare and differ from those of their counterparts in business, public, and educational administration; what criteria are used in selection of administrators; what are the avenues leading to administrative posts; what standards are there by which performance is measured in the different fields; what is the degree of mobility of the executive group; how does the formal and informal decision-making apparatus compare; what is the power structure of the library and how does it differ from, or compare with, other institutional types? These are but a sprinkling of unstudied and researchable comparative issues.

It is time to put to empirical test some of the classic doctrines, or perhaps, myths, and to hold up for examination such statements as "the professional equipment required by the college librarian is different from that required by the public librarian, the high school librarian, even the university librarian,"[21] and "the motivations which bring people into shoe stores, markets, and libraries are not the same, and [that] the satisfactions of the mind and spirit, which are derived from books, make libraries akin to schools and churches."[22]

To stimulate and direct research is a clear and proper function and responsibility of the professional school, for research and teaching should be inseparable if effective practice and instruction are to result. This does not imply that only research and research-founded instruction is important. Technical courses are, of course, needed, but it is in some of the technical areas that research may aid understanding most. Without the transfer of ideas and theories from research to instruction, for most students library education will continue to be a far less stimulating exposure than it might or could be. What is needed is not more schools (in 1953 there were forty-five schools awarding graduate degrees with an average student body of sixty)[23] but schools peopled with faculties and advanced graduate students with the insights, skills, and motivation to improve the educational product.

Research in library administration is equally necessary at the applied level. This need was recognized and discussed as far back as 1939 by Joeckel.[24] The use of applied research as an active management tool in libraries, as it is in industry and government service, is still far too restricted. Several large libraries have experimented here. The Brooklyn Public Library, for example, has carried on a management improvement program for some time.[25] Where applied research has been used by large-scale organizations, the experience has proved many times over that economies are produced which more than offset the personnel costs.

Libraries are nothing more than organizations of people enlisted in a common objective. The larger the library, the more complex the organization and the consequent management problems. What is crucially needed is increased knowledge and understanding of how to accomplish objectives through people. There may well be important differences between books and groceries. But if administration in libraries hopes to rival the administration of supermarkets, there must be more than a better knowledge of books. There must be a more widespread understanding of the issues underlying the ways in which complex organizations, including libraries, function effectively.

FOOTNOTES

[1] Dorothy E. Cole, "Areas for Research in the College Library, *CRL*, XI (1950), 328.
[2] Donald Coney, "Scientific Management and University Libraries," in G. T. Schwenning, ed., *Management Problems*, (Chapel Hill: University of North Carolina Press, 1930), pp. 168-198.
[3] Donald Coney, "Management in College and University Libraries," *Library Trends*, I (1952), 91.
[4] Paul Howard, "The Functions of Library Management," *Library Quarterly*, X (1940), 313-349.
[5] *Ibid.*
[6] Carleton B. Joeckel, ed., *Current Issues in Library Administration*, (Chicago: University of Chicago Press, 1939), Introduction.
[7] Ralph R. Shaw, "Scientific Management in the Library," *Wilson Library Bulletin*, XXI (1947), 349.
[8] Lawrence Clark Powell, "The Gift to Be Simple," *Library Journal*, LXXXII (1957), 314.
[9] *Ibid.*, p. 314.
[10] Lowell Martin, "Shall Library Schools Teach Administration?" *CRL*, VI (1945), 335-340, 345.
[11] Powell, *op. cit.*, 313.

[12] David G. French, "The Utilization of the Social Sciences in Solving Welfare Problems," in *Social Work Practice in the Field of Tuberculosis* (Symposium Proceedings July 27-August 1, 1953), University of Pittsburgh, School of Social Work, 1954, p. 29.
[13] R. C. Martin, "Education for Public Administration," in *Education for the Professions*, U. S. Department of Health, Education and Welfare, Office of Education, 1955, p. 194.
[14] F. C. Mosher, "Research in Public Administration: Some Notes and Suggestions," in *Public Administration Review*, XVI (1956), 178.
[15] "New Program in Administration," *Elementary School Journal*, LV (1955), 311-314.
[16] John Walton, "The Theoretical Study of Educational Administration," *Harvard Educational Review*, XXV (1955), 169.
[17] J. A. Perkins, "Public Administration and the College Administrator," *Harvard Educational Review*, XXV (1955), 216.
[18] Carnegie Corporation of New York, *Annual Report for the Fiscal Year Ended September 30, 1955* (New York, 1956), p. 32.
[19] K. D. Metcalf, *Report on the Harvard University Library: A Study of Present and Prospective Problems* (Cambridge: Harvard University Library, 1955), pp. 120-123.
[20] P. M. Allen, *The Administrative Process: A Comparative Study of Educational and Business Administration*, Ph. D. Dissertation, University of Nebraska, 1956. 147 pp. (Available in microfilm from University Microfilm, Ann Arbor, Michigan, 56-3750.)
[21] W. M. Randall and Francis L. D. Goodrich, *Principles of College Library Administration*. (Chicago: University of Chicago Press, 1936). Introduction.
[22] Powell, *op. cit.*, 314.
[23] U. S. Office of Education, *Education for the Professions* (1955), pp. 128-129.
[24] Joeckel, *op. cit.*, Introduction.
[25] F. R. St. John, "Management Improvement in Libraries," *CRL*, XIV (1953), 174-177.

ABOUT THE AUTHOR—The two primary subject areas which have engaged Paul Wasserman in both his teaching and publication experience are administration and subject bibliography. His present post is as Dean of the recently established Maryland School of Library and Information Services. He served earlier as professor and librarian in the Graduate School of Business and Public Administration at Cornell University until 1965. Before that, he was from 1949 to 1953, assistant to the business librarian and then chief of Science and Industry at the Brooklyn Public Library. He earned a B.B.A. at City College of New York, the M.S.(L.S.) and the M.S. (Economics) from Columbia University and the Ph.D. from Michigan (1960), followed by a post-doctoral year in data processing and information retrieval at Western Reserve (1963-64).
  Paul Wasserman serves as consultant to a number of organizations, including the Gale Research Company, the Public Health Service and the Special Libraries Association, and as advisor to the University of Maryland Library Administrators Development Program. Among his more important publications have been *Information for Administrators* (1956), *Decision-Making: An Annotated Bibliography* (1958) and its *Supplement 1958-1963* (1964), *Measurement and Evaluation of Organizational Performance* (1959), and *The Librarian and the Machine* (1965). He was book review editor of *Administrative Science Quarterly* from 1956-1961, and was editor or co-editor of *Sources of Commodity Prices* (1960), *Directory of University Research Bureaus and Institutes* (1960), *Directory of Health Organizations* (1961), 2nd edition (1965), *Statistics Sources* (1962), 2nd edition (1965), *Consultants and Consulting Organizations* (1965), and *Who's Who in Consulting* (1968). He serves as managing editor of the *Management Information Guide Series* (Gale Research Company), of the *Encyclopedia of Business Information Sources* (in press), and of the Microcard Editions series *Readers in Library and Information Science* of which the present volume is the first to appear.

II
UNDERSTANDING ORGANIZATIONAL BEHAVIOR

The ability of the administrator to perform in a leadership role is tied to his understanding of the nature of his organization and of the values, the goals and the strivings of the human beings he seeks to enlist in achieving the organization's purposes. In order to understand these essential ingredients—the characteristics, the limits of the organizational form, and the culture in which the administrator functions—bureaucracy in all its ramifications must be comprehended. For it is only through such understanding that the real organizational world, its issues, its conflicts, and its nature, may be perceived. And it is only through comprehension of what truly transpires in organizations and why people respond as they do to the conditions of life and work, that an administrator can genuinely direct an enterprise. Organizational understanding serves then as the theory base for practice. These are the issues treated in this section of the volume.

Introduction to Bureaucracy

Libraries are not unlike other organizational forms in this culture. At earlier stages they were very small compared to their modern counterparts just as were companies, schools and hospitals. Recent organizational history has witnessed a dramatic shift to the point where size, complexity, specialization, hierarchical administration, and all the other manifestations of bureaucracy have become widespread and commonplace. As one bureaucratic form, libraries illustrate all of these characteristics. Successful administration of libraries is thus seen in some measure as the capacity of the administrator to understand the nature, the characteristics, the values as well as the dysfunctions of bureaucracy. For to function rationally within a context calls for a clear view of its nature. The selections here introduce the setting and characterize the favorable and unfavorable consequences of performance within it.

Bureaucracy in Modern Society

by Peter M. Blau

This selection is one of the more effective introductions both to the nature of and the reasons for the bureaucratic form, and to the factors which gave rise to it. Why and how bureaucracy works, as well as its shortcomings, are clearly identified. It is shown that while efficiency is a means for seeking the attainment of organizational ends, to become overzealous about efficiency may ultimately reduce the possibility of certain types of organizations to attain these ends. For libraries, the question is seen in the degree to which rituals, when pursued beyond the bounds tolerable by those who use the library, finally destroy the very purpose for which the organization was originally inspired. Blau treats not only the formal structural terms of bureaucracy but also the effect and the influence of the informal organization. Moreover he explains the means employed to counteract the negative consequences or dysfunctions of the bureaucratic form.

WHY STUDY BUREAUCRACY?

"That stupid bureaucrat!" Who has not felt this way at one time or another? When we are sent from one official to the next without getting the information we want; when lengthy forms we had to fill out in sextuplicate are returned to us because we forgot to cross a "t" or dot an "i"; when our applications are refused on some technicality —that is when we think of bureaucracy. Colloquially, the term "bureaucracy" has become an epithet which refers to inefficiency and red tape in the government; but this was not its original meaning, and it is not the way the term will be used in this book.

If you alone had the job of collecting the dues in a small fraternity, you could proceed at your own discretion. But if five persons had this job in a large club, they would find it necessary to organize their work lest some members were asked for dues repeatedly and others never. If hundreds of persons have the assignment of collecting taxes from millions of citizens, their work must be very systematically organized; otherwise chaos would reign and the assignment could not be fulfilled. The type of organization designed to accomplish large-scale administrative tasks by systematically coordinating the work of many individuals is called a bureaucracy. This concept, then, applies to organizing principles that are intended to improve administrative efficiency and that generally do so, although bureaucratization occasionally has the opposite effect of producing inefficiency. Since complex administrative problems confront most large organizations, bureaucracy is not confined to the military and civilian branches of the government but is also found in business, unions, churches, universities, and even in baseball.

While the popular notion that bureaucracies are typically inefficient is not valid, this does not mean that the social scientist can simply dismiss it. The prevalence of this false belief in our society is a social fact that should be explained. In this study, after bureaucratic operations have been analyzed and clarified, such an explanation will be suggested in the last chapter. There we shall see that bureaucratization has implications in a democratic society that engender antagonism toward it. Whereas this antagonism usually results from the ruthless efficiency of bureaucracies, and not from their inefficiency, people often feel constrained to give vent to it by accusing bureaucracies of inefficiency, just as you might call a fellow who made you angry "stupid" even though it was not his lack of intelligence that aroused your anger.

The Rationalization of Modern Life

Much of the magic and mystery that used to pervade human life and lend it enchantment has disappeared from the modern world.* This is

---

SOURCE: Reprinted from Peter M. Blau, *Bureaucracy in Modern Society* (New York: Random House, 1956), Chap. 1, "Why Study Bureaucracy?" pp. 13-25, Chap. 2, "Theory and Development of Bureaucracy," pp. 27-43, and "Footnotes," pp. 119-121, by permission of the publisher.

largely the price of rationalization. In olden times, nature was full of mysteries, and man's most serious intellectual endeavors were directed toward discovering the ultimate meaning of his existence. Today, nature holds fewer secrets for us. Scientific advances, however, have not only made it possible to explain many natural phenomena but have also channeled human thinking. Modern man is less concerned than, say, medieval man was with ultimate values and symbolic meanings, with those aspects of mental life that are not subject to scientific inquiry, such as religious truth and artistic creation. This is an age of great scientists and engineers, not of great philosophers or prophets.

The secularization of the world that spells its disenchantment is indicated by the large amount of time we spend in making a living and getting ahead, and the little time we spend in contemplation and religious activities. Compare the low prestige of moneylenders and the high prestige of priests in former eras with the very different positions of bankers and preachers today. Preoccupied with perfecting efficient means for achieving objectives, we tend to forget why we want to reach those goals. Since we neglect to clarify the basic values that determine why some objectives are preferable to others, objectives lose their significance, and their pursuit becomes an end in itself. This tendency is portrayed in Budd Shulberg's novel *What Makes Sammy Run?* The answer to the question in the title is that only running makes him run, because he is so busy trying to get ahead that he has no time to find out where he is going. Continuous striving for success is not Sammy's means for the attainment of certain ends but the very goal of his life.

These consequences of rationalization have often been deplored, and some observers have even suggested that it is not worth the price.[1] There is no conclusive evidence, however, that alienation from profound values is the inevitable and permanent by-product of rationalization, and not merely an expression of its growing pains. The beneficial results of rationalization—notably the higher standard of living and the greater amount of leisure it makes possible, and the raising of the level of popular education it makes necessary—permit an increasing proportion of the population, not just a privileged elite, to participate actively in the cultural life of the society. This could ultimately lead to a flowering of the arts and other cultural pursuits on a wider scale than that in any earlier period.

Our high standard of living is usually attributed to the spectacular technological developments that have occurred since the Industrial Revolution, but this explanation ignores two related facts. First, the living conditions of most people during the early stages of industrialization, after they had moved from the land into the cities with their sweatshops, were probably much worse than they had been before. Dickens depicts these terrible conditions in certain novels, and Marx describes them in his biting critique of the capitalistic economy.[2] Second, major improvements in the standard of living did not take place until administrative procedures as well as the material technology had been revolutionized. Modern machines could not be utilized without the complex administrative machinery needed for running factories employing thousands of workers. It was not so much the invention of new machines as the introduction of mass-production methods that enabled Henry Ford to increase wages and yet produce a car so cheaply that it ceased to be a luxury. When Ford later refused to make further administrative innovations, in the manner of his competitors, the position of his company suffered, but after his grandson instituted such changes the company manifested new competitive strength. Rationalization in administration is a prerequisite for the full exploitation of technological knowledge in mass production, and thus for a high standard of living.†

Let us examine some of the administrative principles on which the productive efficiency of the modern factory depends. If every worker manufactured a complete car, each would have to be a graduate of an engineering college, and even then he could not do a very good job, since it would be impossible for him to be at once an expert mechanical engineer, electrical engineer, and industrial designer. Besides, there would not be enough people with engineering degrees in the country to fill all the positions. Specialization permits the employment of many less-trained workers, which lowers production costs. Moreover, whereas the jack-of-all-trades is necessarily master of none, each employee can become a highly skilled expert in his particular field of specialization.

What has been taken apart must be put together again. A high degree of specialization creates a need for a complex system of coordination. No such need exists in the small shop, where the work is less specialized, all workers have direct contact with one another, and the boss can supervise the performance of all of them. The president of a large company cannot possibly discharge his managerial responsibility for coordination through direct consultation with each one of several thousand workers. Managerial responsibility, therefore, is exercised through a hierarchy of authority, which furnishes lines of communication between top management and every employee for obtaining information on operations and transmitting operating directives. (Sometimes, these lines of communication become blocked, and this is a major source of inefficiency in administration.)

Effective coordination requires disciplined performance, which cannot be achieved by supervision alone but must pervade the work process itself. This is the function of rules and regulations that govern operations whether they specify the dimensions of nuts and bolts or the criteria to be used in promoting subordinates. Even in the ideal case where every employee is a highly intelligent and skilled expert, there is a need for disciplined adherence to regulations. Say one worker had discovered that he could produce bolts of superior quality by making them one-eighth of an inch larger, and another worker had found that he could increase efficiency by making nuts one-eighth of an inch smaller. Although each one made the most rational decision in terms of his own operations, the nuts and bolts would of course be useless because they would not match. How one's own work fits together with that of others is usually far less obvious than in this illustration. For the operations of hundreds of employees to be coordinated, each individual must conform to prescribed standards even in situations where a different course of action appears to him to be most rational. This is a requirement of all teamwork, although in genuine teamwork the rules are not imposed from above but are based on common agreement.

Efficiency also suffers when emotions or personal considerations influence administrative decisions. If the owner of a small grocery expands his business and opens a second store, he may put his son in charge even though another employee is better qualified for the job. He acts on the basis of his personal attachment rather than in the interest of business efficiency. Similarly, an official in a large company might not promote the best-qualified worker to foreman if one of the candidates were his brother. Indeed, his personal feelings could prevent him from recognizing that the qualifications of his brother were inferior. Since the subtle effects of strong emotions cannot easily be suppressed, the best way to check their interference with efficiency is to exclude from the administrative hierarchy those interpersonal relationships that are characterized by emotional attachments. While relatives sometimes work for the same company, typically they are not put in charge of one another. Impersonal relationships assure the detachment necessary if efficiency alone is to govern administrative decisions. However, relationships between employees who have frequent social contacts do not remain purely impersonal, as we shall see.

These four factors—specialization, a hierarchy of authority, a system of rules, and impersonality—are the basic characteristics of bureaucratic organization. Factories are bureaucratically organized, as are government agencies, and if this were not the case they could not operate efficiently on a large scale. Chapter Two is devoted to a more detailed analysis of bureaucratic structure and the conditions that give rise to bureaucratization. But actual operations do not exactly follow the formal blueprint. To understand how bureaucracies function, we must observe them in action. This is the task of Chapters Three and Four, which are concerned, respectively, with bureaucratic work groups and relationships of authority. After discussing the internal structure and functioning of bureaucracies, we shall turn in the final two chapters to their implications for the society of which they are a part. Specifically, we shall examine the consequences of bureaucratization for social change and for democracy. First, however, the question raised in the title of this introductory chapter should be answered: why study bureaucracy?

The Value of Studying Bureaucracy

Learning to understand bureaucracies is more important today than it ever was. It is, besides, of special significance in a democracy. Finally, the study of bureaucratic organization makes a particular contribution to the advancement of sociological knowledge.

Today Bureaucracy is not a new phenomenon. It existed in rudimentary forms thousands of years ago in Egypt and Rome. But the trend toward bureaucratization has greatly accelerated during the last century. In contemporary society bureaucracy has become a dominant institution, indeed, the institution that epitomizes the modern era. Unless we understand this institutional form, we cannot understand the social life of today.

The enormous size of modern nations and the

organizations within them is one reason for the spread of bureaucracy. In earlier periods, most countries were small, even large ones had only a loose central administration, and there were few formal organizations except the government. Modern countries have many millions of citizens, vast armies, giant corporations, huge unions, and numerous large voluntary associations.[3] To be sure, large size is not synonymous with bureaucratic organization. However, the problems posed by administration on a large scale tend to lead to bureaucratization. As a matter of fact, the large organizations that persisted longest in antiquity and even survived this period, the Roman Empire and the Catholic Church were thoroughly bureaucratized.

In the United States, employment statistics illustrate the trend toward large, bureaucratic organizations. The federal government employed 8000 civil servants in 1820, a quarter of a million fifty years ago, and ten times that number today. If the men in military service are added, nearly 10 per cent of the American labor force, six million people, are in the employ of the federal government. Still larger is the number who work for large-scale private concerns, the extreme example being the American Telephone and Telegraph Company with three-quarters of a million employees. More than three-quarters of the employees in manufacturing work for firms with one hundred or more employees, and even in the retail trades, the bulwark of small business, one-sixth of all employees work for firms of the same size.

A large and increasing proportion of the American people spend their working lives as small cogs in the complex mechanisms of bureaucratic organizations. And this is not all, for bureaucracies also affect much of the rest of our lives. The employment agency we approach to get a job, and the union we join to protect it; the supermarket and the chain store where we shop; the school our children attend, and the political parties for whose candidates we vote; the fraternal organization where we play, and the church where we worship —all these more often than not are large organizations of the kind that tends to be bureaucratically organized.

In a Democracy Bureaucracy, as the foremost theoretician on the subject points out, "is a power instrument of the first order—for the one who controls the bureaucratic apparatus."[4]

Under normal conditions, the power position of a fully developed bureaucracy is always overtowering. The "political master" finds himself in the position of the "dilettante" who stands opposite the "expert," facing the trained official who stands within the management of administration. This holds whether the "master" whom the bureaucracy serves is a "people," equipped with the weapons of "legislative initiative," the "referendum," and the right to remove officials, or a parliament, elected on a . . . "democratic" basis and equipped with the right to vote a lack of confidence, or with the actual authority to vote it.[5]

Totalitarianism is the polar case of such bureaucratic concentration of power that destroys democratic processes, but not the only one. The same tendency can be observed in political machines that transfer the power that legally belongs to voters to political bosses, in business corporations that vest the power that rightfully belongs to stockholders in corporation officials, and in those unions that bestow the power that rightfully belongs to rank-and-file members upon union leaders. These cases lead some writers to contend that the present trend toward bureaucratization spells the doom of democratic institutions. This may well be too fatalistic a viewpoint, but there can be no doubt that this trend constitutes a challenge. To protect ourselves against this threat, while continuing to utilize these efficient administrative mechanisms, we must first learn fully to understand how bureaucracies function. Knowledge alone is not power, but ignorance surely facilitates subjugation. This is the reason why the study of bureaucratic organization has such great significance in a democracy.

The problem of efficiency versus democracy, which will occupy us at length later, can initially be clarified by distinguishing three types of association. If an association among men is established for the explicit purpose of producing jointly certain end-products, whether it is manufacturing cars or winning wars, considerations of efficiency are of primary importance; hence bureaucratization will further the achievement of this objective. However, if an association is established for the purpose of finding intrinsic satisfaction in common activities, say in religious worship, considerations of efficiency are less relevant. When such an association, for instance a religious body, grows so large that administrative problems engender bureaucratization, the pursuit of the original objectives may, indeed, be hampered.[6] Finally, if an association is established for the purpose of deciding upon common goals and courses of action to implement them, which is the function of democratic government (but not that of government agencies), the free expression of opinion must be safeguarded against other considerations, including those of efficiency. Since bureaucratization prevents the attainment of this objective, it must be avoided at all cost. Ideally, organizations of the first type would always be bureaucratized, and those of the last type, never. But one of the difficulties is that many organizations, such as unions, are of a mixed type.

For Sociologists The study of bureaucratic organization is of special significance for sociologists because it helps them in their task of finding an order in the complex interdependencies of social phenomena. The sociologist is concerned with explaining patterns of human behavior in terms of relationships between people and shared normative beliefs of people. For example, to explain why some students get poorer grades than others who are no more intelligent, this sociological hypothesis could be advanced: the former have fewer friends and the discomfort of their social isolation interferes with their work. Let us assume we would actually find that the grades of isolated students are lower than those of the rest. Would that prove the hypothesis? By no means, since the difference could be due to the fact that students who appear stupid in class become less popular, or that radicals (or any other group) are discriminated against by teachers and are also disliked by fellow students.

This problem can be solved in the controlled experiment, which makes it possible to demonstrate that a specific factor has certain effects because all other factors are held constant. If two test tubes have exactly the same content and are kept under the same conditions except that one is heated, the changes that occur in one liquid but not in the other must be the result of heat. Many social conditions, however, in contrast to most physical conditions, cannot be duplicated in the laboratory. Although we can make human subjects feel isolated in an experimental session, this is not the same experience as having no friends in college, and other social conditions, such as international warfare, cannot be reproduced in the laboratory at all. This is a dilemma of social research: controlled conditions are required for the testing of hypotheses, but the artificial situation in laboratory experiments is usually not suitable for this purpose. Not that this is an insurmountable difficulty; techniques have been devised to approximate the analytical model of the controlled experiment outside the laboratory. Still, the larger the number of varying factors in the social situation, the smaller is the chance that explanatory hypotheses can be confirmed.

Bureaucracy provides, as it were, a natural laboratory for social research. The formal organization, with its explicit regulations and official positions, constitutes controlled conditions, and these controls have not been artificially introduced by the scientist but are an inherent part of the bureaucratic structure. To be sure, the daily activities and interactions of the members of a bureaucracy cannot be entirely accounted for by the official blueprint. If they could, there would be no need for conducting empirical studies in bureaucracies, since everything about them could be learned by examining organizational charts and procedure manuals. Several factors in addition to official requirements influence daily operations, which means, of course, that conditions are not as fully controlled as in a laboratory experiment. Nevertheless, the explicit formal organization, the characteristics of which can be easily ascertained, reduces the number of variable conditions in the bureaucratic situation and thereby facilitates the search for and the testing of explanatory hypotheses.

In summary, the prevalence of bureaucracies in our society furnishes a practical reason for studying them; the fact that they endanger democratic institutions supplies an ideological reason; and the contribution their study can make to sociological knowledge provides a scientific reason for undertaking this task.

FOOTNOTES

*The disenchantment of the world is a main theme running through the writings of the German sociologist Max Weber, whose classical analysis of bureaucratic structure will be discussed presently.

[1] See Pitirim Sorokin, *Social and Cultural Dynamics*, New York: American Book Company, 1937-1941. The author traces fluctuations in cultural emphasis on science and rationality, on the one hand, and faith and supernatural phenomena, on the other, from the earliest times to the present, and vigorously condemns the present trend toward rationalization.

[2] *Capital*, Vol. I, Chaps. 26 to 31.

†To be sure, activities of trade unions have greatly contributed to the raising of our standard of living by forcing employers to distribute a larger proportion of their income to workers. Without administrative efficiency in the production and distribution of goods, however, there would be less income to distribute, and fewer goods could be bought with a given amount of income. Moreover, the strength of unions also depends on an efficient administrative machinery.

[3] See Kenneth Boulding, *The Organization Revolution*, New York: Harper & Brothers, 1953.
[4] *From Max Weber: Essays in Sociology*, translated by H. H. Gerth and C. Wright Mills, New York: Oxford University Press, 1946, p. 228.
[5] *Ibid.*, p. 232.
[6] For a fuller discussion of this point, see Charles H. Page, "Bureaucracy and the Liberal Church," *The Review of Religion* 17: 137-50 (1952).

THEORY AND DEVELOPMENT OF BUREAUCRACY

Advancement in any science depends on developments in both theory and empirical research and on a close connection between them. The objectives of science are to improve the accuracy and scope of explanations of phenomena as a basis for better predictability and control. A system of interrelated explanatory propositions is a scientific theory. Not every insight, however, is a scientific proposition; this term refers only to those that have been confirmed in systematic research or can at least be confirmed in future research, which is not the case for all explanations. Toynbee's interpretation of history in terms of challenge and response, for instance, although it may provide new insights into the course of history, cannot be empirically tested, since there is no conceivable factual evidence that would clearly disprove it. An important methodological principle of science holds that only those propositions can be empirically confirmed that indicate precisely the evidence necessary for disproving them.

If undisciplined speculating does not further the advancement of science, neither does random data-collecting. A large number of miscellaneous facts contribute as little to the building of systematic theory as a large number of odd stones contribute to the building of a house. To be sure, unsophisticated fact-finding has its uses, and so does undisciplined imagination, but for empirical research and theoretical insights to serve science, they must be integrated. This requires that theory be precise enough to direct research, and that research be oriented toward establishing theoretical generalizations.

The lesson to be learned from these considerations is that the study of bureaucracy should be governed by a theoretical orientation and should focus upon the investigation of empirical cases. These case studies of bureaucracies, in turn, will help to clarify and refine our theoretical understanding of this social structure and its functioning. Following this procedure, we shall start with Max Weber's famous theory of bureaucracy.

The Concept of Bureaucracy

The main characteristics of a bureaucratic structure (in the "ideal-typical" case*), according to Weber, are the following:

1. "The regular activities required for the purposes of the organization are distributed in a fixed way as official duties."[1] The clear-cut division of labor makes it possible to employ only specialized experts in each particular position and to make every one of them responsible for the effective performance of his duties. This high degree of specialization has become so much part of our socio-economic life that we tend to forget that it did not prevail in former eras but is a relatively recent bureaucratic innovation.

2. "The organization of offices follows the principle of hierarchy; that is, each lower office is under the control and supervision of a higher one."[2] Every official in this administrative hierarchy is accountable to his superior for his subordinates' decisions and actions as well as his own. To be able to discharge his responsibility for the work of subordinates, he has authority over them, which means that he has the right to issue directives and they have the duty to obey them. This authority is strictly circumscribed and confined to those directives that are relevant for official operations. The use of status prerogatives to extend the power of control over subordinates beyond these limits does not constitute the legitimate exercise of bureaucratic authority.

3. Operations are governed "by a consistent system of abstract rules ... [and] consist of the application of these rules to particular cases."[3] This system of standards is designed to assure uniformity in the performance of every task, regardless of the number of persons engaged in it, and the coordination of different tasks. Hence explicit rules and regulations define the responsibility of

each member of the organization and the relationships between them. This does not imply that bureaucratic duties are necessarily simple and routine. It must be remembered that strict adherence to general standards in deciding specific cases characterizes not only the job of the file clerk but also that of the Supreme Court justice. For the former, it may involve merely filing alphabetically; for the latter, it involves interpreting the law of the land in order to settle the most complicated legal issues. Bureaucratic duties range in complexity from one of these extremes to the other.

4. "The ideal official conducts his office... [in] a spirit of formalistic impersonality, '*Sine ira et studio*,' without hatred or passion, and hence without affection or enthusiasm."[4] For rational standards to govern operations without interference from personal considerations, a detached approach must prevail within the organization and especially toward clients. If an official develops strong feelings about some subordinates or clients, he can hardly help letting those feelings influence his official decisions. As a result, and often without being aware of it himself, he might be particularly lenient in evaluating the work of one of his subordinates or might discriminate against some clients and in favor of others. The exclusion of personal considerations from official business is a prerequisite for impartiality as well as for efficiency. The very factors that make a government bureaucrat unpopular with his clients, an aloof attitude and a lack of genuine concern with their problems, actually benefit these clients. Disinterestedness and lack of personal interest go together. The official who does not maintain social distance and becomes personally interested in the cases of his clients tends to be partial in his treatment of them, favoring those he likes over others. Impersonal detachment engenders equitable treatment of all persons and thus fosters democracy in administration.

5. Employment in the bureaucratic organization is based on technical qualifications and is protected against arbitrary dismissal. "It constitutes a career. There is a system of 'promotions' according to seniority or to achievement, or both."[5] These personnel policies, which are found not only in civil service but also in many private companies, encourage the development of loyalty to the organization and *esprit de corps* among its members. The consequent identification of employees with the organization motivates them to exert greater efforts in advancing its interests. It may also give rise to a tendency to think of themselves as a class apart from and superior to the rest of the society. Among civil servants, this tendency has been more pronounced in Europe, notably in Germany, than in the United States, but among military officers, it may be found here, too.

6. "Experience tends universally to show that the purely bureaucratic type of administrative organization... is, from a purely technical point of view, capable of attaining the highest degree of efficiency."[6] "The fully developed bureaucratic mechanism compares with other organizations exactly as does the machine with non-mechanical modes of production."[7] Bureaucracy solves the distinctive organizational problem of maximizing organizational efficiency, not merely that of individuals.

The superior administrative efficiency of bureaucracy is the expected result of its various characteristics as outlined by Weber. For an individual to work efficiently, he must have the necessary skills and apply them rationally and energetically; but for an organization to operate efficiently, more is required. Every one of its members must have the expert skills needed for the performance of his tasks. This is the purpose of specialization and of employment on the basis of technical qualifications, often ascertained by objective tests. Even experts, however, may be prevented by personal bias from making rational decisions. The emphasis on impersonal detachment is intended to eliminate this source of irrational action. But individual rationality is not enough. If the members of the organization were to make rational decisions independently, their work would not be coordinated and the efficiency of the organization would suffer. Hence there is need for discipline to limit the scope of rational discretion, which is met by the system of rules and regulations and the hierarchy of supervision. Moreover, personnel policies that permit employees to feel secure in their jobs and to anticipate advancements for faithful performance of duties discourage attempts to impress superiors by introducing clever innovations, which may endanger coordination. Lest this stress on disciplined obedience to rules and rulings undermine the employee's motivation to devote his energies to his job, incentives for exerting effort must be furnished. Personnel policies that cultivate organizational loyalty and that provide for promotion on the basis of merit serve this function. In other words, the combined effect of bureaucracy's characteristics is to create social conditions which constrain each member of the organization to act in ways that, whether they appear rational or otherwise from his individual standpoint, further the rational pursuit of organizational objectives.

Without explicitly stating so, Weber supplies a *functional* analysis of bureaucracy. In this type of analysis, a social structure is explained by showing how each of its elements contributes to its persistence and effective operations. Concern with discovering all these contributions, however, entails the danger that the scientist may neglect to investigate the disturbances that various elements produce in the structure. As a result, his presentation may make the social structure appear to function more smoothly than it actually does, since he neglects the disruptions that do in fact exist. To protect ourselves against this danger, it is essential to extend the analysis beyond the mere consideration of functions, as Robert K. Merton points out.[8] Of particular importance for avoiding false implications of stability and for explaining social change is the study of *dysfunctions*, those consequences that interfere with adjustment and create problems in the structure.[9]

A re-examination of the foregoing discussion of bureaucratic features in the light of the concept of dysfunction reveals inconsistencies and conflicting tendencies. If reserved detachment characterizes the attitudes of the members of the organization toward one another, it is unlikely that high *esprit de corps* will develop among them. The strict exercise of authority in the interest of discipline induces subordinates, anxious to be highly thought of by their superiors, to conceal defects in operations from superiors, and this obstruction of the flow of information upward in the hierarchy impedes effective management. Insistence on conformity also tends to engender rigidities in official conduct and to inhibit the rational exercise of judgment needed for efficient performance of tasks. If promotions are based on merit, many employees will not experience advancements in their careers; if they are based primarily on seniority so as to give employees this experience and thereby to encourage them to become identified with the organization, the promotion system will not furnish strong incentives for exerting efforts and excelling in one's job. These illustrations suffice to indicate that the same factor that enhances efficiency in one respect often threatens it in another; it may have *both* functional and dysfunctional consequences.

Weber was well aware of such contradictory tendencies in the bureaucratic structure. But since he treats dysfunctions only incidentally, his discussion leaves the impression that administrative efficiency in bureaucracies is more stable and less problematical than it actually is. In part, it was his intention to present an idealized image of bureaucratic structure, and he used the conceptual tool appropriate for this purpose. Let us critically examine this conceptual tool.

Implications of the Ideal-Type Construct

Weber dealt with bureaucracy as what he termed an "ideal type." This methodological concept does not represent an average of the attributes of all existing bureaucracies (or other social structures), but a pure type, derived by abstracting the most characteristic bureaucratic aspects of all known organizations. Since perfect bureaucratization is never fully realized, no empirical organization corresponds exactly to this scientific construct.

The criticism has been made that Weber's analysis of an imaginary ideal type does not provide understanding of concrete bureaucratic structures. But this criticism obscures the fact that the ideal-type construct is intended as a guide in empirical research, not as a substitute for it. By indicating the characteristics of bureaucracy in its pure form, it directs the researcher to those aspects of organizations that he must examine in order to determine the extent of their bureaucratization. This is the function of all conceptual schemes: to specify the factors that must be taken into consideration in investigations and to define them clearly.

The ideal type, however, is not simply a conceptual scheme. It includes not only definitions of concepts but also generalizations about the relationships between them, specifically the hypothesis that the diverse bureaucratic characteristics increase administrative efficiency. Whereas conceptual definitions are presupposed in research and not subject to verification by research findings, hypotheses concerning relationships between factors are subject to such verification. Whether strict hierarchical authority, for example, in fact furthers efficiency is a question of empirical fact and not one of definition. But as a scientific construct, the ideal type cannot be refuted by empirical evidence. If a study of several organizations were to find that strict hierarchical authority is not related to efficiency, this would not prove that no such relationship exists in the ideal-type bureaucracy; it would show only that these organizations are not fully bureaucratized. Since generalizations about idealized states defy testing in systematic research, they have no place in science. On the other hand, if empirical evidence is taken into consideration and generalizations are modified accordingly, we deal with prevailing tendencies in bureaucratic structures and no longer with a pure type.

Two misleading implications of the ideal-type conception of bureaucracy deserve special mention. The student of social organization is concerned with the patterns of activities and interactions that reveal how social conduct is organized, and not with exceptional deviations from these patterns. The fact that one official becomes excited and shouts at his colleague, or that another arrives late at the office, is unimportant in understanding the organization, except that the rare occurrence of such events indicates that they are idiosyncratic, differing from the prevailing patterns. Weber's decision to treat only the purely formal organization of bureaucracy implies that all deviations from these formal requirements are idiosyncratic and of no interest for the student of organization. Recent empirical studies have shown this approach to be misleading. Informal relations and unofficial practices develop among the members of bureaucracies and assume an organized form without being officially sanctioned. Chester I. Barnard, one of the first to call attention to this phenomenon, held that these "informal organizations are necessary to the operations of formal organizations."[10] These informal patterns, in contrast to exceptional occurrences, as we shall see in Chapter Three, are a regular part of bureaucratic organizations and therefore must be taken into account in their analysis.

Weber's approach also implies that any deviation from the formal structure is detrimental to administrative efficiency. Since the ideal type is conceived as the perfectly efficient organization, all differences from it must necessarily interfere with efficiency. There is considerable evidence that suggests the opposite conclusion; informal relations and unofficial practices often contribute to efficient operations. In any case, the significance of these unofficial patterns for operations cannot be determined in advance on theoretical grounds but only on the basis of factual investigations. Before examining such case studies of bureaucracies it is useful to explore the conditions that give rise to bureaucratization.

Conditions that Give Rise to Bureaucratization

To say that there is a historical trend toward bureaucracy is to state that many organizations change from less to more bureaucratic forms of administration. Yet the historical trend itself and the changes in any specific organization are different phenomena. Both are expressions of the process of bureaucratization, but since different conditions account for them, they will be discussed separately.

Historical Conditions One of the historical conditions that favors the development of bureaucracy is a money economy. This is not an absolute prerequisite. Bureaucracies based on compensation in kind existed, for example, in Egypt, Rome, and China. Generally, however, a money economy permits the payment of regular salaries, which, in turn, creates the combination of dependence and independence that is most conducive to the faithful performance of bureaucratic duties. Unpaid volunteers are too independent of the organization to submit unfailingly to its discipline. Slaves, on the other hand, are too dependent on their masters to have the incentive to assume responsibilities and carry them out on their own initiative. The economic dependence of the salaried employee on his job and his freedom to advance himself in his career engender the orientation toward work required for disciplined *and* responsible conduct. Consequently, there were few bureaucracies prior to the development of a monetary system and the abolition of slavery.

It has already been mentioned that sheer size encourages the development of bureaucracies, since they are mechanisms for executing large-scale administrative tasks. The large modern nation, business, or union is more likely to be bureaucratized than was its smaller counterpart in the past. More important than size as such, however, is the emergence of special administrative problems. Thus in ancient Egypt the complex job of constructing and regulating waterways throughout the country gave rise to the first known large-scale bureaucracy in history. In other countries, notably those with long frontiers requiring defense, bureaucratic methods were introduced to solve the problem of organizing an effective army and the related one of raising taxes for this purpose. England, without land frontiers, maintained only a small army in earlier centuries, which may in part account for the fact that the trend toward bureaucratization was less pronounced there than in continental nations, which had to support large armies. Weber cites the victory of the Puritans under the leadership of Cromwell over the Cavaliers, who fought more heroically but with less discipline, as an illustration of the superior effectiveness of a bureaucratized army.[11]

The capitalistic system also has furthered the advance of bureaucracy. The rational estimation of economic risks, which is presupposed in capitalism, requires that the regular processes of the competitive market not be interrupted by external forces in unpredictable ways. Arbitrary actions of political tyrants interfere with the rational calculation of gain or loss, and so do banditry, piracy, and social upheavals. The interest of capitalism demands, therefore, not only the overthrow of tyrannical rulers but also the establishment of governments strong enough to maintain order and stability. Note that after the American Revolution such representatives of the capitalists as Alexander Hamilton advocated a strong federal government, while representatives of farmers, in the manner of Jefferson, favored a weak central government.

Capitalism then promotes effective and extensive operations of the government. It also leads to bureaucratization in other spheres. The expansion of business firms and the consequent removal of most employees from activities directly governed by the profit principle make it increasingly necessary to introduce bureaucratic methods of administration for the sake of efficiency. These giant corporations, in turn, constrain workers, who no longer can bargain individually with an employer they know personally, to organize into large unions with complex administrative machineries. Strange as it may seem, the free-enterprise system fosters the development of bureaucracy in the government, in private companies, and in unions.

These historical conditions were not causes of bureaucracy in the usual sense of the term. Evidently, a large and effective army did not cause bureaucracy; on the contrary, bureaucratic methods of operation produced an effective large army. The need for these methods, however, arose in the course of trying to build such an army without them and helped bring about a bureaucratic form of organization. The qualifying word "helped" is essential. If needs inevitably created ways of meeting them, human society would be paradise. In this world, wishes are not horses, and beggars do not ride. Social needs, just as individual ones, often persist without being met. Knowledge of the conditions that engendered a need for bureaucracy does not answer the question: what made its development actually possible under some circumstances and not under others? The Cavaliers were in need of a better fighting force, as their defeat demonstrates. Why was it not they but the Puritans who organized a disciplined army?

In *The Protestant Ethic and the Spirit of Capitalism*, Weber indirectly answers this question. He shows that the Reformation—especially Calvinism, the religious doctrine of the Puritans—apart from its spiritual significance, had the social consequence of giving rise to this-worldly asceticism, a disciplined devotion to hard work in the pursuit of one's vocation. The Protestant has no Pope or priest to furnish spiritual guidance and absolve him for his sins, but must ultimately rely on his own conscience and faith; this encourages the emergence of self-imposed discipline. The strong condemnation of pleasure and emotions, exemplified by the Puritan "blue laws," generates the sobriety and detachment conducive to rational conduct. Moreover, in contrast to Catholicism and even Lutheranism, Calvinism does not emphasize that the existing order is God's creation but that it has been corrupted by man's sinfulness. Man's religious duty is not to adapt to this wicked world, nor to withdraw from it into a monastery, but to help transform it *pro gloriam Dei* through methodical efforts in his everyday life and regular work. The anxieties aroused by the doctrine of double predestination, according to which man cannot affect his predestined fate or even know whether he will be saved or damned, reinforced the Calvinist's tendency to adopt a rigorous discipline and immerse himself in his work as a way of relieving his anxieties.

Protestantism, therefore, has transplanted the ascetic devotion to disciplined hard work (which must be distinguished from the exertion of effort as a means for reaching specific ends) from monastic life, to which it was largely confined earlier, to the mundane affairs of economic life. Although the explicit purposes of the Reformation were other-worldly and not this-worldly, the psychological orientation it created had the unanticipated consequence of helping to revolutionize the secular world. For without this orientation toward ceaseless effort and rational conduct as intrinsic moral values, Weber argues convincingly, capitalism could not have come into existence, and neither, it should be added, could full-blown bureaucracy have developed, because it too depends on rational discipline.[12]

Structural Conditions The historical conditions that led to the pervasiveness of bureaucracy today do not, of course, explain why some organizations in contemporary society are highly bureaucratized and others are not. These variations raise the problem of the conditions within a given social structure that give rise to its bureaucratization. A recent empirical study is concerned with this problem.

Alvin W. Gouldner investigated the process of bureaucratization in a gypsum plant.[13] After the death of the old manager, the company that owned the plant appointed a man who had been in charge of one of its smaller factories as his successor. The new manager, anxious to prove himself worthy of the promotion by improving productivity, was faced with special difficulties. He was not familiar with the ways of working that had become customary in this plant, had not established informal relations with his subordinates, and did not command the allegiance of workers, who still felt loyal to his predecessor. To marshal the willing support of workers and induce them to identify with his managerial objectives, he attempted to cultivate informal relations with them; but this cannot be done overnight. In the meantime, he found it necessary to discharge his managerial responsibilities by resorting to formal procedures. In the absence of informal channels of communication to keep him informed about the work situation, the new manager instituted a system of regular operational reports for this purpose. Since he did not know the workers well enough to trust them, he closely checked on their operations and ordered his lieutenants to establish strict discipline. When some of these lieutenants, used to the more lenient ways of the former manager, failed to adopt rigorous methods of close supervision, he replaced them by outsiders who were more sympathetic with his disciplinarian approach. These innovations alienated workers and deepened the gulf between them and the manager, with the result that he had to rely increasingly on formal bureaucratic methods of administration.

> The role of the successor . . . confronted Peele with distinctive problems. He had to solve these problems if he wished to hold his job as manager. In the process of solving them, the successor was compelled to use bureaucratic methods. Peele intensified bureaucracy not merely because he wanted to, not necessarily because he liked bureaucracy, nor because he valued it above other techniques, but also because he was constrained to do so by the tensions of his succession.[14]

In the interest of his objective of gaining control over the operations in the plant, it was necessary for the successor to introduce bureaucratic procedures. At the same time, for workers to realize their objective of maintaining some independent control over their own work, it was necessary for them to oppose the introduction of disciplinarian measures. As noted above, the existence of a need does not explain why it is met. In this case, two conflicting needs existed side by side, with the "victor" determined by the power structure in the organization. The powerful position of the manager was responsible for his ability to meet his need by bureaucratizing operations, as indicated by the following comparison with a situation where he was not similarly successful.

This plant consisted of a gypsum mine and a wallboard factory, but the process of bureaucratic formalization was confined to the factory. Stronger informal ties and more pronounced group solidarity prevailed among miners than among factory workers, partly as a consequence of the common danger to which they were exposed in the mine. Miners were highly motivated to work hard, and they had developed their own unofficial system of assigning tasks among themselves; for instance, new miners had to do the dirty jobs. Hence there was less need in the mine for formal discipline and rules prescribing exact duties. Nevertheless, Peele attempted to formalize operating procedures there, too. The strength of their informal organization, however, made it possible for miners, in contrast to factory workers, effectively to resist these attempts. The process of bureaucratic formalization generated by succession in management is not inevitable; collective resistance can arrest it.

The miners, so to speak, had evolved an unofficial bureaucratic apparatus of their own. Their effective informal organization, by regulating their work, took the place of a more formal system of control and simultaneously gave them sufficient power to defeat endeavors to impose a formal system of discipline upon them against their will. Did efficiency suffer? Gouldner implies it did not, although he does not specifically deal with this question. In any case, the conduct of the miners calls attention, once more, to the importance of informal relations and unofficial practices in bureaucratic structures, which is the topic of the next chapter.

FOOTNOTES

*The "ideal type" is discussed later in this chapter.

[1] *From Max Weber: Essays in Sociology*, translated by H. H. Gerth and C. Wright Mills, New York: Oxford University Press, 1946, p. 196. By permission.

[2] Max Weber, *The Theory of Social and Economic Organization*, translated by A. M. Henderson and Talcott Parsons, New York: Oxford University Press, 1947, p. 331.
[3] *Ibid.*, p. 330.
[4] *Ibid.*, p. 340.
[5] *Ibid.*, p. 334.
[6] *Ibid.*, p. 337.
[7] *From Max Weber: Essays in Sociology, op. cit.,* p. 214.
[8] Robert K. Merton, *Social Theory and Social Structure*, Glencoe, Ill.: Free Press, 1949, pp. 21-81.
[9] For a general discussion of functional analysis, see Ely Chinoy, *Sociological Perspective: Basic Concepts and Their Application* (Studies in Sociology), New York: Random House, Inc., 1954. Chap. 5.
[10] Chester I. Barnard, *The Functions of the Executive*, Cambridge: Harvard University Press, 1948, p. 123.
[11] *From Max Weber: Essays in Sociology, op. cit.,* pp. 256-57. The advanced student will have recognized the indebtedness of the foregoing discussion to Weber's (pp. 204-16). It goes without saying that Weber's fund of historical knowledge and his profound theoretical insights about bureaucracy can be acknowledged as outstanding contributions in the field even if one rejects his use of the ideal-type construct.
[12] For a fuller discussion of the unintended effects of Protestantism, see Elizabeth K. Nottingham, *Religion and Society* (Studies in Sociology), New York: Random House, Inc., 1954, pp. 50 ff.
[13] Alvin W. Gouldner, *Patterns of Industrial Bureaucracy*, Glencoe, Ill.: Free Press, 1954.
[14] *Ibid.*, pp. 97-98.

ABOUT THE AUTHOR—Peter M. Blau's first book, *Dynamics of Bureaucracy* (1955), established him as an important contributor to empirical understanding of organizations. Blau has contributed to the further understanding of the dynamics of social and organizational change through both empirical study and theoretical analyses. Most recently with O. D. Duncan, he has analyzed occupational structure in America based upon a sample of over 20,000 men between the ages of 20 and 64 in terms of the stratification system in the society, *The American Occupational Structure* (1967).

Blau was born in Vienna, Austria in 1918. He came to the United States in 1939, received his B.A. from Elmhurst College in 1942, and was naturalized in 1943. He served with the U. S. Army Military Intelligence during World War II. Since receiving his Ph.D. from Columbia in 1952 he has served as a member of the University of Chicago sociology faculty where he is now a professor. A senior postdoctoral fellow of the National Science Foundation in 1962 and a fellow at the Center for the Advancement of Studies in the Behavioral Sciences in 1963, Peter Blau was editor of the *American Journal of Sociology* from 1961 to 1966. For the academic year 1966-67, he was the Pitt Professor of American History and Institutions at the University of Cambridge.

Bureaucratic Structure and Personality

by Robert K. Merton

> *In this now classic piece, Robert Merton briefly characterizes the central characteristics of bureaucratic forms and then strikes to the core of their dysfunctional consequences. Training is thus seen potentially as training for incapacity, particular organizational manifestations are seen to shift the individual to rigid adherence to rules and thereby to a displacement of the organizational goals. Under these terms the bureaucratic design engendered to achieve organizational efficiency may contribute exactly the opposite. The central theme of the paper is the way in which bureaucracy may influence individual behavior to perform in ways inconsistent with the objectives of the organization.*

A formal, rationally organized social structure involves clearly defined patterns of activity in which, ideally, every series of actions is functionally related to the purposes of the organization.[1] In such an organization there is integrated a series of offices, of hierarchized statuses, in which inhere a number of obligations and privileges closely defined by limited and specific rules. Each of these offices contains an area of imputed competence and responsibility. Authority, the power of control which derives from an acknowledged status, inheres in the office and not in the particular person who performs the official role. Official action ordinarily occurs within the framework of pre-existing rules of the organization. The system of prescribed relations between the various offices involves a considerable degree of formality and clearly defined social distance between the occupants of these positions. Formality is manifested by means of a more or less complicated social ritual which symbolizes and supports the "pecking order" of the various offices. Such formality, which is integrated with the distribution of authority within the system, serves to minimize friction by largely restricting (official) contact to modes which are previously defined by the rules of the organization. Ready calculability of other's behavior and a stable set of mutual expectations is thus built up. Moreover, formality facilitates the interaction of the occupants of offices despite their (possibly hostile) private attitudes toward one another. In this way, the subordinate is protected from the arbitrary action of his superior, since the actions of both are constrained by a mutually recognized set of rules. Specific procedural devices foster objectivity and restrain the "quick passage of impulse into action."[2]

The ideal type of such formal organization is bureaucracy and, in many respects, the classical analysis of bureaucracy is that by Max Weber.[3] As Weber indicates, bureaucracy involves a clear-cut division of integrated activities which are regarded as duties inherent in the office. A system of differentiated controls and sanctions are stated in the regulations. The assignment of roles occurs on the basis of technical qualifications which are ascertained through formalized, impersonal procedures (e.g. examinations). Within the structure of hierarchically arranged authority, the activities of "trained and salaried experts" are governed by general, abstract, clearly defined rules which preclude the necessity for the issuance of specific instructions for each specific case. The generality of the rules requires the constant use of *categorization*, whereby individual problems and cases are classified on the basis of designated criteria and are treated accordingly. The pure type of bureaucratic official is appointed, either by a superior or through the exercise of impersonal competition; he is not elected. A measure of flexibility in the bureaucracy is attained by electing higher functionaries who presumably express the will of the electorate (e.g. a body of citizens or a board of directors). The election of higher officials is designed to affect the purposes of the organization, but the technical procedures for attaining these ends are performed by a continuous bureaucratic personnel.[4]

SOURCE: Reprinted from Robert K. Merton, "Bureaucratic Structure and Personality," *Social Forces*, 18 (May, 1940), pp. 560-568, by permission of the University of North Carolina Press.

The bulk of bureaucratic offices involve the expectation of life-long tenure, in the absence of disturbing factors which may decrease the size of of the organization. Bureaucracy maximizes vocational security.[5] The function of security of tenure, pensions, incremental salaries and regularized procedures for promotion is to ensure the devoted performance of official duties, without regard for extraneous pressures.[6] The chief merit of bureaucracy is its technical efficiency, with a premium placed on precision, speed, expert control, continuity, discretion, and optimal returns on input. The structure is one which approaches the complete elimination of personalized relationships and of nonrational considerations (hostility, anxiety, affectual involvements, etc.).

Bureaucratization is accompanied by the centralization of means of production, as in modern capitalistic enterprise, or as in the case of the post-feudal army, complete separation from the means of destruction. Even the bureaucratically organized scientific laboratory is characterized by the separation of the scientist from his technical equipment.

Bureaucracy is administration which almost completely avoids public discussion of its techniques, although there may occur public discussion of its policies.[7] This "bureaucratic secrecy" is held to be necessary in order to keep valuable information from economic competitors or from foreign and potentially hostile political groups.

In these bold outlines, the positive attainments and functions of bureaucratic organization are emphasized and the internal stresses and strains of such structures are almost wholly neglected. The community at large, however, evidently emphasizes the imperfections of bureaucracy, as is suggested by the fact that the "horrid hybrid," bureaucrat, has become a *Schimpfwort*. The transition to a study of the negative aspects of bureaucracy is afforded by the application of Veblen's concept of "trained incapacity," Dewey's notion of "occupational psychosis" or Warnotte's view of "professional deformation." Trained incapacity refers to that state of affairs in which one's abilities function as inadequacies or blind spots. Actions based upon training and skills which have been successfully applied in the past may result in inappropriate responses *under changed conditions*. An inadequate flexibility in the application of skills will, in a changing milieu, result in more or less serious maladjustments.[8] Thus, to adopt a barnyard illustration used in this connection by Burke, chickens may be readily conditioned to interpret the sound of a bell as a signal for food.

The same bell may now be used to summon the "trained chickens" to their doom as they are assembled to suffer decapitation. In general, one adopts measures in keeping with his past training and, under new conditions which are not recognized as *significantly* different, the very soundness of this training may lead to the adoption of the wrong procedures. Again, in Burke's almost echolalic phrase, "people may be unfitted by being fit in an unfit fitness;" their training may become an incapacity.

Dewey's concept of occuaptional psychosis rests upon much the same observations. As a result of their day to day routines, people develop special preferences, antipathies, discriminations and emphases.[9] (The term psychosis is used by Dewey to denote a "pronounced character of the mind.") These psychoses develop through demands put upon the individual by the particular organization of his occupational role.

The concepts of both Veblen and Dewey refer to a fundamental ambivalence. Any action can be considered in terms of what it attains or what it fails to attain. "A way of seeing is also a way of not seeing—a focus upon object A involves a neglect of object B."[10] In his discussion, Weber is almost exclusively concerned with what the bureaucratic structure attains: precision, reliability, efficiency. This same structure may be examined from another perspective provided by the ambivalence. What are the limitations of the organization designed to attain these goals?

For reasons which we have already noted, the bureaucratic structure exerts a constant pressure upon the official to be "methodical, prudent, disciplined." If the bureaucracy is to operate successfully, it must attain a high degree of reliability of behavior, an unusual degree of conformity with prescribed patterns of action. Hence, the fundamental importance of discipline which may be as highly developed in a religious or economic bureaucracy as in the army. Discipline can be effective only if the ideal patterns are buttressed by strong sentiments which entail devotion to one's duties, a keen sense of the limitation of one's authority and competence, and methodical performance of routine activities. The efficacy of social structure depends ultimately upon infusing group participants with appropriate attitudes and sentiments. As we shall see, there are definite arrangements in the bureaucracy for inculcating and reinforcing these sentiments.

At the moment, it suffices to observe that in order to ensure discipline (the necessary reliability of response), these sentiments are often more intense than is technically necessary. There is a margin of safety, so to speak, in the pressure exerted by these sentiments upon the bureaucrat to conform to his patterned obligations, in much the same sense that added allowances (precautionary over-estimations) are made by the engineer in designing the supports for a bridge. But this very emphasis leads to a transference of the sentiments from the *aims* of the organization onto the particular details of behavior required by the rules. Adherence to the rules, originally conceived as a means, becomes transformed into an end-in-itself; there occurs the familiar process of *displacement of goals* whereby "an instrumental value becomes a terminal value."[11] Discipline, readily interpreted as conformance with regulation, whatever the situation, is seen not as a measure designed for specific purposes but becomes an immediate value in the life-organization of the bureaucrat. This emphasis, resulting from the displacement of the original goals, develops into rigidities and an inability to adjust readily. Formalism, even ritualism, ensues with an unchallenged insistence upon punctilious adherence to formalized procedures.[12] This may be exaggerated to the point where primary concern with conformity to the rules interferes with the achievement of the purposes of the organization, in which case we have the familiar phenomenon of the technicism or red tape of the official. An extreme product of this process of displacement of goals is the bureaucratic virtuoso, who never forgets a single rule binding his action and hence is unable to assist many of his clients.[13] A case in point, where strict recognition of the limits of authority and literal adherence to rules produced this result, is the pathetic plight of Bernt Balchen, Admiral Byrd's pilot in the flight over the South Pole.

According to a ruling of the department of labor Bernt Balchen . . . cannot receive his citizenship papers. Balchen, a native of Norway, declared his intention in 1927. It is held that he has failed to meet the condition of five years' continuous residence in the United States. The Byrd antarctic voyage took him out of the country, although he was on a ship flying the American flag, was an invaluable member of an American expedition, and in a region to which there is an American claim because of the exploration and occupation of it by Americans, this region being Little America.

The bureau of naturalization explains that it cannot proceed on the assumption that Little America is American soil. That would be *trespass on international questions* where it has no sanction. So far as the bureau is concerned, Balchen was out of the country and *technically* has not complied with the law of naturalization.[14]

Such inadequacies in orientation which involve trained incapacity clearly derive from structural sources. The process may be briefly recapitulated. (1) An effective bureaucracy demands reliability of response and strict devotion to regulations. (2) Such devotion to the rules leads to their transformation into absolutes; they are no longer conceived as relative to a given set of purposes. (3) This interferes with ready adaptation under special conditions not clearly envisaged by those who drew up the general rules. (4) Thus, the very elements which conduce toward efficiency in general produce inefficiency in specific instances. Full realization of the inadequacy is seldom attained by members of the group who have not divorced themselves from the "meanings" which the rules have for them. These rules in time become symbolic in cast, rather than strictly utilitarian.

Thus far, we have treated the ingrained sentiments making for rigorous discipline simply as data, as given. However, definite features of the bureaucratic structure may be seen to conduce to these sentiments. The bureaucrat's official life is planned for him in terms of a graded career, through the organizational devices of promotion by seniority, pensions, incremental salaries, *etc.*, all of which are designed to provide incentives for disciplined action and conformity to the official regulations.[15] The official is tacitly expected to and largely does adapt his thoughts, feelings, and actions to the prospect of this career. But *these very devices* which increase the probability of conformance also lead to an over-concern with strict adherence to regulations which induces timidity, conservatism, and technicism. Displacement of sentiments from goals onto means is fostered by the tremendous symbolic significance of the means (rules).

Another feature of the bureaucratic structure tends to produce much the same result. Functionaries have the sense of a common destiny for all those who work together. They share the same interests, especially since there is relatively little competition insofar as promotion is in terms of seniority. In-group aggression is thus minimized and this arrangement is therefore conceived to be positively functional for the bureaucracy. However, the esprit de corps and informal social organization which typically develops in such situations often leads the personnel to defend their entrenched interests rather than to assist their clientele and elected higher officials. As President Lowell reports, if the bureaucrats believe that their status is not adequately recognized by an incoming elected official, detailed information will be withheld from him, leading him to errors for which he is held responsible. Or, if he seeks to dominate fully, and thus violates the sentiment of self-integrity of the bureaucrats, he may have documents brought to him in such numbers that he cannot manage to sign them all, let alone read them.[16] This illustrates the defensive informal organization which tends to arise whenever there is an apparent threat to the integrity of the group.[17]

It would be much too facile and partly erroneous to attribute such resistance by bureaucrats simply to vested interests. Vested interests oppose any new order which either eliminates or at least makes uncertain their differential advantage deriving from the current arrangements. This is undoubtedly involved in part in bureaucratic resistance to change but another process is perhaps more significant. As we have seen, bureaucratic officials affectively identify themselves with their way of life. They have a pride of craft which leads them to resist change in established routines; at least, those changes which are felt to be imposed by persons outside the inner circle of co-workers. This nonlogical pride of craft is a familiar pattern found even, to judge from Sutherland's *Professional Thief*, among pickpockets who, despite the risk, delight in mastering the prestige-bearing feat of "beating a left breech" (picking the left front trousers pocket).

In a stimulating paper, Hughes has applied the concepts of "secular" and "sacred" to various types of division of labor; "the sacredness" of caste and *Stände* prerogatives contrasts sharply with the increasing secularism of occupational differentiation in our mobile society.[18] However, as our discussion suggests, there may ensue, in particular vocations and in particular types of organization, the *process of sanctification* (viewed as the counterpart of the process of secularization). This is to say that through sentiment-formation, emotional dependence upon bureaucratic symbols and status, and affective involvement in spheres of competence and authority, there develop prerogatives involving attitudes of moral legitimacy which are established as values in their own right, and are no longer viewed as merely technical means for expediting administration. One may note a tendency for certain bureaucratic norms, originally introduced for technical reasons, to become rigidified and sacred, although, as Durkheim would say, they are *laïque en apparence*.[19] Durkheim has touched on this general process in his description of the attitudes and values which persist in the organic solidarity of a highly differentiated society.

Another feature of the bureaucratic structure, the stress on depersonalization of relationships, also plays its part in the bureaucrat's trained incapacity. The personality pattern of the bureaucrat is nucleated about this norm of impersonality. Both this and the categorizing tendency, which develops from the dominant role of general, abstract rules, tend to produce conflict in the bureaucrat's contacts with the public or clientele. Since functionaries minimize personal relations and resort to categorization, the peculiarities of individual cases are often ignored. But the client who, quite understandably, is convinced of the "special features" of *his* own problem often objects to such categorical treatment. Stereotyped behavior is not adapted to the exigencies of individual problems. The impersonal treatment of affairs which are at times of great personal significance to the client gives rise to the charge of "arrogance" and "haughtiness" of the bureaucrat. Thus, at the Greenwich Employment Exchange, the unemployed worker who is securing his insurance payment resents what he deems to be "the impersonality and, at times, the apparent abruptness and even harshness of his treatment by the clerks.... Some men complain of the superior attitude which the clerks have."[20]

Still another source of conflict with the public derives from the bureaucratic structure. The bureaucrat, in part irrespective of his position with*in* the hierarchy, acts as a representative of the power and prestige of the entire structure. In his official role his is vested with definite authority. This often leads to an actual or apparent domineering attitude, which may only be exaggerated by a discrepancy between his position within the hierarchy and his position with reference to the public.[21] Protest and recourse to other officials on the part of the client are often ineffective or largely precluded by the previously mentioned esprit de corps which joins the officials into a more or less solidary in-group. This source of conflict *may* be minimized in private enterprise since the client can register an effective protest by transferring his trade to another organization within the competitive system. But with the monopolistic nature of the public organization, no such alternative is possible. Moreover, in this case, tension is increased because of a discrepancy between ideology and fact: the governmental personnel are held to be "servants of the people," but in fact they are usually superordinate, and release of tension can seldom be afforded by turning to other agencies for the necessary service.[22] This tension is in part attributable to the confusion of status of bureaucrat and client; the client may consider himself socially superior to the official who is at the moment dominant.[23]

Thus, with respect to the relations between officials and clientele, one structural source of conflict is the pressure for formal and impersonal treatment when individual, personalized consideration is desired by the client. The conflict may be viewed, then, as deriving from the introduction of inappropriate attitudes and relationships. Conflict *within* the bureaucratic structure arises from the converse situation, namely, when personalized relationships are substituted for the structurally required impersonal relationships. This type of conflict may be characterized as follows.

The bureaucracy, as we have seen, is organized as a secondary, formal group. The normal responses involved in this organized network of social expectations are supported by affective attitudes of members of the group. Since the group is oriented toward secondary norms of impersonality, any failure to conform to these norms will arouse antagonism from those who have identified themselves with the legitimacy of these rules. Hence, the substitution of personal for impersonal treatment within the structure is met with widespread disapproval and is characterized by such epithets as graft, favoritism, nepotism, apple-polishing, etc. These epithets are clearly manifestations of injured sentiments.[24] The function of such "automatic resentment" can be clearly seen in terms of the requirements of bureaucratic structure.

Bureaucracy is a secondary group mechanism designed to carry on certain activities which cannot be satisfactorily performed on the basis of primary group criteria.[25] Hence behavior which runs counter to these formalized norms becomes the object of emotionalized disapproval. This constitutes a functionally significant defence set up against tendencies which jeopardize the performance of socially necessary activities. To be sure, these reactions are not rationally determined practices explicitly designed for the fulfilment of this function. Rather, viewed in terms of the individual's interpretation of the situation, such resentment is simply an immediate response opposing the "dishonesty" of those who violate the rules of the game. However, this subjective frame of reference notwithstanding, these reactions serve the function of maintaining the essential structural elements of bureaucracy by reaffirming the necessity for formalized, secondary relations and by helping to prevent the disintegration of the bureaucratic structure which would occur should these be supplanted by personalized relations. This type of conflict may be generically described as the intrusion of primary group attitudes when secondary group attitudes are institutionally demanded, just as the bureaucrat-client conflict often derives from interaction on impersonal terms when personal treatment is individually demanded.[26]

The trend toward increasing bureaucratization in Western society, which Weber had long since foreseen, is not the sole reason for sociologists to turn their attention to this field. Empirical studies of the interaction of bureaucracy and personality should especially increase our understanding of social structure. A large number of specific questions invite our attention. To what extent are particular personality types selected and modified by the various bureaucracies (private enterprise, public service, the quasi-legal political machine, religious orders)? Inasmuch as ascendancy and submission are held to be traits of personality, despite their variability in different stimulus-situations, do bureaucracies select personalities of particularly submissive or ascendant tendencies? And since various studies have shown that these traits can be modified, does participation in bureaucratic office tend to increase ascendant tendencies? Do various systems of recruitment (*e.g.* patronage, open competition involving specialized knowledge or "general mental capacity," practical experience) select different personality types? Does promotion through seniority lessen competitive anxieties and enchance administrative efficiency? A detailed examination of mechanisms for imbuing the bureaucratic codes with affect would be instructive both sociologically and psychologically. Does the general anonymity of civil service decisions tend to restrict the area of prestige-symbols to a narrowly defined inner circle? Is there a tendency for differential association to be especially marked among bureaucrats?

The range of theoretically significant and practically important questions would seem to be limited only by the accessibility of the concrete data. Studies of religious, educational, military, economic, and political bureaucracies dealing with the interdependence of social organization and personality formation should constitute an avenue for fruitful research. On that avenue, the functional analysis of concrete structures may yet build a Solomon's House for sociologists.

FOOTNOTES

[1] For a development of the concept of "rational organization," see Karl Mannheim, *Mensch und Gesellschaft im Zeitalter des Umbaus* (Leiden: A. W. Sijthoff, 1935), esp. pp. 28 ff.

[2] H. D. Lasswell, *Politics* (New York: McGraw-Hill, 1936), pp. 120-21.

[3] Max Weber, *Wirtschaft und Gesellschaft* (Tübingen: J. C. B. Mohr, 1922), Pt. III, chap. 6, pp. 650-678. For a brief summary of Weber's discussion, see Talcott Parsons, *The Structure of Social Action* (New York: McGraw-Hill, 1937), esp. pp. 506 ff. For a description, which is not a caricature, of the bureaucrat as a personality type, see C. Rabany, "Les types sociaux: le fonctionnaire," *Revue générale d'administration*, LXXXVIII (1907), 5-28.

[4] Karl Mannheim, *Ideology and Utopia* (New York: Harcourt, Brace, 1936), pp. 18n., 105 ff. See also Ramsay Muir, *Peers and Bureaucrats* (London: Constable, 1910), pp. 12-13.

[5] E. G. Cahen-Salvador suggests that the personnel of bureaucracies is largely constituted of those who value security above all else. See his "La situation matérielle et morale des fonctionnaires," *Revue politique et parlementaire* (1926), p. 319.

[6] H. J. Laski, "Bureaucracy," *Encyclopedia of the Social Sciences*. This article is written primarily from the standpoint of the political scientist rather than that of the sociologist.

[7] Weber, *op. cit.*, p. 671.

[8] For a stimulating discussion and application of these concepts, see Kenneth Burke, *Permanence and Change* (New York: New Republic, 1935), pp. 50 ff.; Daniel Warnotte, "Bureaucratie et Fonctionnarisme," *Revue de l'Institut de Sociologie*, XVII (1937), 245.

[9] *Ibid.*, pp. 58-59.

[10] *Ibid.*, p. 70.

[11] This process has often been observed in various connections. Wundt's *heterogony of ends* is a case in point; Max Weber's *Paradoxic der Folgen* is another. See also MacIver's observations on the transformation of civilization into culture and Lasswell's remark that "the human animal distinguishes himself by his infinite capacity for making ends of his means." See R. K. Merton, "The Unanticipated Consequences of Purposive Social Action," *American Sociological Review*, I (1936), 894-904. In terms of the psychological mechanisms involved, this process has been analyzed most fully by Gordon W. Allport, in his discussion of what he calls "the functional autonomy of motives." Allport emends the earlier formulations of Woodworth, Tolman, and William Stern, and arrives at a statement of the process from the standpoint of individual motivation. He does not consider those phases of the social structure which conduce toward the "transformation of motives." The formulation adopted in this paper is thus complementary to Allport's analysis; the one stressing the psychological mechanisms involved, the other considering the constraints of the social structure. The convergence of psychology and sociology toward this central concept suggests that it may well constitute one of the conceptual bridges between the two disciplines. See Gordon W. Allport, *Personality* (New York: Henry Holt & Co., 1937), chap. 7.

[12] See E. C. Hughes, "Institutional Office and the Person," *American Journal of Sociology*, XLIII (1937), 404-413; R. K. Merton, "Social Structure and Anomie," *American Sociological Review*, III (1938), 672-682; E. T. Hiller, "Social Structure in Relation to the Person," *Social Forces*, XVI (1937), 34-44.

[13] Mannheim, *Ideology and Utopia*, p. 106.

[14] Quoted from the *Chicago Tribune* (June 24, 1931, p. 10) by Thurman Arnold, *The Symbols of Government* (New Haven: Yale University Press, 1935), pp. 201-2. (My italics.)

[15] Mannheim, *Mensch und Gesellschaft*, pp. 32-33. Mannheim stresses the importance of the "Lebensplan" and the "Amtskarriere." See the comments by Hughes, *op. cit.*, 413.

[16] A. L. Lowell, *The Government of England* (New York, 1908), I, 189 ff.

[17] For an instructive description of the development of such a defensive organization in a group of workers, see F. J. Roethlisberger and W. J. Dickson, *Management and the Worker* (Boston: Harvard School of Business Administration, 1934).

[18] E. C. Hughes, "Personality Types and the Division of Labor," *American Journal of Sociology*, XXXIII (1928), 754-768. Much the same distinction is drawn by Leopold von Wiese and Howard Becker, *Systematic Sociology* (New York: John Wiley & Sons, 1932), pp. 222-25 et passim.

[19] Hughes recognizes one phase of this process of sanctification when he writes that professional training "carries with it as a by-product assimilation of the candidate to a set of professional attitudes and controls, *a professional conscience and solidarity. The profession claims and aims to become a moral unit.*" Hughes, *op. cit.*, p. 762, (italics inserted). In this same connection, Sumner's concept of *pathos*, as the halo of sentiment which protects a social value from criticism, is particularly relevant, inasmuch as it affords a clue to the mechanisms involved in the process of sanctification. See his *Folkways* (Boston: Ginn & Co., 1906), pp. 180-181.

[20] " 'They treat you like a lump of dirt they do. I see a navvy reach across the counter and shake one of them by the collar the other day. The rest of us felt like cheering. Of course he lost his benefit over it. . . . But the clerk deserved it for his sassy way.' " (E. W. Bakke, *The Unemployed Man*, New York: Dutton, 1934, pp. 79-80). Note that the domineering attitude was *imputed* by the unemployed client who is in a state of tension due to his loss of status and self-esteem in a society where the ideology is still current that an "able man" can always find a job. That the imputation of arrogance stems largely from the client's state of mind is seen from Bakke's own observation that "the clerks were rushed, and had no time for pleasantries, but there was little sign of harshness or a superiority feeling in their treatment of the men." Insofar as there is an objective basis for the imputation of arrogant behavior to bureaucrats, it may possibly be explained by the following juxtaposed statements. "Auch der moderne, sei es öffentliche, sei es private, Beamte erstrebt immer und geniesst meist den Beherrschten gegenüber eine spezifisch gehobene, 'ständische' soziale Schätzung." (Weber, *op. cit.*,

652.) "In persons in whom the craving for prestige is uppermost, hostility usually takes the form of a desire to humiliate others." (K. Horney, *The Neurotic Personality of Our Time*, New York: Norton, 1937, pp. 178-79.)

[21] In this connection, note the relevance of Koffka's comments on certain features of the pecking-order of birds. "If one compares the behavior of the bird at the top of the pecking list, the despot, with that of one very far down, the second or third from the last, then one finds the latter much more cruel to the few others over whom he lords it than the former in his treatment of all members. As soon as one removes from the group all members above the penultimate, his behavior becomes milder and may even become very friendly.... It is not difficult to find analogies to this in human societies, and therefore one side of such behavior must be primarily the effects of the social groupings, and not of individual characteristics." K. Koffka, *Principles of Gestalt Psychology* (New York: Harcourt, Brace, 1935), pp. 668-9.

[22] At this point the political machine often becomes functionally significant. As Steffens and others have shown, highly personalized relations and the abrogation of formal rules (red tape) by the machine often satisfy the needs of individual "clients" more fully than the formalized mechanism of governmental bureaucracy.

[23] As one of the unemployed men remarked about the clerks at the Greenwich Employment Exchange: " 'And the bloody blokes wouldn't have their jobs if it wasn't for us men out of a job either. That's what gets me about their holding their noses up.' " Bakke, *op. cit.*, p. 80.

[24] The diagnostic significance of such linguistic indices as epithets has scarcely been explored by the sociologist. Sumner properly observes that epithets produce "summary criticisms" and definitions of social situations. Dollard also notes that "epithets frequently define the central issues in a society," and Sapir has rightly emphasized the importance of context of situations in appraising the significance of epithets. Of equal relevance is Linton's observation that "in case histories the way in which the community felt about a particular episode is, if anything, more important to our study than the actual behavior...." A sociological study of "vocabularies of encomium and opprobrium" should lead to valuable findings.

[25] *Cf.* Ellsworth Faris, *The Nature of Human Nature* (New York: McGraw-Hill, 1937), pp. 41 ff.

[26] Community disapproval of many forms of behavior may be analyzed in terms of one or the other of these patterns of substitution of culturally inappropriate types of relationship. Thus, prostitution constitutes a type-case where coitus, a form of intimacy which is institutionally defined as symbolic of the most "sacred" primary group relationship, is placed within a contractual context, symbolized by the exchange of that most impersonal of all symbols, money. See Kingsley Davis, "The Sociology of Prostitution," *American Sociological Review*, II (1937), 744-55.

ABOUT THE AUTHOR—Robert K. Merton is one of the most widely esteemed American sociologists. He was born into a family of Eastern European immigrants in 1910 and spent his early years in the slums of south Pennsylvania. In 1931 he was awarded his bachelors degree from Temple University and received a Harvard Ph.D. in 1936. With the publication of his article "Social Structure and Anomie" in 1938 his reputation as a promising sociological theorist was firmly established. His research techniques, explained in his 1949 volume, *Social Theory and Social Structure*, were already becoming apparent in his work as a student at Harvard, where he classified thousands of patents issued between 1860 and 1930 as part of a student project and read more than 6000 biographies in fine print in order to prepare his doctoral dissertation. His theoretical concepts are painstakingly developed out of the collection, analysis and classification of many small bits of information.

Merton's teaching career began as an instructor at Harvard and continued at Tulane University. He later accepted a position at Columbia where he is now chairman of the Department of Sociology. Since 1942 he has also held the post of associate director of the Bureau of Applied Social Research there. Merton's writings cover the widest possible spectrum in sociology but his strongest thrust has been in analytical and conceptual contributions. He is known as a perfectionist and sometimes takes years to finish an important piece of work before releasing it for publication. During his distinguished career he has published over a hundred articles and a number of classic volumes.

The Decision-Making Approach

No single manifestation of organizational behavior in recent years has so attracted the attention of behavioral scholars as has the decision-making process. Perhaps this is because the basic elements of decision-making are such a complex mélange of psychological, sociological, philosophical, and technological elements. Each of the disciplines claims the decision process as its own or at least assumes a proprietary interest in its essence. Perhaps no element of administration is so very much at its core as the process of making appropriate choices from among alternatives, or the making of decisions. The literature of decision-making in recent years has burgeoned dramatically. The net result of such zealous analysis has been only to reinforce the notion of the interrelatedness of the several disciplines to the process of choice deliberation. This approach appears to be a particularly viable way to view the processes and to understand the bases for behavior, as well as to identify internal organizational issues in libraries.

A Bibliographical Essay on Decision Making

by William J. Gore and Fred S. Silander

Perhaps the highest order of bibliographic contribution is that synthesis of a literature which relates and interrelates a wide range of publications so as to introduce order and understanding—the bibliographic essay. In the piece which follows the authors have succeeded at the task. They have sifted through a remarkable range of contributions from the sociological, the psychological, and the management science fields, in order to characterize the direction of research and theory in decision-making. The ultimate assessment is that, in spite of an impressive range, the net result is uneven and while certain aspects of decision-making concern have been much studied, other areas have been generally untouched.

It has been said that administration is the critical organizational process, making possible production, procurement, and the rest; that leadership is the heart of administration; and that decision making is the key to leadership. Inherent in these statements are some remarkably accurate characterizations of current administrative theory. One thing they seem to imply is a coherence and a unity in administrative theory which do not seem to exist. When one attempts to assay the literature dealing with a concrete administrative process such as decision making, he discovers this. Divergent approaches to the study of decision making show that there are conflicting conceptions of its nature and function. And these probably are symptoms of a more fundamental conflict in contemporary administrative theory.

Administration and leadership as foci for study have traditionally been the concern of historians, occasional novelists, and students of management, public and private. A generation ago these people had articulated a consistent, rather comprehensive conception of leadership, and especially administration. The *Papers* of Gulick and Urwick, for example, were regarded by many of us as a major conceptual achievement setting forth a twentieth-century theory of organization. Even as these ideas were gaining acceptance, however, the concepts that would replace them were emerging. After World War I, even before the appearance of the *Papers*, industrial sociologists, psychologists, and cultural anthropologists had begun the study of motivation, leadership, communication, and the like. During World War II economists, mathematicians, and statisticians concerned with logistics, war planning, and management of industry-wide planning agencies found themselves analyzing decisional and managerial problems. The war also brought industrial engineers and administrative analysts into management, though they dealt primarily with the more limited, more concrete problems of production and control. In each instance squatters' rights taken fifteen or twenty years ago have been established as homesteads, with the result that the field of management is now an arena where a dozen professions, each armed with its own techniques and framework of concepts and each claiming supporters, contend for the right to see the pattern for management.

Whether this is a desirable state of affairs or not the reader can determine. It seems certain that a vast quantity of ideas, some of them impressive in their quality, have been made available to the practicing administrator. It seems equally certain that the theoretical unity and coherence once ascribed to the *Papers* has been forever destroyed, leaving a kind of conceptual wonderland full of magnificently intricate and promising devices but without any central ordering or organizing concept. It will help to deal with this variety of approaches if decision making is tentatively defined. Although Webster defines it as the settling of a controversy, the term is probably more often used in the sense of making a choice. Just what kind of a choice depends somewhat upon one's conceptual orientation.

Students of formal organization, concerned with structure, authority, and responsibility, often suggest that the choice is presented to an official as a result of some procedure built into the hier-

SOURCE: Reprinted from William J. Gore and Fred S. Silander, "A Bibliographical Essay on Decision Making," *Administrative Science Quarterly*, 4 (June, 1959), pp. 97–121, by permission of the publisher and the authors.

archy which digests the many pressures playing upon it and sifts out for his attention those within his prescribed area of discretion. Frequently more concerned with the politically meaningful question of whether or not the ultimate decision reflects the public will, the scholar is inclined to use the investigation of hierarchical procedures and structural controls as tools for dealing with this question. One of the best public administration texts maintains that "decision-making represents a process where ideas, individuals, events and political considerations are analyzed to meet a problem situation."[2] This might imply that decision making is a process which has its roots far back in organizational experience and is not so much a planned activity as the indigenous and sometimes momentary expression of organizational character in response to a particular demand situation.

What will be labeled the management science approach offers a more rigid conception of the decision-making process. Where the traditionalist assumes that decision making must be at least a reasonable process, and a really logical one when possible, the management scientist, including operations researchers, statistical decision theorists, and industrial engineers, uses rationality as the keystone of his conceptions. Bross's view reflects this emphasis. "Decision-making is . . . the process of selecting one action from a number of alternative courses."[3] Later he states that we have seen decision making evolve from the myth-dominated devil theories of several centuries ago to the rationalistic or scientific basis of the late nineteenth century, and that statistical decision making represents the most powerful of the recent breakthroughs toward more reliable decision making.[4]

Any discussion of decision making must include reference to the conceptions of Herbert Simon of the Carnegie Institute of Technology, who places the decision within the environment of raw organization and its multiplicity of conflicting ideologies, its currents and counter-currents of motive, anxiety, stress, strivings, and satisfactions. It is clear from his classic *Administrative Behavior* that while rational decision-making processes represent the ideal, the organizational context is dominantly nonrational.[5] But one suspects that the more recent *Models of Man* indicates that he accepts the rationalistic imperative and that he is seeking the development of decision-making processes which so maximize rationality that the nonrational impact of the organizational environment is either minimized or negligible.[6]

Snyder, Bruck, and Sapin offer a most useful definition which in many ways reflects the same problems Simon deals with. "Decision-making is a process which results in the selection from a socially defined, limited number of problematical, alternative projects (objectives) of one project intended to bring about the particular future state of affairs envisaged by the decision-makers."[7] Snyder and his associates straddle the gap between the rationalistic presumption of the management scientists and the traditionalists and a third group, the organizational behaviorists. Social scientists studying organizational behavior have adopted the presumption that while rationality is a desirable basis for choice making, given the nature of man, his organizations, and his contradictory emotions and needs, it is not realistic to assume that rationality can become the primary basis of collective choice making.

In his work on the role of the executive, Barnard offers an interpretation which many will find suitable for their own understanding and research.

When decision is involved, there are consciously present two terms—the end to be accomplished and the means to be used. The end itself may be the result of logical processes in which the end is in turn a means to some broader or more remote end; or the immediate end, and generally the ultimate end, may not be a result of logical processes but "given," that is, unconsciously impressed, by conditions, including social conditions past and present and orders of organizations. But whenever the end has been determined, by whatever processes, the decision as to means is itself a logical process of discrimination, analysis and choice—however defective either the factual basis for choice or the reasoning related to these facts.[8]

Most behaviorists would accept this statement and then go on to maintain that administrative decision making is typically an organizational response—launched from and largely determined by collective agreement—to a demand situation. This response is seen by the participants as embodying the values by means of which the organization identifies itself, maintains its structure of roles and patterns of activity, locates its friends and its enemies, and so forth. How much of this is done rationally will vary from organization to organization, but the behaviorist would maintain that it is primarily a rational response in only a few organizations. It is "psycho-logical," but not characteristically logical.

The remainder of this discussion seeks to identify some of the major sources elaborating these two approaches to the analysis of decision making; the rationalistic on the one hand and the behaviorist or organismic on the other.

ORGANISMIC APPROACH

Where the management scientist may conceive of organization as a relatively predictable system of collective action, both the traditionalist and the behaviorist tend to see it as the confluence of several streams of interrelated behavior. If their ultimate aims are similar—everyone is striving toward increased understanding of organization—what the rationalist and the behaviorist actually set down on paper is sufficiently dissimilar so that this is not always apparent. The traditionalist and the behaviorist seem to conceive of a stream of behavior first in terms of its organizational setting, describing it as an interdependent subsystem in a larger system. For example, both the administrative theorist and the management analyst take pains to identify the chain of relationships through which productive activity is tied to public sentiment or consumer demand. This view suggested the term organismic as the title for this section.

Students of formal organization included the organismic element in administrative theory from the beginning. They constructed an extensive body of management ideology that is the immediate foundation of the hierarchies of most of our companies, corporations, and government agencies, as well as the rationale underlying the rise of the professional manager. It is also the source of most of the ideas justifying our position as a leader in management expertise. Such concepts as specialization, chain of command, accountability, efficiency, responsibility, centralization-decentralization, co-ordination, integration, and the like are the kinds of ideas underlying what has been called the managerial revolution.[9]

Since World War I the monopoly of the traditionalists has been threatened, first, by the human relations movement and, following World War II, by the organizational behaviorists. Behaviorists have contributed useful new terms—co-optation, threshold of stress, group syntality; and they have substantially extended the meaning of some others—communication, authority, motivation. Without dwelling on the differences, not to mention incipient conflicts, between these two orientations, one can safely say that they represent vital alternatives to the management science approach.

The Web of Organizational Relationships

One hallmark of the organismic approach is the analysis of organizations within their environments. Most behaviorists and many traditionalists define the organization as a dynamic social organism linked through a web of institutional relationships to the groups, agencies, companies, unions, interests, and publics that constitute its environment. A dominant presupposition is that an organization and its environment are highly interdependent. This mutual dependence has several dimensions, which can be identified by discussing relevant studies.

A pioneering and still worthy conception of organizations as the cells of the larger community is presented in the two Middletown studies by Robert and Helen Lynd.[10] These studies view society as the aggregate of several institutional substructures, each with its characteristic processes and functions. The Lynds examined the economic, family, educational, religious, and recreational institutions in Middletown and then illustrated their joint functioning to meet community-wide needs. By dissecting a community into its component organs, the authors provide a perspective against which the web of relationships of any particular organization can be charted and interdependencies identified. In volume seven of the famous Yankee City study, Warner and his associates develop and apply a similar anatomical technique with considerable success.[11] Where the Lynds found that Middletown's reactions to the boom and depression could be accounted for in terms of the responses implicit in its social mechanisms, Warner and Low trace the impact of the economic revolution of the thirties upon a shoe factory as this revolution took root in the institutions and then the interinstitutional relationships of the community. In both studies it is suggested that organizations must face the future with what they have garnered from the past. And further, that the new, unanticipated demands which periodically confront an organization seldom yield to anything less than creative cross-institutional efforts. Hence the web of institutional relationships is a basis for survival. Jaques and his associates add to this perspective the psychiatrist's concern with the individual in their detailed study of a deliberate policy change in a British factory. They define with rewarding precision the critical links in the invisible chain of interdependencies which tie individual, work group, division, organization, and community into a more or less stable social system.[12]

Paralleling these studies are several more purely theoretical treatises that seek to provide broad frames of reference which represent the dynamics of various types of social systems. The most dramatic, recondite, and controversial of these is the work of Talcott Parsons. Parsons, Bales, and Shils collaborated on the well-known *Working Papers*[13] in *The Theory of Action*. Though the five papers are not presented as more than theory fragments,[14] they must be counted among the most ambitious attempts to present systematically the subtleties and intricacies of social action.

Chapter 5 presents a scheme which assumes that individual and collective motivations are inputs which can be directed toward a number of potential objectives—or, more properly, outlets. A number of dimensions of action which can be taken as co-ordinates of a frame of reference for interpreting action are set down.

Motivational energy entering the system [of action represented by the frame of reference] from an organism cannot simultaneously operate in all the possible processes which go to make up the system. It must be specifically *located*, in the sense that it must be allocated to one or more units of the system .... The dimensional scheme assumes that energy must either be "stored up" in the reservoir or it must be "expended" through transformation into gratification [satisfactions].[15]

Another widely known formal theory is that of Robert Merton.[16] His core conception is functionalism, and his development of the concepts of the function and dysfunction of various organizational behaviors, and their latent as well as manifest functions, has left its mark on much of behavioral science. The field theory of Kurt Lewin is in the same context, though it is less expansive.[17]

Where Parsons, Merton, and Lewin deal with concepts having some universality for society, Homans has constructed an intensive theory representing the dynamics of the small group.[18] His work is especially meaningful for decision making since most decisions are made in and by groups—using this term in its general sense. Homans sees the group as a different species from the organization, for it serves the immediate needs of its members and its clientele. It is prior to these larger organisms in the sense that small groups are the living cells from which organizations are constructed.[19]

Two works reflecting a more restricted attempt to represent the central dynamic of social organisms might be mentioned. In both cases the social organism is government. In point of time Herring's *Public Administration and the Public Interest* comes first.[20] Here the ideas of interdependence, alternative levels of behavior, confined or structured conflict as the norm of organizational behavior, and power are woven together in an early example of functional analysis. Implicit in this conception (as in most others with a functional orientation) is a cycle which begins with felt needs of the citizenry. In a second step these are articulated by pressure and interest groups into latent policy alternatives. In a third step legislative and administrative policy makers legitimatize these as formal governmental goals, and in succeeding steps these are refined, implemented, and translated into action aimed at meeting the original felt needs of the public. David Truman provides a more fully elaborated theory along these same general lines.[21]

This matter of interdependence is common to all of these works. It may involve supplying resources, power, technical assistance, co-operative attacks on common problems, defense against a common antagonist (or potential antagonist), and so forth. In life these interdependencies take the form of interrelationships, which exist because they are (or were) functional—and the more central the function, the higher the interdependence. Two or more formal representatives may be involved. They may work within the limits of a legal agreement (as would a purchasing agent and a sales representative); they may involve individuals who operate as informal liaison officers; or there may be a formal or indigenous "committee" which functions as a linkage mechanism.

In any case the relationships which link an organization with its environment greatly influence its character, its goals, and its opportunities; and the consistency implicit in the total configuration of the commitments embodied in these relationships largely determines the kinds of stresses it will be subject to. Thus relationships which constitute the organization's ties with its environment can reasonably be defined as the ultimate climate of decision making. We shall have to develop refined techniques for representing these if we are to account for the course of the decision-making process. At present such techniques are virtually unknown.

The most striking work on this aspect of organization is Selznick's bench-mark study of TVA.[22] Selznick suggests the term co-optation to represent the "you scratch my back and I'll scratch yours" aspect of any relationship embodying organizational interdependence. His extensive use of the concepts of anticipated and unanticipated consequences of action leads him to discuss the constraints embodied in co-optative relationships, the commitments implicit in them, and finally the mechanisms of maintaining these commitments and enforcing them within the context of a "moving equilibrium."[23]

Almost the only other major works dealing with the organizational environment are aimed primarily at the problem of power, its sources, techniques for generating it, and the like. This thoroughly ambiguous term has a venerable position in the study of organizations. Students from Plato on have understood that power, like money, may not be among the world's most honorable goods but that it is almost impossible to get along without simply because when two men get together the requirements for the emergence of an elemental form of power have been met.

Selznick's study is a valuable source on power. It is significant because for perhaps the first time it systematically treats co-optative power. Where students of formal organization have concerned themselves with formal authority, the formal powers of government, and their control through hierarchal devices, Selznick demonstrates that these extra-formal powers are often the foundation of hierarchal power. Arthur Maass' study of administrative responsibility (and the lack of it) within the Corps of Engineers is also a valuable analysis of power. In pointing up the contradictions confronting an agency attempting to maintain a sense of responsibility to Congress, the executive, and its clientele, Maass emphasizes the role of power as one of the pivotal objectives around which organizational behavior turns.

If, as was the assumption of such pioneer administrative theorists as Gulick, Urwick, and White, organizational objectives could be formulated as a logically consistent set of goals, rationality might indeed be the fulcrum of administration.[24] But as Maass shows, the objectives of many organizations are shot through with dramatic inconsistencies. The result—though this is beyond the scope of *Muddy Waters*—is that there is an ultimate irreducible element of "might makes right" in any administrative decision-making process.

On a highly theoretical plane Lasswell and Kaplan have recognized this.[25] They have tried to provide a frame of reference that brings together and rationalizes the philosophical problem of power, ethics, and reason. David Lilienthal takes account of this problem (though not with such a direct attack as Lasswell and Kaplan) in his commentary on TVA.[26] In both works the authors are concerned with the conflict between the realities of our attempts to institutionalize the manipulation of political power and the ethical imperatives of rationality and the Christian ethic.

These theoretical commentaries on the nature and control of power have a number of empirical counterparts: studies of the distribution of power in groups, communities, and organizations. The most impressive of these is Hunter's representation of the monolithic structure of power in Atlanta.[27] Where sociologists had been studying social stratification and differentiation for some time,[28] Hunter sought to lay bare the anatomy of power in one metropolis. His techniques have now been improved, and numerous similar studies have been made.[29] More important, the theoretical assumptions about community power structures have been reconsidered, and suggestive new formulations are appearing. James March's work stands out, providing operational definitions of power suitable for research and yet sophisticated enough to comprehend the ethical problem.[30] This piece is best considered along with a brilliant analysis by Herbert Simon which well serves as a beginning point for any systematic approach to power.[31] And both of these discussions will be more meaningful if one first reads Dahl's critique of the method-oriented theory of Hunter *et al.* vs. the theory-oriented constructs of scholars like Simon and March.[32]

Organization—The Context of Decision Making

Organizational environment, as discussed above, may be considered as the secondary but immediate structure within which the more intimate structure of the group conditions the choice-making behaviors of the actors. In spite of the impressive theorizing about the small group now available we are still lacking conceptions which account fully for the multitudinous and sometimes contradictory relationships between group structure and decision-making processes. Is the dynamic choice-making behavior separate from the static structure of the group? Or is decision making essentially structure in motion, in much the same way that energy is matter in another state?

Lack of agreement leads to indeterminateness on a more concrete level, but not to a vacuum. There is no question but that the configuration of shared values, the structure of roles that set the relationships between individuals in the group, the reward and penalty systems, the mechanisms of social control, the division of labor, and the technology of a group all have considerable impact upon its decision-making processes. Thus, while questions of the relationship between structure and process and function are not settled, a great deal is known about the fragmentary relationships between particular structural functions and behaviors under given conditions; these bear directly upon the decision-making process.

The research of Peter Blau brings together a great deal of what we know about organizational behavior. His *Dynamics of Bureaucracy* is a fine example of the use of Merton's functionalism as a framework for empirical research. Here the concept of function is defined "as observed consequences of social patterns that change existing conditions in the direction of socially valued objectives."[33] The underlying conceptions are developed further to include latent (unanticipated) as well as manifest functions, the mechanisms through which functional effects are brought about, and the interplay between functional and dysfunctional mechanisms of social change. One of the interesting facets of Blau's study is that he concentrated upon first- and second-level supervision instead of upon the policy makers at the top of the hierarchy.

In many ways Blau provides a precise and more extensive articulation of the landmark work of Roethlisberger and Dickson.[34] This early study provided a blueprint for future investigations.[35]

Two additional studies seeking to treat the broad dynamics of organizational behavior must be mentioned. Bakke's *Bonds of Organization* differs from the studies cited above in that it is not an empirical study.[36] Weiss's *Process of Organization*, which represents a partial exposition of the important work of the Survey Research Center, is data based and is certainly the most rigorous of all of these studies.[37] Chapter headings such as "Processes of Allocation," "Processes of Adaptation and Coordination," and the "Structure of Organization" contain a novel conception of organization as a fusion of crucial behaviors.

Because it has a similar objective Bale's *Interaction Process Analysis* must be mentioned.[38] Here is a highly systematic technique for analyzing the problem-solving processes of a group. There is little doubt but that this device and its successors will become the instruments for advances toward a behavioral decision theory in the next decade. And no researcher can afford not to have scanned this work, for it provides operational categories such as "Asks opinion, Disagrees, Gives orientation, and Gives suggestion."[39]

Alongside these "group-wide" studies are those which focus on one broad dimension of groups. One such dimension is structure, either as role structure or status system. William F. Whyte's analysis of status systems in restaurants is among the most valuable in a field where there have been many studies.[40] Whyte shows how differentiation between roles is one of the foundations of group behavior; i.e., the specialized patterns of individual behavior associated with the role of cook, waitress, vegetable girl, and so on are the foundation of the division of labor within the group; the social interdependencies (an individual in one role must frequently have the co-operation of others to satisfy his own needs) between roles is a major force tending to stabilize role relationships. In any structure of roles there will be points of conflict and the means of handling these are partly a function of the status system. Particularly, the interdependencies within the status system act as dampers, controlling the limits and intensity of most role conflicts.

In one of several reports of his studies Bales points out that consensus among the members of a group on their different statuses is a function of agreement on certain critical values, related to technical aspects of production and to mutual acceptance between leaders and followers within the group.[41]

Benne and Sheats offer a classification of roles according to function. They include productive roles, group-building roles, facilitative roles, and the like.[42] These studies are typical of literally hundreds, and the reader is referred to the survey of the literature by Bendix above.[43]

A second fundamental dimension of the group is its value system. This also has been studied, but much less, under such labels as belief system, ideology, and structure of attitudes. Perhaps the most remarkable work in this area is Alexander Leighton's study of belief systems in an internment camp during World War II.[44] Leighton assumed that beliefs and values are at or near the core of personality. This leads him to the proposition that patterns of shared beliefs are an important basis for the formation of groups. In language that anyone can understand, artfully weaving data and conceptual framework together, Leighton presents an analysis of the dynamics of groups under stress in terms of their belief systems. He considers why one group reacts to the threat of superior authority with aggression and another with withdrawal and how belief systems serve as the reservoirs of experience and as a latent predisposition to action.

De Grazia develops a similar conception of belief systems as a basis for understanding the whole political community.[45] He sees beliefs and systems of belief not only as the framework of society, but as some of the most important manifestations of society. That is, he feels we are not dealing here with the traces on a cardiograph, but we have here a direct view of one of society's vital organs. If we can but develop techniques to chart pulsations of these verbal systems, we can develop diagnostic techniques that can correct pathological patterns before disorganization threatens the functioning of organization.

But De Grazia does not attempt to formulate stable propositions set in empirically grounded frames of reference. For another thorough study of the dynamics of belief and value systems, but one which deals primarily with perception and valuation, Bruner and Postman are suggested.[46] They hold that organizational perception can be represented as a sequence patterned around a manageable number of the total dimensions of reality, organization (relating selective perception to internal configuration of shared values), accentuation (of some perceptions as a preparatory step toward action), and fixation (commitment to a specific interpretation of a perceived situation).[47]

The Decision making Process

Decision making—as a sequence of behaviors—has been placed in perspective against the web of interorganizational relationships and the immediate setting of the group. There remain those works probing the nature of the process itself. Unfortunately these are extremely limited.

In a stimulating "think piece" Robert Dahl suggests that there are four broad classes of decision-making processes: the democratic (where leaders are heavily influenced by nonleaders through such devices as nomination and election), the hierarchical (where leaders are heavily influenced by the structure of the hierarchy itself), the bargaining (where leaders to some degree interdependent with each other exercise reciprocal controls over each other), and the pricing system (though this is qualitatively different from the first three).[48] His central proposition, that "leadership is somewhat specialized and not monolithic, it is bargaining not hierarchical," might well be made a part of the foundation of any future studies. It clearly is a necessary consequence of the "process" approach to the analysis of decision-making in that we presume that decision is not made by one man after receiving all of the facts and alternative courses of action from staff, but by a series of persons—many of them not occupying formal positions—within the hierarchy that happens to be the locale of a particular choice-making episode.[49]

A helpful inquiry into the nature of decision making is Harold Stein's introduction in the Inter-university Case Program casebook.[50] He holds "that the decision itself is fundamentally a process rather than an act, without temporal dimensions."[51] There are no hard and fast rules for piloting the process to a satisfactory conclusion or choice. "Analysis and answer must follow two paths—tactics and values."[52] Finally he suggests that the decisional process must always be analyzed simultaneously as process (group or organizational) and as politics (the interplay of process with organizational environment).

This conception is similar to that of Barnard and Simon.[53] Barnard identifies three executive functions which in effect become processes. These are to maintain organizational communication, to secure essential individual services, and to formulate objectives.[54] But it was Simon who first attempted to formulate what social scientists call an operational statement of the decisional process. Like any attempt to approximate reality, his formulations are too complex to summarize accurately here, but they are essential to anyone seeking to understand decision making.[55]

Still, none of these works presents a fully elaborated operational theory of decision making. Snyder, Bruck, and Sapin attempted a limited formulation in 1954. Their concept of decision as "successive, overlapping definitions of the situation" is an important step toward an operational model. Reflecting Stein's process orientation, they take some pains to present a conception of communication behaviors as the anatomy of the process, including such activities as feedback, restrictive circulation of information, and interaction between communication and authority.[56]

With the exception of several works presenting guides to more effective decision making,[57] and others presenting fragments of theories or merely detailed points of view, such as Durisch's case history of TVA decisions,[58] or Gore's loose process model,[59] one is hard put to suggest other fruitful sources.

Given the absence of materials on decision making as presently defined, one fruitful possibility is to reach over into yet another discipline, experimental psychology, and seek models and concepts from studies of problem solving and thinking. A stimulating work, *A Study of Thinking*, is available.[60] Its chapters include "The Process of Concept Attainment," "Selection Strategies in Concept Attainment," and "Language and Categories." Equally important is the book's two-hundred item bibliography. Another example of the application of psychology to choice making is "Individual Decisions to Undertake Psychotherapy" in this journal.[61] That the claims of advocates of brainstorming and creative thinking are subject to some question is apparent from Taylor's empirical study, "Group Participation, Brainstorming and Creative Thinking," also in *Administrative Science Quarterly*.[62]

THE MANAGEMENT SCIENCE ORIENTATION

The most aggressive probing into decision making techniques has come from those seeking to develop a management science.[63] While traditionalists may accept some compromise of the principle of rationality, many management scientists seek devices and procedures which will reduce both nonrationality and irrationality to negligible factors in decision making. Thus their discussions frequently center on more precise ways of describing the choices confronting management. A good deal of attention is given to the precise definition of alternatives within these choices. And more recently a great deal of attention has been directed toward the identification of the probable "outcomes" of a particular alternative. The expected consequences of each anticipated course of action having been estimated, the critical step is that of maximizing utility or disutility by weighting these outcomes within the values of the organization.

One has the impression that there are those who look toward the time when numerical values, representing estimated outcomes, may be substituted for verbal symbols in a formula representing organizational goals, which would then be solved for a decision. Lest this seem incredible, it should be noted that it was done on a lathe operator's decisions long ago by Fredrich Taylor, and his expectations are becoming a reality through the application of today's more powerful tools to a manager's problems.

If it is accidental that the term management science is almost a simple reversal of scientific management, it is not without significance, for there is a sense in which the current scientific, rationalist movement is essentially scientific management with new, vastly more powerful tools. Where Taylor used algebra, arithmetic, engineering knowledge, and common sense, we find calculus, probability statistics, and the scientific method.

But though the labels are similar and there is a continuity of purpose, it would be misleading to suggest that the current management science movement stems from scientific management. Although it has benefited immeasurably by the ready-made acceptance scientific management inadvertently prepared for it, the management science movement seems more accurately characterized as the confluence of several attempts to apply probability theory. Each attempt has had sufficient identity to acquire a different name, e.g., game theory, statistical decision theory, cybernetics, and operations research. The literature of management science can be conveniently reviewed within a description of three of these fields.

In point of time game theory might claim seniority since Von Neumann conceived the essentials of the theory in 1928. His work went largely unnoticed until the first edition of the *Theory and Practice of Games and Economic Behavior* in 1944 and the standard 1947 edition.[64] This theory suggests that major economic policy decisions can be understood by representing them as games of strategy and chance analogous to poker, bridge, or the like. "In general, a game will have a certain number of players, say n. The game is composed of moves, which are of two types: personal, made by the players, and chance, in which one of several possible outcomes is selected by a chance device." As in poker the distribution of cards between the hands is made by a random device, and the players have certain choices as to how to play their hands. The rules of the game prescribe "the conditions under which players are allowed to make their moves, and thus tend to define the character and the context of the alternative moves open to them."[65]

As a number of writers have pointed out, this amounts to translating a decision into a problem in the strategies of choice. The strategy is applied by a player against nature or competing players. This makes possible the second, and crucial, translation where the principles of probability are used to state a problem as a matter of selecting among alternatives each of whose probable expected consequences has been numerically weighted. Laplace is reputed to have explained statistics as the calculus of common sense. Most exponents of game theory echo his sentiments and add that what Von Neumann did was to provide in this analogy of the game a device for bringing reason directly to bear upon choices previously made intuitively, capriciously, or ignorantly.

The layman who would use this tool runs into an initial difficulty: the theory is most frequently presented in another language—the language of mathematical symbols. Fortunately the literature is now sufficiently extensive to include nonmathematical sources. One who is interested in only a speaking acquaintance with the theory may invest an evening in Arrow's chapter in *The Policy Sciences*, or in McDonald's piece in *Fortune*, "The Theory of Strategy," or in Snyder's discussion in *Research Frontiers in Politics*.[66] For those willing to invest several evenings three nonmathematical books are available. Although Williams' *The Compleat Strategyst, Being a Primer on the Theory of Games of Strategy*[67] has received a good deal of attention, perhaps because of its posture and relatively detailed explanation of specific techniques, Bross's shorter and more general work[68] and McDonald's *Strategy in Poker, Business and War*[69] are both excellent sources. Bross, for example, presents readily understood materials on probability, values, rules for action, sequential decisions, models, and statistical techniques. This would equip most casual readers for a further probing of the subject, and though it does not purport to serve as a systematic survey, Shubik's collection of readings is certainly one of the most useful starting points for many readers.[70]

For those with scientific, mathematical, or statistical training some of the fundamental works on the subject might represent a jumping-off point. The 1947 edition of Von Neumann and Morganstern is already a classic and is almost universally referred to by other students.[71] The two issues of the "Annals of Mathematical Studies" entitled *Contributions to the Theory of Games* must also be counted among the most important basic sources.[72] But as of this moment the most comprehensive and integrated work available is the recently published *Games and Decisions* by Luce and Raiffa. As the authors note,

The over-all outline of this book parallels the original structuring given to the theory by Von Neumann and Morganstern... [though] in the decade since the second edition of their book there have been many additions... and we have tried to include these.... Our emphasis is almost totally on the concepts and so relatively little attention is given to the detailed "solutions" of specific games.

[Finally], our work is strongly colored... by a social science point of view.[73]

The book includes chapters entitled "Utility Theory," "Two-Person Zero-Sum Games," "Two-Person Co-operative Games," "Theories of n-Person Games in Normal Form," "Individual Decision Making under Uncertainty," "Group Decision-Making," and an appendix, "A Probabilistic Theory of Utility." It also contains a highly selective bibliography of four hundred entries. McKinsey's *Introduction to the Theory of Games*,[74] is another useful source.

The line between works on game theory and decision theory is tenuous. Several important sources nominally associated with decision theory suggest the richness and complexity of its underlying mathematical assumptions. The classic work is Abraham Wald's *Statistical Decision Functions*.[75] The work of Von Neumann and Wald is often said to form the theoretical foundations for this whole field. Also helpful are both the collected papers from a RAND seminar in Santa Monica in 1952, *Decision Processes*,[76] and a more restricted work, *Decision Making—An Experimental Approach*.[77] A more concise summary of statistical decision theory has been prepared by Savage,[78] whose work on the foundations of statistics is perhaps the most readable source on decision theory.[79] Again for the mathematically inclined, there are three more comprehensive recent discussions. Vajda has a book which is most worthwhile as a source on linear programming and its uses.[80] And Blackwell and Girshick[81] have prepared a book which treats statistical decision theory with great mathematical sophistication.[82]

For both the layman and the administrative practitioner the literature on operations research may prove rewarding. In approaching operations research one must recognize that (a) it is a new and fluid field, (b) it is heavily reliant conceptually upon game theory and statistical decision theory, and (c) it is often as much influenced by the kind of problems undertaken in the name of operations research as by its theoretical foundations. One may also assume that (a) the field is still seeking general acceptance within industry and government; (b) that there is not a well-defined, professionally enforced pattern and approach (many problems are handled more like research projects than management studies); and (c), though hundreds of concrete applications of operations research techniques have been made, we have probably not yet discovered its full potential nor its real limitations. It is not yet clear, for example, whether a new profession of operations researchers will develop to claim a place among existing top staff functionaries or whether the tools of operations research will be applied by industrial engineers or organization and method analysts. For these reasons there is some tendency for operations research to be what people do in the name of operations research.

Yet several general works reveal considerable agreement upon its major techniques. *Introduction to Operations Research*, by Churchman, Ackoff, and Arnoff, is meant to be a basic textbook (which will yield to the efforts of most laymen). In the first two hundred pages the authors explain the strategy of operations research as "Formulating the Problem," which is to be attacked in terms susceptible to systematic analysis; "Construction of a Model," which represents the central dynamics and alternatives within the problem as defined; "Selection of Decision Criteria"; and "Solution" (in the mathematical sense) of the model. In the remaining four hundred pages four classes of models are described, including inventory, allocation or optimization, waiting time (queuing), and replacement models.[83] In a journal article Ackoff adds routine and sequencing models to this list[84] and notes that information-collecting processes may well lend themselves to mathematical models.

The importance of the model is indicated by the fact that its identification and elaboration seems to be one of two crucial steps, the other being the manipulation of values to produce a precise and internally consistent set of objectives. The model is used as a vehicle for simulating the anticipated choice situation by providing a vicarious testing of alternative subgoals and alternative means of realizing them. Since a model is an abstraction of a complex situation, one soon confronts the inevitable difficulty of determining what elements of the larger process to emphasize in the model. Such problems are presently thwarting much more widespread application of the technique. Kenneth Arrow has done much of the theoretical exploration seeking to penetrate this threshold. His chapter on mathematical models in *The Policy Sciences* is most useful.[85] An introductory discussion of this approach to values appears in *Readings in Game Theory*,[86] but most readers will find it worthwhile to look at his *Social Choice and Individual Values*.[87]

It is no slight to operations research to note that there seems to be a place for more complex and subtle models. The inventory control problem which yields so well to existing models is important because hundreds of thousands of hospitals, department stores, army depots, auto parts houses, and other establishments must cope with it every day. But there are types of decisions, such as the selection of a successor to the chief executive, which are much more vital to organizational survival though they arise much less frequently. If management science is to become the science of decision making, models which comprehend the variables in this sort of decision may be needed.

Perhaps the most popular nonmilitary application of operations research has involved inventory models. Individuals in isolated firms have been working toward systematic techniques of inventory control for a generation. These are nicely summarized by Whitin,[88] but the creation of more refined models has revolutionized this work, and the basic techniques are concisely described in an important article by Laderman, Littaur, and Weiss.[89] Central to this problem is optimizing the ratio of inventory carrying costs to the losses following an inventory shortage. Relatively simple in itself, this becomes a highly complicated matter when one seeks to take account of quantity discounts, limited funds, or production facilities. But these models of "static inventory" problems are elementary in comparison with attempts to devise models that reflect the dynamics of inventory flow problems.[90] An extensive, selective bibliography may be found in *Operations Research*.[91]

A second and more universal class of common managerial problems can be attacked with allocation or optimization models, for which the technical device is linear programming.[92] A typical optimization problem is that of minimizing the costs and maximizing the rate at which empty boxcars are moved to the points where they are to be loaded, taking account, for example, of existing traffic densities on alternative routes. This technique has been applied to hundreds of management problems; among them, optimal staffing patterns given present and anticipated personnel,[93] optimal crop rotation,[94] and optimal bombing patterns.

The relative abundance of literature on linear programming gives testimony to its potential theoretical complexity and its vast potential field of application. Several reliable sources are available for those with a specific problem in mind.[95]

Queuing or waiting-line models are much more restricted devices dealing typically with service situations where the objective is to maximize service and minimize costs by optimizing waiting time and facilities. These models have been applied to the scheduling and flow problems of an airport,[96] the design and provision of capacity in automatic telephone exchanges,[97] and the flow of auto traffic at toll booths and intersections.[98] More comprehensive and detailed discussions may be found in a highly regarded discussion by Kendall.[99]

So-called replacement models are much less widely recognized than these first three, though they may soon receive a great deal of attention because they can provide such determinative and conclusive "solutions." Replacement refers to equipment or facilities, such as machinery, light globes, floors, and trucks. In the case where a light globe is simply replaced when it burns out, the problem is much simpler than when mass replacement is used and maximum average life must be determined. Where equipment is involved, there is the question of the possibility of replacement because of obsolescence in addition to the problem of wearing out. The American Management Association has prepared a summary of problems and principles.[100] Terborgh's treatment of equipment replacement policy will also be useful.[101] Perhaps the most immediately useful source is the chapter "Operations Research" and the accompanying bibliography.[102]

Those unfamiliar with mathematics may have reservations about the mass of symbolism accompanying these various models. Their question is, Why put relatively simple ideas in this complex form? The management scientist seeks to explain on two different levels. In general terms he feels that techniques of mathematical thought embody a higher order of rationality than words or concepts expressed in words. Granting that the nonmathematician is a reasonable individual, his habits of thought may still be short-circuited by unperceived slips in logic—the *non sequitur*, for instance. In one sense science as a whole and mathematics in particular are elaborate rituals designed to forestall faulty reasoning.

Until recently these rituals have had only limited applicability to management decision making because of their cumbersome and over-simplified assumptions. Through the work of Von Neumann and Wald probabilistic devices have been made available so that the power of science can be brought to management. But the immediate justification for these symbols is that they make possible a previously unknown level of rigor in definition. Elements such as product, mission, organizational objective, or authority and relationships like power-over, accountability-to, or communication-with can be given precision which will support a higher level of problem solving because of the increased strength built into their base. It might be noted incidentally that while more precise terms could produce firmer agreement, less ambiguous conceptions of purpose, and much more detailed plans, they may upon occasion induce conflicts which are more intense just because the elbow room possible within more loose definitions has been reduced.

Precision has an even larger implication, however. One of the unique contributions of the manager has always been the contribution of the broad look, the view from the top. Multivariant models now under development could aid immeasurably in the manager's conception of the whole. With the development of N-person game theory and with the unraveling of the problem of representing nonmaterial values in mathematical terms, management science will probably revolutionize day-to-day management.

CONCLUSIONS

First, what was once an emergent, often consistent body of administrative theory has been fractured by new approaches such as human relations, operations research, and democratic management. Concurrently the role of the executive in facilitating organizational unity has been diluted, with the result that organizations have become increasingly effective instruments of production and increasingly impossible places to live and work. It would seem that the former cannot continue indefinitely in defiance of the latter. There is a need for a cogent theory of organization. It is conceivable but improbable that a comprehensive decision theory can emerge in the present chaos of organizational theory.

Secondly, there is a large body of literature dealing more or less directly with some facet of decision making. (A generous list might run to five thousand entries.) The sample of one hundred items included here is a true sample to the extent that it reflects no common core, no universal dimensions. It is probably accurate also in reflecting more concern with technical problems than with fundamental organizational problems, such as role conflict and the pluralism of objectives.

While one might attempt to extract universals from this rather considerable body of literature, it is unlikely that they would receive any general acceptance. In short, the literature dealing with decision making, impressive in relation to one man's ability to deal with it, appears to be uneven and chaotic, and in no respect comprehensive. The themes which occur most frequently (centralization-decentralization, authoritarian vs. democratic leadership, control, "two-way communication," and the like) do not seem to confront many of the central problems. Conversely, critical factors such as a topology of decisions, models of various decisional processes, the function of ideology, and the basis of power and its generation receive only infrequent and inadequate attention.

Finally, though we do not now have anything approaching a theory of decision making, administrative practice remains far behind even those conceptions we do have. Most organizational systems imply an ideology half a century out of date, denying the very existence of modern social science. Thus, inadequate as the literature may be from a conceptual point of view, it contains a vast number of ideas through which organizational effectiveness could be increased simply by throwing off outworn administrative ideologies.

FOOTNOTES

[1] The authors wish to express their appreciation to Professor Paul Wasserman for access to *Decision-Making: An Annotated Bibliography*, published in 1958 by the Graduate School of Business and Public Administration, Cornell University, and to Dr. Martin Shubik for his helpful criticisms.

[2] John M. Pfiffner and Robert V. Presthus, *Public Administration* (3rd ed.; New York, 1953), pp. 50 ff.

[3] Irvin D. Bross, *Design for Decision* (New York, 1953), p. 1.

[4] *Ibid.*, p. 17.

[5] Herbert Simon, *Administrative Behavior* (New York, 1945).

[6] Herbert Simon, *Models of Man* (New York, 1957).

[7] Richard C. Snyder, H. W. Bruck, and Burton Sapin, *Decision-Making* (Princeton, 1954), p. 57.

[8] Chester Barnard, *Functions of the Executive* (Cambridge, 1948), p. 185.

[9] See, for example, Luther Gulick and Lyndall Urwick, eds., *Papers on the Science of Administration* (New York, 1937); Lyndall Urwick, *The Elements of Administration* (New York, 1944); Alvin Brow, *Organizations* (New York, 1945); Paul Holden, L. Fish, and H. Smith, *Top Management Organization and Control* (Stanford, 1941); Leonard D. White, *Public Administration* (rev. ed.; New York, 1939); James D. Mooney, *The Principles of Organization* (rev. ed.; New York, 1947); and Dwight Waldo, *Ideas and Issues in Public Administration* (New York, 1953).

[10] *Middletown* (New York, 1929) and *Middletown in Transition* (New York, 1937).

[11] Lloyd Warner and J. O. Low, *The Social System of a Modern Factory* (New Haven, 1947).

[12] Elliot Jaques, *The Changing Culture of a Factory* (London, 1957).

[13] Glencoe, 1953.

[14] Talcott Parsons, *The Social System* (Glencoe, 1951), provides his conception of an integrated theory.

[15] *Ibid.*, p. 166.

[16] *Social Theory and Social Structure* (Glencoe, 1957).

[17] For a collection of his essays, see *Resolving Social Conflict* (New York, 1948).

[18] George Homans, *The Human Group* (New York, 1950).

[19] Functionalism is well defined by A. R. Radcliffe-Brown, On the Concept of Function in Social Science, *American Anthropologist*, 37 (Nov.-Sept. 1935), pp. 346 ff.

[20] New York, 1936.

[21] *The Governmental Process* (New York, 1953).

[22] Philip Selznick, *TVA and the Grass Roots* (Berkeley, 1949).

[23] Cf. Parsons, Bales, and Shils, *op. cit.*, and David Easton, *The Political System* (New York, 1953), pp. 268-307.

[24] See Gulick and Urwick, *op. cit.* (especially the first paper), and Leonard White, *op. cit.*

[25] Harold Lasswell and Abraham Kaplan, *Power and Society* (New Haven, 1950).

[26] *TVA—Democracy on the March* (New York, 1944).

[27] Floyd Hunter, *Community Power Structures* (Chapel Hill, 1953).

[28] See the discriminating bibliography by Reinhard Bendix and S. M. Lipset, eds., *Class, Status and Power* (Glencoe, 1953).

[29] See Peter H. Rossi, Community Decision Making, *Administrative Science Quarterly* 1 (March 1957), 415-444.

[30] An Introduction to the Theory and Measurement of Influence, *American Political Science Review*, 49 (June 1955), 431-451.

[31] Notes on the Observation and Measurement of Political Power, *Journal of Politics*, 15 (Nov. 1953), 500-516.

[32] Robert A. Dahl, A Critique of the Ruling Elite Model, *American Political Science Review*, 52 (June 1953), 463-470.

[33] Chicago, 1955, pp. 6-12.

[34] Fritz J. Roethlisberger and William Dickson, *Management and the Worker* (Cambridge, 1939).

[35] Fritz J. Roethlisberger, *Management and the Worker* (Cambridge, 1950), pp. 552-568.

[36] New York, 1950.

[37] Ann Arbor, 1956.
[38] Cambridge, 1951.
[39] *Ibid.*, p. 59.
[40] *Street Corner Society* (2nd ed.; Chicago, 1955), *Human Relations in the Restaurant Industry* (1st ed.; New York, 1948), and Social Structure of the Restaurant, *American Journal of Sociology*, 54 (Jan. 1949), 302-310.
[41] Robert Bales, "Role Differentiation in Small Decision-making Groups," in Talcott Parsons and Robert Bales, *Family Socialization and Interaction Process* (Glencoe, 1955).
[42] Kenneth Benne and Paul Sheats, Functional Roles of Group Members, *Journal of Social Issues*, 4 (Spring 1948), 41-49.
[43] Reinhard Bendix and S. M. Lipset, eds., *op. cit.*
[44] *The Governing of Men* (Princeton, 1945).
[45] Sebastian De Grazia, *The Political Community* (Chicago, 1948).
[46] Jerome Bruner and Leo Postman, "An Approach to Social Perception," in Wayne Dennis, ed., *Social Psychology* (Pittsburgh, 1951).
[47] *Ibid.*, pp. 83-114. A most worth-while bibliography is provided.
[48] "Hierarchy, Democracy, and Bargaining in Politics and Economics," in Brookings Lectures, *Research Frontiers in Politics and Government* (Washington, D. C., 1955), pp. 45-69. See also Robert Dahl and Charles E. Lindblom, *Politics, Economics, and Welfare* (New York, 1953).
[49] *Ibid.*, p. 56.
[50] *Public Administration and Policy Development* (New York, 1952), pp. x-xix.
[51] *Ibid.*, p. xiii.
[52] *Ibid.*, p. xvi.
[53] Barnard, *op. cit.*, and Simon, *Administrative Behavior*.
[54] Barnard, *op. cit.*, pp. 220-247.
[55] Simon, *Administrative Behavior*, pp. 220-247. In The Role of Expectations in Business Decision-Making, *Administrative Science Quarterly*, 3 (Dec. 1958), 307-340. Cyert, Dill, and March provide an example of what Simon's Carnegie Technology operation is currently about. This application of the "expectation" concept will interest those concerned with the concrete dynamics of the process.
[56] Snyder, Bruck, and Sapin, *op. cit.*; The theoretical framework of the monograph is given added meaning in The United States Decision to Resist Aggression in Korea, *Administrative Science Quarterly*, 3 (Dec. 1958), 341-378. This analysis of Truman's Korean decision is probably the most ambitious case study yet made.
[57] Sune Carlson, *Executive Behavior* (Stockholm, 1951); Neil Chamberlain, *Management in Motion* (New Haven, 1950); Peter Drucker, *The Practice of Management* (New York, 1954), pp. 251-269; and Manley Howe Jones, *Executive Decision-Making* (Homewood, 1957).
[58] L. I. Durisch and R. E. Lowry, The Scope and Content of Administrative Decision, *Public Administration Review*, 13 (Autumn 1953), 219-226.
[59] William J. Gore, Administrative Decision-Making in Federal Field Offices, *Public Administration Review*, 16 (Autumn, 1956).
[60] Jerome Bruner, Jacqueline Goadnov, and George Austin, *A Study in Thinking* (New York, 1956).
[61] Charles Kadushin, Individual Decisions to Undertake Psychotherapy, *Administrative Science Quarterly*, 3 (Dec. 1958), 379-411.
[62] Donald W. Taylor, Paul C. Berry, and Clifford H. Block, *ibid.* (June 1958), 23-47.
[63] Two new journals carrying the names *Management Science* and *The Journal of the Operations Research Society of America* manifest some of this vigor.
[64] John Von Neumann and Oskar Morganstern (2nd ed.; Princeton, 1947).
[65] Kenneth J. Arrow, "Mathematical Problems in the Social Sciences," in Daniel Lerner and Harold Lasswell, eds., *The Policy Sciences* (Stanford, 1951), pp. 140, 141.
[66] John McDonald, The Theory of Strategy, *Fortune*, 34 (June 1949), 100-110; and Richard Snyder, "Game Theory and the Analysis of Political Behavior," in Brooking's Lectures, *op. cit.*, pp. 70-103.
[67] New York, 1954.
[68] Bross, *op. cit.*
[69] New York, 1950.
[70] Martin Shubik, *Readings in Game Theory and Political Behavior* (New York, 1954). See his more general discussion of decision making in this journal, 3 (Dec. 1958), 289-306, as well.
[71] Von Neumann and Morganstern, *op. cit.*
[72] "Annals of Mathematical Studies," Nos. 24 and 28, in H. W. Kuhn and A. W. Tucker, *Contributions to the Theory of Games* (Princeton, 1950).
[73] New York, 1957.
[74] New York, 1952.
[75] New York, 1950; see also an article by Wald, Review of the Theory of Games, *Review of Economics and Statistics*, 34 (Feb. 1947), 47-52.
[76] R. M. Thrall, C. H. Coombs, and R. L. Davis, eds., *Decision Processes* (New York, 1954).
[77] Donald Davision and Patrick Suppes, *Decision Making* (Stanford, 1957).
[78] L. J. Savage, The Theory of Statistical Decision, *Journal of the American Statistical Association*, 46 (March 1951), 55-67.
[79] L. J. Savage, *The Foundation of Statistics* (New York, 1954).

[80] S. Vajda, *The Theory of Games and Linear Programming* (London, 1956).
[81] David Blackwell and M. A. Girshick, *Theory of Games and Statistical Decisions* (New York, 1954). (Wiley will publish this year an introductory work by Churnoff and Moses on statistical decision theory which will be most useful.)
[82] Included among those sources would be a discussion by the eighteenth century mathematician, David Bernoulli, whose Exposition of a New Theory of the Measurement of Risk, is translated in *Econometrica*, 22 (Jan. 1954), 23-36. This work is seen by some as the birth of the game theory. More modern and comprehensive sources would include Rudolf Carnap, *Logical Foundations of Probability* (Chicago, 1950); Hans Reichenbach, *The Theory of Probability* (Berkeley, 1949); R. E. von Mises, *Probability, Statistics, and Truth* (New York, 1939); W. Feller, *An Introduction to Probability Theory and Its Applications* (New York, 1950); and Savage, *The Foundations of Statistics*.
[83] New York, 1957.
[84] Russell Ackoff, The Development of Operations Research as a Science, *Operations Research*, 4 (June 1956), 265-295. An alternative source is Franklin Lindsay, *New Techniques for Management Decision-Making* (New York, 1958). This discussion is especially useful in the area of concrete application of these techniques.
[85] "Mathematical Models in the Social Science," in Daniel Lerner and Harold Lasswell, eds., *The Policy Sciences* (Stanford, 1951).
[86] Shubik, *op. cit.*, pp. 69-72.
[87] New York, 1951.
[88] T. M. Whitin, *The Theory of Inventory Management* (Princeton, 1953).
[89] J. L. Laderman, S. Littaur, and Lionel Weiss, The Inventory Problem, *Journal of the American Statistical Association*, 88 (Dec. 1953), 717-732.
[90] R. Bellman, I. Glickman, and A. Gross, On the Optimal Inventory Equation, *Management Science*, 2 (Oct. 1955), 83-104.
[91] Churchman, *op. cit.*, pp. 232-234.
[92] A linear function is one where, if three gallons of fuel oil are produced for one dollar, six gallons can be produced for two dollars.
[93] D. F. Votaw and A. Orden, "The Personnel Assignment Problem," in *Symposium on Linear Inequalities and Programming*, Project SCOOP, Hdqts. Air Force (Washington, D. C., 1952).
[94] C. Hindreth and S. Reiter, in T. C. Koopmans, ed., *Activity Analysis of Production and Allocation* (Cowles Commission Monograph 13; New York, 1951).
[95] *Ibid.* Among a number of other helpful sources geared to the layman, see W. W. Cooper, *An Introduction to Linear Programming* (New York, 1953); W. C. Hood and T. C. Koopmans, eds., *Studies in Econometric Method* (Cowles Commission Monograph 14; New York, 1953); Robert Dorfman, Paul Samuelson, and Robert Solow, *Linear Programming and Economic Analysis* (New York, 1958); and a series of two articles by G. B. Danzig, Linear Programming under Uncertainty, *Management Science*, 1 (April-July 1955), 197-207, and G. B. Danzig, Recent Advances in Linear Programming, *Management Science,* 2 (Jan. 1956), 131-145.
[96] R. B. Adler and S. J. Fricker, "The Flow of Scheduled Air Traffic," in *RLE Technical Report*, No. 198 (Cambridge, 1951).
[97] G. S. Berkeley, *Traffic and Trunking Principles in Automatic Telephony* (2nd rev. ed.; London, 1949).
[98] L. C. Edie, Traffic Delays at Toll Booths, *Journal of Operations Research Society of America*, 2 (May 1954), 107-138; and B. D. Breen-Shields, D. Shapiro, and E. Erickson, *Traffic Performance at Urban Street Intersections* (New Haven, 1947).
[99] D. G. Kendall, Some Problems in the Theory of Queuing, *Journal of the Royal Statistical Society,* 8 (June 1951), 151-173. See also B. D. Marshall, "Queuing Theory," in J. F. McCloskey and F. N. Trefethen, eds., *Operations Research for Management* (Baltimore, 1954).
[100] American Management Association, *Tested Approaches to Capital Equipment Replacement* (Special Report No. 1; New York, 1954).
[101] B. Terborgh, *Dynamic Equipment Policy* (New York, 1949).
[102] Churchman, *op. cit.*, pp. 477-516.

ABOUT THE AUTHORS—William J. Gore is professor of political science at the University of Washington. He was born in Oregon in 1924, received his B.A. in 1948 from the University of Washington and his doctorate in 1952 from the University of Southern California. He has served on the faculties of Kansas, Cornell, and Indiana Universities. His latest book, *Administrative Decision Making: A Heuristic Model* (Wiley, 1964) is a highly regarded contribution to the literature of organization theory. In this work, Gore formulates a complex model of decision-making based on empirical studies. He is co-editor with J. W. Dyson of *The Making of Decisions: A Reader in Administrative Behavior* (1964), and with Leroy Hodapp of *Change in the Small Community* (1967).

Fred S. Silander has been, since 1956, in the Department of Economics at DePauw University. He recently served the Middle East Technical University in Ankara, Turkey, where he spent 1965-67 as a Visiting Associate Professor with the Department of Management. In 1960 he received DePauw's "Best Teacher Award." From 1950 to 1955 he was on the faculty of the West Virginia Institute of Technology. Silander received an M.A. in Economics from the University of New Hampshire in 1952, where he had also done his undergraduate work. He served as a research assistant while preparing for his Ph.D. at Cornell University, awarded in 1964, and in 1957-58 was the recipient of a Ford Foundation Fellowship. He is co-author of *Decision Making: An Annotated Bibliography* (1958) and its *Supplement, 1958-1963* (1964).

Fact and Value in Decision-Making

by Herbert A. Simon

One of the volumes which has most influenced scholarship in administration is Herbert Simon's classic Administrative Behavior, *from which the following extract is drawn. The entire monograph is concerned with the decision process in organizations and the principal thesis of the present chapter is the differentiation of factual and ethical elements in decision making. The other important element is the identification of the means of differentiating policy from administrative considerations. No study of decision-making can afford to overlook the very fundamental conceptual postulates which Simon offers in the following piece.*

In Chapter I it was pointed out that every decision involves elements of two kinds, which were called "factual" and "value" elements respectively. This distinction proves to be a very fundamental one for administration. It leads first of all to an understanding of what is meant by a "correct" administrative decision. Secondly, it clarifies the distinction, so often made in the literature of administration, between policy questions and questions of administration. These important issues will be the subject matter of the present chapter.

To ground an answer to these questions on first principles would require that this volume on administration be prefaced by an even longer philosophical treatise. The necessary ideas are already accessible in the literature of philosophy. Hence, the conclusions reached by a particular school of modern philosophy—logical positivism—will be accepted as a starting point, and their implications for the theory of decisions examined. The reader who is interested in examining the reasoning upon which these doctrines are based will find references to the literature in the footnotes to this chapter.

DISTINCTION BETWEEN FACTUAL AND ETHICAL MEANING

Factual propositions are statements about the observable world and the way in which it operates.[1] In principle, factual propositions may be tested to determine whether they are *true* or *false* —whether what they say about the world actually occurs, or whether it does not.

Decisions are something more than factual propositions. To be sure, they are descriptive of a future state of affairs, and this description can be true or false in a strictly empirical sense; but they possess, in addition, an imperative quality— they select one future state of affairs in preference to another and direct behavior toward the chosen alternative. In short, they have an *ethical* as well as a factual content.

The question of whether decisions can be correct and incorrect resolves itself, then, into the question of whether ethical terms like "ought," "good," and "preferable" have a purely empirical meaning. It is a fundamental premise of this study that ethical terms are not completely reducible to factual terms. No attempt will be made here to demonstrate conclusively the correctness of this view toward ethical propositions; the justification has been set forth at length by logical positivists and others.[2]

The argument, briefly, runs as follows. To determine whether a proposition is correct, it must be compared directly with experience—with the facts—or it must lead by logical reasoning to other propositions that can be compared with experience. But factual propositions cannot be derived from ethical ones by any process of reasoning, nor can ethical propositions be compared directly with the facts—since they assert "oughts" rather than facts. Hence, there is no way in which the correctness of ethical propositions can be empirically or rationally tested.

From this viewpoint, if a sentence declares that some particular state of affairs "ought to be," or that it is "preferable" or "desirable," then the sentence performs an imperative function, and is neither true nor false, correct nor incorrect. Since

SOURCE: Reprinted with permission of the Macmillan Company from ADMINISTRATIVE BEHAVIOR: A STUDY OF DECISION-MAKING PROCESSES IN ADMINISTRATIVE ORGANIZATION by Herbert A. Simon. ©Herbert A. Simon 1957.

decisions involve valuation of this kind, they too cannot be objectively described as correct or incorrect.

The search for the philosopher's stone and the squaring of the circle have not been more popular pursuits among philosophers than the attempt to derive ethical sentences, as consequences of purely factual ones. To mention a relatively modern example—Bentham defined the term "good" as equivalent with "conducive to happiness," defining "happiness" in psychological terms.[3] He then considered whether or not particular states of affairs were conducive to happiness, and hence good. Of course, no logical objection can be raised against this procedure: it is here rejected because the word "good" thus defined by Bentham cannot perform the function required of the word "good" in ethics—that of expressing moral preference for one alternative over another. It may be possible by such a process to derive the conclusion that people will be happier under one set of circumstances than under another, but this does not prove that they *ought* to be happier. The Aristotelian definition—that something is good for man which makes him correspond more closely with his essential nature as a rational animal[4]—suffers from the same limitation.

Thus, by appropriate definitions of the word "good" it may be possible to construct sentences of the form: "Such a state of affairs *is good*." But from "good" defined in this way it is impossible to deduce "Such a state of affairs *ought to be*." The task of ethics is to select imperatives—ought-sentences; and this task cannot be accomplished if the term "good" is defined in such a way that it merely designates existents. In this study, therefore, words like "good" and "ought" will be reserved for their ethical functions, and will not be predicated of any state of affairs in a purely factual sense. It follows that decisions may be "good," but they cannot, in an unqualified sense, be "correct," or "true."

The Evaluation of Decisions

We see that, in a strict sense, the administrator's decisions cannot be evaluated by scientific means. Is there no scientific content, then, to administrative problems? Are they purely questions of ethics? Quite the contrary: to assert that there is an ethical element involved in every decision is not to assert that decisions involve only ethical elements.

Consider the following passage from the *Infantry Field Manual* of the United States Army:

> Surprise is an essential element of a successful attack. Its effects should be striven for in small as well as in large operations. Infantry effects surprise by concealment of the time and place of the attack, screening of its dispositions, rapidity of maneuver, deception, and the avoidance of stereotyped procedures.[5]

It is difficult to say to what extent these three sentences are meant as factual propositions, and to what extent they are intended as imperatives, that is, as decisions. The first may be read purely as a statement about the conditions for a successful attack; the third may be interpreted as a listing of the conditions under which a state of surprise is achieved. But binding together these factual sentences—providing them with connective tissue, so to speak—is a set of expressed and implied imperatives, which may be paraphrased thus: "Attack successfully!" "Employ surprise!" and "Conceal the time and place of attack, screen dispositions, move rapidly, deceive the enemy, and avoid stereotyped procedures!"

In fact, the paragraph can be rephrased in another way, separating it into three sentences, the first ethical, the others purely factual:

1. Attack successfully!
2. An attack is successful only when carried out under conditions of surprise.
3. The conditions of surprise are concealment of the time and place of attack, etc.

It follows that the decisions that a military commander makes to screen the dispositions of his troops contain both factual and ethical elements, for he screens the dispositions *in order* to *effect* "surprise," and this *in order* to attack successfully. Hence, there is one sense in which the correctness of his decisions can be judged: it is a purely factual question whether the measures he takes *in order* to accomplish his aim are appropriate measures. It is not a factual question whether the aim itself is correct or not, except in so far as this aim is connected, by an "in order," to further aims.

Decisions can always be evaluated in this relative sense—it can be determined whether they are correct, given the objective at which they are aimed—but a change in objectives implies a change in evaluation. Strictly speaking, it is not the decision itself which is evaluated, but the purely factual relationship that is asserted between the decision and its aims.[6] The commander's decision to take particular measures in order to attain surprise is not evaluated; what is evaluated is his factual judgment that the measures he takes will, in fact, attain surprise.

This argument may be presented in a slightly different way. Consider the two sentences: "Achieve surprise!" and "The conditions of surprise are concealment of the time and place of attack, etc." While the first sentence contains an imperative, or ethical, element, and hence is neither true nor false, the second sentence is purely factual. If the notion of logical inference be extended so as to apply to the ethical as well as the factual element in sentences, then from these two sentences a third may be deduced: "Conceal the time and place of attack, etc.!" Thus, with the mediation of a factual premise (the second sentence), one imperative can be deduced from another.[7]

The Mixed Character of Ethical Statements

It should be clear from the illustrations already put forth that most ethical propositions have admixed with them factual elements. Since most imperatives are not ends-in-themselves but intermediate ends, the question of their appropriateness to the more final ends at which they are aimed remains a factual question. Whether it is ever possible to trace the chain of implementation far enough to isolate a "pure" value—an end that is desired purely for itself—is a question that need not be settled here. The important point for the present discussion is that any statement that contains an ethical element, intermediate or final, cannot be described as correct or incorrect, and that the decision-making process must start with some ethical premise that is taken as "given." This ethical premise describes the objective of the organization in question.

In administration, the mixed character of the ethical "givens" is usually fairly obvious. A municipal department may take as its objective the providing of recreation to the city's inhabitants. This aim may then be further analyzed as a means toward "building healthier bodies," "using leisure time constructively," "preventing juvenile delinquency," and a host of others, until the chain of means and ends is traced into a vague realm labeled "the good life." At this point the means-ends connections become so conjectural (e.g. the relation between recreation and character), and the content of the values so ill defined (e.g. "happiness"), that the analysis becomes valueless for administrative purposes.[8]

The last point may be stated in a more positive way. In order for an ethical proposition to be useful for rational decision-making, (a) the values taken as organizational objectives must be definite, so that their degree of realization in any situation can be assessed, and (b) it must be possible to form judgments as to the probability that particular actions will implement these objectives.

The Role of Judgment in Decision

The division of the premises of decision into those that are eithical and those that are factual might appear to leave no room for judgment in decision-making. This difficulty is avoided by the very broad meaning that has been given to the word "factual": a statement about the observable world is factual if, in principle, its truth or falsity may be tested. That is, if certain events occur, we say the statement was true; if other events occur, we say that it was false.

This does not by any means imply that we are able to determine in advance whether it is true or false. It is here that judgment enters. In making administrative decisions it is continually necessary to choose factual premises whose truth or falsehood is not definitely known and cannot be determined with certainty with the information and time available for reaching the decision.

It is a purely factual question whether a particular infantry attack will take its objective or fail. It is, nevertheless, a question involving judgment, since the success or failure will depend upon the disposition of the enemy, the accuracy and strength of artillery support, the topography, the morale of the attacking and defending troops, and a host of other factors that cannot be completely known or assessed by the commander who has to order the attack.

In ordinary speech there is often confusion between the element of judgment in decision and the ethical element. This confusion is enhanced by the fact that the further the means-end chain is followed, i.e. the greater the ethical element, the more doubtful are the steps in the chain, and the greater is the element of judgment involved in determining what means will contribute to what ends.[9]

The process by which judgments are formed has been very imperfectly studied. In practical administration it may be feared that confidence in the correctness of judgments sometimes takes the place of any serious attempt to evaluate them systematically on the basis of subsequent results. But further consideration of the psychology of decision-making will have to be postponed to a later chapter.[10]

Value Judgments in Private Management

The illustrations used thus far in this chapter have been drawn largely from the field of public administration. One reason for this is that the problem of value judgments has been more fully explored—particularly in relation to administrative discretion and administrative regulation—in the public than in the private field. There is, in fact, no essential difference on this topic between the two. Decisions in private management, like decisions in public management, must take as their ethical premises the objectives that have been set for the organization.

There are important differences between public and private management, of course, in the types of organizational objectives that are set up and in the procedures and mechanisms for establishing them. In public administration final responsibility for determining objectives rests with a legislative body; in private management, with the board of directors, and ultimately with the stockholders.[11] In both fields serious problems have arisen as to the means to be used in implementing the responsibility of these control bodies.[12] It is to this problem that we turn next—again directing our attention particularly to the field of public administration. A little translation of terms should suffice to make most of the discussion applicable to the stockholder-management relationship.

POLICY AND ADMINISTRATION

In practice, the separation between the ethical and the factual elements in judgment can usually be carried only a short distance. The values involved in administrative decisions are seldom final values in any psychological or philosophical sense. Most objectives and activities derive their value from the means-ends relationships which connect them with objectives or activities that are valued in themselves. By a process of anticipation, the value inhering in the desired end is transferred to the means. The product of a manufacturing process is valued by its producers for its convertibility into money (which in turn has value only in exchange) and by its purchasers for the values to be derived from its consumption. Just so, the activities of a fire department, or a school system, are valued ultimately for their contribution to human and social life, and they retain their value only so long as they serve those more final ends.

To the extent that these intermediate values are involved, valuation includes important factual as well as ethical elements. Since the results of administrative activity can be considered as ends only in an intermediate sense, the values that will be attached to these results depend on the empirical connections that are believed to exist between them and the more final goals. To weight properly these intermediate values, it is necessary to understand their objective consequences.

At best it might be hoped that the process of decision could be subdivided into two major segments. The first would involve the development of a system of intermediate values, and an appraisal of their relative weights. The second would consist in a comparison of the possible lines of action in terms of this value system. The first segment would obviously involve both ethical and factual considerations; the second segment could be pretty well restricted to factual problems.

As already pointed out, the reason for making a division of this sort lies in the different criteria of "correctness" that must be applied to the ethical and factual elements in a decision. "Correctness" as applied to imperatives has meaning only in terms of subjective human values. "Correctness" as applied to factual propositions means objective, empirical truth. If two persons give different answers to a factual problem, both cannot be right. Not so with ethical questions.

Vagueness of the "Policy and Administration" Distinction

Recognition of this distinction in the meanings of "correctness" would lend clarity to the distinction that is commonly made in the literature of political science between "policy questions" and "administrative questions." These latter terms were given currency by Goodnow's classical treatise, *Politics and Administration*,[13] published in 1900. Yet, neither in Goodnow's study nor in any of the innumerable discussions that have followed it have any clear-cut criteria or marks of identification been suggested that would enable one to recognize a "policy question" on sight, or to distinguish it from an "administrative question." Apparently, it has been assumed that the distinction is self-evident—so self-evident as hardly to require discussion.

In *The New Democracy and the New Despotism,* Charles E. Merriam sets forth as one of the five principal assumptions of democracy "the desirability of popular decision in the last analysis on basic questions of social direction and policy, and of recognized procedures for the expression of such decisions and their validation in policy."[14] As to the exact scope and nature of these "basic questions," he is less explicit:

> It may be asked, Who shall decide what are "basic questions," and who shall determine whether the ways and means of expressing the mass will are appropriate and effective? We cannot go farther back than the "general understandings" of the community, always the judge of the form and functioning of the legal order in which the system is set.[15]

Similarly, Goodnow, in the original statement of the roles of politics and administration in government, fails to draw a careful line between the two. In fact, he comes perilously close to identifying "policy" with "deciding," and "administration" with "doing." For example:

> ... political functions group themselves naturally under two heads, which are equally applicable to the mental operations and the actions of self-conscious personalities. That is, the action of the state as a political entity consists either in operations necessary to the expression of its will, or in operations necessary to the execution of that will.[16]

And again:

> These two functions of government may for purposes of convenience be designated respectively as Politics and Administration. Politics has to do with policies or expressions of the state will. Administration has to do with the execution of these policies.[17]

At a later point in his discussion, however, Goodnow retreats from this extreme position, and recognizes that certain decisional elements are included in the administrative function:

> The fact is, then, that there is a large part of administration which is unconnected with politics, which should therefore be relieved very largely, if not altogether, from the control of political bodies. It is unconnected with politics because it embraces fields of semi-scientific, *quasi*-judicial and *quasi*-business or commercial activity–work which has little if any influence on the expression of the true state will.[18]

Without embracing Goodnow's conclusion regarding the desirability of removing some portions of administration from political control, we may recognize in this third statement an attempt on his part to segregate a class of decisions which do not require external control because they possess an internal criterion of correctness. The epistemological position of the present volume leads us to identify this internal criterion with the criterion of factual correctness, and the group of decisions possessing this criterion with those that are factual in nature.

In discussions of administrative discretion from the point of view of administrative law there has sometimes been a tendency to deny that there exists any class of factual questions which possess a unique epistemological status. Neither Freund nor Dickinson is able to find a justification for administrative discretion except as an application of decisions to concrete instances, or as a transitory phenomenon confined to a sphere of uncertainty within which the rule of law has not yet penetrated.[19]

To be sure, the two men offer different suggestions for the gradual elimination of this area of uncertainty. Freund relies upon the legislature to restrict discretion by the exercise of its function of policy determination.[20] Dickinson thinks that administrative discretion can gradually be replaced by general rules to be formulated by the courts, as principles gradually emerge to view from a given set of problems.[21] Neither is willing to admit any fundamental difference between the factual and normative elements involved in law-finding, or to see in that difference a justification for discretionary action.

The courts have come somewhat closer to a recognition of this distinction, through their separation of "questions of fact" from "questions of law" places in the latter category a great many factual issues—especially when "jurisdictional facts" and "constitutional facts" become "questions of law."[22] This is not the place, however, to discuss the whole problem of judicial review. These brief comments serve merely to illustrate the lack of any general agreement as to the fundamental difference between factual and value questions in the field of administrative law.

Opposed to the view that discretion is inherently undesirable, is the equally extreme view that *all* administrative decisions can safely be guided by the internal criteria of correctness, and that legislative control can be supplanted by the control which is exercised by the fellowship of science.[23] Our own analysis exposes the fallacy of an argument that declares decisions to be all factual as clearly as it refutes an argument that declares them to be all ethical.

The position to which the methodological assumptions of the present study lead us is this: The process of validating a factual proposition is quite distinct from the process of validating a value judgment. The former is validated by its agreement with the facts, the latter by human fiat.

Legislator and Administrator

Democratic institutions find their principal justification as a procedure for the validation of value judgments. There is no "scientific" or "expert" way of making such judgments, hence expertise of whatever kind is no qualification for the performance of this function. If the factual elements in decision could be strictly separated, in practice, from the ethical, the proper roles of representative and expert in a democratic decision-making process would be simple. For two reasons this is not possible. First, as has already been noted, most value judgments are made in terms of intermediate values, which themselves involve factual questions. Second, if factual decisions are entrusted to the experts, sanctions must be available to guarantee that the experts will conform, in good faith, to the value judgments that have been democratically formulated.

Critics of existing procedures for enforcing responsibility point to the high degree of ineffectiveness of these procedures in practice.[24] But there is no reason to conclude that the procedures are inherently valueless. First, for the reasons already explained, self-responsibility of the administrator is no answer to the problem. Second, the fact that pressure of legislative work forbids the review of more than a few administrative decisions does not destroy the usefulness of sanctions that permit the legislative body to hold the administrator answerable for *any* of his decisions. The anticipation of possible legislative investigation and review will have a powerful controlling effect on the administrator, even if this potential review can be actualized only in a few cases. The *function* of deciding may be distributed very differently in the body politic from the *final authority* for solving disputed decisions.

It would not be possible to lay down any final principles with regard to a subject so controversial, and so imperfectly explored.[25] Nevertheless, if the distinction of factual from ethical questions is a valid one, these conclusions would seem to follow:

1. Responsibility to democratic institutions for value determination can be strengthened by the invention of procedural devices permitting a more effective separation of the factual and ethical elements in decisions. Some suggestions will be offered along these lines in later chapters.

2. The allocation of a question to legislature or administrator for decision should depend on the relative importance of the factual and ethical issues involved, and the degree to which the former are controversial. A proper allocation will become increasingly possible, without overburdening the legislature, to the extent that point 1 above is successfully carried out.

3. Since the legislative body must of necessity make many factual judgments, it must have ready access to information and advice. However, this must take the form not merely of recommendations for action, but of factual information on the objective consequences of the alternatives that are before the legislative body.

4. Since the administrative agency must of necessity make many value judgments, it must be responsive to community values, far beyond those that are explicitly enacted into law. Likewise, though the function of making value judgments may often be delegated to the administrator, especially where controversial issues are not involved, his complete answerability, in case of disagreement, must be retained.

If it is desired to retain the terms "policy" and "administration," they can best be applied to a division of the decisional functions that follows these suggested lines. While not identical with the separation of "value" from "fact," such a division would clearly be dependent upon that fundamental distinction.

It would be naive to suggest that the division of work between legislature and administrator in any actual public agency will ever follow very closely the lines just suggested. In the first place the legislative body will often wish, for political reasons, to avoid making clear-cut policy decisions, and to pass these on to an administrative agency.[26] In the second place the administrator may be very different from the neutral, compliant individual pictured here. He may (and usually will) have his own very definite set of personal values that he would like to see implemented by his administrative organization, and he may resist attempts by the legislature to assume completely the function of policy determination, or he may sabotage their decisions by his manner of executing them.

Nevertheless, it would probably be fair to say that the attainment of democratic responsibility in modern government will require an approximation to those lines of demarcation between legislature and administrator that were outlined above.

A Note on Terminology

Before concluding this chapter, it should be pointed out that the term "policy" is often used in a much broader and looser sense than the meaning given here. In private management literature, particularly, "policy" often means either (a) any general rule that has been laid down in an organization to limit the discretion of subordinates (e.g. it is "policy" in B department to file a carbon of all letters by subject), or (b) at least the more important of these rules, promulgated by top management (e.g. an employee is allowed two weeks' sick leave per year). In neither of these usages is it implied that policy has any ethical content. Serious ambiguity would be avoided if different terms were used for these three concepts—the one discussed in preceding paragraphs, and the two listed just above. Perhaps the ethical premises of management could be called "legislative policy"; the broad non-ethical rules laid down by top management, "management policy"; and other rules, "working policy."

In addition to these several kinds of policy, or authoritatively promulgated rules, there are to be found in almost every organization a large number of "practices" which have not been established as orders or regulations, and which are not enforced by sanctions, but which are nevertheless observed in the organization by force of custom or for other reasons. Often, the line between policy and practice is not sharp unless the organization follows the "practice" (or "policy") of putting all its policies in writing.

CONCLUSION

This chapter has been devoted to an explanation of the distinction between the value elements and the factual elements in decision-making. It has been shown, furthermore, that this distinction is the basis for the line that is commonly drawn between questions of policy and questions of administration.

In the next chapter, the anatomy of decision will be further examined, with special reference to the concept of "rationality" in decision-making. The emphasis will remain upon the logical rather than the psychological aspects of decision.

FOOTNOTES

[1] The positivist theory as to the nature of scientific propositions is discussed at length by Charles W. Morris, *Foundations of the Theory of Signs*, and Rudolf Carnap, *Foundations of Logic and Mathematics*, in International Encyclopedia of Unified Science, vol. I, nos. 2 and 3 (Chicago: University of Chicago Press, 1937 and 1938); P. W. Bridgman, *The Logic of Modern Physics* (New York: Macmillan Co., 1937); Rudolf Carnap, "Testability and Meaning," *Philosophy of Science*, 3: 420–471 (Oct. 1936), and 4: 2–40 (Jan., 1937); Rudolf Carnap, *The Logical Syntax of Language* (New York: Harcourt, Brace & Co., 1937); Alfred J. Ayer, *Language, Truth, and Logic* (London: Victor Gollancz, 1936).

[2] Two recent treatments are Ayer, *op. cit.*, and T. V. Smith, *Beyond Conscience* (New York: McGraw-Hill Book Co., 1934).

[3] Jeremy Bentham, *An Introduction to the Principles of Morals and Legislation* (Oxford: Clarendon Press, 1907), p. 1.

[4] Aristotle, "Nicomachean Ethics," bk. I, chap. vii, 12–18, in *The Basic Works of Aristotle*, ed. by Richard McKeon (New York: Random House, 1941).

[5] *Complete Tactics, Infantry Rifle Battalion* (Washington: Infantry Journal, 1940), p. 20.

[6] This point of view is developed by Jorgen Jorgensen in "Imperatives and Logic," *Erkenntnis*, 7: 288–296 (1938).

[7] In fact the usual laws of inference do not appear to hold strictly in deducing one imperative from another. For a number of discussions of the possibility of a logical calculus for imperatives and attempts to construct a rigorous calculus, see the following: Karl Menger, "A Logic of the Doubtful: On Optative and Imperative Logic," *Reports of a Mathematical Colloquium* (Notre Dame, Indiana, 1939), series 2, No. 1, pp. 53–64; K. Grue-Sörensen, "Imperativsätze und Logik: Begegnung einer Kritik," *Theoria*, 5: 195–202 (1939); Albert Hofstadter and J. C. C. McKinsey, "On the Logic of Imperatives," *Philosophy of Science*, 6: 446–457 (1939); Kurt Grelling, "Zur Logik der Sollsätze," *Unity of Science Forum*, Jan., 1939, pp. 44–47; K. Reach, "Some Comments on Grelling's Paper," *Ibid.*, Apr., 1939, p. 72; Kalle Sorainen, "Der Modus und die Logik," *Theoria*, 5: 202–204 (1939); Rose Rand, "Logik der Forderungssätze," *Revue internationale de la Theorie du droit* (Zurich), New Series, 5: 308–322 (1939).

[8] See the excellent discussion of this point by Wayne A. R. Leys in "Ethics and Administrative Discretion," *Public Administration Review*, 3: 19 (Winter, 1943).

[9] Leys, *op. cit.*, p. 18, points out that this confusion has been present in most of the literature on administrative discretion.

[10] Barnard, *op. cit.*, presents an interesting, but perhaps too optimistic, view of the "intuitive" element in administrative decision, in an Appendix, "Mind in Everyday Affairs," pp. 299–322.

[11] In chap. vi arguments will be presented that the true analogue of the legislative body is the customer rather than the stockholder.

[12] The private-management literature on this topic, while for the most part relatively recent, is growing rapidly. See for example Beardsley Ruml, *Tomorrow's Business* (New York: Farrar & Rinehart, 1945); Robert A. Brady, *Business as a System of Power* (New York: Columbia University Press, 1943); or Robert Aaron Gordon, *Business Leadership in the Large Corporation* (Washington: Brookings Institution, 1945).

[13] Frank J. Goodnow, *Politics and Administration* (New York: Macmillan Company, 1960).
[14] Charles E. Merriam, *The New Democracy and the New Despotism* (New York: McGraw-Hill Book Co., 1939), p. 11.
[15] *Ibid.*, p. 39.
[16] Goodnow, *op. cit.*, p. 9.
[17] *Ibid.*, p. 18.
[18] *Ibid.*, p. 85.
[19] Ernst Freund, *Administrative Powers over Persons and Property* (Chicago: University of Chicago Press, 1928), pp. 97–103; John Dickinson, *Administrative Justice and the Supremacy of Law in the United States* (Cambridge: Harvard University Press, 1927), *passim*.
[20] Freund, *op. cit.*, pp. 98–99.
[21] Dickinson, *op. cit.*, pp. 105–156.
[22] Freund, *op. cit.*, pp. 289–299; Dickinson, *op. cit.*, pp. 307–313.
[23] C. J. Friedrich stresses the value of the "fellowship of science" in enforcing responsibility. He does not propose, however, to dispense with the device of legislative control. See "Public Policy and the Nature of Administrative Responsibility," in *Public Policy, 1940* (Cambridge: Harvard University Press, 1940), pp. 3–24. Cf. John M. Gaus, "The Responsibility of Public Administration," in *The Frontiers of Public Administration*, ed. Gaus, White, and Dimock (Chicago: University of Chicago Press, 1936), pp. 26–44.
[24] Cf. Friedrich, *op. cit.*, pp. 3–8. It should be pointed out again that Friedrich does not propose to dispense with democratic control, but to supplement it with other sanctions.
[25] I. G. Gibbon treats of this question in "The Official and His Authority," *Public Administration*, 4: 81–94 (Apr., 1926), arriving at conclusions substantially in agreement with those set forth here.
[26] This point is ably discussed by Leys, *op. cit.*, pp. 20–22.

ABOUT THE AUTHOR–Herbert A. Simon, see p. 14.

Decision Making in Libraries

by Mary Lee Bundy

> *The concepts advanced in Herbert Simon's* Administrative Behavior *are here applied to professional decision-making in libraries. In analyzing library processes, a number of professional and administrative issues are identified. The argument for local cataloging to meet unique local needs is attacked. In many colleges and universities a key professional decision, book selection, remains in the hands of the faculty. But until control of this function is gained, improved status for college librarians appears difficult of attainment. While the analysis serves to assault the myths which surround professional practice and claims, the writer believes that analysis of professional decisions would provide insights necessary for curriculum modification in library education.*

While such classic concepts of organization as line and staff and span of control still have operational value in setting up a library's internal organization and operation, they fail to explain much of what goes on inside any organization. Modern day organizational and administrative theory recognizes that people do not perform like automatons nor do they stay put like pins on the organizational chart. Theorists have turned to a study of the decision-making which occurs in organizations as a better way to understand organizational behavior.

Such an analysis from the administrator's point of view includes the study of where in his organization decisions relating to its operation should best be made. (This may be only indirectly related to the formal placement of responsibility and authority. If a man has his secretary set up and handle his files without either direction or review, then it is she and not he who is making the decisions relevant to those files.)

The placement of decision making responsibility should take into consideration such aspects as the knowledge required to make the decision. At what point in the organization is this knowledge available at the time it is needed? What channels of communication can be devised to get the necessary information to the point at which it will be needed? How can the administration be assured that decisions made at various points in the organization have as a common base an understanding and acceptance of the organization's goals, plans, and current policies?

Dependent on his place in the organization, the individual decision maker will have particular viewpoints, loyalties, and pressures acting to influence his decisions. These and the information available to him and his understandings and commitments to the goals of the organization explain his final decisions. His successful performance will depend on his ability to examine his possible choices, predict the consequences of the various decisions open to him, and select the alternative which at a given point in time will best facilitate the attainment of the goals of his organization.

It is the purpose of this paper to take the concept of decision making introduced in the foregoing and apply it to certain decisions peculiar to the operation of libraries. Excluded in this analysis are decisions related to general organizational matters except as they relate to the particular decisions selected for study. Also outside the direct scope of the paper are the external forces which influence internal decision making. The writer begins with a generalized concept of the function of a library as being to provide its public with access to knowledge. The decisions are examined at one end of the decision making process—the point at which action occurs and the over-all decision making process is examined only in relation to this final decision making task.

The writer did not attempt a refined analysis but rather intends generally to cover professional decision making in three instances for purposes of showing the value to the professional, the administrator, and the profession of this way of examining professional behavior in libraries. The writer's observations are based on professional experience and personal observation rather than on any planned research design and investigation. Some aspects explored here have been thoroughly cov-

SOURCE: Reprinted from Mary Lee Bundy, "Decision Making in Libraries," *Illinois Libraries,* 43 (Dec., 1961), pp. 780-793, by permission of the Illinois State Library.

ered in the literature, others not at all. A number of pieces are put together here within the theoretical framework developed in order to present a more total if admittedly unbalanced and, in parts, sketchy picture.

The article is written in a negative vein and ignores much of the current experimentation and thinking going on in the profession. Its intent, however, is to contribute to, rather than disregard, the re-examination and soul-searching taking place in response to new and increasing demands on our libraries and their systems and procedures. Nor does the writer wish in any way to belittle the many fine libraries which are obviously keyed to the interests of their communities and whose operations are characterized by a high degree of rational behavior.

The decisions identified as critical decisions made in libraries are: (1) the decision to purchase a book; (2) the decisions related to cataloging a book; and (3) the decisions clustered around the act of helping the patron locate needed information. These are some, but not all of the important professional decisions made in libraries. The cumulation of these decisions over a period of time, however, determines to a great extent the effectiveness of the library in meeting its goals; or, in fact, where its goals have never been precisely defined, these decisions account for the function which the library fulfills in its community.

It is the author's thesis that these are professional decisions requiring the exercise of individual judgment and discretion; but that many times they are not backed by the necessary professional knowledge and understandings and ability to apply this knowledge in an individual situation. Instead they represent unconsciously formulated concepts of the function of the library and the role of the professional and fail to distinguish between these underlying value judgments and assumptions and the factual basis for arriving at decisions.

This failure to perceive what the professional task is and to call on a body of knowledge for the purpose of reaching a desired end in a given situation explains why library science remains at the "common sense" stage of development. It will not progress until it has explored the functions of libraries and its various processes and procedures in terms of meeting these functions.

In the absence of a basis and a framework for his decision making, the professional making decisions in libraries is placed in a continual state of conflict between the impossible to which the librarian gives lip service—that libraries serve all the needs of all their publics—and the reality that libraries to most people on most matters are a minor source of information, that in more cases than not the library may be failing to meet the needs of those who do try to use it and that he himself is not adequately performing the job required of him. The professional is thus uneasy in his role and one expression of this uneasiness is discouragement with the profession and with the work he is called on to do day by day. In the meantime, libraries may be slipping into a third-class or lower position in their communities without a conscious decision to take or accept this position and the limited amount of support which inevitably accompanies it. This paper does not seek to resolve this situation, but simply to describe it in such a way that it is capable of solution.

SELECTING A BOOK

The basis for the selection of books in a library determines the type or types of knowledge or information required of the persons making selection decisions. If one criterion for selection is merit of the work, then knowledge of the subject is demanded. This would encompass knowledge of the publications, authors, and publishers in the field.

But before this knowledge can be brought into play there must be a prior decision to select a book on this particular subject. This would seem to require knowledge of the informational needs of the library's various publics. This is, however, still an inadequate basis for selecting a book on this subject and not another. All the informational needs and interests of the library's public cannot be represented equally in the collection. Some basis must be established for proportionately representing these needs.

For this purpose a hierarchy of decisions may be called for. At the top level of the organization a statement or statements of functions of the library and the translation of these functions into a selection policy for the library, which includes the proportionate representation of each subject field in the library's collection, must be made.

While this narrows the task of the decision maker down to that of selecting within a particular field, it still does not tell him what type of book to purchase. Additional guidelines are needed. What particular clientele will use books on this subject—students, faculty, research people? For what purposes? To gain historical perspective, to keep currently informed? What will be the over-all expected volume of use? Answers to some of these questions may be incorporated in general statements of selection, but each subject field will need this type of delineation as well. The characteristics of the literature and the costs of its publications must also be figured.

The decision is yet more complex. If the aim of the library is to provide access to knowledge, then a decision whether to give preference to actual materials or to bibliographies and indexes which provide access to materials must also be made. The decision should also be backed by actual knowledge of the whereabouts and accessibility of the material if it is wanted and the frequency with which it will be needed.

Knowledge of current publication is also needed. The selector must know what is available from the universe of publication. This requires setting up a system whereby he will automatically have brought to his attention the published works in a field. He also needs assistance in evaluating these works obtained by reviews or by arrangements with faculty or other subject specialists to examine publications.

He must also consider not only current acquisitions but also gaps in his collection. For this purpose the acquisition of checklists, guides, and recommended reading lists would seem necessary. Some arrangement for checking the collection against such guides should be arranged to discover gaps in terms of the stated objectives of a particular library. He also has other methods for reviewing the degree to which his selection is a success. He can arrange to be informed on all requests for material which could not be supplied by the library.

He is, of course, making far more than the decision to purchase a particular book. If the library program has continuity and order in it, then the selection decision sets in motion a series of automatic decisions. It is to be cataloged and added to the collection. If the library has an active program for calling materials to the attention of the public it may be announced, exhibited, and called to the attention of a patron.

Other decisions relevant to the book would seem to be a part of the selection process. Should the magazine be bound? At what point should a book be considered for storage or withdrawal, i.e., how long is the book needed in the collection? Is the need such that added copies are required?

The selection process can be automatically simplified by use of several devices. It may be decided to purchase automatically all works of an agency. The decision to subscribe to a periodical generally becomes an automatic decision unless some method is set for review of the decision.

The task of the administrator is, then, to translate the goals and directions of his college or community into a statement of objectives which realistically admits that all needs cannot be met equally, to translate these objectives into guidelines for the selection of materials which provide for continuity and logic in the development of the library's collection, then to arrange for the necessary "watch" to be kept of all relevant subject fields and for selection decisions to be made by people who are in a position to obtain the knowledge necessary to make the decisions, to establish a procedure whereby knowledge of publication and need is transmitted to these people and to arrange for a method of periodical review and evaluation of the collection and the degree to which it is meeting the needs of the public.

In the absence of such administrative direction, the book selector must himself limit his choices. He may decide to buy in terms of what he considers the quality of what is being published. He may establish what he believes to be the needs of his clientele on the basis of his experience. His position in the organization and his own system of values will enter into his choices. He can maintain consistency in his own method of selection of materials, but he cannot be assured that his choices, except in a one-man library, will be related to the total efforts of the organization to meet the needs of its community.

When the value judgments which belong at the top of the organization are placed at points in the organization where they should not properly be assumed, the result is likely to be a collection which meets the needs of a few people well; most, indifferently; and some, not at all. When librarianship has advanced to the point that it is aware of the library's position in the whole information network of its community, when it is aware of the flow of information through its community whether it be the towns and cities of America or the scholarly and scientific community and can see the consequences of its decisions relevant to maintaining collections and purchasing materials, then a library's requests for its budget will rest on surer ground and its policies and selection procedures be more surely designed to realize its goals.

CATALOGING A BOOK

Recognizing that the selection may be organized to provide for a later review and co-ordination of individual selection decisions, and ignoring decisions relating to selection of dealer and the priority given for sending out orders, the next important decision required is the decision whether or not to catalog a book. Most frequently this is probably set by policy and does not have an individual review. This policy is perhaps most frequently based on format of material rather than on worth or value to the collection, i.e., books may be automatically cataloged, reports relegated to a reports file, pamphlets to yet another system.

Gifts may be fed into the collection without going through the same selection points as books on the same subject or subjected to the same criteria for addition since the material will not cost the library anything to obtain. (The subsequent cost of adding the material to the collection, the cost of maintenance and space problems raise questions as to the merit of making this distinction.)

Assuming the material is to be cataloged, the individual cataloger probably does not have to decide whether to purchase the cataloging cards of a central agency. Presumably this is also a standing decision made for the library based on availability of cards, urgency of getting materials to the shelves, and relative costs involved—or simply the need to release time for other tasks. If cards are obtained or if the library subscribes to the LC proof sheets which are used as the beginning point in cataloging, then the task of the cataloger begins with the cataloging of the book done by a prior decision maker. He must decide whether to accept the decisions made by this first cataloger, who described, classified, and assigned subject headings to the book.

If he reviews the classification decision it will be on the basis of whether this is the number assigned to other works on the subject in his library. He may have a policy regarding the edition of the classification scheme used for books on a particular subject decided by his library. But if he interprets his task as one of keeping all books on a subject together in his collection, he must face the fact that his library like libraries of any age, have books on this subject scattered in the collection because of earlier use of shorter numbers, variations in interpretation of the content of books, and changes made in classification schemes. Should he reclassify a considerable portion of books on the subject to bring them together at one point with the book he is presently cataloging? This decision has probably already been made for him. The library probably has set up some future time and possibly even has some continual process for gradually reclassifying materials so as not to slow up current cataloging with this task. So he must assign the current number being used for books on this subject, or if none has been set, do so, and note that he has done this for future books which may be added. In deciding on the degree of "closeness" of classification he will give to a book he considers such factors as amount of material already in the collection on this subject and amount likely to be added. He too would seem to need guidelines of expected growth of collection in various areas as well as knowledge of publication output.

He, like the person who first suggested the number, has other dilemmas. The book does not fall neatly in one number. It could be placed in two and possibly three places and he is limited to one physical location. On what basis does he decide in favor of one and not the others? Knowledge of the relative numbers of people who look on the shelves for books in or near the various possible classifications he might assign? Consideration of the actual physical disposition of materials in the library? Acceptance of the fact that access to his collection cannot be gained by scanning shelves anyway and that his primary task is to assign a number which identified this book once the patron has first identified this as a library book he would like to examine?

His task in one way is easier when it comes to subject headings, for here he has more than one choice. Does he review the work of the first cataloger in terms of the degree to which the subjects assigned actually describe the contents of the book? He has a guideline here. Subject headings should be as specific as possible. References are made from the general unused heading to the specific. But specific to whom? To the librarian? To the subject specialist? How often is the terminology used in subject heading guides out of date? How often do they fail to keep up with specialization within a subject area? What is happening to departmental libraries in the university system when they must use standard headings and classification totally unsuited to their particular clientele and their literature?

Furthermore, isn't the process actually more frequently one of contorting a subject heading to fit a book or jamming a book into a heading which does not really describe its contents? Or does the cataloger assign a heading under which he thinks a person searching for information would look? How does he know what people with what needs this book would satisfy and what headings they would look under? Can he both select a heading which describes a particular book and at the same time arrive at a heading which will allow other books to be added?

Does he limit his choices to that of a standard guide for subject headings used by his library? When does he make the decision to add another heading instead? He may examine periodical indexes or call on his own knowledge of the field for new terms which need to be incorporated into his subject heading guide. He may add additional headings not selected by the first cataloger with the attendant "see" references and "see also" references. If he admits that he has no more basis for changing or adding headings than the first cataloger, then his task is to use his common sense and get on with the cataloging so that the book will reach the shelves as quickly as possible. (Unless some method has been found for the library to balance its input with its cataloging output, then another cataloging decision to be made is the priority to be given to materials in cataloging them. Is it part of the selection process to state that some materials are needed more quickly than others? How does this interfere with other methods for arranging materials for the most expeditious flow through the technical services department?)

For his choice of "main entry" he has again guide lines, a system of rules, which while they conflict with each other can be resolved by entry under still another agency or author who might be the one responsible for the work. At this point the basis for his choice can be to maintain the consistency of the system and do the same as has been done before with other publications of the same author or agency. Lacking any clear direction in his rules or any precedent in his library he must search for one elsewhere. Having found a basis for his decision somewhere and further rationalized it, he can now proceed.

The cataloger may make some individual decisions. He may decide whether or not to make a contents note or an analytic card for a part of a book or series. In deciding on an analytic is his decision based on knowledge of the importance of this part of the work? On what else is in the collection on this subject and how important it is that this part be revealed to the library's clientele? In his decision based on knowledge of other indexes and checklists which will get the user to this main work? If his task is not to reveal in some way the parts of his collection, what is it? What level of entry to information in the library is he responsible for making?

General policies may have been established regarding making analytics. Were they based on knowledge of the results of making them or not making them in terms of the time and therefore money involved? Were they based on knowledge of the loss involved and agreement with reference to make up for this lack? Or has there been a gradual limiting of the function of the card catalog in the process of cutting the work down to a size that can be handled by the staff—while the department still continues other procedures which also have not been subjected to any empirical study of either need or results.

Granted that the cataloger cannot be expected to have a method for determining the success with which he catalogs every book, does the library have a method for evaluating the success with which the catalog is meeting the needs of its users? Does cataloging get feedback from the reference department on difficulties in use, breakdown in the system, unnecessary time and delay in search which could be solved by adding a card? Or is it assumed that responsibility now rests with the reference staff to instruct the user properly in the use of this tool?

The cataloger may have accepted the cataloging of another person, based on a set of rules and headings for which there is no proof of effectiveness in meeting the needs of users, whose application is subject to great variation, without consideration of the other means of access available to this publication and without any method established for the review of policies and procedures.

Or he may, in the supposed interests of cataloging for the needs of his clientele, spend needless time reviewing the decisions made at the Library of Congress since he has no further basis for changing them than there was for making them in the first place except his judgment against that of another. If inability or inconsistency in applying the rules at the Library of Congress is a major problem, shouldn't this be corrected at the Library of Congress in preference to having thousands of catalogers throughout the country revise its work? If the problem is the need to adjust cards to keep the historical system of the individual library intact, doesn't the cost of maintaining the system demand a serious consideration of ways by which the value of a central cataloging service can be fully realized? If the cataloger does have a method for identifying needs peculiar to his library and to particular clientele, how does he know that he will not destroy the logic and consistency of the whole system in his attempt to meet them?

The individual cataloger would seem to be sitting in the box which catalogers have created for themselves, carrying out an abortive process whose results are unknown. Unable to understand the intricacies and demands of the system, head librarians attempt to keep costs down by suggesting simplifying and reducing parts of the cataloging process. Head catalogers attempt to hold the line in the face of the threat to destroy whatever effectiveness the system still has but are caught by their inability to see beyond the particular functions assumed by their own department and the particular system they support. Materials like serials which cannot be fitted into the existing system without change produce new departments. Somewhere a load and a responsibility is being passed on to a public services department and a loss suffered by the library's users.

Librarianship would seem to need an understanding and ability to generalize concerning the informational needs of its various publics. It needs, too, a way of deriving its part in the whole process by which access to knowledge is supplied. This would require a sophisticated concept of the whole bibliographic process and a study of its various parts in their relation to the whole process. Administrators should view their catalog as only one tool in the library which performs the function of providing access to information—including such special systems as documents collections, pamphlet files and reference files built to do the job the catalog has failed to do as well as the printed indexes and bibliographies which first inform the user of the existence of materials.

In terms of these various direct and indirect access points to the collection, what specific functions does the catalog need to serve? Once having developed specific functions for the catalog, the cataloging process can be re-examined and the internal organization of the library be designed to facilitate the production, storage and flow of indexing information in the library. It could be that our static cataloging system which requires continual re-doing should be replaced by a system built for change. As we push the frontiers of knowledge in all directions, deal with new concepts, new specialties and shifts in emphasis in interest and research, a general and stationary system is archaic.

We may reduce or resolve the inevitable conflict which presently exists where one department is geared to maintaining the most expeditious flow of materials through processing and another to meeting the needs of the library's users. The solution often suggested of having catalogers work with the public and reference staff spend part time in cataloging helps each understand the other better. But to whom do the personnel grant their primary loyalty—the system or the public? This would appear to be the dilemma of librarians until their system is more nearly related to their public and to the other means by which people are given access to knowledge.

In the meantime, public services personnel should sympathize with the cataloger who bristles when they attempt to tell him of one more case where something was found in the collection but could not be located through the catalog for they are suggesting to him what he must continually have bordering on his consciousness—that the system to which he must pay slavish devotion does not meet the claims made for it—that it is not in fact an adequate index to the library's collection and that in his daily cataloging he is continually faced not with choices but rather a dilemma.

HELPING THE USER

This third decision is actually a cluster of decisions which surrounds the act of helping the user to locate information in the library. This decision is considered from the point at which help is given the user although this may not be the officially designated point at which the user is to receive his information—or the user's first point of contact. (This is in fact a major administrative problem. Having deposited the collection and its various indexes in places considered most appropriate, the user must next be connected with them. If he does not get to the point where immediate access is to be found, who is responsible for seeing that he gets what he came for? The first person he asks? A central information point? Or is it his responsibility to get around the system once it is set up?)

The help he receives may vary from merely directional "pointing" to the tool to use, to the actual supplying of the information needed. The decision as to how far to go in meeting the needs of the user may be based on policies regarding help to be given to various types of users or to an overall policy regarding the degree to which the library will be active in meeting the needs of its clientele. Policy may be based in part at least on the type of question asked—informational questions which can be answered quickly may be supplied. More detailed literature searches may receive only directional guidance, the user being expected to conduct the actual search. The degree of help given may vary with the form of request. Requests received over the telephone may be automatically supplied, person-to-person requests going instead through a process of categorizing the clientele or otherwise making an estimate of the importance of the question. Pressure of time and limitations of staff may in many cases be the actual reason for the relative amounts of time and help given to different users.

If the library is operating within a policy of helping users based on clientele let us examine the basis for the policy and its actual outcome in practice. Perhaps the most common rule of thumb in the college library is the "Students learn to help themselves. We don't do their work for them." The philosophy underlying this policy is that use of the library in connection with school work is a learning experience whereby the student operating under motivation supplied by an instructor becomes familiar with libraries and the tools which assist him to locate knowledge.

Let us see how this operates in practice. A student appears with a request for information pertaining to a certain subject. He is referred to the card catalog or the *Reader's Guide*. What is the basis for this referral—also whether or not to go with him or send him? Knowledge of the assignment, its purposes, scope and objectives with regard to the library-end of the assignment? This would seem to require in any instance that the librarian be aware in advance or immediately determine the assignment, how best the material can be located in the library and knowledge of the student, his background and previous library experience. Without this knowledge and without a definite procedure for locating this knowledge and without procedures for assisting the student, the librarian cannot be said to be taking any active part in the learning process involved.

Daily practice if it is to be meaningful and capable of evaluation should be related to a planned program for the library to carry out its part in the instructional program. This would include a definition of the library's part in the whole educational program of its college, including any primary responsibility for teaching students how to locate and use knowledge and the tools of knowledge as well as its auxiliary role in the instructional program. The appropriate methods for implementing its goals can then be selected —individual instruction, library courses, tours, lab sessions in the library, exhibits and displays and—at another level—planning curriculum and course content with instructors, working out the division of responsibility for teaching the literature and bibliography of a field with each department and arranging to be informed about library related assignments. A vital part, ideally at least, would be knowledge of the student as an individual, his interests, his background and his progress as it relates to the library program.

Treating a question as simply an answer to be determined by the librarian through the collection without regard to its part in the instructional program, the librarian has to make a choice in the selection of tools he uses or has the user use to get his answer. One basis for the selection of tools and the approach used to answer the question is knowledge of the depth and level of information desired. This may be obtained by asking the user a series of questions. What questions these are, i.e., the patron-librarian relationship has never been formalized in our literature and library school courses too often assume what we all know is not true, that the user has accurately defined his information problem in terms that relate it to the literature which will answer it.

Another type of knowledge which comes into play in the process of helping the user is knowledge of the tools which provide access to knowledge from the card catalog to other bibliographical tools. This kind of knowledge comes through training and use of the tools. Related to both is the subject knowledge necessary to help the user define his informational need and to select the appropriate tools which will lead him to the desired information. Supposedly this knowledge is added to currently by the librarian who examines not only bibliographical tools but also new books, periodicals in the various fields, keeps up with current developments, changes in terminology. (In many ways this kind of knowledge is the same as required for the initial selection of materials.) Which type of knowledge—clientele, subject or bibliographical—is needed and in what proportions again must be resolved if the proper internal organization is to be established.

There is a further decision on whether to limit

the supplying of information to that which exists in recorded form or to conceive of the function of the library as obtaining solutions to information problems in whatever form the necessary information is stored. On the basis of the library's philosophy on this it will have set up or not set up a series of liaison relationships with other agencies and departments in its community to which it will turn.

In the assistance to the user, then, there is a mixture of decisions, some are value judgments about the degree and type of attention to be given the user, some are factual based on knowledge of the literature and the user, requiring continual application, modification and re-evaluation in each individual situation. From the administrator's viewpoint, of interest is the proportion of questions being successfully answered, an analysis of instances when the user did not receive the help needed for purposes of analyzing reasons for this failure. (What proportion of information searches even come to the attention of a staff member is often not known.) Without a follow-up on performance the reference librarian cannot know whether it is his skill which failed, the collection, its tools or knowledge itself which has not met the needs of a person.

Neither a librarian nor a library should exist in a constant state of doubt regarding the extent to which it is fulfilling its objectives. And one point in time to examine the success of the system is when its clientele approach a librarian for assistance. (We do of course still have the comfortable knowledge that the system with and without direct intervention did produce helpful information as evidenced by our circulation figures even if what, why, when and how remains a mystery.)

No administration can afford to ignore continually the "front line" messages coming from its clientele which signal the need for change. For when any organization refuses to make a necessary change it does not stand still but actually takes a step toward instability. And librarianship needs the richness of experience of those who work directly with the public for it is they who have the feel of the pulse of "grass roots" America, of students at the point of learning and of scholars as they imbibe from the past and prepare to pass into new frontiers. The library schools, in particular, must be sensitive to evolving librarianship if they are to contribute rather than hamper our professional development.

A number of elements necessary to providing library service would seem to be lacking—an adequate and meaningful philosophy of librarianship, a way of conceptualizing our function within which to set and examine our operations and again, basic information about the informational needs and use made of information by the various elements in our community. Perhaps most importantly, we need acceptance of responsibility for meeting some portion of the informational needs of our community—one which demands that we look beyond the day-to-day service given those who come in our doors to the total community we serve. When we have accepted and defined our responsibilities we will be prepared to select our methods and procedures on the basis of the degree to which they help us fulfill our obligations. Such futile arguments as a-v versus the book and the value of using the public media or becoming a part of the political process of our communities will be replaced by a rational selection of the best means to accomplish the goals we have set for ourselves.

CONCLUSION

Librarians, then, throughout the libraries of the country are sitting at various points in their library organization doing jobs which require them to make the decision to buy a book, assign subject classification and guide cards in a catalog, and help users to locate information. The knowledge required to make these decisions and the appropriate skills involved in obtaining and utilizing this knowledge would appear to be the logical content of the library science course. An examination of the basis for making these decisions, a screening out of knowledge which can best be acquired on the job, would leave the knowledge, skills and understandings which should be provided in the professional training program. This examination of the decisions made in libraries would also help in the separation of the professional from the non-professional task, enabling the present often arbitrary distinctions to become real distinctions based on level of performance.

The administrator needs in turn an understanding of the process by which policies and planning are determined and the methods for ensuring the proper placement, staffing, and direction of professional decision making in a library. He needs, of course, general administrative skills and background understandings of organizations and their application to libraries but this aspect should, it would seem, be the distinctive part of administrative training in library science.

The profession needs, if libraries are to take on any common functions and directions, an underpinning in philosophy and purposes of libraries and procedures for the derivation of specific objectives in any particular situation. Here, too, it would seem that the library school curriculum could provide the common base. Finally methods must be developed for both individual and organizational evaluation of performance if the profession is to develop from a simple art practiced by a group of devotees to a professional status.

A study of decision making in libraries appears, then, to offer advantages to the profession, the librarian, and the library administrator. In the development of professional curriculum, certainly neither the historical nor strictly theoretical approaches can offer what the study of the critical decisions made in libraries can, although there is a need for the purely theoretical approach as well as the empirical and each has much to gain from the other. Studies of basic techniques and codes might also benefit from an examination of their part in professional decision making.

The library administrator can immediately relieve both his and his staff's anxieties and uncertainties by exploring with them their respective parts in the process of professional decision making in libraries. He can begin to distinguish between basic conflicts "built" into the system and personal feuds. The profession can be taken out of the position of being merely resistant or buffeted by forces requiring change, spending its energies instead productively.

If we fail to approach our tasks in a rational manner will not some portion of our public eventually see through our disguises and defenses and perceive this lack of conscious and deliberate decision making? They might suggest that funds allocated for library support are not being wisely spent. If the library profession can first define and then tackle its major problems in a rational manner and from an understanding of the human elements involved, if it can explore the value system on which it rests its claims for support, it cannot fail to find a receptive clientele and group of supporters for the American public badly needs an institution which is dedicated to the free flow of information and ideas and which is efficient in carrying out this obligation to society.

ABOUT THE AUTHOR—Mary Lee Bundy has been both a practicing librarian and a library educator. Her first professional library degree was earned at the University of Denver. Her professional experience is in reference and administration and she was for several years at the Rensselaer Polytechnic Institute. Since receiving her doctorate in library science from the University of Illinois in 1960, she has devoted a major portion of her time to research activity. One of her prime interests is public library development activity; she has studied a number of new developments for the Illinois State Library, the Missouri State Library, the Massachusetts Division of Library Extension and the Maryland Division of Library Extension. These include a study of voting behavior on a library issue, central processing, library boards, regional library systems development and public library use. She is currently a professor at the University of Maryland School of Library and Information Services having joined that faculty in the first year of the School's operation in 1965. Previously she was a professor at the Library School at the State University of New York at Albany. Recent articles include "Conflict in Libraries," *College and Research Libraries*, July, 1966, "Metropolitan Public Library Use," *Wilson Library Bulletin*, May, 1967, "Factors Influencing Public Library Use," *Wilson Library Bulletin*, December, 1967, "Professionalism Reconsidered," *College and Research Libraries*, January, 1968.

Organizational Dynamics

Just as the individual must find adaptive mechanisms in order to function within the bureaucracy, so will there be strains and pressures for adaptive mechanisms within which to pursue organizational goals to advantage. Two central issues are considered in the pieces which follow. These concentrate upon organizational strains which arise out of the very nature of the bureaucracy—as a consequence of hierarchy and specialization of functions, and as a consequence of different views of what should be the library's objectives.

Hierarchy, Specialization, and Organizational Conflict

by Victor A. Thompson

>*A number of salient points are made here—one that is particularly germane for library administrators is the conflict between the hierarchical structure and the role of the technical specialist. Consequences include organizational deference to authority rather than to expertise, and a status system which rewards administrative performance more adequately than professional contributions. To the extent that professional decisions are frequently group decisions, innovative and hierarchical views are seen to be in direct conflict. Furthermore, and this is as true in libraries as in other organizations, in order to receive greatest rewards and incentives, the specialist is forced to shift to a hierarchical role. The alternative is to become reconciled to remaining as a technical or professional functionary while others enjoy greater bureaucratic rewards.*

Many elements undoubtedly combine to make up that particular ordering of human behavior which we call bureaucratic organization, but two are of rather obvious and particular importance. These are the social process of specialization and the cultural institution of hierarchy. A great deal of insight into these organizations can be gained by tracing out the relations between specialization and hierarchy. Particularly, many underlying tensions or conflicts can be illuminated in this fashion.

Modern bureaucracy attempts to accommodate specialization within an hierarchical framework. A hierarchy is a system of roles—the roles of subordination and superordination—arranged in a chain so that role 1 is subordinate to role 2; 2 is superordinate to 1 but subordinate to 3; and so forth until a role is reached that is subordinate to no other role (but perhaps to a group of people, such as a board of directors or an electorate).

A role is an organized pattern of behavior in accordance with the expectations of others. Social scientists often refer to the pattern of expectations as a person's social position—his rights and duties in a particular interactional situation—and his role as behavior appropriate to his position.

Roles are cultural items and are learned. The roles of subordinate and superior (i.e., man–boss roles) are likewise learned cultural patterns of behavior transmitted from generation to generation.

We will refer to these roles in shorthand fashion as hierarchical roles.

Defining position as a system of rights and duties in a situation of interaction, and role as behavior appropriate to a position, we will first turn our attention to a discussion of the rights and duties associated with hierarchical roles.

First let us consider the role of a "superior"—the superordinate role. When a person is designated as the "boss," what does this mean? In the first place, it means that he has a right to veto or affirm the organizationally directed proposals of his subordinates, subject to no appeal. Furthermore, the superior's rights include a near-absolute power over the organizational ambitions and careers of subordinates, such as raises or promotions. Although there are many promotional arrangements, nearly all depend heavily and ultimately on the kind word from the "boss."[1]

Hierarchical relations overemphasize the veto and underemphasize approval of innovation. Since there is no appeal from the superior's decision, a veto usually ends the matter. An approval, however, will often have to go to the next higher level where it is again subject to a veto. Thus, an hierarchical system always favors the *status quo*. In a collegiate body, individual members have a free constituency to which they can appeal and get a hearing. However, even in collegiate bodies (e.g., legislatures) there is some hierarchy, and so the

---

SOURCE: Reprinted from Victor A. Thompson, "Hierarchy, Specialization, and Organizational Conflict," *Administrative Science Quarterly*, 5 (March, 1961), pp. 485-521, by permission of the publisher and the author. Original publication bore the following note: "This article is condensed from chs. iii and iv of *Modern Organization* (New York, Alfred A. Knopf, Inc., in press)."

status quo is also favored in these bodies. The advantage is on the side of those who oppose innovations (e.g., new legislation); the advantage is on the side of the veto. (Here we do not refer to collegiate bodies which are hierarchical creations such as a Russian Soviet).

The superior is generally considered to have the right to expect obedience and loyalty from his subordinates.[2] Although Weber thought that the separation of public (i.e., organizational) from private (i.e., personal) rights and duties was one of the hallmarks of modern bureaucracy, bureaucratic demands upon subordinates extend to many aspects of their personal lives.[3] The right to obedience is only another aspect of the right to command. It should be noted that this is the right to command autocratically and arbitrarily, as Weber indicated. Although there are many superiors who do not supervise autocratically and arbitrarily, they nevertheless have the right to do so.

The superior has the right to monopolize communication, both official communication between the unit and the outside world and communication between the members of the unit. The right to monopolize outgoing communication is often expressed by the insistence upon "going through channels" and bitter resistance to the use of specialist, nonhierarchical channels. The right to dominate internal communication is less often pressed. In autocratically supervised units, however, communication often comes close to a one-way, star-shaped pattern—a restriction of communication to the superior-subordinate relationship only.

The superior has the right to deference from his subordinates, the right to be treated with extra care and respect. What makes this right significant is that it is one-way. The superior has a right to be somewhat insensitive as to subordinates' personal needs.[4] The ranking of roles with regard to the amount of deference due them is what we mean by the "status system." Although specialties are also status ranked, by far the most visible and virile ranking in organization is ranking according to hierarchical position. Thus, the status system of an organization corresponds very closely to the hierarchy of superior-subordinate roles. It will be discussed below.

From these primary rights of the superior flow, logically, certain secondary rights—the right to determine the personnel of the unit and its organizational form; the right to initiate activities (set the unit's goal) and to assign them (confer jurisdiction); the right to settle conflicts (make decisions). His power of command makes it possible for him to create nonhierarchical authority by ordering his subordinates to submit to the influence of persons other than himself in various specialized areas—the delegation of authority. In this way the propriety of specialist influence can be assured.

The rights associated with hierarchical positions are cultural givens. Actual behavior associated with these positions will be modified by personality, any one person being more or less authoritarian than another. Actual behavior may also be modified by the social process within the groups of people which compose the organization. Thus a superior may form strong affective attachments to his subordinates; he may identify with them. Having become their friend, so to speak, he will find he has assumed the duties of friendship, most of which are at war with his hierarchical rights and usually with his duties to his superior. In extreme cases of this kind, a specific individual may engage in almost no behavior appropriate to his hierarchical position; he may not enact his hierarchical role. It is not unusual in such a situation for a person so entrapped to be considered useless by the hierarchy and to be replaced. Perhaps most people in hierarchical positions find their roles compromised in this fashion to a greater or lesser degree.

Above what might be considered a market minimum, the good things, the satisfactions which the organization has to offer, are distributed according to hierarchical rank, hence status rank. These goods, in addition to money, include deference, power, interesting activities and associations, inside knowledge, conveniences, and the like. Because these goods are distributed according to status rank, and access to any rank is controlled by hierarchical position, these positions acquire great power even over those who might not recognize all the rights of the position as they have been outlined above. Likewise, these positions become great personal prizes as means to personal (as opposed to organizational) ends, and as such are the objects of a constant struggle.[5]

The superordinate role is chiefly characterized by rights. If it has duties, they constitute the correlatives of subordinate rights. On the other hand, the subordinate role is chiefly characterized by duties—all those duties which constitute the correlatives of the superordinate's rights. They are the duties of obedience, of loyalty, of deference; the duty to accept a superior's veto without attempting to appeal around him (is anything more organizationally immoral than attempting to "go around" a superior?); and so on. In our modern democratic culture there are demands for rights of subordinates—rights to personal dignity, to be treated on the basis of merit, to extraorganizational freedom from organizational superiors. All of these "rights" are ambiguous because they conflict with superordinate rights, and this conflict has not yet been worked out in our culture. That is to say, the doctrines of democracy and liberalism which underlie our state have made almost no impact upon our bureaucratic organizations. The only nonlabor-union movement in this direction has been the attempt by some personnel people to introduce rudimentary elements of procedural due process into the bureaucracy; but because of the persistence of the old role definitions and the actual power of hierarchies the assurance of procedural due process is problematical in any particular organization and more or less dependent upon the personalities or connections of the people involved.

Since a large part of the role behavior associated with hierarchical positions is concerned with deference or prestige, it would be well to take a closer look at the status system. Prestige has been defined as the invidious value of a role.[6] We have defined the "status system" as a hierarchy of deference ranks and seen that it corresponds to the hierarchy of subordinate-superordinate roles. Although positions can be differentiated without ranking, they are usually ranked.[7]

Since a person's hierarchical position is a matter of definition, of defined rights and duties, it should be clear at the outset that any special deference paid to the incumbent may constitute a confusion of person and role. That is to say, a person may be entitled to deference by virtue of one or more of his qualities, but his role is not one of his qualities. A person is perceived by others, however, through his roles, his public or perceived personality being the sum of his various roles.[8]

The confusion of office (role) and person is a very old phenomenon; it was part of the charismatic pattern. In fact, status can be regarded as the continuation of charismatic attitudes and practices. It has often been noted that people impute superior abilities to persons of higher status.[9] Furthermore, this imputed superior ability is generalized into a halo of general superiority. Thus, persons of very high status are called upon to help solve problems of every conceivable kind—problems about which they could have no knowledge whatsoever. In public affairs, this halo effect of status requires high-status persons to speak out on all sorts of matters from a position of almost complete ignorance. They are, therefore, forced to develop plausible-sounding jargons and propositions which come to constitute pseudo technologies in terms of which many of our public problems must be publicly analyzed and discussed.[10] If, with this handicap, real solutions are found to these problems, they must be found by unsung "staff" specialists who must perforce solve the problems in ways which do not jolt the pseudo technologies too profoundly.

It has already been pointed out that status has a dominant position in the distributive system. Studies with small groups show that high-status persons get the most satisfactions from such groups.[11] Studies of military behavior suggest that high-status persons are more interested in preserving the system of status ranking than are low-status persons.[12] Above a certain level it would seem that salaries are to some, rather large, extent a function of status—the higher the status, the higher the salary. In fact, it would seem that salaries operate chiefly as symbols of status rank.[13] That the perquisites and conveniences of the work situation are distributed according to status rather than organizational need is common knowledge, and it has been argued that they are distributed in inverse ratio to need.[14] These perquisites also act as symbols and, along with other symbols such as salaries, methods of payment, clothing, insignia, titles, and the like, help to maintain the status system by increasing its visibility.[15] The amount of deference a person receives is made manifest by the good things others give him, and so, in one sense, the status system *is* the distributive system.

We have said that a hierarchical position carried with it rights to a certain amount of deference. But the system of deference ranking, the status system, while it corresponds to the hierarchical system, is much more than a hierarchy of deference rights. These rights are owed by a group of subordinates, but a person's status spreads its influence over a much broader area. Furthermore, the amount of prestige attached to hierarchical positions increases as we go up the hierarchy at what would appear to be an "abnormal" rate. The status system appears to have a "quasi-neurotic" character.[16] This element of exaggeration in status systems has both structural and psychological determinants.

Cognitive stability is promoted if one's superior by definition is perceived as one's superior in abilities.[17] The subordinate's self-image is protected by the same mechanism.[18] The superordinate position and the person who occupies it are perceptually merged.

The superior's restriction of the subordinate's freedom and his power to frustrate the subordinate's ambitions result in hostilities. The hostilities are not compatible with acts of submission, and they create guilt. Consequently, according to Eric Fromm, they are suppressed and replaced by admiration.[19] My superior is wonderful, and I neither need to be ashamed of submission to him nor need I try to be equal to him in any way. If Fromm is correct, hierarchical status may be partly a result of "reaction formation."

Furthermore, the person as perceived by others is the result of his many roles. His prestige relates to the perception of his roles. Prestige is more easily maintained when there is considerable vagueness about a person's roles—about what he actually does. On the other hand, a person whose prestige is based on what he actually can do must constantly struggle to maintain it.[20] That is to say, charismatic status rank is both more sure and more general than status rank based upon a specialty. Incumbents of high office are held in awe because they are in touch with the mysteries and magic of such office; they are "on the inside,"[21] have "inside information," and so forth. Since one knows less and less about the activities of superordinates the farther away on the hierarchy they are, the more the awe in which he holds them and consequently the greater their prestige or status. Thus it is difficult for workers to impute superior qualities to their foremen because they know fairly well what the foremen do, both at work and away from work. The same is not true for men higher up.[22] In this sense, status rank is a function of ignorance. The hierarchy is a highly restricted system of communication with much information coming in to each position, but the amount sent out to subordinates is subject to the control of the incumbent and always limited, for strategic reasons or otherwise. There results an increasing vagueness as to the activities at each level as one mounts the hierarchy, and this vagueness supports the prestige ranking which we call the status system.

Experimental studies with small groups indicate that stratification (invidious ranking) in such groups is positively correlated with leader dominance behavior and negatively correlated with leader membership behavior.[23] Hierarchical roles are simply institutionalized dominance. The status system is thus seen as inseparable from the hierarchy. Furthermore, groups seem to have a process or mechanism similar to homeostasis in biology. If one member of the group engages in tension-producing behavior, the others act so as to reduce tension.[24] Thus if the rights of deference are pushed by a group's superior (if he "pulls rank"), tension may be reduced by acceding to the superior's demands. Communication blockages between the superior and the group reduce its influence over him so that the group must usually adjust to the superior rather than the reverse. Supporting this deference-building process is the cultural norm in our society that a person's presentation of himself should be taken at face value.[25] Thus, the role relations between superior and subordinates create a situation where there is almost no limit to the expansion of the superior's prestige except the prestige rank of the superior at the next level.

People vary greatly in their needs for dominance and for status. One would expect a sort of natural selection to bring into hierarchies persons with great dominance and status needs. Persons whose dominance needs are satisfied by mastery over materials rather than people will probably become specialists of some kind. Others may satisfy their dominance needs by identifying with their organization superior, thereby reinforcing his drive to dominance and status. Whereas specialists are always subordinate, a hierarchical position always includes a superordinate role and hence a chance to dominate people.[26] Given the group adjustment mechanism of homeostasis and the natural selection by the hierarchy of people with great status and dominance needs, the exaggerated character of the status system becomes intelligible, since people with great status needs can get just about as much deference as they demand if they occupy hierarchical positions.

It has often been noted that there are few operational performance standards for hierarchial positions.[27] Incumbents can never be sure "how well they are doing." This insecurity increases as one goes up the hierarchy. Furthermore, as one mounts the hierarchy, his activities have less and less specialist content and become more and more purely hierarchical role playing.[28] What specialist content remains at very high levels relates only to the particular organization he is in and has to do mostly with its history, its organization and methods, and the idiosyncracies of some of its personnel, clients, or suppliers. Thus, as one goes up the hierarchy, he has less and less value for other organizations.[29] The result of these two conditions —lack of operational performance standards and lack of opportunities in other organizations—make for great anxiety. This anxiety is most likely to express itself in conformism—which means conformism to the wishes of the boss. The resulting neurotic overemphasis on pleasing the boss further inflates the deference system and modifies upwards the boss' self-evaluation and consequent demands for deference.

Prolonged enactment of a role reacts upon the personality.[30] People become what they do. Thus the deference accorded a person who performs a hierarchical role gradually modifies his self-characterization and hence his self-projection. He comes to feel that the deference is due him by right, that he truly is a superior person, and the deference system is further inflated.

The inflation at the upper end of the status system results in a deflation at lower levels. Since the status system controls distribution, the organization gives a great deal at the top and very little at the bottom.[31] It has often been observed that at the middle and lower-middle reaches of the hierarchy, concern with status and the symbols of status reaches an almost pathological intensity.[32] At these points people with great dominance and status needs find less than enough to satisfy their needs because so much has been allocated to the positions above. The status system skews the distribution system.

We have shown that hierarchical roles, as culturally defined, have strong charismatic elements connected with them. Current conceptions of organization are clearly based upon charismatic assumptions concerning these roles. It will be recalled that current formulations of bureaucratic organization (which we have called "monistic" and Weber "monocratic") conceptualize organization entirely in terms of hierarchy, as follows:

1. The person in each hierarchical position is told what to do by the person in the hierarchical position above him, and by no one else. He in turn, and he alone, tells his subordinates what to do. They, and they alone, do the same for their subordinates. These instructions establish the division of work, namely the organization. The authority to do anything is cascaded down in this way, and only in this way, by the process of delegation.

2. Each subordinate is guided (supervised or directed) in carrying out these instructions by his superior and no one else, who, in turn, is guided in this guiding by his superior and no one else, etc.

3. Each superior "controls" his subordinates in carrying out the instructions by holding them responsible for compliance with the instructions or with performance standards associated with them. The subordinates are responsible to their superior, and no one else; he, in turn, is responsible to his superior and no one else; etc. Thus all authority comes from the top and is cascaded down by progressive delegations, while responsibility comes from the bottom and is owed to the next superior and to no one else.[33]

This monistic formulation is based upon charismatic assumptions at various points. It is assumed that the superior, at any point in the hierarchy, is able to tell his subordinates what to do, and to guide them in doing it. That is, it is assumed that he is more capable in all of his unit's activities than any of his subordinate specialists who perform them. The concept of responsibility for results assumes the ability or capacity to determine the results (or else the responsibility is merely ritualistic). The concept of unity of command or influence denies the relevance of the nonhierarchical expertise within the organization; the hierarchy of subordinate-superior roles, the "line of command," is sufficient. When these assumptions of superordinate ability are viewed against the background of the increasing range of activities subordinate to hierarchical positions at successively higher stages in modern bureaucracy, the assumptions clearly leave the realm of objective reality and become charismatic.

The monistic concept has other weaknesses. It is unable to account for specialization. More specifically, it cannot account for the delegation of nonhierarchical authority. The existence of such authority is consequently denied or hidden by fictions (e.g., "staff only advises; it does not command"). Furthermore, the monistic concept asserts that hierarchical authority is created by delegation from above, whereas, as we have seen, it is a cultural item, compounded from the culturally derived roles of the superior and the subordinate.

The monistic concept, since it is based entirely upon the institution of hierarchy and completely ignores the fact of specialization, naturally confuses rights with abilities—for example, the right to make decisions with the ability to do so. This confusion of rights with abilities results in the popular journalistic presentation of the actions of organizations, including states, as the actions of their top officials. It also encourages elitist interpretations of society.

Hierarchical roles began to develop at times and under conditions when it was credible to think of the chief as the most capable person. Under these circumstances, vast rights became associated with the role. The belief in unusual powers of persons who perform such roles—charisma—has continued in the form of the status system. Although specialization has enormously changed the circumstances of organized action, modern organization theory, and to a considerable extent practice, is fixated on the system of hierarchical roles. The fact and implications of specialization are hardly recognized.

In modern bureaucracy specialization is incorporated into the older hierarchical framework. Consequently, our problem is to describe and explain the interactions between specialist and hierarchical roles and the kind of order resulting therefrom.

The behavior of people in organizations is purposive in two senses. First, this behavior must be minimally oriented to a common (organizational) purpose or it would not be meaningful to speak of an organization. Second, behavior within organizations is oriented to personal goals. Consequently, we are interested in role interaction in the promotion of organizational goals and in the pursuit of personal goals. The first interest stresses capacities (abilities, powers), while the second stresses tastes, i.e., motivation.

Activities and relations oriented to the objective, externalized goals of the organization stress instrumental considerations. These activities and relations reflect an institutional framework characterized by specificity of function and the norms of rationalism and universalism. They grow out of specialization and out of advancing science and technology. On the other hand, the relations most closely associated with personal goals in bureaucratic structures stress rights or authority rather than instrumental considerations. These relations are characterized by diffuseness of function (in relation to personal goals) and particularism. They are the relations of hierarchy. The subordinate's obligations to his superior which rise out of his dependence upon the superior for the satisfaction of his personal goals (needs, satisfactions, motivations, and so on) are diffuse and ill-defined; and since objective standards governing the relationship tend to be absent (e.g., bills of rights) particularistic norms appear in their place (who one knows, mannerisms, appearance, out-of-office behavior, and so on).[34] The institutional pattern of functional diffuseness and particularism associated with our hierarchical relations is older than the pattern of functional specificity and universalism associated with specialization. Bureaucracy is thus seen to be compounded of the old and the new, of hierarchy and specialization.

We have defined a specialist as a person skilled in a number of programs—fairly complex sets of organized activities of a practical nature. As problem-solving mechanisms, organizations can be viewed as a breakdown (factoring) of a general problem (accomplishing the organizational goal) into simpler and more specific sets of organized activities until actual programs are reached. New problems for an existing organization are likewise factored. If this factoring is done in defiance of existing specialties (hence programs), new and usually unacceptable specialties are created with all their implicit problems of tension, co-operation, and co-ordination. Such factoring would not be freely undertaken by specialists and could thus be only an act of authority. For these reasons, problem factoring, hence the definition of organization structure, is being forced into specialist hands (though note; the hierarchical role includes the right to do this job and it is almost universally claimed as an "executive function" by writers). The overwhelming need for co-ordinated (hence co-operative) activities among specialists makes this development inevitable.

Associated with the factoring of the organization's goal is the delegation of jurisdictions (i.e., the creation of nonhierarchical authority relations). Previously we emphasized the principal system of authority in organization—the hierarchy. The authority relations of hierarchy are the relations of a superior to a subordinate. The superior's right to command, however, makes it possible for him to create (delegate) nonhierarchical authority relations. He can command his subordinates to accede to the influence of another person in some defined area or specialty. He can therefore centralize activities or create interdependencies.[35] Since this power of a superior is not necessarily restricted by any formula or operational standard, it is essentially political power—the personal power to confer favors. To the extent that this power is exercised in accordance with the needs of specialization, it constitutes a *pro forma* legitimizing of a technical reality, an official promulgation of a technically existing interdependence.

Although the making of assignments—the setting of goals or purposes—is almost universally designated an "executive function," programs are for the most part activated by received information or the proceduralized flow of work, unless new programs (innovations) are called for. Although approval (legitimizing) of innovations is a superordinate right, innovation is actually a specialist function. Innovation is a specialist function not only because new programs come from specialist organizations and educational curricula, but also because they are suggested by the interpretation of incoming raw data, an activity which of necessity is specialist. (Particular executive positions often combine specialist and superordinate roles.) The *approval* of innovations must, of necessity (i.e., if organization goals are to be achieved), be determined by confidence in the sources of innovation and the order of their appearance.[36] If the approval is based upon the technical adequacy of the proposal, necessarily a specialist determination, the right of approval becomes a formality only.

The adequacy of problem solving within organizations depends upon the adequacy of communication as well as upon the skills available. We have already pointed out that the interdependence of specialists is made more tolerable if communication between them is adequate, and this fact exerts pressure for developing specialized languages and useful shorthand categories for classifying large amounts of information. The relation between adequate and reliable communication and the tolerance of interdependence also exerts pressures for the creation of specialist communication channels beyond the formal channel of the hierarchy. Not only has specialization resulted in an intolerable overloading of the formal channels, but they are no longer technically adequate for much of the communication. Furthermore, these channels are notoriously unreliable because of opportunities and motives for suppression and censorship at each communication station (hierarchical position). Most problem-solving communication, consequently, takes place through specialist communication channels. These communication channels are generally not officially recognized and legitimatized by organization hierarchies, so that most problem-solving communication is either "illegal" and surreptitious or its existence repressed from official consciousness (i.e., notice) by means of myths and fictions.

Since problem solving in organizations is a specialist activity, it is a group rather than an individual activity. A decision by a group of specialists must be almost unanimous, and modern organizations try to make decisions about organization goals by unanimous groups.[37] In matters involving the personal goals or ambitions of employees, however, autocratic hierarchical decision is still the rule. Although group decision is an inevitable result of specialization (hence interdependence), it is also a result of the perceived need for group decision. Thus, there may be and probably usually is more group consultation in modern bureaucratic organizations than the objective facts of interdependence warrant.[38] This overworking of group processes, the exaggeration of interdependence, appears to result from conditions within the hierarchy rather than from specialization.[39] Since the hierarchy, by definition, is an allocation of rights rather than abilities, this emphasis on the right to be consulted, the right of review, is understandable. The relation of the hierarchical role to the decisional process is a relation of right (competency or jurisdiction). "Has everyone with a legitimate interest been consulted?" Furthermore, the more joint decision is engaged in, the more the immediate superior will be called upon to settle differences, and hence the greater his influence will be. When only single recommendations can reach him, he becomes largely a captive of his organization. It is not surprising, therefore, that the superior will see the need for joint decision whether it exists or not and that he may be tempted to create technically unnecessary interdependence by delegating authority in defiance of the criteria of specialization. However, in addition to the right to be consulted, and desire for enhanced influence, excessive insistence upon joint decision reflects insecurity growing from dependence upon specialists, which increases both in time and with elevation in the hierarchy.

Although, in general, group decision can be greatly superior to individual decision as a problem-solving device,[40] bureaucratic structure severely limits the effectiveness of the group process. For the small-group-thinking process to be most effective, a substantial degree of group cohesion is required. This cohesion greatly increases the ability of the group members to accept and back up affectively one another's analyses and suggestions.[41] It minimizes autocratic procedures and behavior which create tensions, dry up spontaneity and creativity, and attack co-operativeness.[42] Although many spontaneous, nonhierarchical, informal group discussions constantly take place in organizations, the decisions which commit the organization, the official ones, take place in hierarchically structured situations including hierarchically structured groups. Although attempts are often made to hide the hierarchical structure in the formal group-decision process, to pretend that it is not there,[43] the hierarchy is *in fact* present and all group participants know it. Consequently, because of hierarchical control over personal goals, everything said and done in the group situation must be evaluated from the standpoint not only of its relation to the organization's goals but also of its relation to personal goals. In bureaucracy, ideas do not stand on their merits alone.[44] It is not only an opinion or an idea that wins but also a man. The situation is inherently competitive rather than co-operative, and, as Kurt Lewin has pointed out, competition attacks group solidarity and consequently the ability of the group to employ specialization in pursuit of the group goal.[45]

An organizational decision-making group is ostensibly a small problem-solving group and so all the experimental data concerning the latter are relevant to the former. These data roughly indicate that the problem-solving process goes through three stages[46]—orientation (the statement of the problem, definitions, and the like), evaluation (setting up the relevant values and norms), and control (attempts to influence decision or solution). It is necessary to get agreement at each phase before a joint decision at the control end can be achieved. One of the prerogatives of the superior position in hierarchically structured groups is to monopolize the orientation phase—to define the problem ("we are meeting here for the following purpose"). If the problem is thus hierarchically defined, the resulting decision cannot be called a group decision. Although in specific cases particular superiors may forego the exercise of this right, common experience indicates that the right is frequently claimed. Such a hierarchical statement of the problem will almost certainly have inarticulate premises relating to personal goals (or informal group goals), and this fact contributes to the difficulty of obtaining an effective solution.

In a nonstratified group, positive and negative responses of other members act as controls over participants both in the direction of goal accomplishment and of eventual consensus (true group decision). In the stratified (hierarchical) group, high status or prestige protects a person from group influence but increases the power of his own positive and negative reactions as controls over others in the group. The group must therefore yield to him.

It has been observed in experimental groups that the perception of leadership (who is the leader?) is related to the quantity of activity rather than its quality.[47] Furthermore, as groups increase in size, a larger and larger proportion of the activity is addressed to the perceived leader, and he addresses himself more and more to the group as a whole. The process tends to become one of informal lecture with questions and answers (with the familiar rimless wagon-wheel or star pattern of communication). In the formal organizational group, the position of "leader" is predefined—he is the person with the highest hierarchical position.[48] Thus, even apart from the *rights* of his position there is a strong tendency for him to dominate the group process.

In a group with considerable cohesion, "questions provide a means of turning the process into the instrumental-adaptive direction of movement, with a low probability of provoking an affective reaction, and are an extremely effective way of turning the initiative over to the other."[49] Questions, however, prevent the asker from improving his status because the initiative is given to another and so are much less likely to be used in a competitive, stratified group.

In the experimental group without formal structure, the idea man is most disruptive of group equilibrium and hence is most likely to arouse hostility. He is also most likely to be perceived as the group leader. In the formally structured group, the idea man is doubly dangerous. He endangers the established distribution of power and status, and he is a competitive threat to his peers. Consequently, he tends to be suppressed.[50]

These potential weaknesses in the group thinking process in formally structured groups raise the question of how effective organization decisions are made in our modern bureaucracies. Four possible answers suggest themselves, all of which are no doubt true to some extent. First, the problems taken up for formal group decision may not usually have a high degree of importance to the organization's success, and a *de facto* delegation of important decisions to specialist, informal group processes actually takes place. Secondly, it is likely that a considerable degree of self-restraint in the exercise of hierarchical decisional rights must be and usually is practiced.[51] In the third place, it is possible that formal bureaucratic decisions are not as effective as they could be.[52] And, finally, much of the effective decisional process in organization is camouflaged by myths and fictions to give it an apparent consistency with the culturally sanctioned rights of hierarchy.

Durkheim said that specialization as an adjustment to achieve a more satisfactory life involves not only a function which reduces competition but also one suited to a person's constitution or tastes.[53] Thus the organization must be capable of satisfying personal goals. It is not only a distribution of powers (capacities and rights) designed to promote an official system of values but also a means toward personal goals.[54]

The ability of an organization to satisfy the personal needs and motives of all its participants is compromised by the definitions of hierarchical roles. Job satisfaction depends upon the degree of skill involved, the variety of activities, the degree of autonomy, the consistency of the job with the individual's self image, and the predictability of work relations. These elements of job satisfaction may come into conflict with hierarchical rights to assign activities and to supervise them. The right of arbitrary command may conflict with cultural norms of independence, and the right to unusual deference, with norms of equality and dignity. Thus, the self-images of subordinates are endangered.[55]

Within the hierarchy, the opportunities for job satisfactions other than the exercise of authority are particularly scarce, and increasingly so as one mounts the hierarchy, since the specialist element in such jobs becomes increasingly attenuated. Consequently, hierarchical positions are more instrumental to other goals such as power, money, and prestige. With the decline in specialist content goes the possibility of operational performance standards. Since the distribution of the more formal and obvious personal rewards of power, money, and prestige is the prerogative of a superior, the satisfaction of such personal goals requires conformity to a superior's demands whatever they may be. Thus "brown-nosing," hypocrisy, "false personalization,"[56] are endemic in modern bureaucracies and especially in those areas where the instrumental satisfactions of work (skill satisfactions) are not so available, namely the upper reaches of the hierarchy. Anxiety generated by the nonoperational demands of superiors and the actual dependence upon subordinates often expresses itself in a preference for "bureaucratic" practices—excessive formalism and impersonality, strict compliance with rules and regulations, close supervision.[57]

The full exercise of hierarchical rights results in autocratic rule, or "bureaucratic" supervision as the term "bureaucratic" was used in the previous paragraph. Whereas a person in a hierarchical position can be expected to dislike the insecurity of his own position and the application of autocratic practices to himself, he may be less sensitive to his subordinates' reactions to such practices, may even need to impose autocratic discipline as an outlet for aggressions necessarily repressed in his role as subordinate.[58] Many studies testify to the deleterious effect which autocratic supervision has on the satisfactions (personal goals) of participants.[59]

The superior's right to monopolize official communication can be particularly damaging to personal satisfactions or goals. As Lewin has pointed out, denial of pertinent information to participants prevents a cognitive structuring of the situation and results in emotionalism, lack of direction, alienation, and conflict.[60] Furthermore, the denial of information, by concealing the relation between activities and the larger group objectives, denies the satisfactions of knowing one is part of a larger, important, co-operative effort. Although the hierarchical role does not *require* the withholding of information, it does condone a certain insensitivity to subordinate needs. Furthermore, the strategic considerations surrounding hierarchical competition and the need to protect the legitimacy of the positions[61] counsel caution in the distribution of information, both to subordinates and to others.

We pointed out above that the currently prevalent concept of organization, the monistic concept, was essentially a formalization of the institution of hierarchy. The monistic concept gives rise to practices and relationships that duplicate childhood to a considerable extent. In monistic theory and somewhat less in practice, each individual in the organization (except the top man) is subordinate to a parentlike figure who instructs, reviews, admonishes, reproves, praises, criticizes, evaluates, supports, rewards, and punishes, thereby duplicating much of the experience of childhood. This denial of adulthood is surely one of the more painful aspects of modern organization.[62] Furthermore, we suspect that performing the role of the parentlike figure would be equally painful for mature, sensitive adults. It may not usually be performed very faithfully.

The most serious impact of the hierarchical system upon the achievement of personal goals within organizations results from its appropriation of the definition of success in our culture. Since the time of the Reformation, success in Western civilization has been interpreted in competitive and individualistic terms of relative social prestige or status.[63] Wealth has long been a dominant symbol of status. As we have shown above, status or social prestige, with all its symbols, including income, has become largely a monopoly of the hierarchy in modern bureaucracy. Bureaucratic hierarchy has inherited the rights and privileges of the early charismatic leader and his retainers, the traditionalistic king and his nobility, and the entrepreneurial owner-manager and his familial protégés. Consequently, to be socially defined as "successful" in our culture, one must proceed up some hierarchy. To have public recognition and esteem, hence self-esteem, one must succeed hierarchically. This situation is painful for the specialist. Even if he is the kind of person who can satisfy his dominance needs by mastering a skill rather than people, he will be denied "success" unless he gives up his specialty and enters hierarchical competition.[64] The converse of the hierarchical appropriation of success is the derogation of intellect, imagination, and skill so prevalent in modern bureaucracy.[65]

As pointed out above, the status system, which apportions prestige largely according to hierarchical position, skews the distribution of personal satisfactions other than those related to work—such satisfactions as power, income, deference, interesting opportunities and associations. This tendency is reinforced by the fact that persons in hierarchical positions have greater opportunities to manipulate the organization in the interest of personal goals.[66] These opportunities result from the superior's strategic power to satisfy or frustrate the personal goals of others in the organization unit, from his ability to control the flow of official communication, from his hierarchical rights *in re* subordinates (for example, the institutionalized plagiarism involved in the obligation to use the boss' signature); and from the fact that superiors cannot practically be subjected to very close supervision by *their* superiors. The resulting maldistribution causes a sense of injustice within organizations and suspicion of the upper hierarchy (the "management").[67] This general sense of injustice reduces the willingness and ability to co-operate, thereby sabotaging the promise of specialization.

This damage to co-operativeness is increased by the hierarchical appropriation of success. Employees of our modern organizations are culturally conditioned to expect promotions for good work. With some exceptions in professional specializations (e.g., junior chemist to chemist to senior chemist), promotions are defined as improvement in hierarchical rank. But the number of hierarchical positions decreases rapidly, and so opportunities for promotions, so defined, are extremely limited. Furthermore, above a very low level of actual operations, "merit" becomes an essentially subjective judgment of superiors, despite the attempted quantification of formal performance-rating schemes.[68] Furthermore, above very low hierarchical levels, the admission of new persons into the hierarchy is best described as sponsorship and co-optation. The crucial questions are not merit and ability in the ordinary sense, but the compatibility and loyalty of the newcomers from the standpoint of the existing "management team" ("is he our kind?").[69] The result of these various considerations is that many persons of great merit according to one set of criteria will nevertheless be "failures" in our society. Since they have been led to expect promotion for good work, they will interpret their nonpromotion as rejection by superiors and the organization as a whole. As March and Simon point out, this feeling of rejection is less painful if the persons involved do not identify with the organization.[70] Thus, the definitions and structures of modern bureaucratic organizations are not compatible with a high degree of organization identification and resulting co-operativeness, further sabotaging the promise of modern specialization.

The foregoing discussion of the relations between specialist and hierarchical roles in the accomplishment of organizational and personal goals provides a basis for the analysis of conflict in modern organizations. Concerning conflict in industrial bureaucracy, Melville Dalton has said: "Approached sociologically, relations among members of management in the plants could be viewed as a general conflict system caused and perpetuated chiefly by (1) power struggles ... from competition between departments ... ; (2) drives ... to increase ... status; (3) conflict between union and management; and (4) the staff-line friction."[71] Without in any way disagreeing with Dalton we view the pattern of intraorganizational conflict as arising from the interactions between the principal behavior systems in these organizations—the system of rights (authority), the system of deference (status), the system of specialization (the distribution of abilities) which governs the pattern of technical interdependence, and the system of communicative interaction which governs the pattern of identifications. We will discuss conflict under three general organizing topics: (1) conflict due to the violation of role expectations; (2) conflict concerning the reality of interdependence; and (3) conflict arising from blocks to spontaneous communication.

The newer specialties in organizations are usually lumped together conceptually under the name "staff specialist." A number of upsetting relations arise from these new specialities. In the first place, they threaten older specialties with the loss of functions or the addition of new unwanted ones. Especially is this so if the centralizations involved in the new specialties result from the exercise of the hierarchical prerogative to assign duties (create jobs) rather than from the social advance of specialization.[72] Apart from such acts of power, however, the new specialty must achieve social accreditation before it is accepted.

Advancing specialization upsets status expectations as well as vested interests in functions. Specialization, by giving a function to everyone, brings persons of low and high status into interdependent relations, thereby violating the status expectations of the latter.[73]

The "staff" threat to function and status is particularly acute with regard to hierarchial positions low enough down to contain specialist content.[74] In fact, the conflict arising from these new specialties is usually designated as the line (hierarchy) versus staff conflict. Since specialties eventually win legitimacy one way or another, they acquire authority of a nonhierarchical kind which invades the domain of hierarchical authority. In this way there arises a growing discrepancy between expected authority and actual authority which lies at the heart of the line-staff conflict. Mechanisms of hierarchical protection against this threat of specialization are many, but here we wish only to call attention to the universally adopted devices of derogating staff importance ("line is more important than staff") and of attempting to suppress recognition of the unpalatable features of the relation by the use of fictions ("staff only advises; it does not command").

Much conflict in organizations concerns the reality of interdependence (or the need for joint decision). As we pointed out above, part of this conflict is due to differing perceptions of reality between persons in specialist and hierarchical positions. The need for the new specialty, hence the new interdependence, may also be questioned by existing specialists because of fear of loss of function. More important from the standpoint of conflict in organizations is disagreement as to the need for new interdependence which arises when rights (competencies) are allocated in disregard of technical criteria. As pointed out above, one of the rights of hierarchical positions is the right to delegate rights (authority). Thus, it is possible for rights (e.g., the right to review or be consulted) to be distributed in a manner inconsistent with the distribution of ability. It is possible for competencies to be defined in defiance of the needs of specialization.

The existence of the authority to defy the needs of specialization, the possibility of pure acts of political power, creates the possibility for interpersonal and intergroup competition for authority (e.g., jurisdiction). An ambitious person may bring more activities, hence people, under his jurisdiction and thereby increase his power and status by two methods. He may contrive to get himself promoted to a higher hierarchical position, or he may get rights reallocated so as to increase his jurisdiction. The first method, being more legitimate, is less likely to arouse conflict, but, as we have seen, promotional opportunities are inherently scarce in relation to demand and may not in any case be available to a particular person because of the sponsorship system prevailing in the organization. Thus the second method, that of expanding jurisdiction, may be the only one practically available. Furthermore, if a given group of subordinates seeks status vicariously through identification with its superior and organizational unit, its influence will be in the direction of expansion of jurisdiction. Once again, as pointed out above, since the hierarchy is more impressed by the need for joint decision than are others in the organization, its defenses against attempts to expand jurisdiction are weakened, resulting in much unnecessary interdependence in bureaucracy. Since expansion of one jurisdiction often means the diminution of another, this method of increasing status produces conflict.

It is likely that newer specialties are more expansionist than old ones, deprived as they are of the full measure of their expected status and function because of lack of full acceptance.[75] If the new centralization (specialization) is an act of hierarchical power rather than a result of the advance of specialization, expansionism probably reflects an attempt to allay the inevitable insecurity associated with an imbalance between authority and ability (the right to be consulted versus the ability to make a contribution). However, expansionism may also reflect simply the attempt by a newer specialty to realize a full measure of function consistent with its technical promise. In this latter case, free interaction between the new and the old will eventually cure the cause of conflict, allowing the new to demonstrate its validity and hence the need for the new interdependence.[76] However, conflict arising from resistance to the interdependence resulting from pure power plays can only be eliminated by a redefinition of jurisdictions to the actual needs of specialization, or by defeatist acceptance of the new jurisdictions. In the latter case, any change in the distribution of political power in the organization (power which comes from the personal support of persons with power) will likely be followed by more or less intense activity seeking to reallocate rights of jurisdiction. In this way, an allocation of rights by arbitrary authority creates an unstable and potentially explosive situation.

A common form of the conflict concerning the reality or need for interdependence is that which sometimes arises over the joint use of means. When centralization is undertaken to allow full employment of the latest specializations in skills or equipment, the minor conflicts from joint use which arise because of some inevitable degree of scarcity are not important and are easily resolved without destroying co-operation. The amount of denial and frustration involved can be shown to be necessary and thus acceptable. When the centralization of means is an act of power, however, frustrations arising from the interdependence cannot be made acceptable because they cannot be demonstrated to be necessary. Attempts to ameliorate the conflict by the permanent, full-time assignment of subunits of means to each client cannot remove the instability in the situation, disclosing as it does the fact that the centralization in question is purely a matter of right, of authority, with none of the requirements of specialization involved. Whenever it is technically possible permanently to assign subunits of means, it is technically possible to decentralize.

To illustrate our point, suppose Miss Brown is the subordinate of Mr. Jones and that she is his stenographer. The organization then decides to centralize stenography by creating a stenographic pool. Miss Brown is transferred to the pool but, to avoid conflict over the joint use of means, she is permanently assigned to Mr. Jones. Her technical relation to Mr. Jones is the same; she is his stenographer. Her authority relationship, however, has been changed. She is now the subordinate of Mrs. Smith, the pool chief, rather than Mr. Jones. The centralization was a pure act of authority. Only authority relations were involved.

We should point out that part of the difficulties which arise from centralization can be traced back to the monocratic character of the hierarchical institution. We have said that activities are frequently centralized to assure full employment of the latest specialization in skills or equipment by concentrating demand for them. If the new specialist could be a member of several organization units instead of one, this centralization of activities would not be necessary. It is held that such multiple membership would violate the principle of "unity of command" and must hence be avoided. The reason it is avoided is that it is incompatible with the institution of hierarchy. It would place the specialist in the subordinate relationship with more than one superior. He would have more than one *boss*. While a person can be placed in a subordinate relation to several nonhierarchical authority positions, and always is so placed in modern bureaucracy, he cannot be placed in a subordinate relationship to more than one boss. The rights of the superordinate role preclude more than one boss. The hierarchical institution is monocratic. Among the many suggestions which Frederick Taylor made, his suggestion for several "functional foremen" for each operator was never taken seriously by management. Such an arrangement would attack the very heart of the institution of hierarchy.

Apart from conflicts due to role invasion and the reality of interdependence, the system of communicative interaction also affects the amount and kind of conflict. A great deal of communication works toward a common conception of reality and the sharing of goals. Conversely, blocks to such interaction result in differentiation of reality perception and of goals.[77] The pattern of the distribution of these blocks in modern bureaucracy produces a pattern of groups—clusters of people who, by virtue of frequent and free interaction, share goals and reality perceptions.

The pattern of interaction is determined by the principal behavior systems in organizations. Involved are the systems of authority, status, and specialization (the system of technically necessary interdependence in regard to the organization's goal). The pyramidal distribution of hierarchical rights tends strongly to create groups composed of subordinates and a superior with a wagon-wheel pattern of communication.[78] The hierarchical control of official communication tends to divide the organization into management (hierarchy) and employees (labor). The status system, with its blocks to interaction between strata, reinforces this division and both together alienate the group —"employees"—from the organization as a whole. Shared goals and reality perceptions do not easily extend across this barrier.

Hierarchical control of official communication in conjunction with the status system subdivides the whole organization into status strata. Although there are status strata among purely specialist positions (e.g., junior classification analyst, analyst, and senior analyst), and general status divisions between clerical and professional and blue-collar and white-collar, the heavily emphasized status divisions correspond to hierarchical rank. Status blocks to interaction between strata prevent the development of common goals and perceptions of reality, creating some degree of alienation from the organization, strata by strata, diminishing as one goes up the hierarchy of strata. This alienation within the hierarchy is reduced by two factors. First, mobile individuals, expecting to climb to high positions, try to adopt, or appear to adopt, the values and reality perceptions of higher levels.[79] Second, through the practice of sponsorship, certain likely individuals at lower levels are chosen early and "groomed" for high management positions.[80] By virtue of these various forces and mechanisms, the "management group" is actually much smaller than everyone in supervisory positions, and, in fact, it is customary these days to speak of a still smaller "inner cabinet" or "top management" composed of the head of the organization and his immediate subordinates.

The system of specialization requires the interaction of persons whose specialties must be harmonized in order to achieve the organization goal. This interaction is restricted both by the distribution of authority, hierarchical and delegated, and by the groupings formed by the official communication system. The superior's right to be the sole source of influence over subordinates ("unity of command"), his right to be fully appraised of what is going on (supervision), his right to monopolize communication, his right to the loyalty of his subordinates, all restrict free interaction between subordinate specialists of one organization unit and those of another. Reinforcing these restrictions are the demands of the individual's immediate work group (fellow subordinates and possibly his superior) that he share and give effect to their values and perceptions of reality. Although his status grouping may also interfere with communication with a lower-level specialist, it is our belief that this factor is not serious in purely specialist interaction.[81]

Despite these blocks, interaction is technically necessary. And since no formal-unit work group or status strata could contain all the relevant specialties, specialist interaction must take place across formal-unit and status-strata lines. As mentioned above, this necessary interaction carves out specialist channels of communication, and hence channels of influence, of a semi-illegal nature. More important, it leads to the sharing of values and reality perceptions between the specialists—to multiple group membership—and hence, perhaps to divided loyalties, doubts, and guilts. Inter-unit conflict becomes internalized in the individual. All these effects are likely to be reinforced by the specialist's dependence upon specialist lines and channels for personal satisfactions of status and function, unless he is willing to forego his specialty and enter hierarchical competition. Finally, we should point out that the dimensions of the dilemma of specialist interaction are qualified by the importance of the interdependence, by whether the interdependence involves functional necessities or only working convenience (e.g., the clearance of proposed new programs versus the installation of an additional telephone extension).[82]

The bases of intraorganizational conflict can be summarized in a few general propositions, as follows:[83]

1. Conflict is a function of disagreement over the reality of interdependence.
    1.1. Lack of agreement about the reality of interdependence arises from lack of acceptance of specialties.
        Lack of acceptance of specialties results from lack of accreditation of specialties, which, in turn, is a function of
        1.1.1. their newness, or
        1.1.2. the creation of specialties by acts of authority in defiance of technical criteria.
    1.2. Lack of agreement about the reality of interdependence is also a function of differing perceptions of reality. These differing perceptions are a function of position in
        1.2.1. the authority system,
        1.2.2. the status system, and
        1.2.3. the system of person-to-person communication (the group system).
2. Conflict is a function of the degree of disparity between authority (the right to be consulted) and the ability to contribute to goals. This disparity arises from
    2.1. Growing dependence upon specialists (a function of the process of specialization) while hierarchical role definitions change more slowly; and
    2.2. The allocation of rights (delegation) in disregard of the needs of specialization (acts of sheer authority).
3. Conflict is a function of the degree of status violation involved in interaction.

3.1. Status violation results from advancing specialization and consequent growing interdependence of high- and low-status positions—from positional claims to deference, on the one hand, and the fact of dependence upon specialists, on the other.
4. Conflict is made more or less intense by the relative importance of the interdependence to the success of the organization.
5. Finally, conflict is a function of the lack of shared values and reality perceptions (identifications), which are, in addition to personalities,
    5.1. A function of the lack of spontaneity and freedom in communicative interaction, which is
        5.1.1. a function of the resistance to penetration from without of the principal behavior systems—the authority system, the status system, and the technical system (specialization).

In short, conflict arises from growing inconsistencies between specialist and hierarchical roles. Whereas there are other bases for conflict, it is likely that they could be easily managed under a regime of specialist solidarity based upon the mutual recognition of the need for interdependence.

The conflict between specialist and hierarchical roles has generated mechanisms of role defense. From the standpoint of the hierarchical role, defense involves the securing and maintenance of the legitimacy of the role. Here we only wish to set forth briefly some of the mechanisms of specialist role defense.

We have already mentioned that in order to claim "success," as culturally defined, the specialist must give up his specialty and enter hierarchical competition. A person who chooses this course of action must adopt the values of the managerial group to which he aspires. This "anticipatory socialization" enables such a person to avoid the worst consequences of specialist-hierarchical conflict.[84] Merton has pointed out that a specialist not wishing to follow this path may adopt a sort of schizoid separation of his roles, maintaining his own values privately and relating himself to the organization solely in his specialist or technical capacity. Thus he refuses to take any responsibility for the use or nonspecialist consequences of his advice, regarding such matters as "policy questions" to be handled by the "administrative people." Much specialist training, especially of engineers, contains a liberal amount of preparation for such a subaltern status.[85]

We have also pointed out that specialists engaged in organization problem solving consistently evade official prescriptions in order to get the job done, especially in the matter of communication. This evasion of official prescriptions also takes place in the lower levels of the hierarchy where hierarchical positions contain a good deal of specialist content, perhaps mostly specialist content.[86]

An increasingly used device of specialist role protection is the formation of local, state, and national associations of specialists. These associations compensate to some extent for lack of rights of appeal from hierarchical vetoes by providing a "free constituency" to which vetoed items may be presented.[87] Although some professional associations may function as devices of managerial control of specialists (perhaps some engineering associations have so functioned in the past), it would seem that most of them severely limit managerial control by specifying just how their members may be employed in organizations.[88] In short, they are devices for protecting specialist status and function.

Where a particular skill is concentrated under one or a few employers (that is, in a specific organization), efforts of the skill group to protect its status and function are more effective, resulting in distinctive career groups and peculiar "problems of personnel administration." Examples of such career groups in government organization are: the Forest Service, the Geological Survey, social workers, police, firemen, school teachers, public health workers. Protective activities of such groups result in strong attachments to the careers and the organizations through which they are pursued, emphasis upon objective or proceduralized distribution of recognition (status), life commitments to the careers, a long-range program for the whole career, and the like.[89]

Finally, we should mention that pressures for "due process" proceduralized protection of organization employees have specialist rather than hierarchical origins. They originate both in the new specialties of personnel administration and in the employee associations (whether they be called unions or professional societies).

The resolution of conflict in modern organization is made difficult by the fact that conflict is not formally recognized, hence legitimated. To legitimate conflict would be inconsistent with the monocratic nature of hierarchy. It would require formal bargaining procedures. Modern organizations, through the formal hierarchy of authority, seek an "administered consensus."[90] Conflict resolution, therefore, must occur informally by surreptitious and somewhat illegal means. Or else it must be repressed, creating a phony atmosphere of good feeling and superficial harmony.

FOOTNOTES

[1] See Norman Powell, *Personnel Administration in Government* (Englewood Cliffs, 1956), pp. 395-398; also see Harold J. Leavitt, *Managerial Psychology* (Chicago, 1958), pp. 259-262; Wilbert E. Moore, *Industrial Relations and the Social Order* (2d, ed.; New York, 1951), p. 143.

[2] Note the widespread reaction against the late Senator McCarthy's assertion that public officials owe their first loyalty to the United States, not to their bureaucratic superiors. For the same reasons there has been considerable criticism of the Nuremberg trials of war criminals because the command of a superior officer was not accepted as a defense.

[3] See William H. Whyte, Jr., *The Organization Man* (New York, 1957).

[4] Moore, *op. cit.*, pp. 183-184, says this insensitivity of superiors in regard to needs of subordinates is the cause of much trouble in organizations. Harold Leavitt says superiors generally resist the introduction of objective performance standards because they interfere with the superiors' right to dominate the situation, to command respect, to rule the roost (*ibid.*, p. 261).

[5] For a discussion of the various psychological "goods" or advantages enjoyed by the person with superior power in a relationship, see John W. Thibaut and Harold H. Kelley, *The Social Psychology of Groups* (New York, 1959), pp. 116-119.

[6] Kingsley Davis, A Conceptual Analysis of Stratification, *American Sociological Review*, 7 (1942), 309-321.

[7] Robert K. Merton, *Social Theory and Social Structure* (rev. ed.; Glencoe, 1957), p. 315.

[8] G. H. Mead, *Mind, Self, and Society* (Chicago, 1934); Theodore R. Sarbin, "Role Theory," in Gardner Lindzey, ed., *Handbook of Social Psychology* (Cambridge, Mass., 1954); Davis, *op. cit.*

[9] See Chester I. Barnard, "Functions and Pathology of Status Systems in Formal Organizations," in William Foote Whyte, ed., *Industry and Society* (New York, 1946).

[10] See Cecil A. Gibb, "Leadership," in Lindzey, *op. cit.*, p. 905. See also R. T. LaPiere and P. R. Farnsworth, *Social Psychology* (New York, 1936), pp. 308-309; and Norton E. Long, The Local Community as an Ecology of Games, *American Journal of Sociology*, 64 (1958), 251-261. The pressure upon high-status people to speak out plausibly on a great range of subjects has given rise to a new and highly paid profession—the ghost writers. See Daniel M. Burham, Corporate Ghosts, *Wall Street Journal*, Jan. 4, 1960, p. 1.

[11] Robert F. Bales, "The Equilibrium Problem in Small Groups," in Talcott Parsons, Robert F. Bales, and Edward A. Shils, *Working Papers in the Theory of Action* (Glencoe, 1953).

[12] Samuel Stouffer et al., *The American Soldier*, I (Princeton, N. J., 1949), pp. 391 ff.

[13] See Moore, *op. cit.*, p. 125. Washington and Rothschild do an effective job of refuting arguments that the existing pattern of executive compensation has a purely utilitarian function in relation to organization goals. *Compensating the Corporation Executive* (New York, 1951).

[14] Fritz Roethlisberger, *Management and Morale* (Cambridge, Mass., 1941), p. 77; Victor A. Thompson, *The Regulatory Process in OPA Rationing* (New York, 1950), p. 323.

[15] See Barnard, *op. cit.* See also Thibaut and Kelley, *op. cit.*, ch. xii. They equate the status system with the distributive system.

[16] With regard to the military status system, Ralph H. Turner says: "However, through their charisma officers are generally held in far greater awe than their actual powers or inclinations warrant, and a lesser officer is often afraid even to suggest to a superior that his request is not in keeping with regulations" (The Navy Disbursing Officer, *American Sociological Review*, 12 [1947], 342-348).

[17] See works by F. Heider, for example, Social Perception and Phenomenal Causality, *Psychological Review*, 51 (1944), 358-374.

[18] Barnard, *op. cit.* The difficulties encountered when orders must be taken from persons perceived as having lower status are well illustrated by interpersonal problems of chefs and waitresses. See William Foote Whyte, *Human Relations in the Restaurant Industry* (New York, 1948).

[19] *Escape from Freedom*, pp. 165-166. On the ambivalence generated by the authority relationship, see also G. Murphy, *Personality* (New York, 1947), pp. 845-846; and Krech and Crutchfield, *Theory and Problems of Social Psychology* (New York, 1948), p. 421.

[20] See Norman Miller, "The Jewish Leadership of Lakeport," in Gouldner, ed., *op. cit.*, pp. 206-207.

[21] Philip Selznick, An Approach to a Theory of Bureaucracy, *American Sociological Review*, 8 (1943), 323.

[22] See Henri de Man, *Joy in Work* (London, 1929), pp. 200-204.

[23] Gibb, *op. cit.*, p. 899.

[24] *Ibid.*, p. 901.

[25] See Erving Goffman, *The Presentation of Self in Everyday Life* (Garden City, 1959).

[26] According to Eric Fromm, this fact contributed much to the Nazi's success in Germany, *op. cit.*, ch. vi, esp. pp. 236-247. The elaborate Nazi hierarchy provided opportunities for domination and submission for many authoritarian personalities with their combination of sadistic and masochistic characteristics.

[27] Moore, *op. cit.*, p. 143; also James G. March and Herbert A. Simon, *Organizations* (New York, 1958), p. 63. Of course, a particular office may include specialist as well as hierarchical activities, and operational performance standards for the former may be available.

[28] This loss of functions to specialists has been noted by many writers. See for example, Leavitt, *op. cit.*, pp. 266, 269, 238; Moore, *op. cit.*, p. 76; and Reinhard Bendix, *Work and Authority in Industry* (New York, 1956), pp. 226 ff.

[29] See March and Simon, *op. cit.*, p. 102.

[30] Merton, *op. cit.*, ch. vi, "Bureaucratic Structure and Personality." See also Willard Waller, *The Sociology of Teaching* (New York, 1932).

[31] See Barnard, *op. cit.*

[32] Moore, *op. cit.*; Carl Dreyfuss, *Occupation and Ideology of the Salaried Employee*, tr. by Eva Abramovitch (New York, 1938).

[33] For examples of this monistic concept in organization theory see: Mary Cushing Howard Niles, *Middle Management* (New York, 1941); Marshall E. Dimock, *The Executive in Action* (New York, 1945); L. C. Marshall, *Business Administration* (Chicago, 1921); Paul E. Holden, Lounsberry S. Fish, and Hubert L. Smith, *Top Management Organization and Control* (Stanford, 1941); first Hoover Commission Report (Washington, D. C., 1949).

[34] See Peter B. Hammond, "The Functions of Indirection in Communication," in *Comparative Studies in Administration*, ed. by staff of the Administrative Science Center, University of Pittsburgh, Pittsburgh, 1959.

[35] Nonhierarchial authority differs from hierarchical authority in the following ways: (1) it is more specific; (2) it relates to organizational rather than personal goals; (3) it can be withdrawn without destroying the position; (4) it is always subject to formal appeal; and (5) it is organizationally rather than culturally defined (i. e., it is peculiar to the organization rather than the culture).

[36] See March and Simon, *op. cit.*, p. 188; also Thompson, *op. cit.*, pp. 303 ff.

[37] See Moore, *op. cit.*, p. 124, n. 14; March and Simon, *op. cit.*, p. 118; Gordon, *Business Leadership in the Large Corporation* (Washington, D. C., 1945), pp. 99 ff.; W. H. Whyte, *op. cit.* Consultants are probably brought in because unanimity cannot be obtained (Moore, *op. cit.*, p. 124).

[38] Note W. H. Whyte's complaints on this score.

[39] March and Simon say that the felt need for joint decision increases as one goes up the hierarchy. They feel that since the chief legitimation of hierarchy is co-ordination, the hierarchy is likely to see the need for co-ordination whether or not it exists (*op. cit.*, p. 124).

[40] See E. L. Thorndyke, The Effect of Discussion upon the Correctness of Group Decisions when the Factor of Majority Influence is Allowed For, *Journal of Social Psychology*, 9 (1938), 342-362; and Thibaut and Kelley, "Experimental Studies of Group Problem Solving Process," in Lindzey, ed., *op. cit.*

[41] For example, see M. Deutsch, An Experimental Study of the Effects of Cooperation and Competition upon Group Processes, *Human Relations*, 2 (1949), 199-232; K. Back, The Exertion of Influence through Social Communication, *Journal of Abnormal Psychology*, 46 (1951), 9-23; S. Schachter, Deviation, Rejection and Communication, *Journal of Abnormal Psychology*, 46 (1951), 190-207.

[42] See Kurt Lewin, *Resolving Social Conflict* (New York, 1948); L. Cock and J. R. P. French, Jr., Overcoming Resistance to Change, *Human Relations*, 1 (1948), 512-532; D. McGregor, Conditions of Effective Leadership in the Industrial Organization, *Journal of Consulting Psychologists*, 8 (1944), 55-63; and R. Lippitt and R. K. White, "The Social Climate of Children's Groups," in R. G. Barker, J. S. Kounin, and H. F. Wright, eds., *Child Behavior and Development* (New York, 1943), pp. 485-508.

[43] For example, "brainstorming," or the Harwold Group Thinkometer which allows each participant to press a button for "yes," "no," or "maybe," thus not endangering his position in the organization with open discussion.

[44] See Lyman Bryson, Notes on a Theory of Advice, *Political Science Quarterly*, 66 (1951), 321-329. On the problem-solving superiority of groups low in self-oriented need, see N. T. Fouriezos, M. L. Hutt, and H. Guetzkow, Measurement of Self-Oriented Needs in Discussion Groups, *Journal of Abnormal Social Psychology*, 45 (1950), 682-690.

[45] *Resolving Social Conflicts.*

[46] See Robert F. Bales, "The Equilibrium Problem in Small Groups," in *op. cit.*, pp. 111-163.

[47] *Ibid.*

[48] See W. H. Crockett, Emergent Leadership in Small, Decision-Making Groups, *Journal of Abnormal Psychology*, 51 (1955), 378-383.

[49] Bales, *op. cit.*, p. 127.

[50] Note the growing antipathy to idea men, to brilliance, that pervades our bureaucracies. The average person who will *get along* with others and *go along* with the system is preferred. See W. H. Whyte, *op. cit.*, pp. 143 ff.

[51] See Chester I. Barnard, *The Function of the Executive* (Cambridge, Mass., 1938), pp. 193-194. He says the "fine art" of executive decisional ability is knowing when *not* to decide.

[52] Note March and Simon's contention that satisficing rather than maximizing norms are usually applied to organization decisions, and that the approval of proposals is as much a function of their source and timing as of their utility (*op. cit.*, pp. 140-141, 188).

[53] *The Division of Labor in Society* (Glencoe, 1947), pp. 374-375.

[54] On this point see especially the works of Chris Argyris, for example, The Individual and Organization: Some Problems of Mutual Adjustment, *Administrative Science Quarterly*, 2 (1957) 1-22, and "Understanding Human Behavior in Organizations: One Viewpoint," in Mason Haire, ed., *Modern Organization Theory* (New York, 1959), pp. 115-154.

[55] March and Simon summarize the observed bases of job satisfaction (*op. cit.*, pp. 76-77, 94-97). Expectations of independence, equality, and dignity, being cultural, will vary from country to country. Their impact upon organization will, hence, also vary. See Stephan A. Richardson, Organizational Contrasts on British and American Ships, *Administrative Science Quarterly* (1956).

[56] The term is from *The Lonely Crowd* (New Haven, 1950), by David Riesman, Nathan Glazer, and Reuel Denney; see pp. 303-305. See also Harold Leavitt, *op. cit.*, p. 264, and Moore, *op. cit.*, pp. 142-145.

[57] Anxiety has been defined as a vague, nonspecific fear resulting from threats to values basic to the integrity of the personality (Rollo May, *The Meaning of Anxiety* [New York, 1950], p. 191). The values in question in our society are those related to social prestige or status. Status in our society is largely a function of hierarchical position; but so is *loss* of status. Consequently, acute anxiety is a normal condition within the bureaucratic hierarchy.

[58] See Fromm, *op. cit.*

[59] This statement applies to a society where expectations of democratic treatment predominate. Where people have been brought up to expect autocratic supervision, it would probably not apply. See Gibb, *op. cit.*, pp. 910-912.

[60] *Ibid.*

[61] Leavitt says that equalitarian, multichannel communication nets are best but are seldom used because they conflict with hierarchical prerogatives (*op. cit.*, p. 204).

[62] See Leavitt, *op. cit.*, pp. 264-265, and Argyris, *op. cit.*, pp. 18-21.

[63] See May, *op. cit.*, pp. 215 ff.; also Abram Kardiner, *The Psychological Frontiers of Society* (New York, 1945). Since the dominant symbol of status has been money, "success" in America is usually equated with "making money." See Irvin Gordon Wyllie, *The Self-Made Man in America* (New Brunswick, 1954); Kenneth S. Lynn, *The Dream of Success* (Boston, 1955); Richard D. Moiser, *Making the American Mind* (New York, 1947).

[64] See Moore, *op. cit.*, ch. vi; Riesman, *op. cit.*, pp. 154-155; and Alvin W. Gouldner, *Patterns of Industrial Bureaucracy* (Glencoe, 1954), p. 226.

[65] See W. H. Whyte, *op. cit.*, ch. x and *passim*.

[66] See Philip Selznick, An Approach to a Theory of Bureaucracy, *American Sociological Review*, 8 (1943). The office, because of its advantages, comes to be regarded as an end rather than a means. For this process in labor unions, see A. J. Muste, "Factional Fights in Trade Unions," in J. B. S. Hardman, ed., *American Labor Dynamics* (New York, 1928).

[67] Many people report this general sense of injustice resulting from the hierarchically skewed distribution system. See, for example, Barnard, "The Functions and Pathology of Status Systems in Formal Organizations," in *op. cit.*; Moore, *op. cit.*, p. 184; Roethlesberger, *op. cit.*, p. 77; Peter Drucker, *The New Society: The Anatomy of the Industrial Order* (New York, 1950), pp. 92-95.

[68] See Norman J. Powell, *op. cit.*, chs. xi and xvi; Moore, *op. cit.*, p. 143; and Leavitt, *op. cit.*, pp. 259-262.

[69] See note 79, below; also C. Wright Mills, *The Power Elite* (New York, 1957), ch. vi. Since the operationality of performance standards declines as we go up the hierarchy (see Moore, *op. cit.*, pp. 140-143, and March and Simon, *op. cit.*, p. 63), the superior's rights with relation to the subordinate's ambitions or personal needs become more and more analogous to political power; the process of climbing the hierarchy or "getting ahead" becomes more and more a political process; and the kind of person who can succeed at this game becomes more and more like the political type. On this point generally, see Harold Lasswell, *Politics: Who Gets What, When, How* (New York, 1936).

[70] *Op. cit.* p. 74. See also R. C. Stone, Mobility Factors as they Affect Workers' Attitudes and Conduct toward Incentive Systems, *American Sociological Review*, 17 (1952), 58-64.

[71] Conflicts between Line and Staff Managerial Officers, *American Sociological Review*, 15 (1950), 342-351. He points out that the intensity of the conflict was exaggerated because recognition of the conflict had to be repressed.

In the following discussion we do not wish to leave the impression that we believe conflict, per se, is bad.

[72] Dalton's study showed only 50 per cent of staff people doing work related to their college training, thereby casting doubt on the validity of some of the specializations.

[73] In Dalton's study, staff specialties were the new ones, and these specialists were much younger than others in the organization on the average. "Line" resistance was especially pronounced.

[74] Dalton, *op. cit.*; Moore, *op. cit.*, ch. vi.

[75] Dalton says that staff people have less chance of hierarchical advance and hence must engage in empire building activities.

[76] It should be noted that specialist organizations may block this free interaction and thus slow up the integration of the new with the old and the adjustment of the old to the new for considerable periods of time. The activities of building trades unions are notorious examples of this process, but the same elements are at work, for example, in medical resistance to a redefinition of nurses' roles. See Harvey L. Smith, Contingencies of Professional Differentiation, *American Journal of Sociology*, 63 (1958), 410-414.

[77] See March and Simon, *op. cit.*, pp. 124-129.

[78] Under strictly autocratic practices, the pattern of communication would be star-shaped; little group identification would result. As the group composed of supervisor and subordinates becomes more cohesive, the structure of the communication pattern changes until it is difficult to tell who is the formal head and, in fact, most communication may eventually be directed to a person other than the appointed head—to an "informal leader." When this development occurs, the formal head has accepted the obligations of group membership and has rejected his hierarchical duties and forfeited his hierarchical rights.

[79] See Merton, *op. cit.*, ch. ix, "Continuities in the Theory of Reference Groups and Social Structure."

[80] See Mills, *op. cit.*, ch. vi; Everett C. Hughes, Queries concerning Industry and Society Growing Out of Study of Ethnic Relations in Industry, *American Sociological Review*, 14 (1949), 218-220; Orvis Collins, Ethnic Behavior in Industry: Sponsorship and Rejection in a New England Factory, *American Journal of Sociology*, 51 (1946), 293-298; Joseph W. Eaton, Is Scientific Leadership Selection Possible? *American Journal of Sociology*, 52 (1947), 523-535. E. L. Thorndike, *Human Nature and the Social Order* (New York, 1940); W. R. Kornhauser, The Negro Union Official: A Study of Sponsorship and Control, *American Journal of Sociology*, 57 (1952), 443-452; Melville Dalton, Informal Factors in Career Achievements, *American Journal of Sociology*, 56 (1951), 407-415.

[81] We are arguing, for example, that a senior economist will have little difficulty dealing with a junior statistician in

another unit who can actually perform some service that an economist requires. For the chief of the economics section to deal with the same junior statistician would be more painful.

[82] It should be noted, however, that trivia may have great symbolical significance. Much of the conflict in organizations has a trivial origin.

[83] We should emphasize again that we are discussing *only* organizationally generated phenomena. Conflict also results from extraorganizational influences such as the general social conditioning that shapes personality, conflicting group affiliations, racial and religious attitudes, and the like.

[84] See Merton, *op. cit.*, pp. 265-271. Conscious, opportunistic adoption of managerial values is likely to involve the specialist in difficulties with his peers who will regard him as "pushy," a "climber," a person "bucking for a promotion," an "upstart," and even a "renegade" (Merton, *ibid.*).

[85] *Ibid.*, chs. vii, xvii. Others have pointed out that technical specialists are generally easy for power seekers to manipulate. See Hans H. Gerth and C. Wright Mills, A Marx for the Managers, *Ethics*, 3 (1941-1942), 200-215. The specialized training acts as a blinder to other aspects of experience. Veblen referred to this phenomenon as "trained incapacity."

[86] See Melville Dalton, Unofficial Union-Management Relations, *American Sociological Review*, 15 (1950), 611-619. This study shows that lower-level management officials and lower-level union officials both evade the prescriptions of their respective hierarchies in order to solve their mutual problems. See also Charles Hunt Page, Bureaucracy's Other Face, *Social Forces*, 25 (Oct. 1946), 88-94.

[87] On this point see Bryson, *op. cit.*; Selznick, *TVA and the Grass Roots* (Berkeley, 1949), esp. pp. 145-147; and David Truman, *The Governmental Process* (New York, 1951), *passim*. Because ideas are not considered on their merits alone in bureaucratic organizations, it would seem reasonable to argue that these "free constituencies" are a necessary condition of organization success in the long run.

[88] Note, for example, how the Group for the Advancement of Psychiatry seeks to determine the activities of the various specialists in mental institutions. The role of the social worker is defined in the GAP Report Number 16; the role of the "Consultant Psychiatrist in a Family Service for Welfare Agency," in GAP Letter Number 259; and so on.

[89] See Wallace S. Sayre and Frederick C. Mosher, *An Agenda for Research in Public Personnel Administration* (Washington, D. C., 1959), pp. 37-42.

[90] The term was suggested to me by Robert V. Presthus.

ABOUT THE AUTHOR—Victor A. Thompson is another behavioral scholar in the field of public administration who found that classical explanations of administration bore very little relation to what actually transpired in organizations and determined to help remedy the situation for future students. All his writings are concentrated upon the attempt to bring theory into line with practice through empirical evidence. His first volume reported on *The Regulatory Process in OPA Rationing* (1950) in which he drew directly upon his experience as an administrator in the Office of Price Administration. He collaborated with Herbert Simon and Donald Smithburg in the preparation of the widely used textbook *Public Administration* (1950). The inspiration and material for his more recent volume, *Modern Organization* (1961), grew out of the exchange of ideas during seminars he conducted at Chicago's Center for Programs in Government Administration involving more than 1,500 government executives.

Victor Thompson received his B.A. from the University of Washington and his Ph.D. from Columbia University in 1949. He has been a consultant to a number of government agencies while serving on the faculties of the University of Texas, Illinois Institute of Technology and Syracuse University. At present he is Professor of Political Science at the University of Illinois.

Conflict in Libraries

by Mary Lee Bundy

The author originally turned to organization theory to understand her own working experience in libraries. While much library conflict is undoubtedly personal in nature, her experience and that of others suggested that there were other common causes at work, and that the outcome of conflict was heavily structured in favor of the status quo. Perhaps the most serious question is the degree to which organizational arrangements in libraries make them receptive or unreceptive to change.

Her proposed restructuring of libraries may not resolve the conflict between what appears to be the two types of people in libraries—those who are people and service oriented, and those whose commitment is to the maintenance of the system. The need is to help libraries distinguish between their means and their goals for this confusion permits excessive amounts of time and resources to be spent perpetuating present practice at the expense of the service goal. Her thesis is that this fact, coupled with the interal preoccupation with personal and power relationships, effectively circumvents and retards needed change in libraries.

THE PROBLEM

Conflict is a fact of existence. It exists whenever and wherever people come together to work. Some types of conflict encourage strong vitality and exert the right kinds of pressures to meet the objectives of an organization. Other kinds of conflict, however, work in reverse. They act to sap the energy of an organization, to subvert its goals—and can even endanger its existence.

Conflict has been given major attention in management literature, but it has been largely neglected in the literature of library administration. This article is devoted to the analysis of conflict in the library situation with particular attention focused on its undesirable aspects. While practical solutions are proposed, its chief purpose is to develop understanding of the causes and consequences of conflict in libraries.

Librarians frequently attribute conflict to "problem" staff, yet individuals can leave the library and the conflicts persist. All libraries are likely to have similar conflicts for they are often caused by common organizational forces in the library environment. Chief among them is departmentalization and hierarchial organization. Groups other than formal organizational groups also conflict with each other. Older and newer staff members typically disagree on important questions. Since conflict has organizational causes, it can—and indeed it must—be dealt with on an organizational basis.

This paper undertakes to deal with a complex and highly volatile subject because of its implications for library development. It draws upon management literature and speaks in management terms. What is truly at stake here, however, is professionalism itself. Librarianship gives major attention to the organization of its physical materials. It must give equal attention to the organization of its human resources, if the reason for material flow—service—is to be realized. This article attempts to explain why service objectives are often subordinated to other considerations.

In the ensuing discussion several organizational concepts are used. Hierarchy or bureaucratic organization refers to the pyramidal structure characterized by the "chain of command" where each person has one person to whom he reports who in turn reports to someone higher in the heirarchy. Professional organizations are discussed and a distinction made between professional and semi-professional organizations.

Organization, as it is used here, refers both to the formal organization and to informal aspects of organization, those outside the formal structure. One way to examine informal groupings is in terms of interest groups, that is, of people who

---

SOURCE: Reprinted from Mary Lee Bundy, "Conflict in Libraries," *College and Research Libraries*, 27 (July, 1966), pp. 253-262, by permission of the Association of College and Research Libraries.

have common goals and act together at least part of the time to achieve these goals. The informal organization also includes people who hold "power"; these are, by definition, people in the organization who decide what goes on. As will be developed, power is only partly a function of authority granted by the administrative organization. Professionalism is considered here in terms of what constitutes professional behavior in the various organizational relationships of librarians.

TECHNICAL SERVICES VS. PUBLIC SERVICES

Dividing into departments achieves the important advantage of specialization, but departmentalization also immediately establishes the conditions of conflict. The various departments must compete with each other for a share of limited resources. Since their work is interrelated in many ways, the success of one is partly dependent on the success of another. Each department develops its own specific goals which may conflict with those of other departments.[1]

Every department in a library can conflict with every other, but the most serious and also the major divisional conflict in libraries is usually between technical services and public services. For processing units the goal becomes one of efficiency—the greatest output in least time. Of equal, if not greater, importance to them is the maintenance of their systems and procedures. These goals can and do conflict with public services' goals to serve the user.

Since processing departments are perennially behind, the priorities they assign to processing materials influences the degree of public service possible. Few processing departments have an organized plan for processing in an order based on user needs. They may "rush" specific requests, although they often do so reluctantly. Important new statistical sources essential to reference service, for example, may be lost for days as they wend their way through processing with other less urgently needed materials.

Improving the speed of processing would alleviate this problem. But the order of processing materials is only one aspect of the conflict. In making decisions relevant to the degree and type of cataloging to be given materials, efficiency considerations and conformity to existing practices can also be in opposition to service needs. These aspects may have more long-term effects if only because it is more difficult to detect when service requirements are not being met.

One reason for processing policies and procedures not being geared to service needs is that processing units are frequently isolated from the first-hand experience with users and their needs for materials. Generally libraries have not been successful in devising organized ways to feed back to technical services information on the success of their operation. Technical services tend to let their systems and procedures become ends in themselves. Public services departments can try individually and on a departmental basis to get changes or decisions which will improve service, but—and this is the crux of the matter—they will not always be successful because technical services have an equal position in the line operations of the library. Therefore, service needs cannot automatically win. Library goals are, under such circumstances, subordinated to a means operation in the library.

It can be disputed whether cataloging is a goal or a means toward goals, but the intellectual or professional character of the operation cannot be disputed. Within technical services departments, however organized, cataloging too must deal with pressures of physical processing activities which can be in opposition to professional standards of excellence. Certainly in the medium-sized operation catalogers are sometimes forced to give major attention to processing problems at the expense of time they would normally give to cataloging questions and problems. The professional services in libraries are, under such circumstances, and by the way work is arranged, forced to take second place to the operations which should in effect serve them.

HIERARCHY

Library schools, teaching in the classical administration tradition, have taught librarians the advantage of bureaucratic organization. This type of organization does achieve important advantages in locating responsibility, directing communications, and assuring coordination. But bureaucracy also has limitations inherent in it.

By its nature, advancement in hierarchial systems depends on pleasing superiors. "What the boss wants" enters into the decisions of subordinates. There is a distinct tendency for people not to communicate events or information which may reflect poorly upon them. Personal motives inevitably enter into relations with superiors.

Indeed, this facet is built into the hierarchial structure which dispenses rewards as a way to win loyalty and ensure compliance. There are times, of course, when doing what the boss wants is not in the best interest of the library.

There is conflict in any bureaucracy which employs specialists.[2] Some decisions can only be made by people with a particular expertise. Yet the specialist who has the knowledge to make the decision may not occupy the position in the hierarchy assigned for this decision. This is particularly true as organizations get more specialized. No administrator can have the knowledge required to handle all the complex technical matters which come to him because policy, change, or money is involved. Administrators may call on individuals or on groups for advice, reserving the final decision for themselves, but if they habitually follow this advice, their decision-making power in effect is going into the hands of the specialist.

One reason heads of organizations resist this is that the specialist sometimes makes his decisions on a different basis from that used by the administrator. He uses technical criteria and may or may not have the immediate organizational objectives in mind in making his decisions. This conflict may be seen operating with scientists employed in government and industry.

Many library administrators think they allow for full exploration of a topic by professional staff, but the impact of status is nevertheless present. This may be observed in a library staff meeting. Junior members hesitate to express their opinions frankly in the presence of their department heads. However much administrators like to think their meetings are democratic, the decision-making actually rests on how supervisors feel and not upon the consensus of the professional staff.

Because of these limitations, professional organizations take over certain areas of decision-making. A professional organization is one in which what the majority of the professionals do is the major goal of the organization. In these organizations, typically, the professional group through full group participation and through their representation on committees takes over the decisions relating to the goals of the organization. The administration concerns itself with means decisions and activities (those involving economy and efficiency and auxiliary services not central to the enterprise, such as business affairs). An administrative hierarchy still exists, but there is actually a sharing of power between the professional group and the administration.

It is important that this division of authority be achieved. Since professional organizations are non-profit in nature, there is no test of success in the competitive market place. Their activities are difficult to measure. Control groups naturally seek to keep costs down. Since need cannot be proved, it is important to have a professional group insisting on standards as a counterpressure to pressures for economy.

Library administrators, coming from the ranks of the professional, should also be expected to fight for standards, and they do. But they are directly susceptible to external pressures. Their job depends on getting along with control groups. They need a strong counterforce from the professionals. Too, the administrator is fundamentally loyal first to the administration for whom he works. The professional's major commitment is to his clientele and to his internalized set of professional standards and ethics.

Most libraries probably fall into the classification of semiprofessional organizations. A semiprofessional organization is characterized by the fact that its professional group has *not* achieved control in matters relating to goals and standards. Means or economic considerations characteristically dominate goals considerations. Ways and means become ends in themselves. Substantive questions having to do with the intellectual side of the enterprise are either ignored or downgraded by leaving them to staff down the line who do not have the authority to make decisions and carry them out. Consider again the library staff meetings in which ways and means and routine matters dominate discussions. Few academic library staffs engage in defining service goals and in working out plans to achieve them.

Hierarchy and change. Another aspect of hierarchy which acts against professional goals has been implied. People in hierarchies tend to act to protect their position or status. When a change is proposed they examine and act on it in terms of how it will affect their status. This means that new ideas and proposals do not get the free and critical appraisal they require. Rather, people in hierarchies tend to be strongly committed to the status quo. Innovation frequently can be made only after long struggle or not at all. The absence of conflict in the face of social conditions requiring internal change becomes dangerous.[3] Professionals can also resist change for the same reasons or because they fear they cannot perform in new ways. Management can be also effectively stymied by a staff unreceptive to change.

Why do librarians not demand greater voice in library affairs? One reason is that they have not diagnosed the problem in these terms. Another is that librarians are more "employee" than "professionally" oriented, feeling their obligation is to "go along." They have no strong commitment to their clientele or to standards. These obligations are normally the basic loyalty of a professional group and constitute the reason the professional, either individually or in groups, takes action and assumes power over certain types of organizational decisions.[4] If the professional person in a professional organization does not see the need and assume these responsibilities, all other arguments for his professional status become academic.

SPECIAL INTERESTS

There are other special interest groups in the library which are in conflict with the formal administration or with other groups in the library. One of these groups is the "old community."

The old community. The old community consists of people who have been on the library staff many years. They may have long-standing differences with each other, but they are held together on important issues by a common commitment to the status quo. There are many good reasons for this. To a new person change is an opportunity to show his worth. An older staff member may feel that changes cast a bad reflection on him, that advocacy of change shows a lack of appreciation for the accomplishments of the past. The newcomer brings outside experience and a fresh viewpoint to a situation. The older staff member is more likely to be settled in his notions. Past disappointments may have caused him to lower the level of his aspirations. The older staff member in most libraries is likely to be conservative in his outlook, to see the library as a passive rather than an active service. He simply will not see the need for, nor the appropriateness of, certain kinds of innovations.

Conflict between older and newer staff members in libraries is common and has varying consequences, depending on a number of factors, but if the majority of the staff are older members it is likely that they will successfully resist efforts of newer staff. All change is not necessarily good and all new staff members are not change agents, but change is normally introduced through new staff; often they are hired for this specific purpose. Administrative approval, however, cannot wholly gainsay the conservative and uncooperative attitude of a staff. It can form an effective force against desirable change in libraries.

Informal power. All power, of course, is not in the formal organization. There are people whose position does not account for the amount of influence they have in library matters. People can hold power for several reasons. Some people get power simply because they have been around a long time. Much of what goes on in organizations is not written down. People who hold information about the organization's business wield power in the way they provide or withhold it. Another type of power enjoyed in libraries is that of the group which has the special confidence of the head librarian. These are the people upon whom he relies and to whom he turns for advice. The "in-group" need not be those who report immediately to him. It is more likely to be the people with whom he habitually shares his lunch or breaktime. Librarians also have natural leaders, people who have won the respect and confidence of the staff. Since they speak for the staff, management must take their point of view into account in decision making.

It is not necessary to attempt to probe further into the complex topic of power relations in organizations, but it should be emphasized that individuals and groups outside the official hierarchy do have power. One result of having power is to seek to hold it. As many new librarians have discovered, what looks like getting a new and minor change actually turns into a power struggle with the "in-group" or with individuals with power who resist the change. Making many library changes depends on whether those furthering them can secure a position of influence or power in the library. It should also be noted that department heads can and do resist efforts for change from upper level administration. A head librarian can be blocked by his subordinates who subtly or directly resist his authority.

This discussion of special interests in libraries would not be complete without including two other groups in libraries which cross formal departmental lines. Neither is relatively powerful; both are likely to be dissatisfied.

The subprofessional. Subprofessional levels were established in libraries for the worthy purpose of relieving professional staff of routine, nonprofessional work. But this class system, nevertheless, creates conflict. No matter how well the subprofessional performs, he can never join the ranks of the professional—and far better paid—class.

Further, in many libraries the distinction between what the two groups do is highly arbitrary. A subprofessional can carry a position of nearly equal responsibility at half the pay, as he sees it, only because he has not been to library school. Some professionals achieve much of their professionalism by looking down on the non-professional. Under these conditions, whether or not it is openly expressed, the subprofessional is likely to feel considerable resentment. A democratic staff association alleviates but does not solve the problem.

Junior staff. The junior professional staff member has two strikes against him; he is probably relatively new and he has no organizational status. Further, he is probably kept doing subprofessional work for an excessively long period of time. He is likely to be similarly restricted in his outside professional activities, for library associations are also slow to accept newcomers and are influenced by status in making committee appointments at any very high level. Librarians have been acutely conscious of their lack of status, particularly in the academic community. Yet librarians themselves give their junior entrants into the profession something far less than the colleague relationship they deserve.

OTHER ASPECTS

The individual and the organization. Actually, any individual has a struggle with the organization in which he works. In going to work, he must give up a certain amount of independence. Organizations naturally seek to take as much of his time as possible. He has other group memberships besides the library and is therefore pulled between the various groups for which he has a loyalty and which have a claim on his time and effort.

Some jobs get so monotonous, so devoid of opportunity to use imagination or initiative, that they impair the human beings' growth forces.[5] In the interest of efficiency libraries have reduced some people to doing jobs which are overwhelmingly monotonous and fatiguing. This is not only true for stack readers. Many professional jobs in libraries, in the interest of "mass production," approach this level. It is important to treat any human being as an individual and to provide him with opportunities for growth, but for librarians to be stymied in this fashion is the antithesis of professionalism.

Excessive authoritarianism. Under excessive authoritarianism all the weaknesses of bureaucracy are magnified. Orders, threats, and criticisms characterize communications with staff. People are treated like cogs in a machine. Basic feelings and rights of employees are disregarded. This is a sorry state for any library and whatever the outward appearance, fear, interpersonal hostility, and resentment are present. People are forced to act simply to protect themselves. They cannot act freely in the best interest of the library. Indeed, they would be criticized if they did, for compliance and conformity are the essential demands of this type of administration.[6]

The external environment. The impact of pressures from control and support groups to keep costs down has already been noted. The external environment affects the internal library situation in other ways as well. Organizations which occupy positions of low regard and status in their community, which is sometimes true of libraries, can be expected to be less receptive to new ideas, to be less likely to welcome and explore innovations. Being treated like semiprofessionals by their community reinforces their own semiprofessional behavior.

What a professional organization hopes from its community is that it will provide challenges and give it support and encouragement. When the opposite is true, the attitude of the community will complement and give support to the more conservative elements inside. Under such circumstances these conservative elements may be quite accurately reflecting what the community wants in the way of service and expects from its librarians.

The external environment of any library contains some elements which are sympathetic and concerned with library development. In the academic community, faculty committees can be expected to concern themselves with and support service improvements. These groups are not equally effective and often represent special interests. They can become critical of the way the library operates.

Any organization should arrange to be influenced by its environment in the form of planned-for data about the community and about its effectiveness and satisfaction with its services. Yet most libraries have little more than a highly impressionistic, individual, and probably distorted idea of how satisfied their community is with their services. This failure adequately to take the community into account in internal decision-making defeats service objectives and can be politically dangerous. As has been indicated, the failure of librarians to build strong professional-clientele relationships and give first loyalty to that clientele is a major reason for their not being pressed sufficiently for service improvements.

An examination of internal conflict in libraries therefore identifies the groups and interests whose attitudes and activities decide whether or not a library gives good service. Processing-service relationships and administrative-professional relationships, as they now exist in many libraries, let "means" become "ends." In the absence of a strong professional voice, economy considerations lower service standards. Intellectual aspects are downgraded. Formal and informal organizational elements conspire to defeat proposals for change and growth. The basis for much decision-making in libraries is personal or is power motivated, in opposition to the best interest of the library. This is not the organizational setting for maintaining a high level of professional service. It can perhaps only be changed significantly by changing the ways of organizing work into divisions and by changing the way power is distributed in libraries.

SOLUTIONS

One organizational structure that might contribute to the accomplishment of these changes is modeled after and closely parallels that of institutions of higher education. Libraries could be restructured to group professional activities together and then organizationally designate them as the central activity of the organization. This could be done by assigning other activities to a staff or service relationship to them, as shown in Figure 1.

Within the subject divisions, the professional activities of selection, indexing (cataloging), reference, and readers advisory service would be performed. As a library grows, these divisions would have one head occupying much the same position as an academic vice president holds in a university. Under these broad subject divisions, various subunits or further specialization of effort could develop. Units might be further subdivided by subject—chemistry, etc. (Departmental libraries would fall within the jurisdiction of the appropriate division.) Or, some staff might spend full time on indexing materials; others operate primarily in readers service. Departments would be run on the relatively democratic basis of teaching departments in a university where, regardless of rank, every faculty member has an equal voice and an equal vote.[7]

A second informal framework should also be established. Permanent professional committees crossing departments, such as indexing committees and selection committees, would function. These committees would concern themselves with common problems and with areas where common policies are desirable. The decisions made by these groups would be more or less binding on the organization. Professional staff would also be represented by advisory committees to the head librarian to advise from the professional point of view on such aspects as personnel policies. Similarly, auxiliary units would have professional advisory committees concerned with service implications of their various activities. The auxiliary units

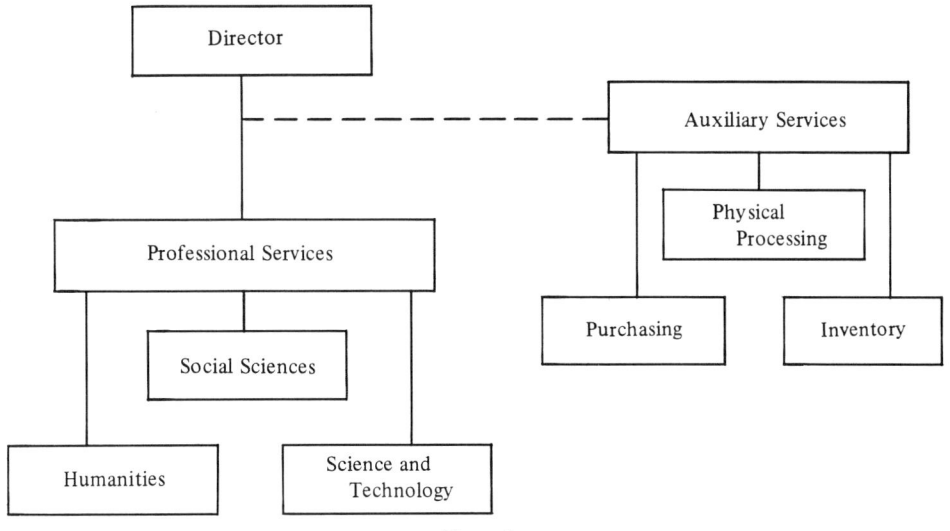

Figure 1.

would bear to the central departments the same relationship as business offices do to academic teaching departments.

The auxiliary units, as libraries grow larger, could encompass a variety of specialties such as data processing personnel. Competent nonprofessionals could find here a career advancement ladder, for the upper positions in auxiliary services would carry high salaries commensurate with responsibility for important, complex, but not professional services.

These changes could not be "paper" changes only. They would have to involve an actual relinquishing of authority by administrators and an acceptance of responsibility on the part of professional staff. Further, they would mean a major redirection of professional effort away from the routines of library operation. Administrators would lose a measure of control but in the process would achieve their ultimate goals. The quality of administrative leadership would be a critical factor in whether or not libraries succeeded in becoming first-class professional organizations.

New relationships among groups would have to be worked out. Libraries would have to find new ways to resolve conflict between divergent points of view under this more democratic form of administration. Building the relationship of auxiliary services with professional services would be a major task. The respective decision-making prerogatives of administrators and professional staff can only be partially distinguished. Their interrelationship in achieving goals is critical and would involve continued negotiations and compromise. Service standards would have to bend— but not bow—to economic realities. Systems and procedures would be modified in terms of user needs, but they would not be abandoned before user demands on the system.

In such a structure as is here described there would be more conflict in the sense of questioning, intensive scrutiny, and the consideration of a wider range of alternative courses of action. Where a library staff is largely conservative, however, this viewpoint can still prevail. Informal power will still exist, although the basis for it may change somewhat. Certainly, staff who have the respect and trust of their colleagues will formally and informally have much to say about what goes on.

What would be accomplished is that powerful growth forces would be released to offset the restrictive forces described earlier. We would have made clear to ourselves and eventually to our users what constitutes the nature of the library enterprise. Libraries would be expected to refocus their endeavor on their service character. Staff time would have been released to serve clientele. By limiting the range of subject areas with which they dealt, professionals could develop the competency to conduct clientele relationships at a truly professional level. On a group basis, professional staff could concern itself with, and engage in, defining purposes and developing programs to achieve these purposes. Out of discussion and deliberation should come a commitment on the part of all members to make them work. These goals would also form the basis for resolving conflict in the best interest of the library. A climate for decision-making could grow which values critical inquiry more highly than present structures. Individual ambition could be better harnessed to the improvement of the library. With these orientations, libraries might be expected to realize a potential of service and of support for that service far beyond any that has been previously known.

Certainly many libraries have made advances in these directions. Many already divide by some subject arrangement, although the majority still keep technical services in the line operation, and cataloging functions within this unit. Many public libraries have largely resolved this aspect of the problem by removing their processing from the immediate library to a central processing center. Many libraries, particularly medium-sized libraries, enjoy a high degree of democracy in working out their affairs, but most have been attempting to cope with organizational forces which inhibited and hampered them. The central issue is not democracy versus bureaucracy; it is whether or not librarians are prepared to assume responsibilities and arrange their organizational life to permit the performance of a service which can be labeled professional.

What is the alternative? In all but backwash situations, libraries of every size are going to be pressed for increased service. Under the conditions described earlier, libraries will respond with rigidity. This will intensify the criticism of control and clientele groups and create internal working conditions even less tolerable than those now existing. Eventually, the entire library enterprise could be placed in jeopardy. In the face of present and future demands on libraries, a fundamental reassessment and realignment of existing organizational relationships in libraries would appear imperative.

FOOTNOTES

[1] For a discussion of intergroup conflict see: J. G. March and H. A. Simon, *Organizations* (New York: Wiley, 1963), p. 121.

[2] For one presentation of this conflict see: V. A. Thompson, "Hierarchy, Specialization and Organizational Conflict," *Administrative Science Quarterly*, V (March 1961), 485-521.

[3] Presthus deals with this aspect in a more general social context. Organizations tend to stress conformity rather than difference. In the face of social and technological pressures for change they frequently respond with inflexibility. Yet, survival depends on critical inquiry into patterns of organization, thought, and behavior. With critical inquiry, the quality of decision is sharpened. Without it, decision-making rests dangerously on tradition and on status. R. Presthus, *The Organizational Society* (New York: Knopf, 1962), p. 287-94.

[4] Etzioni suggests another reason. In his characterization of the semiprofessions, he points out that the majority of their members are women and women may be more submissive to authority. A. Etzioni, *Modern Organizations* (New Jersey: Prentice, 1964), p. 89. We may also find part of the explanation in the relatively passive personality of librarians. See A. L. Brophy and G. M. Gazda, "Handling the Problem Staff Member" *Illinois Libraries*, XLIII (December 1961), 750-63 for an analysis of the personality of librarians.

[5] Argyris contends there are basic incongruencies between the growth trends of a healthy personality and the requirements of the formal organization. Frustration, conflict, failure, and short term perspective are the resultants. C. Argyris, *Personality and Organization* (New York: Harper, 1957).

[6] In a "before and after" study, Guest explores staff feelings and attitudes under an authoritarian regime. R. H. Guest, *Organizational Change: The Effect of Successful Leadership* (Homewood, Ill.: Irwin, 1962).

[7] See J. D. Millett, *The Academic Community* (New York: McGraw-Hill, 1962), for an exploration of the academic organizational structure.

ABOUT THE AUTHOR—Mary Lee Bundy, see p. 94.

III
THE SEARCH FOR RATIONALITY

In the attempt to condition the organization to achieve its sought-for ends, a number of characteristic activities and processes form the basic elements. Inherent is the need to concentrate upon determining the goals and purposes, the administrative processes through which the organization strives to achieve its objectives, the utilization of the resources of authority, personnel and finance, and the communication mechanisms employed within and without the organization. Creative administration concentrates upon the desired and sought-after ends for which the organization exists. This is not a problem for libraries alone, but for other organizations, even including nations and societies. For, to center exclusively and ever more zealously upon particular problems, one at a time and in isolation, is to lose the sense of the purpose for which the organization was begun. Matters of technique are less fundamental than ordering the priorities of the organization. As a library administrator concentrates upon the symptoms of a problem, as for example whether to shift to book catalogs, the problem is examined as though it were purely a technical issue; but the more fundamental and root problem—the nature of the services and the collections and the intended purposes to which they are put—frequently not only goes undiscussed, it is furthermore obscured by the preoccupation of the administrator with technique. Once a policy has been established, too frequently administration is viewed to be a sort of technically and administratively preordained determinism. If administration becomes cumbersome, we build in new levels of function. If one element of service is viewed by a vociferous clientele to be inadequate, it is reinforced, while others remain untouched. It is not intended here to minimize the importance of techniques and procedures, of adequate appropriation, or of adaptive managerial skills, but only to suggest that concentration solely upon problem issues tends to divert attention from the fundamental direction in which the organization is or should be moving. Such pragmatic orientation is a reflection of the highly applied and instrumental approach too frequently taken by administrators, within which the goals and values are not only taken for granted but are naturally assumed to be valid and relevant for all time. But it is the very failure to examine values and goals which brings down upon organizations, libraries among them, the critical problems which they must ultimately face.

Formulation of Objectives

It seems almost ludicrous to stress the essential nature of goal specification. Yet to formulate objectives with precision, to achieve consensus upon their priorities, and understanding of their implications, constitutes one of the most arduous tasks faced by those who assume leadership roles. Here is the explanation for the vagueness and ambiguity of the objectives of countless organizations, libraries prominent among them. The difficulties of forging goals are staggering; but the costs and the hazards to organizations in avoiding or evading the issue are very great. The readings which follow explain why this is so.

The Objectives of a Business

by Peter F. Drucker

In this chapter Peter Drucker identifies the primary measures relevant to the establishment of objectives in an organization. While he concentrates upon the corporate organization, the lesson of these remarks is just as relevant to the library form. This classic contribution elaborates the reasons why objectives are necessary if the survival and effectiveness of an organization are to be achieved. Particularly relevant are the comments made upon market standing and innovation. While libraries may have traditionally been viewed to be like public utilities having no competition, it is clear that competitive pressures from alternative information purveying organizations now make such presumed insulation from competitive pressure illusory. The need to fashion a balanced set of objectives and to constantly review such choices over time is nowhere made more explicit than in the piece which follows.

Most of today's lively discussion of management by objectives is concerned with the search for the one right objective. This search is not only likely to be as unproductive as the quest for the philosopher's stone; it is certain to do harm and to misdirect.

To emphasize only profit, for instance, misdirects managers to the point where they may endanger the survival of the business. To obtain profit today they tend to undermine the future. They may push the most easily saleable product lines and slight those that are the market of tomorrow. They tend to short-change research, promotion and the other postponable investments. Above all, they shy away from any capital expenditure that may increase the invested-capital base against which profits are measured; and the result is dangerous obsolescence of equipment. In other words, they are directed into the worst practices of management.

To manage a business is to balance a variety of needs and goals. This requires judgment. The search for the one objective is essentially a search for a magic formula that will make judgment unnecessary. But the attempt to replace judgment by formula is always irrational; all that can be done is to make judgment possible by narrowing its range and the available alternatives, giving it clear focus, a sound foundation in facts and reliable measurements of the effects and validity of actions and decisions. And this, by the very nature of business enterprise, requires multiple objectives.

What should these objectives be, then? There is only one answer: *Objectives are needed in every area where performance and results directly and vitally affect the survival and prosperity of the business.* These are the areas which are affected by every management decision and which therefore have to be considered in every management decision. They decide what it means concretely to manage the business. They spell out what results the business must aim at and what is needed to work effectively toward these targets.

Objectives in these key areas should enable us to do five things: to organize and explain the whole range of business phenomena in a small number of general statements; to test these statements in actual experience; to predict behavior; to appraise the soundness of decisions when they are still being made; and to enable practicing businessmen to analyze their own experience and, as a result, improve their performance. It is precisely because the traditional theorem of the maximization of profits cannot meet any of these tests—let alone all of them—that it has to be discarded.

At first sight it might seem that different businesses would have entirely different key areas—so different as to make impossible any general theory. It is indeed true that different key areas require different emphasis in different businesses—and different emphasis at different stages of the development of each business. But the areas are the same, whatever the business, whatever the economic conditions, whatever the business's size or stage of growth.

There are eight areas in which objectives of

SOURCE: "The Objectives of a Business" from THE PRACTICE OF MANAGEMENT by Peter F. Drucker. Copyright 1954, by Peter F. Drucker. Reprinted by permission of Harper & Row, Publishers, Incorporated.

performance and results have to be set:

Market standing; innovation; productivity; physical and financial resources; profitability; manager performance and development; worker performance and attitude; public responsibility.

There should be little dispute over the first five objectives. But there will be real protest against the inclusion of the intangibles: manager performance and development; worker performance and attitude; and public responsibility.

Yet, even if managing were merely the application of economics, we would have to include these three areas and would have to demand that objectives be set for them. They belong in the most purely formal economic theory of the business enterprise. For neglect of manager performance and development, worker performance and public responsibility soon results in the most practical and tangible loss of market standing, technological leadership, producitivity and profit—and ultimately in the loss of business life. That they look so different from anything the economist—especially the modern economic analyst—is wont to deal with, that they do not readily submit to quantification and mathematical treatment, is the economist's bad luck; but it is no argument against their consideration.

The very reason for which economist and accountant consider these areas impractical—that they deal with principles and values rather than solely with dollars and cents—makes them central to the management of the enterprise, as tangible, as practical—and indeed as measurable—as dollars and cents.

For the enterprise is a community of human beings. Its performance is the performance of human beings. And a human community must be founded on common beliefs, must symbolize its cohesion in common principles. Otherwise it becomes paralyzed, unable to act, unable to demand and to obtain effort and performance from its members.

If such considerations are intangible, it is management's job to make them tangible by its deeds. To neglect them is to risk not only business incompetence but labor trouble or at least loss of worker productivity, and public restrictions on business provoked by irresponsible business conduct. It also means risking lack-luster, mediocre, time-serving managers—managers who are being conditioned to "look out for themselves" instead of for the common good of the enterprise, managers who become mean, narrow and blind for lack of challenge, leadership and vision.

How to Set Objectives

The real difficulty lies indeed not in determining what objectives we need, but in deciding how to set them.

There is only one fruitful way to make this decision: by determining what shall be measured in each area and what the yardstick of measurement should be. For the measurement used determines what one pays attention to. It makes things visible and tangible. The things included in the measurement become relevant; the things omitted are out of sight and out of mind. "Intelligence is what the Intelligence Test measures"–that well-worn quip is used by the psychologist to disclaim omniscience and infallibility for his gadget. Parents or teachers, however, including those well aware of the shakiness of its theory and its mode of calculation, sometimes tend to see that precise-looking measurement of the "I.Q." every time they look at little Susie–to the point where they may no longer see little Susie at all.

Unfortunately the measurements available to us in the key areas of business enterprise are, by and large, even shakier than the I.Q. We have adequate concepts only for measuring market standing. For something as obvious as profitability we have only a rubber yardstick, and we have no real tools at all to determine how much profitability is necessary. In respect to innovation and, even more, to productivity, we hardly know more than what ought to be done. And in the other areas—including physical and financial resources— we are reduced to statements of intentions rather than goals and measurements for their attainment.

For the subject is brand new. It is one of the most active frontiers of thought, research and invention in American business today. Company after company is working on the definition of the key areas, on thinking through what should be measured and on fashioning the tools of measurement.

Within a few years our knowledge of what to measure and our ability to do so should therefore be greatly increased. After all, twenty-five years ago we knew less about the basic problems in market standing than we know today about productivity or even about the efficiency and attitudes of workers. Today's relative clarity concerning market standing is the result not of anything inherent in the field, but of hard, concentrated and imaginative work.

In the meantime, only a "progress report" can be given, outlining the work ahead rather than reporting accomplishment.

Market Standing

Market standing has to be measured against the market potential, and against the performance of suppliers of competing products or services—whether competition is direct or indirect.

"We don't care what share of the market we have, as long as our sales go up," is a fairly common comment. It sounds plausible enough; but it does not stand up under analysis. By itself, volume of sales tells little about performance, results or the future of the business. A company's sales may go up—and the company may actually be headed for rapid collapse. A company's sales may go down—and the reason may not be that its marketing is poor but that it is in a dying field and had better change fast.

A maker of oil refinery equipment reported rising sales year after year. Actually new refineries and their equipment were being supplied by the company's competitors. But because the equipment it had supplied in the past was getting old and needed repairs, sales spurted; for replacement parts for equipment of this kind have usually to be bought from the original supplier. Sooner or later, however, the original customers were going to put in new and efficient equipment rather than patch up the old and obsolescent stuff. Then almost certainly they were going to go to the competitors designing and building the new equipment. The company was thus threatened with going out of business—which is what actually happened.

Not only are absolute sales figures meaningless alone, since they must be projected against actual and potential market trends, but market standing itself has intrinsic importance. A business that supplies less than a certain share of the market becomes a marginal supplier. Its pricing becomes dependent on the decisions of the larger suppliers. In any business setback—even in a slight one—it stands in danger of being squeezed out altogether. Competition becomes intense. Distributors in cutting back inventories tend to cut out slow-moving merchandise. Customers tend to concentrate their purchases on the most popular products. And in a depression the sales volume of the marginal supplier may become too low to give the needed service. The point below which a supplier becomes marginal varies from industry to industry. It is different in different price classes within the same industry. It has marked regional variations. But to be a marginal producer is always dangerous, a minimum of market standing always desirable.

Conversely, there is a maximum market standing above which it may be unwise to go—even if there were no anti-trust laws. Leadership that gives market dominance tends to lull the leader to sleep; monopolists have usually foundered on their own complacency rather than on public opposition. For market dominance creates tremendous internal resistance against any innovation and thus makes adaptation to change dangerously difficult. Also it almost always means that the enterprise has too many of its eggs in one basket and is too vulnerable to economic fluctuations. There is, in other words, an upper as well as a lower margin—though for most businesses the perils of the former may appear a good deal more remote.

To be able to set market-standing objectives, a business must first find out what its market is—who the customer is, where he is, what he buys, what he considers value, what his unsatisfied wants are. On the basis of this study the enterprise must analyze its products or services according to "lines," that is, according to the wants of the customers they satisfy.

All electric condensers may look the same, be the same technically and come off the same production line. Market-wise, condensers for new radios may, however, be an entirely different line from condensers for radio repair and replacement, and both again quite different from the physically indistinguishable condensers that go into telephones. Condensers for radio repair may even be different lines if customers in the South judge their value by their resistance to termites, and customers in the Northwest by their resistance to high humidity.

For each line the market has to be determined—its actual size and its potential, its economic and its innovating trends. This must be done on the basis of a definition of the market that is customer-oriented and takes in both direct and indirect competition. Only then can marketing objectives actually be set.

In most businesses not one but seven distinct marketing goals are necessary:

1. The desired standing of existing products in their present market, expressed in dollars as well as in percentage of the market, measured against both direct and indirect competition.
2. The desired standing of existing products in new markets set both in dollars and percentage points, and measured against direct and indirect competition.
3. The existing products that should be abandoned—for technological reasons, because of market trend, to improve product mix or as a result of management's decision concerning what its business should be.
4. The new products needed in existing markets—the number of products, their properties, the dollar volume and the market share they should gain for themselves.
5. The new markets that new products should develop—in dollars and in percentage points.
6. The distributive organization needed to accomplish

the marketing goals and the pricing policy appropriate to them.

7. A service objective measuring how well the customer should be supplied with what he considers value by the company, its products, its sales and service organization.

At the least the service objective should be in keeping with the targets set for competitive market standing. But usually it is not enough to do as well as the competition in respect to service; for service is the best and the easiest way to build customer loyalty and satisfaction. Service performance should never be appraised by management guesses or on the basis of occasional chats the "big boss" has with important customers. It should be measured by regular, systematic and unbiased questioning of the customer.

In a large company this may have to take the form of an annual customer survey. The outstanding job here has probably been done by General Motors; and it explains the company's success in no small degree. In the small company the same results can be achieved by a different method.

In one of the most successful hospital-supply wholesalers, two of the top men of the company—president and chairman of the Board—visit between them two hundred of the company's six hundred customers every year. They spend a whole day with each customer. They do not sell—refuse indeed to take an order. They discuss the customer's problems and his needs, and ask for criticism of the company's products and service. In this company the annual customer survey is considered the first job of top management. And the company's eighteen-fold growth in the last twelve years is directly attributed to it.

Innovation

There are two kinds of innovation in every business: innovation in product or service; and innovation in the various skills and activities needed to supply them. Innovation may arise out of the needs of market and customer; necessity may be the mother of innovation. Or it may come out of work on the advancement of skill and knowledge carried out in the schools and the laboratories, by researchers, writers, thinkers and practitioners.

The problem in setting innovation objectives is the difficulty of measuring the relative impact and importance of various innovations. Technological leadership is clearly desirable, especially if the term "technology" is used in its rightful sense as applying to the art, craft or science of any organized human activity. But how are we to determine what weighs more: one hundred minor but immediately applicable improvements in packaging the product, or one fundamental chemical discovery which, after ten more years of hard work, may change the character of the business altogether? A department store and a pharmaceutical company will answer this question differently; but so may two different pharmaceutical companies.

Innovating objectives can therefore never be as clear and as sharply focused as marketing objectives. To set them, management must first obtain a forecast of the innovations needed to reach marketing goals—according to product lines, existing markets, new markets and, usually, also according to service requirements. Secondly, it must appraise developments arising or likely to arise out of technological advancement in all areas of the business and in all of its activities. These forecasts are best organized in two parts: one looking a short time ahead and projecting fairly concrete developments which, in effect, only carry out innovations already made; another looking a long time ahead and aiming at what might be.

Here are the innovation goals for a typical business:

1. New products or services that are needed to attain marketing objectives.
2. New products or services that will be needed because of technological changes that may make present products obsolete.
3. Product improvements needed both to attain market objectives and to anticipate expected technological changes.
4. New processes and improvements in old processes needed to satisfy market goals—for instance, manufacturing improvements to make possible the attainment of pricing objectives.
5. Innovations and improvements in all major areas of activity—in accounting or design, office management or labor relations—so as to keep up with the advances in knowledge and skill.

Management must not forget that innovation is a slow process. Many companies owe their position of leadership today to the activity of a generation that went to its reward twenty-five years or so ago. Many companies that are unknown to the public will be leaders in their industry tomorrow because of their innovations today. The successful company is always in danger of living smugly off the accumulated innovating fat of an earlier generation. An index of activity and success in this field is therefore indicated.

An appraisal of performance during the last ten years serves well for this purpose. Has innovation in all the major areas been commensurate with the market standing of the company? If it has not, the company is living off past achievements and is eating up its innovating capital. Has the company developed adequate sources of innovation for the future? Or has it come to depend on work done on the outside—in the universities, by other businesses, maybe abroad—which may not be adequate to the demands of the future?

Deliberate emphasis on innovation may be needed most where technological changes are least spectacular. Everybody in a pharmaceutical company or in a company making synthetic organic chemicals knows that the company's survival depends on its ability to replace three quarters of its products by entirely new ones every ten years. But how many people in an insurance company realize that the company's growth—perhaps even its survival—depends on the development of new forms of insurance, the modification of existing forms and the constant search for new, better and cheaper ways of selling policies and of settling claims? The less spectacular or prominent technological change is in a business, the greater is the danger that the whole organization will ossify; the more important therefore is the emphasis on innovation.

It may be argued that such goals are "big-company stuff" suitable for General Electric or for General Motors, but unnecessary in the small business. But although the small company may be less in need of a complete and detailed analysis of its needs and goals, this means only that it is easier to set innovation objectives in the smaller business—not that the need for objectives is less. In fact, the managements of several small companies I know assert that the comparative simplicity of planning for innovation is one of the main advantages of small size. As the president of one of them—a container manufacturer with sales of fewer than ten million dollars—puts it: "When you are small, you are sufficiently close to the market to know fairly fast what new products are needed. And your engineering staff is too small to become ingrown. They know they can't do everything themselves and therefore keep their eyes and ears wide open for any new development that they could possibly use."

Productivity and "Contributed Value"

A productivity measurement is the only yardstick that can actually gauge the competence of management and allow comparison between managements of different units within the enterprise, and of different enterprises. For producitivity includes all the efforts the enterprise contributes; it excludes everything it does not control.

Businesses have pretty much the same resources to work with. Except for the rare monopoly situation, the only thing that differentiates one business from another in any given field is the quality of its management on all levels. And the only way to measure this crucial factor is through a measurement of productivity that shows how well resources are utilized and how much they yield.

The Wall Street exercise of comparing the profit margin of Chrysler and General Motors is actually meaningless. General Motors manufactures most of the parts of the car; it buys only the frame, fhe wheels and the brake. Chrysler until recently was an assembler; it made nothing but the engine which is but a fraction of the value of the car. The two companies are entirely different in their process mix. Yet both sell a complete car. In the case of G.M. the bulk of the sales price is compensation for work done by G.M.; in the case of Chrysler the bulk of the sales price is paid out again to independent suppliers. The profit G.M. shows is for 70 per cent of the work and risk, the profit Chrysler shows is for 30 or 40 per cent of the work and risk. Obviously General Motors must show a much bigger profit margin—but how much bigger? Only an analysis of productivity which would show how the two companies utilize their respective resources and how much profit they get out of them, would show which company did the better managing job.

But such a yardstick is needed also because the constant improvement of productivity is one of management's most important jobs. It is also one of the most difficult; for productivity is a balance between a great variety of factors, few of which are easily definable or clearly measurable.

We do not as yet have the yardstick we need to measure productivity. Only within the last few years have we found a basic concept that even enables us to define what we have to measure—the economist calls it "Contributed Value."

Contributed Value is the difference between the gross revenue received by a company from the sale of its products or services, and the amount paid out by it for the purchase of raw materials and for services rendered by outside suppliers. Contributed Value, in other words, includes all the costs of all the efforts of the business and the entire reward received for these efforts. It accounts for all the resources the business itself contributes to the final product and the appraisal of their efforts by the market.

Contributed Value is not a panacea. It can be used to analyze productivity only if the allocation of costs which together make up the figures is economically meaningful. This may require major reforms in the accountant's traditional concepts, figures and methods. We have to give up such time-honored practices as the allocation of "overhead" on a percentage basis "across the board" which makes realistic cost analysis impossible. We have to think through what depreciation charges are supposed to do—charge for the use of capital, measure the shrinkage in value of the equipment, or provide for its eventual replacement; we cannot be satisfied with a "rule of thumb" percentage depreciation allowance. In short, we have to focus accounting data on management's needs in running a business, rather than on the requirements of tax collector and banker, or on the old wives' tales so many investors imbibe at their security analyst's knee and forever after mistake for financial wisdom.

Contributed Value will not measure productivity resulting from balance of functions or from organization structure, for these are qualitative factors rather than quantitative ones, and Contributed Value is strictly a quantitative tool. Yet, the qualitative factors are among the biggest factors in productivity.

Within these limitations, however, Contributed Value should make possible, for the first time, a rational analysis of productivity and the setting of goals for its improvement. In particular it should make possible the application to the systematic study of productivity of new tools such as the mathematical methods known as "Operations Research" and "Information Theory." For these tools all aim at working out alternative courses of action and their predictable consequences. And the productivity problem is always one of seeing the range of alternative combinations of the various resources, and of finding the combination that gives the maximum output at minimum cost or effort.

We should therefore now be able to tackle the basic productivity problems.

When and where is the substitution of capital equipment for labor likely to improve productivity, within what limits and under what conditions? How do we distinguish creative overhead, which cuts down total effort required, from parasitical overhead, which only adds to costs? What is the best time utilization? What the best product mix? What the best process mix? In all these problems we should no longer have to guess; we can find the right answer systematically.

The Contributed Value concept should show us clearly what the objectives for productivity are:

1. To increase the ratio of Contributed Value to total revenue within the existing process. This is simply another way of saying that the first goal must be to find the best utilization of raw materials or of services bought.
2. To increase the proportion of contributed value retained as profit. For this means that the business has improved the productivity of its own resources.

Physical and Financial Resources

What resources objectives are needed and how progress toward them is to be measured differs for each individual business. Also objectives in this area do not concern managers throughout the enterprise as do the objectives in all other areas: the planning for an adequate supply of physical and financial resources is primarily top management's job; the carrying out of these plans is mainly the job of functional specialists.

Yet, physical and financial resources are too important to be left out of consideration. Any business handling physical goods must be able to obtain physical resources, must be sure of its supply. Physical facilities—plants, machines, offices—are needed. And every business needs financial resources. In a life-insurance company this may be called "investment management," and it may be more important even than marketing or innovation. For a toy wholesaler the problem may simply be one of obtaining a seasonal line of credit. Neither, however, can operate unless assured of the financial resources it needs. To set objectives without planning for the money needed to make operations possible is like putting the roast in the oven without turning on the flame. At present objectives for physical resources, physical facilities and supply of capital are only too often taken as "crash decisions" rather than as carefully prepared policies.

One large railroad company spends a lot of time and large amounts of money on traffic forecasts. But a decision to spend ten million dollars on new equipment was taken in a board meeting without a single figure to show what return the investment would bring or why it was necessary. What convinced the Board was the treasurer's assurance that he could easily raise the money at low interest rates.

A notable exception in respect to physical resources is the long-range forest-building policy of Crown-Zellerbach, the West Coast pulp and paper manufacturer. Its aim is to make sure that the company can stay in business by providing the timber supply it will need in the future. Since it takes fifty years or more to grow a mature tree, replacement of cut trees involves investing today capital that will not pay off until the year 2000. And since the company expects the trend of pulp and paper consumption to continue to rise sharply, mere replacement is not enough. For every tree cut today, two are being planted to become available in fifty years.

Few companies face a supply problem of Crown-Zellerbach's proportions. Those that do usually realize its importance. All major oil companies work on the finding and exploration of new oil wells. The large steel companies, too, have begun to make the search for new iron-ore reserves a systematic, planned activity. But the typical business does not worry enough about tomorrow's supply of physical resources. Few even of the big retailers have, for instance, anything comparable to the planned and systematic development of "sources" that is so important an activity in Sears, Roebuck. And when the Ford Motor Company announced a few years ago that it would systematically build up suppliers for its new West Coast assembly plants, the purchasing agent of a big manufacturing company considered this a "radical innovation." Any manufacturer, wholesaler, retailer, public utility or transportation business needs to think through the problem of its physical resources, and spell out basic decisions.

Should the company depend on one supplier for an important material, part or product? There may be a price advantage because of bulk purchases; in times of shortage a big and constant buyer may get priority; and the close relationship may result in a better design or in closer quality control. Or should the company find several suppliers for the same resource? This may make it independent; it minimizes the danger of being forced to close down because of a strike at a single supplier; it may even lead to lower purchase prices as a result of competition between several suppliers. A cotton-textile manufacturer has to decide whether he should attempt to outguess the cotton market or try, in his buying policy, to average out fluctuations in cotton price, and so forth.

Whatever the decision, objectives should aim at providing the physical supplies needed to attain the goals set for market standing and innovation.

Equally important is good facilities planning. And it is even rarer. Few industrial companies know when to stop patching up an old plant and start building a new one, when to replace machines and tools, when to build a new office building. The costs of using obsolete facilities are usually hidden. Indeed, on the books the obsolete plant or machine may look very profitable; for it has been written down to zero so that it looks as if running it involved no cost at all. Most managers know, of course, that this is pure fallacy; but it is not easy to free ourselves completely from the spell of arithmetical sleight of hand.

Yet, clearly, both undersupply of facilities and their oversupply are extremely dangerous. Physical facilities cannot be improvised; they must be planned.

The tools for the job are available today. They have been developed above all by Joel Dean, the Columbia business economist.[1] They are simple enough to enable every business, large or small, to decide what physical facilities and equipment it needs to attain its basic goals, and to plan for them.

This, of course, requires a capital budget. And this raises the questions: How much capital will we need, and in what form; and where will it come from?

The life-insurance companies have had capital objectives for a long time. They know that they have to obtain a certain amount of money each year to pay off their claims. They know that this money has to come from the income earned on their invested reserves. Accordingly they plan for a certain minimum rate of return on these investments. Indeed, "profit" in a life-insurance company is essentially nothing but the excess of investment earnings over the planned minimum return.

Other examples of capital-supply planning are those of General Motors, DuPont and the Chesapeake and Ohio Railroad. And the American Telephone and Telegraph Company, as already mentioned, considers this so important a job as to justify the full-time attention of a senior member of top management.

But, on the whole, managements do not worry over capital supply until the financial shoe pinches. Then it is often too late to do a good job. Such vitally important questions as: should new capital be raised internally by self-financing, borrowed long-term or short-term, or through stock issue, not only need careful thought and study; they largely determine what kinds of capital expenditure should be undertaken. Decisions on these questions lead to conclusions regarding such vital matters as pricing, dividend, depreciation and tax policy. Also, unless answered in advance, the company may well fritter away its available capital on the less important investments only to find itself unable to raise the capital for vital investments. In far too many companies—including some big and reputedly well-managed ones—failure to think through capital supply and to set capital objectives has stunted growth and nullified much of the management's brilliant work on marketing, innovation and productivity.

How Much Profitability?

Profit serves three purposes. It measures the net effectiveness and soundness of a business's efforts. It is indeed the ultimate test of business performance.

It is the "risk premium" that covers the costs of staying in business—replacement, obsolescence, market risk and uncertainty.[2] Seen from this point of view, there is no such thing as "profit"; there are only "costs of being in business" and "costs of staying in business." And the task of a business is to provide adequately for these "costs of staying in business" by earning an adequate profit—which not enough businesses do.

Finally, profit insures the supply of future capital for innovation and expansion, either directly, by providing the means of self-financing out of retained earnings, or indirectly, through providing sufficient inducement for new outside capital in the form in which it is best suited to the enterprise's objectives.

None of these three functions of profit has anything to do with the economist's maximization of profit. All the three are indeed "minimum" concepts—the minimum of profit needed for the survival and prosperity of the enterprise. A profitability objective therefore measures not the maximum profit the business can produce, but the minimum it must produce.

The simplest way to find this minimum is by focusing on the last of the three functions of profit: a means to obtain new capital. The rate of profit required is easily ascertainable; it is the capital-market rate for the desired type of financing. In the case of self-financing, there must be enough profit both to yield the capital-market rate of return on money already in the business, and to produce the additional capital needed.

It is from this basis that most profitability objectives in use in American business today are derived. "We shoot for a return on capital of 25 per cent before taxes," is accountant's shorthand way of saying: "A return of 25 per cent before taxes is the minimum we need to get the kind of capital we want, in the amounts we need and at the cost we are willing to pay."

This is a rational objective. Its adoption by more and more businesses is a tremendous step forward. It can be made even more serviceable by a few simple but important refinements. First, as Joel Dean has pointed out,[3] profitably must always include the time factor. Profitability as such is meaningless and misleading unless we know for how many years the profit can be expected. We should therefore always state anticipated total profits over the life of the investment discounted for present cash value, rather than as an annual rate of return. This is the method the capital market uses when calculating the rate of return of a bond or similar security; and, after all, this entire approach to profit is based on capital-market considerations. This method also surmounts the greatest weakness of conventional accounting: its superstitious belief that the calendar year has any economic meaning or reality. We can never have rational business management until we have freed ourselves from what one company president (himself an ex-accountant) calls "the unnecessary tyranny of the accounting year."

Second, we should always consider the rate of return as an average resulting from good and bad years together. The business may indeed need a profit of 25 per cent before taxes. But if the 25 per cent are being earned in a good year they are unlikely to be earned over the life time of the investment. We may need a 40 per cent return in good years to average 25 per cent over a dozen years. And we have to know how much we actually need to get the desired average.

The tool for this is also available today. It is the "break-even point analysis" (best described by Rautenstrauch and Villiers in their book *The Economics of Industrial Management*, (New York: Funk and Wagnall's, 1949). This enables us to predict with fair accuracy the range of returns under various business conditions—especially if the analysis is adjusted to express both changes in volume and in price.

For small and simple businesses this capital-market concept of the minimum profitability required is probably adequate. For the large business it is not sufficient, however, for the rate of return expected is only one factor. The other is the amount of risk involved. An investment may return 40 per cent before taxes but there may be a 50 per cent risk of failure. Is it a better investment than one returning 20 per cent with practically no risk?

Shooting for a 25 per cent return before taxes may be good enough for existing investments, investments that have already been made irrevocably. But for new decisions management needs to be able to say: "We aim at a ratio of 1.5 to 1, 1.33 to 1, or 1.25 to 1 between anticipated return after all costs (including those of capital) and estimated risk." Otherwise a rational capital investment policy cannot be worked out.

And without a rational capital-investment policy, especially in the big business, no real budget is possible. It is a necessity for effective decentralization of management; for without it central management will always manage its components by arbitrarily granting or withholding capital and arbitrarily centralizing the management of cash. It is a prerequisite of the spirit of management; without it lower management will always feel that its best ideas get lost in the procedural maze of the Appropriations Committee "upstairs."

A rational capital-investment policy sets the range for management decisions. It indicates which of the alternative ways of reaching marketing, innovation and productivity goals should be preferred. Above all, it forces management to realize what obligations it assumes when making decisions. That our business managers have for so long been able to manage without such a policy is as amazing a feat of navigation as Leif Erickson's feat in finding his way back to Vineland across the Atlantic without map, compass or sextant.

A capital-investment policy must be based on a reasonably reliable assessment of the ratio between return and risks. These risks are not statistical risks like the odds at the roulette table or the life expectancies of the actuary, which can always be calculated. Only one of the four "costs of staying in business" is a statistical risk: replacement. It is no accident that it is the only one that is being handled as a cost, called variously depreciation, amortization or replacement reserve. The other three—each of which is a more serious risk than replacement—are essentially not predictable by what happened in the past; that is, they are not predictable statistically. They are the risks of some new, different, unprecedented occurrence in the future.

Still we can today reduce even these risks to probability forecasts—though only with a fairly large margin of error. Several of the large companies are apparently doing work in the field; but the systematic job has yet to be done.

The real problem concerning profitability is not however what we should measure. It is what to use for a yardstick.

Profit as percentage of sales—lately very popular in American business—will not do, for it does not indicate how vulnerable a product or a business is to economic fluctuations. Only a "break-even point" analysis will do that.

"Return on invested capital" makes sense, but it is the worst of all yardsticks—pure rubber of almost infinite elasticity. What is "invested capital"? Is a dollar invested in 1920 the same thing as a dollar invested in 1950? Is capital to be defined with the accountant as original cash value less subsequent depreciation? Or is it to be defined with the economist as wealth-producing capacity in the future, discounted at capital-market interest rates to current cash value?

Neither definition gets us far. The accountant's definition makes no allowance for changes in the purchasing power of the currency nor for technological changes. It does not permit any appraisal of business performance for the simple reason that it does not take the varying risks of different businesses into account, does not allow comparison between different businesses, between different components of the same company, between the old plants and the new plants, etc. Above all, it tends to encourage technological obsolescence. Once equipment is old enough to have been written down to zero, it tends to look much more profitable on the books than new equipment that actually produces at much lower cost. This holds true even during a deflationary period.

The economist's concept of invested capital avoids all this. It is theoretically perfect. But it cannot be used in practice. It is literally impossible to figure out how much future wealth-producing capacity any investment made in the past represents today. There are too many variables for even the best "electronic brain." There are far too many unknowns and unknowables. To find out even what would be knowable would cost more than could possibly be gained.

For these reasons a good many management people and accountants now incline toward a compromise. They would define "invested capital" as the amount it would cost today to build a new organization, a new plant, new equipment with the same productive capacity as the old organization, plant and equipment. Theoretically this, too, has weaknesses—it would, for instance, greatly distort profitability in a depression period when new equipment prices and building costs are low. But the main difficulties are practical. For replacement assumptions, besides being not too reliable, are difficult to make; and even minor changes in the assumed basis will lead to wide divergences in the end results.

There is, in other words, no really adequate method as yet. Perhaps the most sensible thing is not to search for one but to accept the simplest way, to realize its shortcomings and to build safeguards against its most serious dangers.

I have therefore come to advocate a method which has little in theory to commend it: to measure profitability by projecting net profit—after depreciation charges but before taxes—against original investment at original cost, that is, before depreciation. In inflationary periods the original investment figures are adjusted roughly for the rise in costs. In deflationary periods (this method has still to be tested in one) original investment figures would similarly be adjusted downward. In this way a uniform investment figure can be arrived at in roughly comparable dollars every three or five years, regardless of the date of the original investment or the purchasing power of the original money. This is admittedly crude; and I cannot defend it against the argument advanced by a friend that it is no better than painting over a badly rusted spot. But at least the method is simple; and it is so crude that it will not fool any manager into mistaking for precision what, like all "return on invested capital" figures, no matter how obtained, is at best a rough guess.

The Remaining Key Areas

Little needs to be said here about the three remaining key areas: manager performance and development, worker performance and attitude, and public responsibility. For each is dealt with in later parts of this book.

However, it should be clear that performance and results in these areas cannot be fully measured quantitatively. All three deal with human beings. And as each human being is unique, we cannot simply add them together, or subtract them from one another. What we need are qualitative standards, judgment rather than data, appraisal rather than measurements.

It is fairly easy to determine what objectives are needed for *manager performance and development*. A business—to stay in business and remain profitable—needs goals in respect to the direction of its managers by objectives and self-control, the setting up of their jobs, the spirit of the management organization, the structure of management and the development of tomorrow's managers. And once the goals are clear, it can always be determined whether they are being attained or not. Certainly the examination of the spirit of management, proposed in Chapter 13 below, should bring out any significant shortfall.

No one but the management of each particular business can decide what the objectives in the area of *public responsibility* should be. As discussed in the Conclusion of this book, objectives in this area, while extremely tangible, have to be set according to the social and political conditions which affect each individual enterprise and are affected by it, and on the basis of the beliefs of each management. It is this that makes the area so important; for in it managers go beyond the confines of their own little world and participate responsibly in society. But the overriding goal is common for every business: to strive to make whatever is productive for our society, whatever strengthens it and advances its prosperity, a source of strength, prosperity and profit for the enterprise.

We are in a bad way, however, when we come to setting objectives for *worker performance and attitude*. It is not that the area is "intangible." It is only too tangible; but we know too little about it so far, operate largely by superstitions, omens and slogans rather than by knowledge.

To think through the problems in this area and to arrive at meaningful measurements is one of the great challenges to management.

The objectives in this area should include objectives for union relations.

If this were a book on industrial society, the union would figure prominently (as it does indeed in my *New Society*). In a book on the *Practice of Management* the union is only one of many outside groups and forces management deals with—suppliers, for instance. But it is a powerful outside force. It can through wage demands wreck the business, and through a strike deprive management of control. The management of any unionized company therefore needs definite long-range objectives for its union relations. If it leaves the initiative in labor relations entirely to the union, it can be said not to manage at all.

Unfortunately that has been precisely the way too many of our managements have conducted their labor relations in the last fifteen or twenty years. They have left the initiative to the union. They have usually not even known what to expect in the way of union demands. They have, by and large, not known what the union is, how it behaves and why it behaves as it does. When first told that certain union demands are about to be made, the typical management refuses to listen. It is sure that the demand will not be made—for the simple reason that it does not consider it justified. Then, when the demand is made, management tends to turn it down as "impossible" and as "certain to ruin the business," if not our free enterprise system. Three days to three years later management caves in, accepts the demand, and in a joint statement with the union leader hails the agreement as a "milestone in democratic labor relations." This is not management; it is abdication.

What union-relations objectives should be concretely goes beyond the scope of this book. But they should first focus on returning the initiative to management. This requires that management must know how a union operates and why. It must know what demands the union will make and why; indeed it must be able to anticipate these demands so as to make their eventual acceptance beneficial to the enterprise or, at the least, harmless to it. Above all, it must learn to make demands itself; as long as the union alone makes demands, management will remain the passive, the frustrated, the ineffectual partner in the relationship.

Union relations, no matter how important, are however only a small and peripheral part of the management of work and worker. Yet, in the main areas we simply do not even know whether the things we can measure—turnover, absenteeism, safety, calls on the medical department, suggestion system participation, grievances, employee attitudes, etc.,—have anything at all to do with employee performance. At best they are surface indications. Still they can be used—in some companies are being used—to build an Employee Relations Index. And though we can only guess what such an index measures, at least the systematic attempt to find out what goes on in the work force focuses management's attention on what it could and should do. While no more than the merest palliative it serves at least to remind managers of their responsibility for the organization of the worker and his work. Admittedly this is hardly even a stopgap, perhaps only an acknowledgment of ignorance. The goal must be to replace it by real objectives which are based on knowledge.

The Time-Span of Objectives

For what time-span should objectives be set? How far ahead should we set our targets?

The nature of the business clearly has a bearing here. In certain parts of the garment business next week's clearance sale is "long-range future." It may take four years to build a big steam turbine and two more to install it; in the turbine business six years may be "immediate present" therefore. And Crown Zellerbach is forced to plant today the trees it will harvest fifty years hence.

Different areas require different time-spans. To build a marketing organization takes at least five years. Innovations in engineering and chemistry made today are unlikely to show up in marketing results and profits for five years or longer. On the other hand a sales campaign, veteran sales managers believe, must show results within six weeks or less; "Sure, there are sleepers," one of these veterans once said, "but most of them never wake up."

This means that in getting objectives management has to balance the immediate future—the next few years—against the long range: five years or longer. This balance can best be found through a "managed-expenditures budget." For practically all the decisions that affect the balance are made as decisions on what the accountant calls "managed expenditures"—those expenditures that are determined by current management decision rather than by past and irrevocable decisions (like capital charges), or by the requirements of current business (like labor and raw material costs). Today's managed expenditures are tomorrow's profit; but they may also be today's loss.

Every second-year accountancy student knows that almost any "profit" figure can be turned into a "loss" by changing the basis of depreciation charges; and the new basis can usually be made to appear as rational as the old. But few managements—including their accountants—realize how many such expenditures there are that are based, knowingly or not, on an assessment of short-range versus long-range needs, and that vitally affect both. Here is a partial list:

Depreciation charges; maintenance budgets; capital replacement, modernization and expansion costs; research budgets; expenditures on product development and design; expenditures on the management group, its compensation and rewards, its size, and on developing tomorrow's managers; cost of building and maintaining a marketing organization; promotion and advertising budgets; cost of service to the customer; personnel management, especially training expenditures.

Almost any one of these expenditures can be cut back sharply, if not eliminated; and for some time, perhaps for a long time, there will be no adverse effect. Any one of these expenditures can be increased sharply and for good reasons, with no resulting benefits visible for a long time. By cutting these expenditures immediate results can always be made to look better. By raising them immediate results can always be made to look worse.

There are no formulas for making the decisions on managed expenditures. They must always be based on judgment and are almost always a compromise. But even a wrong decision is better than a haphazard approach "by bellows and meat ax": inflating appropriations in fair weather and cutting them off as soon as the first cloud appears. All managed expenditures require long application; short spurts of high activity do not increase their effectiveness. Sudden cuts may destroy in one day what it took years to build. It is better to have a modest but steady program of employee activities than to splurge on benefits, lush company papers and plant baseball teams when times are good, only to cut down to the point of taking out the soap in the washrooms when orders drop 10 per cent.[4] It is better to give the customer minimum service than to get him used to good service only to lay off half the service force when profits go down. It is more productive to spend 50,000 dollars each year for ten years on research than to spend, say, two millions one year and nothing the next nine. Where managed expenditures are concerned, one slice of bread every day is better than half a loaf today and none tomorrow.

Almost every one of these expenditures requires highly skilled people to be effective. Yet, first-rate people will not remain with a business if their activity is subject to sudden, unpredictable and arbitrary ups and downs. Or if they stay, they will cease to exert themselves—for "what's the use of my working hard if management will kill it anyhow." And if the meat ax cuts off trained people during an "economy wave," replacements are hard to find or take a long time to train when management, applying the bellows, suddenly decides to revive the activity.

Decisions concerning managed expenditures themselves are of such importance for the business as a whole—over and above their impact on individual activities—that they must not be made without careful consideration of every item in turn and of all of them jointly. It is essential that management know and consciously decide what it is doing in each area and why. It is essential that management know and consciously decide which area to give priority, which to cut first and how far, which to expand first and how far. It is essential finally that management know and consciously decide what risks to take with the long-run future for the sake of sort-term results, and what short-term sacrifices to make for long-run results.

A managed-expenditures budget for a five-year period should show the expenditure considered necessary in each area to attain business objectives within the near future—up to five years or so. It should show the additional expenditure considered necessary in each area to maintain the position of the business beyond the five-year period for which concrete objectives are being set. This brings out the areas where expenditures are to be raised first if business gets better, and those where they are to be cut first if business turns down; it enables management to plan what to maintain even in bad times, what to adjust to the times, and what to avoid even in a boom. It shows the total impact of these expenditures on short-range results. And finally it shows what to expect from them in the long range.

Balancing the Objectives

In addition to balancing the immediate and the long-range future, management also has to balance objectives. What is more important: an expansion in markets and sales volume, or a higher rate of return? How much time, effort and energy should be expended on improving manufacturing productivity? Would the same amount of effort or money bring greater returns if invested in new-product design?

There are few things that distinguish competent from incompetent management quite as sharply as the performance in balancing objectives. Yet, there is no formula for doing the job. Each business requires its own balance—and it may require a different balance at different times. The only thing that can be said is that balancing objectives is not a mechanical job, is not achieved by "budgeting." The budget is the document in which balance decisions find final expression; but the decisions themselves require judgment; and the judgment will be sound only if it is based on a sound analysis of the business. The ability of a management to stay within its budget is often considered a test of management skill. But the effort to arrive at the budget that best harmonizes the divergent needs of the business is a much more important test of management's ability. The late Nicholas Dreystadt, head of Cadillac and one of the wisest managers I have ever met, said to me once: "Any fool can learn to stay within his budget. But I have seen only a handful of managers in my life who can draw up a budget that is worth staying within."

Objectives in the key areas are the "instrument panel" necessary to pilot the business enterprise. Without them management flies by the "seat of its pants"—without landmarks to steer by, without maps and without having flown the route before.

However, an instrument panel is no better than the pilot's ability to read and interpret it. In the case of management this means ability to anticipate the future. Objectives that are based on completely wrong anticipations may actually be worse than no objectives at all. The pilot who flies by the "seat of his pants" at least knows that he may not be where he thinks he is. Our next topic must therefore be the tools that management needs to make decisions today for the results of tomorrow.

FOOTNOTES

[1] See especially his *Capital Budgeting* (New York: Columbia University Press, 1951) and his brilliant article: "*Measuring the Productivity of Capital*," in the January 1954 issue of the *Harvard Business Review*.
[2] For a discussion of these terms see my *New Society*, (New York: Harper & Bros., 1950), especially Chapter 4.

[3] Most effectively in the *Harvard Business Review* article mentioned above.
[4] Lest this be considered hyperbole, it actually happened, in this country, and in 1951.

ABOUT THE AUTHOR—Despite his disclaimer that "I have no desire to run a corporation," Peter F. Drucker has had a role in contributing to such giant organizations as General Motors, General Electric, Sears Roebuck, and to the federal government, in his role as management consultant. His particular area of concentration is long range planning, problem solving and decision making. It is here that his analytical competence and wide background are most effectively exploited. Peter Drucker was born in Vienna, Austria, in 1909; in 1927 he went to Germany to study law at the University of Hamburg and at the University of Frankfurt, obtaining his LLD. in 1931. In 1933 Drucker emigrated to England and served as an economist with an investment banking house in London. When he came to the United States in 1937 it was as advisor to British banks and investment trusts and as correspondent for several British newspapers. The publication of his book, *The End of Economic Man* (1939), and a number of articles analyzing Nazi Germany established his reputation and enabled him to set up independent offices as a private consultant. Since that time he has served as a faculty member at a number of universities and his services are in wide demand as a lecturer to management groups. Since 1950 he has been professor of management at the Graduate Business School of New York University. Drucker has written a number of important books and his *The Practice of Management* (1954) is widely regarded as the basic primer of corporate management.

The Administration of Libraries

by John Walton

> *No more economic and insightful suggestion of the goal of the library than the following brief statement can be advanced. Walton identifies the fact that the library goal is to find a balance between those procedures needed to insure effective functioning short of over-ritualizing and thus interference with the purpose for which the library was established. The contribution of the effective administrator is seen in finding that precise balance which tolerates minimal routine and maximum utility for the library program.*

Administration is an activity that attaches itself to all organizations. As organizations increase in size, and in the number, complexity, and urgency of the functions they perform, they demand more, and more efficient, administration.

The relationships between the administrative function and the intrinsic purpose of an organization is not only complicated and obscure; the fact that such a relationship exists, and that it may be the source of considerable conflict, has not been frankly recognized. Trite statements about administration being a service function, and the failure to recognize its real nature and task have contributed to the tendency to confuse the administrative activity with everything and anything else the organization may be doing. If, as we assume, administration is *sui generis*, an activity concerned largely with the survival and maintenance of an organization, then it is possible that the intrinsic functions of some organizations may be incompatible with administration.

The administration of university libraries is not unlike educational administration in general, not unlike the administration of research institutions, art museums, and other organizations, the intrinsic functions of which seem to require a great deal of freedom, inefficiency, and lack of precise schedules. On the other hand, such organizations require for their survival an increasing amount of administration. Few of them can afford to operate inefficiently. A university librarian, for example, must provide for the maximum of freedom, convenience, and accesssibility in the use, withdrawal, and exchange of books, records, and fugitive materials, if the library is to serve the academic community. At the same time he works under the severe necessity of reducing the loss of books, of being economical in the use of staff and supplies, and efficient in ordering, cataloguing, and keeping accounts. The two functions may well be antithetical.

If such a conflict is inherent in the institutionalization of various scholarly and creative activities, we may inquire how it can be reduced to a minimum. Apparently no answers are available in the literature on administration. Certainly we cannot expect libraries, research institutions, and similar institutions to become smaller and less complex; nor can we expect administrative necessities to decrease. It is true that some educational organizations may deliberately choose to remain small, but libraries can hardly make this choice. Decentralization has been proposed as a means of avoiding excessive administrative control, but this procedure increases the complexity of the organization through greater geographical diversity, duplication of materials, and the necessity for more staff. Probably no entirely satisfactory answer to this problem can be found, but the first step toward any kind of a solution is the recognition that such a problem exists.

In line with the above theory of aministration, studies might be undertaken to determine how much the intrinsic purposes of libraries and similar organizations are hampered by the increase of administrative efficiency, and also, how much administrative efficiency is decreased by adherence to practices that seem to be necessary for the intrinsic functions of the organization. At some point a reasonably adequate degree of administrative efficiency might allow for an acceptable amount of freedom in the operation of the intrinsic functions.

SOURCE: Reprinted from John Walton, "The Administration of Libraries," *Johns Hopkins University Ex Libris*, 16 (Nov., 1957), pp. 1-2, by permission of the Johns Hopkins University and the author.

Some sacrifice in both is probably inevitable; it could be accepted with full recognition of the demands of complex organizations. As things stand now the librarian is equally responsible for two incompatible objectives.

ABOUT THE AUTHOR—John Walton is a distinguished educator concerned basically with upgrading the profession and the practice of teaching. His most recent publication is a general methods textbook *Toward Better Teaching in the Secondary Schools* (1966) in which he describes teaching as "the process by which new (i.e., unknown to the learner) information, skills or habits are related to those that are familiar or established." He is also author of *Administration and Policy-Making in Education* (1960) in which he formulates a modified professional role for educators.

John Walton was born in Fleming County, Kentucky, in 1910; after receiving his M.A. in 1936 from the University of Kentucky, he was employed as teacher, principal, and superintendent of public schools in Manchester, Ohio, until the war. He served as a special agent in the United States Army Counter-Intelligence Service during the Second World War. He received his Ph.D. from Johns Hopkins University in 1950 where he is now professor and chairman of the Department of Education.

Methodology for the Formulation of Objectives in Public Libraries

by Paul Wasserman

> *In this selection objective formulation is viewed to be a central task fundamental to the ultimate assessment or evaluation of organizational performance as practiced in libraries. The problems of delineating choices are viewed from several vantage points and are seen to be common to all forms of public organization including libraries. There follows an elaboration of some of the more formidable barriers to a clear and unambiguous determination of objectives in public libraries which have served to deter their precise elaboration.*

THEORETICAL BASES OF EVALUATION OF LIBRARY PERFORMANCE

If the phenomena of measurement and evaluation in library service are to be understood, analyzed and appraised, the theoretical bases for such procedures must first be laid. While there is an abundance of literature in the field of librarianship which reflects a long-standing and continued preoccupation with the ideas, means and methods of library performance appraisal, this represents only a tangential stream from the larger body of theoretical literature in the broader and more inclusive field of public administration. Our concern at the outset, then, is to seek to understand the underlying theory and philosophy of measurement and evaluation before turning our attention to the applied area of library administration.

For our purposes, it appears reasonable to take as a point of departure contemporary public administration theory which has been conditioned during a long evolutionary process by the contributions of ethics and philosophy. Fundamentally, the search for organizational measurement instruments is tied to the philosophical and ethical quest for ideals of social and community action.

THE ETHICAL BASE

In essence, the preliminary question is how are decisions governing the allocation and use of public resources to be made? Put another way, the same question would ask where, that is in which agency, institution, control body, community group, or individual administrator, the responsibility for defining objectives which are in the public interest, is to be lodged. For many public service functions, including libraries, legislators, in devising statutes and regulations, have traditionally failed to prove more than broad public policies.

As Leys has put it:

Legislative power is delegated in a few fields where the legislature and the public find themselves unable to define either the rule or the criterion of action. These are the subjects on which most of those in the community do not even know the results which they desire.[1]

Library service, like social welfare and education, is a field of public service where the legislative standard is indefinite in the sense of being vague. These fields are characterized by a common lack of clearly articulated public or private notions as to what constitutes good service. Consequently, administration in these areas often constitutes an area of great discretionary power not only over the means, which would be common to most fields of effort, but over the ends or purposes of organizational activity, as well.

In the field of public library service, the usual pattern is for legislative or executive public officials to vest the authority to direct the program in a library board. Acting under the jurisdiction of such bodies, library administrators tend to exercise what one writer terms "value-neutral"[2] technical judgment. That is, the authority of the administrator is the authority of the expert. What is lacking under such a control mechanism is a theory of the

---

SOURCE: Paul Wasserman, "Toward a Methodology for the Formulation of Objectives in Public Libraries: An Empirical Analysis" (unpublished Ph.D. Dissertation, University of Michigan, 1960), Chap. 1, "Theoretical Bases of Evaluation of Library Performance," pp. 1–5, Chap. 2, "Design for the Research Study," pp. 6–12.

public interest, other than the notion that the exercising of professional expertness in the area of service will automatically result in fulfilling the public will.

Such a control mechanism, however, fails to square with the question of public responsibility. For how is it then to be determined what really is in the public interest—is it to a citizen majority, to the groups most affected by an agency's performance, to the administrator's idea of the public interest, or to the definitions of the professional group which he represents? When faced with the need to choose objectives, or alternatives for program purposes, administrators may, and inevitably do, choose one or more of these possibilities to corroborate their judgments. In the absence of clearly stated and generally agreed-to objectives and goals, performance may be rationalized through the selection of the most convenient value prop.

DEFINITIONS OF OBJECTIVES

Until the values, objectives and goals of organizational activity are clearly articulated, evaluation or assessment of performance is impossible. It is generally conceded that clear identification of organizational goals is the most difficult, but also the most crucial element in the evaluation process. As an illustration, a public library may establish as one of its goals ". . . service to meet the frequent informational and research needs of its community."[3] Before this objective is susceptible of measurement and subsequent evaluation, it must be further and more specifically defined lest a review of this criterion reflect the reviewer's biases about what constitutes the proper level, extent and type of "informational and research needs" of the community in question.

Equally obviously, difficulty arises when one organization seek to pursue, as is inevitable in a multi-purpose public institution, several courses simultaneously. Shall the public library serve the adult educational needs of the community, shall it satisfy the public appetite for recreational reading, or both? What is the relative importance of these two fundamentally incompatible goals? The performance of the organization in seeking to accomplish these goals may be assessed once a detailed and generally agreed-to program and its specifications is drawn, but measurement and evaluation can never suggest which course of action is to be preferred, or what order of priority each goal should receive. Such problems evoke the earlier issue of social values and public responsibility, and in the absence of political clarification, there is seldom a clearly spelled out and universally understood definition of a library's purposes.

Unfortunately, a community's library goals and objectives are neither simple nor readily identifiable. What is more, the goals of the individual professional practitioner (the librarian) may, in practice, differ from those of the library director, which may, in turn, differ from the goals of the library user. Without general agreement and understanding of objectives for use in the measurement of success or failure, evaluation has little meaning for the various individuals concerned.

Because it is so difficult to define objectives clearly in universally agreed-to and understood terms, measurement of performance and evaluation of its results becomes a difficult and frequently impossible task. Simon has put it this way:

In order for an ethical proposition to be useful for rational decision-making, a) the values taken as organizational objectives must be definite, so that the degree of realization in any situation may be assessed, and b) it must be possible to form judgments as to the probability that particular actions will implement these objectives.[4]

Due to the difficulties enumerated, few libraries have attempted to specify their goals in the elusive tangible terms which are amenable to measurement. There is, in fact, a real and basic question as to whether or not the total objectives of an individual library program can be so specified as to lend themselves to effective and unbiased appraisal without preliminary research. The achievement of agreement on goals and criteria of success, when it is not specified in statute or regulation, is of fundamental importance. However, such agreement may never be achieved without effective research aimed at ascertaining the extent to which there is agreement among board members, administrators, librarians and public users and non-users as to what properly constitutes the proper organizational goals. As a matter of fact, in an individual institution such research almost inevitably must precede the development of accurate measurement means, since if no agreement can be reached on the objectives and goals of the library's services, there can never be agreement upon success or failure of performance. Here, in fact, is in sum the rationale for the methodological analysis which forms the essence of this study.

UNIVERSAL IMPLICATIONS

The issues thus far discussed appear most meaningful, perhaps, when considered in terms of public libraries. Value issues, however, and the need to gage and assess results, loom equally large in other settings. It is hardly less relevant to focus clearly and evaluate effectively in the school, the company, or the university library. Furthermore, the need for clarification of objectives as the key sequence in the measurement process, would appear to be equally significant in other types of public institutions. Hence the concerns of the present analysis may be identified with the universal issues of public administration. Perhaps then, the implications of the research method developed here may prove equally of interest to the student of public administration as of library administration.

DESIGN FOR THE RESEARCH STUDY

The preceding chapter has detailed the broad philosophical complexities in the attempt to assess performance in public organizations. Following upon this, the impetus for the research to be described develops out of the need for an effective instrument to aid in the identification of an individual institution's objectives. However, further complications arise due to pragmatic and abstract problems inherent in striving to articulate a particular public library's goals.

BARRIERS TO OBJECTIVE FORMULATION

Many basic conflicts reside in the hazy twilight zone between theory and practice. Only some of the most salient will be specified hereafter.

I *The dilemma of the public library serving "educational" versus "recreational" community needs and interests.* The annals of librarianship are a continuing testament to this dichotomy. From the first white paper[5] down to the Public Library Inquiry[6] and beyond, the battle rages fiercely on. Martin has stated the issue in this way:

Two schools of thought concerning basic purposes can be identified in the literature of public librarianship. They are characterized all too frequently and inaccurately by the symbols "education" and "recreation," or by "giving the people what they want" versus "giving them what they should have." More carefully defined, the controversy is between a policy of book selection and service based on a consensus of public demand as expressed by numerical requests alone and a policy based on some evaluation of requests in terms of presumed social or personal benefits. It is an oversimplification to say that one group wants to supply trash while the other wants to force serious literature on unsuspecting readers. One group believes that the public library is maintained by government to serve the people; the other, that it is maintained to serve the people for certain social ends.[7]

II *Ambivalence in the attitudes of public librarians as between the quality standards proposed by their national professional body and the practical day-to-day demands of library users.* Here the conflict arises out of what may be termed the imbalance between the continually evolving standards for professional practice and the urge to "give the customer what he wants." Bernard Berelson sums it up as follows:

On the one hand, public librarians have a set of actual objectives which have developed historically, which have been accepted traditionally, and which have been expressed in practice. They may not always be articulated—indeed, it is their peculiar province not to be—but they are nonetheless there as guides for a whole range of library activities ... Then, on the other hand, there is a group of professed objectives, skillfully formulated by official bodies, which express the higher aspirations for professional service. When a request for objectives is made, they are brought forward. Thus, just as many lawyers will tell you that their objective is to see justice done, whereas they are actually out to win cases, so many librarians will tell you that education is their objective, when they are busy trying to increase circulation.[8]

III *The pluralistic composition and the pluralistic attitudes of the public library's clientele.* The issue is, of course, that of how to reconcile the library's program with the needs or interests of its constituency. Put another way, this is the problem of how to order each segment of the community into a ranking scale of hierarchy of importance. For, as Berelson again suggests:

There is no such thing as "the library's public".... There is no single public of library users; there are several publics. The several publics of the library are the several distinctive groups which make distinctive demands for library materials. There is a public of high school students who mainly want from the public library what their school libraries cannot adequately supply. There is a public mainly composed of housewives and white collar workers who want "some light reading." There is a public of business representatives who want specific and isolated pieces of information from the library files. There is a public of ambitious young people who hope to use the library in their drive for occupational mobility. There is a public of serious-minded people concerned with serious-minded materials on a variety of topics who find in the library what they cannot get elsewhere. There is a public of miscellaneous people with leisure and "nothing else to do." There are other publics.[9]

IV *The pluralistic patterns of library service officially prescribed by the national professional association.* How shall the library allocate its limited funds, time and talent among the impressive set of roles in which it is cast by the American Library Association?

The public library as an institution exists to provide materials which communicate experience and ideas from one person to another. Its function is to assemble, preserve, and make easily and freely available to all people the printed and other materials that will assist them to:
 Educate themselves continuously
 Keep pace with progress in all fields of knowledge
 Become better members of home and community
 Discharge political and social obligations
 Appreciate and enjoy works of art and literature
 Develop their creative and spiritual capacities
 Make such use of leisure time as will promote personal and social well being
 Contribute to the growth of knowledge.[10]

V *The absence of a philosophy of public library service which might reinforce the position of each library.* American librarianship has been characterized all through its evolution by a staunch disregard for theoretical issues, by a practiced posture of immunity toward external social forces and by a deep distaste for fashioning a coherent public library point of view. Instead, the accent has been on the continuing rationalization of pragmatic library practice. Butler points out the costs:

A professional philosophy would give to librarianship that directness of action which can spring only from a complete consciousness of purpose. Certainly it will make a great difference for communal welfare whether this public agency is conceived as a necessary and normal social element, or as a supererogatory benefaction to fortunate individuals. By the one view the service will be rendered as an obvious duty, by the other it may easily degenerate to bureaucratic favoritism. It will make a great difference for library extension whether the proposed institution is considered an essential part in the machinery of public education or as provision for certain incidental elegancies of life. The one opinion will inspire immediate action at public cost, the other will defer to the chances of private munificence. It will make a great difference whether the librarian is regarded as a public official, or merely as the holder of a desirable position. By the one theory he must be selected for his professional education, experience, and efficiency, by the other it may be for pity or personal obligation. It will make a great difference to the young man hesitating in the choice of his career whether he believes that librarianship is a profession or an occupation. It will make an equal difference in the quality of his training whether the school looks upon his future activity as the administration of a public trust or as the correct supervision of a routine procedure. And so the tale might easily be continued, but, after all, it should require no long argument to convince anyone who will consider this matter seriously that an understanding of the social theory of the library will contribute to its successful administration.[11]

VI *The dilemma of a public service institution which seeks to be all things to all men.* Founded upon the concepts of democracy, and based upon the literal interpretation of equal educational opportunity for all, the public library strives to fill the boundless and indefinite need of providing service to all; to the whole public, and to all its constituent parts—the student, the scholar, the retired, the homemaker, and so on. In complex modern times which witness a continuing geometric accretion of specialized knowledge in specialized fields, can any agency with inelastic resources keep pace with every special field of demand? Kelley had already anticipated this problem more than twenty-five years ago:

Is it to be expected that public libraries can ever offer the kind of selective service that will satisfy the needs of specialists and scholars of various kinds? Can their book collections or the service which they render cover the whole field of knowledge, as was formerly assumed to be their function, before specialization had resulted in extreme subdivision of subject matter? We have found that specialized libraries, ante-dating and co-existing with public libraries, continue to be devoted to definite fields of subject matter, with the function of meeting the needs of special groups of patrons who are equipped to carry on investigations in these fields. Very special libraries, covering all sorts of specific subjects, have been called into existence by the requirements of smaller and more homogeneous groups and have assumed functions which public libraries, on the whole, have never attempted to fill.[12]

VII *The public library has no line structural relationship to aid in identifying its objectives.* Where the library forms the working laboratory of a company, the study center of a school or college, or the research core of university or research institute, the library program may take its administrative cue from the purposes and goals of the parent institution. In the public library this cannot be done simply because objectives are scarcely articulated by municipalities, and, even if they were, there is a serious question of whether the library program could mesh into this framework. For while objective formulation in a university is replete with potential hazards, a public library's mandate can never be so clear as the following:

The library is not an end in itself. Essential services and technical operations should be kept in the background and administered in such a way as to promote the attainment of the educational objectives of the institution. The major function of the library is to support the administrative and educational policies of the university of which it is a part.[13]

VIII *The potential strategic dysfunction of a single clearly articulated set of institutional objectives.* In the absence of a stated set of institutional goals, a library may adhere to whichever objectives suit its convenience for a specific political purpose. Consequently, there may be fashioned a set of budgetary objectives, internal operating objectives, public pronouncements, ideas of the agency's administrator, and so on. All may be applied as needed for different purposes, and turned on and off at the will of the librarian. A specific set of goals which were to be universally identified with the library, would perhaps foreclose such administrative maneuverability.

The almost inevitable consequence of the overbearing host of deterrents which has been specified (and of other lesser obstacles which have not been) has been the paucity of formulations of objectives in individual libraries. Even if it were to be conceded that a library's book selection policy may play a major role in, or even be closely synonymous in many respects with an overall statement of library objectives, the existence of even statements of book selection policy are isolated and rare.[14] For, every empirical study which inquires, determines that policy statements practically do not exist in public libraries.[15] And while the lack of objectives is often lamented, and even implored for in the Association's standards statement—"The program of each public library should be focused upon clear and specific objectives.... Each public library should adopt a written statement of clear and specific objectives,"[16] the number of libraries to boast such documents remains very few.

FOOTNOTES

[1] Wayne A. R. Leys, "Ethics and Administrative Discretion," *Public Administration Review,* III, No. 1 (Winter 1943), 19.

[2] Glendon A. Schubert, Jr., "The Public Interest in Administrative Decisionmaking: Theorem, Theosophy or Theory?" *American Political Science Review,* LI, No. 2 (June 1957), 347.

[3] American Library Association, Coordinating Committee on Revision of Public Library Standards, Public Libraries Division, *Public Library Service: A Guide to Evaluation with Minimum Standards* (Chicago: American Library Association, 1956), p. 27.

[4] Herbert A. Simon, *Administrative Behavior* (New York: Macmillan, 1955), p. 50.

[5] Great Britain, House of Commons, *Report from the Select Committee on Public Libraries: together with the Proceedings of the Committee, Minutes of Evidence and Appendix.* July 23, 1849.

[6] Robert D. Leigh, *The Public Library in the United States* (New York: Columbia University Press, 1950).

[7] Lowell A. Martin, "The Desirable Minimum Size of Public Library Units" (unpublished Ph.D. dissertation, Graduate Library School, University of Chicago, 1945), p. 17.

[8] Lester Asheim, ed., *A Forum on the Public Library Inquiry* (New York: Columbia University Press, 1950), pp. 61-62.

[9] Bernard Berelson, with the assistance of Lester Asheim, *The Library's Public: A Report of the Public Library Inquiry* (New York: Columbia University Press, 1949), pp. 133-134.

[10] American Library Association, Coordinating Commitee on Revision of Public Library Standards, Public Libraries Division, *Public Library Service: A Guide to Evaluation with Minimum Standards* (Chicago: American Library Association, 1956), p. 31.

[11] Pierce Butler, *An Introduction to Library Science* (Chicago: University of Chicago Press, 1933), pp. 103-104.

[12] Grace O. Kelley, "The Democratic Function of Libraries," *Library Quarterly,* IV, No. 1 (January 1934), 12-13.

[13] Louis R. Wilson and Maurice F. Tauber, *The University Library: the Organization, Administration and Functions of Academic Libraries* (2nd ed; New York: Columbia University Press, 1956), p. 22.

[14] Although not non-existent, particularly in the public libraries of the largest American cities. For selected abstracts from several extant large metropolitan library book selection statements, and of a complete statement for a smaller city library, see Mary Duncan Carter and Wallace John Bonk, *Building Library Collections* (New York: Scarecrow Press, 1959), pp. 212-223.

[15] Recent testimony will be found in American Library Association, Committee on Intellectual Freedom, "Book Selection," *The PLD Reporter,* No. 4, October 1955.

[16] American Library Association, Coordinating Committee on Revision of Public Library Standards, Public Libraries Division, *Public Library Service: A Guide to Evaluation with Minimum Standards* (Chicago: American Library Association, 1956), p. 24.

ABOUT THE AUTHOR—Paul Wasserman, see p. 40

Controlling and Reappraising

The process of programming an organizational plan calls for the setting of standards and the enforcement of the conduct of the activity. Control is thus viewed as the means of insuring the desired response as well as the definition of its meaning. Control therefore is seen as action designed to insure that operating norms are established which will serve as the basis for the individuals who play roles in the organization, and also as a basis against which to evaluate. The setting of standards and the enforcement of such standards are involved in the process of elaborating the methodology of control. A whole range of organizational implements are employed for such purposes. The danger inherent in control practice is the tendency which controls exert to become purposes in and of themselves. Moreover the control process is never complete within itself but must also have built into it the constant and continuing reappraisal of organizational attainment to insure that it is continuously consistent with the organization's objectives. Control is achieved through the effective exploitation of those economic and human incentives necessary to accomplish the purposes of the organization.

Some Social Processes for Control

by Robert A. Dahl and Charles E. Lindblom

> *Perhaps the most salient contribution of this highly original selection is the issue of where, that is in whose hands organizational controls ultimately reside. The case for social and psychological controls which are not the same as the punitive potential of the administrator is skillfully demonstrated. Perhaps the most important lesson is the very limited degree of reliance which can or may be placed upon direct command in the control of human behavior.*

Calculation is only one of two major components of rational social action. The other is control, the subject of this chapter. All economies, such as the United States, Great Britain, and the USSR, are combinations of various elemental techniques of control. Differences between the economy of one country and that of another—say, the United States and the Soviet Union—cannot be explained, as is often assumed, by saying that each relies on a different technique of control. For the elementary techniques of control are present in all complex economies. The difference lies in the combination. Just as the same three or four chemical elements may produce quite different compounds depending on the quantities of each that are used, so too different combinations of four basic control techniques will produce economies as different (and as similar) as those of the United States and the USSR. Indeed, it will be shown that the basic methods of control tend to be combined into certain typical constellations of politico-economic techniques and the economies of different countries are really different combinations of these politico-economic techniques.

I. SOME CHARACTERISTICS OF CONTROL

Control Reducible to Direct Control

A quick check with one's own experience will corroborate four important aspects of control. First, large units of indirect control such as a corporation, a trade union, or the stock market, usually consist of many small units of direct control. To say that the corporation president controls the responses of the plant foreman is a useful abstraction, meaning that the responses of the plant foreman are functionally dependent on the acts of the corporation president. But even in an enterprise of a few hundred people, the corporation president usually finds it necessary to control the plant foreman through an intermediate chain of other individuals. This intermediate chain is necessary because the number of people that any one person can act on *directly* is usually small, although of course the number varies with different individuals, different situations, and different tasks. Hence because generals, corporation presidents, bureau chiefs, party leaders, and other executives all find it impossible to exercise direct control over more than a handful of the participants in their organizations, they must work through chains of direct control if they are to control these people at all.

Consequently, the elemental techniques of control examined in this chapter are techniques of *direct* control; in the last analysis chains of control in every economic order, political society, or other human organization are reducible to links of direct control. So that this will not be forgotten, hereafter in this chapter we capitalize Control whenever we mean *direct* control. In this sense, Control is always a direct relationship between two or more human beings. In loose language, A Controls the responses of B if A's acts cause B to respond in a definite way. To put it in stricter but more cumbersome language: *B is Controlled by A to the extent that B's responses are dependent on A's acts in an immediate and direct functional relationship.*

Controllers and Superiors Not Identical

Second, the controller (the one who Controls) and the subordinate (the one who is Controlled)

SOURCE: "Some Social Processes for Control" from POLITICS, ECONOMICS, AND WELFARE by Robert A. Dahl and Charles E. Lindblom. Copyright 1953, by Harper & Row, Publishers, Incorporated. Reprinted by permission of Harper & Row, Publishers, Incorporated.

are not always identical with the prescribed or even the usual superior and subordinate. Often the nominal subordinate Controls his nominal superior; indeed, this is probably inevitable in any complex organization. The nominal subordinate has a thousand opportunities to exert Control over his superior; the superior must rely on the judgment of his nominal subordinate in certain decisions, or the superior deliberately grants discretion to the nominal subordinate and accepts his decisions as binding, or the subordinate negotiates with another employer in order to induce his superior to grant him a raise. Nor is it only a matter of a nominal subordinate's Controlling his superior. Sometimes X, the nominal subordinate of A, is the actual subordinate of B.

PRESCRIBED AND OPERATING ORGANIZATIONS. This discrepancy between nominal and actual superior or subordinate is one instance of a common phenomenon that may be called the discrepancy between prescribed and operating organizations. A *prescription* is any implied or explicit instruction that a particular act or set of acts ought to be performed. When one or more individuals instruct some people to engage in certain stable, persistent, and repetitive relationships, their instructions can be said to constitute a prescribed organization or (since technically the instructions do not constitute an organization at all) a prescribed charter for an organization.[1] There can be as many prescribed organizations, therefore, as there are prescribers.

Any observable, actual, real-life behavior we call *operating* behavior when we wish to distinguish it from prescribed behavior. Thus one can distinguish prescribed and operating charters, norms, codes, goals, and organizations.

For a great variety of reasons, relationships in operating organizations are rarely identical with those set forth in prescription. Four common reasons are:

1. Prescriptions can rarely anticipate all possible situations that will arise. Hence new relationships grow up that, for a time, are not found in any set of prescriptions and may never be incorporated into the official prescriptions of superiors.

2. Prescriptions may conflict; the operating organization cannot fit them all. In the Hawthorne works studied by Roethlisberger and Dickson, the organization prescribed by top officials conflicted with what actually developed and came to be implicitly prescribed by workers.

3. To be effective, prescriptions may require techniques of control that are in fact lacking for any one of a vast number of reasons, including such possibilities as these: there are technical difficulties such as communication; control is held by others who employ it to nullify the prescriptions in question; social indoctrination and habituation have failed to cultivate the necessary responses; etc., etc.

4. Prescriptions may be intended for propaganda, morale, public relations, psychological warfare, deceit, etc., rather than as a genuine organizational charter.

Control is Often Not Intended

Third, much control is unintended. The boss who comes to work in a grumpy mood may not intend to induce his secretary to treat him gently; yet the responses of a good secretary are as definitely Controlled as if the boss had deliberately asked her to smooth the way a little more than usual that day. Consumers who buy a commodity may not intend to control the activities of producers; but often they do so more effectively than if they had commanded producers to behave in some particular way. Writers on planning have usually neglected unintended control on the false assumption that it is in some way the negation of rational social action.

Control On Continuum With Autonomy

Fourth, Controlled behavior may best be thought of as lying at one end of a continuum of which the other end is autonomous behavior. Autonomy is the absence of immediate and direct Control. An individual's responses are autonomous or uncontrolled to the extent that no other people can bring about these responses in a definite way. More precisely: *With respect to A, B's responses are autonomous to the extent that they are not dependent on the acts of A in an immediate and direct functional relationship.*

Thus responses may be autonomous with respect to some people but Controlled by others; or responses may be entirely autonomous in the sense that no other people can bring them about. In either case, however, autonomous action can be an important part of coordinated effort to bring about some desired state of affairs. For the question is whether the autonomous actions are predictable by those who seek coordination. Many autonomous actions are determined mostly by an apparently unique combination of events in which the individual finds himself at some given moment. Because such actions cannot be predicted, they cannot be scheduled. But autonomous responses are often habitual and repetitive, and hence predictable to individuals who cannot Control the responses. Such responses can be scheduled as a part of the coordinated actions of several people. Thus because German artillery units were usually quite methodical in their interdicting fire on a road junction outside their observation, after first timing the enemy artillery fire to discover the safe intervals Allied troops could often move their vehicles safely.

II. CONTROL THROUGH THE SUBJECTIVE FIELD

To Control people one must produce responses in them. To produce responses in others, usually one must act on their subjective "field" of awareness, that is, each individual's own special conscious and unconscious awareness of the universe made up of the self and its relations with other objects, resources and capacities, feelings of reward and deprivation, symbols and expectations.[2] One may, of course, act on some elements in an individual's field to influence other elements.

Other Methods

There are ways of producing responses in other people, to be sure, that do not involve acting on their psychological "field." But these ways are not very important in social behavior, and assuredly not in rational social action. For example, you can physically manipulate other people as you might any inanimate object, a stick, a stone, a stream, a machine. The terms "force" and "violence" are sometimes used as if they were equivalents of physical manipulation. Actually what one usually means when he says that force or violence is an important method of controlling others is this: Some people control others by making them fearful of severe punishment if they do not obey. Even when torture is used to produce pain which in turn induces confession, the action is ultimately successful only because it acts on the psychological field of the victim.[3]

In politico-economic action Control to all intents and purposes means action on psychological fields. Admittedly, as with so many useful distinctions, physical manipulation, manipulation of psychophysical capacities, and action on psychological fields all lie along a continuum; but the differences in real life are gross enough so that hereafter Control may safely be taken to require action on the psychological field.

Ways of Acting On a Person's Field

How one can penetrate the field in order to produce a response is a matter of some controversy and ambiguity among contemporary psychologists. Nevertheless, one must make assumptions; and it is probably best if they are made explicit.

There appear to be several possible ways of acting on an individual's field. One is to *change his resources and capacities* for rewarding or penalizing others, and in this way altering his expectations, and hence his responses. When a politician is put in or out of office, his resources for influencing public policy are significantly altered. In economic life one can change an individual's behavior by increasing or decreasing his money.

But the principle system for altering a person's field and so Controlling his responses is to influence his *expectations of rewards and deprivations*, or, as these will be variously called in this book, his incentives, or his gratifications, gains, satisfactions, or goal achievement, and his punishments, losses, penalties, costs, or dissatisfactions. One's incentives may be altered by teaching him that a given stimulus (or signal, communication, cue, or item of information) will be followed by certain rewards or deprivations, and that a particular response will avoid the deprivation or win the reward. The signals or communications that induce actions may or may not constitute rewards or deprivations by themselves.

Specifically, then, one can Control another person's field by acting on his information, signals, communications, cues, or symbols and thereby affecting his expectations about rewards or deprivations; or one can act on the rewards and deprivations that actually operate on the subordinate, thereby affecting his expectations; or one can act on both.[4]

III. FOUR BASIC CONTROL TECHNIQUES

For our purposes it is convenient to distinguish four techniques of Controlling others by acting on their fields to produce a response. First, one may act on another's field without intending to do so; we call this spontaneous field Control. If one reads that the price of a particular stock is rising, the information may directly stimulate a pleasurable feeling of well-being in one who owns the stock; to one who does not own the stock, the information may provide no such gratification. But in both cases the reader might take the information as a cue to buy more of the stock in the expectation of future rewards.

Second, one may deliberately manipulate another's field by command. Third, one may deliberately manipulate another's field by means other than command. These three relationships, it is evident, are all unilateral; symbolically they are A $\longrightarrow$ B relationships. But many relationships are reciprocal, that is, two or more people manipulate the fields of one another; symbolically the reciprocal relationship may be expressed as A $\longleftrightarrow$ B or A $\longleftrightarrow$ B, etc.[5]

$$A \searrow \swarrow B$$
$$C$$

Spontaneous Field Control

THREE PARADOXES. Spontaneous Control of another person's field is perhaps the most paradoxical of all the Control techniques. First paradox: it is a basic Control technique in all social organizations, yet many people do not even think of it as a form of Control. Second paradox: it is sometimes the most tyrannical Control to which a person is ever subjected in his entire lifetime, yet to anarchists the society of perfect freedom operates entirely with spontaneous field Controls. Third paradox: because it is unintended rather than deliberate Control, it can be pictured as the antithesis of planning, yet it is one of the most important techniques of Control and therefore of rational social action.

What is this paradoxical Control technique? It works this way: Often when you act, as unintended by-products of your behavior you produce signals about rewards or deprivations or even the rewards and deprivations themselves; these signals, rewards, and deprivations influence another person's expectations of rewards and deprivations. He responds in an attempt to avoid the threatened deprivations or secure the expected gratifications; yet you did not deliberately seek to produce his response. Thus his response is functionally dependent on your original act; unintentionally you Control his response. This is spontaneous field Control.[6]

This technique of Control is strategically important to rational social action in economic affairs because, as we shall see later, it is fundamental to the operation of a price system. Other Control techniques also operate in a price system, but spontaneous field Control plays a crucial part.

BOTH TYRANNICAL AND FREE. One can now understand the three paradoxes of spontaneous field Control. It is sometimes tyrannical because it is so hard to escape; among family, neighbors, colleagues, employees, superiors, acquaintances—wherever one goes a network of spontaneous field Controls envelops him. Moreover, many of the gratifications and deprivations it dispenses are of exceptional importance to the human organism: love and hate, affection and hostility, friendship and enmity, respect and contempt, sometimes money and power. Because these incentives are so intense, one will strive mightily to avoid the deprivations and gain the gratifications; but often one must choose between a heavily penalized response and an alternative that may be only slightly less penalizing to him. This is "tyranny," i.e., a severe deprivation of one's freedom by others.

By contrast, anarchists, looking for a voluntary system of social order, could mistakenly identify spontaneous field Control as a noncoercive substitute for state-enforced commands because they did not always see either that it was Control or that it could be tyrannical. They did not always see it was Control because, like the secret ink described in our boyhood detective novels, it is invisible by the usual tests: There are no commands, no articulated directives, no evident statutes or laws, no specified judicial systems, no prisons for violators. Yet their anarchist society could be as coercive as the "social" tyrannies of Main Street, which would also pass these inadequate tests.

WHY "PLANNERS" DISCOUNT IT. One can also see why writers on planning have often been hostile to spontaneous field Controls. For one thing, spontaneous field Controls seem relatively unpredictable and erratic. If you substitute commands for spontaneous field Controls, the planner implies, order will prevail over chaos. Then again, to socialist and even to many nonsocialist planners, spontaneous field Controls seem identical with a private, competitive economy or laissez-faire capitalism; laissez-faire capitalism they think is evil; therefore spontaneous field Controls are evil. Those who hold to this view deny that spontaneous field Controls are Controls at all, hence they see that the worker or consumer is controlled by command and manipulation but are blind to spontaneous field Controls over the entrepreneur. Consequently, just as the neoclassical economists exaggerated the role spontaneous field Controls could play in a market economy, so planners have often romanticized the possibilities of command and manipulation of fields as substitutes for spontaneous field Controls.

WHY IT DOES NOT SEEM TO BE CONTROL. Why does spontaneous field Control often not seem to be Control? Observers may simply fail, like the anarchists, to "see" Control operating because there are no commands, explicit laws, specialized enforcement agents, judges, or recognized means of punishment. Controllers may fail to see it because they do not intend the Controlled action and hence their attention is focused elsewhere. Even those who are controlled may not "feel" the Control for these reasons. Moreover, any Controls create an atmosphere of permissiveness if the deprivations are slight, if they emphasize rewards rather than deprivations, or if they create a variety of rewards and deprivations among which one may choose in performing the desired response. In principle, command can also operate this way, but usually it does not, for reasons that will become clear in a moment. Hence both spontaneous and manipulated field Controls often give the Controlled individual a feeling that he is performing an autonomous action.

WHY IT IS UBIQUITOUS. Why is spontaneous field Control so commonplace and universal? There are a great variety of reasons for its ubiquity. Some but not all of these also explain the universality of the other forms of Control. The main reasons are:[7]

1. The cues, gratifications, and deprivations are inevitably created by basic human relationships in fundamental human organizations, such as family, kin group, neighborhood, work place, market, friendship group, religious association.

2. It is also a universal control technique because many of the gratifications and deprivations through which it operates are deep-seated wants and avoidances of the human organism: love, affection, respect, solidarity, friendship, for example. To achieve these rewards, often the subordinate literally wants to be Controlled. For example, many people avidly long to make responses that will earn them love and avoid hate.

3. It is universal because many vital goals can be achieved only by spontaneous field Control. Although its symbols, rewards, and penalties can be and often are manipulated deliberately, there appears to be a certain degree of psychological incompatibility between deliberate manipulation and some of the important gratifications. If one constantly attempts deliberately to manipulate his loves, hates, affections, friendships, and respect in order to Control others, the value of his love, friendship, and respect tends to depreciate: Control thereupon declines. An element of spontaneity seems to be necessary to valued love, friendship and respect relations.

Parenthetically, and as corroborative evidence of this last point, one common criticism Americans make of their own culture is the widespread tendency to "prostitute" or "corrupt" these highly valued gratifications through deliberate manipulation in advertising, speeches, business "friendships," corporate recruitment and promotion policies, the false joviality and conviviality of the Rotary Club, etc. The result is a serious depreciation in the value of the act; i.e., it ceases to stimulate intense gratification, or even much of a sense of deprivation when it is lost.

4. It is universal because it is quickly learned. Because, as we have just seen, the human organism in most cultures is powerfully motivated to earn the rewards and avoid the deprivations frequently employed in spontaneous field Control, the required responses tend to be learned quickly. Children, for example, speedily learn to respond appropriately to such things as facial expressions, intonations, pitch and volume of voice, choice of words, physical stance.

5. It is universal because spontaneous field Control can be unusually sensitive; compared with it the other techniques are crude and imprecise. In roles where sensitive responses are needed, or the appropriate response requires adjustment to relatively small changes in social stimuli, rewards, and penalties, spontaneous field Control may be necessary. To civilize or socialize a child is in great part to teach him to submit readily to spontaneous field Controls. Jane Austen's novels indicate that the elaborate courtesy of the eighteenth-century gentry in England was mainly a matter of spontaneous field Control. In contemporary society, too, many roles require the individual to subordinate himself to spontaneous field Controls: orators, lawyers, teachers, hostesses, secretaries, and even parents must learn to make sensitive and minutely adjusted responses to by-product stimuli, rewards, and penalties of others.

6. It is universal because it is simple, economical, and easily created. Deliberate calculation and

deliberate control of relevant consequences are often felt to be added costs. At the very least, they require additional effort from people. People tend to indulge in deliberate calculation and control, therefore, only when failures to do so appear to be penalizing. To the extent that spontaneous field Control is a way of avoiding deliberate calculation and control, the creation of specialized machinery for enforcement, and specialized organs deliberately devoted to coördinating social activity, it has a kind of *prima-facie* case in its favor.

7. It is ubiquitous because, as we saw, it can be "permissive." Though as we have seen it need not necessarily do so, it may permit a sense of "free choice." To many people in many cultures this feeling is desired in itself. In addition, the existence of this state of mind may help make for enthusiasm and initiative, qualities also often regarded as desirable.

8. Finally, spontaneous field Control can often be employed, and perhaps usually is, in a bilateral or multilateral relationship. If it begins as a unilateral relationship, often it is easily converted into a bilateral one. Consequently, people may be able to Control one another without damaging subjective equality. Although subjective equality is not a universally demanded goal, in any societal organization where subjective equality is highly valued, spontaneous field Controls will be widely used in bilateral and multilateral relationships. Even in a highly oligarchical societal organization there would be some demand for subjective equality among the oligarchs, and among the subordinates.

Manipulated Field Control

Very often a spontaneous field Control is potentially a manipulated field Control. The young child's cries bring the mother to its crib. At first the Control is spontaneous. But soon the child learns that a cry will be followed by mother's attention; then it cries whenever it wants attention. The child now operates a manipulated field Control. Or again: for years consumers buy in the market with no intention of controlling prices. Then a period of inflation alerts them to the rising cost of living; they stage buyers' strikes in an attempt to bring down prices. Now they operate manipulated field Controls. Another example: oligopolists control each other through manipulated field Controls. Or still again: at one time in the United States the rate of interest was little more than a price paid for the use of capital; it was fixed by multilateral spontaneous field Controls. Only on rare occasions was it deliberately manipulated, as when Biddle and the Second Bank of the United States created a crisis in a vain attempt to frighten Jackson and the Bank's enemies. Today, the Federal Reserve Board relies heavily on the rate of interest to manipulate the fields of bankers, businessmen, and consumers.

WHAT IT IS. A manipulated field Control, then, is deliberate action on another person's field (by means other than command) in order to secure a definite response, by manipulating signals about rewards and deprivations, or by manipulating rewards and deprivations themselves, or both. Thus the subordinate's expectations about rewards and deprivations are affected; and he responds so as to secure the expected rewards or avoid the expected deprivations.

WHY IT IS UBIQUITOUS. Deliberate manipulation of another's field by acting on information, rewards, and deprivations appears to be as universal, widespread, and comprehensive as spontaneous field Control, and for many of the same reasons:

1. The cues, gratifications, and deprivations of ordinary day-to-day life can be used in this way.

2. Highly ranked gratifications and deprivations can be manipulated to *some* extent. Affection, love, respect, sympathy, hostility, encouragement, friendship, and status are to some extent manipulated as gratifications and deprivations in a wide variety of human groups. But perhaps two instrumental goals, power and income, are most easily manipulated for purposes of Control. Both can be manipulated in relatively fine gradations; they can be used to establish chains of control for large numbers of people; and, because in many societies they are instrumental to a wide variety of prime and other instrumental goals, they are highly effective as rewards and penalties.

3. Because of the importance of the goals used as gratifications and deprivations, the required responses tend to be quickly learned.

4. The Control can be used in a rather sensitive way.

5. Manipulation through cues, gratifications, and deprivations can—though it need not—stimulate feelings of "free choice" and evoke enthusiasm and initiative.

DIFFERENCES. Yet these similarities do not mean that the differences between spontaneous and manipulated field Controls are not often very great. In one respect they are significantly different. It is difficult for one person or a small group of people to coördinate the activities of large numbers of people through spontaneous field Controls or chains of such Controls; leaders are unlikely to generate the appropriate rewards, penalties, and communications simply as by-products of their own behavior. A social organization operating mostly through spontaneous field Controls would necessarily either be very small or highly dispersed and decentralized. By contrast, deliberate manipulation of expectations through information, rewards, and deprivations opens up possibilities for centralized control by the few over the many. In every large, centralized organization manipulated field Controls must play a highly significant role.

Command

The two Control techniques we have described so far are universal, widespread, comprehensive; probably they are components in almost all Control relationships found in the real world. As compared with these, command is an important but marginal system. For the number of actions Controlled by command seems to be relatively small in most human organizations.[8]

WHAT IT IS. What does one mean by a command? Is there a difference, as popular language implies, between being "asked" to do something and being "commanded" to do it? Although command is not always used in any single sense, a distinct shade of meaning is usually associated with the word: to give a command is to threaten someone with deprivations if he does not obey. And this is the way in which we use the term in isolating command as a third major technique of Control that needs special attention. To put it precisely: *To command is to Control the response of a subordinate exclusively by virtue of a penalty prescribed by the Controller for nonperformance of an implied or stipulated directive, so that the subordinate expects that his failure to respond as directed will result in the initiation of penalties by his superior.*[9]

COMMAND IS MARGINAL. Like the anarchists, many people confuse law with command and command with Control; they see the great number of acts stipulated by law in a modern society and conclude that command is everywhere. But laws are merely in the *form* of commands; they *appear* to be commands because on their face they do no more than prescribe penalties for nonperformance of certain directives stated in the body of the law.

Yet as modern students of the sociology of law point out, the form of the law does not explain why most people obey the law; it only explains why a relatively small number of people obey it. To explain why most people obey laws one needs to examine a complex body of rewards and deprivations through spontaneous and manipulated field Controls that are not invoked by courts but by family, friends, teachers, neighbors, acquaintances, colleagues, superiors, nominal subordinates, and so on. Hence the common paradox of the sociologists: "If a law is not supported by the mores of the community, it is ineffectual; if it is, the law is unnecessary." The paradox is false, of course, because although it is marginal, command can be catalytic. But the paradox correctly suggests the limited role of command in law enforcement.[10]

WHY COMMAND IS MARGINAL. Why is command usually restricted to a relatively small number of acts? For one thing, command usually requires prior training in order to teach the signals, the correct responses, and the appropriate penalties for failure to perform the response. To train people efficiently it is usually necessary to reward them. Hence to establish a command system and keep it going with new recruits often requires one or more of the other Control techniques.

Moreover, for a variety of reasons the fact that pure command imposes deprivations and offers no rewards seriously restricts its utility as a Control technique:

1. Nominal subordinates have no incentive to obey the command if they can devise a way to escape the penalties. (If there is any incentive other than fear of penalties, then a pure Command technique no longer exists.) Hence a considerable amount of ingenuity and energy will tend to be diverted into avoiding commands and escaping the penalties. The failure of prohibition in the United States is a case in point.

2. Command in the limited sense used here is difficult to legitimize. For if an individual is rewarded by his conscience for obeying an order, in the strict sense an element of manipulation of field has been blended with the command Control. It is true, however, that one may intellectually accept the necessity of command as part of a total network of Controls and accept the command as legitimate even if obedience to the particular command is motivated by no expectations of rewards.

3. Because command is difficult to legitimize,

it requires specialized machinery for detection, enforcement, and meting out punishment. Specialized machinery is costly.

4. Although the evidence is not entirely clear, it appears that in a pure command situation there is little incentive to industry, enthusiasm, loyalty, innovations, creativity, drive. Dictatorships, military organizations, and other hierarchical systems therefore employ other Control techniques in order to produce responses of this kind. Even slavery is rarely a *pure* command system; yet slavery has usually proved less productive than "free" labor.

5. Because command only imposes deprivations, it is inherently frustrating. Yet relations between controllers and subordinates are certain to be strained if the controller has nothing to offer his subordinates except deprivations. Such a relationship obviously endangers the minimum agreement necessary for organizational stability. A pure command society—one entirely ridden by fear—would seriously threaten social stability.

6. For all these reasons, therefore, superiors themselves find it unprofitable and inefficient to rely exclusively on command. The institution of a system of rewards is an obvious method of minimizing the disadvantages of command. Even totalitarian leaders find it efficient to introduce rewards, e.g., Stakhanovism.

Then, too, many of the most highly ranked goals cannot be obtained by command. As has already been shown, love, affection, respect, friendship, dignity, and solidarity require manipulated field Controls at the very least, and often spontaneous field Controls. Hence thousands of day-to-day relationships are immune to command. Command can only destroy such relationships; it can never achieve them.

Finally, command is possible only under conditions of social organization that prevent subordinates from fleeing the reach of the superior. "The conditions in which many primitive peoples live, afford one safeguard against any form of oppression, and that is the possibility of a group or even an individual separating from the community and forming a settlement of their own."[11] Under these conditions penalties for disobedience must be administered with extreme care and hence command is curtailed.[12] Even in contemporary societies, the more "voluntary" a group—that is, the more easily a member can withdraw and achieve his goals in an alternative group—the less reason any member has for obeying a command, and therefore the more limited the capacity of leaders to achieve Control through command. As will be shown in a later chapter, this social fact is of extraordinary importance as a condition for polyarchy.

Reciprocity

In the real world Control is rarely unilateral.[13] As we have already pointed out, spontaneous Control of another's field is quite commonly employed by two or more people in a bilateral or multilateral relationship. Yet even in hierarchical organizations there are many situations in which people can employ command or manipulated field Controls, or both, against one another. Such a bilateral or multilateral relationship, in which two or more people are Controlling one another through command or manipulation of fields or both, we shall call reciprocity.

Given goals such as subjective equality, democracy, and freedom, reciprocity is a Control technique of vital importance. If Control of human beings by human beings cannot be eliminated, reciprocity is an alternative to anarchy. And if great inequalities in control are undesirable, reciprocity is an alternative to tyranny.

IV. CONTROL AND COÖRDINATION

These four fundamental techniques of Control —spontaneous field Control, manipulated field Control, command, and reciprocity—are the building blocks from which all social systems are constructed.

Limits on Direct Control

Yet these Control techniques are not always sufficient to bring about a desired state of affairs. For one thing, the physical universe can be manipulated only within limits. Although these limits are widening rapidly, as everyone knows they are still narrow. In the face of a widespread drought throughout Asia no Controls could prevent mass starvation.

The social universe is also refractory. As with the physical universe, the limits within which the social universe can be controlled are widening but still narrow. Totalitarian leaders relying heavily on command and centralized manipulation of field are frequently just as much thwarted by human personalities and social organization as polyarchal societies relying heavily on reciprocity. Then, too, there is the eternal dilemma of means and ends. For just as a totalitarian commitment to unilateral control as a means rules out a number of important ends that can be maximized only through reciprocity and spontaneous field systems, so too a democratic commitment to ends allowable only by reciprocity and spontaneous field systems rules out some of the means of control available to totalitarians. Moreover, in every society important areas of individual autonomy are never effectively breached by direct controls. Hence the limits on control, like the limits on rational calculation, are so great that only marginal changes can sensibly be expected from attempts at rational social action, whether in totalitarian or in polyarchal societies.

Methods of Roundabout Control

Nevertheless, even when a desired state of affairs cannot be brought about in the first instance by Control or a chain of control over particular acts, what is desired can sometimes be brought about by indirection.

1. AFFECTING PERSONALITY. Where particular desired acts cannot now be produced, Control can be used in the first instance to *affect personalities*, so that later either an individual's responses produce the desired results or Controls may then be employed that would be unworkable with his present personality. Thus polyarchal societies are possible only because, in the first instance, Controls are used to indoctrinate and habituate individuals in the kinds of responses subsequently needed to operate polyarchy.

2. AFFECTING ROLES. Control can be used in the first instance to *affect roles*. When a person is faced with a particular agenda (schedule of things-to-be-done) or a class of agendas, he may act in a particular way; if his responses when faced with a particular agenda or class of agendas are more or less habitual and repetitive, then these responses may be said to make up his role.[14] A prosecuting attorney has a role different from that of a defense lawyer. A judge's role is not that of an attorney. Depending upon whether the agenda calls for prosecuting an alleged criminal, defending him, or insuring him a fair trial, the same man tends to make quite different responses.

Control is necessary in the first instance to indoctrinate an individual so that he will later play his role in some desired way. An individual must be taught the kinds of autonomous responses he should make and the kinds of Controls he should accept in the roles he is expected to play in life. In the United States many people are taught responses appropriate to the businessman's role with their first newspaper route, magazine sales, church bazaar, or household chore. Many of these responses subsequently become autonomous. The individual learns, for example, that in his business role he should not apply the precepts of Christian charity stressed in a number of his nonbusiness roles. He is taught to play a variety of apparently conflicting roles by compartmentalizing each of them. Thus responses he would find abhorrent or idiotic in one role seem just and sensible in another.

3. AFFECTING AGENDAS. Control may also be used in the first instance to achieve a subsequent desired result by *affecting the agenda*. This is a matter of affecting the kind of decision that must be made and perhaps changing the people who need to make the decision. For example, some of the aids to rational calculation also make possible changes in an agenda. Thus, to delegate some decisions to others or to quantify the value of alternatives in comparable units can also change the agenda and permit Control where it was difficult or impossible before.

To change the agenda is one of the most dramatic and far-reaching methods of government economic planning in war and mobilization. During mobilization and war when raw materials, machinery, and consumer goods are no longer allocated through the price system but by government priorities and direct allotments, the agendas of businessmen and government leaders are profoundly altered. Businessmen and government leaders face a vast new agenda of complex decisions that hitherto were made by no one individual or committee. Government leaders in particular are required to make centralized decisions of staggering complexity, allocating steel, copper, aluminum, and dozens of other materials in a tremendous variety of raw, semifinished, and finished states to the manufacture of an even greater number of semifinished and finished products.

The decisions to be made are of such magnitude that no one individual or committee could possibly make them all; hence, after the agenda is initially changed by substituting government priorities and allocations for the price system, individuals and committees in top policy-making positions continue to change their own agendas by decentralization. The central administrative problem facing leaders in a war economy is to discover the minimum agenda for themselves that is compatible with the need for centralized decision and the maximum agenda compatible with their own capacities. The continual reorganization of war agencies is a long experiment with the agenda.[15]

V. SOME CONDITIONS FOR EFFECTIVE CONTROL

Often the conditions that make for effective Control are absent. What are some of the most important conditions?

Consistency Between Controller's and Sub-Ordinate's Goals

First, the goals of the would-be controller must be consistent with at least some of the goals of the individual he hopes to Control. It is as easy to exaggerate the pliability of human personalities as to underestimate it. In recent years Marxism, Leninism, behaviorism, advertising, early propaganda studies, and the dissemination of anthropological knowledge about diverse cultures all have fostered the erroneous conclusion that human beings can be made in almost any mold; and further that in cases where immediate Control is limited, one merely needs to Control the rearing of the next generation.

But men are not infinitely pliable.[16] In every society some people stubbornly persist in seeking goals that conflict with their would-be controllers. Primitive societies, though relatively homogeneous as compared with our own, have to cope with deviants; and they handle their deviants in a variety of ways, at one extreme accepting them as magicians or medicine men and at the other extreme subjecting them to torture, exile, or execution. In any society deviants present something of a problem. If controllers deal vigorously with them this action often creates goal conflicts with still other people. Yet if the recalcitrants are permitted to go their way, they may influence others.

Adequate Rewards and Penalties

Second, controllers need an adequate system of rewards and penalties. Yet it is often impossible for would-be controllers to create such a system even where there are no ineradicable conflicts in goals. For they may lack knowledge and resources. We have already stressed the role of rewards and penalties in Control, and it seems superfluous to do more at this point than emphasize it again as a formally necessary condition.

Internalized Rewards and Penalties

FUNCTION OF THE CONSCIENCE. Not all the rewards and deprivations to which a person responds are external. The source of many rewards and deprivations is internal, in the sense that these rewards and deprivations are inflicted by the self on the self in such forms as shame, pride, self-respect, anxiety, or self-approval. Such internalized rewards and deprivations constitute the individual's conscience (or superego). Because these rewards and deprivations are internalized, once they are built into the individual they are not easily manipulated.

Hence great social effort is invested in building into people some particular type of conscience. A heavy investment in training the supergos of people in a social organization often pays rich dividends because of two vital functions carried on by the conscience.

AS SURROGATE CONTROL. First, the conscience is useful as a surrogate control; this fact makes it possible for superiors to repose enough confidence in subordinates to grant them discretion. For example, the Atomic Energy Commission in effect has at its disposal a vast amount of "patronage" in the form of contract awards to private corporations for the design, construction, and operation of its facilities. The Joint Congressional Committee, the Budget Bureau, and the White House might have created an extensive supervisory system to insure that contracts were fairly awarded; but such a system would be cumbersome and costly to administer. So far, extensive external supervision over contract awards has been avoided; in effect, confidence in the consciences of the commissioners and their employees permits Congress and the President to grant a large measure of discretion to the commission.

It is not too much to say that the operations of many organizations—industrial, commercial, governmental, religious, educational—would initially come to a halt if superiors could place no reliance on the consciences of subordinates. To function at all, these organizations would have to be made much more centralized and hierarchical; the gains of decentralization and discretion would largely be lost.

AS SOURCE OF LEGITIMACY. A closely related function of the conscience is to help establish legitimacy. Control is legitimate to the extent that it is approved or regarded as "right."[17] The test of "rightness" may be rather conscious, articulated, logically structured norms (such as theory of the appropriate role of judicial review in a democratic order). Or the test may be the less conscious, more incoherent norms with less logical structure and abstract theory, the "feeling" of what is right and wrong in a given instance. The second is more inaccessible to manipulation than the first; it is more clearly the domain of the conscience. Because it is more inaccessible, controllers are often unable to achieve many of the responses they seek.

Because legitimacy is tested subjectively, what is legitimate Control to a controller may be illegitimate to a subordinate; what is legitimate to one subordinate may not be legitimate to another. Partly because of this complexity, partly because of the multiple superiors of modern pluralistic societies, and partly because of the breakdown of consistent belief systems,[18] clear-cut legitimacy is probably much rarer in modern Western societies than in the past or in many primitive societies. Thus Control, like so many other social phenomena, tends to be ranged between the pure polar types of legitimacy and illegitimacy. A decade after Pearl Harbor Americans were still sharply divided over the legitimacy of Roosevelt's Control over foreign policy decisions during the year preceding the Japanese attack.

Legitimacy is not indispensable to all Control. Nevertheless lack of legitimacy imposes heavy costs on the controllers. For legitimacy facilitates the operation of organizations requiring enthusiasm, loyalty, discretion, decentralization, and careful judgment. It is difficult to imagine how the atomic bomb could have been designed, developed, and constructed in the time it was if every participant of the Manhattan Engineer District had regarded General Groves' Control as entirely illegitimate.

Appropriate Identification

The way in which one identifies himself with others is often crucial in determining how, and indeed whether, he can be induced to respond in a way desired by someone else.[19] Yet, because it is internalized, like the conscience, it is not easy to manipulate.

One's planes of identification may facilitate or frustrate Control. The small child exerts Control over the parent partly because it is so easy for the parent to identify with the child. The docility of white-collar workers in business organizations no doubt partly stems from their tendency to identify themselves with their superiors. But in recent years urban workers have evidently identified themselves more and more with one another; the plane of identification with business leaders has snapped.[20] Workers are therefore more responsive to working-class leaders, less responsive to business leaders.

One important consequence of altering a role is often to alter one's identifications, the "self" at the focus of attention and striving. In his various roles as son, friend, father, husband, neighbor, club member, retail purchaser, business executive, and voter, the individual may have rather different identifications. Controls one submits to as father he would find intolerable as business executive, and vice versa. His identifications in the act of buying a lamb roast, a set of matched irons, a car, or a house may be rather different from one another, and even more different from his identifications in the act of voting in a polling booth, a town meeting, or a legislative body.

Thus identification can impose stubborn restraints on Control; and often controllers can do little more than accept the identifications of their subordinates as given, and alter their own Controls accordingly.

Communications

Finally, Control requires effective transmission of cues, signals, stimuli, or information. In the interwar years the competitive price system was looked on with a certain disdain by many reformers and planners. Experience with hierarchical coordination of national economies during wartime and in postwar reconstruction in some countries—particularly in Great Britain—has stripped some of the glamour from hierarchy, however, and has restored a little to the price system. One important reason for this change in mood is the realization that hierarchial coordination of a national economy imposes such a staggering burden on communications that the dilemma of central coordination vs. decentralized discretion is never satisfactorily resolved. By comparison the ease of coordination through the price system in some circumstances seems rather more attractive to many "national planners" than it did during the interwar years when they were still unfamiliar with this problem of hierarchical coordination.

Sometimes one important reason for changing

an agenda is to make possible a different system for transmitting information. Thus to change the agenda from hierarchical allocations of raw materials in wartime to allocations through a competitive price system is to work a profound change in the system of communications.

These, then, are some of the critical prerequisites of Control. Once stated, they seem rather formal and obvious. But sometimes it is easier to forget the obvious than the obscure.

VI. FREEDOM, EQUALITY, RATIONALITY, AND CONTROL

Freedom and Control

There is no necessary blood feud between freedom and control. On the contrary, freedom requires control. As we have shown in a previous chapter, freedom often requires social organization. Yet every social organization is a system of controls. It follows that freedom must often require some system of controls.

One may reach the same conclusion by another route. Most of us have highly valued goals we cannot achieve unless we are able regularly to secure the response of others; regularly to secure the response of others is to Control them; hence our own freedom requires each of us to Control some others in certain respects. Conversely, some of our goals like friendship and love cannot be achieved unless we allow others to Control us in some respects.[21]

Sometimes freedom is confused with autonomy—the absence of Control. But if what we have just said is true, freedom cannot be identical with autonomy. (Possibly the controversy over "freewill" vs. "determinism" might be more meaningful if cast in terms that carefully distinguished autonomy, Control, and freedom.) To be sure, autonomous actions may sometimes be necessary to one's freedom because occasionally one's goals cannot be attained except by autonomous action. Many aesthetic satisfactions are of this kind. But whenever one's own goals require the responses of others, to rely on autonomous action is to frustrate one's own freedom.

What, then, is the bearing on freedom of the four techniques of Control discussed earlier in this chapter?

FREEDOM AND SPONTANEOUS FIELD CONTROL. As has already been shown, spontaneous field Controls are among the most tyrannical most of us ever know. Because such important gratifications and deprivations as love and hate or respect and contempt are dispensed through spontaneous field Controls, possibly no other system of control can be so frustrating, so oppressive. Literature and real life are both full of the tyrannies of the family, the neighbors, the small town, the office, one's colleagues, relatives, even friends operating through spontaneous field Controls. It is doubtful whether even command can wreck the harm of some spontaneous field Controls; for spontaneous field Controls can, and often do, provoke overwhelming frustration, anxiety, despair, hatred; permanently wreck personalities; and create the sufferings of neurotics and psychotics. In the last analysis, probably far more people are in mental institutions and prisons because of spontaneous field Controls than because of command.

The very fact that spontaneous field Control is unintentional is often the source of its tyrannies. Controllers do not even know they are responsible for the misery of their victims. The checks imposed by sympathetic identification may therefore be missing or come too late. Yet, unlike command, spontaneous field Controls need not frustrate the goals of the subordinate. Unlike command, and like certain forms of manipulated field Controls, some forms of spontaneous field Controls are compatible with the freedom both of controller and of subordinate. No doubt it is because spontaneous field Controls *can* in some circumstances lead to the mutual freedom of subordinates and controllers that Controls of this kind are so often implicitly identified with freedom; a possible condition of freedom is wrongly taken as a sufficient condition.

MANIPULATED FIELD CONTROL. Much the same can be said of manipulated field Controls. There is no one-for-one relation between manipulated field Controls and freedom. Whether they increase or decrease freedom depends upon the situation, the specific kind of manipulated field Controls used in that situation, and whose freedom is under consideration.

But the ways in which one can manipulate the field of another have significantly different consequences for freedom. Two sets of alternatives are particularly important: (1) whether one manipulates symbols of reality in order to clarify or to confuse individuals' understanding of reality and (2) whether one manipulates the field of an individual with rewards or with deprivations. Let us examine both of these sets of alternatives from the standpoint of the individual controlled.

1. Manipulating symbols of reality in order to control others may be done in two ways (these are really ends of a continuum), which have usually been valued quite differently in the Greco-Roman culture and its derivatives. The effort to manipulate symbols in order to clarify the subordinate's understanding of reality—i.e., to provide him with expectations that will prove to be correct when he acts in accordance with them—has usually been highly valued by the norms of Western societies. Parents, teachers, political leaders, and others are expected to rely heavily on this method of manipulated field Control. But one may also manipulate symbols of reality in order to transmit false expectations, as is often done in propaganda, advertising, and political campaigns. Although widely practiced, and in recent generations developed to a high art, this type of manipulated field Control conflicts violently with certain persistent norms of Western culture.

Men like Jefferson have urged widespread education, dissemination of correct information, discussion, freedom of speech, and freedom of press all as necessary instruments to individual freedom. Their assumption has been that these institutions are necessary if people are to obtain a correct understanding of reality. The better individuals comprehend reality, they further assume, the more efficiently they can attain their goals. The more efficiently people can attain their goals, the more liberated they are. Hence in the liberal democratic view there is a direct connection between one's freedom and his understanding of reality.

Even if early liberal democrats like Jefferson and Paine employed an excessively rationalistic psychology, modern psychology lends strength to their basic assumption. Because ignorance of reality is an important source of frustrating actions, ignorance does diminish freedom. Perhaps the most enslaved people in any society are the neurotics; and the neurotic is in one sense a person who has learned a false view of the reality around him.

To be sure, if reality itself is frustrating, then merely to understand it will not make one free. The child living in a disreputable slum with embittered, quarreling parents will not be liberated simply by being made to understand his immediate environment and the world beyond. In social life, sometimes an individual is less frustrated if he does *not* know what his fellows think of his actions.

Yet despite these difficulties, the liberal democratic view is basically sound. For if reality is frustrating, the need is not merely to understand it but to change it. And if reality is frustrating there is a powerful motivation for changing it. To understand reality, then, is to increase the chances for changing it in desired ways. To understand reality even when it is frustrating is often a necessary condition for an increase of freedom.

An unbridgeable gulf divides the case of the liberal democrat from the case of Dostoevski's Grand Inquisitor. Reality is often inherently so frustrating (runs the attack on the liberal case) that people can survive only with myths. To manipulate symbols in order to confuse reality is better for mankind than to increase their understanding, it is said, because understanding will only multiply their despair. Only a very short step divides the Grand Inquisitor from Lenin's "Truth is a bourgeois virtue."

The liberal democratic case rests on the premise that, even if ignorance may decrease frustration in the short run, in the long run ignorance will significantly increase frustration by reducing one's capacity for dealing effectively with reality. And if it be said that the deceptions are only to be temporary, the liberal democrat will reply that controllers who can impose "temporary" deceptions are almost certain to be in a position of control from which they can convert temporary deceptions into permanent ones.

The liberal democratic case is, then, an argument for scientific investigation, freedom of inquiry, and a belief that truth is openended.

2. As for the second set of alternatives, manipulated field Controls that employ rewards clearly grant more freedom to the Controlled individual than command can ever do; for command is inherently frustrating to the subordinate. But even without commanding an individual, one can manipulate the field of a subordinate by affecting the deprivations that actually operate on him. This is not to command him, because the individual does not have the expectation that the controller will initiate certain prescribed penalties for his failure to obey some specific directive of the controller.

Whether manipulation of operating penalties is more or less frustrating than command, it is impossible to generalize. Because command is a more ostensible, direct, person-to-person relationship, perhaps it can offend status, self-respect, and dignity of individuals more than does manipulation of operating penalties. Manipulation of field seems to be more suitable for creating "permissive" situations, i.e., situations in which a particular response is attained although the individual can choose among a variety of rewards and penalties. On the other hand, manipulation of operating penalties can create frustration and despair merely because the subordinate cannot always clearly identify and attack the controller (even if only secretly). Thus the question must be left unsettled. This fact in itself has some significance, because sometimes it is assumed that to act on operating penalties must inevitably lead to greater freedom than to command.

COMMAND. In appraising command it is particularly vital to distinguish the freedom of subordinate, of controller, and of third parties. For if the freedom of the subordinate were the only concern, then command would rarely be used. For command is a method of Control by threats of deprivation; it directly and necessarily reduces the immediate freedom of the subordinate. The other control techniques *can* be used in such a way as to increase the immediate freedom both of controllers and of subordinates. Command never can directly increase the freedom of the subordinate; the freedom of the controller is always attained at the immediate expense of the subordinate. For the subordinate can never earn any immediate rewards for what he does; he can only escape deprivations. Hence, in a pure command situation the subordinate does not seek goals rewarding to himself; he can only seek goals rewarding to the controller.

Yet if the freedom of the subordinate is always infringed by command, the freedom of the controller or of third parties sometimes requires it. Take the suppression of crime. Not, of course, that impulses to criminality are mainly controlled by command. As we have already indicated, command in the form of law, prescribed penalties, police, courts, and prisons is a marginal factor in controlling criminality. Yet few of us would dispense with command; for we do want to use it against the marginal human beings who can be inhibited from criminality only by the expectation of judicial penalties, or by imprisonment and the actual limitation of the criminal's resources for committing crimes.

RECIPROCITY. Unlike command, reciprocity need not inherently limit the freedom of any participant. But wherever there is less than complete agreement on goals among all the participants in a reciprocal arrangement someone's freedom is bound to be restrained. Hence reciprocity is mainly important to freedom as a system for arriving at decisions as to whose freedom will be permitted or curtailed, and by how much, in cases of conflict.

CONCLUSION. Thus even a short examination of the relationships between freedom and the four control techniques shows that no one of them is more indispensable to freedom than the others and no one of them is inherently more productive of freedom than the others. This is, we think, an important conclusion. For there is a tendency to assume that one type of Control is intrinsically superior to the others; or that from goals like political equality and freedom one can logically establish the superiority of, say, reciprocity over command. This, as has been shown, is false.

The most one can say—and this too is important —is that command always infringes the freedom of subordinates and the other techniques need not. A society concerned with maximizing freedom must therefore be inventive in discovering effective alternatives to command. But it must be equally inventive in discovering effective alternatives when the other control techniques infringe upon freedom.

And in all situations where democracy is a dominant goal, reciprocal Controls are necessary among the participants. Command and manipulated field Controls are unilateral. The Control relationship they make possible is inherently an unequal one; the subordinate is not the political equal of the controller. Hence reciprocal Controls are the only tolerable ones among political equals *qua* political equals. Not only reciprocity but maximum reciprocity is required. Any deviation from maximum reciprocity means political inequality.

Subjective Equality

Like political equality, subjective equality is not always a goal to be maximized. This difficult and admittedly ambiguous goal, it will be recalled, was stated this way: *Wherever in any specific situation in which more people rather than less can have the opportunity to achieve their goals, the decision is for the greater number rather than for any lesser number.* Thus a relationship of subjective equality requires in general that rewards and deprivations be distributed more or less equally.

COMMAND. If one considers only the relationship between controller and subordinate, clearly pure command inherently violates subjective equality. For pure command, remember, can inflict only deprivations on the subordinate, whereas the controller is usually in a position to reward himself through the actions of his subordinate. Hence command increases the opportunity for the opportunity for the controller to attain his goals at the expense of the subordinate's opportunities. The subordinate must do the bidding of the controller or suffer punishment; the subordinate's own goals—aside from his desire to escape punishment—are neglected. For to the extent that the subordinate gains anything by the action, other than an escape from punishment initiated by the controller, he is rewarded; and if he is rewarded, something more than a pure command relationship must exist.

MANIPULATED AND SPONTANEOUS FIELD CONTROLS. Unlike the case with political equality, manipulated and spontaneous field Controls may or may not violate subjective equality. Any unilateral Control does create the possibility, of course, that the subordinate may suffer at the expense of the controller. But neither manipulated nor spontaneous field Controls *need* to produce this result. For the controller can use these Controls to grant rewards to the subordinate. Hence, the subordinate can maximize some of his goals within such a relationship.

RECIPROCITY. As a practial matter, however, some element of reciprocity is the best guarantee that Controls will be used to reward the individuals controlled. Any unilateral relationship is potentially exploitative. The crucial guarantee that rewards and deprivations will be distributed on something like an equal basis is the fact of mutual Control. Alike in intimate personal relationships such as love and friendship and in the more impersonal relationships of work place, store, town hall, and federal office building, what makes for subjective equality is the fact that each participant exercises some Control over the other.

So far we have been concerned only with the subjective equality of the individual Controlled. As was seen in the case of freedom, however, one cannot appraise the utility of a Control technique only from that standpoint; for one must also consider the controller and any third parties who may be affected. Then too, one's appraisal is likely to vary with one's concern over the outcome of a specific decision.

In many cases involving the action of other people one has little concern with the outcome of a specific decision; yet one might have a strong preference that the outcome, whatever it might be, should not significantly violate subjective equality among the participants. In such cases it is logical merely to rule out any relationship that will significantly violate subjective equality.

In practice, a tremendous variety of social relationships is disposed of in this way. No particular outcome is demanded by third parties. But the relationship is regulated so that A can Control B only if B expects to gain by it; any relationship where A can Control B only at B's expense is ruled out by various laws and regulations. Indeed, laissez-faire liberalism was hardly more than an application of this idea to all or nearly all economic relationships. And the changes from laissez faire to the modern highly regulatory state are a result not so much of an abandonment of the rule as of a growing belief that the rule could not be realistically applied to many situations. For laissez faire actually permitted much more unilateral control by entrepreneurs over workers and consumers than the theory recognized. The modern regulatory state is an attempt, then, not to arrive at specific decisions by government action, but to rule out relationships that significantly violate subjective equality.

Rationality and Control

To achieve a variety of goals as complex as those of Chapter 2, a more or less rational society, it should now be clear, would need to use all four Control techniques in a formidable array of different combinations and permutations. To describe all the combinations needed would take not a book but an encyclopedia of many volumes. Even if all the needed combinations were known, and certainly they are not, even to list them would doubtless take as many pages as there are in this book. In the rest of this volume we content ourselves with describing some of the major combinations most relevant to problems of government economic planning.

Before turning to these, however, it may be worth while to indicate in summary from the necessary relationships between the four Control techniques and the goal-scheduling devices discussed in the previous chapter. For the way in which a group of people schedules goals is dependent on its choice of Control techniques; and conversely, the Control techniques a group employs are dependent on its choice of goal-scheduling devices:

1. To schedule goals through:
   - Voting or implicit voting — requires — Reciprocity
   - Market choices or other spontaneous choices — requires — Spontaneous field Control
   - Delegation — requires — Command and/or manipulated field Control

2. Conversely, Control by:
   - Reciprocity — requires — Voting or implicit voting
   - Spontaneous field Control — requires — Market choices or other spontaneous choices
   - Command and/or manipulated field Control — requires — Delegation

A look at these relationships reinforces our previous conclusion. Because goals like those of Chapter 2 require all of the scheduling devices listed above, it follows that they also require all of the Control techniques. Conversely, because goals like those of Chapter 2 require all of the Control techniques, it follows that they also require all of the scheduling devices.

One final warning: Even when one knows the goals he wants to achieve, it is often difficult to decide intelligently which Control technique, or which combination of Control techniques, to employ. There are two main reasons for this difficulty. First, rarely can anyone know all the relevant consequences of using one Control technique rather than another. Indeed, there is one vital set of consequences about which relatively little is known, and these are the long-run consequences for the personalities of the people involved.[22] Hence choosing one technique or combination is to some extent groping in the dark. Second, one technique can often be converted into another, thus interjecting an indeterminate element in the decision, for not only must one calculate the probable consequences of one technique as against another in a given situation; one must also try to calculate both the likelihood that one technique will be converted into another and the probable consequences of such a change. In the past, laissez-faire liberals sometimes ignored this point. Under the benevolent jurisdiction of Say's Law, which ruled out mass unemployment and the consequent exploitation of labor, they often failed to see that in depression the entrepreneur was able to Control his employees by command with little reciprocal restraint. Labor was not in fact mobile; nor did a worker always have alternative employment; and in the worst circumstances, he rented a company house and went into debt at a company store. Hence, an unscrupulous employer possessed a large element of Control; he could direct the workers to accept certain working conditions on penalty of severe, unilateral deprivations if the workers refused. Thus an ostensible system of reciprocal Controls was converted into a command system.

One must always reckon with this possibility. One crucial test of governmental techniques, for example, is supplied not by normal operations but by crisis. For in crisis and its aftermath a society discovers the forms into which its governmental techniques can be converted.

FOOTNOTES

[1] F. J. Roethlisberger and W. J. Dickson called this the "formal" organization, in *Management and the Worker*, Harvard University Press, Cambridge, 1939, p. 558. Others have sometimes spoken of the "formal" organization, although there is by no means consistency in the usage of that term. Chester Barnard, for example, appears to use "formal organization" in a different sense in *The Functions of the Executive*, Harvard University Press, Cambridge, 1938, p. 4; and see Herbert A. Simon, *Administrative Behavior*, The Macmillan Company, New York, 1947, pp. 147–149. Because of these ambiguities, we have chosen what we think is the more descriptive term, "prescribed."

[2] The term "field" as used here is meant only as we have defined it, and should not be taken as an attempt to approximate its meaning in physics, in the sociology of Karl Mannheim, or in the psychological theories of Kurt Lewin. This caution applies to all the terms used in this chapter. Wherever possible we have deliberately restricted ourselves to elementary assumptions common to most or all psychological theories. Although our language is eclectic, no one should read into our terms the specific definitions of the psychologists with whom some of the terms are commonly associated.

[3] Another possibility is to act directly on a person's psychophysical capacities by surgery, drugs, and the like. Soviet techniques for extracting confession, by depriving an individual of sleep and keeping him on a starvation diet, might also be put in this category. Although this method, and possibly the development of some of the newer drugs, may vastly enhance the possibilities of direct psychophysical manipulation, for the purposes of this book these methods may be ignored..

[4] It may also be possible, as some eminent psychologists believe, to influence behavior by manipulating the objects or symbols in the individual's environment, even if the individual's expectations of rewards and deprivations are in no way affected. However, we have not found it necessary to make use of this assumption and in the rest of the book it is ignored.

[5] The following is a schematic summary of the relation of the four Control techniques:

Unilateral   Multilateral
Spontaneous field Control = Spontaneous field Control
Manipulated field Control ⎫
Command   ⎬ = Reciprocity

[6] Use of the word "spontaneous" does not mean that the actions of the controller are uncaused. The controller's actions may themselves be produced by the Control of others. Even if autonomous, presumably they are caused by interaction with nonhuman objects in the environment, or by built-in personality factors, etc. Neither the term "spontaneous" nor the term "autonomous" is intended to imply that any human action is uncaused.

[7] Spontaneous field Control in a price system is a special case. All the reasons given here do not necessarily apply to it.

[8] In different language, this has been pointed out by other observers. Cf. *The Sociology of Georg Simmel* (translated, edited, and with introduction by Kurt H. Wolff), Free Press, Glencoe, Ill., 1950, pp. 182-183; Charles Merriam, *Political Power, Its Composition and Incidence,* McGraw-Hill Book Co., New York, 1934, pp. 22 ff.

[9] Command in this sense appears to be rather similar to what Harold Lasswell and Abraham Kaplan mean by power. "Power is . . . the process of affecting policies of others with the help of (actual or threatened) severe deprivations for nonconformity with the policies intended." See their *Power and Society,* Yale University Press, New Haven, 1950, p. 76.

[10] The USSR may offer an exception to what we have said about the marginal character of command. Unfortunately, the information necessary to a sound judgment is inadequate. The Soviet Union probably gives a more prominent role to control through command than any other society has ever done. Yet in the three great control hierarchies—party, secret police, and administrative bureaucracy—rewards are manipulated in the form of power, status, and income. Soviet citizens are also manipulated by propaganda—in part, no doubt, to render them more amenable to command.

[11] Gunnar Landtman, *The Origin of the Inequality of the Social Classes,* University of Chicago, Chicago, 1938, p. 320. Cf. also Richard Thurnwald, *Werden, Wandel, und Gestaltung von Staat und Kultur im Lichte der Volkerforschung,* in *Die Menschliche Gesellschaft,* Vierter Band, Walter de Gruyter & Co., Berlin and Leipzig, 1935, pp. 86 ff.

[12] "Among the Kiwai Papuans . . . there is no one to hinder malcontents from going away . . . . If among the Kayans of Borneo, some portion of a tribe are dissatisfied with the conduct of their chief, they leave their former village. . . . Among the Punans, also, in case of disagreement, one or more of the members of the band may refuse to accept the judgment of the leader and of the majority; he or they will withdraw from the community. . . . ." Gunnar Landtman, *op. cit.,* p. 320.

[13] Cf. *The Sociology of Georg Simmel,* p. 185, and Herbert Goldhamer and Edward A. Shils, "Types of Power and Status," *The American Journal of Sociology,* September, 1939, p. 178.

[14] See Talcott Parsons and Edward A. Shils, *Toward a General Theory of Action,* Harvard University Press, Cambridge, 1951, p. 23. Parsons and Shils emphasize the expectations of self and others, rather than the repetitive responses as the distinguishing characteristic of role. We have found the present concept more convenient for our purposes.

[15] There is no clear dichotomy dividing Control over particular acts in order to achieve the immediate cooperation of others from Control over particular acts that in the first instance affect personality, roles, or agenda, because (a) there is always some time lag between the action of a Controller and the responses of a subordinate, (b) the desired response from the subordinate is usually preceded by some intervening responses, and (c) it is not always easy to decide whether a response is unique or repetitive.

[16] For example, "Though every biological fact is given a social meaning, the stuff provided by heredity is not infinitely plastic." Clyde Kluckhohn and Henry A. Murray, "A Conception of Personality," in Kluckhohn and Murray (eds.), *Personality in Nature, Society and Culture,* Alfred A. Knopf, New York, 1949, p. 107. And see Clark L. Hull, *Principles of Behavior,* Appleton-Century-Crofts, New York, 1943, pp. 59-60; Otto Klineberg, *Social Psychology,* Henry Holt and Co., New York, 1940, pp. 160-162; George P. Murdock, "The Common Denominator of Cultures," in Ralph Linton (ed.), *The Science of Man in the World Crisis,* Columbia University Press, New York, 1945, pp. 127-129; Gardner Murphy, *Personality,* Harper & Brothers, New York, 1947, pp. 127-129, 620, et seq.; Edward Chace Tolman, "Motivation, Learning, and Adjustment," *Proceedings,* American Philosophical Society, vol. 84, 1941, pp. 543-550.

[17] The concept of legitimacy has been strangely neglected in American political science. Herbert A. Simon, Donald W. Smithburg, and Victor A. Thompson have recently helped to restore it, in *Public Administration,* Alfred A. Knopf, New York, 1950.

[18] Karl Mannheim, *Diagnosis of Our Time,* Kegan Paul, Trench, Trubner & Co., London, 1943, pp. 17 ff.; Alexander H. Leighton, *The Governing of Men,* Princeton University Press, Princeton, 1946, pp. 322-325; Sebastian de Grazia, *The Political Community,* University of Chicago Press, Chicago, 1948, *passim.*

[19] In political science the most extensive use of the concept of identification is in the various works of Harold Lasswell. With respect to the subject at hand, however, cf. Herbert A. Simon, *op. cit.,* chap. 10. The term "identification" has been used in various ways, but the most suitable for our purposes is the one by Simon: "A person identifies himself with a group when in making a decision he evaluates the several alternatives of choice in terms of their consequences for the specified group." *Ibid.,* p. 205.

[20] This is strongly indicated by a comparison of Lynd's two studies of Middletown. See Robert S. Lynd, *Middletown,* Harcourt, Brace and Co., New York, 1929, and *Middletown in Transition,* Harcourt, Brace and Co., New York, 1937.

[21] Confusion over the relationship between freedom, control, and autonomy is sometimes compounded by a failure to distinguish the freedom of (1) the subordinate, (2) the controller, and (3) others affected by the actions of the subordinate or controller.

[22] Some relevant questions are raised but few are answered in our final chapter.

ABOUT THE AUTHORS—Robert A. Dahl and Charles E. Lindblom. "As political scientists, they are economically literate; as economists, they are politically sophisticated. They are thinking about real problems from all sides... Accordingly, they produce better sociology than is generally available nowadays." So wrote C. Wright Mills in his review of the volume from which the present chapter has been drawn. The book resulted when, following a period begun six years earlier, upon discovering that they both were conducting graduate seminars whose contents overlapped on the topic of 'planning,' Robert Dahl and Charles E. Lindblom decided to pool their efforts and conduct the seminars jointly. This close and conscientious collaboration on every session and every topic led to the ideas incorporated in their book.

Robert A. Dahl is primarily a theorist whose observations are derived from and subject to empirical verification. His work is characterized by his concentration on the realities of the political milieu. Before assuming his present role as Sterling Professor of Political Science at Yale, held since 1964, Dahl was the Eugene Meyer Professor from 1955 to 1964. He has been a Guggenheim Fellow, and a Fellow at the Center for Advanced Studies in the Behavioral Sciences and a Ford Foundation Research Professor. In 1955 he was Walgreen Lecturer at the University of Chicago. He serves at present as President of the American Political Science Association. Dahl completed his undergraduate work at the University of Michigan, and received his Ph.D. from Yale in 1940. With the exception of the war years his entire academic career has been spent at Yale. He has contributed to many journals and is author of *Who Governs?* (1961), *Modern Political Analysis* (1963) and edited *Political Opposition in Western Democracies* (1966).

Charles E. Lindblom received his B.A. from Stanford University in 1937 and his Ph.D. from the University of Chicago in 1945. Having taught previously at the University of Minnesota from 1939 to 1946, he came to Yale in 1946 where he serves now as professor of economics and political science. His publications include *Unions and Capitalism* (1949), *A Strategy of Decision* (with David Braybrooke) (1963), *The Intelligence of Democracy* (1965) and *The Policy Making Process* to be published during 1968.

Assessment of Results

The process of administration is no more effective than the capacity of the organization for making assessments about whether or not it is achieving its sought-for ends. Yet the success or failure of performance is perhaps the most unattainable measure to achieve in reviewing the performance of organizations. In part the problem is magnified by the incapacity of organizations to address themselves to the inherent aims and purposes for which they exist. The development of criteria needed for assessing accomplishment in other than the value-free quantitative indicators is elusive and frustrating. Yet without the attempt to evaluate achievement, only the crudest yardsticks of program effectiveness in libraries or in any other kind of organization are possible. Under these terms what is a "good" or "bad" library is the personal judgment of whoever exercises such judgment based upon the criteria which he alone has fashioned since the organization will not have evolved such criteria as a basis for such assessment. While the task of measuring organizational results is not susceptible of simple measurement, it is so fundamental to rational organizational procedures that it must be energetically pursued in any agency which strives to enhance the intelligent attainment of organizational goals.

Measuring Municipal Activities: Public Libraries

by Clarence E. Ridley and Herbert A. Simon

The concern of this contribution is with those functions of public libraries which are susceptible of measurement. It is interesting to note that in the twenty-five year period which has elapsed from the time when this work was first published, the sophistication of library administration has not advanced beyond the mechanisms then available for evaluating performance. Potential uses and applications of registration data, information about book stock, conditions of support and other factors were related to the feasibility of evaluating the public library contribution. Effectiveness and efficiency are differentiated. The first is seen as the contribution of the organization toward its desired ends and the second the relative success which the organization achieves in economic use of its resources.

The American Library Association in 1933 developed a statement of the objectives of library service. These objectives were conceived to be (1) to provide the means for self-education and recreational reading, (2) to give education and advice in the use of library materials, (3) to diffuse information and ideas necessary to the present welfare and future advancement of the community, and (4) to strengthen and extend appreciation of cultural and spiritual values in life.[1]

The first two aims can be measured objectively in terms of specific activities; the last two are measurable only in terms of a certain set of social values which will determine *what* ideas, information, and cultural and spiritual values are most significant for the advancement of the community. We shall refer to the first two ends as specific, the latter two as ultimate objectives.

In terms of ultimate objectives the library becomes a factor in providing wide opportunities for recreational and informational reading on all sides of life's experience.[2] The problem of measuring ultimate objectives can be solved only when adequate measurements are developed for specific objectives. The latter in turn must be broken down so that each aspect may be examined separately. By such analysis the adequacy and inadequacy of existing standards can be determined and new standards developed.

STANDARDS OF PERFORMANCE IN USE TODAY

There are today two statistical standards widely used to measure library service; those developed by the American Library Association, and the minimum standards for public libraries in New York developed by the State Education Department of the University of the State of New York.[3] Most of the units discussed in this paper have their basis in these two sets of standards. The American Library Association standards include criteria of lending service, books and miscellaneous stock, personnel, salaries, and financial data. The New York standards are somewhat more comprehensive, employing a larger number of criteria and setting separate standards for each of nineteen population classes of cities.

Each year the American Library Association compiles statistical tables based upon returns from libraries in many districts of the United States and Canada.[4] Comparison of one's own statistics with those of other institutions should be of great value to the administrator. A variation from the norms of other institutions is no proof that anything is wrong, but it may be an indication of a need for analysis.[5]

The tools developed for the measurement of public libraries by these two agencies have great

SOURCE: Reprinted from Clarence E. Ridley and Herbert A. Simon, *Measuring Municipal Activities: A Survey of Suggested Criteria for Appraising Administration* (2d ed. rev.; Chicago: The International City Manager's Association, 1943), Chap. 10, "Public Libraries," pp. 46-51, by permission of the publisher and the authors. Original publication bore the following note: "The writers acknowledge their indebtedness to Miss Henrietta Rybczynski who collaborated in preparing this chapter and to Harland A. Carpenter, New Bedford Free Public Library; Mary D. Clark and Margery C. Quigley, Free Public Library, Montclair, New Jersey; Julia Wright Merrill and Carl H. Milam, American Library Association; Arnold Miles, American Municipal Association; and Louis R. Wilson, Graduate Library School, University of Chicago, who contributed many valuable suggestions during the course of preparation."

potentiality for the improvement of the organizational and internal administrative aspects of our public libraries. These potentialities would be more completely realized if a greater degree of co-operation could be secured from municipal libraries in the compilation of requested data.

ANALYSIS OF PERFORMANCE UNITS

Before statistics have any real meaning for measurement in terms of service, interpretative instruments must be devised in the light of the purposes which the library is attempting to serve. The types of services rendered by the public library are educational, recreational, and cultural. Reasonably adequate service has been defined as including: (1) a main library with reading room facilities; (2) special provision for children; (3) lending; (4) reference; (5) periodicals; (6) such branches and other distributing agencies as the area and topography of the city may require.[6] Of increasing importance are the special co-operative services a library undertakes in order to make available its materials to other agencies in the city, especially the schools, and to show them how they can enrich their programs with the use of books.

Since the prime objective of modern library service is purposeful use, whether the object of use is recreational, educational, or cultural, the first criterion to be used in the measurement of service should provide some method for breaking down total lending service into its *circulation* and *informational* aspects.

Circulation. The most commonly used measuring rods for determining the nature of the circulation are circulation per capita and per borrower, per cent of children's circulation to the total circulation, and per cent of non-fiction circulation to the total circulation. Registration is generally measured as the per cent of population registered as borrowers.

Gross and per capita circulation figures are only rough measures of the actual quality of circulation and may obscure more than they reveal by confusing quantity with quality. Composition of circulation may be analyzed according to the size of the book collection and expressed as a percentage distribution of circulation according to fiction and non-fiction.[7] By combining the corresponding data on book stock and circulation the annual rate of circulation of book stock may be determined.[8] If a library has an adult non-fiction stock of 1,000 books and books are withdrawn 3,000 times in the course of a year the average use per volume in that stock is three times. This figure computed for the various types of books indicates which type in proportion to its numbers is most frequently withdrawn.[9]

These figures, however, give no indication of the quality of the books that are being circulated. Before circulation figures have any qualitative significance for revealing the kind of reading that is being done by the patrons of a library, they must be refined so that different types of books can be given different weight. A book is not a constant unit. The content value of adult non-fiction is not equal to that of adult fiction.

The problem now becomes one of establishing some kind of weighting system on the basis of the content value of the books. But a book that fulfills a recreational value may not fill an educational one although undoubtedly there are books which combine elements of information, recreation, and culture. The relative value of subject matter in the last analysis will be determined by individual preference and the needs, interests, and literary sophistication of the community; and the estimate will not be the same for all communities nor for all individuals.

However, if the book stock is improved and circulation shows an increase, content value can be roughly measured by the direction in which the community develops. Thus if a community garden club is furnished with the best available information on plant nurture and there is a marked improvement in the appearance of the community as a result of the efforts of the members of the club, it is safe to say that the library which satisfied that interest is giving better service than one in which the information was not available.

It may be that the weighting system used to measure the content value of books at first will be crude and arbitrary; nevertheless a step in the right direction will have been taken even with the attempt. Refinement and greater accuracy will inevitably follow.

Registration. The registration of borrowers indicates the number of persons who are privileged to withdraw books for home use. This count, however, is not synonymous with the number of active borrowers, for some registrants fail to withdraw books at all.

If the library is to serve both the community and the individual something must be known concerning the needs of both. The librarian should attempt to answer such questions as:

1. What groups in the population are heavy readers?

2. What groups make little use of the libraries?
3. What types of reading are of special interest to a particular group?
4. On what subjects are the heaviest demands made?[10]

Library users can be classified according to: (1) name or registration number; (2) sex; (3) occupation; (4) age; (5) grade of student; (6) fraternal affiliation, clubs, church, etc.; (7) number of fiction and nonfiction types withdrawn; (8) Dewey class number of types withdrawn.

By the use of a spot map showing the location of registered borrowers the extent and direction of the library's penetration is indicated.[11] The spot map reveals what classes of people have library cards and leads the way to an investigation of why other classes stay away.

Book Collection. Most recent pronouncements on public library standards include the provision of "a broad collection of books on a wide range of subjects," based on the expectation of varied needs and interests within the community.[12] The standard because of its indefiniteness necessitates certain supplementing if the ability of a library to fulfill it is to be assessed. Thus in order to undertake an evaluation of service potentialities as indicated by book collection, it is necessary to devise a measuring instrument. Something more than a mere measure of size is desirable, for a patently large book stock in itself offers no guarantee of high qualitative standards.[13]

A primary analysis of the book stock would be in terms of adult-juvenile and fiction-non-fiction. But for more careful study, a more elaborate breakdown would be necessary.

Wight and Carnovsky in their study of Westchester County, New York, employed a book-list, the *Standard Catalogue*, whose volumes are selected objectively enough to have equal application in libraries with common ends to be used as a test of the quality of the *adult non-fiction* stock.[14]

Many of the titles may have substitutes. But if a library fails to have available a large proportion of the starred items, in all probability it is falling short of offering the quality of service which would be possible with the provision of such titles.

A similar instrument used by the same persons to test the quality of the *reference* service must be supplemented by an evaluation of the resourcefulness of the personnel, for a library that fails to make available the tools which have been devised as short cuts and first aids in reference service is falling short of providing one of the essentials for the highest type of such service. How extensive such provision should be must depend to a great extent on local demands.[15] The measuring instrument used to evaluate the *periodical* collection was based upon *Walters' Periodicals* for the small library.[16]

The value of these lists used to measure adult non-fiction, reference, and periodicals lies principally in the clues which they offer as to the gaps that exist in the collections and the direction in which future expenditures should be made.

An approach from a more positive aspect has been developed by the Sub-committee on Measuring Reference Service of the American Library Association. A study was conducted under the auspices of this committee in nine libraries of various sizes and wide geographical distribution to determine the number of questions and types of questions asked at the information desk.[17] From entries of the books most frequently found to contain the desired answers to reference questions, a list of titles was compiled to supplement the list of reference books most used in Boston branches. Such a list is particularly valuable because it is based on known need rather than conjecture.

Both aspects of the maintenance of the book stock in a library, book buying, and book elimination should base their technique upon expressed need.[18] Through careful notation of the number and kinds of questions asked, the number of requests for a particular volume, careful analysis of the predominant community interests, a continuous study of book lists, and current book reviews the librarian can intelligently decide upon what will be the most valuable addition to the book stock. Older books must justify their tenancy in the open shelves on the same basis.

An important factor that must be taken into consideration is the presence of other libraries in the community. A survey was conducted in an eastern city recently, to determine what other book supplies were available and how large these other supplies were. By means of the information gathered through the survey the library was able to improve its service by eliminating as much duplication as possible by co-operating with these other book stocks and to direct its expenditure toward rounding out community needs.

Service. Public library service in the last analysis is to be measured in terms of satisfied borrowers. The modern librarian has no interest in books that stay on the shelf. His task is to get books into circulation. A book in circulation may not necessarily mean an idea in somebody's head, but it is as close to the consummation as the librarian's services can get.[19]

The modern librarian must be prepared to satisfy the needs of a reading public which demands information on every subject from how to feed guppies to the fundamental social and economic problems of the day. He must be able to answer these questions by directing the reader to the right material.

But how is the modern librarian to determine the result of directing a reader's attention to a particular volume? He can do this first by maintaining a record of the questions asked by individual borrowers. To determine satisfaction in terms of service he must not only maintain a record as to the number and kinds of questions asked and the time required in answering them but must also follow up the initial request by making inquiries as to the results of answering particular requests. With an adequate staff certain members of it can be responsible for individual borrowers on repeated occasions. Comparisons should be made between different reactions. The human element involved naturally makes a vast difference in the answers made in each case so it is preferable to investigate as large a number of cases as possible.[20]

The ratio of questions asked to questions satisfactorily answered will serve then as a partial measure of the quality of service in terms of satisfaction, and an analysis of the time consumed will give a further basis for a study of the adequacy of replies and the efficiency of staff members. But the librarian is faced with still another side to this service question. Are not the answers to some questions more valuable than others as measured in terms of social consequences? To the satisfaction of what kinds of demands should energy be directed?

What is the relative value in terms of social consequences of concentrating effort upon opening the world of books to the unlettered rather than satisfying the needs of those whose appetite for books has been already sharpened in the educational or experiential processes? Is it more profitable socially to provide escape through reading for those faced with serious problems or is it best to discover what those problems are and direct the readers' attention to the kind of reading material which will throw light upon them?

The solution of these problems is not simple. Their answers will be decided largely by underlying social and philosophical values. And the library which improves its service on the basis of expressed needs enters this field of values when it decides what needs it is most important to fill with available resources.

MEASURES OF EFFORT AND COST

The library that sets for its measurement unit the satisfaction of expressed need becomes more than a place to house books. Such a library must be manned by a competent, alert, intelligent, and adequate staff. The size of this staff and the proportion of the library's budget which must be expended on salary will be determined in part on the number of requests for information and guidance in purposeful reading which is demanded in a given library. A continuous record of the number of requests of both types can be used as a guide to determine how large the professional staff should be.

No fixed proportion can prevail between the numbers of professional and clerical workers, nor between the amounts which are to be expended for salaries and books. This will vary both according to the relative concentration of the demands and the size of the library.[21] The professional staff should be adequate to give competent reading guidance at all hours. The adequacy of this staff is one test for the quality of service.

Library service requires the support of the taxpayer. Continued support must come through wise expenditure of funds. One way of testing the wisdom of expenditures is through the installation of a cost accounting system which shows unit costs for the comparative analysis of similar types of services at approximately uniform standards of quality.

MEASUREMENT OF EFFICIENCY

Reduction of expenditures to a unit basis allows certain conclusions to be drawn as to the efficiency of performance. In an analysis of the expenditures of an institution the most commonly expressed units are: (1) expenditures per capita of the population served; (2) expenditures per registered borrower; (3) expenditures per volume circulated.

On the evidence of the expenditures alone there is no indication of whether a high unit figure represents a high quality of service which is worth the amount expended, or on the other hand whether it indicates extravagance, inefficient operation, or an administrative unit not well suited to the function served. Conversely, a low figure may represent relatively efficient service or a paucity in the specialized service of the library such as a trained staff, sufficient reference facilities, and purchase of new books or failure of the library to provide comfortable quarters. For the nature of the library service is such that unit figures cannot be reduced beyond certain limits without impairing the quality of the product.[22] Data on unit expenditure must be interpreted in the light of the amount and quality of the service provided.

Efficiency of book buying activities might be measured by comparing quality of the book collection as measured by some of the devices suggested above, with the size of the collection. "Circulation per volume" has a similar significance.

CONCLUSIONS AND PROSPECTS

Three phases of library performance seem adaptable to measurement—at least in part: circulation, book stock, and service. The standards suggested by the American Library Association and the State Education Department of New York provide a rather objective basis of measuring the quantitative aspects of the first two activites. Techniques have also been developed in library surveys for roughly determining the quality of the book stock. Measurement of the third activity, service, is still in a highly experimental stage, but seems to offer the greatest promise of development in the near future, provided that library objectives can be definitely formulated; for of all the levels of measurement, it comes closest to a determination of the actual *results* which the library is accomplishing.

FOOTNOTES

[1] "Standards for Public Libraries," *Bulletin of the American Library Association,* November, 1933. A more detailed enumeration of objectives will be found in "A National Plan for Libraries," *Bulletin of the American Library Association,* February, 1935.
[2] A. S. Cutter, "Measurements in School Library Service," *Bulletin of the American Library Association,* February, 1937.
[3] "Standards for Public Libraries," *Bulletin of the American Library Association,* November, 1933, and *Minimum Standards of Service of Public Libraries of New York State* (University of the State of New York, State Education Department).
[4] An arrangement is now being worked out among the American Library Association, the United States Bureau of Education, and a number of state library agencies for the co-operative collection of uniform statistics.
[5] "Statistical Data and Their Use in the College Library," *Bulletin of the American Library Association,* April, 1936.
[6] Wilson and Wight, *County Library Service in the South* (University of Chicago Press, 1935).
[7] Wight and Carnovsky, *A Study of Library Service in Westchester County, New York* (American Library Association, 1936), p. 35.
[8] *Op. cit.,* p. 81.
[9] *Op. cit.,* p. 84.
[10] Wight and Carnovsky, *op. cit.*
[11] Quigley and Marcus, *Portrait of a Library* (Appleton-Century, 1936), p. 84.
[12] Wight and Carnovsky, *op. cit.*
[13] It must be emphasized that evaluating the book *collection* is a very different problem from evaluating *circulation.* In the former case we are judging the capacity of the collection to meet demands upon it. In the latter, we are appraising the demands themselves—that is, the reading tastes of the community.
[14] Wight and Carnovsky, *op. cit.*
[15] *Op. cit.,* p. 67.
[16] *Op. cit.,* p. 20.
[17] "Annual Report of the American Library Association," *Bulletin of the American Library Association,* May, 1936, p. 403.
[18] Quigley and Marcus, *Portrait of a Library.*
[19] Bryson, "Can We Afford to Read Books?" *Survey Graphic,* May, 1936, p. 327.
[20] Quigley and Marcus, *Portrait of a Library.* p. 107.
[21] "Annual Report of the American Library Association," *Bulletin of the American Library Association,* May, 1936, p. 761.
[22] Wight and Carnovsky, *op. cit.,* p. 99.

ABOUT THE AUTHORS—While serving as executive director of the International City Manager's Association, Clarence E. Ridley's contributions to city management included the development of standards of measurement for municipal services, the *Municipal Year Book,* the development of a series of comprehensive manuals used for training officials already on the job, and the initiation of the Management Information Service designed to provide advice on municipal problems to subscribing cities.

Ridley was born in Michigan in 1891, received a B.S. at the University of Michigan in 1914, spending the next four years as assistant engineer at Flint, Michigan. There followed a two year period of service as city engineer and water superintendent at Port Arthur, Texas. In 1921 he was awarded a masters degree in economics and public administration at Columbia University and then spent four years as city manager of Bluefield, West Virginia. He subsequently studied public administration at Syracuse University and was awarded his Ph.D. in 1927. He was the first choice for the executive directorship of the International City Managers' Association when its first full-time paid official was engaged and served in this capacity from 1929 until his retirement in 1957.

For the biographical sketch on Herbert A. Simon, see p. 14.

Measuring Performance in a Special Library

by Paul Wasserman

In this piece the essential task of measurement is seen as the development of clear cut and measurable goals. The specific problem of measuring library service when it exists only to support the requirements of the overall organization is considered in detail. A central thesis is that no standards can assess the individual administrator or the contribution of his work, other than those which involve the language and the logic of the program he directs.

There is an interesting definition making the rounds about administrative functions (including measurement of performance). It's said to be "like a blind man, in a dark room, groping around for a black cat that isn't there." It's true—this measurement issue *is* difficult, it *is* elusive, it *is* frustrating and nobody has all the answers. Why then measure or even try to measure? Primarily, perhaps, because there is no other equally rational criterion for evaluating performance. If the special library is really an active agency in any institution which strives to attain a set of realistic goals, inevitably its accomplishment must be demonstrated, its utility assessed and its reason for existence endorsed. Without demonstrable, visible proof of its attainment using an acceptable managerial-type yardstick, the library (this department which defies accounting responsibility because it cannot be subjected to a break-even analysis) becomes an inevitable target of cost-conscious managements which wield that frightening instrument of internal destruction—the budget-cutting scalpel.

It *is* most difficult to measure and assess the company library for here is a department that produces no tangible, clear-cut identifiable product. Instead, its traffic is in ideas, absolutely the most nebulous of all the components that comprise a company's final product. From a purely economic standpoint, how does one calculate the "value-added" of so elusive, so intangible a raw material as facts that shape decisions and ideas that generate ultimate action? But the problem is not unique—it is also faced by the public relations department, by advertising, by research and by every other functional facility in industry which cannot demonstrate its end product in concrete and tangible terms.

Defining Purposes And Goals

First there must be purpose. Without a clearly conceived rationale for its existence, the library in industry is on shaky ground. The library is only one of many agencies in a larger complex. As the total organization strives to achieve its goals, so the internal agencies reflect these goals in a program of activities aimed at achieving these total objectives. How does one determine objectives?

In some situations, this is easier than in others. The best illustration of single-minded purposeful activity I know is reflected in the story of the lady shoplifter who frequented a popular priced Chicago department store. Day after day she was caught and sent on her way. (This was pre-recession before violations were being prosecuted.) "Why," she was asked, "don't you try some other place? Why don't you go to another store for a change?" "Go somewhere else?" she asked witheringly, "Go somewhere else? Where else could I get such bargains?"

A library must be a purposeful activity. Why is there a library in the organization? Why and how was the library begun? What exactly is the library's role? How does the library's purpose mesh into the total organization's goals? Perhaps the most striking difference among special libraries is the number of different ways in which these questions can be answered in different organizations. And rightly so, since the library program grows out of, supports and fosters the total program of the organization in which it functions. The types of organizations are legion, and each effective library program will be tailored to the specifications of the parent organization.

One thing is certain. Until the objectives of any

SOURCE: Reprinted from Paul Wasserman, "Measuring Performance in a Special Library—Problems and Prospects," *Special Libraries*, 49 (Oct., 1958), pp. 377–382, by permission of the Special Libraries Association. Originally presented before the Business Division, June 12, 1958, at the 49th SLA Convention in Chicago, Illinois.

library are clearly and unequivocally set out, ultimate assessment or evaluation of its performance is impossible. Who is to decide the library's role? A very frequent pattern is for the librarian to formulate the goals. Ideally, however, the process of formulating objectives is one in which all of the interested parties play a distinct role—company officials, professional staff, library users and non-users, in fact everyone who controls the technical functions of the library as well as everyone for whom the library is intended. Goals are usually neither simple nor readily identifiable. Library goals may change as total organizational goals change. Frequently, the objectives of the librarian will differ from management or from users or both, and unless differences are reconciled fruitful effort is endangered.

What are some of the problems of formulating these goals? One of them is certainly that of trying to obtain agreement among everyone concerned. If there is no agreement about why the library exists, then it will surely be impossible to gain agreement about the success or failure of its performance. This means securing the facts and the points of view of all the parties at interest. Differences in points of view when the facts are once known can lead to disappointment. For example, there's a little boy of five or six who often shows up around our house before lunch. Usually he is sent along and told to return later, but one day I remember he was invited to stay for lunch. He was greatly pleased at the prospect and immediately went to the phone to call his mother for permission. While he talked with her I could see his face drop and the tone of his voice change. It was clear that he was terribly disappointed about the outcome, and when he put down the receiver he turned to us with a very dejected look and explained that "my mother said I already had my lunch."

There *may* be disappointments in getting other points of view about exactly what the library's role should be. But only after agreements on goals and criteria of success are achieved can evaluation have meaning.

Another problem is to define goals in explicit terms. Vague, general, non-specific objectives will not serve. Ultimately, the value assumptions of the library must reflect in clear and unmistakable meanings exactly what it attempts to achieve. These value assumptions must be in line with the ultimate purposes of the parent body. To say that the library will "meet the informational needs of company personnel" is not enough. Exactly what is the level, extent and type of informational need to be met—does it include research, fact finding, recreation? The operating program will be shaped in the image of the library's avowed purposes. Only as these purposes emerge in sharp, clear-cut and specific terms can a sound program be evolved.

Still another problem is the need to order the library's purposes into a hierarchy of objectives based upon the degree of their importance. Such ranking will help influence the allocation of resources to specific tasks in some order of priority. This is further complicated by the need to pursue several purposes simultaneously. For example, shall the library focus on the research needs of company personnel (reflected in abstracting, title page reviewing and the like) or shall it seek to provide facts and data on demand, or both, and if so what should be the relative degree of concentration? What is the order of importance in the organization of the several different goals? It is clear that a sound operating program cannot proceed without the understanding that grows out of an analysis of which courses of action to pursue, their relative order of priority and specific definitions of purpose in clear and unmistakable terminology.

Specifically, I am suggesting that measurement must proceed from first establishing the goals; these must be arranged into a hierarchy of broad philosophical goals at the top and then grouped below as a series of specific and limited goals, which taken all together aim toward realization of the ultimate objectives. These goals presuppose agreement amongst all who are concerned with the library—not merely the librarian. The limited objectives must be spelled out in clear, operating, functional terms.

Measurement Problems

It is only after this very difficult process of determining goals and their hierarchy has been concluded that it becomes possible to consider the instruments with which to accomplish the objectives. It is during this stage that technical expertise comes into play. For this is, in fact, a basic function of the professional—to determine the most effective means of accomplishing the agency's ultimate ends. The variables, the alternatives are many. One crucial measure of administrative talent is the way in which the librarian considers alternate means and evolves an active program or allocates his resources so as to expeditiously achieve the agreed-to aims of his program.

One point should be introduced here in setting the problem in true perspective. Measurement of library attainment is similar to measuring other types of organizational endeavors. There are differences, of course, but the problem is not unique to libraries, and it would be a mistake to review the situation as if it were. Ultimately, in measurement, there is the problem of determining what change or advantage accrues from the service. There are really two important measurement questions here. First, there is the adequacy of performance. How does performance and its results meet the organization's service needs? Second, what is the efficiency of the service? How do the results compare with the most effective use of resources? In these terms, adequacy is seem as the absolute measure of accomplishment. Efficiency is accomplishment relative to available resources.

In one sense of the term efficiency, organizational measurement is simply the sum total of the measurement of each individual's performance. Work measurement, that is the relative attainment of the individual as assessed against a standard for his function, when cumulated into an aggregate work measurement score, becomes a total measure of accomplishment. This is the logical evolution of the scientific management concept, which assesses each individual performer against a set benchmark, extended to cover a total organization. One very key element, however, is that efficiency of performance or individual and organizational work measurement are really meaningful yardsticks only as the functions which they measure contribute to the total organization's goals. Five hundred cards typed in one day is far more efficient than 400 in the same period, but unless this process is compatible with the library's purpose, efficiency is meaningless. Unless it is clear that *this* is the way to achieve the result, rather than by photographing or some alternative device, then efficiency of individual performance may be suspect.

One of the specific performance characteristics to be measured is the degree of change, or the results of the program. Exactly what change or advantage accrues to the organization due to the library service? What is the actual effect of the service on its users? Or put another way, what are the results achieved as compared to the prospects without library service?

The simplest measure is the straight tabulation of use: how many books, how many inquiries, how many bibliographies compiled and so on. Statistics is a historical and comparative yardstick in widespread use. Unfortunately, it has only limited application because we have not yet learned to equate raw numbers with qualitative accomplishment. We can report that the number of acquisitions rose 15 per cent, or that the average number of readers a day rose from 73 to 79, but until use is equated with achievement, measureable achievement, the tabulations fail to prove valuable. At this point in the development of our techniques, the nearest thing to the value indicator is the successful study or succession of case studies—detailed accounts of specific illustrations of the use of library resources including facts, reference, research, books—which functioned as the raw material or catalytic agent of tangible accomplishment in the organization. Finally, a device must be developed that will rate varying types of effort and provide a scale against which to measure results.

Measurement is of course simplest when statistics of activity are available or accessible. When statistical data is less accessible, then modified working standards apply. In really obscure areas there are usually general rules of thumb. As it becomes more possible to sharpen definitions of objectives in very specific terms and as statistical facts governing activity become available, standards evolve to more exact specifications.

There are really many different ways of measuring. It may be recalled, for example, that there are various ways of estimating the weight of a pig. One is to look at the pig and make a guess of it. Another one consistent with the scientific method was suggested in this manner: one should obtain a plank, an oak plank of precise length, 16 feet; balance that across a sharp edge until it is perfectly balanced; put the pig on the end of the plank and then on the other end pile rocks; when the plank comes up to a perfectly horizontal position so that by measurement it is shown to be perfectly horizontal one estimates the weight of the rocks and he then knows how heavy the pig is.

Another way of looking at measurement is as a marketing problem—that is, if we conceive of library service primarily as library use. Here we are concerned with what is the market opportunity. Who are the library's clientele and what are the dimensions of this potential group? The distinction between prospects and users is eliminated—the difference between fruitful and unfruitful users is accentuated. In marketing, such a procedure would call for reasonably complicated techniques employing the arrangement of customers geographically, checking against directories and credit sources, delineation of sales territories and the like. In special library service within an organization these procedures are unnecessary. Rosters of personnel are available; the market is geographically pinpointed. Assessments of potential and active accounts can be based upon organizational values of productivity, hierarchy, and so forth. Product lines (reference services, abstract bulletin and the like) and distribution channels (telephone service, periodical routing) can be evolved in response to the pressures and needs of the market. This is simply another way of ordering the problem of achieving maximum accomplishment within any given set of resources and another way of assessing effectiveness of performance along rational line.

Another problem in measurement is terminology. Terminological difference leads to all kinds of confusion as the following story proves. A certain plumber wrote to the Health Bureau in New York saying that he had been using hydrochloric acid with great success. The Bureau wrote back saying hydrochloric acid was extremely efficacious but left a noxious residue, and so he replied saying he was glad they agreed with him. They wrote again using similar language, and he replied back saying he was still glad they agreed with him, so they wrote again saying "Don't use hydrochloric acid; it eats hell out of the pipes!"

Measurement implies relationships. That is, to measure is to relate something to a standard and to determine by observation what the degree of effectiveness or completeness is. In measuring the "effectiveness" of a library exactly what and how much is being reviewed must be specified. If by effectiveness we mean that every question asked in the library is answered, then performance is a function of number of times succeeded. Nebulous questions like "Is this a good library or an effective library?" can never be resolved. The real problem of measurement is less one of attaining the right answers than it is of asking the right questions. This is old hat to any librarian who knows almost instinctively that the most important step in solving a problem is to state the problem correctly or ask the right question.

Another of the problems of measuring special library performance is the heterogeneous nature of the enterprise. If it is clear that the library program must be shaped to maintain consistency with the objectives of its parent organization, because of the myriad forms, types and purposes of these organizations, it is very doubtful that outside the organization guidelines can be of much use.

At this point I must confess that it is virtually impossible to treat measurement without alluding to standards. In the public library, and even the university library, national bodies may devise usable broad performance benchmarks which may have local applicability. Even these standards are vague, general and strongly modified in each institution to conform to the local situation. Perhaps their greatest utility lies in demonstrating to trustees and officials that professional guidelines do exist, so that local effort may be patterned after the ideal recommendations. For business organizations, however, even if outside standards were derived, the same pressures for conforming, which exist in public and university bodies, would not be true here. The ultimate question in a company or other non-educational organization is the measure of performance—the value added by the library to the company's idea or product flow. This objective, I suspect, may never quite be equated with a library service value scheme originating outside the organization which might propose alternative guidelines.

Still another problem of measurement is that obviously not everything is measurable. It has been suggested that we do not know the specific gravity of honesty, the atomic weight of integrity or why a silent smile often rings more decibels of emotional response than a hollow laugh. And I suspect that if we *could* measure everything, the world would be a pretty humdrum place.

Another complication arises in that often results may be readily determined, but frequently these results may not be concluded to relate to the library's goals. For example, if a research inquiry causes a two-hour study of a problem, how can it be determined that the resultant data is related to the library's goals and not, as is sometimes the case, to resolve an academic argument that arose at lunch? And again, if library use increases, provided this is a sought after goal, can it be certain that increased use stems from an improved internal library program and not from some other external pressures in the organization, such as a slackening of work in a department which provides more free time for study?

The real question here is that of determining what change or advantage accrues to the organization due to the library program. That is, what is the effect of the services on the users? This is a comparative analysis. In effect this question asks what was the result of the service as compared to what results would be without the service? The accomplishment *is* elusive. No one has yet discovered how to gage accurately and precisely the effect of an idea on a creative man or the relationship between finding the facts that spark an idea and the ultimate sale or product design, and these are the raw materials of our library craft. But conversely, unless we can find the instruments of measurement, our efforts are liable to be criticized or even dismissed as intangible and unnecessary.

Evaluating Library Service

If we attempt to review library service in the same way in which research is assessed, what do we find? Corporate research usually begins with clear-cut definitions of research objectives, technical feasibility of the work, careful market evaluation, economic justification of investment and finally a comparison of expenditure with competitive enterprise. And how often, in special libraries, do we stop short of the last two factors—economic justification of investment in the program and comparison of expenditures with libraries in comparative institutions?

Are there actually any positive universal answers here? There would appear to be at least two, anyway. First, is there in writing, in clear and specific terms, a statement of the library's fundamental goals, objectives and philosophy, with respect to its functioning in the organization? Is it understood and agreed to by all library staff, management and clientele? Does the person responsible for the library's service, by example and in active contacts within the organization of subordinates, superiors and others, support and insist upon the application of this philosophy to all levels of performance? And second, is this broad planning implemented in the actual functioning of the library in the clarification and delineation of duties, responsibilities, work movements, details, familiarity with policy by all, and all of the other standard parts of sound personnel policy?

Measuring is really a process of relating, usually by determining a numerical relationship to a generally recognized standard. Other forms of relating are also possible and profitable. But relating is not possible until concepts are defined in concrete terms. What does "effectiveness" mean in a given organization? If effectiveness is to be measured, we must narrow down what we mean by effectiveness and broaden what we mean by measure to include other forms of relating.

Unfortunately, there are no standards or other factors that can be used to assess the individual librarian or the contribution of his work other than those which involve the program he directs. The librarian applies his skills, knowledge and technology to accomplish the results and achieve the objectives which are tied to the organization's goals and needs. While we are concerned with his leadership, without which the library resources are non-productive, we are concerned only with his leadership as one factor which brings the library toward attainment of its purpose. The total effort is the real concern.

Now it will be noted that I have raised many more questions than I have answered in the course of my remarks. In the measurement of organizational performance, there are, unfortunately, more questions than there are answers. There is the story told of old emeritus professor Abercrombie at a fine old eastern university who spent the better part of a black moonless night in the village imbibing. On his way home he had a little trouble finding his lodging. He finally approached a house that looked like his but he wasn't quite sure; it was dark and his vision was blurred. He strode up to the door and knocked. After a long wait, the housekeeper came to the door and said "Yes?" Professor Abercrombie peered at her and said, "Is this the home of Professor Abercrombie?" The housekeeper blinked out at him and said, "Why . . . why aren't you Professor Abercrombie?" The old professor drew himself up to his full height and bellowed "Madam, I am here tonight to ask the questions, not to answer them!" In final defense, I can only reiterate more feebly than Professor Abercrombie, I am here to ask the questions, not to answer them.

ABOUT THE AUTHOR—Paul Wasserman, see p. 40

IV
MANAGEMENT OF RESOURCES

The administrative process functions only when the policy ends of the organization are pursued through the application of its resources: people, authority, financial capability and control, and communications systems. In this view, these elements are the crucial determinants in the attainment of goals, and the task of the administrator is seen as his capacity to manage these resources with wisdom, imagination and courage. The writings will clearly reflect the fact that such capability stems far more from understanding than manipulative capacity and that in each of these elements, both formal and informal processes are at work.

Authority

Seemingly, authority relationships are clear and unambiguous and consequently they are often too simply viewed. But actually the matter is infinitely more complex. While the basic elements are the manifestations of behavior between those holding supervisor and subordinate positions, these are conditioned by many factors such as the nature of the organization, the personalities and working style of the individuals and the professional orientations of the work group. Because bureaucracies are characterized by hierarchical arrangement, clear understanding of both the formal and informal authority relations of organizations, form part of the essential equipment of the sophisticated library administrator.

The Theory of Authority
by Chester I. Barnard

> *While Barnard was not necessarily advocating more democratic forms of administration, his analysis challenges the traditional view of authority. In essence, he identifies the fact that it is those supervised who control the situation. His classic statement clarifies the subtleties of the relationships and as a consequence he is among the more important writers who forced a reassessment of traditional assumptions about authority acceptance. This view engendered much of the behavioral research about organizations by sociologists, psychologists and other students of organizations during the last three decades.*

In this chapter we consider a subject which in one aspect relates to the "willingness of individuals to contribute to organizations," the element of organization presented in the preceding chapter; and in a second aspect is the most general phase of the element "communication."

I. THE SOURCE OF AUTHORITY

If it is true that all complex organizations consist of aggregations of unit organizations and have grown only from unit organizations, we may reasonably postulate that, whatever the nature of authority, it is inherent in the simple organization unit; and that a correct theory of authority must be consistent with what is essentially true of these unit organizations. We shall, therefore, regard the observations which we can make of the actual conditions as at first a source for discovering what is essential in elementary and simple organizations.

I

Now a most significant fact of general observation relative to authority is the extent to which it is ineffective in specific instances. It is so ineffective that the violation of authority is accepted as a matter of course and its implications are not considered. It is true that we are sometimes appalled at the extent of major criminal activities; but we pass over very lightly the universal violations, particularly of sumptuary laws, which are as "valid" as any others. Even clauses of constitutions and statutes carrying them "into effect," such as the Eighteenth Amendment, are violated in wholesale degrees.

Violation of law is not, however, peculiar to our own country. I observed recently in a totalitarian state under a dictator, where personal liberty is supposed to be at a minimum and arbitrary authority at a maximum, many violations of positive law or edict, some of them open and on a wide scale; and I was reliably informed of others.

Nor is this condition peculiar to the authority of the state. It is likewise true of the authority of churches. The Ten Commandments and the prescriptions and prohibitions of religious authority are repeatedly violated by those who profess to acknowledge their formal authority.

These observations do not mean that all citizens are lawless and defy authority; nor that all Christians are godless or their conduct unaffected by the tenets of their faith. It is obvious that to a large extent citizens are governed; and that the conduct of Christians is substantially qualified by the prescriptions of their churches. What is implied is merely that which specific laws will be obeyed or disobeyed by the individual citizen are decided by him under the specific conditions pertinent. This is what we mean when we refer to individual responsibility. It implies that which prescriptions of the church will be disobeyed by the individual are determined by him at a given time and place. This is what we mean by moral responsibility.

It may be thought that ineffectiveness of authority in specific cases is chiefly exemplified in matters of state and church, but not in those of smaller organizations which are more closely knit or more concretely managed. But this is not true. It is surprising how much that in theory is authori-

---
SOURCE: Reprinted by permission of the publishers from Chester I. Barnard THE FUNCTIONS OF THE EXECUTIVE Cambridge, Mass.: Harvard University Press, Copyright, 1938, by the President and Fellows of Harvard College; 1966 by Grace F. Noera Barnard.

tative, in the best of organizations in practice lacks authority—or, in plain language, how generally orders are disobeyed. For many years the writer has been interested to observe this fact, not only in organizations with which he was directly connected, but in many others. In all of them, armies, navies, universities, penal institutions, hospitals, relief organizations, corporations, the same conditions prevail—dead laws, regulations, rules, which no one dares bury but which are not obeyed; obvious disobedience carefully disregarded; vital practices and major institutions for which there is no authority, like the Democratic and Republican parties, not known to the Constitution.

II

We may leave the secondary stages of this analysis for later consideration. What we derive from it is an approximate definition of authority for our purpose: Authority is the character of a communication (order) in a formal organization by virtue of which it is accepted by a contributor to or "member" of the organization as governing the action he contributes; that is, as governing or determining what he does or is not to do so far as the organization is concerned. According to this definition, authority involves two aspects: first, the subjective, the personal, the *accepting* of a communication as authoritative, the aspects which I shall present in this section; and, second, the objective aspect—the character in the communication by virtue of which it is accepted—which I present in the second section, "The System of Coördination."

If a directive communication is accepted by one to whom it is addressed, its authority for him is confirmed or established. It is admitted as the basis of action. Disobedience of such a communication is a denial of its authority for him. Therefore, under this definition the decision as to whether an order has authority or not lies with the persons to whom it is addressed, and does not reside in "persons of authority" or those who issue these orders.

This is so contrary to the view widely held by informed persons of many ranks and professions, and so contradictory to legalistic conceptions, and will seem to many so opposed to common experience, that it will be well at the outset to quote two opinions of persons in a position to merit respectful attention. It is not the intention to "argue from authorities"; but before attacking the subject it is desirable at least to recognize that prevalent notions are not universally held. Says Roberto Michels in the monograph "Authority" in the *Encyclopaedia of the Social Sciences*,[1] "Whether authority is of personal or institutional origin it is created and maintained by public opinion, which in its turn is conditioned by sentiment, affection, reverence or fatalism. Even when authority rests on mere physical coercion it is *accepted*[2] by those ruled, although the acceptance may be due to a fear of force."

Again, Major-General James G. Harbord, of long and distinguished military experience, and since his retirement from the Army a notable business executive, says on page 259 of his *The American Army in France*:[3]

> A democratic President had forgotten that the greatest of all democracies is an Army. Discipline and morale influence the inarticulate vote that is instantly taken by masses of men when the order comes to move forward—a variant of the crowd psychology that inclines it to follow a leader, but the Army does not move forward until the motion has "carried." "Unanimous consent" only follows cooperation between the *individual* men in the ranks.

These opinions are to the effect that even though physical force is involved, and even under the extreme condition of battle, when the regime is nearly absolute, authority nevertheless rests upon the acceptance or consent of individuals. Evidently such conceptions, if justified, deeply affect an appropriate understanding of organization and especially of the character of the executive functions.

Our definition of authority, like General Harbord's democracy in an army, no doubt will appear to many whose eyes are fixed only on enduring organizations to be a platform of chaos. And so it is—exactly so in the preponderance of attempted organizations. They fail because they can maintain no authority, that is, they cannot secure sufficient contributions of personal efforts to be effective or cannot induce them on terms that are efficient. In the last analysis the authority fails because the individuals in sufficient numbers regard the burden involved in accepting necessary orders as changing the balance of advantage against their interest, and they withdraw or withhold the indispensable contributions.

III

We must not rest our definition, however, on general opinion. The necessity of the assent of the individual to establish authority *for him* is inescapable. A person can and will accept a communication as authoritative only when four conditions simultaneously obtain: (*a*) he can and does understand the communication; (*b*) *at the time of his decision* he believes that it is not inconsistent with the purpose of the organization; (*c*) *at the time of his decision* he believes it to be compatible with his personal interest as a whole; and (*d*) he is able mentally and physically to comply with it.

(*a*) A communication that cannot be understood *can* have no authority. An order issued, for example, in a language not intelligible to the recipient is no order at all—no one would so regard it. Now, many orders are exceedingly difficult to understand. They are often necessarily stated in general terms, and the persons who issued them could not themselves apply them under many conditions. Until interpreted they have no meaning. The recipient either must disregard them or merely do anything in the hope that that is compliance.

Hence, a considerable part of administrative work consists in the interpretation and reinterpretation of orders in their application to concrete circumstances that were not or could not be taken into account initially.

(*b*) A communication believed by the recipient to be incompatible with the purpose of the organization, as he understands it, could not be accepted. Action would be frustrated by cross purposes. The most common practical example is that involved in conflicts of orders. They are not rare. An intelligent person will deny the authority of that one which contradicts the purpose of the effort as *he* understands it. In extreme cases many individuals would be virtually paralyzed by conflicting orders. They would be literally unable to comply—for example, an employee of a water system ordered to blow up an essential pump, or soldiers ordered to shoot their own comrades. I suppose all experienced executives know that when it is necessary to issue orders that will appear to the recipients to be contrary to the main purpose, especially as exemplified in prior habitual practice, it is usually necessary and always advisable, if practicable, to explain or demonstrate why the appearance of conflict is an illusion. Otherwise the orders are likely not to be executed, or to be executed inadequately.

(*c*) If a communication is believed to involve a burden that destroys the net advantage of connection with the organization, there no longer would remain a net inducement to the individual to contribute to it. The existence of a net inducement is the only reason for accepting *any* order as having authority. Hence, if such an order is received it must be disobeyed (evaded in the more usual cases) as utterly inconsistent with personal motives that are the basis of accepting any orders at all. Cases of voluntary resignation from all sorts of organizations are common for this sole reason. Malingering and intentional lack of dependability are the more usual methods.

(*d*) If a person is unable to comply with an order, obviously it must be disobeyed, or, better, disregarded. To order a man who cannot swim to swim a river is a sufficient case. Such extreme cases are not frequent; but they occur. The more usual case is to order a man to do things only a little beyond his capacity; but a little impossible is still impossible.

IV

Naturally the reader will ask: How is it possible to secure such important and enduring coöperation as we observe if in principle and in fact the determination of authority lies with the subordinate individual? It is possible because the decisions of individuals occur under the following conditions: (*a*) orders that are deliberately issued in enduring organizations usually comply with the four conditions mentioned above; (*b*) there exists a "zone of indifference" in each individual within which orders are acceptable without conscious questioning of their authority; (*c*) the interests of the persons who contribute to an organization as a group result in the exercise of an influence on the subject, or on the attitude of the individual, that maintains a certain stability of this zone of indifference.

(*a*) There is no principle of executive conduct better established in good organizations than that orders will not be issued that cannot or will not be obeyed. Executives and most persons of experience who have thought about it know that to do so destroys authority, discipline, and morale.[4] For reasons to be stated shortly, this principle cannot ordinarily be formally admitted, or at least cannot be professed. When it appears necessary to issue orders which are initially or apparently unacceptable, either careful preliminary education, or persuasive efforts, or the prior offering of effective inducements will be made, so that the issue will not be raised, the denial of authority will not occur, and orders will be obeyed. It is generally recognized that those who least understand this fact—newly appointed minor or "first line" executives—are often guilty of "disorganizing" their groups for this reason, as do experienced executives who lose self-control or become unbalanced by a delusion of power or for some other reason. Inexperienced persons take literally the current notions of authority and are then said "not to know how to use authority" or "to abuse authority." Their superiors often profess the same beliefs about authority in the abstract, but their successful practice is easily observed to be inconsistent with their professions.

(b) The phrase "zone of indifference" may be explained as follows: If all the orders for actions reasonably practicable be arranged in the order of their acceptability to the person affected, it may be conceived that there are a number which are clearly unacceptable, that is, which certainly will not be obeyed; there is another group somewhat more or less on the neutral line, that is, either barely acceptable or barely unacceptable; and a third group unquestionably acceptable. This last group lies within the "zone of indifference." The person affected will accept orders lying within this zone and is relatively indifferent as to what the order is so far as the question of authority is concerned. Such an order lies within the range that in a general way was anticipated at time of undertaking the connection with the organization. For example, if a soldier enlists, whether voluntarily or not, in an army in which the men are ordinarily moved about within a certain broad region, it is a matter of indifference whether the order be to go to A or B, C or D, and so on; and goings to A, B, C, D, etc., are in the zone of indifference.

The zone of indifference will be wider or narrower depending upon the degree to which the inducements exceed the burdens and sacrifices which determine the individual's adhesion to the organization. It follows that the range of orders that will be accepted will be very limited among those who are barely induced to contribute to the system.

(c) Since the efficiency of organization is affected by the degree to which individuals assent to orders, denying the authority of an organization communication is a threat to the interests of all individuals who derive a net advantage from their connection with the organization, unless the orders are unacceptable to them also. Accordingly, at any given time there is among most of the contributors an active personal interest in the maintenance of the authority of all orders which to them are within the zone of indifference. The maintenance of this interest is largely a function of informal organization. Its expression goes under the names of "public opinion," "organization opinion," "feeling in the ranks," "group attitude," etc. Thus the common sense of the community informally arrived at affects the attitude of individuals, and makes them, as individuals, loath to question authority that is within or near the zone of indifference. The formal statement of this common sense is the fiction that authority comes down from above, from the general to the particular. This fiction merely establishes a presumption among individuals in favor of the acceptability of orders from superiors, enabling them to avoid making issues of such orders without incurring a sense of personal subserviency or a loss of personal or individual status with their fellows.

Thus the contributors are willing to maintain the authority of communications because, where care is taken to see that only acceptable communications in general are issued, most of them fall within the zone of personal indifference; and because communal sense influences the motives of most contributors most of the time. The practical instrument of this sense is the fiction of superior authority, which makes it possible normally to treat a personal question impersonally.

The fiction[5] of superior authority is necessary for two main reasons:

(1) It is the process by which the individual delegates upward, or to the organization, responsibility for what is an organization decision—an action which is depersonalized by the fact of its coördinate character. This means that if an instruction is disregarded, an executive's risk of being wrong must be accepted, a risk that the individual cannot and usually will not take unless in fact his position is at least as good as that of another with respect to correct appraisal of the relevant situation. Most persons are disposed to grant authority because they dislike the personal responsibility which they otherwise accept, especially when they are not in a good position to accept it. The practical difficulties in the operation of organization seldom lie in the excessive desire of individuals to assume responsibility for the organization action of themselves or others, but rather lie in the reluctance to take responsibility for their own actions in organization.

(2) The fiction gives impersonal notice that what is at stake is the good of the organization. If objective authority is flouted for arbitrary or merely temperamental reasons, if, in other words, there is deliberate attempt to twist an organiza-

tion requirement to personal advantage, rather than properly to safeguard a substantial personal interest, then there is a deliberate attack on the organization itself. To remain outside an organization is not necessarily to be more than not friendly or not interested. To fail in an obligation intentionally is an act of hostility. This no organization can permit; and it must respond with punitive action if it can, even to the point of incarcerating or executing the culprit. This is rather generally the case where a person has agreed in advance in general what he will do. Leaving an organization in the lurch is not often tolerable.

The correctness of what has been said above will perhaps appear most probable from a consideration of the difference between executive action in emergency and that under "normal" conditions. In times of war the disciplinary atmosphere of an army is intensified—it is rather obvious to all that its success and the safety of its members are dependent upon it. In other organizations, abruptness of command is not only tolerated in times of emergency, but expected, and the lack of it often would actually be demoralizing. It is the sense of the justification which lies in the obvious situation which regulates the exercise of the veto by the final authority which lies at the bottom. This is a commonplace of executive experience, though it is not a commonplace of conversation about it.[6]

II. THE SYSTEM OF COÖRDINATION

Up to this point we have devoted our attention to the subjective aspect of authority. The executive, however, is predominantly occupied not with this subjective aspect, which is fundamental, but with the objective character of a communication which induces acceptance.

I

Authority has been defined in part as a "character of a communication in a formal organization." A "superior" is not in our view an authority nor does he have authority strictly speaking; nor is a communication authoritative except when it is an effort or action of organization. This is what we mean when we say that individuals are able to exercise authority only when they are acting "officially," a principle well established in law, and generally in secular and religious practice. Hence the importance ascribed to time, place, dress, ceremony, and authentication of a communication to establish its official character. These practices confirm the statement that authority relates to a communication "in a formal organization." There often occur occasions of compulsive power of individuals and of hostile groups; but authority is always concerned with something *within* a definitely organized system. Current usage conforms to the definition in this respect. The word "authority" is seldom employed except where formal organization connection is stated or implied (unless, of course, the reference is obviously figurative).

These circumstances arise from the fact that the character of authority in organization communications lies in the *potentiality of assent* of those to whom they are sent. Hence, they are only sent to contributors or "members" of the organization. Since all authoritative communications are official and relate only to organization action, they have no meaning to those whose actions are not included within the coöperative system. This is clearly in accord with the common understanding. The laws of one country have no authority for citizens of another, except under special circumstances. Employers do not issue directions to employees of other organizations. Officials would appear incompetent who issued orders to those outside their jurisdiction.

A communication has the presumption of authority when it originates at sources of organization information—a communications center—better than individual sources. It loses this presumption, however, if not within the scope or field of this center. The presumption is also lost if the communication shows an absence of adjustment to the actual situation which confronts the recipient of it.

Thus men impute authority to communications from superior positions, provided they are reasonably consistent with advantages of scope and perspective that are credited to those positions. This authority is to a considerable extent independent of the personal ability of the incumbent of the position. It is often recognized that though the incumbent may be of limited personal ability his advice may be superior solely by reason of the advantage of position. This is the *authority of position*.

But it is obvious that some men have superior ability. Their knowledge and understanding regardless of position command respect. Men impute authority to what they say in an organization for this reason only. This is the *authority of leadership*. When the authority of leadership is combined with the authority of position, men who have an established connection with an organization generally will grant authority, accepting orders far outside the zone of indifference. The confidence engendered may even make compliance an inducement in itself.

Nevertheless, the determination of authority remains with the individual. Let these "positions" of authority in fact show ineptness, ignorance of conditions, failure to communicate what ought to be said, or let leadership fail (chiefly by its concrete action) to recognize implicitly its dependence upon the essential character of the relationship of the individual to the organization, and the authority if tested disappears.

This objective authority is only maintained if the positions or leaders continue to be adequately informed. In very rare cases persons possessing great knowledge, insight, or skill have this adequate information without occupying executive position. What they say ought to be done or ought not to be done will be accepted. But this is usually personal advice at the risk of the taker. Such persons have influence rather than authority. In most cases genuine leaders who give advice concerning organized efforts are required to accept positions of responsibility; for knowledge of the applicability of their special knowledge or judgment to concrete *organization* action, not to abstract problems, is essential to the worth of what they say as a basis of organization authority. In other words, they have an organization personality, as distinguished from their individual personality,[7] commensurate with the influence of their leadership. The common way to state this is that there cannot be authority without corresponding responsibility. A more exact expression would be that objective authority cannot be imputed to persons in organization positions unless subjectively they are dominated by the organization as respects their decisions.

It may be said, then, that the maintenance of objective authority adequate to support the fiction of superior authority and able to make the zone of indifference an actuality depends upon the operation of the system of communication in the organization. The function of this system is to supply adequate information to the positions of authority and adequate facilities for the issuance of orders. To do so it requires commensurate capacities in those able to be leaders. High positions that are not so supported have weak authority, as do strong men in minor positions.

Thus authority depends upon a coöperative personal attitude of individuals on the one hand; and the system of communication in the organization on the other. Without the latter, the former cannot be maintained. The most devoted adherents of an organization will quit it, if its system results in inadequate, contradictory, inept orders, so that they cannot know who is who, what is what, or have the sense of effective coördination.

This system of communication, or its maintenance, is a primary or essential continuing problem of a formal organization. Every other practical question of effectiveness or efficiency—that is, of the factors of survival—depends upon it. In technical language the system of communication of which we are now speaking is often known as the "lines of authority."

II

It has already been shown[8] that the requirements of communication determine the size of unit organizations, the grouping of units, the grouping of groups of unit organizations. We may now consider the controlling factors in the character of the communication system as a system of objective authority.

(*a*) The first is that *channels of communication should be definitely known.* The language in which this principle is ordinarily stated is, "The lines of authority must be definitely established." The method of doing so is by making official appointments known; by assigning each individual to his position; by general announcements; by organization charts; by educational effort, and most of all by habituation, that is, by securing as much permanence of system as is practicable. Emphasis is laid either upon the position, or upon the persons; but usually the fixing of authority is made both to positions and, less emphatically, to persons.

(*b*) Next, we may say that *objective authority requires a definite formal channel of communication to every member of an organization.* In ordinary language this means "everyone must report to someone" (communication in one direction) and "everyone must be subordinate to someone" (communication in the other direction). In other words, in formal organizations everyone must have definite formal relationship to the organization.[9]

(*c*) Another factor is that *the line of communication must be as direct or short as possible.*

This may be explained as follows: Substantially all formal communication is verbal (written or oral). Language as a vehicle of communication is limited and susceptible of misunderstanding. Much communication is necessarily without preparation. Even communications that are carefully prepared require interpretation. Moreover, communications are likely to be in more general terms the more general—that is, the higher—the position. It follows that something may be lost or added by transmission at each stage of the process, especially when communication is oral, or when at each stage there is combination of several communications. Moreover, when communications go from high positions down they often must be made more specific as they proceed; and when in the reverse direction, usually more general. In addition, the speed of communication, other things equal, will be less the greater the number of centers through which it passes. Accordingly, the shorter the line the greater the speed and the less the error.

How important this factor is may be indicated by the remarkable fact that in great complex organizations the number of levels of communication is not much larger than in smaller organizations. In most organizations consisting of the services of one or two hundred men the levels of communication will be from three to five. In the Army the levels are: President, (Secretary of War), General, Major-General, Brigadier-General, Colonel, Major, Captain, Lieutenant, Sergeant, men—that is, nine or ten. In the Bell Telephone System, with over 300,000 working members, the number is eight to ten.[10] A similar shortness of the line of communication is noteworthy in the Catholic Church viewed from the administrative standpoint.

Many organization practices or inventions are used to accomplish this end, depending upon the purpose and technical conditions. Briefly, these methods are: The use of expanded executive organizations at each stage; the use of the staff department (technical, expert, advisory); the division of executive work into functional bureaus; and processes of delegating responsibility with automatic coördination through regular conference procedures, committees for special temporary functions, etc.

(*d*) Another factor is that, in principle, *the complete line of communication should usually be used.* By this is meant that a communication from the head of an organization to the bottom should pass through every stage of the line of authority. This is due to the necessity of avoiding conflicting communications (in either direction) which might (and would) occur if there were any "jumping of the line" of organization. It is also necessary because of the need of interpretation, and to maintain responsibility.[11]

(*e*) Again, the *competence of the persons serving as communication centers, that is, officers, supervisory heads, must be adequate.* The competence required is that of more and more *general* ability with reference to the work of the entire organization the more central the office of communication and the larger the organization. For the function of the center of communication in an organization is to translate incoming communications concerning external conditions, the progress of activity, successes, failures, difficulties, dangers, into outgoing communications in terms of new activities, preparatory steps, etc., all shaped according to the ultimate as well as the immediate purposes to be served. There is accordingly required more or less mastery of the technologies involved, of the capabilities of the personnel, of the informal organization situation, of the character and status of the subsidiary organizations, of the principles of action relative to purpose, of the interpretation of environmental factors, and a power of discrimination between communications that can possess authority because they are recognizably compatible with *all* the pertinent conditions and those which will not possess authority because they will not or cannot be accepted.

It is a fact, I think, that we hardly nowadays expect individual personal ability adequate to positional requirements of communication in modern large-scale organization. The limitations of individuals as respects time and energy alone preclude such personal ability, and the complexity of the technologies or other special knowledge involved make it impossible. For these reasons each major center of communication is itself organized, sometimes quite elaborately. The immediate staff of the executive (commanding officer), consisting of deputies, or chief clerks, or adjutants, or auxiliaries with their assistants, constitute an executive unit of organization only one member of which is perhaps an "executive," that is, occupies the *position* of authority; and the technical matters are assigned to staff departments or organizations of experts. Such staff departments often are partly "field" departments in the sense that they directly investigate or secure information on facts or conditions external to the organizations; but in major part in most cases they digest and translate information from the field, and prepare the plans, orders, etc., for transmission. In this capacity they are advisory or adjutant to the executives. In practice, however, these assistants have the function of semi-formal advice under regulated conditions to the organizations as a whole. In this way, both the formal channels and the informal organization are supplemented by intermediate processes.

In some cases the executive (either chief or some subordinate executive) may be not a person but a board, a legislature, a committee. I know of no important organizations, except some churches and some absolute governments in which the highest objective authority is not lodged in an *organized* executive group, that is, a "highest" unit of organization.

(*f*) Again, *the line of communication should not be interrupted during the time when the organization is to function.* Many organizations (factories, stores) function intermittently, being closed or substantially so during the night, Sundays, etc. Others, such as army, police, railroad systems, telephone systems, never cease to operate. During the times when organizations are at work, in principle the line of authority must never be broken; and practically this is almost, if not quite, literally true in many cases. This is one of the reasons which may be given for the great importance attached to hereditary succession in states, and for the elaborate provision that is made in most organizations (except possibly small "personal" organizations) for the temporary filling of offices automatically during incapacity or absence of incumbents. These provisions emphasize the non-personal and communication character of organization authority, as does the persistent emphasis upon the *office* rather than the *man* that is a matter of indoctrination of many organizations, especially those in which "discipline" is an important feature.

The necessity for this is not merely that specific communications cannot otherwise be attended to. It is at least equally that the *informal* organization disintegrates very quickly if the formal "line of authority" is broken. In organization parlance, "politics" runs riot. Thus, if an office were vacant, but the fact were not known, an organization might function for a considerable time without serious disturbance, except in emergency. But if known, it would quickly become disorganized.

(*g*) The final factor I shall mention is that *every communication should be authenticated.* This means that the person communicating must be known actually to occupy the "position of authority" concerned; that the position includes the type of communication concerned—that is, it is "within its authority"; and that it actually is an authorized communication from this office. The process of authentication in all three respects varies in different organizations under different conditions and for different positions. The practice is undergoing rapid changes in the modern technique, but the principles remain the same. Ceremonials of investiture, inaugurations, swearing-in, general orders of appointment, induction, and introduction, are all essentially appropriate methods of making known who actually fills a position and what the position includes as authority. In order that these *positions* may function it is often necessary that the filling of them should be dramatized, an essential process to the creation of authority *at the bottom*, where only it can be fundamentally—that is, it is essential to inculcate the "sense of organization." This is merely stating that it is essential to "organization loyalty and solidarity" as it may be otherwise expressed. Dignifying the superior position is an important method of dignifying *all* connection with organization, a fact which has been well learned in both religious and political organizations where great attention to the subjective aspects of the "membership" is the rule.

This statement of the principles of communication systems of organizations from the viewpoint of the maintenance of objective authority has necessarily been in terms of complex organizations, since in a simple unit organization the concrete applications of these principles are fused. The principles are with difficulty isolated under simple conditions. Thus, as a matter of course, in unit organizations the channels of communication are known, indeed usually obvious; they are definite; they are the shortest possible; the only lines of authority are complete lines; there is little question of authentication. The doubtful points in unit organization are the competence of the leader, never to be taken for granted even in simple organizations; and whether he is functioning when the organization is in operation. Yet as a whole the adequately balanced maintenance of these aspects of simple leadership is the basis of objective authority in the unit organization, as the maintenance of the more formal and observable manifestations of the same aspects is the basis of authority in the complex organizations.

III. RECONCILIATION WITH LEGALISTIC CONCEPTIONS

Legalistic conceptions of authority, at least somewhat different from those we have presented, seem to have support in the relations between superior and subsidiary organizations. A corporate organization, for example, is subject to the law of the state. Is not this a case where authority actually does come down from the top, from the superior organizations? Only in exactly the same sense that individuals accept objective authority, as we have described it. A subsidiary or dependent organization must accept law to give law its authority. Units of organization, integrated complexes of organization, and dependent organizations, make and must make the subjective decision of authority just as individuals do. A corporation may and often does quit if it cannot obey the law and still have a net reason for existence. It is no more able to carry out an unintelligible law than an individual, it can no more do the impossible than an individual, it will show the same inability to conform to conflicting laws as the individual. The only difference between subsidiary, or dependent, unit and group organizations and individuals is that the denial of authority can be made directly by the individual, and either directly or indirectly by the unit, group, or dependent or subsidiary complex. When it is direct, the effect of the law or order upon the organization as a whole is in point; when it is indirect the effect is on the individuals of whose efforts the whole is made up. Thus no complex can carry out a superior order if its members (either unit organizations or individuals) will not enable it to do so. For example, to order by law working conditions which will not be accepted by individual employees, even though the employer is willing, is futile; its authority is in fact denied. The employees quit, then the organization ends.

But in the final analysis the differences are not important, except occasionally in the concrete case. The subsidiary organization in point of fact derives most of its authority for most of its action from its own "members" individually. They may quit if they do not accept the orders, no matter what the "ultimate" authority; and no absolute or external authority can compel the necessary effort beyond a minimum insufficient to maintain efficient or effective organization performance. An important effect of the ascription of legalistic origin of a part of the formal authority of subsidiary and independent organizations has been its obscuring of the nature of the real authority that governs the greater part of the coöperative effort of such organizations.

There is, however, a considerable quantitative difference in the factor of informal organization, that is, the factor of public opinion, general sentiment. This is not a difference of principle, but merely one of the relationship of the size of the informal organization relative to the individual or formal group. A strong individual can resist the domination of opinion if it is confined to a small number; but rarely if there is in question the opinion of an overwhelming number, actively and hostilely expressed. Now the size of any subsidiary organization is small compared with the informal organization that permeates the State; and this wide informal organization will usually support "law and order" regardless of merits if the question at issue is minor from its point of view. The pressure on the subjective attitude of individuals or on that of subsidiary or dependent organizations is strong ordinarily to induce acceptance of law in an "orderly" society.

But this informal support of objective authority of the State depends upon essentially the same principles as in the case of ordinary organizations. Inappropriateness of law and of government administration, lack of understanding of the ultimate basis of authority, indifference to the motives governing individual support, untimely or impossible legislation, as is well known destroy "respect for law and order," that is, destroy objective political authority. In democracies the normal reaction is to change law and administration through political action. But when majorities are unable to understand that authority rests fundamentally upon the consent of minorities as well as of majorities, or when the system is autocratic or absolute, the liquidation of attempted tyranny is through revolution or civil war. Authority lies always with him to whom it applies. Coercion creates a contrary illusion; but the use of force *ipso facto* destroys the authority postulated. It creates a new authority, a new situation, a new objective, which is granted when the force is accepted. Many men have destroyed all authority as to themselves by dying rather than yield.

At first thought it may seem that the element

of communication in organization is only in part related to authority; but more thorough consideration leads to the understanding that communication, authority, specialization, and purpose are all aspects comprehended in coördination. All communication relates to the formulation of purpose and the transmission of coördinating prescriptions for action and so rests upon the ability to communicate with those willing to coöperate.

Authority is another name for the willingness and capacity of individuals to submit to the necessities of coöperative systems. Authority arises from the technological and social limitations of coöperative systems on the one hand, and of individuals on the other. Hence the status of authority in a society is the measure both of the development of individuals and of the technological and social conditions of the society.

FOOTNOTES

[1] New York: Macmillan.
[2] Italics mine.
[3] Boston: Little, Brown and Co., 1936.
[4] Barring relatively few individual cases, when the attitude of the individual indicates in advance likelihood of disobedience (either before or after connection with the organization), the connection is terminated or refused before the formal question arises.

It seems advisable to add a caution here against interpreting the exposition in terms of "democracy," whether in governmental, religious, or industrial organizations. The dogmatic assertion that "democracy" or "democratic methods" are (or are not) in accordance with the principles here discussed is not tenable. As will be more evident after the consideration of objective authority, the issues involved are much too complex and subtle to be taken into account in *any* formal scheme. Under many conditions in the political, religious, and industrial fields democratic processes create artificial questions of more or less logical character, in place of the real questions, which are matters of feeling and appropriateness and of informal organization. By oversimplification of issues this may destroy objective authority. No doubt in many situations formal democratic processes may be an important element in the maintenance of authority, i.e., of organization cohesion, but may in other situations be disruptive, and probably never could be, in themselves, sufficient. On the other hand the solidarity of some coöperative systems (General Harbord's army, for example) under many conditions may be unexcelled, though requiring formally autocratic processes.

Moreover, it should never be forgotten that authority in the aggregate arises from *all* the contributors to a coöperative system, and that the weighting to be attributed to the attitude of individuals varies. It is often forgotten that in industrial (or political) organizations measures which are acceptable at the bottom may be quite unacceptable to the substantial proportion of contributors who are executives, and who will no more perform their essential functions than will others, if the conditions are, to them, impossible. The point to be emphasized is that the maintenance of the contributions necessary to the endurance of an organization requires the authority of *all* essential contributors.

[5] The word "fiction" is used because from the standpoint of logical construction it merely explains overt acts. Either as a superior officer or as a subordinate, however, I know nothing that I actually regard as more "real" than "authority."

[6] It will be of interest to quote a statement which has appeared since these lines were written, in a pamphlet entitled "Business—Well on the Firing Line" (No. 9 in the series "What Helps Business Helps You," in *Nation's Business*). It reads in part: "Laws don't create Teamplay. It is not called into play by law. For every written rule there are a thousand unwritten rules by which the course of business is guided, which govern the millions of daily transactions of which business consists. These rules are not applied from the top down, by arbitrary authority. They grow out of actual practice—from the bottom up. They are based upon mutual understanding and compromise, the desire to achieve common ends and further the common good. They are observed *voluntarily*, because they have the backing of experience and common sense."

[7] See Chapter VII, p. 88.
[8] Chapter VIII, "The Structure of Complex Formal Organizations," beginning at p. 106.
[9] In some types of organizations it is not unusual, however, for one person to report to and to be subordinate to two or three "superiors," in which case the functions of the superiors are defined and are mutually exclusive in principle.
[10] Disregarding the corporate aspects of the organization, and not including board of directors.
[11] These by no means exhaust the considerations. The necessity of maintaining personal prestige of executives as an *inducement to them* to function is on the whole an important additional reason.

ABOUT THE AUTHOR—Chester I. Barnard (1886-1961) was one of those modern rarities who, having achieved success as a practicing executive in the business world, then shifted over to theoretical and conceptual pursuits and achieved even greater eminence as a theorist in the world of academia. Forced to fend for himself at an early age, Barnard put himself through school, receiving a B.A. in 1906 from Mt. Hermon College in Massachusetts. He withdrew after three years of graduate study at Harvard, not because of financial difficulty—but because of a basic disagreement over a course prerequisite. In 1909 he went to work for American Telephone and Telegraph Company as a translator and rose rapidly through the ranks to become the youngest chief executive in the Bell Telephone System in 1927, a position he held for twenty-one years. From this base Barnard applied his talents to a wide range of fields. He was especially active in voluntary organizations, serving as president of the USO during its developmental period, 1942–1945. He coauthored with Robert Oppenheimer the policy-forming State Department Report on International Control of Atomic Energy.

Overshadowing these efforts were his contributions to the literature of management, taking the form of his first work *The Functions of the Executive* (1938). Since that time the volume has become a classic of organizational theory. Barnard was first to treat the organization as a decision-making system and to recognize the importance of such aspects of it as communication and the informal organization. His concepts were distilled not only out of common sense and experience but through extensive study on his own initiative and close contact with Harvard University where he often lectured. His work has had an important influence upon the contemporary generation of organization scholars and most notably upon Herbert Simon who acknowledges Barnard's contribution to his own writing.

Authority Structure and Organizational Effectiveness

by Amitai Etzioni

Etzioni postulates that if goals and authority structure in an organization are incompatible, goals will be modified in such a way that means become part of the goals themselves. He suggests further that in professional organizations, traditional staff and line concepts will be reversed so that staff officers carry out the major goal orientated activities of the organization while line officials perform the more traditional service role equated with staff.

The overriding issue is the degree to which libraries adhere to the authority structure of the bureaucratic or the professional type organization. The crucial question is the degree to which the professionals tolerate final authority over their professional functions and the substance of their work from the administrative hierarchy. For the consequence would ultimately be to undermine the goal for which the organization was established, and this would inevitably endanger the conditions under which professionals can properly function. The final effect would thereby be a disorientation of the organization and of its professional class as well as a reduction in the relevance of the organization's program and service.

Organizations are co-ordinated human efforts to realize specific goals. But in all organizations there is eternal strain which limits the scope and degree to which organizational goals can be attained. A major interest of the student of organizations is to determine the conditions under which attainment of such goals is promoted or hindered. One important factor determining the degree of goal realization is the nature of the authority structure of the organization. If the orientation of this structure is compatible with the organizational goals, the probability that these goals will be achieved is greater than in organizations where this is not the case.[1] In bureaucracies where the goals and the authority structure are incompatible, it is likely that the goals will be modified. Goals originally considered secondary may become of primary importance in the organization's activity; means may become ritualized, that is, conceived of as parts of the goals themselves; and activities which were considered illegitimate when the organization was established may become part of the goal structure.[2]

This paper is devoted to a discussion of this issue in terms of three different perspectives on the authority structure of complex organizations: (a) the relationships between staff and line, (b) the role of the organizational head, and (c) the functions of the authority center.

AUTHORITY STRUCTURE AND INSTITUTIONALIZATION OF GOALS

The study of organizations has proceeded mainly on two levels.[3] Studies are devoted either to case descriptions and analysis or to high-level generalizations and speculations on organizations in general. There is relatively little systematic examination on the middle level, as, for example, the study of various types of organizations.[4] Propositions believed to hold for all organizations have to be tested separately for each organizational type. Such examinations might show that assumed generalizations hold true only for certain types of organizations.[5] In this paper several such propositions will be scrutinized in an attempt to show that they cannot be applied to professional organizations. The three major generalizations to be discussed are as follows: (a) In the ultimate analysis staff authority is subordinated to line authority. (b) Organizational units, especially the organization as a whole, are therefore headed by managers and not by experts. (c) Organiza-

SOURCE: Reprinted from Amitai Etzioni, "Authority Structure and Organizational Effectiveness," *Administrative Science Quarterly*, 4 (June, 1959), pp. 43-67, by permission of the publisher and the author.

tions have one and only one ultimate center of authority.

Staff and Line

There are two approaches to the relationship between staff and line. According to one approach the staff has no direct authority whatsoever. It advises the executive (line authority) on what action to take. The staff in itself does not issue orders and is not responsible for action. According to the second approach the staff, while advising the line on various issues, also takes responsibility for limited areas of activity.[6] In spite of important differences between the two approaches both agree that staff authority is subordinate to line authority, and they tend to identify line with managers or administrators and staff with experts and specialists. While it is obvious that there are some staff functions which are not carried out by experts and that there are some experts among the line personnel, it is suggested that there is a high correlation between line and managers and between staff and experts.

What is the relation between these two groups and the organizational goals? Managers are generally considered as those who have the major (line) authority because they direct the major goal activity. Experts deal only with means, with secondary activities. Therefore it is functional for them to have none, or only limited (staff), authority.

Manager and expert are the two major terms used in this paper. Therefore a few lines will be devoted here to some conceptual clarification. Managers and experts may be differentiated from four points of view: (a) role structure, (b) personality, (c) background, mainly in terms of educational and occupational experience, and (d) normative orientations.

The *role* of the expert is to create and institutionalize knowledge. The role of the manager is to integrate (create or maintain) organizational systems or subsystems from the point of view of the institutional goals and needs.[7] The expert typically deals with symbols and materials (although there are many who disagree with this point of view).[8] The manager deals with people. The two role types require different *personality* types. The expert who has intensive knowledge in a limited area, tends to have a restricted perspective. The manager has extensive, though limited, knowledge of many areas, and the resulting broad perspective is essential for his role.

Experts are committed to abstract ideas and therefore tend to be unrealistic, whereas managers are more practical. Managers are skilled in human relations; experts are temperamental.[9]

Managers and experts differ in *background*. Experts usually have higher educations than managers and tend to enter their first job at a later age and at higher initial salaries. They often start at relatively high positions in the hierarchy but are limited in the range of their mobility. Managers enter their first job at a younger age, with less education, and at lower positions, but they move upward faster than the experts and some of them eventually get higher than any expert.[10] Whereas many experts remain more or less restricted to the same organizational functions, the typical manager is assigned to a large variety of tasks in what is called the process of broadening.

Managers' *orientations* differ considerably from those of experts. Managers are more committed or loyal to their specific organization than are experts.[11] Experts are often primarily oriented toward their professional reference and membership groups. While managers are often committed to the organization's particular goals, experts are committed to the scientific and professional ethos regardless of the particular needs and goals of their institution.[12]

Obviously though there is a high correlation among these four variables, they are not inevitably associated. Two major mechanisms explain how the correlation is maintained. First of all there is *selective recruitment*. People with managerial personalities and background are recruited to managerial roles, and those with the personalities and education of experts tend to enter staff positions. The second mechanism is *role adaptation*. People who enter roles which are initially incompatible with their personalities often adjust to their new roles. Whether they had latent tendencies to act in accordance with the new role or whether the new role meant deep changes in their personality structure need not to be discussed here. In both cases the actors will adjust to their new roles. In such adjustment the process of broadening produces managers from initial specialists; a parallel process produces semiexperts from managers who entered managerial roles in professional organizations. These processes explain in part also why there is no perfect correlation among the four variables discussed above. For example, people with the background of experts may fulfill managerial roles.

Institutional Heads

It is one of the basic characteristics of bureaucratic organizational structures to have one and only one center of authority. This is often vested in the role of the head of the organization. He is seen as the top of the chain of command, as the ultimate authority in the internal structure and as ultimately responsible for the organizational activity relative to external structures such as the community and the government. Institutional heads are often symbols of identification for members and employees of the organization.[13] Customers and other outsiders, such as the personnel of other organizations, tend to identify an organization with the organizational head. Institutional heads are in a strategic position to influence the implementation of proclaimed organizational goals.[14]

All organizations need to integrate their various activities into one operating whole.[15] This function is partially fulfilled by the organizational head. Since integrating is a managerial role, it follows that managers and not experts will head organizations. We shall return to this point.

Organizations Are Monocratic

As noted above, bureaucratic organizations have one center of authority.[16] This is one of the important characteristics which differentiate bureaucracies from feudal regimes.[17] This does not mean that all activities are directed from one center. Authority is often delegated. Organizations can be compared with respect to the degree to which authority is centralized. But even in decentralized organizations there is one center of authority where final decisions are made and conflicts among lower authorities can be resolved. The monocratic structure is one of the more important reasons why bureaucracies are considered as the most effective form of organization. Such a structure enables the top central authority, which is often strongly committed to the organizational goals, to retain control of much of the organizational activity.

On the basis of existing theory, then, one would hold three expectations: (a) Managers have the major (line) authority whereas experts deal with secondary activities, and therefore have only limited (staff) authority. (b) Institutional heads have to be manager oriented because their role is a role of system integration. If an expert-oriented person were to hold this role, the system would be alienated from its goals and might even eventually disintegrate because some functions would be overemphasized while others would be neglected. (c) Organizational goals can be maintained more effectively in organizations with one center of authority.

The rest of this paper will be devoted to an attempt to show that these generalizations apply to some organizations but not to others.

THE PRIVATE BUSINESS: AN AFFIRMATION

The organizational goal of private business is to make profits. The major means are production and exchange. While experts deal with various aspects of the production and exchange process, that is, with means such as engineering, labor relations, quality control, and marketing, the manager is the one who co-ordinates the various activities in such a way that the major organizational goal will be maximized. Profit making is his responsibility. That seems to be one of the reasons why modern corporations prefer to have people with administrative experience as top executives rather than former specialists such as engineers. In a study of the chief executives of American industry in 1950 administration was found to be the principal occupation of 43.1 per cent; finance the field of only 12.4 per cent; 11.8 per cent were defined as entrepreneurs; and only 12.6 per cent had been engineers.[18] People with scientific background such as research workers are even less likely to become heads of private business. Only about 4 per cent of the presidents of American corporations had such a background.[19] Corporations have different types of heads at different periods in their life cycle. But the heads are usually not experts at any period.

In general the goals of private business are consistent with managerial orientations. The economic goals of the organization and the bureaucratic orientations of the managerial role have in common the orientation toward rational use of means and development of rational procedures to maximize goals which are considered as given.[20] The social and cultural conditions that support modern economic activities also support modern administration.

When people with strong expert orientations take over the managerial role of the institutional head, a conflict between the organizational goals and the expert orientation can be predicted. The case described in *Executive Suite*, where the design engineer with strong craftsman commitments takes over the presidency of a private corporation, should be considered atypical.[21] Usually commitment to professional values runs counter to the economic values of the organization.[22]

Homans reports an interesting case in which the influence of the experts was greater than it is in most corporations.[23] He discusses an electrical equipment company, which was owned, managed, and staffed by engineers. Management, which was in the hand of manager-oriented engineers, suffered from pressure toward professional values from the design engineers. The design engineers in the eyes of management were "prima donnas" and "temperamental," terms often used by management to describe experts. Furthermore, they were indifferent "to the general welfare of the company", that is, to profit making, as "shown by their lack of concern with finance, sales, and the practical needs of the consumer and by their habit of spending months on an aspect of design that had only theoretical importance." This caused considerable tension between the managerial and expert-oriented groups, tension to which this company was especially sensitive because of its high dependence on expert work and the special structure of ownership. A power struggle resulted, ending with a clearer subordination of the design engineers (staff) to the managerial engineers (line). This was mandatory "if the company was to survive and increase its sales," as Homans puts it. The treasurer (a nonexpert in this context) became the most influential member of the new management. In short, in a corporation where the experts had a strong power position, the existence of the organization was threatened, considerable internal tension was generated, and finally the organizational structure was changed toward a more usual structure with a clearer subordination of the experts. In other words, the organizational authority structure was made more compatible with the goals of the organization. Manager orientations and the institutional goals of private business seem to match. When an expert orientation dominates, this is dysfunctional to the organizational purposes.

To sum up, the study of private business as an organization can be seen as an affirmation of the three generalizations of organizational theory presented above. Managers direct the major goal activities and have the major authority; experts deal with means and are in minor and subordinated authority positions. The organizational heads are manager oriented, and there is only one internal center of authority. All business organizations studied, including such decentralized organizations as General Motors and Bata seem to have one center of authority.[24]

PROFESSIONAL ORGANIZATIONS: A NEGATIVE CASE

The rest of this paper will be devoted to an examination of the relations between goals and authority structure in professional organizations from the three points of view discussed above. An attempt will be made to show that the three generalizations do not apply and therefore can no longer be seen as valid generalizations of organizational theory. The assumption of universal applicability seems to have been made initially because organizational theory was developed mainly on the basis of observation and analysis of governmental and private business bureaucracies. Although it cannot be demonstrated here, we would like to suggest that it is doubtful whether the generalizations apply to political organizations such as parties and trade unions, to religious organizations such as churches and monasteries, and to many other organizations.[25]

Professional Organizations–Definition

Professional organizations are organizations whose major goal is to institutionalize knowledge and to sustain its creation. Knowledge is created in research organizations (such as the Rand Corporation), spread in schools, created and spread in universities, and applied in hospitals.[26] Knowledge is also created and institutionalized in organizations other than professional ones, but only in professional organizations are these functions the predominant goals.

Staff and Line in Professional Organizations

We would like to suggest that in professional organizations the staff-expert line-manager correlation, insofar as such a correlation exists at all, is reversed. Although manager orientations are suitable for the major goal activities in private business, the major goal activity of professional organizations is, in its nature, expertness. Managers in professional organizations are in charge of secondary activities; they administer *means* to the major activity carried out by experts. In other words, if there is a staff-line relationship at all, experts constitute the line (major authority) structure and managers the staff. Managers give advice about the economic and administrative implications of various activities planned by the professionals. The final internal decision is, functionally speaking, in the hands of the various professionals and their decision-making bodies. The professor decides what research he is going to undertake and to a large degree what he is going to teach; the physician determines what treatment should be given to the patient.

Administrators may raise objections to planned activities. They may point out that a certain drug is too expensive or that a certain teaching policy will decrease the number of students in a way that endangers the financing of a university. But functionally the professional is the one to decide whether to accept these limitations on his discretion and whether the administrator is right in bringing up his limited point of view. It is of interest to note that some of the complaints usually launched against experts in private business are launched against administrators in professional organizations: they are said to lose sight of the major function of the organization in pursuit of their specific limited responsibilities. Experts in private business are sometimes criticized as being too committed to science, craftsmanship, and abstract ideas; administrators in professional organizations are deplored because they are too committed to their specialties—efficiency and economy.

Many of the sociological characteristics of experts and managers in private business cannot be found in professional organizations. Experts enter professional organizations younger and at lower positions (namely, as students, research assistants, or interns) than managers do. Although the range of mobility of managers is usually relatively limited, a professional is more likely to reach the top position of the institutional head.

In private business overinfluence by experts threatens the realization of organizational goals, sometimes even the organization's existence. In professional organizations overinfluence by the administration is considered as ritualization of means, undermining the goals for which the organization has been established, and endangering the conditions under which knowledge can be created and institutionalized (as for instance, academic freedom).

Institutional Heads—A Role Conflict

The role of the institutional head in professional organizations constitutes a dilemma. It is a typical case of institutionalized role conflict.[27] On the one hand the role should be in the hand of an expert in order to ensure that the orientation of the head will match organizational goals. An expert at the head of the authority structure will mean that expert activity is recognized as the major goal activity and that the needs of professionals will be more likely to receive understanding attention. On the other hand organizations have functional requisites that are unrelated to their specific goal activity.[28] Organizations have to obtain funds to finance their activities, recruit personnel to staff the various functions, and allocate the funds and personnel which have been recruited. Organizational heads must know how to keep the system integrated by giving the right amount of attention and funds to the various organizational needs, including secondary needs.[29] An expert may endanger the integration of the professional organization by over-emphasizing the major goal activity, neglecting secondary functions, and lacking skill in human relations. Thus the role of head of professional organizations requires two incompatible sets of orientations, personal characteristics, and aptitudes. If the role is performed by either a lay administrator or a typical expert, considerable organizational strain can be expected.

So far the organizational needs have been discussed. The severity of the dilemma is increased because of the motivational structure of typical experts. Most successful experts are not motivated to become administrators. Some would refuse any administrative role, including that of university president or hospital chief, because of their commitment to professional values and professional groups and because they feel that they would not be capable of performing the administrative role successfully. Even those professionals who would not reject the distinguished and powerful role of organizational head avoid the administrative roles that are training grounds and channels of mobility to these top positions. Thus many academicians refuse to become deans and try to avoid if possible the role of department chairman. Those who are willing to accept administrative roles are often less committed to professional values than their colleagues.[30] The same can be said about administrative appointments in hospitals. Thus, for instance, in the mental hospital studied by Stanton and Schwartz the role of administrative psychiatrist is fulfilled at the beginning of the training period. It is considered an undesirable chore that must be endured before turning to the real job. Psychiatrists who complete their training tend to withdraw to private practice. From other studies, especially those of state mental hospitals, it appears that those who stay are often less competent and less committed to professional values than those who leave.[31]

Institutional Heads—Some Functional Solutions

There are various functional solutions to this dilemma. By far the most widespread one is the rule of the semiexpert. The semiexpert is a person who combines an expert background and education with a managerial personality and role. Goal as well as means activities seem to be handled best when such a person is the institutional head. Because of his personal characteristics he is likely to be skilled in handling the needs and requests of his former colleagues as well as those of the administrative staff.

There are two major sources of semiexperts. One is the experts themselves. Some professionals feel that they have little chance of becoming outstanding experts in their field. Often the same people find that they are relatively more skilled in administrative activities. Thus they gravitate toward administrative jobs by participating on committees and taking minor administrative roles, and some eventually become top administrators. In contrast to the popular belief, most university presidents seem to be former experts. Wilson found that out of the 30 universities he studied 28 had presidents who had been professors, albeit none a very eminent scholar.[32] It seems that academicians who are inclined to take administrative jobs or are organization oriented, not only publish less in quantity and quality after they have entered administrative positions, but also tended to publish less before they accepted such jobs.

Of the heads of mental hospitals cited in a recent study, 74.2 per cent are physicians. Although there is no study on their professional eminence as compared to that of private practitioners, there is reason to believe that the heads of mental hospitals do not include the most successful psychiatrists.[33] Only about 22 per cent of the heads of general hospitals are physicians.[34] Where these are full-time jobs, the statement made about the heads of mental hospitals seems to apply here also. Although about 90 per cent of elementary and high-school principals have been teachers,[35] it has been pointed out that a poor teacher who occupies himself with administrative action is more likely to be promoted than a successful, child-focused teacher.[36]

The second source of semiexperts is special training agencies. In recent years there has been a movement toward developing more and more specialized administrators, such as hospital administrators and educational administrators, and lately it has been suggested that research administrators be trained. Twelve per cent of heads of short-term general hospitals, 10.9 per cent of long-term general hospitals, and 6.5 per cent of mental hospitals are graduates of such courses.[37] Moreover, a considerable number of teachers return to universities to take courses in administrative education before they become school principals.

The advantages of specialized administrators over lay administrators are obvious. They are trained for their peculiar role and have considerable understanding of the organization in which they are about to function before they enter it. They are sensitized to the special tension of working with professionals, and they share some of their professional values. On the other hand they are less prepared for their role than semiexperts from the first source, who have a deeper indoctrination with professional values, command more professional respect, and have more social ties with professionals than the semiexperts produced in university courses. It is therefore of interest that the first type of semiexpert is much more common than the second type. This may be due to the fact that such administrators have been trained only recently and that it takes time for these new trainees to work their way up in the various organizations. But it could also be explained partially by the fact that the first type is more functional.

A third way of solving the dilemma is found when an expert board nominates and supervises a lay administrator who runs the organization. Thus expert and managerial goals are taken into account, yet segregated with reference to individuals. The arrangement, which is the way most proprietary hospitals are run, seems to function relatively more effectively when those who are on the board constitute a large proportion of the professional staff of the organization. The major reason why this arrangement seems to be quite rare is that it means that the professionals must take financial and administrative responsibilities for the organization—responsibilities which they often are not in a position or not inclined to take.

It is important to distinguish between an institutional head and an institutional figurehead. Since the institution needs legitimation in the eyes of the personnel, clients, and community, and this legitimation has to be of a professional type, there is a tendency to nominate as institutional head a well-known expert. Although this means in some cases that an expert takes over control of the organization, much more frequently it means that an expert is lost and becomes a semiexpert (see the discussion of role adaptation) or that the expert is the figurehead and some other person actually has primary authority. In this analysis we are referring to the real and not the nominal institutional head.[38]

Lay Administrators

Although most professional organizations are controlled by experts or semiexperts of one type or another, some professional organizations are controlled by lay administrators. By lay administrators we mean administrators who have no training in the major goal activities of the organization. This holds for 2 out of the 30 universities studied by Wilson, for less than 10 per cent of schools, for 20.5 per cent of the mental hospitals, and for about 38 per cent of the general hospitals.[39]

The strain created by lay administrators in professional organizations has been discussed above. When the hierarchy of authority is in adverse relation to the hierarchy of values, there is always a danger that the hierarchy of values will be reversed. Of course there are many other factors which may have such a distorting influence; all that is suggested here is that lay administrators are more likely to cause strain than are other administrators.

The major function of mental hospitals is to cure the patient; however, mental hospitals are often custodial institutions which serve as places to keep the patients so that they will not endanger or disturb the society.[40] Although some custodial activities are an essential part of the means that the mental hospital has to apply in order to fulfill its therapeutic function, there is a constant danger that the means will become a major focus of its activities. Thus a mental patient will be transferred from closed to open ward, not when it is best for his recovery, but when it is most convenient for the staff or when he will be the smallest nuisance to the community if he escapes. As has been pointed out in a number of studies, the therapeutic goals seem to be what Selznick termed "precarious values."[41]

A similar strain seems to exist in some general hospitals. Overmanagement can occur when the administrator forgets that the chief purpose of the hospital is to care for the sick. Some hospitals are so bound down with "red tape" that professional care is handicapped by multiplicity of documentation, compilation of unimportant statistics and unwarranted restriction upon the discretion of the professional and technical staff.[42]

A similar distortion of the relation between goals and means seems to occur in some vocational schools.[43] These schools are established in order to train pupils in vocations which they will pursue in later years, but the predominant function of the institutions is often to keep teenagers off the street. As long as they fulfill this function, little attention is paid to the quality of the teachers, the adequacy of the equipment, and the relation between the vocations which the school teaches and those which the market can absorb.

Universities constitute a more complicated case. Whereas in the two cases discussed above the legitimate function is neglected and emphasis is put on means, here the dilemma is different. A secondary goal threatens to become the major goal. Although there is some controversy as to what constitute the primary and what the secondary goals of outstanding universities, it seems fair to conclude that a majority of the members of professional communities would see research as primary and teaching as secondary. This is well reflected in the prestige and promotion systems.[44] But there is constant danger that the university will respond to pressures to give more money and attention to teaching and less to research.[45]

There are many sources for these conflicting strains. Some values seem to be more precarious than others to begin with. Professionals themselves may generate such pressures; for, example, some physicians see in the hospital a research institution and try to refuse or to discharge uninteresting cases. The community in the form of the alumni association, the chamber of commerce, and the board of trustees is another source of these strains. But the head of the institution has a strategic position in this important institutional conflict. If he is in sympathy with the primary institutional goals, he can do much to neutralize the conflicting pressures and to mobilize the forces that support the primary institutional goals. If he himself joins those who try to give primacy to secondary goals, or ritualize means, or introduce illegitimate goals (as when, for instance, profit making becomes the primary goal of a hospital or patients who are mentally or physically ill are made to do the aides' work), the probability that the institutional goals will be distorted becomes very great indeed. Professional institutions are characterized by the fact that they cater to values which are usually upheld by the professional. Hence a lay administrator with a strong bureaucratic orientation seems to be more likely to endanger the professional goals than a semiexpert or an expert-oriented institutional head.

Center of Authority

Line and staff analysis as well as bureaucratic theory assumes that there is one major structure of authority (the line).[46] It may be very complicated and have many branches but it always has one center of authority where final decisions are made and conflicts can be resolved.[47] The main authority line is directly related to the primary goal activity of the organization and only indirectly to secondary (means) activities.

In professional organizations there seems to be no line in such a sense. This has been pointed out before, and it has been suggested that this means that professional organizations have a functional structure of authority. As Moore has pointed out, this concept is far from being a clear one.[48] It usually refers to the fact that low-level actors are subordinated to two or more authorities at a time, each authority being responsible for a limited area of action. The hospital, for instance, has been cited as an organization with two lines of authority, one professional and one administrative,[49] and therefore it is suggested that it be seen as a functional organization.

We would like to suggest that in professional organizations there are indeed two types of authority but only the nonprofessional one is structured in a bureaucratic way with a clear line and center of authority. Various department heads (office, custodians, campus police, hospital kitchen, and the like) are subordinated to the administrative director and through him (in smaller institutions, directly to) the head of the organization. This line is responsible mainly for secondary activities. Thus we suggest that in professional organizations the staff, or personnel performing secondary activities, are administrators, clerks, and laborers and that this is the only part of the organization which has a clear line structure. The professionals who conduct the major goal activity do not form an authority structure in the regular sense of the term.

As far as research is concerned, each faculty member is to a very large extent free from any direct control by superiors. This holds to a large degree for the substance of his teaching as well. The physician's absolute authority over the treatment given to his patient is a well-known fact. Teachers in elementary and secondary schools are more closely supervised than university professors. There are visits in the classrooms and prescribed textbooks. But this supervision is far more lax and limited than any line supervision in industry, for instance. It is of special interest to note that principals try to avoid as much as possible their obligation to supervise the teachers. Principals devote, according to one study, 57.7 per cent of their time to administrative work, 26.6 to clerical work, and only 13.3 to supervision.[50] In short, while there is an administrative line in professional organizations for secondary activities, there is no clear line in the major goal activities and to a large degree each professional is left to rely on his judgment, that is, he has final authority.

Of course, there are many other sources of control than line orders and direct supervision of performance. For example, a great variety of rewards and sanctions encourage conformity; informal pressures are exerted by peers and others. But most of these mechanisms function also in nonprofessional organizations in addition to supervision, so that one can say that there is less control in professional organizations than in other organizations. Moreover, as far as the major goal activity is concerned, such control does not take the form of a clear hierarchy with superiors who issue orders and require performance reports. This does not hold to the same extent for students, research assistants, and interns who have a status similar to semiprofessionals and are not part of the collegiate organizational structure.

There are three areas of activity in professional organizations: (a) major goal activities carried out by professionals and almost completely under the authority of the professional who performs the activity or directs the semiprofessionals and nonprofessionals who perform it, (b) secondary activities performed by administrators and nonprofessional personnel under their control, and (c) secondary activities performed by the professionals. The latter include writing reports, preparing statistics, participating in public relations activities, and allocating facilities. In this third area there is sometimes a clear hierarchy and administrative predominance, and therefore there is room to misunderstand the nature of the professional organization and to see the professionals as part of an administrative line structure. But as far as a hierarchy exists in this realm, it is limited to what are primarily secondary activities; as far as the main goal activities are concerned, there is considerable autonomy. In other words the professional organizations are service organizations for professionals, who follow in the organizational contexts the values which as professionals they are committed to, namely, professional autonomy and immunity.

It is of interest to note that Weber suggested that the basis of bureaucratic authority is technical knowledge.[51] Parsons distinguished two types of authority: power authority (the power of a clerk over a subordinated clerk or over a client) and authority of knowledge (the authority of the professional private practitioner over his client).[52] There seems to be a basic incompatibility between expert orientation and bureaucratic orientation. This is circumvented in private business and in some other organizations by giving the expert functional autonomy in a limited area while subordinating him in major goal activities and decisions. In professional organizations this solution would be dysfunctional to the organizational goals. Therefore a different authority structure is constructed. Professional organizations are turned into service organizations to individuals and teams of professionals. The limited lines of authority which exist are mainly devoted to secondary activities involving service personnel and the service (nonprofessional) activities of the professionals.

STAFF AND LINE IN DIFFERENT PROFESSIONAL ORGANIZATIONS

Goal Structure

Professional organizations also differ considerably from the point of view of the relationships between goals and authority structure. One important factor is the goals themselves. The creation of knowledge seems to require more institutionalization of professional values than does the spreading of knowledge. This is one reason why academic freedom is more institutionalized in universities than in other schools. The application of knowledge seems to enjoy as much, if not more, institutionalized protection than the creation of knowledge, but for different reasons. Creation requires freedom in order not to limit the inquiry. Application requires immunity in order to protect the practitioners from the consequences of unsuccessful applications. Thus from the point of view of goals, universities and hospitals are closer to the ideal type of professional organization than schools.

There are interesting differences among general and mental hospitals in this respect. The general hospital's status as a therapeutic organization is well established and therefore in general it has the required freedom and immunity. It can afford to have laymen as its head, semiprofessionals as its major personnel, and professionals imported from the outside. The mental hospital legitimation is less established for the clientele as well as for the semiprofessional staff.[53] Therefore the incorporation of the professional into the structure of the organization itself is functionally required.

Externalization versus Internalization

Another important differentiating factor is the division of labor between the professional organization and other organizations. All organizations rely to some degree for the fulfillment and regulation of some of their functions on other organizations and collectivities.[54] The point of interest here is which functions are handled by the professional organization and which are externalized. The more that professional functions are internalized, and administrative functions are externalized, the closer the organization comes to the ideal type of professional organization. Thus the school is from this perspective a highly professional organization. It has few administrative problems to begin with because it is not a total institution.[55] It relies considerably on families, community, social workers, police, and others to administer most of the nonprofessional needs of its clients. Hospitals, on the other hand, have to take care of most of the nonprofessional needs of their patients. Most of the professionals (physicians) are not part of the staff.[56] Hospitals therefore have a much higher percentage of nonprofessional staff and many more administrative problems.[57] Universities are from this viewpoint similar to schools. Boarding schools, on the other hand, are very different in their personnel structure and administrative problems because they are total institutions.[58]

Research organizations are highly professional considering their goal of creation of knowledge.[59] Their structure differs considerably in terms of the externalization versus the internalization of nonprofessional functions. Some research organizations are incorporated into university structures to a high degree, as for instance the Institute of Industrial Relations at the University of California. These research organizations usually serve mainly as service organizations to professionals (supply space, secretaries, and statistical clerks) with only a limited research policy of their own. Other research organizations are relatively more indepenpendent and have to finance their activities themselves, as for instance the Stanford Research Institute. This type usually has a stronger administrative policy.

On the other end of the continuum are research organizations that are incorporated in nonprofessional and even authoritarian organizations such as the armed forces. As several interesting studies show, there seems to be considerable confusion in the structure of these research organizations.[60] Military principles of organization and behavior are mixed with professional ones.[61] Strict observation of the protocol of the military hierarchy is demanded in some situations, and professional collegial relations are encouraged in others. The heads of many research organizations in the United States armed forces are experts or semiexperts. This can be explained in part by the fact that, although these research units are total organizations on the one hand, they rely to a large degree on other military units for supply and regulation of many of their nonprofessional needs on the other hand.[62] Thus administrative problems are minimized.

Of special interest from this point of view is a study which examines the effect of nationalization on the organizational structure of hospitals in England.[63] The study shows that, when administrative responsibilities were taken over by higher-level administrative units, the heads of single hospitals became more professionally oriented. This can be compared to the relationships between the superintendent's office and the school principal. As more administrative tasks are taken over by the superintendent, the principal can devote more time and energy to his professional function: improving the quality of teaching.

Mono versus Multiple Professions

A third factor which impinges on the balance between professionals and administrators and on the relationship between this balance and the process of goal implementation is the number of professions co-operating in one organization and their mutual attitudes. The greater the number and the stronger the tensions among the various professions, the greater is the need for a neutral administrator as final authority. The grammar school is from this point of view on one end of the continuum, with one professional group, the teachers. The university is on the other end, with a large number of professions. When there is strong rivalry among various groups of faculty, as for instance between humanities and natural sciences, a layman is often more functional as a university president than a professional. In general the university administrator functions often as an arbitrator among different professional groups (departments).[64] There is of course the danger, as in the political realm, that the administrator will create an alliance with one "party," but this seems to be rare because there are usually many small "parties" rather than two camps and alliance with one of them would not give the administrator too much help.

Hospitals are in the middle of the continuum. General hospitals are closer to the school from this point of view because they are dominated by one profession. Mental hospitals are closer to the universities because of their multiprofessional nature, with an uneasy dominance by psychiatrists. The overlapping functions of psychiatrists, clinical psychologists, psychiatric social workers, and physical therapists, as well as the different schools of treatment, make a neutral administrator and administration highly functional in some mental hospitals.

Private versus Public Organizations

One of the most important dimensions along which further study of the problems discussed here has to be developed is the question of the ownership of the professional organizations and the ways they are financed. Many professional organizations are financed partially through contributions or from tax money, and clients' fees play very different roles in the various organizations. In some cases they have no role at all; in others they are dominant criteria for action. Another aspect of the same problem is the way the professionals are rewarded. In some cases they are paid salaries, in others fees, by the organization or by the clients. These factors impinge on the relationships between the administrators and the professionals because they determine to a considerable degree who is representing the profit goal of the organization.

From the viewpoint of professional goals, the distorting potentials of a lay administrator seem to be highest in those "private" organizations where professionals are salaried. On the other hand, in those public organizations where the professionals are not salaried and the administrators represent public interests, the distorting potential may be minimized. Between these two poles exists a whole gamut of alternatives, which have yet to be explored.

CONCLUSION

The relationship between organizational goals and authority structures has been discussed from the standpoint of the influence of authority orientations on goal implementation. The application of three generalizations of administrative theory to professional organizations has been examined:

(a) It has been suggested that in professional organizations staff and line concepts, to the degree that they can be applied at all, have to be reversed. The major (line) goal activity is carried out by experts. Managers have staff functions, that is, serve the major goal activities. (b) Institutional heads are either experts, semiexperts (former experts or specialized administrators), or lay administrators. It seems that the most functional heads from the point of view of organizational goals are the semiexperts. Whether former experts or specialized administrators are preferable has to be determined by further research and experience.

Professional organizations are monocratic organizations only with regard to service activities. The authority structure of the major goal activities is highly dispersed. To a large extent the final authority over research, substance of teaching, and therapy is in the hands of the individual professional. Thus professional organizations are either service institutions to professionals who are not an integral part of the organization, or service organizations in which professionals function with a high degree of self-determination.

FOOTNOTES

[1] See J. G. March and H. A. Simon *Organizations* (New York, 1958), p. 195.

[2] Studies of police forces will illustrate this point.

[3] The terms organization and institution will be used interchangeably. In all cases the reference is to large and complex organizations which have a *formal* structure, thus excluding such social organizations as the family and the community.

[4] This point is elaborated somewhat further in the author's Industrial Sociology: The Study of Economic Organizations, *Social Research,* 25 (Autumn 1958), 303–324.

[5] For an example of comparative analysis or organizations that takes into account the limitations of these "generalizations," see James D. Thompson and Frederick L. Bates, Technology, Organization, and Administration, *Administrative Science Quarterly,* 2 (1957), pp. 325–343; James D. Thompson and William J. McEwen, Organizational Goals and Environment: Goal-setting as an Interaction Process, *American Sociological Review,* 23 (1958), pp. 23–31.

[6] On the two approaches see H. A. Simon, D. W. Smithburg, and V. A. Thompson, *Public Administration* (New York, 1956), pp. 280–295; also A. W. Gouldner, *Patterns of Industrial Bureaucracy* (Glencoe, 1954), pp. 224–228.

[7] The roles of managers will be discussed here only with regard to the internal functions of the organization. Their roles with regard to environment will be disregarded because of space limitations.

[8] Experts can be arranged in a continuum from the less to the more skilled in human relations. Chemists, for instance, are on the average less skilled from this point of view than labor relations experts. See L. E. Danielson, Management's Relations with Engineers and Scientists, *Proceedings of Industrial Relations Research Association,* Tenth Annual Meeting, 1957, pp. 314–321.

[9] See Robert Dubin, *Human Relations in Administration* (New York, 1951), pp. 113–138.

[10] For a comparison, see M. Dalton, Conflicts between Staff and Line Managerial Officers, *American Sociological Review,* 15 (1950), 342–351; and C. A. Myers and J. G. Turnbull, Line and Staff in Industrial Relations, *Harvard Business Review,* 34 (July–Aug. 1956), 113–124.

[11] For a case study which brings out this point, see A. H. Stanton and M. S. Schwartz, *The Mental Hospital* (New York, 1954).

[12] A. W. Gouldner, Cosmopolitans and Locals: Toward an Analysis of Latent Social Roles, *Administrative Science Quarterly,* 2 (1957), 444–480.

[13] The University of Liverpool, *The Dock Worker* (Liverpool, 1951), pp. 95–96.

[14] See Philip Selznick, *Leadership in Administration* (Evanston, 1957).

[15] See Talcott Parsons, "Some Ingredients of a General Theory of Formal Organization," in Andrew W. Halpin, ed., *Administrative Theory in Education* (Chicago, 1958).

[16] For a discussion of this point, see M. Weber, *The Theory of Social and Economic Organization* (Glencoe, 1947), p. 337; Herbert A. Simon, "Decision-Making and Administrative Organization," in R. K. Merton, A. P. Grey, B. Hockey, and H. C. Selvin, eds., *Reader in Bureaucracy* (Glencoe, 1952), pp. 185–194.

[17] See G. Mosca, *The Ruling Class* (New York, 1939).

[18] M. Newcomer, *The Big Business Executive* (New York, 1955), p. 92.

[19] See G. H. Copeman, *Leaders of British Industry* (London, 1955), p. 136.

[20] See H. A. Simon, A Comparison of Organizational Theories, *Review of Economic Studies,* 20 (1952–1953), 40–48.

[21] See E. Larrabee and D. Riesman, "The Role of Business in 'Executive Suite,' " in B. Rosenberg and D. M. White, eds., *Mass Culture* (Glencoe, 1957), pp. 325–340.

[22] See Thorstein Veblen, *The Engineers and the Price System* (New York, 1921), esp. pp. 70–81.

[23] George C. Homans, *The Human Group* (New York, 1950), pp. 369–414.

[24] See George Friedman, *Industrial Society* (Glencoe, 1955), pp. 325–329.

[25] For some insights and information on the relations between staff and line which seem not to match the "general" model, see on trade unions, H. L. Wilensky, *Intellectuals in Labor Unions* (Glencoe, 1956); on prisons, R. H. McCleery, *Policy Change in Prison Management* (East Lansing, 1957), esp. p. 27; Harvey Powelson and Reinhard Bendix, Psychiatry in Prison, *Psychiatry*, 14 (1951), 73-86; Donald R. Cressey, Achievement of an Unstated Goal: An Observation on Prisons, *Pacific Sociological Review*, Fall, 1958, 43-49; on the armed forces, James D. Thompson, Authority and Power in "Identical" Organizations, *American Journal of Sociology*, 62 (1956), 290-301; on advertising agencies, Martin Mayer, *Madison Avenue, U.S.A.* (New York, 1958), esp. pp. 102-104.

[26] Spreading and applying knowledge are the two major dimensions of the process of institutionalization of knowledge.

[27] On this concept, see N. Gross, W. S. Manson, and A. W. McEackern, *Explorations in Role Analysis* (New York, 1958); Melvin Seeman, Role Conflict and Ambivalent Leadership, *American Sociological Review*, 18 (1953), 373-380; S. A. Stouffer and J. Toby, Role Conflict and Personality, *American Journal of Sociology*, 56 (1951), 395-406.

[28] Talcott Parsons, A Sociological Approach to the Theory of Organization, *Administrative Science Quarterly*, 1 (1956), 63-85, 225-234.

[29] On the concept of organizational needs, see P. Selznick, Foundations of the Theory of Organizations, *American Sociological Review*, 13 (1948), 25-35.

[30] Gouldner, Cosmopolitans and Locals.

[31] Ivan Belknap, *Human Problems of a State Mental Hospital* (New York, 1956).

[32] L. Wilson, *The Academic Man* (New York, 1942), p. 85.

[33] L. Block, Ready Reference of Hospital Facts, *Hospital Topics*, 34 (April 1956), p. 23. From statistics quoted by E. A. Kennard one seems warranted in concluding that out of 39 mental hospitals studied the heads of 35 were psychiatrists. See M. Greenblatt, D. J. Levinson, and R. H. Williams, eds., *The Patient and the Mental Hospital* (Glencoe, 1957), p. 45.

[34] See Block, *op. cit.*, pp. 121, 136. See also T. Burling, E. M. Lentz, and R. N. Wilson, *The Give and Take in Hospitals* (New York, 1956), esp. pp. 51, 53.

[35] F. M. Farmer, The Public High School Principalship, *Bulletin National Association of Secondary School Principals*, 32 (1948), 82-91; see p. 83.

[36] This point has been made by J. Ben-David in private communication with the author. Some indirect evidence is supplied in J. Ben-David, "The Professions and the Social Structure in Israel," unpublished Ph.D. dissertation, Hebrew University, Jerusalem, 1955.

[37] Block, *op. cit.*

[38] For an interesting case of such a situation and its consequence for the problems discussed here, see M. Greenblatt, R. H. York, and E. L. Brown, *From Custodial to Therapeutic Patient Care in Mental Hospitals* (New York, 1955), pp. 42-43.

[39] See notes 34 and 35.

[40] See Greenblatt, York, and Brown, *op. cit.*, and M. Greenblatt, D. J. Levinson, and R. H. Williams, eds., *The Patient and the Mental Hospital* (Glencoe, 1957), esp. p. 320.

[41] Selznick, *op. cit.*, pp. 119-133. For an interesting case study which deals with this problem in another professional organization, see B. R. Clark, *Adult Education in Transition: A Study of Institutional Insecurity* (Berkeley, 1956).

[42] C. U. Letourneau, The Evaluation of Hospital Management, Part III, *Hospital Management*, 81 (1956), 41-44.

[43] A nonscientific but quite insightful discussion of this problem in vocational schools is included in E. Hunter's novel, *Blackboard Jungle* (New York, 1956).

[44] See T. Caplow and R. J. McGee, *The Academic Marketplace* (New York, 1958).

[45] For a case study of such a pressure, see Hans L. Zetterberg, "A College for Adults" (forthcoming).

[46] See Max Weber, "The Essentials of Bureaucratic Organizations: An Ideal-Type Construction," reprinted in Merton, Gray, Hockey, Selvin, eds., *Reader in Bureaucracy*, pp. 18-27, esp. p. 24.

[47] See the author's A Case of Functional Differentiation of Elites, *American Journal of Sociology*, 65 (March 1959), 476-487.

[48] W. E. Moore, *Industrial Relations and the Social Order* (rev. ed.; New York, 1951), pp. 77-84. See also H. G. Hodges, Management of Universities, *Southern Economic Journal*, 19 (1952), 79-89.

[49] H. L. Smith, Two Lines of Authority Are One Too Much, *Modern Hospital*, 84 (1955), 54-64. See also J. Henry, The Formal Structure of a Psychiatric Hospital, *Psychiatry*, 17 (1954), 139-151.

[50] P. B. Jacobson, *Duties of School Principals* (New York, 1941), pp. 18-19.

[51] Weber, *op. cit.*, pp. 335, 337.

[52] T. Parsons, Introduction in Weber, *The Theory of Social and Economic Organization*, pp. 58-60, n. 4.

[53] See A. H. Stanton and M. S. Schwartz, *The Mental Hospital* (New York, 1954); and William Caudill, *The Psychiatric Hospital as a Small Society* (Cambridge, 1958).

[54] See March and Simon, *op. cit.*, pp. 70-76.

[55] On this concept, see E. Goffman, On the Characteristics of Total Institutions, *Proceedings of the Symposium of Preventive and Social Psychiatry* (Washington, D. C., 1957).

[56] In a study which compares two types of hospitals we see that English hospitals under local authority which employ medical staff are administered by medical superintendents, whereas voluntary hospitals which do not employ any full-time medical senior personnel are administered by lay administrators. See C. Sofer, Reactions to Administrative Change, *Human Relations*, 8 (1955), 291-316.

[57] The hospitals discussed here are "regular," cure-oriented hospitals. The more the hospital serves additional professional goals—as, for instance, teaching and research—the more it will tend to internalize professionals and become administered by M.D.s. See Burling, *op. cit.*, pp. 76-77.

[58] On the organizational structure of boarding schools, see the author's The Organizational Structure of "Closed" Educational Institutions in Israel, *Harvard Educational Review*, 27 (1957), 107-125.
[59] See C. Y. Clock, Some Implications of Organization for Social Research, *Social Forces*, 30 (1951), 129-134.
[60] See the special issue on research administration of the *Administrative Science Quarterly*, 1 (Dec. 1956); and H. A. Shepard, The Value System of a University Research Group, *American Sociological Review*, 19 (1954), 456-462.
[61] W. J. McEwen, Position Conflict and Professional Orientation in a Research Organization, *Administrative Science Quarterly*, 1 (1956), 208-224.
[62] It is reported that of 20 laboratories studied all the heads were expert oriented. See H. Baumgartel, Leadership Style as a Variable in Research Administration, *Administrative Science Quarterly*, 2 (1957), 347; see also C. Shepard and P. Brown, *ibid.*, 1 (1956), 345-346; and McEwen, *op. cit.*, pp. 220-221.
[63] See Sofer, *op. cit.*, esp. p. 299.
[64] See Richard H. Sullivan, Administrative-Faculty Relationships in Colleges and Universities, *Journal of Higher Education*, 27 (June 1956), 325.

ABOUT THE AUTHOR—Amitai Etzioni, although at present heavily committed to the utilization of his sociological competence to the cause of world peace, has made a number of important contributions to the broad field of sociology and to the literature of organization and administration. His 1964 volume, *Modern Organizations*, presents a view of current research and conceptual thinking in the field of organizational behavior. His book, *Studies in Social Change* (1966), is a collection of essays in which he applies his extensive knowledge of international politics to an analysis of change in social systems.

Etzioni, born in Cologne, West Germany in 1929, attended Hebrew University where he worked in the kibbutzim project and received his B.A. in 1954, his M.A. in 1956. He came to the University of California at Berkeley to work on his doctorate, where he studied under Bendix, Selznick and Lipset. Since receiving his Ph.D. in 1958, he has been associated with Columbia University where he teaches and carries out research. He has just published a new volume on social and political theory, *The Active Society* (1968). He is a member of the Institute of War and Peace Studies and serves on the editorial boards of *American Sociological Review* and *Administrative Science Quarterly*.

A Purchase of Mechanical Dictation Equipment

by Kenneth R. Shaffer

> *This case is simple and complex at the same time. On its surface it appears to be a clear cut and unambiguous situation in which the board member is exercising his authority and punishing the librarian for using only her own judgment. But more questions are asked than answered in the elaboration of this simple situation. Individual readers must hypothesize on circumstances not detailed and reconcile the problem based upon their own individual construction of the information which is presented. Yet it is clearly a case which allows the issue of librarian/board authority relations to be explored. It forms an interesting contrast to the reading which follows hereafter.*

Miss Winston came to the D— Public Library as its head two years ago. D— is a town of approximately 40,000 in the Midwest and the public library has been well supported and well administered almost from its beginnings. Miss Winston has done a good job as director and has enjoyed fine relations with her board of trustees and staff in her development of the library and its services to the city.

Customarily, each year, Miss Winston prepares a budget request divided into various categories which include the following: books and periodicals, binding, personnel, equipment and replacement, travel and contingency. These estimates she brings to Mr. Furness, the chairman of the finance committee of the board of trustees who, after going over them with her and making any changes that seem necessary, places them before the entire board for consideration and approval. Following this action on the part of the board, the budget is sent to the mayor of the city who incorporates it in his larger budget for all municipal operations, and ultimately it is approved by the city council. The approved budget is then returned to the board and the board in turn authorizes the librarian to proceed with expenditures during the coming year within the limits of the budget. The board, however, reserves for itself the *post facto* approval of all expenditures so that in advance of each of the twelve monthly board meetings Miss Winston provides a list of purchases together with a statement of unexpended budgetary balances This document is usually handled in a *pro forma* kind of way by the board and for many years—including years before Miss Winston's coming to the library—the board had never questioned expenditures made by the library head.

Because Miss Winston had found it very difficult to hire competent secretarial assistance, she decided some time ago to purchase mechanical dictation equipment. This would permit her to engage a typist, rather than a secretary who could take shorthand, and would make available not only a much larger number of candidates for such positions but also enable her to attract them to the library under better financial inducements than if she were attempting to hire a person with complete secretarial skills. She carefully studied various types of dictation equipment and finally decided that for her purposes Brand A would be best. This cost $535 for both dictation and transcription equipment and since she had ample funds in her equipment budget to care for such an item, she placed an order and eventually received the item. The company through which the equipment was purchased was slow in presenting its bill so she received the bill for payment some two months after she had received the equipment and had enjoyed its use. The bill was paid by the city, and Miss Winston duly listed it among expenses to be brought to the attention of the board for its *post facto* approval at its next meeting. This document customarily was forwarded to Mr. Furness who was the member of the board serving as chairman of the finance committee and who always asked to receive it approximately a week before the fall meeting of the board.

But shortly thereafter, Mr. Furness telephoned asking if he could come over to the library and see Miss Winston. She assured him that she would be

---

SOURCE: Reprinted from Kenneth R. Shaffer, *Twenty-Five Cases in Executive-Trustee Relationships in Public Libraries* ("Case Studies in Library Administration"; Hamden, Conn.: Shoe String Press, 1960), Chap. 5, "A Purchase of Mechanical Dictation Equipment," pp. 58–61, by permission of the Shoe String Press, Inc., and the author.

delighted and in a few minutes he appeared with the list of expenditures which had been sent to him only two days before. Speaking rather abruptly, it seemed to Miss Winston, Mr. Furness said, "I'd like to ask you about the item here for Brand A dictation equipment, Miss Winston. What is this all about?"

Miss Winston explained the difficulties in hiring people with full secretarial skill and explained that the equipment was intended to solve this problem. She said that she had been enjoying the use of the equipment for two months and found that it had met all her expectations.

Mr. Furness, however, took a different view of the matter. "The board cannot approve the purchase of this equipment, Miss Winston," he said. "You have had no authorization from us to go ahead in this purchase and you had better return the equipment and ask for a full refund of its cost to the city. The board will not go along with what seems to me to be a rather serious indiscretion—at least, a serious breach of judgment."

Miss Winston explained that she did not realize that any prior approval on the part of the board might be necessary. She pointed out that it had never before been necessary with regard to purchases of books, other types of equipment, or the engagement of personnel, and she said that it did not occur to her that it would be necessary for dictation equipment. She said furthermore that it would probably be impossible to return the equipment for refund since she had been using it for two months.

Mr. Furness answered by saying that the equipment item in the budget had been approved by the board for the purchase of regular library equipment such as catalog files, typewriters, book trucks, and other items used in library operation. He said that dictation equipment did not come within this category and that, therefore, the board would not approve of the transaction. He finally said, "This, of course, will come up before the board, but I think I had better warn you that I feel sure the board will react exactly as I have as chairman of its finance committee."

At a meeting of the board, three days later, the matter did come up and was presented by Mr. Furness in brief but complete form. He explained his own reservations as chairman of the finance committee, and finally made a motion as follows:

That the board of trustees of the D—Public Library not approve the purchase of dictation equipment costing $535 made by the librarian and that the librarian be instructed to return the equipment to the company from which it was purchased for a full refund of the original purchase price.

Miss Winston of course was both dismayed and angry at this turn of events. Although the matter had come before the board in a seemingly casual way, it was evident that members of the board had had the matter discussed with them by Mr. Furness prior to the meeting. In any case, they voted unanimously to approve Mr. Furness' resolution and proceeded to other items on the agenda of the meeting.

* * *

How would you evaluate this situation from the standpoint of Miss Winston and from the standpoint of the board?

If you were Mr. Furness or if you were a member of the board, and if you believed that the equipment should not have been purchased in the first place, as Mr. Furness so believes, what action other than the resolution quoted in the case would you recommend the board take? What are the issues involved in such a situation beyond the matter of the purchase of the equipment?

What would you recommend that Miss Winston do and why?

ABOUT THE AUTHOR—Kenneth R. Shaffer has concentrated most of his working life upon library education, and particulary to the library school program at Simmons College where he is Director of the School of Library Science and of the college library. To improve the preparation of students, Shaffer has adapted the Harvard business school case method to the study of library science. This work has resulted in books on personnel administration, executive-trustee relationships in public libraries, and the book collection in public and academic libraries.

Shaffer received his B.A. in English in 1935 from Butler University, accepted employment with the Indiana State Library in Indianapolis and soon became head of the acquisition department. He holds a University of Illinois B.S. and served as Assistant Director of the Indiana University Library from 1941-1945. He assumed responsibility for the direction of the program of the American Book Center for War Devastated Libraries in 1945. At Simmons, since 1946, Shaffer plays an active role as consultant on library planning and architecture both in the United States and abroad.

Personnel

Perhaps no element of administration is as essential to the achievement of the organization's ends as that of the effective use and utilization of human resources. In its essence the competence of the administrator is gauged by his capacity to effectively direct, encourage and manage the human beings who work with him toward the achievement of the organization's goals. The role of the human being in organization affairs is of course an underlying theme through all of this volume and so here only two selections have been drawn from the vast body of literature dealing with personnel management. The first identifies positively human needs and aspirations in the workplace and the second relates some of these issues to the library.

The Human Side of Enterprise

by Douglas M. McGregor

> *No construct in the theory of organization and administration has received more attention than Douglas McGregor's propositions—theory X and theory Y. In essence McGregor is pleading for a work role and conditions of employment designed to free the member of the work team from close supervision and to allow for the assumption of freedom and responsibility necessary to further the mental health of the individual and to give him a clearer stake in his role in the organization. This view commits management to the development of maturity in the work force through the acceptance of positive assumptions about human nature.*

It has become trite to say that the most significant developments of the next quarter century will take place not in the physical but in the social sciences, that industry—the economic organ of society—has the fundamental know-how to utilize physical science and technology for the material benefit of mankind, and that we must now learn how to utilize the social sciences to make our human organizations truly effective.

Many people agree in principle with such statements; but so far they represent a pious hope—and little else. Consider with me, if you will, something of what may be involved when we attempt to transform the hope into reality.

I

Let me begin with an analogy. A quarter century ago basic conceptions of the nature of matter and energy had changed profoundly from what they had been since Newton's time. The physical scientists were persuaded that under proper conditions new and hitherto unimagined sources of energy could be made available to mankind.

We know what has happened since then. First came the bomb. Then, during the past decade, have come many other attempts to exploit these scientific discoveries—some successful, some not.

The point of my analogy, however, is that the application of theory in this field is a slow and costly matter. We expect it always to be thus. No one is impatient with the scientist because he cannot tell industry how to build a simple, cheap, all-purpose source of atomic energy today. That it will take at least another decade and the investment of billions of dollars to achieve results which are economically competitive with present sources of power is understood and accepted.

It is transparently pretentious to suggest any *direct* similarity between the developments in the physical sciences leading to the harnessing of atomic energy and potential developments in the social sciences. Nevertheless, the analogy is not as absurd as it might appear to be at first glance.

To a lesser degree, and in a much more tentative fashion, we are in a position in the social sciences today like that of the physical sciences with respect to atomic energy in the thirties. We know that past conceptions of the nature of man are inadequate and in many ways incorrect. We are becoming quite certain that, under proper conditions, unimagined resources of creative human energy could become available within the organizational setting.

We cannot tell industrial management how to apply this new knowledge in simple, economic ways. We know it will require years of exploration, much costly development research, and a substantial amount of creative imagination on the part of management to discover how to apply this growing knowledge to the organization of human effort in industry.

May I ask that you keep this analogy in mind—overdrawn and pretentious though it may be—as a framework for what I have to say this morning.

SOURCE: Reprinted from *Leadership and Motivation* by Douglas McGregor, pp. 3–20, by permission of the MIT Press, Cambridge, Massachusetts. Copyright 1966 by the Massachusetts Institute of Technology. First published in *Adventure in Thought and Action*, Proceedings of the Fifth Anniversary Convocation of the School of Industrial Management, Massachusetts Institute of Technology, Cambridge, April 9, 1957.

Management's Task: Conventional View

The conventional conception of management's task in harnessing human energy to organizational requirements can be stated broadly in terms of three propositions. In order to avoid the complications introduced by a label, I shall call this set of propositions "Theory X:"

1. Management is responsible for organizing the elements of productive enterprise—money, materials, equipment, people—in the interest of economic ends.
2. With respect to people, this is a process of directing their efforts; motivating them, controlling their actions, modifying their behavior to fit the needs of the organization.
3. Without this active intervention by management, people would be passive—even resistant—to organizational needs. They must therefore be persuaded, rewarded, punished, controlled—their activities must be directed. This is management's task—in managing subordinate managers or workers. We often sum it up by saying that management consists of getting things done through other people.

Behind this conventional theory there are several additional beliefs—less explicit, but widespread:

4. The average man is by nature indolent—he works as little as possible.
5. He lacks ambition, dislikes responsibility, prefers to be led.
6. He is inherently self-centered, indifferent to organizational needs.
7. He is by nature resistant to change.
8. He is gullible, not very bright, the ready dupe of the charlatan and the demagogue.

The human side of economic enterprise today is fashioned from propositions and beliefs such as these. Conventional organization structures, managerial policies, practices, and programs reflect these assumptions.

In accomplishing its task—with these assumptions as guides—management has conceived of a range of possibilities between two extremes.

The Hard or the Soft Approach?

At one extreme, management can be "hard" or "strong." The methods for directing behavior involve coercion and threat (usually disguised), close supervision, tight controls over behavior. At the other extreme, management can be "soft" or "weak." The methods for directing behavior involve being permissive, satisfying people's demands, achieving harmony. Then they will be tractable, accept direction.

This range has been fairly completely explored during the past half century, and management has learned some things from the exploration. There are difficulties in the "hard" approach. Force breeds counterforces: restriction of output, antagonism, militant unionism, subtle but effective sabotage of management objectives. This approach is especially difficult during times of full employment.

There are also difficulties in the "soft" approach. It leads frequently to the abdication of management—to harmony, perhaps, but to indifferent performance. People take advantage of the soft approach. They continually expect more, but they give less and less.

Currently, the popular theme is "firm but fair." This is an attempt to gain the advantages of both the hard and the soft approaches. It is reminiscent of Teddy Roosevelt's "speak softly and carry a big stick."

Is the Conventional View Correct?

The findings which are beginning to emerge from the social sciences challenge this whole set of beliefs about man and human nature and about the task of management. The evidence is far from conclusive, certainly, but it is suggestive. It comes from the laboratory, the clinic, the schoolroom, the home, and even to a limited extent from industry itself.

The social scientist does not deny that human behavior in industrial organization today is approximately what management perceives it to be. He has, in fact, observed it and studied it fairly extensively. But he is pretty sure that this behavior is *not* a consequence of man's inherent nature. It is a consequence rather of the nature of industrial organizations, of management philosophy, policy, and practice. The conventional approach of Theory X is based on mistaken notions of what is cause and what is effect.

"Well," you ask, "what then is the *true* nature of man? What evidence leads the social scientist to deny what is obvious?" And, if I am not mistaken, you are also thinking, "Tell me—simply, and without a lot of scientific verbiage—what you think you know that is so unusual. Give me—without a lot of intellectual claptrap and theoretical nonsense—some practical ideas which will enable me to improve the situation in my organization. And remember, I'm faced with increasing costs and narrowing profit margins. I want proof that such ideas won't result simply in new and costly human relations frills. I want practical results, and I want them now."

If these are your wishes, you are going to be disappointed. Such requests can no more be met by the social scientist today than could comparable ones with respect to atomic energy be met by the physicist fifteen years ago. I can, however, indicate a few of the reasons for asserting that conventional assumptions about the human side of enterprise are inadequate. And I can suggest—tentatively—some of the propositions that will comprise a more adequate theory of the management of people. The magnitude of the task that confronts us will then, I think be apparent.

II

Perhaps the best way to indicate why the conventional approach of management is inadequate is to consider the subject of motivation. In discussing this subject I will draw heavily on the work of my colleague, Abraham Maslow of Brandeis University. His is the most fruitful approach I know. Naturally, what I have to say will be overgeneralized and will ignore important qualifications. In the time at our disposal, this is inevitable.

Physiological and Safety Needs

Man is a wanting animal—as soon as one of his needs is satisfied, another appears in its place. This process is unending. It continues from birth to death.

Man's needs are organized in a series of levels—a hierarchy of importance. At the lowest level, but preeminent in importance when they are thwarted, are his physiological needs. Man lives by bread alone, when there is no bread. Unless the circumstances are unusual, his needs for love, for status, for recognition are inoperative when his stomach has been empty for a while. But when he eats regularly and adequately, hunger ceases to be an important need. The sated man has hunger only in the sense that a full bottle has emptiness. The same is true of the other physiological needs of man—for rest, exercise, shelter, protection from the elements.

A satisfied need is not a motivator of behavior!

This is a fact of profound significance. It is a fact which is regularly ignored in the conventional approach to the management of people. I shall return to it later. For the moment, one example will make my point. Consider your own need for air. Except as you are deprived of it, it has no appreciable motivating effect upon your behavior.

When the physiological needs are reasonably satisfied, needs at the next higher level begin to dominate man's behavior—to motivate him. These are called safety needs. They are needs for protection against danger, threat, deprivation. Some people mistakenly refer to these as needs for security. However, unless man is in a dependent relationship where he fears arbitrary deprivation, he does not demand security. The need is for the "fairest possible break." When he is confident of this, he is more than willing to take risks. But when he feels threatened or dependent, his greatest need is for guarantees, for protection, for security.

The fact needs little emphasis that since every industrial employee is in a dependent relationship, safety needs may assume considerable importance. Arbitrary management actions, behavior which arouses uncertainty with respect to continued employment or which reflects favoritism or discrimination, unpredictable administration of policy—these can be powerful motivators of the safety needs in the employment relationship *at every level* from worker to vice president.

Social Needs

When man's physiological needs are satisfied and he is no longer fearful about his physical welfare, his social needs become important motivators of his behavior—for belonging, for association, for acceptance by his fellows, for giving and receiving friendship and love.

Management knows today of the existence of these needs, but it often assumes quite wrongly that they represent a threat to the organization. Many studies have demonstrated that the tightly knit, cohesive work group may, under proper conditions, be far more effective than an equal number of separate individuals in achieving organizational goals.

Yet management, fearing group hostility to its own objectives, often goes to considerable lengths to control and direct human efforts in ways that are inimical to the natural "groupiness" of human beings. When man's social needs—and perhaps his safety needs, too—are thus thwarted, he behaves in ways which tend to defeat organizational objectives. He becomes resistant, antagonistic, uncooperative. But this behavior is a consequence, not a cause.

Ego Needs

Above the social needs—in the sense that they do not become motivators until lower needs are reasonably satisfied—are the needs of greatest significance to management and to man himself. They are the egoistic needs, and they are of two kinds:

1. Those needs that relate to one's self-esteem—needs for self-confidence, for independence, for achievement, for competence, for knowledge.
2. Those needs that relate to one's reputation—needs for status, for recognition, for appreciation, for the deserved respect of one's fellows.

Unlike the lower needs, these are rarely satisfied; man seeks indefinitely for more satisfaction of these needs once they have become important to him. But they do not appear in any significant way until physiological, safety, and social needs are all reasonably satisfied.

The typical industrial organization offers few opportunities for the satisfaction of these egoistic needs to people at lower levels in the hierarchy. The conventional methods of organizing work, particularly in mass production industries, give little heed to these aspects of human motivation. If the practices of scientific management were deliberately calculated to thwart these needs—which, of course, they are not—they could hardly accomplish this purpose better than they do.

Self-Fulfillment Needs

Finally—a capstone, as it were, on the hierarchy of man's needs—there are what we may call the needs for self-fulfillment. These are the needs for realizing one's own potentialities, for continued self-development, for being creative in the broadest sense of that term.

It is clear that the conditions of modern life give only limited opportunity for these relatively weak needs to obtain expression. The deprivation most people experience with respect to other lower-level needs diverts their energies into the struggle to satisfy *those* needs, and the needs for self-fulfillment remain dormant.

III

Now, briefly, a few general comments about motivation:

We recognize readily enough that a man suffering from a severe dietary deficiency is sick. The deprivation of physiological needs has behavioral consequences. The same is true—although less well recognized—of deprivation of higher-level needs. The man whose needs for safety, association, independence, or status are thwarted is sick just as surely as is he who has rickets. And his sickness will have behavioral consequences. We will be mistaken if we attribute his resultant passivity, his hostility, his refusal to accept responsibility to his inherent "human nature." These forms of behavior are *symptoms* of illness—of deprivation of his social and egoistic needs.

The man whose lower-level needs are satisfied is not motivated to satisfy those needs any longer. For practical purposes they exist no longer. (Remember my point about your need for air.) Management often asks, "Why aren't people more productive? We pay good wages, provide good working conditions, have excellent fringe benefits and steady employment. Yet people do not seem to be willing to put forth more than minimum effort."

The fact that management has provided for these physiological and safety needs has shifted the motivational emphasis to the social and perhaps to the egoistic needs. Unless there are opportunities *at work* to satisfy these higher-level needs, people will be deprived; and their behavior will reflect this deprivation. Under such conditions, if management continues to focus its attention on physiological needs, its efforts are bound to be ineffective.

People *will* make insistent demands for more money under these conditions. It becomes more important than ever to buy the material goods and services which can provide limited satisfaction of the thwarted needs. Although money has only limited value in satisfying many higher-level needs, it can become the focus of interest if it is the *only* means available.

The Carrot and Stick Approach

The carrot and stick theory of motivation (like Newtonian physical theory) works reasonably well under certain circumstances. The *means* for satisfying man's physiological and (within limits) his safety needs can be provided or withheld by management. Employment itself is such a means, and so are wages, working conditions, and benefits. By these means the individual can be controlled so long as he is struggling for subsistence. Man lives for bread alone when there is no bread.

But the carrot and stick theory does not work at all once man has reached an adequate subsistence level and is motivated primarily by higher needs. Management cannot provide a man with self-respect, or with the respect of his fellows, or with the satisfaction of needs for self-fulfillment. It can create conditions such that he is encouraged and enabled to seek such satisfactions *for himself,* or it can thwart him by failing to create those conditions.

But this creation of conditions is not "control." It is not a good device for directing behavior. And so management finds itself in an odd position. The high standard of living created by our modern technological know-how provides quite adequately for the satisfaction of physiological and safety needs. The only significant exception is where management practices have not created confidence in a "fair break"—and thus where safety needs are thwarted. But by making possible the satisfaction of low-level needs, management has deprived itself of the ability to use as motivators the devices on which conventional theory has taught it to rely—rewards, promises, incentives, or threats and other coercive devices.

Neither Hard nor Soft

The philosophy of management by direction and control—*regardless of whether it is hard or soft*—is inadequate to motivate because the human needs on which this approach relies are today unimportant motivators of behavior. Direction and control are essentially useless in motivating people whose important needs are social and egoistic. Both the hard and the soft approach fail today because they are simply irrelevant to the situation.

People, deprived of opportunities to satisfy at work the needs which are now important to them, behave exactly as we might predict—with indolence, passivity, resistance to change, lack of responsibility, willingness to follow the demagogue, unreasonable demands for economic benefits. It would seem that we are caught in a web of our own weaving.

In summary, then, of these comments about motivation:

Management by direction and control—whether implemented with the hard, the soft, or the firm but fair approach—fails under today's conditions to provide effective motivation of human effort toward organizational objectives. It fails because direction and control are useless methods of motivating people whose physiological and safety needs are reasonably satisfied and whose social, egoistic, and self-fulfillment needs are predominant.

IV

For these and many other reasons, we require a different theory of the task of managing people based on more adequate assumptions about human nature and human motivation. I am going to be so bold as to suggest the broad dimensions of such a theory. Call it "Theory Y," if you will.

1. Management is responsible for organizing the elements of productive enterpirse—money, materials, equipment, people—in the interest of economic ends.

2. People are *not* by nature passive or resistant to organizational needs. They have become so as a result of experience in organizations.

3. The motivation, the potential for development, the capacity for assuming responsibility, the readiness to direct behavior toward organizational goals are all present in people. Management does not put them there. It is a responsibility of management to make it possible for people to recognize and develop these human characteristics for themselves.

4. The essential task of management is to arrange organizational conditions and methods of operation so that people can achieve their own goals *best* by directing *their own* efforts toward organizational objectives.

This is a process primarily of creating opportunities, releasing potential, removing obstacles, encouraging growth, providing guidance. It is what Peter Durcker has called "management by objectives" in contrast to "management by control."

And I hasten to add that it does *not* involve the abdication of management, the absence of leadership, the lowering of standards, or the other characteristics usually associated with the "soft" approach under Theory X. Much on the contrary. It is no more possible to create an organization today which will be a fully effective application of this theory than it was to build an atomic power plant in 1945. There are many formidable obstacles to overcome.

Some Difficulties

The conditions imposed by conventional organization theory and by the approach of scientific management for the past half century have tied men to limited jobs which do not ultilize their capabilities, have discouraged the acceptance of responsibility, have encouraged passivity, have eliminated meaning from work. Man's habits, attitudes, expectations—his whole conception of membership in an industrial organization—have been conditioned by his experience under these circumstances. Change in the direction of Theory Y will be slow, and it will require extensive modification of the attitudes of management and workers alike.

People today are accustomed to being directed, manipulated, controlled in industrial organizations and to finding satisfaction for their social, egoistic, and self-fulfillment needs away from the job. This is true of much of management as well as of workers. Genuine "industrial citizenship"—to borrow again a term from Drucker—is a remote and unrealistic idea, the meaning of which has not even been considered by most members of industrial organizations.

Another way of saying this is that Theory X places exclusive reliance upon external control of human behavior, while Theory Y relies heavily on self-control and self-direction. It is worth noting that this difference is the difference between treating people as children and treating them as mature adults. After generations of the former, we cannot expect to shift to the latter overnight.

V

Before we are overwhelmed by the obstacles, let us remember that the application of theory is always slow. Progress is usually achieved in small steps.

Consider with me a few innovative ideas which are entirely consistent with Theory Y and which are today being applied with some success:

Decentralization and Delegation

These are ways of freeing people from the too-close control of conventional organization, giving them a degree of freedom to direct their own activities, to assume responsibility, and, importantly, to satisfy their egoistic needs. In this connection, the flat organization of Sears, Roebuck and Company provides an interesting example. It forces "management by objectives" since it enlarges the number of people reporting to a manager until he cannot direct and control them in the conventional manner.

Job Enlargement

This concept, pioneered by I.B.M. and Detroit Edison, is quite consistent with Theory Y. It encourages the acceptance of responsibility at the bottom of the organization; it provides opportunities for satisfying social and egoistic needs. In fact, the reorganization of work at the factory level offers one of the more challenging opportunities for innovation consistent with Theory Y. The studies by A.T.M. Wilson and his associates of British coal mining and Indian textile manufacture have added appreciably to our understanding of work organization. Moreover, the economic and psychological results achieved by this work have been substantial.

Participation and Consultative Management

Under proper conditions these results provide encouragement to people to direct their creative energies toward organizational objectives, give them some voice in decisions that affect them, provide significant opportunities for the satisfaction of social and egoistic needs. I need only mention the Scanlon Plan as the outstanding embodiment of these ideas in practice.

The not infrequent failure of such ideas as these to work as well as expected is often attributable to the fact that a management has "bought the idea" but applied it within the framework of Theory X and its assumptions.

Delegation is not an effective way of exercising management by control. Participation becomes a farce when it is applied as a sales gimmick or a device for kidding people into thinking they are important. Only the management that has confidence in human capacities and is itself directed toward organizational objectives rather than toward the preservation of personal power can grasp the implications of this emerging theory. Such management will find and apply successfully other innovative ideas as we move slowly toward the full implementation of a theory like Y.

Performance Appraisal

Before I stop, let me mention one other practical application of Theory Y which—while still highly tentative—may well have important consequences. This has to do with performance appraisal within the ranks of management. Even a cursory examination of conventional programs of performance appraisal will reveal how completely consistent they are with Theory X. In fact, most such programs tend to treat the individual as through he were a product under inspection on the assembly line.

Take the typical plan: substitute "product" for "subordinate being appraised," substitute "inspector" for "superior making the appraisal," substitute "rework" for "training or development," and, except for the attributes being judged, the human appraisal process will be virtually indistinguishable from the product inspection process.

A few companies—among them General Mills, Ansul Chemical, and General Electric—have been experimenting with approaches which involve the individual in setting "targets" or objectives *for himself* and in a *self*-evaluation of performance semi-annually or annually. Of course, the superior plays an important leadership role in this process—one, in fact, which demands substantially more competence than the conventional approach. The role is, however, considerably more congenial to many managers than the role of "judge" or "inspector" which is forced upon them by conventional performance. Above all, the individual is encouraged to take a greater responsibility for planning and appraising his own contribution to organizational objectives; and the accompanying effects on egoistic and self-fulfillment needs are substantial. This approach to performance appraisal represents one more innovative idea being explored by a few managements who are moving toward the implementation of Theory Y.

VI

And now I am back where I began. I share the belief that we could realize substantial improvements in the effectiveness of industrial organizations during the next decade or two. Moreover, I believe the social sciences can contribute much to such developments. We are only beginning to grasp the implications of the growing body of knowledge in these fields. But if this conviction is to become a reality instead of a pious hope, we will need to view the process much as we view the process of releasing the energy of the atom for constructive human ends—as a slow, costly, sometimes discouraging approach toward a goal which would seem to many to be quite unrealistic.

The ingenuity and the perseverance of industrial management in the pursuit of economic ends have changed many scientific and technological dreams into commonplace realities. It is now becoming clear that the application of these same talents to the human side of enterprise will not only enhance substantially these materialistic achievements but will bring us one step closer to "the good society." Shall we get on with the job?

ABOUT THE AUTHOR—Douglas M. McGregor (1960-1964), having had experience during the depression years in organizing and supervising a shelter for transient laborers founded by his father, went on to graduate work at Harvard, where in 1935 he completed his doctorate in psychology. He served there as a faculty member until 1937 when he was brought to MIT as part of that university's efforts to broaden the education of engineering students by introducing them to behavioral insights. At MIT he was appointed executive director of the Industrial Relations Section. During this period he shifted his focus from basic research to essay and general writing bringing into play his capacity for lucid and compelling writing. When the presidency of Antioch College, an institution noted for its unique innovations in student self-government, became vacant, McGregor was chosen for the post. From 1948 to 1954 he served in this capacity, staunchly defending the college's policies of liberalism and free speech in the face of charges of Communist infiltration. In 1954 McGregor returned to MIT as Sloan Professor of Industrial Management. At other times in his career McGregor served as an analyst and arbitrator for the Labor Department and as director of industrial relations for the Dewey & Almy Company. He was a well known consultant, industrial educator and promoter and prosecutor of research into organizational arrangements. In a volume by W. G. Bennis and Edward H. Shine, with Caroline McGregor, *Leadership and Motivation* (1966), McGregor's achievements are underscored through the selection of his more prominent essays detailing the changing role of corporate management through the effective use of human beings in industry.

Handling the Problem Staff Member

by Alfred L. Brophy and George M. Gazda

Essentially, the piece which follows affords a review of the research which has been done on personality characteristics of librarians. The writers' basic approach to dealing with the question of the "problem" staff member is a situational one. The task of the organization is to provide a working environment which meets basic human needs but further to match personality types with work roles. While advice is given as to how to treat the truly "problem" staff member, the key issue raised is the attractiveness of working conditions in libraries. A problem inherent here is that library administrators as well as librarians may be intolerant of characteristics which do not fit the bureaucratic mold. For enforcement of a working milieu which strives for congeniality, homogeneity and conformity may excise out the innovator and the change agent.

All occupations contain a certain number of problem employees—persons who are not meeting the requirements of their positions either because of an unfavorable work environment, or as a result of improper occupational placement, or as an expression of an inadequate personality. While few estimates are available of the number of such employees, some studies have found that personality problems alone result in vocational maladjustment for approximately 25 per cent of the work force.[1] To point out further the extent of vocational maladjustment, many studies of workers' subjective feelings toward their jobs have found that on the average about 12 per cent are actively dissatisfied,[2] and that about 54 per cent would choose a different occupation if they could relive their lives.[3]

This paper discusses the problem employee with special reference to the profession of library science, reviews research on personality characteristics of librarians, and suggests ways of handling the problem employee so that he may become a more effective member of the staff. A selected bibliography is also provided for readers desiring a more extended treatment of personnel management, vocational psychology, and personality dynamics.

DISTINGUISHING PROBLEM STAFF MEMBERS FROM PROBLEM SITUATIONS

An employee may be a "problem" for any one or more of a number of overt reasons. The quality of his work performance may be very poor or his working speed may be excessively slow. He may have a poor record of absenteeism or tardiness, or otherwise disregard the regulations of the library. He may, on the other hand, be noted as a "problem" because of inability to maintain good interpersonal relations with supervisors, co-workers, or clientele.

Many such people not only create dissatisfaction in others who are inconvenienced by their inadequate work performance but also feel dissatisfied themselves, because of their inability to function effectively on their jobs and/or because of generalized unhappiness. They may, therefore, be considered "problems" both overtly, in the eyes of others, and subjectively, in their own eyes. There is not always, however, a direct relationship between vocational satisfaction and quality of performance,[4] so it should not be supposed that the ineffective worker will always be unhappy about his work, or that the dissatisfied worker will always be ineffective.

Problem behavior in some cases does not reflect a misplaced or emotionally upset employee, but rather represents a fairly direct response to a problem situation, in which it is the inadequacy of the work environment rather than of the person that needs to be corrected. One should consider the possibility that a problem situation exists if a large number of employees in a single work group manifest problem behavior.

The most humane approach in dealing with problem staff members would be to investigate first their working conditions. This must be done carefully, for if the staff members feel threatened by the supervisor or administration, it is unlikely

SOURCE: Reprinted from Alfred L. Brophy and George M. Gazda, "Handling the Problem Staff Member," *Illinois Libraries,* 43 (Dec., 1961), pp. 760-763, by permission of the Illinois State Library and the authors.

that the survey will obtain useful, frank, and honest responses. It would also be useless to survey workers' satisfaction if the one seeking the information did not have the power or the intention to change conditions. Only when the climate is right will individuals feel free to tell how they really feel about working conditions.

THE PERSONALITY AND NEEDS OF THE LIBRARIAN

What are man's basic needs? Through what means does man satisfy his basic needs? These questions are relevant to the topic under discussion for it is likely that problem people have many unfulfilled needs. Maslow[5] has provided us with a listing of the basic needs in terms of their hierarchy of prepotency. These basic needs are: (1) the physiological needs; (2) the safety needs; (3) the belongingness and love needs; (4) the needs for self-esteem and esteem of others; (5) the need for self-actualization; (6) the needs to know and to understand; and (7) the aesthetic needs.

The above listing is in the usual order of potency. Before one can satisfy higher order needs he first must satisfy the lower needs such as the physiological needs. Maslow believes that the person who has been able to satisfy his basic needs tends to be self-reliant, serene, and tolerant of frustration, while those who have suffered repeated frustrations are more inclined to aggressiveness and more susceptible to neurosis.

Although psychologists are not in agreement with respect to a single acceptable theory of personality, some aspects of Maslow's theory seem especially adaptable to this discussion. Roe has borrowed heavily from Maslow in her *The Psychology of Occupations*. She has expressed herself as follows:

> The application of this theory to occupational psychology is fairly obvious. In our society there is no single situation which is potentially so capable of giving some satisfaction at all levels of basic needs as is the occupation . . .
> Occupations as a source of need satisfaction are of extreme importance in our culture. It may be that occupations have become important in our culture just because so many needs are so well satisfied by them. Whether the relation is causal or not, and if so which is cause and which is effect, does not particularly matter. It is probably a sort of feedback arrangement anyway. What is important is that this relationship exists and is an essential aspect of the value of the occupation of the individual.[6]

Research by Centers[7] on sources of satisfaction in work lends support to the occupational relevance of Maslow's theory. For our purposes, Centers' most important finding was his discovery that the major motives which workers in business, professional, and white-collar occupations seek to fulfill in their jobs are the desires for self-expression, independence or freedom from supervision, interesting experience, and the opportunity to be of service to others.

If we are to provide any insights which will be helpful to those who have the occasion to deal with problem staff members, then our discussion needs to be related to the personality of the librarian. Research is very limited with respect to the unique personality characteristics of the librarian. In fact, research which has attempted to delineate personality types for occupations has usually been inconclusive. One reason for this state of affairs is that individuals with a wide range of personalities and abilities can be successful in an occupation, and another reason is that many different kinds of positions exist within a single occupation. Still another reason is that personality tests are not highly valid.

Two research reports shed light on ways in which the librarian may be unique and how this uniqueness may contribute to the nature of his problems. Bryan in *The Public Librarian*[8] interpreted some findings of the Inquiry study which were based on questionnaire returns and test data from approximately 2,400 practicing public librarians selected from forty-seven libraries. The ratio of professional librarians to subprofessional personnel was three to one. Of the 2,400 librarians in the basic sample, 92 per cent were women. This sample was representative of the librarian population throughout the country. The tests employed in the Inquiry were the Guilford-Martin Inventory of Factors GAMIN, a personality questionnaire, and the Strong Vocational Interest Blank. The tests were analyzed only for the professional librarians.

The second study is a Ph.D. dissertation by Douglass entitled *The Personality of the Librarian*.[9] Douglass selected as his experimental group 125 men and 400 women enrolled during the school year 1947-1948 in seventeen of the thirty-six library schools accredited at that time by the American Library Association. An additional twenty men were later added as subjects for one of the personality tests. The group consisted mainly of graduate students; only 8 per cent reported junior or senior status. Of the remaining, 84 per cent held bachelor's degrees and 8 per cent the master's or the doctor's. The control group was composed of graduate students in other fields matched for age, sex, marital status, educational background, etc. Douglass administered to his subjects a personal data questionnaire and five personality inventories, the Minnesota Multiphasic Personality Inventory (MMPI), the Allport-Vernon Study of Values, the Allport-Allport A-S Reaction Study, the Terman-Miles Attitude Interest Analysis Test, and the Bernreuter Personality Inventory.

Both the Douglass study and the Inquiry investigated the distinctive characteristics of the librarian. Bryan made the following observations based on data obtained from the GAMIN for male professional public librarians only.

> As compared with the average male university student, the typical male librarian is rather submissive in social situations and less likely to show qualities of leadership. He is within the normal range of masculinity in his attitudes and interests but he tends to lack confidence in himself and to feel somewhat inferior. His feelings of inferiority, however, seem not to worry him excessively, for he experiences less than average nervous tension and irritability. He shows no great drive for overt activity, but is normally sedentary for his age. On the whole, he seems to have made a reasonably good adjustment to life, and one might guess that stomach ulcers would not be his occupational disease.[10]

The female professional public librarian was described by Bryan, on the basis of the GAMIN scores, as follows:

> The typical female librarian has a personality profile that is remarkably similar to that of her male colleague. As compared with the average woman university student, she is submissive in social situations, lacks self-confidence, feels inferior, has an average amount of drive for overt activity, and feels a normal degree of nervous tension and irritability. She is normally feminine in her attitudes and interests. Like the typical male librarian, she seems reasonably well adjusted.[11]

It should be noted that the norm group of university students for the GAMIN provided a questionable comparison group for the librarian subjects, because of the difference in age, and possible other differences.

Bryan[12] observed some interesting differences in personality profiles between married and single librarians. The married men as a group, compared with the unmarried men, included a larger percentage who scored low on general pressure for overt activity, a larger percentage who scored high on masculinity of attitudes and interests and on self-confidence, and a larger percentage who showed a lack of nervous tension and irritability. There was no difference in scores on social ascendancy. Married women as a group scored higher on overt activity level, social ascendancy, self-confidence, and feminity than did unmarried women. A larger number of married women than of single women experienced a high nervous tension and irritability.

From the Strong Vocational Interest Blank, Bryan[13] observed that the female librarians as a group scored highest in the occupation "librarian," thus indicating that their pattern of interests was most similar to that of successful female librarians. The females' Strong scores also showed that their interests were similar to those of artists, authors, and office workers. The results of the Strong suggested that the female librarians did not have interests like those of psychologists, buyers, home economics teachers, YWCA secretaries, and physical education teachers.

According to Bryan, females in administrative positions, as a group, scored somewhat higher on the scale for "librarian" than did the female professional assistants. This is consistent with Strong's observations that individuals successfully engaged in certain occupations are differentiated from those in the same occupation who are not as successful.

At the time of the Inquiry study, Strong had not established norms for male librarians. Of the thirty-four occupations for which norms were available, Bryan[14] observed that the interests of the men were most like those of musicians. The interests of the male professional librarians were also similar to those of authors and journalists, public administrators, advertising men, and printers. The male librarians' interests were unlike those of sales managers, accountants, policemen, purchasing agents, carpenters, and forest service men. These findings on interests of the male librarians should be considered tentative, since the number of males who returned usable Strong Blanks was very small.

On the whole Bryan found that the men's interests ranged over a broader area than those of the women. Male and female librarians shared a common interest in literary and artistic occupations, but the men were found to score relatively high on five occupations outside of their own field, whereas the women as a group did not score particularly high on any occupation, including "librarian."

On the basis of questionnaire data, Bryan concluded that librarians ". . . as a group predominantly identified with the genteel, bookish, aesthetic tradition and that their preferences and their special knowledge are in the fields of literature, languages, history, arts, and the humanities generally rather than in the scientific-technological and politico-economic specialties and concerns of our time...."[15]

Although Douglass' dissertation was not completed until 1957 the data were gathered in 1947-48, a period of time included within the Inquiry study, which was launched in 1946 and which extended for two and one-quarter years. The populations of the two studies were somewhat different. Douglass studied library students enrolled in graduate library training, whereas the Inquiry studied practicing public librarians. The Inquiry sample averaged several years older than the Douglass sample, the median age of the Inquiry sample being about forty-two, whereas the median age for males and females in the Douglass study was thirty and twenty-five, respectively. In the Douglass study 39 per cent of the men were married while only 10 per cent of the women were married.

On the basis of the test results, Douglass[16] characterized the modal librarian as described below. Caution is advised in interpreting these findings, as some of them are based on trends only and not on clear-cut differences.

Orderliness. To a significant degree the group was characterized by orderliness and accompanying traits of meticulousness and neatness. These traits were somewhat more pronounced in the women than in the men.

Conscientiousness. Both males and females in the library school group were found to be highly conscientious—more so than the control or comparison group.

Sense of responsibility. The male librarians were characterized by a greater sense of responsibility than were the males in the control group. There was no significant difference between the female groups.

Conservation and conformity. Librarian students possessed these characteristics to an exceptional degree. Douglass labeled librarians perfectionists who are somewhat overly critical and inclined toward rigidity in attitudes and modes of thinking and behavior.

Ascendance, motivation, and drive. The data revealed the library student as weak in the dynamic qualities associated with social ascendance and leadership. He seemed to lack vigor, strong motivation and drive, and imaginative thinking.

Introspection and self-sufficiency. The library student was found to have a strong trend toward introspection, preoccupation with subjective feelings, and self-sufficiency. The females appeared to be more self-sufficient than the males.

Sociability and interest in people. The test data revealed that the library students were not the "out-going" sort. Their interests in people were not of an emotional or spontaneous nature but rather tended to be idealized and intellectual. Douglass characterized the library student as aloof and impersonal with respect to people.

Interests and values. The interests of the male library student were observed to be more feminine than masculine insofar as they were more concerned with the literary, the aesthetic, and the otherwise more "cultural" aspects of life. The value system of the male library student, as compared with the average graduate student, was more strongly oriented toward the theoretical, the aesthetic, and the social, and more weakly oriented toward the economic, political, and the religious values.

The value system of the female library student, as compared with the average graduate student, was found to be very strong in the social and religious values and weaker in the economic and political values.

Anxiousness and neuroticism. The test data on the library students did not characterize them as being unduly anxious or, by inference, neurotic.

Keeping in mind the differences between the two populations studied and the different instruments employed in the Inquiry and in the Douglass study, we nevertheless would like to point out wherein there is concurrence.

Both Bryan and Douglass found that librarians as a group were lower than their respective control groups with respect to leadership qualities and self-confidence. Bryan and Douglass also concurred that librarians' interests were higher than control groups in the aesthetic and more "cultural" aspects of life and lower in the scientific-technological and politico-economic aspects. In general, both Douglass and Bryan agreed that librarians are suited by temperament and background for the occupation in which they are engaged.

Douglass[17] concluded that the library profession exercises a selective influence in recruiting its members and that the behavior patterns of librarians have been established before entering library school. It seems necessary, therefore, to discuss in what ways the occupation of librarian affords or does not afford the opportunity for librarians to meet their unique and general needs.

Bryan[18] found that more than two thirds of the professional librarians in the Inquiry sample reported inadequate financial return as the greatest disadvantage in choosing librarianship as a career. Insufficient opportunity for advancement was the second most frequently reported reason for dissatisfaction with library work. A limited income certainly restricts the extent to which the physiological and safety needs are satisfied and also limits the development and satisfaction of the higher order needs of which Maslow speaks. Inadequate opportunity for advancement would appear to limit the satisfaction of the needs for self-esteem, and its subsidiaries, the desires for achievement and independence, and for status and recognition. Perhaps this situation contributes to the librarian's lack of self-confidence and leadership. The frustration of the self-esteem needs likely accounts for Bryan's observations regarding female librarians who held middle administrative positions without much chance for advancement to the few top positions held by a disproportionate number of men. These women expressed greater disappointment in their life work than any of the other librarians.

The needs to be a group member and to give and receive love can be satisfied in part by one's occupation.[19] The low sociability of aloof and impersonal attitude observed by Douglass in his sample, coupled with lack of confidence and submissiveness in social situations observed by both Douglass and Bryan, would seem to reduce the satisfaction of membership needs and of the need to give and receive love.

Bryan[20] found that 64 per cent of the Inquiry sample of the unmarried professional women and 79 per cent of the single subprofessional women said that they would like to marry. Furthermore, 39 per cent of both these groups of women would like not only to marry, but also to give up their library work and devote themselves to homemaking. When one considers that approximately 90 per cent of librarians are female, that only one in four is married, and of those not married two thirds to three fourths desire marriage, then there seems to be good reason to look to the possibility of a large pool of problem staff members coming from those females suffering from frustrations of the unmarried state. The lack of opportunity to wed for large numbers of females must indeed be negatively reflected in their self concepts, and must frustrate needs for belongingness and love and needs for esteem.

Occupation is the major determinant of socioeconomic status in our culture,[21] and one's need for esteem is at least partially fulfilled through his social and economic status. Therefore, one's occupational status is obviously a potential source of gratification or frustration of his esteem needs. There seems to be little doubt that librarianships have not, in the past, provided high economic status for librarians. The expected result would be lowered self-esteem for the librarian, since individuals often judge their own worth in terms of their value as reflected by the larger community. The future, however, appears to be brighter because of increased salaries.

Many librarians' esteem needs are probably frustrated and thwarted as a result of poor personnel management and poor personnel classification schemes, which, though perhaps somewhat improved today, were found by Bryan[22] to be inadequate in the late forties. We must caution the reader that some of the inability to secure need fulfillment may be a result of the types of person entering library work and that improving such things as salaries, tenure, retirement, and working conditions, may be only a partial solution.

Because of librarians' strong aesthetic needs and literary interests, it is important to ask whether their jobs provide outlets for these motives. There is little evidence on this point other than informal subjective reports of librarians. Most library positions probably do provide some gratification of aesthetic interests and desires, if only because of the physical setting of the occupation and the fact of its being, in a very literal sense, book-related. For the subprofessional librarian, however, routine clerical duties are apt to crowd out opportunities for aesthetic fulfillment, and for the professional librarian administrative and public contact responsibilities are likely to do the same.

The need for self-actualization, *i.e.*, the need to express one's potentialities in one's living, has in recent years been recognized by many psychological theorists as the major human motive, and has been regarded as subsuming all other needs. Fulfillment of the need for self-actualization in one's work also has recently been hypothesized to be the main means of attaining vocational adjustment. If a job provides an opportunity for the worker to act as the kind of person he believes he is, in a way consistent with the role he would really like to assume at work, then he will tend to feel happy in it.[23]

This being the case, more is required than that a particular librarian's position allow fulfillment of the needs and interests that most people hold in common and that are characteristic of the modal librarian. For maximum vocational adjustment, the position must also provide outlets for the unique needs, interests, values, and other traits of the individual. Where a job is inappropriate because of failure to fulfill unique traits, the situation may be extremely difficult to correct, both because the traits that are being frustrated may not be recognized, and because it may be virtually impossible to adapt the position to the peculiar needs of the staff member.

UNDERSTANDING THE EMOTIONALLY DISTURBED STAFF MEMBER

Unique traits of the individual worker may be well-integrated in the personality of the person, and serve healthy adaptive functions for him. Unique traits may, on the other hand, suggest the presence of emotional disturbance that may interfere with vocational adjustment. It is impossible in a short space to treat even superficially all the varieties of behavior that are characteristic of the conflicted or emotionally disturbed personality. The reader is referred to texts in mental hygiene and abnormal psychology included in the bibliography for extended discussion of the development and dynamics of psychological maladjustment.

A major feature of emotional disturbance is the occurrence of feelings and behavior that are not appropriate to the external circumstances of the person. Thus, an employee, when given a helpful suggestion by a skilled supervisor, may respond with irritability or outright hostility. It is this inappropriate, inefficient, strained quality that makes behavior often seem inexplicable and frustrating, and, in some cases, bizarre. Yet, we can always be sure that no matter how strange behavior appears to the outsider, to the person himself it is always appropriate to his perception of his situation and it always implements his understanding at the moment of the best way to act. In the example above, the worker may perceive himself as competent, but may be implicitly threatened by inadequacy feelings, so that outside assistance is regarded as something that must be combated. It is difficult to change such behavior because it is based on perceptions that have been learned over many years and that are now regarded as reality by the perceiver. It is helpful, however, in trying to understand behavior, to attempt to see how the individual looks at himself and the world, how, in effect, he perceives things. Then, his behavior will usually make more sense to the outsider. In trying to understand inappropriate behavior, you should, then, endeavor to understand the person's perceptions, and what purpose his actions have in their light. At times, behavior may be more an expression of anxiety than an attempt to accomplish some goal, but it is always consistent with the person's perceptions.

Four signs may be used as an aid in evaluating disturbed behavior. One or more of these symptoms may suggest that a staff member will require special attention if he is to work effectively: (1) subjective feelings of being ill-at-ease, anxiety, depressed mood; (2) poor social relationships; (3) inefficient use of abilities and other capacities; and (4) inadequate evaluation of reality, distorted perception of self and others. (In extreme cases, the disturbed reality relationship may be one of loss of contact with the real world that most people are responsive to, and a corresponding withdrawal into a self-created world of fantasy.)

It should be stressed that there is not a clear line between emotional normality and abnormality, and that it would be unwise to draw conclusions about the presence of personality disturbance from the above signs alone. In appraising personality, modern psychologists and psychiatrists no longer focus on specific symptoms, such as compulsive handwashing and hysterical paralysis, but instead study pervasive personality manifestations, such as emotional rigidity, shallowness, and variability.

SUGGESTIONS FOR HANDLING THE PROBLEM STAFF MEMBER

The first step in a program of management of problem employees is actually a preventive measure that should be used as early as possible. This step, which requires continuing attention from the administration of the library, is to provide a working environment that comes as close as possible to meeting the basic human needs discussed earlier. The social structure of the organization should be planned in such a way that the members of the staff are able to relate their contributions to the overall activity, and so that they are accorded respect within the larger social unit of the library.[24] The need for improvement in library organization is shown by Bryan's finding that about half of professional assistants believed that they were given too little opportunity for participation in policy determination.[25]

Both the over-all situation and specific components of the situation, such as the quality of supervision, should be reviewed to see whether they allow gratification of desires for self-expression, independence, interesting experience, and being of service to others.[26] And an even more basic requirement, as Maslow's theory suggests, is the provision of adequate salaries, pension systems, and improved schedules of working hours. Many advances need to be made in this area because of the widespread failure to develop modern personnel programs in libraries.

Kahn and Katz[27] report research which shows that effective leaders in a variety of work situations can be distinguished from less successful leaders. The effective leaders tended to assume the expected supervisory functions more frequently than did the less effective leaders, and yet more often delegated authority and developed group cohesiveness, and were generally more employee-centered and less production-oriented in their approach to their supervisees. Their behavior contributed toward the establishment of a supportive personal relationship between themselves and the members of their work group.

The second step in dealing with a problem staff member is to make certain that the problem is not one of improper placement. The staff member should possess the necessary ability and training for his position, and the position should furthermore be one that allows him to "be" the kind of person he would like to be in his work. If the problem behavior appears to be a result of deficiencies in this area or of inconsistencies between what the position requires and what the person desires, then the needed training should be obtained, or transfer to a more appropriate position should be considered. Professional vocational counseling may be desirable in cases where change in career appears indicated. Improvements may be needed in selection procedures and training and in position classification and promotion policies.

In-service training may be desirable both as a means of education in technical developments in library science, and as a way of improving communication between staff and administrators. Organized group discussion and counseling may be of value in improving staff relationships and ability to handle mutual problems. One research study, for example, found that teachers showed trends toward increased general adjustment as a result of counseling in a group setting.[28]

If the problem behavior persists even after the above steps have been taken, then it is likely that the behavior is not an adaptive response to a problem situation but rather an idiosyncratic expression of the staff member's personality. The situation is in this case allowing potential need gratification, the person's characteristics and the demands of his position are reasonably well matched, and we are left with the question as to how we can help the individual to recognize the opportunities to fulfill his needs and to live out his desired role in his position. Often in such cases, while the staff member recognizes no realistic problems of discrepancy between the kind of role he would like to play in his work and the role his position allows, he still feels inadequate or unhappy with himself. He might, therefore, be dissatisfied in almost any occupation. His problem is one of inner strain and conflicted attitudes toward himself.

There are various approaches possible in helping the problem employee whose inadequacies arise largely from the nature of his own personality. It is almost always desirable from a humane point of view and as a mental health effort to assist problem employees to continue in productive roles as workers, and it is also frequently the practical thing to do in the light of the experience and ability that these employees may offer. Sometimes the problem employee can be helped while on the job through special efforts of supervisors to understand him and to accept his work, or to make minor modifications in his job.

A basic principle to remember in helping the problem employee on the job is that change in the direction of becoming a more adequate employee, or a more adequate person in general, is most likely to occur under conditions of freedom from threat. This fact is not believed by many supervisors, teachers, and parents, but it does represent the best opinion of modern psychology.

Unfortunately, it is sometimes difficult to establish an atmosphere of freedom from threat with a problem employee. He may expect to be terminated or at least criticized for his shortcomings, and his supervisor may indeed feel provoked to treat him in this way. But, if the problem employee is to be freed to change, to relax his ineffective defenses to the point where he can see better ways of acting, he will have to be placed under conditions of reduced strain, threat, and anxiety. This is true even though the problem employee's behavior appears superficially to result from irresponsible lack of concern.

It is very difficult to determine what specific modifications should be made in a given job situation to accommodate it to a particular employee. The best recommendation that can be made without intensive study of the individual staff member is to provide the sort of environment discussed above that allows fulfillment of the needs that are important for virtually all people, and to reinforce this situation by establishing an atmosphere of acceptance and respect for the employee, together with the "quiet expectation" that the employee *will* do well. (People tend to behave in accordance with your expectations—a phenomenon that the sociologists have termed "the self-fulfilling prophecy.")

Some industrial firms have in recent years established counseling services within their organizations, modeled after the famous program of the Western Electric Hawthorne plant.[29] Such services, existing as they do within the firm, can conveniently be used earlier and with less serious problems than can counseling facilities outside the organization. Only fairly large firms find it feasible to establish such programs, however. Smaller organizations ordinarily have to rely on more informal counseling by supervisors who lack training in counseling and psychotherapy, and on the services of outside agencies such as community mental hygiene clinics.

Where problem cases do not improve under the above conditions, or where the behavior problems seem so severe that immediate psychiatric help appears desirable, a supervisor may wish to refer a staff member for diagnostic evaluation and treatment. Such diagnostic and advisory services have been used occasionally by some businesses for many years,[30] and there is some evidence that even brief treatment of rather seriously disturbed employees can result in improved work adjustment.[31] Careful selection of consultants is required in order to obtain both competent personality appraisal and knowledgeable consideration of the demands of the work situation. A community mental health clinic that will apply the knowledge of its staff of psychiatrists, psychologists, and social workers to problems of personal and vocational adjustment may be the best source of help. Assistance may also be obtained from psychologists in the new specialty of counseling psychology, which uses the insights of both vocational counseling and clinical psychology. Some private practitioners in clinical psychology and in psychiatry also possess the necessary skills and experience to be of assistance with problems of vocational maladjustment. If the problem is more a result of a problem situation or of ineffective selection, placement, and training, personnel psychologists, occupational sociologists, or management consultants may have important contributions to make. If the problem is one of severe personality disorder, psychiatric help will be needed for the individual, even though by itself this may do nothing to correct a job situation that may have aggravated the person's emotional problem.

SUMMARY

Problem employees occur with relative frequency in most work situations. A variety of steps may be taken to assist them to become more effective workers and also to prevent the emergence of work problems in other staff members.

1. The work situation should be planned so as to allow fulfillment of basic human needs such as depicted by Maslow and Centers.
2. Effort should be taken to insure proper occupational placement in the light of the individual's abilities, interests, personality, values, and role aspirations.
3. Orientation and training appropriate to the individual staff member's position should be instituted.
4. Supervisors should endeavor to establish an atmosphere of genuine acceptance and respect for the members of the staff, but also to explain the duties and responsibilities of each position as clearly as possible to the person who holds the position.
5. Insofar as is consistent with the requirements of the institution, the staff member should be allowed to modify his job so as to be more in line with his traits.
6. Problem employees whose performance does not improve under the above conditions may be referred to an outside agency for counseling or for other help with their adjustment.

BIBLIOGRAPHY

Personnel Management

Bryan, Alice I., *The Public Librarian* (New York: Columbia University Press, 1952).
Cantor, N., *Employee Counseling* (New York: McGraw-Hill, 1945).
Fay, Adra M., *Supervising Library Personnel* (Chicago: American Library Association, 1950).
Fromm, E., *The Sane Society* (New York: Rinehart, 1955).

Gordon, T., "Group-Centered Leadership and Administration," In C. R. Rogers, *Client-Centered Therapy* (Boston: Houghton Mifflin, 1951), ch. 8.

Heckmann, I. L., Jr., and Huneryager, S. G., (Eds.), *Human Relations in Management* (Cincinnati: South-Western, 1960).

Martin, L.,(Ed.), *Personnel Administration in Libraries* (Chicago: University of Chicago Press, 1946).

Mayo, E., *The Social Problems of an Industrial Civilization* (Boston: Harvard University Graduate School of Business Administration, 1945).

Stebbins, Kathleen B., *Personnel Administration in Libraries* (New York: Scarecrow Press, 1958).

Vocational Psychology and Sociology

Caplow, T., *The Sociology of Work* (Minneapolis: University of Minnesota Press, 1954).

Miller, D. C. and Form, W. H., *Industrial Sociology* (New York: Harper, 1951).

Roe, Anne, *The Psychology of Occupations* (New York: Wiley, 1956).

Super, D. E., *The Psychology of Careers* (New York: Harper, 1957).

Personality Dynamics

Combs, A. W. and Snygg, D., *Individual Behavior* (Rev. ed.; New York: Harper, 1959).

Shaffer, L. F., & Shoben, E. J., Jr., *The Psychology of Adjustment*. (2nd ed.; Boston: Houghton Mifflin, 1956).

White, R. W., *The Abnormal Personality* (2nd ed.; New York: Ronald, 1956).

FOOTNOTES

[1] R. Fraser, *The Incidence of Neurosis Among Factory Workers* (London: H. M. Stationery Office, 1947).
V. V. Anderson, *Psychiatry in Industry* (New York: Harper, 1929).

[2] H. A. Robinson and R. P. Connors, "Job Satisfaction Researches of 1959," *Personnel Guid. J.,* 1960, 39, 47-52.

[3] F. Herzberg; B. Mausner; R. O. Peterson and Dora F. Capwell, *Job Attitudes: Review of Research and Opinion* (Pittsburgh: Psychological Services of Pittsburgh, 1957).

[4] A. H. Brayfield and W. H. Crockett, "Employee Attitudes and Employee Performance," *Psychol. Bull.,* 1955, 52, 396-424.

[5] A. H. Maslow, *Motivation and Personality* (New York: Harper, 1954), Chapter 5.

[6] Anne Roe, *The Psychology of Occupations* (New York: Wiley, 1956), pp. 31-33.

[7] R. Centers, "Motivational Aspects of Occupational Stratification," *J. Soc. Psychol.,* 1948, 28, 187-217.

[8] Alice I. Bryan, *The Public Librarian* (New York: Columbia University Press, 1952).

[9] R. R. Douglass, The Personality of the Librarian (Ph.D. dissertation, University of Chicago, 1957).

[10] Bryan, *op. cit.,* p. 43.

[11] *Ibid.*

[12] *Ibid.,* pp. 43-44.

[13] *Ibid.,* p. 123.

[14] *Ibid.,* p. 125.

[15] *Ibid.,* p. 442.

[16] Douglass, *op. cit.,* pp. 122-125.

[17] *Ibid.,* p. 121.

[18] Bryan, *op. cit.,* p. 129.

[19] Roe, *op. cit.,* p. 32.

[20] Bryan, *op. cit.,* p. 37.

[21] W. L. Warner; Marchia Meeker; and K. Eels, *Social Class in America* (Chicago: Science Research Associates, 1949).

[22] Bryan, *op. cit.,* p. 440.

[23] D. E. Super, *The Psychology of Careers* (New York: Harper, 1957) ch. 13.
A. L. Brophy, "Self, Role, and Satisfaction," *Genet. Psychol. Monogr.,* 1959, 59, 263-308.
R. H. Schaffer, "Job Satisfaction as Related to Need Satisfaction in Work," *Psychol. Monogr.,* 1953, 67, No. 14.

[24] E. Mayo, *The Social Problems of an Industrial Civilization* (Boston: Harvard University Graduate School of Business Administration, 1945).

[25] Bryan, *op. cit.,* p. 276.

[26] Centers, *op. cit.*

[27] R. L. Kahn and D. Katz, "Leadership Practices in Relation to Productivity and Morale," In D. Cartwright and A. Zander (Eds.), *Group Dynamics* (Evanston, Illinois: Row, Peterson, 1953), ch. 41.

[28] G. Gazda and M. Ohlsen, "The Effects of Short-Term Group Counseling on Prospective Counselors," *Personnel Guid. J.,* 1961, 39, 634-638.

[29] F. J. Roethlisberger and W. J. Dickson, *Management and the Worker* (Cambridge: Harvard University Press, 1939).
[30] Anderson, *op. cit.*
[31] A. L. Brophy and Paula O. Horowitz, "Improving Poor Work Adjustment Through Psychodiagnostic Evaluation," *Ment. Hyg.*, N.Y., 1961, 45, 46-52.

ABOUT THE AUTHORS—Alfred L. Brophy is a counseling psychologist and associate professor of psychology at the U. S. Coast Guard Academy in New London, Connecticut. He received his B.A. from Harvard in 1952 and completed his professional training in counseling psychology at Columbia University, receiving his M.A. in 1953 and his Ph.D. in 1957. While completing work for his doctorate at Columbia, he interned at Veterans Administration Hospitals in New York, New Jersey, and Massachusetts. From 1957 to 1959 he served as clinical psychologist for the U. S. Public Health Service in Washington, D. C. He subsequently held teaching positions at Richmond Professional Institute, College of William and Mary, where he was associate professor of psychology from 1959 to 1961, and at the University of Illinois, Urbana, where he was associate professor of educational psychology before assuming his present position in 1964. Brophy's major interests are in vocational and psychotherapeutic counseling and occupational psychology; his writings have appeared in a number of leading professional journals, including the *American Psychologist*, *Genetic Psychology Monographs*, and *Mental Hygiene*.

George M. Gazda centers his research and teaching activity primarily in the field of Guidance and Counseling. He holds undergraduate and master's degrees from Western Illinois University and completed his doctorate at the University of Illinois in 1959. He was Assistant Professor of Education at Illinois, later at the University of Missouri, followed by a period from 1964–67 as Associate Professor at the University of Georgia. Since 1967 he has been Professor of Education at the University of Georgia, where he also is engaged in efforts with the Department of Psychiatry and Neurology in the Medical College of Georgia. Gazda's principal publications include the *Handbook of Guidance Services* (1966), *Innovations to Group Psychotherapy* (1968), *Basic Approaches to Group Psychotherapy and Group Counseling* (1968), and *Group Guidance: A Critical Incidents Approach* (1968).

Finance and Budgetary Controls

A central determinant of the effectiveness of an organization will be not only the volume of economic resources accessible to it, but the mechanisms which it employs in the effective exploitation and utilization of these resources. For budgetary control and financial management are the keys to efficient utilization of those dollars invested in the organization for the attainment of its ends. Because there is no scientific basis for the "proper content" of an organization's budget and since the process of seeking and utilizing resources is inevitably a sequence of struggle and compromise, the effective administrator is attuned to the subtleties, the nuances, the behavioral and the organizational ramifications of the process. Librarians have not always been comfortable with or effective at the task of financial management. Yet, there can be little argument that in organizations of growing scale, skill in gaining access to and monitoring appropriately the resources of the organization becomes an increasingly essential requisite. One selection cannot be expected to foster sophistication about the budgetary process, but it may serve to underscore the key political and behavioral elements.

The Study of Budgeting

by Frederick C. Mosher

>*The essential contribution of this piece is to analyze and carefully detail the underlying principles as well as the key problems relating to effective budgetary management in the public sector. Perhaps nowhere is the essential point and purpose of the budget process better detailed than in this selection. The most central issue identifies that while budgets traffic in dollars, they are the result of human interaction, human deliberative processes and human administration.*

The understanding of budgeting in its totality presents difficult problems to the student. It is a field in which several different social science disciplines are concerned and have made their contributions. But the disciplines do not quite come together. Bringing them into a meaningful context is no simple job. It involves mastering and relating their different approaches and interests, their differing degrees of abstraction and specificity, their varieties of technique, and their jargons. Few persons if any have accomplished the task to their satisfaction.

Political scientists, among the first in the field, have long been concerned with the problems involved in control of fiscal affairs, the relations of the legislature and the executive in this field, the constitutional and legal bases of fiscal activities generally and of budgeting in particular. They have given much attention to the organization of the Executive as it relates to budgeting among other things, to the Bureau of the Budget, and particularly to the organization and processes of Congress for appropriations and revenues. There have also been scattered discussions of substantive issues in the budget incident to studies of various fields of public policy such as foreign aid and social welfare.

Modern public administration, an outgrowth and still, by most definitions, a part of political science, has since its birth about half a century ago concentrated its attention in the field of budgeting upon formal organizational arrangements and procedures. Its accent has been upon the mechanism, the calendar, the forms and justifications, the classification of accounts, and the system of responsibilities. It has pushed the development of program planning, work measurement, cost accounting, and reporting. Probably more than any other field, it is responsible for the rationalist concept in budgeting and for the model form now generally accepted for the budget process on the administrative side.

The economists and their ancestors, the political economists, were involved in one phase of public fiscal affairs for many, many decades and even centuries. Most of the classical economists from Adam Smith on studied public finance, but their primary concern was its effect upon the nonpublic economy. Their major field of interest was upon revenues and taxation with accent upon the incidence of taxes. It was not until relatively recently, about two decades ago, that much attention was directed to the expenditure side of the budget or to the application of economic principles and techniques to public financial management. The tremendous acceleration of economists' activity in the public sphere was, of course, stimulated by the recovery experiments of the New Deal and later the problems of economic and financial management of the war economy and the efforts toward postwar planning. Specific concern with the Federal budget as an economic problem was stimulated by the development of the Fiscal Division of the Bureau of the Budget and, later, of the Council of Economic Advisers, and by the invention of such new devices as the national economic budget and the consolidated cash budget. Probably more than any other group, the economists are contributing to the understanding of, and policy relating to, the Federal budget as a totality, the interrelationships of Federal fiscal activity with

---

SOURCE: Reprinted from Frederick C. Mosher, *Program Budgeting: Theory and Practice with Particular Reference to the U. S. Department of the Army* (Public Administration Service, 1954), Chap. 1, "The Study of Budgeting," pp. 1–18, by permission of the publisher.

the private sector of the economy, and the implications and impact of various major budgetary programs and policies. Their concern is more with substance and economic policy in the budget, less with procedural and political power aspects.

The fourth professional field which has been importantly concerned in public budgeting is that of accounting, vaguely related on one side with economics and on the other with public administration. Although accounting has served governments since time immemorial, it is probably safe to say that current emphasis in accounting thought and practice is in the area of business rather than public finance. There are intrinsic differences between the two, and the Federal accounting system, developed on foundations laid down by Alexander Hamilton, is in many ways unique unto itself. Much of the current ferment about reforms of the Federal financial system is being stimulated and led by the accounting fraternity, and part of it at least is characterized by the effort to adapt private accounting practice to the Federal system. Accounting concern extends well beyond the forms and techniques of keeping books, the classifications of accounts, the financial reports and controls. The accounts are the basis of budget estimates, in large part the informational base for evaluation and decision on budgetary questions, and the source of authority for budgetary expenditures. The classifications of accounts and the way they are related to programs, functions, and organizations, are highly significant in decision-making and management generally. The current drive in the direction of accrual accounting, costing, revolving funds, and consumer budgeting importantly affect organization, program, and the entire system of responsibility.

Other disciplines have contributed only fragmentarily to our understanding of budgeting. It is particularly unfortunate that those social sciences in the general field of social relations, such as anthropology, sociology, and social psychology, have not used the budget process as a laboratory for some of their approaches and hypotheses. There is a conspicuous need for exploration of the significance of institutional arrangements and of interpersonal relationships in budgeting.

The obvious disparity in the aspects of the various approaches is particularly significant in the study of budgeting, because the very essence of this activity is in bringing aspects together, in providing links between program and action, between policy and administration, and between an infinite multiplicity of detail and a few understandable and generalized issues. It is two movements, following each other in sequence but going in opposite directions: a movement of synthesizing and generalizing, and a reverse movement of particularizing. The concentration upon the generalized issues at one end or upon the specific details at the other misses the vital character of the phenomenon as a whole.

BUDGETING AS COMMUNICATION

Another way of expressing this is that budgeting is a device whereby the same phenomena and the same ideas are progressively translated into differing levels of meaning. If one were to ask a carpenter who is at work on a house what he is doing, he might reply, "I am pounding these nails into these boards," or, "I am helping to build this house." It is vastly improbable that he would say "I am expending these nails and these boards and depreciating this hammer," though such an answer would be correct from the accounting standpoint. If he had a broader frame of reference, he might answer, "I am part of an industry which provides the places where people can live and work and thus build the future prosperity and happiness for all of us." These do not exhaust his possible correct answers. He might say that he was simply carrying out the blueprint provided him by the contractor; or that he was only practicing his trade; or that he was abiding by the policies and regulations of his union; or that he was earning the wherewithal to provide his family with food, clothing, and shelter.

Obviously, all these answers, while technically accurate, would not be equally appropriate or useful. Their propriety would depend heavily upon the source of, and reason for, the inquiry. It is also probable that the nature of the reply would depend upon the carpenter himself—his own view of his activity and his trade and particularly his perception of the inquirer and the latter's motivations.

The budget process permits, and to some extent compels, objectivity in the perception of information. This it does by formalization, by standardizing the categories of information that will be considered and the form of their presentation, and by prescribing specifically against the introduction of certain kinds of personal and institutional considerations. In reference to our carpenter analogy, the attempt is made to minimize the carpenter's subjective considerations—as well as those of the inquirer—in framing the answer to the question.

The budget process also serves as a device whereby the carpenter's answer may be translated into a level of meaning useful and significant to consideration and decision by the inquirers at successively broader levels of cognizance. Thus it may be put together with the answers of a great many other carpenters, plumbers, electricians, and other builders. The kind of meaning appropriate to each successive level may well be, and to some extent probably should be, different from the ones below and above it. In more specific terms, we might imagine the information having to do with a carpenter's activities and the plans for his future work in the Army Corps of Engineers. Does the budget process provide the information necessary for planning and decision at the level of his foreman? the project director? the District Engineer? the Division Engineer? the Chief of Engineers? the Chief of Staff? the Secretary of the Army? the Bureau of the Budget? the President? the Congress? It is evident that the information necessary and appropriate to the kinds of decisions at many of these levels differs not only in its extent and in its detail, but also in kind. This applies to the accumulating or estimating part of the process and also to the reverse part of the process, the allocation and allotment of resources into increasingly specific purposes and accounts.

There are, of course, a variety of ways to translate information in both the synthesizing and the "spreading" processes. The ways in which it is done importantly affect the kinds of treatment and kinds of decisions that can be made at various levels. Furthermore, it can and usually must be done in various different ways at the same time for the same items of information. This is why budgetary classification has always assumed an important role; in one sense, it is the essence of the rationale of the recent strivings toward "performance budgeting."

The importance of the two-way movement approach to budgeting is directly related to the factor of organizational size and functional heterogeneity. The greater the size and complexity, the greater is the factor of organizational distance, the more difficult is the communication, and the greater are the disparities in points of view and kinds of considerations brought to bear upon the same information at different levels. Furthermore, in large organizations, the possibility of effective consideration of details progressively declines as the information moves up the levels of hierarchy. A significant factor in our present budgetary problems is that we have inherited from the past budgetary practices and philosophy which were originally developed for organizations of far less size and complexity. For example, it may be perfectly appropriate for a town council in a small town to consider the job of an individual carpenter, his wage and his habits of economy or profligacy in the use of boards and nails. But for the President or the Congress to give similar attention to the Corps of Engineers carpenter at Camp Drum would be inappropriate, useless, and in fact impossible on any systematic basis. Budgetary information and budgetary classifications must be tailored to the needs, the scope, and the areas of effective decision at various levels in large organizations.

PURPOSES AND PRINCIPLES OF BUDGETING

The budget process thus presented is primarily a system of communications, regularized and cyclical. Its purposes fall into two logical categories: first, the bringing of information to the proper level for the making of decisions—a category in governmental policies, programs, and objectives, which we may roughly classify as policy; and, second, the providing of information both upward and downward so that those decisions will be properly carried out—a category we may roughly classify as administrative.

Its potential value in the first connection is tremendous and unique. It is the only device invented in democratic governments which does, or can do, all of the following things:

1. Bring about a regular, periodic reconsideration and reevaluation of government purposes and objectives.
2. Facilitate a comparative evaluation of different purposes and programs in relation to each other and in relation to their relative costs.
3. Provide a basis for examining the total role of the government and its cost, in relation to the private sector of the economy, and thus for tailoring the governmental program to the society and the economy as a whole.
4. Provide a periodic link among the administrative organizations, the Executive, the Congress, and segments of the public, and thus an important basis of democratic information and discussion and of democratic control of governmental activities.

The second category of budgetary purposes involves its use as an instrument for carrying out public policy legally, honestly, and efficiently. In this function it:

1. Provides the legal basis for the expenditure of funds.
2. Provides the framework for public accounts and fiscal accountability.
3. Makes possible systematic re-examination of internal operations from the standpoint of efficiency and economy.
4. Facilitates delegation of operating as well as financial authority and responsibility, while providing the basis for central controls.

It is probable that the greater part of budgetary theory and of budgetary principles have been dedicated to the second, or administrative, type of purpose. In fact there appears to be fairly widespread agreement on what these principles are. Many of them are expressed in the literature on budgeting. Presented below, for yardstick purposes and without any attempt to develop new, or criticize old, principles of budgeting, is a synthesis of some of the "doctrines" of budgetary administration that are most pertinent to large governmental organization.

A first principle is the principle of responsibility: that officials be held responsible for the performance of their assigned functions and the utilization of resources for that purpose; and that they not be held responsible for either more or less than the scope of their authority over activities and resources. The primary responsibility for the allocation and consumption of resources, whether they be in the form of funds or goods and services purchased and paid for elsewhere, is vested in the using organization.

A second principle is that authority and responsibility be delegated to the operating echelon where activities are performed and resources are utilized. Administration, and the responsibility therefore, should be "on the spot," not "absentee."

A third principle is that officials held responsible for performance should have a primary voice in the planning of how their activities will be performed and in estimating the resource requirements necessary to perform them. Such plans and estimates must be reviewed and adjusted by higher authority, and the planning official should be called upon to support and defend his plans. But basically the functions of planning and carrying out plans within approved missions should be vested at the same echelon.

A fourth principle is that the operating official should derive his authority and responsibility from one and only one higher unit. And this unit should be the source both of his program and his resources to perform that program. His plans and estimates should go to that unit; his directives and resources should come from it; and his accountability for performance should be to it.

A fifth principle is that fiscal responsibility and responsibility for other resources be merged with program responsibility at every echelon and not follow separate and unrelated or poorly related channels.

A sixth principle is that methods and criteria be established and utilized to hold operating officials accountable for results in relation to costs. This requires the measurement of work and of costs, the development of standards, and the comparison of work and costs with like activities outside and inside the agency and from year to year.

A seventh principle is that each official with responsibility be made in fact, responsible; that is, that he have a stake in and an incentive for exercising his responsibilities in an effective and efficient manner. Positively, this means that he should anticipate a reward for a job well done; negatively, a penalty for one poorly done. Ultimately, the system of responsibility must be tied in with the personnel system.

THE CONTEXT OF BUDGETING

The purposes and the principles enumerated above are, it is thought, useful generalizations for the evaluation of budget systems. And they are so used in this document. But it should be borne in mind that they are generalized; they are abstract; and they are impersonal. They are meaningful and useful only to the extent that they are applied to organizations and institutions which are themselves understood. Budgeting, like other social processes, is a human undertaking, carried on by people who are subject to a wide variety of influences and motivations. The process itself can be examined, evaluated, and improved only to a minor degree unless there is appreciation of the totality of the situations and the environment within which it is carried on. This contextual framework is of tremendous importance in national budgeting and perhaps particularly military budgeting, and its significance is commonly underestimated.

In an article published late in 1952, D. W. Brogan, eminent British political scientist, chided the American people for what he termed "The Illusion of American Omnipotence."[1] He referred to our recent disposition to attribute to ourselves, and more particularly to certain allegedly treacherous or incompetent leaders, full responsibility for the course of world events. He pointed out that if we assume American blame for the fall of Czechoslovakia or the revolution of China, we must also assume that the United States had within its power to determine the social and political developments in these countries and elsewhere in the world. He did not dispute that American policy may influence and perhaps modify events far from our shores. But the thought that we, or a few of our leaders, could halt or reverse the forces of change in China, developing out of a revolution that started with our blessings a quarter of a century ago, reflects, according to Brogan, a conceit that may be frustrating and demoralizing to ourselves and dangerous to our relations with others.

This same illusion, or at least a very parallel

one, was illustrated during the course of the 1952 election campaign after Adlai Stevenson's remark that the extent of possible budget cuts would depend most heavily upon decisions made in Moscow. This suggestion of a restriction upon unlimited American discretion over a matter of domestic as well as international import attracted virulent attack. One suspects that the attack was effective. Yet the truth of the statement, however repugnant to national pride and however impolitic, could hardly be more obvious. The tendency in American attitudes and thought noted by Mr. Brogan in the field of foreign affairs is related to, and probably an outgrowth of, a widespread confidence in American mastery over our own internal affairs and destiny. The idea of omnipotence, identified with a relatively small number of political and administrative leaders, is a significant feature in our political culture. It is a source of strength and of challenge. "Nothing is impossible." Yet it also begets misunderstanding and frustration. Our national public life seems to be a machine-gun staccato of day-to-day climaxes, each linked with a few well-known names of public figures. It becomes difficult for the student, let alone the radio-listening public, to link the gun shots together, to find the strands of meaning which can make out of a series of actions a course, or a trend, or a direction of events. The imputation to the aimers and firers of the guns—the decision-makers—of omnipotence in aiming and timing the gunfire implies a freedom in their action which in many cases is quite unreal. This, of course, encourages us later on to hold them responsible for consequences, or alleged consequences, of events over which, in fact, they may have had little or no control.

There is no question that, with the expanding role of government in our national and international life, with the increasingly interlocking and interdependent structure of our society, and with the apparent centralization of political power in a relatively few officials, leadership in the governmental sphere has assumed a crucial and decisive role. What is left out of the focus upon these leaders, so dramatized by the press and the other media of mass communications, is that their decisions and pronouncements, including those affecting the budget, must grow out of a context that is full of unknowns, of prior commitments, and of influences that are relatively uncontrolled. The freedom of action of a President, or of a subcommittee of Congress, at any given moment in time is limited, and the degree to which the limitation is recognized is a measure of the sense of responsibility of the official or the group of officials involved.

Parts of the context are the large *areas of crucial importance to future plans which are unknown or relatively unresponsive to control.* These factors are particularly significant in military budgeting. The plans and capabilities of potential enemies, cited above in reference to Adlai Stevenson's statement, are perhaps the most significant. Future technical developments in the design of weapons are increasingly subject to planning and control but still constitute an area of high uncertainty. Industrial development and productivity, the potentialities of allies, and defensive ability to ward off bomb attacks on our industrial centers all introduce elements of uncertainty, varyingly responsive to public planning and control.

A second important element conditioning budgetary decision-making is that of *time*. It has become a popular recreation, unsuccessfully formalized in the legislative budget provision of the Legislative Reorganization Act of 1946, to settle in advance upon an expenditure figure for the coming fiscal year. There seems here to be an assumption that a President or a Congress has discretion for any given year to determine upon a figure of 90 or 80 or 70 or 50 billion dollars as a desirable budget. No President and no Congress can escape from the past, whether or not it is of his or its own making. A large part of the annual expenditure budget is in fact legally committed at least one year before the budget year. The Congress which went into office in January, 1953, for example, made appropriations for the fiscal year ending June 30, 1954, but a major proportion of the expenditures of that year already had been appropriated or otherwise committed by prior Congresses. The decisions which Congress made in the spring of 1953 will influence importantly the expenditures of fiscal year 1955, but the 83rd Congress will probably adjourn permanently soon after the beginning of that fiscal year, to be succeeded by the 84th Congress. Of course Presidents and Congresses can and do make important and crucial decisions affecting the next following budget year and even affecting the current one. But in public financial affairs, as in public policy matters, there is a continuity, an "on-going-ness," not easy to interrupt. The bulk of national programs and the national budgets which reflect their costs fall in this category.

The past is parent to the present and also, to a

considerable degree, to the future. Current governmental authorities can interpret the past, can juggle the records of it, but they can not change it. The social, economic, and political forces that have grown out of the past and have given rise to public policies for the present do not, except under the pressure of total emergencies, cease or reverse themselves. A great many of these are legally or morally protected: service on the public debt, fulfillment of obligations for foreign aid, payment on social security, payment to contractors for goods and services, and retirement to civil servants. Others, amendable in legislation and appropriations, remain responsive to the forces and the needs which procreated them: build-up of the military establishment, support for farm prices, services to veterans, Federal aid in social welfare, highways, and many others. The degree of commitment, legal, political, and moral, of course varies widely among different programs. An important qualification for the statesman and the administrator is his awareness and understanding of these factors. It is indispensable to his determination of the points at which current actions will be both possible and desirable, the pace at which they should be accomplished, and the effects which may reasonably be expected.

Our political leaders seldom have the opportunity to "start from scratch." More often, their actions are of the order of accelerating or decelerating or changing the direction of programs and of movements. When they do initiate new undertakings, it is usually in response to forces and to needs that have been developed and articulated for a considerable period of time. Many, perhaps most, of their significant innovations require years, terms of office, and decades for full accomplishment. Roosevelt's TVA, a product of more than a decade of political gestations, did not complete even its physical program during his lifetime, even though he spent more than three terms in the White House. Truman's Point Four was just getting away from "home base" as he vacated office, a full four years to the day from the time of his original proposal. The military build-up, begun soon after the outbreak of hostilities in Korea, will not achieve its primary objective until 1955 or 1956, at which time it will be under the direction of a different President as well as a different Congress from those who initiated it.

The appreciation of the temporal context of budgeting is made more difficult because it is accomplished in periodic cycles. One of the distinguishing features, and one of the principal values, of the budget is that it recurs every year on a calendar basis, forcing a systematic reexamination of public policies and activities. The Constitution, the laws, and the necessities of official accountability have compelled a somewhat artificial division of time, for public purposes, into discrete fiscal years that end and begin at midnight of June 30. The fiscal year is indeed a very real and important matter in public administration and it has great program and operational significance, probably more than might be desirable. Practically all agency programs are geared to it, as is a large part of the procedure of Congress. In the fiscal realm, it has been frequently dramatized by the unseemly obligation of uncommitted funds in late June; by the dying agencies which must go out of business by the end of the fiscal year; by the occasional failures of Congress to appropriate funds in time and the payless paydays of Federal employees.

The fiscal year is unquestionably a convenient and necessary device for administrative, accounting, and public control purposes. But to the extent that it encourages thinking of each year as an "autonomous" unit in time, independent of the year that preceded and the year that will follow, it is deceptive. Most public porgrams are growing or declining or maintaining an even keel through the months and years. Midnight of June 30 has no magic significance to the needs, the demands, and the reasons for public services. In fact, many fiscal and administrative inventions have been motivated at least partially by the desire to minimize the disruptive effects of fiscal-year autonomy—the distinction of obligations from expenditures, contract authorizations, corporation budgets, revolving funds, permanent appropriations, and "no-year" appropriations.

But the most important effect of "fiscal-year thinking" is its encouragement of the feeling that the administrative and legislative powers in a given year have complete authority and responsibility for the fiscal-year budget as such; that it must be considered and treated as an entity. Many of the most important decisions that go into the annual budget affect the expenditures for the fiscal year for which the budget is made and announced moderately, slightly, or not at all. The emphasis placed upon the totals for the fiscal year under consideration detracts from the interest in, and understanding of, the longer-run implications and impact of these decisions. And the anticipation of this overstress upon fiscal-year totals by the decision-makers themselves must certainly affect the determinations that they make. If these officials are considered authoritative with respect to the oncoming fiscal-year budget and responsible for it, they will probably be at least tempted to make it as politically palatable as they can, even when it means transferring unpleasant surprises to the future. An indirect effect of the concept of executive-legislative omnipotence when it is coupled with that of annuality of the budget is to encourage short-run as against long-run thinking and planning.

A third important factor in the context of budget decisions is that of *the institutions and the organizations* involved in the process of budget-making and execution. It is no accident but an important governmental symbolism that the estimates which the President annually transmits to the Congress are widely known as "The President's Budget." The attachment of complete and final responsibility in the President is a fundamental and essential fact in our system of government and administration. But it would be a mistake to assume that the President personally produced the budget, or even that his office and his Bureau of the Budget produced it. The budget is a product of the entire administration. Decisions, small and large but cumulatively of real importance, are made by officials six to ten echelons away from the President. The legislative and the administrative heads can and do make crucial judgments on specific substantive questions raised by the budget process. But even in this activity they are very largely dependent upon the information which is presented to them and the manner and the form in which it is presented. They can influence the way decisions of others are made and the content of the decisions in many direct and many more indirect ways. But it is most important to appreciate that their means are the influencing of behaviors, attitudes, and motivations of other people, associated more or less distantly, rather than the making of all the decisions themselves.

The key requisites for the administrator and the legislator in budgeting are that they be adequately equipped with information to make the best possible decisions on the matters which they, from their particular vantage points, should make; and that they equip those below them with the perspectives and the objectives necessary to the making of the best decisions at their respective levels. The budget process is essentially a system of communications—perhaps the most highly developed and comprehensive formal system of communications in American government. The importance of the communications aspect increases with the size and complexity of the organization, for size implies distance between operating levels and administrative and legislative levels. If budget planning and control are relatively centralized, their wisdom and effectiveness depend heavily upon the operational information conveyed to central levels. If they are relatively decentralized, democratic control and responsibility depend upon the effectiveness with which objectives and perspectives may be conveyed from central to operating levels and assimilated by the latter. In either case, imperfections in communication detract from the true authority of the leaders and from the effective scope of their responsibility.

It is not enough that a President, a Congress, or a department head sincerely want to do the "right" thing, nor that they make wise decisions on the matters they should decide at their level, nor that procedures and organizational arrangements be perfected whereby such matters, and only such, reach them. It is equally important that they be able effectively to influence the decisions of subordinates in accordance with their understandings of problems and objectives. The degree of responsibility often associated with administrative heads by the press and the public is unreal and even impossible. For the leader must work with and through organization, a process which is usually difficult, subtle, and gradual. The pronouncement by spokesmen for the Hoover reports of 3 billion dollars of waste in the Federal establishment did not eliminate the waste. Similarly, the judgment of a President, a department head, or a bureau chief that there was waste in his establishment would not automatically eliminate it, even if the source of the waste were specifically identified. Some people in the organization first have to be stimulated to take action—and for many important areas of alleged waste, action would be required of thousands and even hundreds of thousands of personnel. The military chief of one of the service departments, concerned about the extravagant use of electricity because personnel failed to turn off the unused lights in their rooms and offices, suggested that an order be drafted for his signature directing all personnel to decrease their use of lights by 10 per cent. He dropped the idea when subordinates advised him that such an order would be unenforceable. If a four-star officer cannot direct such a simple change in behaviors of subordinates, who can? And what other recourse does he have to influence their motivations and behaviors in accordance with a need which he can observe and feel?

A going organization is a great package of systems, traditions, habits, values and beliefs, relationships, and behavioral patterns. In the main, these are inevitable elements of cooperative effort, and desirable ones. They form the basis for predictable behaviors, for group and individual reliability, for personal security and group morale. They also constitute resistances and insurance against rapid change. An understanding of the institutional forces, their relative strengths and meanings in the minds of the people linked by them, is essential to the effective management and control of an agency's program and budget. The institutions provide the framework within which and through which—in some degree, by which and for which—budgets are formed and executed. The budget process itself and the organizational arrangements for budgeting may now be regarded as highly institutionalized. But the significance of the institutional context of budgeting is far broader and deeper than this. The grades, ranks, compensation, and specializations of personnel; the methods and procedures of working together; the goals and aspirations of groups; the accustomed patterns of formal and informal organization; the configurations of power within the organization; and even the missions and established programs—all of these affect and are affected by the budget and must be reckoned with by the administrator or legislator seeking changes.

A fourth element of the context of public budgeting may be termed *the human or interpersonal factor.* Though budgets and their supporting documents are almost deadly in their impersonality, and though the official process is highly formalized, all budget decisions are made by human beings as individuals or in association, working with and sometimes against each other. The record and the literature in the field unfortunately provide little in the way of description of the actual processes by which most budgetary decisions are reached. We see the official "position" that resulted and the formal reasons for it, but we can only imagine the course of the path to the "position." The very rigors and formalities of the process probably protect the budget from many possible abuses on purely personal bases. Yet there is reason to believe that the ambitions, professional interests, pride, and even pet foibles and prejudices of individuals find their way into estimates, as well as into the use of appropriated funds. There are cases of mutual "back-scratching" and "log-rolling" within the administrative structure as well as within Congress and between the two.

It is dangerous to generalize about the prevalence and impact of the human factor in budgeting. But it may be worth noting certain interpersonal situations which appear to be both widespread and significant. For example, it is probable that most administrators tend to identify their personal progress and welfare with that of their programs and organization. To some extent, the strength and security of an organization is associated with its size, the rank of its personnel, and the amount of funds available to it. The importance and indispensability of an administrator's program and organization appears, and probably should appear, greater to him than to those in other organizations or to those at higher levels who must balance the demands of many different units. There is thus normally, though not universally, a fairly constant pressure for expansion from both organizational and personal sources.

A second factor working in the same direction has been termed the law of anticipated reactions. An administrator expecting higher echelons to cut his estimates will insure himself against serious damage by building them up to the maximum that he can reasonably defend—and sometimes beyond it. To the outsider this appears as "padding" and "empire-building," but the perpetrator can rationalize it as only common sense and self-protection. It is not unknown that budgets be padded as a favor to reviewing bodies; it gives them an opportunity to make and proclaim cuts without real damage. Indeed, the very expectation of budget review may encourage budget padding.

One view of budgeting is that it is a system of orderly competition in which the competition occurs not in the market place but in the councils of higher authority. Each administrator is competing with his associates for his share of the "pie," and the pie is usually not big enough to go around. But, as in private enterprise, combinations in restraint of competition are not uncommon, and they are about as difficult to deal with. Strong unitary agencies may develop a solid budgetary position in advance, stifling internal competition in order to present a united front before—and against—the next higher echelon, the Bureau of the Budget, and Congress. The same phenomenon sometimes occurs at the bureau level, the regional level, even the division level within agencies. The tendency is undoubtedly strengthened when the administrative personnel within the unit are strongly bound together by a common core of doctrine, professionalism, and career identification through the personnel system. Such restraints to free internal competition are a major problem in public budgeting, particularly in the military services, because they make intelligent review at higher levels more difficult and virtually force the top reviewing bodies to operate below their proper levels—or "give up the ghost."

Partly because of its competitive nature, the budget process tends to accentuate and dramatize conflicts and antagonisms between individuals and groups. In fact, it generates some of its own. Differences and conflicting objectives as between organizations, professional groups, echelons, field and headquarters, and staff and line, are probably a normal and, by and large, constructive part of the governmental environment. The budget process sometimes removes the protective clothing from the competitors and reduces these conflicts to a naked struggle for power or survival. Such struggles within agencies, or between them and the Bureau of the Budget or a Congressional subcommittee, may leave deep-seated hostilities in the minds of the participants, which are communicated to others in the organization. This potential hostility is endemic in many agencies, and has led at least one Federal budget officer privately to describe Federal budgeting as a process of mutual and endless suspicion of the other fellow. Budgeting is not merely an objective search for "truth"; it is a struggle between differing points of view and competing programs. And not least among the qualifications of an administrator and a budget officer are their abilities as tacticians and gladiators in the budget process.

Most of the human elements in the context of Federal budgeting are less theatrical than those mentioned above, but they are nonetheless important and probably more prevalent. Not a few budgeteers can probably call to mind without difficulty examples of professional or "line" officers who are typically resentful and resistant to real substantive questioning by nonprofessionals. They and their politically appointed superiors can probably recall their frustrations in trying to penetrate the plans and estimates of career-minded substantive officers. A fact attendant upon a good many budget review processes is the reluctance of a reviewer to analyze critically the estimates of an officer of higher rank or status, particularly when the future career of the former may be influenced by the latter.

Group relationships and friendships, particularly those that are reinforced by professional, working association, are often a significant influence even when unacknowledged. An example is the sometimes close professional tie between budget examiners at different echelons of the same organization. The efforts of some budget offices to clothe their activities with legitimacy by identifying themselves with the status and position if not the person of the top officers have effects on the way the process itself progresses, as do their sometimes parallel efforts to enshroud their determinations with secrecy. The impact of individual personalities upon the budget is frequently great: for example, the Patton-type administrator—dominant, aggressive, prone to "crash" decisions—who leaves to his harried staff the picking up of the pieces, the finding of funds for decisions already made, and the justification of the deeds. In contrast, there is the passive administrator, frustrated, bewildered, or, in some cases, fascinated by the red tape, to whom program becomes subordinate to process.

In the military services, these kinds of phenomena are complicated by the problems involved in civil-military relationships, the emphasis upon ranks and statuses, the officer-enlisted relationship, the regular-reserve relationship, and the officer rotation policy.

One other cluster of factors in the context of budgeting is the whole system of *political, economic, and social forces and pressures* working on the budget process from outside the organizations concerned, as well as from a combination of internal-external relations at various echelons. These are not discussed at length here, partly because they have been extensively explored in other studies.[2] Obviously, major budgetary policies reflect administrative and legislative responses to the total political situation, the current state of alarm, interest, or apathy of the public, the economic situation, the conditions and trend in prices, and other factors. The influences of producers and suppliers, of local groups seeking military construction, of private social and professional groups are equally well recognized.

THE BUDGET AND RATIONALITY

The foregoing paragraphs have dwelt upon some of the principal kinds of factors that make up the environment in which national budgets are developed and administered. These included the unknown and uncontrollable or only partially controllable factors; time and its impact upon present budgetary behavior; organizational and institutional factors; personal and interpersonal factors; and political, social, and economic forces.

One intent of this presentation has been to indicate the boundaries of complete freedom of action and decision upon the budget at any one time. More positively, statesmen can be more effective if they recognize the totality of the conditions and forces affected in and by the budget. The discussion is thus to be considered less as a formulation of limitations than as an extension of the area of effective action. An understanding of the full context should help in focusing attention upon those points at which action decisions may truly be decisive.

Public administration has to do with social change, its direction, its speed, sometimes its prevention. The job of the politically responsible official is to bring about change in directions deemed desirable, or to stop it when undesirable. In determining what is or is not desirable, he is to some extent dependent upon public organizations themselves. Part of his responsibility is simply to assure that such organizations are responsive to changes in program needs. Another part is to utilize effectively the instruments that are available to bring about change in desired directions. And this requires understanding of all the factors entering into institutional behavior, the full context of governmental decision and action.

The complexities and the apparent contradictions of public budgeting should not be construed as arguments for an approach of either opportunism or determinism. The budget process remains one of the supreme examples of rationality in government. This is, in many ways, its principal feature. And it is proper to assume that those immediately concerned with it are, with few exceptions, capable and desirous of making their decisions in a rational manner. In budgetary terms, they will act favorably on proposals of which the social benefits, total or marginal, are expected to exceed the costs, and vice versa.

In public affairs, only a part of either costs or benefits can be measured precisely in dollar figures. It is often more than difficult, it is metaphysical, to weigh short-term dollar costs against long-term social benefits or short-term benefits against long-term costs. It is hardly possible to give dollar values to benefits and costs that are largely social, institutional, or purely "human." Nonetheless valuations, or at least judgments, on such questions *are made* and almost *have to be made* in the budget process. It is at least to be hoped that such judgments will be better informed and wiser ones if they are reached with an understanding of how the budget proposals have been originated and processed and if the "actor," the judge himself, appreciates the context within which he himself is operating.

It is equally important that those of us in the audience see how the budget actions are taken "in depth," looking beyond and behind the dramatic and well-publicized episodes that dominate the stage from time to time. In perhaps no other organization in the national government is examination and analysis to this end more demanding in its challenge or potentially more rewarding than in the military establishment, to which the remaining chapters principally pertain.

FOOTNOTES

[1] *Harper's Magazine,* December, 1952, pp. 21-8.

[2] Few subjects in the field of budgeting and appropriations have had more extensive treatment. See, for example, David B. Truman, *The Governmental Process* (New York: Alfred H. Knopf, 1951), especially his Chapter VIII on "The Ordeal of the Executive." In fact, a considerable part of the literature on politics and interest groups deals with this problem. The historical study by Lucius Wilmerding, *The Spending Power* (New Haven: Yale University Press, 1943), discusses this subject frequently. A large part of the work by Arthur Maass, *Muddy Waters: The Army Engineers and the Nation's Rivers* (Cambridge: Harvard University Press, 1951), deals with this problem in an area close to, though not covered by, this study. Finally, we should refer to two primary references in this field: Pendleton Herring, "The Politics of Fiscal Policy," *Yale Law Journal,* March, 1938, pp. 724-45; and Paul H. Appleby, "The Influence of the Political Order," *American Political Science Review,* April, 1948, pp. 272-83.

ABOUT THE AUTHOR—Frederick C. Mosher has concentrated most of his career in the field of public administration. He received his B.A. from Dartmouth in 1934, and later on an M.S. from Syracuse University. From 1934 to 1949 Mosher served in a variety of posts with increasing responsibility in government. During World War II he served first as a civilian and later as a Major in the headquarters of the Army Air Force. His first position was as a research assistant with TVA, and when he began his teaching career in 1949, he shifted over from the post of Chief of the Division of Organization of the Department of State. He also has held posts with the Public Administration Clearing House, the Los Angeles City Civil Service Department, and with UNRRA. In 1953 he received a D.P.A. degree from Harvard University, since which time he has served as a member of the faculty at Syracuse University, the University of Bologna from 1957–1959, and he is now a professor at the University of California, Berkeley.

From 1953 to 1956 Mosher was editor-in-chief of the *Public Administration Review,* a medium to which he has also contributed frequently. He is the author of *City Manager Government in Rochester, New York* (1939), *Conference Planning and Management* (1940), *Program Budgeting* (1954), *Elementi di Scienza dell 'Amministrazione* (1959). He is co-author of *Features and Problems of the Federal Civil Service* (1954), *The Costs of American Governments* (1964), *Government Reorganizations: A Case Book* (1967), and *Democracy and the Public Service* (1968).

Communication

Perhaps one of the most difficult issues faced by administrators is the need to provide within the organizational framework both a hierarchical and interpersonal structure to convey clearly and unambiguously in both directions precisely what is going on. Yet no organization yet conceived is organized to fully achieve this optimum end. Resort is had to many techniques and practices. In some instances the formal communication structure may itself constitute a delimiting factor in the transmission of knowledge within the organization and outside the organization—sometimes intentionally and sometimes unintentionally.

In the annals of management literature no topic has received more attention than methods of facilitating communication. Formal communications have the limit of all of the constraints that other bureaucratic forms are heir to. Informal communication is almost precisely the same as social communication. At the extreme there is the process of rumor, sometimes unconsciously the method in an organization and sometimes a substitute only by default. Effective management of communication within the organization begins with an understanding of its central relevance to the attainment of the organization's ends and its correlation with morale.

Barriers and Gateways to Communication

Carl R. Rogers and F. J. Roethlisberger

> *The central thesis here is that the major restraint in communication is the tendency to insert evaluative a priori judgement to situations. Much of the difficulty in understanding between management and non-managerial personnel can be attributed to difficulties which each group has had in accepting and listening to the perspective of the other party at issue. This selection identifies how such impediments constitute a barrier both in interpersonal as well as intergroup relationships. The lessons of the selection are clear and unambiguous and are as relevant to library organizations as to any other form of human effort in which there are several views of the world on the part of those who must interact and strive for mutual understanding.*

Part I

It may seem curious that a person like myself, whose whole professional effort is devoted to psychotherapy, should be interested in problems of communication. What relationship is there between obstacles to communication and providing therapeutic help to individuals with emotional maladjustments?

Actually the relationship is very close indeed. The whole task of psychotherapy is the task of dealing with a failure in communication. The emotionally maladjusted person, the "neurotic," is in difficulty, first, because communication within himself has broken down and, secondly, because as a result of this his communication with others has been damaged. To put it another way, in the "neurotic" individual parts of himself which have been termed unconscious, or repressed, or denied to awareness, become blocked off so that they no longer communicate themselves to the conscious or managing part of himself; as long as this is true, there are distortions in the way he communicates himself to others, and so he suffers both within himself and in his interpersonal relations.

The task of psychotherapy is to help the person achieve, through a special relationship with a therapist, good communication within himself. Once this is achieved, he can communicate more freely and more effectively with others. We may say then that psychotherapy is good communication, within and between men. We may also turn that statement around and it will still be true. Good communication, free communication, within or between men, is always therapeutic.

It is, then, from a background of experience with communication in counseling and psychotherapy that I want to present two ideas: (1) I wish to state what I believe is one of the major factors in blocking or impeding communication, and then (2) I wish to present what in our experience has proved to be a very important way of improving or facilitating communication.

Barrier: The Tendency to Evaluate

I should like to propose, as a hypothesis for consideration, that the major barrier to mutual interpersonal communication is our very natural tendency to judge, to evaluate, to approve (or disapprove) the statement of the other person or the other group. Let me illustrate my meaning with some very simple examples. Suppose someone, commenting on this discussion, makes the statement, "I didn't like what that man said." What will you respond? Almost invariably your reply will be either approval or disapproval of the attitude expressed. Either you respond, "I didn't either; I thought it was terrible," or else you tend to reply, "Oh, I thought it was really good." In

---

SOURCE: Reprinted by permission of the publishers from Fritz J. Roethlisberger & Carl R. Rogers HARVARD BUSINESS REVIEW Cambridge, Mass.: Copyright, 1952, by the President and Fellows of Harvard College. This article will appear in the forthcoming MAN-IN-ORGANIZATION, by Fritz J. Roethlisberger, to be published by the Belknap Press of Harvard University Press. Original publication bore the following note: "Mr. Rogers' and Mr. Roethlisberger's observations are based on their contributions to a panel discussion at the Centennial Conference on Communications, Northwestern University, October 1951."

other words, your primary reaction is to evaluate it from *your* point of view, your own frame of reference.

Or take another example. Suppose I say with some feeling, "I think the Republicans are behaving in ways that show a lot of good sound sense these days." What is the response that arises in your mind? The overwhelming likelihood is that it will be evaluative. In other words, you will find yourself agreeing, or disagreeing, or making some judgment about me such as "He must be a conservative," or "He seems solid in his thinking." Or let us take an illustration from the international scene. Russia says vehemently, "The treaty with Japan is a war plot on the part of the United States." We rise as one person to say, "That's a lie!"

This last illustration brings in another element connected with my hypothesis. Although the tendency to make evaluations is common in almost all interchange of language, it is very much heightened in those situations where feelings and emotions are deeply involved. So the stronger our feelings, the more likely it is that there will be no mutual element in the communication. There will be just two ideas, two feelings, two judgments, missing each other in psychological space.

I am sure you recognize this from your own experience. When you have not been emotionally involved yourself and have listened to a heated discussion, you often go away thinking, "Well, they actually weren't talking about the same thing." And they were not. Each was making a judgment, an evaluation, from his own frame of reference. There was really nothing which could be called communication in any genuine sense. This tendency to react to any emotionally meaningful statement by forming an evaluation of it from our own point of view is, I repeat, the major barrier to interpersonal communication.

Gateway: Listening with Understanding

Is there any way of solving this problem, of avoiding this barrier? I feel that we are making exciting progress toward this goal, and I should like to present it as simply as I can. Real communication occurs, and this evaluative tendency is avoided, when we listen with understanding. What does that mean? It means to see the expressed idea and attitude from the other person's point of view, to sense how it feels to him, to achieve his frame of reference in regard to the thing he is talking about.

Stated so briefly, this may sound absurdly simple, but it is not. It is an approach which we have found extremely potent in the field of psychotherapy. It is the most effective agent we know for altering the basic personality structure of an individual and for improving his relationships and his communications with others. If I can listen to what he can tell me, if I can understand how it seems to him, if I can see its personal meaning for him, if I can sense the emotional flavor which it has for him, then I will be releasing potent forces of change in him.

Again, if I can really understand how he hates his father, or hates the company, or hates Communists—if I can catch the flavor of his fear of insanity, or his fear of atom bombs, or of Russia—it will be of the greatest help to him in altering those hatreds and fears and in establishing realistic and harmonious relationships with the very people and situations toward which he has felt hatred and fear. We know from our research that such empathic understanding—understanding *with* a person, not *about* him—is such an effective approach that it can bring about major changes in personality.

Some of you may be feeling that you listen well to people and yet you have never seen such results. The chances are great indeed that your listening has not been of the type I have described. Fortunately, I can suggest a little laboratory experiment which you can try to test the quality of your understanding. The next time you get into an argument with your wife, or your friend, or with a small group of friends, just stop the discussion for a moment and, for an experiment, institute this rule: "Each person can speak up for himself only *after* he has first restated the ideas and feelings of the previous speaker accurately and to that speaker's satisfaction."

You see what this would mean. It would simply mean that before presenting your own point of view, it would be necessary for you to achieve the other speaker's frame of reference—to understand his thoughts and feelings so well that you could summarize them for him. Sounds simple, doesn't it? But if you try it, you will discover that it is one of the most difficult things you have ever tried to do. However, once you have been able to see the other's point of view, your own comments will have to be drastically revised. You will also find the emotion going out of the discussion, the differences being reduced, and those differences which remain being of a rational and understandable sort.

Can you imagine what this kind of an approach would mean if it were projected into larger areas?

What would happen to a labor-management dispute if it were conducted in such a way that labor, without necessarily agreeing, could accurately state management's point of view in a way that management could accept; and management, without approving labor's stand, could state labor's case in a way that labor agreed was accurate? It would mean that real communication was established, and one could practically guarantee that some reasonable solution would be reached.

If, then, this way of approach is an effective avenue to good communication and good relationships, as I am quite sure you will agree if you try the experiment I have mentioned, why is it not more widely tried and used? I will try to list the difficulties which keep it from being utilized.

Need for Courage. In the first place it takes courage, a quality which is not too widespread. I am indebted to Dr. S. I. Hayakawa, the semanticist, for pointing out that to carry on psychotherapy in this fashion is to take a very real risk, and that courage is required. If you really understand another person in this way, if you are willing to enter his private world and see the way life appears to him, without any attempt to make evaluative judgments, you run the risk of being changed yourself. You might see it his way; you might find yourself influenced in your attitudes or your personality.

This risk of being changed is one of the most frightening prospects many of us can face. If I enter, as fully as I am able, into the private world of a neurotic or psychotic individual, isn't there a risk that I might become lost in that world? Most of us are afraid to take that risk. Or if we were listening to a Russian Communist, or Senator Joe McCarthy, how many of us would dare to try to see the world from each of their points of view? The great majority of us could not *listen;* we would find ourselves compelled to *evaluate,* because listening would seem too dangerous. So the first requirement is courage, and we do not always have it.

Heightened Emotions. But there is a second obstacle. It is just when emotions are strongest that it is most difficult to achieve the frame of reference of the other person or group. Yet it is then that the attitude is most needed if communication is to be established. We have not found this to be an insuperable obstacle in our experience in psychotherapy. A third party, who is able to lay aside his own feelings and evaluations, can assist greatly by listening with understanding to each person or group and clarifying the views and attitudes each holds.

We have found this effective in small groups in which contradictory or antagonistic attitudes exist. When the parties to a dispute realize that they are being understood, that someone sees how the situation seems to them, the statements grow less exaggerated and less defensive, and it is no longer necessary to maintain the attitude, "I am 100% right and you are 100% wrong." The influence of such an understanding catalyst in the group permits the members to come closer and closer to the objective truth involved in the relationship. In this way mutual communication is established, and some type of agreement becomes much more possible.

So we may say that though heightened emotions make it much more difficult to understand *with* an opponent, our experience makes it clear that a neutral, understanding, catalyst type of leader or therapist can overcome this obstacle in a small group.

Size of Group. The last phrase, however, suggests another obstacle to utilizing the approach I have described. Thus far all our experience has been with small face-to-face groups—groups exhibiting industrial tensions, religious tensions, racial tensions, and therapy groups in which many personal tensions are present. In these small groups our experience, confirmed by a limited amount of research, shows that this basic approach leads to improved communication, to greater acceptance of others and by others, and to attitudes which are more positive and more problem-solving in nature. There is a decrease in defensiveness, in exaggerated statements, in evaluative and critical behavior.

But these findings are from small groups. What about trying to achieve understanding between larger groups that are geographically remote, or between face-to-face groups that are not speaking for themselves but simply as representatives of others, like the delegates at Kaesong? Frankly we do not know the answers to these questions. I believe the situation might be put this way: As social scientists we have a tentative test-tube solution of the problem of breakdown in communication. But to confirm the validity of this test-tube solution and to adapt it to the enormous problems of communication breakdown between classes, groups, and nations would involve additional funds, much more research, and creative thinking of a high order.

Yet with our present limited knowledge we can see some steps which might be taken even in large groups to increase the amount of listening *with* and decrease the amount of evaluation *about.* To be imaginative for a moment, let us suppose that a therapeutically oriented international group went to the Russian leaders and said, "We want to achieve a genuine understanding of your views and, even more important, of your attitudes and feelings toward the United States. We will summarize and resummarize these views and feelings if necessary, until you agree that our description represents the situation as it seems to you."

Then suppose they did the same thing with the leaders in our own country. If they then gave the widest possible distribution to these two views, with the feelings clearly described but not expressed in name-calling, might not the effect be very great? It would not guarantee the type of understanding I have been describing, but it would make it much more possible. We can understand the feelings of a person who hates us much more readily when his attitudes are accurately described to us by a neutral third party than we can when he is shaking his fist at us.

Faith in Social Sciences. But even to describe such a first step is to suggest another obstacle to this approach of understanding. Our civilization does not yet have enough faith in the social sciences to utilize their findings. The opposite is true of the physical sciences. During the war when a test-tube solution was found to the problem of synthetic rubber, millions of dollars and an army of talent were turned loose on the problem of using that finding. If synthetic rubber could be made in milligrams, it could and would be made in the thousands of tons. And it was. But in the social science realm, if a way is found of facilitating communication and mutual understanding in small groups, there is no guarantee that the finding will be utilized. It may be a generation or more before the money and the brains will be turned loose to exploit that finding.

Summary

In closing, I should like to summarize this small-scale solution to the problem of barriers in communication, and to point out certain of its characteristics.

I have said that our research and experience to date would make it appear that breakdowns in communication, and the evaluative tendency which is the major barrier to communication, can be avoided. The solution is provided by creating a situation in which each of the different parties comes to understand the other from the *other's* point of view. This has been achieved, in practice, even when feelings run high, by the influence of a person who is willing to understand each point of view empathically, and who thus acts as a catalyst to precipitate further understanding.

This procedure has important characteristics. It can be initiated by one party, without waiting for the other to be ready. It can even be initiated by a neutral third person, provided he can gain a minimum of cooperation from one of the parties.

This procedure can deal with the insincerities, the defensive exaggerations, the lies, the "false fronts" which characterize almost every failure in communication. These defensive distortions drop away with astonishing speed as people find that the only intent is to understand, not to judge.

This approach leads steadily and rapidly toward the discovery of the truth, toward a realistic appraisal of the objective barriers to communication. The dropping of some defensiveness by one party leads to further dropping of defensiveness by the other party, and truth is thus approached.

This procedure gradually achieves mutual communication. Mutual communication tends to be pointed toward solving a problem rather than toward attacking a person or group. It leads to a situation in which I see how the problem appears to you as well as to me, and you see how it appears to me as well as to you. Thus accurately and realistically defined, the problem is almost certain to yield to intelligent attack; or if it is in part insoluble, it will be comfortably accepted as such.

This then appears to be a test-tube solution to the breakdown of communication as it occurs in small groups. Can we take this small-scale answer, investigate it further, refine it, develop it, and apply it to the tragic and well-nigh fatal failures of communication which threaten the very existence of our modern world? It seems to me that this is a possibility and a challenge which we should explore.

Part II

In thinking about the many barriers to personal communication, particularly those that are due to differences of background, experience, and motivation, it seems to me extraordinary that any two persons can ever understand each other. Such reflections provoke the question of how communication is possible when people do not see and assume the same things and share the same values.

On this question there are two schools of thought. One school assumes that communication between A and B, for example, has failed when B does not accept what A has to say as being fact, true, or valid; and that the goal of communication is to get B to agree with A's opinions, ideas, facts, or information.

The position of the other school of thought is quite different. It assumes that communication has failed when B does not feel free to express his feelings to A because B fears they will not be accepted by A. Communication is facilitated when on the part of A or B or both there is a willingness to express and accept differences.

As these are quite divergent conceptions, let us explore them further with an example. Bill, an employee, is talking with his boss in the boss's office. The boss says, "I think, Bill, that this is the best way to do your job." Bill says, "Oh yeah!" According to the first school of thought, this reply would be a sign of poor communication. Bill does not understand the best way of doing his work. To improve communication, therefore, it is up to the boss to explain to Bill why his way is the best.

From the point of view of the second school of thought, Bill's reply is a sign neither of good nor bad communication. Bill's response is indeterminate. But the boss has an opportunity to find out what Bill means if he so desires. Let us assume that this is what he chooses to do, i.e., find out what Bill means. So this boss tries to get Bill to talk more about his job while he (the boss) listens.

For purposes of simplification, I shall call the boss representing the first school of thought "*Smith*" and the boss representing the second school of thought "*Jones*." In the presence of the so-called same stimulus each behaves differently. Smith chooses to *explain*; Jones chooses to *listen*. In my experience Jones's response works better than Smith's. It works better because Jones is making a more proper evaluation of what is taking place between him and Bill than Smith is. Let us test this hypothesis by continuing with our example.

What Smith Assumes, Sees, and Feels

Smith assumes that he understands what Bill means when Bill says, "Oh yeah!" so there is no need to find out. Smith is sure that Bill does not understand why this is the best way to do his job, so Smith has to tell him. In this process let us assume Smith is logical, lucid, and clear. He presents his facts and evidence well. But, alas, Bill remains unconvinced. What does Smith do? Operating under the assumption that what is taking place between him and Bill is something essentially logical, Smith can draw only one of two conclusions: either (1) he has not been clear enough, or (2) Bill is too damned stupid to understand. So he either has to "spell out" his case in words of fewer and fewer syllables or give up. Smith is reluctant to do the latter, so he continues to explain. What happens?

If Bill still does not accept Smith's explanation of why this is the best way for him to do his job, a pattern of interacting feelings is produced of which Smith is often unaware. The more Smith cannot get Bill to understand him the more frustrated Smith becomes and the more Bill becomes a threat to his logical capacity. Since Smith sees himself as a fairly reasonable and logical chap, this is a difficult feeling to accept. It is much easier for him to perceive Bill as uncooperative or stupid. This perception, however, will affect what Smith says and does. Under these pressures Bill comes to be evaluated more and more in terms of Smith's values. By this process Smith tends to treat Bill's values as unimportant. He tends to deny Bill's uniqueness and difference. He treats Bill as if he had little capacity for self-direction.

Let us be clear. Smith does not see that he is doing these things. When he is feverishly scratching hieroglyphics on the back of an envelope, trying to explain to Bill why this is the best way to do his job, Smith is trying to be helpful. He is a man of goodwill, and he wants to set Bill straight. This is the way Smith sees himself and his behavior. But it is for this very reason that Bill's "Oh yeah!" is getting under Smith's skin.

"How dumb can a guy be?" is Smith's attitude, and unfortunately Bill will hear that more than Smith's good intentions. Bill will feel misunderstood. He will not see Smith as a man of goodwill trying to be helpful. Rather he will perceive him as a threat to his self-esteem and personal integrity. Against this threat Bill will feel the need to defend himself at all cost. Not being so logically articulate as Smith, Bill expresses this need, again, by saying, "Oh yeah!"

What Jones Assumes, Sees, and Feels

Let us leave this sad scene between Smith and Bill, which I fear is going to terminate by Bill's either leaving in a huff or being kicked out of

Smith's office. Let us turn for a moment to Jones and see what he is assuming, seeing, hearing, feeling, doing, and saying when he interacts with Bill.

Jones, it will be remembered, does not assume that he knows what Bill means when he says, "Oh yeah!" so he has to find out. Moreover, he assumes that when Bill said this, he had not exhausted his vocabulary or his feelings. Bill may not necessarily mean one thing; he may mean several different things. So Jones decides to listen.

In this process Jones is not under any illusion that what will take place will be eventually logical. Rather he is assuming that what will take place will be primarily an interaction of feelings. Therefore, he cannot ignore the feelings of Bill, the effect of Bill's feelings on him, or the effect of his feelings on Bill. In other words, he cannot ignore his relationship to Bill; he cannot assume that it will make no difference to what Bill will hear or accept.

Therefore, Jones will be paying strict attention to all of the things Smith has ignored. He will be addressing himself to Bill's feelings, his own, and the interactions between them.

Jones will therefore realize that he has ruffled Bill's feelings with his comment, "I think, Bill, this is the best way to do your job." So instead of trying to get Bill to understand him, he decides to try to understand Bill. He does this by encouraging Bill to speak. Instead of telling Bill how he should feel or think, he asks Bill such questions as, "Is this what you feel?" "Is this what you see?" "Is this what you assume?" Instead of ignoring Bill's evaluations as irrelevant, not valid, inconsequential, or false, he tries to understand Bill's reality as he feels it, perceives it, and assumes it to be. As Bill begins to open up, Jones's curiosity is piqued by this process.

"Bill isn't so dumb; he's quite an interesting guy" becomes Jones's attitude. And that is what Bill hears. Therefore Bill feels understood and accepted as a person. He becomes less defensive. He is in a better frame of mind to explore and re-examine his own perceptions, feelings, and assumptions. In this process he perceives Jones as a source of help. Bill feels free to express his differences. He feels that Jones has some respect for his capacity for self-direction. These positive feelings toward Jones make Bill more inclined to say, "Well, Jones, I don't quite agree with you that this is the best way to do my job, but I'll tell you what I'll do. I'll try to do it that way for a few days, and then I'll tell you what I think."

Conclusion

I grant that my two orientations do not work themselves out in practice in quite so simple or neat a fashion as I have been able to work them out on paper. There are many other ways in which Bill could have responded to Smith in the first place. He might even have said, "O.K., boss, I agree that your way of doing my job is better." But Smith still would not have known how Bill felt when he made this statement or whether Bill was actually going to do his job differently. Likewise, Bill could have responded to Jones in a way different from my example. In spite of Jones's attitude, Bill might still be reluctant to express himself freely to his boss.

The purpose of my examples has not been to demonstrate the right or wrong way of communicating. My purpose has been simply to provide something concrete to point to when I make the following generalizations:

(1) Smith represents to me a very common pattern of misunderstanding. The misunderstanding does not arise because Smith is not clear enough in expressing himself. It arises because of Smith's misevaluation of what is taking place when two people are talking together.

(2) Smith's misevaluation of the process of personal communication consists of certain very common assumptions, e.g., (a) that what is taking place is something essentially logical; (b) that words in themselves apart from the people involved mean something; and (c) that the purpose of the interaction is to get Bill to see things from Smith's point of view.

(3) Because of these assumptions, a chain reaction of perceptions and negative feelings is engendered which blocks communication. By ignoring Bill's feelings and by rationalizing his own, Smith ignores his relationship to Bill as one of the most important determinants of the communication. As a result, Bill hears Smith's attitude more clearly than the logical content of Smith's words. Bill feels that his individual uniqueness is being denied. His personal integrity being at stake, he becomes defensive and belligerent. As a result, Smith feels frustrated. He perceives Bill as stupid. So he says and does things which only provoke more defensiveness on the part of Bill.

(4) In the case of Jones, I have tried to show what might possibly happen if we made a different evaluation of what is taking place when two people are talking together. Jones makes a different set of assumptions. He assumes (a) that

what is taking place between him and Bill is an interaction of sentiments; (b) that Bill—not his words in themselves—means something; (c) that the object of the interaction is to give Bill an opportunity to express freely his differences.

(5) Because of these assumptions, a psychological chain reaction of reinforcing feelings and perceptions is set up which facilitates communication between Bill and him. When Jones addresses himself to Bill's feelings and perceptions from Bill's point of view, Bill feels understood and accepted as a person; he feels free to express his differences. Bill sees Jones as a source of help; Jones sees Bill as an interesting person. Bill in turn becomes more cooperative.

(6) If I have identified correctly these very common patterns of personal communication, then some interesting hypotheses can be stated:

(a) Jones's method works better than Smith's, not because of any magic, but because Jones has a better map than Smith of the process of personal communication.

(b) The practice of Jones's method, however, is not merely an intellectual exercise. It depends on Jones's capacity and willingness to see and accept points of view different from his own, and to practice this orientation in a face-to-face relationship. This practice involves an emotional as well as an intellectual achievement. It depends in part on Jones's awareness of himself, in part on the practice of a skill.

(c) Although our colleges and universities try to get students to appreciate intellectually points of view different from their own, very little is done to help them to implement this general intellectual appreciation in a simple face-to-face relationship—at the level of a skill. Most educational institutions train their students to be logical, lucid, and clear. Very little is done to help them to listen more skillfully. As a result, our educated world contains too many Smiths and too few Joneses.

(d) The biggest block to personal communication is man's inability to listen intelligently, understandingly, and skillfully to another person. This deficiency in the modern world is widespread and appalling. In our universities as well as elsewhere, too little is being done about it.

(7) In conclusion, let me apologize for acting toward you the way Smith did. But who am I to violate a long-standing academic tradition!

ABOUT THE AUTHORS—The name of Carl R. Rogers is identified with client-centered psychotherapy. In his own terms this is client-oriented and the patient's role is to search for his own insights and solutions, while the therapist empathizes and elucidates but does not manipulate. Rogers was born in Illinois in 1902. He entered Union Theological Seminary after his graduation from the University of Wisconsin in 1924, but he was unwilling to commit himself to a field where he was "required to believe in a specific doctrine," and he withdrew. At Union Theological he became interested in psychology but questioned the tools and doctrines to which he was exposed. Taking issue with both the experimental psychologists and the Freudian perspective, he began to formulate his own approach. His primary focus was children. His Ph.D. in Psychology from Teachers' College, Columbia in 1931 led to work with the Society for Prevention of Cruelty to Children in Rochester, New York. He published *Measuring the Personality Adjustment in Children* (1931) and *Clinical Treatment of the Problem Child* (1939). At the University of Rochester he lectured in the Sociology rather than the Psychology Department, reflecting the skepticism of colleagues in his own discipline.

From 1940 to 1945 Rogers taught Counseling and Psychotherapy at Ohio State. He served as Director of Counseling at the United Service Organization from 1944-45 and established and directed the Counseling Center at the University of Chicago from 1945 to 1957. During this time he co-authored *Counseling with Returned Servicemen* (1946), wrote *Client Centered Therapy* (1951) and co-authored *Psychotherapy and Personality Change* (1954). He has been Visiting Professor at UCLA, Harvard, and Occidental College. In 1957 he joined the University of Wisconsin faculty as Professor of Psychology and Psychiatry. In 1962 he was a Fellow at the Center for Advanced Study of the Behavioral Sciences, and in 1964 he became a Resident Fellow of the Western Behavioral Sciences Institute at La Jolla, California. A recent book was *On Becoming a Person* (1961). He was editor and co-author of *The Therapeutic Relationship: A Study of Psychotherapy with Schizophrenics* (1967). Rogers helped found the American Association for Applied Psychology, which he has served as president and he has also been president of the American Psychology Association (1946) and the Academy of Psychotherapy (1956-67). He holds numerous awards and honors

Since 1950, Fritz J. Roethlisberger has been Wallace B. Donham Professor in the Harvard Graduate School of Business Administration. He has written extensively in the field of human relations. *Management and Morale* was published in 1941. Roethlisberger was the co-author of *Management and the*

Worker (1939), *Training for Human Relations* (1954), *The Motivation, Productivity, and Satisfaction of Workers: A Prediction Study* (1958) and *Counseling in an Organization* (1966). He has been the recipient of many honors. In 1956 he received the Taylor Key Award from the Society for the Advancement of Management, and in 1959, the Harvard Ledlie Prize. He also was awarded an honorary doctorate from the St. Gall (Switzerland) School of Economics, Business, and Public Administration. Born in New York in 1898, Roethlisberger received his undergraduate degree from Columbia, and then moved to Boston, where he received a B.S. from MIT in 1922, and an M.A. from Harvard in 1925. He joined the Harvard faculty in 1927 and retired officially in 1967. A volume of Roethlisberger's essays will be published in 1968 by Harvard University Press to be called *Man-In-Organization* and he is engaged at present in writing his autobiography.

Aspects of Upward Communications in a Public Library

by Millicent D. Abell

This report points up a number of common tendencies of organizations. Typically they fill their communication channels (and their time) with the routine, the trivial and the immediate at the expense of the more important. The impact of status on receptivity to communication is also seen as a factor. Thus the relative merit of ideas can be less consequential than the status of those expressing them.

This is a report presented in terms of communications. The situation could also be explained in power terms; that is an analysis of communications serves to reveal a basic struggle between a new head librarian and the older members of the staff. The "human relations" school of management views the employee as wanting merely an opportunity to communicate with management, to have his point of view expressed. This situation confirms what studies in other settings have shown, that groups and individuals in organizations are not that naive and that they frequently can and will deliberately withhold information to achieve their own goals.

The last two decades have witnessed the growth of a significant body of literature on theory and research on organizations—their parts, their wholes, their likenesses and diversities. Some has been given widespread and significant practical application. This literature has, as in other disciplines, added to the sum of knowledge and led to new considerations for research; of particular importance to librarians is the fact that much of organizational theory, as perceived or intuited by the library administrator, is at best out-of-date, at worst little known or valued. Many reasons can be cited for this state of affairs. One is that in libraries, as in schools and other similar organizations, it is often assumed that the good librarian, like the good teacher, will automatically become the good administrator, whereas the skills and knowledge involved in the two positions are in many respects quite different.

Another factor is that organizational theory and research have rarely been applied or discussed in terms of the library. As a result, the busy working librarian or library administrator has little opportunity to acquaint himself with the ways in which his organization can be studied, defined, and improved through the utilization of a literature which has been developed by the social scientists.

It is the purpose of this essay to discuss a part of this body of knowledge which deals with communications within an organization. A small field study will be described and used to illustrate some of the problems revealed by an investigation of communications.

The significance of an internal communications study for the library cannot be overstated. Researchers and theoreticians agree that one of the processes indispensable to an organization is that of communication. One writer has argued that communication "... is the essence of organized activity and is the basic process out of which all other functions derive." (*1*, p. 313) Other writers speaking in the framework of modern organization theory, consider communications as one of the linking activities which serve to hold all of the various parts of an organizational system together. (*7*, p. 21) Certainly an organized system of information exchange is necessary to other essential organizational functions, such as the setting of goals, the exercise of control, the adjustment of procedures, the establishment of coordination, and the like.

SOURCE: Reprinted from Millicent D. Abell, "Aspects of Upward Communications in a Public Library," *Social and Political Aspects of Librarianship: Student Contributions to Library Science*, ed. by Mary Lee Bundy and Ruth Aronson (Albany School of Library Science, State University of New York at Albany, 1965), pp. 91–99, by permission of the publisher. Original publication bore the following note: "Based on a study conducted by the writer with Mary Lee Bundy."

Many organizations which have been studied extensively—certain businesses, units of government, and the military—have fairly definite hierarchical patterns. Their major communications patterns can, therefore, be analyzed largely in terms of the authority structure. It is, moreover, this hierarchical view, first stated by Max Weber over 40 years ago, which widely pervades and restricts the thinking of administrators.

The many criticisms of Weber's principles of bureaucracy and the myriad theories which have developed during the intervening years cannot properly be examined here. Suffice it to say that many modern organizational theorists, while acknowledging the multitude of characteristics common to all organizations, do differentiate among types of organizations. Limiting our discussion to service organizations, we shall identify the library as an organization with a professional orientation, as opposed to a bureaucratic orientation. That is to say that those who do the distinctive and significant work of the library, the librarians, tend to be more influenced by their loyalty to the wider profession than by their loyalty to the administration of their own particular organization. They have more interest in maintaining their identification with their professional group at large and in gaining the support and approval of their peers than they do in obtaining the approval of their administrative superiors. (2, pp. 60-74)

The extent to which librarians have achieved professional status is not our immediate concern here. We can at least grant that librarians perform services at a level which draws upon their personal knowledge and skills more than it does on direct orders and supervision from someone placed above them in the traditional line of authority. In addition, it is obvious that library staffs have many more horizontal relationships than vertical ones. A third factor which works against the use of a hierarchical arrangement as a communications channel in the library is well-known to us all. The staff is usually quite small in proportion to the tasks to be performed and, therefore, there is a greater tendency to rely on informal and spontaneous communications for the exchange of information.

Thus one assumption prevalent in library administrative circles—that a clear hierarchical structure ideally exists in every organization and that communications will automatically flow along its lines—seems to be unwarranted.

Nevertheless, attention must be paid to vertical communication within the library for several reasons. It is essential to the administrator if he is to fulfill the typical management functions, such as planning, coordination, and control. In spite of the communications habits of an organization and the extensive opportunities for informal communications within the library the communications patterns can be affected by the top management, the head librarian. By the establishment of clear-cut lines of authority and by specific assignments of information-exchange functions, the librarian-administrator can have some effect on both the formal and informal communication systems. (6, p. 235) It need hardly be argued that management cannot reach the point of absolute control of the communications system, even were this desirable. There is a viability to the spontaneous informal system with an organization. In addition, both communications theory and power theory are insufficiently developed to be applied in a given situation with any reasonable certainty of results. (3, pp. 148-49)

Vertical communication is often considered in terms of its direction. Everyone is familiar with the nature and importance of downward communication and accepts the necessity for studying the means of making it more effective. It is the way in which the head librarian informs the staff of the goals, policies, needs, and administrative procedures of the organization.

Upward communication, on the other hand, is less appreciated and less understood; yet it is of crucial importance to effective organizational functions. (Many of the ideas in the following section were drawn from an article by Earl G. Planty and William Machaver. (4)) Its values accrue to the head librarian and to the staff. The head librarian can, through effective upward communication, learn how receptive the staff might be to new ideas which he is planning to transmit; he can also learn, after the fact, how well understood and effective his communications were. The head librarian can also earn the appreciation and loyalty of his staff if he shows himself open to and interested in their questions, problems, and ideas. Furthermore, the ideas themselves, the professional stimulation and information vital to decisions that an administrator can receive from the staff, are of particular importance in a professional organization, such as the library.

At the same time, the importance of upward communication to the staff should not be overlooked. Any staff member needs to feel that his ideas are valued by the organization. This is particularly true of the professional staff who need to feel that their expertise is being utilized in organizational decision-making in order for them to continue to function as professionals—to view their jobs in terms of the potentialities, not the routines. Furthermore, the staff benefits from the emotional satisfaction which can result from opportunities to freely question and complain about administrative procedures. It is generally better for the organization if this can be done in an upward rather than a horizontal direction.

It is this aspect of communications, the upward system in a medium-sized public library, which was recently studied by the writer. The focus was on the communications flowing directly from the staff to the director. The means, type, frequency, and personnel involved in the communications were noted. The writer attempted to determine some of the communications patterns in this library and to define the barriers to communications.

The communications were investigated in two ways: first, the daily patterns and individual attitudes were studied through a self-reporting system and interviews; second, the formal written reports and forms were examined.

In general, during the six working days studied, it was found that the head librarian was involved in some form of communication most of his working day. Over 93 percent of his contacts with his staff were in face-to-face conversations. It should be noted here that few contacts of this type can be characterized as strictly upward or downward; only those which include upward communication were included. The other contacts were fairly evenly divided between telephone calls and written notes.

Of the fifteen staff members who had contacts with him during this period, the associate director and the secretary, as might be expected, had the greatest number of contacts with the director. Other supervisory personnel in the building which houses the director's office averaged about one contact a day, except for the Senior Reference Librarian who had only one contact with the director during the whole period. Four of the five branch library heads were also limited to only one contact. Significantly, those staff members not directly responsible to the director averaged more contacts with him than did those directly responsible, with the exception of the office staff.

Typical of the style of the director in this library was the fact that he initiated over half of the contacts. Furthermore, over 70 percent took place somewhere other than his office.

The content of most of the contacts was routine and immediate in nature. About half of them were strictly administrative. Almost all of the others dealt with library operations, chiefly circulation matters and some on-going library-sponsored programs. The remainder were social or otherwise concerned with matters outside the library. Rarely were new ideas or professional planning mentioned.

There are some, but relatively few, formalized communications procedures. For example, there is a monthly staff meeting. The one meeting observed was largely devoted to a change in registration regulations. At the end of the meeting time was provided for individual staff members to report on their activities, but this system seemed to be too limited and haphazard to produce much information. Furthermore, the junior staff members were mostly silent throughout the meeting with participation mainly by those few with superior status.

A few other regular meetings are held. There are two book selection meetings a week, which are sometimes attended by the director. Although they were not observed, it was reported that they serve to keep the director in touch with branch clientele interests and also provide an opportunity for discussion of branch administrative problems. The occasional reference meetings, involving those who share the reference desk assignments, are almost entirely limited to routines.

The written reports regularly seen by the director are the monthly circulation and financial reports and the annual departmental and branch reports. Records of other data are kept, some of which are potentially quite useful, but generally are not analyzed nor forwarded with regularity to the director.

In summary, those things being communicated upward in this library are primarily routine in content. While a large part of the communications of the director are with his two immediate associates, he averages fewer contacts through regular organizational channels than through those that circumvent the formal structure. While he and some of his staff members assert that he is perhaps too accessible, partially because of the physical location of his office, it was seen that most of the contacts were initiated by him, away from his office.

A number of weaknesses are evident through this examination of the communications system. One might view them as weaknesses in the functioning of the system itself or as symptomatic of other factors of poor functioning in the organization. This point will be discussed later. At any rate, some of the failures are these. The director feels overly burdened with routine communications. Several staff members hesitate to communicate ideas which might be of value. Some staff members seem to feel that the director is overly occupied with trivia. Most of the staff feel that they are properly concerned only with what occurs within the confines of their own departments and do not communicate about the library as a whole. The director does not trust nor rely upon his formal communications channels.

What are some of the barriers to upward communications which might contribute to these and similar problems? The suggestions below will be based on the findings of the study and the knowledge and experiences of the writer with other libraries, public and academic. The communications barriers can be grouped as follows: those involving the library organization itself; those involving the head librarian; and those involving the staff. Suggestions of some of these barriers were found in Planty. (*4*, pp. 134-49)

Among the barriers inherent in the organizational structure, physical distance is an obvious and significant factor. Where branch libraries are involved, almost no communication will be sent upward unless there is a regular procedure for doing so. As was seen in this study, communication with the branches is quite infrequent. It should also be noted that it is trivial, dealing with such matters as a minor physical alteration and the demonstration of some new peg boards. It is apparently easy to lose the sense of unity binding a branch to a main library through the lack of personal contact between branch head and head librarian.

It was noted earlier that most libraries have less rigidly hierarchical structures than many other kinds of organizations. As a result problems of dilution, distortion, or delay as the information rises through channels are less likely to occur. At the same time this lack of rigid structure may contribute to a tendency to downgrade the necessity for certain formal reporting systems. On the other hand, the administrator may incorrectly assume that a hierarchical structure and its companion formal reporting system are inherent in the organization. In either case, information can fail to flow through oversight or lack of mutual understanding about what is important for the head librarian to know. Both conditions seemed to exist in the library situation described above. As was stated, the formal communications system does not satisfy the administrator's needs as he percieves them.

The barriers involving the head librarian depend in large part upon his philosophy and style of administration. If he values the attitudes and opinions of his staff as being essential to his own proper functioning, he will, of course, devote more time and attention to his communications system than he would if he believed that he could function effectively without an upward flow of communications.

In the study under discussion, the director's deep commitment to certain of his own plans is known but not shared by other members of the staff. This had led to mutual caution in a number of relationships and to the director's tendency to encourage more communication from those staff members who are in sympathy with his objectives than from the others. By his own admission he attempts to manipulate his staff to achieve his own objectives, having resigned the attempt to maintain meaningful communications with them. Through this attitude, he may stifle both valuable new ideas and the free expression of dissatisfactions on the part of his staff. He also loses the opportunity to continue to explain the reasons for his own positions to a relatively open-minded and interested listener. Rogers asserts that the tendency to evaluate and let emotions become involved, rather than listening with understanding, is the major barrier to all communications. (*5*)

The director's apparent desire to avoid conflict through avoidance of dissenters is an indication of certain characteristics of his administrative style which can also be detected in his accessibility. Most staff members testify to his unusual graciousness and availability; some consider it excessive for the good of the organization. Paradoxically, this high level of accessibility seems to serve at times as a barrier to communication. The director has a tendency to get over-involved in routines and trivial conversation at the expense of time that might be spent receiving more significant communications.

One of the most common barriers to upward communication in a library is the failure of the head librarian to make decisions or take action within a reasonable length of time. This is a characteristic of the director which was cited by several members of his staff. When no decision was made regarding some of their ideas, staff members began to think that the raising of issues, such as proposing new services in their departments, was a waste of effort.

Finally there is a barrier which represents the constant temptation of every busy head librarian. It is the tendency to equate the absence of upward communication with smooth operation. If the staff is not communicating, however, it is much more likely that something is wrong with the communications system than that all is right with the library. It is certainly true in the situation which we are viewing that those who communicate least are those who seem to have the least dynamic views of their own jobs and of the library as a whole, and thus the least sense of the importance of upward communication.

Most of the barriers to upward communication which primarily involve the library staff revolve around considerations of status. In many situations, including the one under study, the barriers stem from a sense of the superior-subordinate relationships. Several of the staff members feel considerable hesitation in seeking out and taking the time of the head librarian. In general, the staff members' facilities and opportunities for communicating upward are not as extensive as are those for downward communications. As noted earlier in this paper, junior staff members seldom express themselves in meetings without special encouragement.

Furthermore, the staff member is usually more apprehensive about the reaction to his communication than is the supervisor. He tends to think that it is better to say nothing at all than to risk undesirable consequences. Such consequences could range from a personally unfavorable reaction through a decision which would increase the workload of the staff member. A number of times staff members stated that they had not pursued casual suggestions for fear of increasing their workloads. The barriers of apprehension are particularly strong, of course, when the staff member has bad news or a mistake to report—there is a distinct tendency in organizations to filter out information with a negative connotation on its way upward.

By virtue of their status as professionals, the professional staff of a library is likely to encounter a number of barriers to communication with administrators. In the particular library under study, the inclination toward professional, rather than institutional, orientation among the staff is relatively weak. Nevertheless, it should be noted that if a professional feels that his independent judgment is being threatened by management, he may withhold information from the administrators. In general, the professional can be expected to feel detached from administrative authority. (2, pp. 244-7)

In the situation studied, there are two related factors of much greater effectiveness in blocking upward communications. Several of the senior staff members have been associated with the library for many years; the director has been there for a relatively short time. Resistance to positive programs suggested by the director is evident among these senior members. They are, therefore, not likely to pass upward information which might facilitate change. Furthermore, since they do not share or even, in many respects, know or understand his goals, they do not themselves have a clear understanding of what information needs to be communicated. The result of this division of interests can not help but dampen the enthusiasm of the director and undoubtedly puts limitations on his communicating with his staff.

This last difficulty leads to a primary consideration in the discussion of communications systems. The structure of the communications system is closely tied to the structure and type of organization in which it exists. At the same time, its content and its effectiveness cannot really be evaluated except in terms of the organizational goals. Where the formal structure of an organization is ill-defined or amorphous, as is true in most libraries, the communications system tends to be informal. This situation often requires more attention from the administrator than would a more formalized system.

Beyond this, as two communications researchers have said, "... the principal effort of organizational activities is the making of favorable conditions for the achievement of certain goals." (1 p. 312) Administrators can study their organizational structures thoroughly, but genuine evaluation is not possible in the absence of clearcut goals. In particular, the upward communications system may function perfectly well in transmitting information about on-going routines, but it will not transmit information necessary to the success of the organization unless there is staff-wide acceptance and understanding of organizational goals. The definition and understanding of these goals is, of course, more difficult in a library than in a profit-oriented organization. The library can, and often does, continue to exist while functioning in an almost habitual fashion, but its ability to function more effectively, to make its presence felt in its community and to engender support, depends in large part on its organizational self-understanding.

BIBLIOGRAPHY

1. Bavelas, Alex and Dermot Barrett, "An Experimental Approach to Organizational Communication," in I. L. Heckmann and S. G. Huneryager, *Human Relations in Management*, Cincinnati, Southwestern Publishing Co., c1960, pp. 310–317.
2. Blau, Peter M. and W. Richard Scott, *Formal Organizations: A Comparative Approach,* San Francisco, Chandler Publishing Co., c1962.
3. Long, Norton E., "Administrative Communication," in Sidney Mailick and Edward H. Van Ness, eds., *Concepts and Issues in Administrative Behavior*, Prentice-Hall, c1962, pp. 137–149.
4. Planty, Earl G. and William Machaver, "Stimulating Upward Communication," in M. Joseph Dooher and Vivienne Marquis, eds., *Effective Communication on the Job*, N. Y.: American Management Association, c1956, pp. 134–49.
5. Rogers, Carl R. and F. J. Roethlisberger, "Barriers and Gateways to Communication," in I. L. Heckman, and S. G. Hunneryager, *Human Relations in Management*, Cincinnati, Southwestern Publishing Co., c1960, pp. 297–309.
6. Rubenstein, Albert H. and Chadwick J. Haberstroh, eds., *Some Theories of Organization*, Homewood, Ill.: The Dorsey Press, c1960.
7. Scott, William G., "Organization Theory: An Overview and Appraisal," in Joseph A. Litterer, *Organizations: Structure and Behavior*, New York: Wiley, c1963, pp. 13–26.

ABOUT THE AUTHOR—Millicent D. Abell is a graduate of Colorado College where she received her A.B. in 1956. She also has an M.A. from Columbia University with a major in psychology, as well as an M.L.S. from the Library School of the State University of New York at Albany. It was while a student in this program that Mrs. Abell participated in the study reported here. She has also been in the past Assistant Dean of Women at the University of Arizona.

V

THE STRUGGLE FOR EXISTENCE

A very misleading view of administration would be fostered if this reader were to be devoted exclusively to the internal administration of libraries. At higher levels of administration particularly, the task of the administrator must be viewed as largely a political one. It has been estimated that as much as eighty percent of the time of the public library administrator is spent on the library's political relationships and we believe this would hold true—if to a somewhat lesser extent or in less obvious ways—with library administrators in other settings.

Yet it is characteristic of librarians to eschew discussion if not active involvement in politics and things political, as if to suggest that understanding of the political world in which the library functions is to be equated with subscribing to the power motive. Such a view is naive and can be disastrous. Libraries do not function alone; they are dependent on agencies in their environment for support. And for this reason, external factors are key determinants in shaping their goals and influencing their success. Political sophistication will become increasingly important for every type of library as they enter more serious competition with alternative agencies and as they plot out new service areas and seek to reach new clienteles in new ways. For these reasons, an entire section of this volume is devoted to the "politics of administration." Because several political scientists have viewed the public library from their disciplinary vantage point, this part of the reader more than any other, has the advantage of literature and research bearing directly upon libraries.

Introduction to the Political Process

The view of politics presented here is a dynamic rather than static one, politics being viewed as a process which occurs both in and out of formal government. In this section the group basis of politics is introduced and the political process is examined in the context of city government. Community power and power structure are also introduced. The approaches presented thus escape the bounds of legalistic considerations to more nearly explain the process by which decisions are made whether in the public or institutional setting. The concepts presented appear to the editors to be extremely useful ways for librarians to conceptualize their communities and their part in its political life.

The Public Library as a Pressure Group

by Phillip A. Monypenny

> *Phillip Monypenny's article introduces this section because it provides at the start a review of the group basis of politics. This approach seems to the editors to be a particularly viable way for librarians to conceptualize their communities and their part in its political life. It is here that we also find a reaffirmation of the potential of the public library in clearer and more hopeful terms and specifications than have been typically articulated by those in or of librarianship.*

The conception of group pressures as a means of understanding and describing the world of politics was first put forward over fifty years ago. Although the full length works which have exploited this idea have been few, it has nevertheless entered into the popular as well as the professional literature of politics as an explanation of a wide variety of phenomena. The only fault to be found with this wide acceptance is that like most popularizations it presents a simplified version of the original in which much of its possible value is lost. In the popular version "group" becomes organization, and "pressure" becomes lobbying.

The fundamental assertion of Arthur Bentley,[1] who originated the conception, was that government cannot be separated in its operation from the general operation of society, which works through group rather than individual action, and that the power of government to shape the actions of men is essentially the power of those groups in society who support and, indeed, originate its action. The official structure of government has power because of the social interests which are incorporated in its action. For Bentley, therefore, the political world was best described as a sort of elastic medium in which ever changing forces, representing the interests men seek through government, work in various, often contradictory, directions and governmental policy incorporates the direction of the dominant forces.

Neither Bentley nor his successor have told us much about the dimensions of this world, except in the common sense terms of particular groups and particular interests. The furthest Bentley went was to suggest that groups vary in intensity of action, technique, and in number of members and that their degree of success in competition with each other depends on their relative standing in these traits. There is an important if obvious truth in this. Groups equal in number may be most unequal in political effect because one is more active than another, better able to mobilize its members, more skillful in operating the machinery of political decision. There is an implied truth: if we deal with these groups and interests as forces, then forces in total or partial opposition diminish each other's effectiveness and the end result is a modification of original demands in the governmental policies which finally emerge.

In the latest and most recent use of this general thesis to describe the political system surrounding the national government, David Truman has told us a great deal about particular groups and their relative ability to achieve their purposes in the several branches of the national government which are treated as alternate arenas of action and decision.[2] In his early chapters he tells us about the formation of organizations of all kinds; their roles in the lives of their members and their internal policy making processes. He describes in some detail several large national associations which are continuously active in politics such as the AFL-CIO, the American Farm Bureau Federation, the United States Chamber of Commerce, and the American Medical Association. Admirable as this account is, an attempt to relate sociology and psychology to politics and to use the growing literature about the great private organizations interested in politics, it exhibits the most common modification of Bentley's original statement, the interpretation of the term "group" as meaning an organization or association, a finite number of particular human beings in an ordered relationship. In the *Process of Government*, "group" was equivalent to such abstract terms as "force" or "mass" or "vector"; it indicated a direction of

---

SOURCE: Reprinted from Phillip Monypenny, "The Public Library as a Pressure Group," *Illinois Libraries,* 43 (Dec., 1961), pp. 720–730, by permission of the Illinois State Library and the author.

effort without specifying the exact character of the active agents. The utility of such general terms which have a wide variety of possible specific contents is obvious in a number of scientific fields. "Cell" is such a term in biology, "plant" or "firm" in economic theory, "system" in engineering or physics, "culture" in anthropology.

The advantages of Bentley's use of "group," which we shall follow in the rest of this paper, is evident if we consider another term he used, "representation." Representation is not a matter of structure, as in the election of representatives to a legislature. Rather it is an identity of purpose or goal between some element in the population and the action of some official or agency. You are represented when what you want is done. It is in this sense that Donald Kingsley uses "Representative Bureaucracy" as part of the title of his study of the administrative class of the British Civil Service.[3] Thus a "group" may comprise official and unofficial persons because of their identity of outlook even though there are no organizational ties between them and no apparent communication. The unofficial members of the group are nevertheless "represented" by the official members.

Since so many social processes which transmit information or attitudes, which indicate appropriate conduct, which serve to form opinion, through which something we call a movement is started, are unobservable except for the effects which they create, the advantage of avoiding premature specificity is obvious. There are interests in any society which are so pervasive that they need no particular organization in order to have effect on governmental action. It is easy to assign the rejection of a proposal for expenditure to the efforts of a taxpayers organization without recognizing that the legislators who made the adverse decision may well share the organization's outlook and are in no need of outside stimulus to vote as they do.

The foregoing is a very indirect way of getting to the public library as a pressure group. However, without indicating both our use of the term and the theoretical outlook implicit in it, a useful discussion is difficult. The active agency in any political issue which concerns library service is certainly not just the particular proponents of the action, whether librarians or friends of the library. Those who make the proposal and work for it are only the most visible part of a larger group much of which is probably unknown to the public leaders. To use an analogy not original with me, it is the underwater mass of an iceberg which wrecks the ship; and, in estimating the effect of public campaign, political leaders are always attempting to estimate the size of the interested public which is not directly visible. The problem of the proponents of any public cause is the number, intensity and technique of their own group in relationship to the opposition which is pursuing a contrary purpose.

This conception of politics accepts conflict as the chief form of political action and assumes opposition for almost every political proposal. The practical questions of politics are always questions about conflicts: what the opposition is likely to be, who the available allies are, how to get the maximum effect of whatever support one has. Implicit also is the limited character of most conflicts; they arise over particular projects, have as active or passive participants only those who are sensitive to the issues in conflict. Conflict divides on particular matters people who may be united on other matters. The final implication is that governments may be expected to respond to any demand, by however few people it is made, if there is no appreciable opposition. Therefore much of the daily substance of politics is of apparent concern to relatively small numbers of persons and the world of politics permits very fluid alliances among those who share temporarily some common concern.

After every legislative session in Springfield or in Washington the newspapers make much of the total number of bills introduced, of the great numbers passed. The impression is created that we are strangling in this legislative output. A review of the measures passed will show that great numbers of them are of interest to very few people indeed, that most are not in any degree matters of controversy, that only a few issues arise in a session which arouse the effort and attentions of considerable numbers of persons and are, to that degree, matters of serious conflict.

Where do public libraries, state and local, stand in this political universe of contending groups? A few things are apparent; libraries have had enough support to get recognition as governmental activities, authorized by specific statutes, most often supported by separate property tax levies; they have had enough support to get federal aid, though in very limited amounts; librarians have been able to get legal prescription of minimum standards of training for employment in public libraries in a great many states. So much for support. Since they make demands on public funds, libraries face an opposition of varying intensity to any expansion of expenditure, particularly an expansion which will require tax increases. In a great many states public libraries have been supported from very early times by "pegged" statutory levies which continue indefinitely without change unless there is an extraordinary authorization such as a referendum vote. Librarians and library patrons are consequently unaccustomed to seeing themselves as competitors for public funds and have not equipped themselves to enter the competition.

In entering the competition they may make unwelcome discoveries. Public libraries, as a local government activity, are part of the complex structure and politics of local government. Proposals for legislation affecting public libraries go into a system of decision in which there are sharply opposed interests, well mobilized and organized, well provided with spokesmen in the legislature itself. The opposition to increased property tax levies which has risen to such a degree that there is virtually an absolute barrier to proposals which would increase property tax authorizations, is only the most obvious of the interests adverse to much library legislation. There are also structural interests in local government which are connected closely with political party operations and the inter- and intra-party competition for office. These structural interests further ramify to connect with issues and policies which are currently being contested in the domain of the various local governmental units. These interests are active in every proposal for the change of service areas, whether they are for schools or roads or libraries, and in every proposal for change in the organization of governing structures of the various local units. Since the leadership of these local government structural interests, county, township, and special district officers, and their representatives, are among the most active persons in local party structures, it follows that their influence in the legislature is enormous.

To be a part of local government, to seek to promote a service which is administered through local government, thus has its great disadvantages. The new burdens of local government units are notorious, and the question of local government structure is constantly an issue, whether in the form of abolishing or merging units, or transferring functions and services to larger units. As we have indicated, the proposals for change not only threaten to displace office holders who are persons of consequence in the politics of their areas; they indirectly affect hotly contested issues of local policy; liquor control (county or township and village option), county zoning versus unrestricted private development of land, traditional township road policy, versus the presumptive rationality of country highway planning. The current rate of activity in this area keeps the various interests mobilized and ready for action.

As a local government activity, or a local government unit, public libraries cannot escape the polarities which arise within the general field of local government legislation. If library units are permitted to escape present tax limits, if they consolidate into larger service units, if service is transposed from smaller units to the counties, then similar changes may take place in other fields. The opposition in one area is likely to be transferred to the other. The cost of the library unit and of library service may be small. However, the vast potential forces which revolve around existing local government organization, functions, and taxing powers, even if mobilized only to a slight degree, may be large enough to defeat the relatively small forces which libraries as local services are able to deploy. Library legislative goals nearly always mean more money, whether from local or state government and the creation of larger service areas, whether through consolidation, transfer of function, or contractual arrangement. The parallel to the issues which arise with respect to other local government activities is all too complete.

The world of the state library is not a wholly different one. Its mere existence argues support; the size of its appropriation is a fair measure of the degree of support. More significantly, the state library has come to occupy that relationship to public library service throughout the state that other state agencies occupy with respect to their local government counterparts.

It provides consultative services, may have some regulatory powers, extends financial support directly and indirectly. Like other state agencies, the state library has two areas of political interest—its own survival as an organization, the services it provides directly to a various public; and the interest of local library service for which it is surrogate. The group of services it provides, the financial resources of which it disposes, are an indication of a very significant support for library service as an activity of state government, the indication of a well-established state library interest.

By the same token, the support given implies that a corresponding opposition has been overcome. The source of the opposition is obvious enough. Primarily it consists of opposition to increased state expenditure, which, well led and well mobilized, has nevertheless been unable to prevent the steady growth of state expenditure and taxes. Secondarily perhaps, there is a sort of indirect opposition—the relative priority which is given to library expenditure in relation to any other state. Libraries are currently in the position of asking for more money, both to increase their own services and to underwrite local services, so their engagement with the opposition to expenditure is continuous. If they have a low priority, in the minds of those who allocate funds, they are the weak point in the state budget on which the anti-expenditure forces will converge.

It is not our purpose here to pursue a separate discussion of state and local library interests, however. Rather we are concerned with pro-library interests as a common enterprise. In looking at the common enterprise, what is striking in the deployment of forces is that the push for support has been transposed to successively higher government levels. This is worth noting of itself, and because it may shed some light on the pro-library interest and its relative standing as a competitor in the struggle to determine governmental policy.

In some states we have state aid, in all states indirect subvention in the form of consultative services, centralized services, book loans, the extension of reference service. Since 1956 we have had federal aid, and the authority for this has recently been renewed even though part of the argument for the original act was that it was a demonstration and would come to an end once new services won expanded state and local financing. This shift of the focus of political effort to higher governmental levels may be regarded as an example of political technique, in the Bentleyan sense in which technique is power. It is a technique which has been used since the early days of the republic by those who found local or state government unresponsive. The reason for resort to higher levels is not only the inadequacy of local resources, though that is a frequent argument. Rather the larger governmental unit seems to offer more advantageous conditions to the proponents of some kinds of programs, and it is worth our while to see what these advantages are.

The present extent and organization of public library service imply that it has no such large public as public education or traffic control. Federal grants to education are comparatively trifling, yet total expenditures on elementary, secondary, and higher education have grown at an astonishing rate, almost all of it state and local revenue. Although state aid has grown at the largest rate, local expenditure has also grown to a quite remarkable degree. Here, the economy group has been routed, leaving small victories only for those who sought to shift the burden of increased cost to other than the general property tax (the principal local government revenue source). They have not in fact reduced property taxes, though they have undoubtedly minimized their increase. Considering the concurrent increase in the expenditures of state government for highways and for welfare, the record is a remarkable one. It makes the position of the public library as a poor cousin stand out the more remarkably. Certainly, considering the small total expenditure of libraries, resort to federal financing was necessary for other reasons than the absolute unavailability of state and local funds.

The weak bargaining position of the public libraries is the more remarkable if we consider that they do reach a substantial portion of the public with their services; they play a significant part in the autobiographical reminiscences of many of our intellectual and political leaders, they have an obviously important potential role in the individual and social search for knowledge which is a striking characteristic of our time. What is the character of the library public that it has done no better?

If we look at the obvious social characteristics of the library public we may develop some elements of an answer. As members of that public or that interest, we must count the library staffs, the library users, and the lay persons who participate in library government as members of boards of trustees. It has been noted that users are a comparatively small group out of the whole population, that a disproportionate number are children, who do not vote, that a disproportionate number are women, and, moreover, single women, that the relative proportions of the highest and lowest sectors of the socio-economic scale are low. On the other hand the library staffs are an educated group, well organized, capable of knowing the political system in which they work, and able through their organizations to mobilize at the appropriate point in it. Their capacity for political action is strikingly indicated by the Library Services Act of 1956. I do not know the detailed history of that act, though it was apparently a long time in being born. However, the hearings in the House on the Act in the years of its passage, and in 1960 the year of its renewal, are an impressive tribute to the skill with which the campaign for it was conducted.[4]

At these hearings there were virtually no opposition witnesses, though there were a few rather nasty anti-library tracts submitted. With one exception in 1956, and with no exceptions which I could see in 1960, the subcommittees conducting the hearing were the most enthusiastic proponents of the legislation. The number of members of Congress induced to testify in support of the bill, or to submit statements, particularly in 1960, is astonishing. The cross section of respectable society represented by the friendly witnesses was most appealing; the amount of data worked up for their statements by state librarians and state library associations was most impressive. Except for a few professional library spokesmen, most of the witnesses could not be said to have a personal or professional interest in the bills before the committee, yet their presentation of the library situation in their own states and communities was utterly disarming. The whole record demonstrates an astonishing organized effort prior to the hearings. The logistical arrangements alone, for getting witnesses to the place of hearing at the appropriate moment, must have been demanding. The record of witnesses and statements also demonstrates a most sagacious understanding of what arguments, what personal and social qualities are most appealing to members of Congress and to the press which reports these affairs.

From what has happened in other fields—child welfare, wildlife and wilderness conservation, maternal and child health, anti-bill board legislation—one gets the impression that groups whose leadership and explicit membership is somewhat similar to that of the pro-library group have been more successful in Washington than in most of the state capitals. Some elements of this success are quite tangible. A small segment of the population, well educated and politically aware, with a limited budget, and limited facilities for reaching the population at large, can afford one competent spokesman in a Washington office, can organize their politically effective members into one significant campaign, drawing on their whole national resources. Divided among fifty states they do not have the talent in depth, the money, or the skilled manpower to do as well.

One may speculate also that the members of Congress who are full-time at their jobs, living in a rather cosmopolitan world, aware of a wide range of political events and interests, are more open to communication about matters of limited general appeal than are members of state legislatures, who spend a few months a year at best on their immediately legislative tasks. However, there is another advantage in Washington which has nothing to do with the characteristics of political groups or of members of Congress: the national budget is an enormous pool of funds and significant increases in the expenditures for some functions can be made without notable financial strain. The decision not to construct a single aircraft carrier, after authorization and initial appropriation, would release several times more funds than have been spent since the passage of the Library Services Act. This advantage as a place to win financial support, state capitals also have, over all except the largest local government units.

The apparent advantage which small literate well-organized groups, with access to the more elite media of national opinion, have at the national level is an indication of their handicaps in the smaller political arenas. The school people, largely defeated in Washington, have done magnificently well in the states and in local districts. Are libraries like natural wildernesses, the concern only of small groups of intensively alert and poetically articulate people? Few of us sojourn in wildernesses. If we did, the wilderness would die. Many of us find their mere existence as evocative as poetry and this gives the supporters of wilderness protection much of their influence. But do we dream of library shelves which we never see, and never really expect to see?

Obviously there is something of this in the support for libraries. To have the possibility of exposure to great minds is probably a more real goal for many than the actual exposure. The more that this is so, the more I suspect the library will be forced to compete only in those arenas in which intellect and skill in argument will win support, albeit on a small scale. The many tiered leadership and membership required to compete at all levels of government, to get support through any set of taxes which has an element of flexibility in it, will not be available to the public library.

Yet this is not the necessary limit of political support for library objectives. If library boards, as a Wisconsin study shows, have an extremely high proportion of women as members (divided, for reasons the study does not say, between housewives and club women) a membership of women has not been incompatible with success in many campaigns.[5] Not in vain do the advertisements say, "Never underestimate the power of a woman." The League of Women Voters, the National Congress of Parents and Teachers, the General Federation of Womens' Clubs, the American Association of University Women, already allied with library organizations in a number of fights, are most able campaigners for the things in which their members and their leaders believe deeply.

The users of libraries may not be as numerous among the highest and lowest social strata as they are in the middle levels. However, the latter, despite their numbers, are not active or well led, and the former are not numerous, so that their normally great weight in our councils is overcome by number on issues about which many feel strongly. The middle classes provide most of our political leadership, most of our civic leadership, and monopolize whatever general prestige movie stars and sports heroes do not dispose of. They are alert, in communication with each other, hence capable of concerted action, and reasonably knowing in political matters. Perhaps what the library needs, to use its potential position more effectively, is to increase the identifications of its services with the aspirations of its users. At its best, the library offers knowledge rather than entertainment, and knowledge is still power. It offers the emotional catharsis of art, not only in words but in sounds and pictures. It permits growth beyond the formal limits of schools. It is relevant to every community enterprise and to every individual purpose. Even the art of love might grow in depth and tenderness with poetry and song. As more superficial needs for knowledge and for recreation are met by other means, more challenging and fruitful vistas open.

The prospects, in the long run, are that the impasses of governmental policy caused by the balance of the forces for expenditure and against taxation will shift somewhat. Beyond the simple needs of food and shelter and transportation, there is an increasing range of discretionary expenditures. Despite the increasing bite of taxes, people should still find it advantageous to spend somewhat more for public services which increase fullness of individual life, despite the heavy charge of services which provide insurance against catastrophe. Despite the present heavy tribute to government which we all pay, most of us are able to provide our families with material conveniences and comforts beyond the dreams of our depression-ridden youth. There is a limit to the consumption of motor cars and washing machines, television sets and even four lane highways at several million dollars a mile. Given the growth of the economy and of personal income of which the business and economic experts are so confident, there should be more funds for libraries and art museums, for parks and playgrounds, and perhaps for theatres as well. From the standpoint of an economy of effort and material, the public library has an enormous advantage over the large personal library which all too few can have and which must be largely unread, given the other preoccupations of its owner.

The evidence of the ability of those who support library service to achieve governmental goals is the Library Services Act itself. The original indifference to it vanished like snow in a southern wind as the campaign for it took hold. In the individual states there have been similar victories, some resting on the prestige and skill of a single political leader who makes the library cause his own, more often the work of a strong alliance of like-minded people, exploiting various organizational connections and personal relationships to expand their base. I think that the present library leadership, both professionals and interested laymen, is equal to the task, that the size and geographic spread of library organizations is most appropriate to what has to be done.

To reach a larger public that is now quite uninvolved, I think that the libraries will have to open up new lines of service. They must let the school boards know how much of the daily assignments of school pupils could not be completed without local public library resources, they must show the Chamber of Commerce how much marketing and industrial location information is contained in the available statistical reference works. They must show the businessman interested in new opportunities how much technical and financial data is available from the library's books and periodicals. They must show the officers of local government how many of their problems are discussed in standard works. They can help the wage earner interested in a new career find the materials for his own retraining, and assist the endless varieties of women's clubs to see how much of interest the library has for their members in cultural and public affairs, and even in domestic science fields. The library is potentially an ally in every civic campaign, in every kind of individual and group educational activity, in every effort to create new individual and group horizons. In estimating the success of any pressure group one has to ask not only how much it can demand but how much it has to offer. The library and its friends cannot do much with money and not too much with votes, but services of a most profound and flexible character it certainly can provide.

We have ignored in this essay the anti-intellectualism and the suspicion of books and those who write and use them, which has been an affliction to libraries at times and places in this country. The resistance of all forms of education in response to attack is more impressive than the preoccupation of the headline writers with the attacks they would suggest. However, the primary problem of libraries in the political arena does not lie here. It lies in securing the financial resources and legal authorizations necessary to extend a level of library service that library leadership regards as adequate. The winning of these things will demonstrate a base of popular support which makes the enemies of free inquiry a mere temporary inconvenience.

FOOTNOTES

[1] Arthur F. Bentley, *The Process of Government* (Chicago: The University of Chicago Press, 1908.) Reprinted at various times by the Principia Press, Bloomington, Indiana.

[2] David B. Truman, *The Governmental Process* (New York: Knopf, 1951.) Other significant books which utilize the Bentley insights are: E. P. Herring, *Group Representation Before Congress* (Baltimore: Johns Hopkins Press, 1929); *Public Administration and the Public Interest* (New York: McGraw Hill, 1936), by the same author; Betram M. Gross, *The Legislative Struggle* (New York: McGraw Hill, 1953.)

[3] J. Donald Kingsley, *Representative Bureaucracy* (Yellow Springs, Ohio: Antioch Press, 1944.)

[4] U. S. 84th Congress, 1st Session, House of Representatives, Committee on Education and Labor, *Federal Aid for Library Service in Rural Areas, Hearing before the Subcommittee,* etc. May 26-27, 1955 (Washington: U. S. Government Printing Office, 1955); 86th Congress, 2nd Session, House of Representatives, Committee on Education and Labor, *Extension of the Library Services Act, Hearings before the Subcommittee,* etc., March 25-April 7, 1960 (Washington: Government Printing Office, 1960.)

[5] Ruth Bauman, *Facing the 60's, the Public Library in Wisconsin, A Report to the Wisconsin Library Commission,* Parts I and II (Madison, Wisconsin: University of Wisconsin, Bureau of Government, February, 1961.)

ABOUT THE AUTHOR—Phillip A. Monypenny is a political scientist whose primary fields of interest are public administration and policy formulation, and civil-military relations in policy formulation. He has also contributed to scholarship and the literature of librarianship. Since 1947 Monypenny has been a member of the University of Illinois faculty. Prior to this time, he had been on the faculty of City College, New York, and served in the armed forces. From 1946 to 1947 he was a Visiting Professor in Puerto Rico. From 1963 to 1965 Monypenny served as Editor of the *Midwest Journal of Political Science.* He is currently on the Council of the American Society for Public Administration.

Monypenny is at present chairman of a committee of the American Association of University Professors conducting an investigation of "Faculty Responsibility for the Academic Freedom of Students." In 1961/62 the American Association of State Libraries sponsored a study to obtain basic information on all state agencies providing library services and to establish standards for state libraries. Monypenny was director of the survey, and edited its report volume, *Library Functions of the States* (1965).

The Political Function

by Edward C. Banfield and James Q. Wilson

> The writers present here the importance of the political function of government, that is, the management of conflict. They argue that the political basis for decision-making may at times best serve the public interest even when "efficiency" and the service function must be sacrificed. Librarians will note their use of the placement of a public library branch as illustrative of this thesis. This piece provides a sophisticated introduction to the major participants, the issues and the process of politics in city government.

The future of the city and the great forces affecting it are talked about in after-dinner speeches sometimes, but they rarely occupy the serious attention of practical men. The questions that *do* occupy their attention are usually of a more immediate and limited kind. Such questions may or may not matter to the community as a whole, but their importance to particular interests is usually great or even crucial, and it is this that brings them to the fore in a practical way. The questions that give rise to most city politics are the following: (1) Who is to be elected to office? (2) Where is some specific facility to be located? (Usually the struggle is between neighborhoods, each trying to *avoid* having the facility for fear that it will displace families, attract "undersirable" people, or depress local property values.) (3) How are taxes to be apportioned? (4) Which agency or official is to be in charge of a particular matter? (5) Is an existing policy or practice to be changed? (6) At what levels are certain services to be supported, and how is the budget to be distributed? (7) What is to be the bias of the police in its treatment of organized crime, labor disputes, and racial incidents?

MANAGING CONFLICT

A government serves two principal functions. One is that of supplying those goods and services—for example, police protection and garbage removal—which cannot be (or at any rate are not) supplied under private auspices. This is its "service function." The other function—the "political" one—is that of managing conflict in matters of public importance.

Since the two functions are performed at the same time by the same set of institutions, they are often concretely indistinguishable. A mayor who intervenes in a dispute about the location of a new public library manages a service at the same time that he settles a conflict, but he usually is thought of, and thinks of himself, as doing a single thing—"running the city government." One function may at times be much more conspicuous than the other. In some cities, the service function is decidedly subordinate to the political one; decisions generally turn on the struggle of politicians, parties, and interest groups for some advantage. In other cities, politics seems to be entirely absent; there are no conflicts and no struggles for power; matters are decided, at least seemingly, on purely technical grounds.

The city without politics is held up as a shining example by some writers on local government. Many people believe that politics in any sphere is pointless and wasteful, a pathological disturbance of social life.

This attitude may arise from a general distaste for conflict and a feeling that matters ought always to be decided reasonably and without contention. A writer on public school administration, for example, upholds this view in the following characteristic terms: "One criterion of how well a school board functions is the extent to which its members agree among themselves. If they are in fair agreement of what the school board should do and about what the duties of the superintendent should be, then, when it comes to making a decision, they will spend little time disagreeing about basic values, about what their jobs actually entail,

---

SOURCE: Reprinted by permission of the publishers from Edward C. Banfield & James Q. Wilson CITY POLITICS Cambridge, Mass.: Harvard University Press, Copyright, 1963, by the President and Fellows of Harvard College and the Massachusetts Institute of Technology.

and devote their energies to solving the problem at hand."[1]

Another reason for disliking politics is that political decisions are often based on considerations entirely unrelated to the merits of the issue. Of course the politician *claims* that his decision is based solely on grounds of efficiency: for example, he favors a certain site for the library "because it will be most convenient to users." But the observer suspects that the *real* grounds of the decision are self-serving or party-serving—that the politician wants the library there because its being there would gain him votes.

It does not necessarily follow, however, that if a politician acts from self-interest he inevitably sacrifices the public interest. Nor is it necessarily true that the public interest is best served by treating the service function of government as more important or more worthy than the political one. It is entirely possible that in some circumstances it is more important to manage conflict than to make the most "efficient" use of resources. If the politician's self-interest leads him to put the library in what the contending interests regard as an acceptable compromise site, he may serve a more useful social function than he would if he decided on purely disinterested grounds to put it where it would be most convenient. Many people's cast of mind is essentially unpolitical, however, and they find it hard to see how the politician's self-interest can serve the public or how any sacrifice of the service function can be justified by any gain in the political one.

City government especially, many people think, ought to be free of politics. In this view, the government of a city differs from other governments, or *should* differ from them, in that it exists solely for the sake of the service function. Cleaning streets, running schools, and collecting garbage ought to be no more controversial, and therefore no more political, than selling groceries. There will be politics in the city government (according to this view) only if it is "injected from the outside"; to prevent this, city government ought to be insulated from state and national government, which are bound to be affected with politics. This is the general idea behind nonpartisanship, and it is one which has greatly affected local government in the United States.

At least two good arguments can be made in support of this view. One is that because of the city's inferior position in the federal system (a matter to be discussed in Chapter 5), all conflicts of real importance must be settled at a higher level.

The great questions of the day and, for that matter, most that are not great, cannot fruitfully be discussed by the city council. Such questions as can usefully be discussed by it (for example, the location of the new library) ought to be decided on their merits, which means that considerations of efficiency (the service function) ought to be paramount.

The other argument that can be made is that there are ordinarily no inherent conflicts in the city—no conflicts, that is, which are not the result of politics rather than the cause of it. This is indeed sometimes the case in fairly small, middle-class cities. Where everybody is pretty much agreed on fundamentals, there is certainly much to be said for leaving the choice of means to technicians. In sizable cities, however, there is rarely this agreement on fundamentals. Moreover, even in those places, small or large, where matters are left to technicians, conflict may arise, for the technicians themselves have different and more or less incompatible professional ends. Park, school, and traffic technicians, for example, may disagree about street layouts; and, in the end, politics—albeit generally not under that name—must decide.

Whether one likes it or not, politics, like sex, cannot be abolished. It can sometimes be repressed by denying people the opportunity to practice it, but it cannot be done away with because it is the nature of man to disagree and to contend. We are not saying that politics arises solely from the selfish desire of some to have their way, although that is certainly one source of it. The fact is that even in a society of altruists or angels there would be politics, for some would conceive the common good in one way and some in another, and (assuming the uncertainties that prevail in this world) some would think one course of action more prudent and some would think another.[2]

Whether it is generally desirable to try to repress conflict may also be doubted. Civilized people have a distaste for it because in the ordinary personal relations of life it involves selfishness, deceit, and strong and unpleasant emotions like hate. On the wider stage of political life, however, it does not necessarily involve these. Political struggle is often noble and highminded. To repress it, moreover, is to discourage or prevent some people from asserting their needs, wants, and interests. One can imagine a political system in which there is no struggle because the people in disagreement know that their efforts to exercise influence would have no effect upon events. In such a case politics is absent, but so also are the conditions of progress.

Where there exists conflict that threatens the existence or the good health of the society, the political function should certainly take precedence over the service one. In some cities, race and class conflict has this dangerous character. To govern New York, Chicago, or Los Angeles, for example, by the canons of efficiency—of efficiency *simply*—might lead to an accumulation of restlessness and tension that would eventually erupt in meaningless individual acts of violence, in some irrational mass movement, or perhaps in the slow and imperceptible weakening of the social bonds. Politics is, among other things, a way of converting the restless, hostile impulses of individuals into a fairly stable social product (albeit perhaps a revolution!) and, in doing so, of giving these impulses moral significance.

This suggests another reason why the management of conflict is a social function of the greatest importance. Political struggle, even the seemingly trivial kind that so often exists in the cities, is frequently a part of the rhetoric by which society discusses the nature of the common good and the meaning of justice and virtue. The location of a housing project may not be of much intrinsic importance. But such a question becomes endowed with very great importance when in the course of controversy larger issues are connected with it symbolically or ideologically; then the housing matter is the vehicle for the discussion of, say, racial justice and ultimately of justice itself. Society creates its ideals, as judges make laws, by deciding particular cases in the light of general principles. It is only as general principles are brought into contact with particular cases that the principles have meaning.

Finally, politics is a way by which politicians and others get the power they must have to govern. In the American political system, legal authority is so widely distributed that an official —say a mayor—usually lacks authority to do very much. By "playing politics" he in effect borrows additional authority and he also acquires other means of exercising influence. Part II of this book describes at length the process by which power (that is, legal authority plus other means of exercising influence) is assembled in the city. It will suffice here to point out that generating some of the power without which the authorities could not govern is an indispensable function of politics.

POLITICS AS PLAY

In America, perhaps more than any where else, politics is also a form of play—a game. *Play* is any activity that is enjoyed for itself and not as a means to some end. A *game* is play that is carried on under rules. Much of our city politics fits these definitions. The ends that are in conflict are often not "really" valued by the players: they are not valued, that is, except for the purposes of the game. To put it still another way, the players value the ends about which they contend *in order that* they may enjoy the game. Much local office seeking, for example, cannot be understood on any assumption other than that people are having fun.

The origins of Tammany Hall, the once powerful Democratic machine in New York City, illustrate the point very well. At the end of the Revolutionary War, certain troops serving under Washington discarded their patron saint, St. George, and adopted instead "St. Tammany." Tamanend had been a noted Indian chief who was supposed to have died at the age of 107 after making a great record as a statesman. The soldiers put on a big celebration to mark the change of patrons. They erected a liberty pole and dressed themselves as Indian warriors with feathers and bucktails. According to Matthew Breen: "From the huge wigwam, which was adorned as befitted the abode of a great chief, came forth the representative of St. Tammany, dressed in the most artistic Indian fashion. To the assembled multitude, composed of civilians as well as soldiers, he gave a 'long talk' on the duty of the hour, dilating upon the virtues of courage, justice, and freedom; after which the warriors danced and caroused far into the night."[3]

Celebrations of this sort occurred in Pennsylvania and elsewhere for several years and then, in 1789, the Tammany Society was organized in New York City. It elected a presiding officer or Grand Sachem and twelve lesser sachems, adopted Indian ceremonies, divided the year into "moons," and issued calls for meetings "one hour after the setting of the sun."

There was an element of seriousness in the Tammany Society, but this does not mean that it was not mostly horseplay. Play is boring, even for little children, unless it can be made serious. Anyone who is a member of a fraternity or lodge knows that exalted purposes are essential to sustain the nonsense.

The "game" and "work" elements of a political incident may therefore be difficult or impossible to separate in some instances, but the distinction is important for analysis nevertheless, because it helps to explain behavior which would be otherwise inexplicable. It also points to a possible danger for society. For although it may be safe to treat make-believe as real, it probably is not safe to treat what is real as make-believe; a politics which is an "interesting game" may in some circumstances be radically unsuited to serve the most important function of politics, the management of conflict that is *real*.

ACTORS IN CITY POLITICS

It is characteristic of the American political system that everyone has a right and even a positive obligation to "get in on the act" of running the government. As heirs to the Protestant tradition, a great many Americans believe that they owe a debt of service to the community; participating in public affairs is one of the ways in which these Americans discharge their obligation to "do good." As heirs of the frontier and of Jacksonian democracy, they believe, too, that the ordinary citizen is qualified to decide any matter of public importance. And, as we have just seen, politics in America has always been a form of mass entertainment. For all these reasons and more, the public business is everybody's business to an extent that would astonish other democratic peoples, even the English.

However, most participation in the affairs of the city is by groups and organizations rather than by individuals. Or, to put it properly, it is by individuals acting in group or organizational roles. The individual appears as a "person" on election day to choose between this candidate and that and sometimes to say "yes" or "no" to a few propositions on the ballot. At most other times, "persons" are of little account; groups and organizations are the principal actors.

An exception must be made to this in the case of towns and very small cities. Here formal organizations concerned with governmental affairs may not exist. Informal groupings—crowds, cliques, and circles formed around leading men—take the place of formal organizations to some extent. Whether by themselves or in cliques, individuals are relatively more important in the politics of smaller cities, or else—the two possibilities are by no means exclusive—the level of participation is lower.

Arthur Vidich and Joseph Bensman found this to be the case in a village (which they called Springdale) in upper New York State.[4] Meetings of the village trustees are dull and almost meaningless. There is scarcely ever any new business, projects are rarely undertaken, and few decisions are made. The trustees do what they absolutely must, but avoid whatever they can. Far from seeking power, they seem to shun it. When the trustees act, it is always unanimously; no one ever dissents. Before the vote, however, the "debate" on the issue is long, rambling, uninformed, and inconclusive. No one wants to commit himself or to disagree with his colleagues.

Beneath the surface of Springdale, there are many matters about which some citizens feel concern. The tax assessments have never been reviewed, despite obvious inequities. Some homeowners and some farmers are disturbed about the lack of adequate roads and street lights, deficiencies in the removal of garbage and snow, and occasional failures in water pressure. Others want the town to try to attract industry, and still others are upset by certain school policies. These matters rarely develop into public issues, however, and they almost never lead to governmental action. The one opportunity effectively to challenge the system—the annual election of village trustees—is carefully controlled to prevent struggles for power. Local elections are held at different times from state and national ones; this reduces turnout and keeps partisan issues from affecting village affairs. The polls are open for only four hours; this further discourages participation, particularly by the commuters who work during the day in nearby cities and may not entirely share the village ethos. Out of about four hundred who are eligible, no more than thirty-five vote, and on occasion as few as fifteen. Slates are made up after consultation with everyone "who counts" and are rarely opposed.

This pattern is characteristic of many small places. It can be explained on several grounds. For one thing, there is not much at stake in small-town politics; no large formal organizations are concerned in it and, since the governing body spends very little, citizens and taxpayers have little to gain or lose by what it does. For another thing, the leaders of the town depend for support upon personal associations and friendships and being "good fellows," not upon interest groups and organized constituencies. The most important consideration, however, is probably that the intimacy of small-town life makes harmony, or at least the appearance of it, almost indispensable. Where everyone is in frequent face-to-face contact with almost everyone else, it is essential that all be on good terms. People in such a town have learned from experience that controversies are particularly bitter when they involve "persons" as distinguished from "representatives of organizations." Nothing in small-town politics is as important to most people, consequently, as the preservation of peace and harmony and the maintenance of easy personal relations. The style of this politics therefore reflects this view of things. The tacitly accepted rule of unanimity and the rambling, pointless character of public discussion, for example, are both functional; they insure that no one will be put on the spot, as they probably would be if there were split votes, firm positions, and clear arguments. To put the matter more generally, the function of politics in the small towns is less to resolve issues than, by suppressing them, to enable people to get along with each other while living together in very close contact. In sizable cities, of course, this need does not exist.

In a community which is relatively compact and homogeneous, the idea of a common good tends to be widely shared. Few citizens identify themselves with organizations having rival interests in community politics. There is little need for "interest balancing" and, in any case, it is considered wrong and even immoral. Since the maintenance of organizations is not at stake, there is more likely to be discussion of what is "best for the community." The views of people who are especially disinterested, well-informed, and intelligent, and who represent in a marked degree the ethos of the community, are considered particularly relevant and those of people who speak for special interests are considered irrelevant or are given little weight. Even in the largest and most heterogeneous cities, of course, some issues may be decided largely on the basis of what is "best for the community," and even there some individuals (though usually not many) hold themselves aloof from organizational identifications in order to have the authority that goes with impartiality.[5]

From time to time the search for the common good under arrangements designed to suppress conflict breaks down. When this happens, politics in the small community tends to be more bitter, more divisive, and more explosive than politics in the large city. Issues, once they "break through" social restraints, are likely to polarize the community into hostile camps. James S. Coleman has described the impact of such issues as fluoridation, desegregation, and school policy on various small communities. There are few, if any, large impersonal organizations which seek to mitigate the conflict in order to preserve themselves. There are no established channels for the expression of disagreement. Since organized interests are not involved, issues tend to become ideological and their settlement imposes heavy strains on the social fabric.[6] James G. Coke has noted that protests and calls for remedial civic action are "endemic in the large, but weak and episodic in the small" metropolitan centers; the larger the city, he says, the more likely it is to have its attention called to social problems and the more likely also to deal with problems by making rules rather than by treating cases individually; the application of rules, he thinks, is likely to lead to conflict.[7]

The participation of individuals in politics probably tends to be reduced where strong organizations exist, because organizations are apt to push individuals out and to pre-empt the field of controversy for themselves. This happens because organizations are impelled by a dynamic, immanent in the process of organization, to select and manage issues in ways that individuals do not.

The organizations which participate in big-city politics are of two general sorts, permanent and *ad hoc*. The *ad hoc* ones are, of course, those that come into being to participate in a particular issue and then either dissolve or else convert themselves into permanent ones.

The permanent organizations which play continuing roles in city politics are of five general kinds: (1) the press; (2) other business firms, especially department stores and the owners and managers of real estate; (3) the city bureaucracies; (4) voluntary (or "civic") associations; and (5) labor unions. Each of these will be treated later in a separate chapter.

Except for the press, which concerns itself with the whole spectrum of civic activity, the permanent and *ad hoc* organizations which participate in city politics usually confine themselves to rather narrow ranges of subject matter. Wallace Sayre and Herbert Kaufman classify nongovernmental groups in New York City by frequency of intervention and scope of influence.[8] On their chart, the quadrant representing high frequency and broad scope is very sparsely populated, containing only the press, the League of Women Voters, and the Citizens' Union. That representing high frequency and narrow scope is heavily populated, and the organizations in it (concerned mainly with health, education, and welfare) tend to be permanent. That representing broad scope and low frequency is almost empty. The remaining quadrant, representing low frequency and narrow scope, is heavily populated with *ad hoc* bodies—letterhead organizations that quickly come and quickly go.

Any organization must offer a continuous stream of incentives to elicit the activities that it requires from its members or other "contributors" (taxpayers, customers, patrons). In large, permanent, formal organizations these incentives are largely pecuniary (e.g., salary) or at least material. But the maintenance of such organizations depends also upon their ability to offer certain nonmaterial incentives, such as prestige, association with pleasant or interesting people, and the opportunity to "do good." If it is to grow, or even to survive, every organization must offer a suitable mixture of such incentives—material, nonmaterial, or both—and it must offer them in sufficient quantity and without interruption.[9]

Voluntary associations (such as welfare organizations and housing and planning associations) rely mainly upon nonmaterial incentives, especially opportunities to "serve the community," to mix with "important people," to engage in activity which is "interesting." Because they must provide such incentives in order to survive, associations of this sort are always in search of "good program material," that is, topics or issues which will bring the right people together and arouse in them the enthusiasm needed to sustain the organization. The range of suitable program material is in the nature of the case limited.[10]

HOW ISSUES ARISE AND ARE HANDLED

These considerations help to explain how political issues arise in the city and how they are handled after they arise. Sometimes an issue is created by a politician in the course of his effort to get or keep office. Sometimes they arise because a voluntary association has put in motion certain legal machinery—as, for example, when a civic group gets enough signatures on a petition to compel the city to hold a referendum on a new city charter. More commonly, however, they arise in response to the maintenance and enhancement needs of large formal organizations. These are not, as a rule, voluntary associations. Typically they are organizations which offer mainly material rather than nonmaterial incentives (i.e., which must meet a payroll). The manager of such an organization sees some advantage in changing the status quo. He proposes changes. Other large formal organizations are threatened by the proposed changes. They oppose them, and a controversy which involves public authorities takes place.

One of the authors of this book found that the six city-wide controversies that occurred in Chicago in a two-year period could be analyzed in these terms.[11] In one case, a large private hospital felt threatened by heavy demands for service from low-income Negroes. Its managers proposed that the county build a public hospital nearby. This idea was opposed by the existing county hospital, a very large institution on the other side of the city. The two principal antagonists, both large organizations depending mainly upon material incentives, gathered about them various allies. The private hospital, for example, was supported by the Welfare Council, an association of organizations dealing with welfare matters; by a civic-minded millionaire; and by the newspapers. In the other Chicago cases, the prime-mover organizations were the city and county welfare departments, a university, a forest preserve district, a transit authority, a department store, and a newspaper.

Sometimes an issue is created, so to speak, out of thin air by an organization that is searching for program material. One of the Chicago cases, for example, arose when the *Chicago Tribune,* anxious to demonstrate its power and to memorialize its late editor and publisher, Colonel Robert R. McCormick, fought a long, hard, and successful battle to have an exhibition hall built under public auspices on the lake front. When the editor was asked why the paper had made such a fuss about the hall, he replied:

Why did we put so much time into this? Because it's good for the city. But partly from selfish motives too. We want to build a bigger Chicago and a bigger *Tribune.* We want more circulation and more advertising. We want to keep growing, and we want the city to keep growing so that we can keep growing.

We think the community respects a newspaper that can do things like that. People will go by that hall and say, "See that? The *Tribune* did that singlehanded." That's good for us to have them say that.

If it hadn't come off—if those lawsuits had turned out wrong—it would not have been good. It's good that people should think that their newspaper is powerful. It's good that it be powerful.[12]

When a large organization is the prime mover in a civic controversy, the chief executive of the organization normally plays a crucial role in development of the controversy. In the struggle between the private and the public hospital in Chicago, the chief strategists on both sides were the medical superintendents of the hospitals. In the case of the exhibition hall the strategists were the editor of the *Tribune* and the owner of a private amphitheater which would be damaged by competition from the new hall.

The chief executives of the prime-moving organizations do not ordinarily appear in the matter conspicuously. They much prefer the background. They are used to doing things through subordinates. Unless they are newspaper executives they are reluctant, for reasons of public relations, to have their organizations involved openly in controversies. For example, when the University of Chicago decided to do something drastic about the spread of blight in its neighborhood, it set up the Southeast Commission. This was largely controlled by the university—that is, by the chancellor and his subordinates—but it had a separate board of directors and a separate letterhead, and could at least claim to be "broadly based" and representative of "the whole community."[13]

This is what often happens. The principally affected, or prime-moving, organization sets up a "front" organization like the Southeast Commission, or else it gets voluntary associations to "front" for it. For the voluntary association there are usually definite advantages in such an arrangement; the prime-moving organization not only supplies it with good program material but, perhaps, with financial assistance as well.

Local government agencies—city departments and special-function districts, for example— are often the prime-moving organizations, and they therefore commonly foster close, continuing relationships with at least one voluntary association which can be depended upon to "front" for them when necessary. We are in the habit of thinking that pressure groups use public agencies, and of course they often do. But the influence commonly runs the other way as well, the public agency using the pressure group, and there are a good many cases where the "pressure group" exists solely to be used by the public agency.

The public agitation of a civic issue is likely, therefore, to be carried on by co-opted voluntary associations which pass resolutions, testify before legislative committees, issue press releases, wait on the mayor, and then at the end of the year give testimonial dinners to acclaim themselves for "civic leadership."

The elected officials, who of course have the authority to decide matters, watch the maneuvers of the prime-moving organizations and their co-opted agents with critical attention. They know well enough what is going on behind the scenes and they know approximately how many—if any —votes the organizations may be able to swing. Usually they wait as long as possible before making a decision. They know that as long as they do nothing they are probably safe, and, anyway, they want to allow time for public opinion to form. When a magazine writer suggested to Mayor Richard J. Daley of Chicago that the mayor had never in his whole life committed himself to anything whatsoever until he absolutely had to, the mayor laughed. "That's a pretty good way to be, don't you think?" he said. "Pretty good way to run any business."

But this tendency to let proposals affecting city affairs arise and be fought over by non-governmental organizations (or at any rate by organizations which do not have responsibility for the city government as a whole) is not merely an expression of the politician's shrewdness. In the United States, the public takes the view that the elected official ought not to make and impose a policy of his own; instead, he should preside over and exercise final authority in a struggle among private and partial interests in which they try to get their policies adopted. This explains, perhaps, why the mayor of Minneapolis, the politics of which is as different from that of Chicago as could be imagined, follows the same strategy as Mayor Daley. According to Alan Altshuler, the mayor of Minneapolis does not actively sponsor anything: "He waits for private groups to agree upon a project. If he likes it, he endorses it. Since he has no formal power with which to pressure the Council himself, he feels that the private groups must take responsibility for getting their plans accepted."[14]

Sometimes (and, as we shall suggest later, more frequently now than in the past) mayors do create issues. Several, for example, have taken the initiative on urban renewal. This seems to be most often the tactic of a mayor who takes office without much prior civic achievement to point to and without a strong party organization to produce votes for him. Sometimes it is an ambitious man's response to a situation in which general dissatisfaction with the local government has afforded an opportunity for spectacular, visible (and popular) innovation. But the advantages in being a bold, vigorous leader—if, indeed, they are real and not based on misconceptions—are fleeting; often, after a first wave of mayor-initiated programs, the situation returns to normal and the mayor finds that discretion is the better part of valor.

That the seriousness with which an issue is taken depends so much upon considerations of organizational maintenance and enhancement has wide implications for the political life of the city. What happens in those matters in which no organization's maintenance is involved? What happens in those which do not afford good program material to the voluntary associations and the press? Such matters are not likely to come to public attention at all. It is easy to think of examples of matters that might be issues but almost never are. Municipal justice is one. In several cities, large organizations have a stake in the enforcement, or non-enforcement, of building and housing codes, and accordingly this particular kind of court case is often in the news in these cities. But so far as we know there are no large organizations in any city with a stake in seeing that justice is done in, say, cases of breaches of the peace or vagrancy, and the quality of justice in these is therefore hardly ever the subject of a civic controversy.

For example, a study of vagrancy law in Philadelphia showed that it was seriously abused.[15] At certain times of the year, the police force conducted "drives" to keep "undesirables" out of some areas. In a typical day at the courts, fifty-five vagrancy cases were heard within fifteen minutes. Four defendants were tried, found guilty, and sentenced within seventeen seconds. "In each of these cases the magistrate merely read off the name of the defendant, took one look at him and said, 'Three months in the House of Correction.'" Some who were discharged were told to get out of Philadelphia or out of certain sections of it. After being discharged, some defendants were kept to mop up the building for a couple of hours because work was "good for them," but if one of them contributed a dollar or more to the magistrate's favorite charity (collected in a Heart Fund box), he was permitted to leave at once. These "drives" were given extensive newspaper coverage. The *Philadelphia Inquirer* in particular ran editorials and stories under headings like "Get the Bums Off the Streets and Into Prison Cells." When the newspaper publicity let up, magistrates became less harsh and would often dismiss the cases with a joke. Justice, however, was still largely hit or miss. "When you get tired of seeing their faces," one magistrate said, "you send them to correction."

The author of the study concluded that "the only reason such administration is tolerated" is that the defendants involved "are too poor or too weak to assert their obvious rights." No doubt this was the ultimate reason. But the proximate one was that no large organizations—except perhaps the newspapers, which were on the other side—had any maintenance or enhancement interest at stake in the situation.

FOOTNOTES

[1] Neal Gross, *Who Runs Our Schools?* (New York: John Wiley and Sons, 1958), p. 85.
[2] Yves R. Simon, *The Philosophy of Democratic Government* (Chicago: University of Chicago Press, 1951), chap. i.
[3] Matthew P. Breen, *Thirty Years of New York Politics Up-To-Date* (Boston, 1899), p. 34.
[4] Arthur Vidich and Joseph Bensman, *Small Town Politics in Mass Society* (Princeton, N. J.: Princeton University Press, 1958), chaps. v-viii.
[5] Edward C. Banfield, *Political Influence* (New York: Free Press of Glencoe, 1961), p. 250.
[6] James S. Coleman, *Community Conflict* (Glencoe, Ill.: Free Press, 1959), p. 4.
[7] James G. Coke, "The Lesser Metropolitan Areas of Illinois," *Illinois Government*, no. 15, November 1962, published by the Institute of Government and Public Affairs, University of Illinois, Urbana, Ill.
[8] Wallace S. Sayre and Herbert Kaufman, *Governing New York City* (New York: Russell Sage Foundation, 1960), p. 79.
[9] See Chester I. Barnard, *The Functions of the Executive* (Cambridge, Mass.: Harvard University Press, 1938).
[10] Martin Meyerson and Edward C. Banfield, *Politics, Planning, and the Public Interest* (Glencoe, Ill.: Free Press, 1955), pp. 144-145.
[11] Banfield, *Political Influence;* see especially chap. ix.
[12] *Ibid.,* p. 231.
[13] Peter H. Rossi and Robert A. Dentler, *The Politics of Urban Renewal* (New York: Free Press of Glencoe, 1961), pp. 72-84.

[14] Alan Altshuler, *Minneapolis City Politics Report* (Cambridge, Mass.: Joint Center for Urban Studies, 1959, mimeo), pp. 14-15.
[15] Caleb Foote, "Vagrancy-Type Law and Its Administration," *University of Pennsylvania Law Review,* vol. CIV (1956), p. 603.

ABOUT THE AUTHORS—Edward C. Banfield, a specialist on the problems of cities, is Henry Lee Shattuck Professor of Urban Government at Harvard University. He was formerly on the faculty of the University of Chicago, where he received his Ph.D. Banfield was born in 1916 in Bloomfield, Connecticut. His nonacademic experience includes several years as an Information Specialist for the Farm Security Administration.

Many of Banfield's books are concerned with urban problems. *Politics, Planning and the Public Interest* (with Martin Meyerson) (1955) and *Political Influence* (1961) deal with Chicago. *Boston, the Job Ahead* (also with Meyerson) (1966) is written for the layman; several chapters were first published as public service advertisements in the Boston newspapers. Banfield is co-author (with James Q. Wilson) of *City Politics* (1963) and editor of *Urban Government* (1961), a book of readings. *Big City Politics* (1965), Banfield's latest book, is based on data collected by the Joint Center. But Banfield is not concerned exclusively with urban affairs. In 1951 he published *Government Project*, the case history of a cooperative farm in Arizona. *The Moral Basis for a Backward Society* was issued in 1958. The data for this study were obtained when Banfield and his wife spent 1954-55 in a village in southern Italy. Through interviewing, they studied the influence of political culture on economic development.

The focus of James Q. Wilson's research has been the political and sociological phenomena of cities. A member of the Harvard Department of Government since 1961 and a professor since 1967, he is also on the research staff of the Harvard-MIT Joint Center for Urban Studies. Wilson was born in Denver in 1931 and attended the University of Redlands. After service with the Navy, he was a graduate student at the University of Chicago from 1956 to 1959, from which he received his Ph.D. in political science. From 1959 to 1961 he was on the faculty of the University of Chicago. In addition to being the co-author of *City Politics,* Wilson has written *Negro Politics; The Search for Leadership* (1960); *The Amateur Democrat: Club Politics in Three Cities* (1962), and edited *Urban Renewal; the Record and the Controversy* (1966) and *City Politics and Public Policy* (1968).

Power and Community Structure

by Peter H. Rossi

This paper offers an introduction to one of the most exciting areas of research in local government—the study of community power and power distribution. Rossi's article serves to identify major studies up to the time of its writing and details one conceptual way of ordering and explaining variations in power structure among cities. It goes without saying that the public library administrator must develop an understanding of informal as well as formal power elements in his community. Yet the literature of librarianship has still to identify this aspect of public administration. A relevant ethical question is whether libraries should seek to gain the support of an elite who may actually control decision-making in a community. For then would they not actually be encouraging forms of governance which fall far short of the democratic ideal?

This paper deals with some structural characteristics of local communities which are relevant to their power structures and decision making processes. The ideas presented constitute a theory both in the sense of a conceptual scheme and in the sense of a set of propositions, albeit only loosely interrelated. The theory has its origins both in the growing body of literature on the power structures of local communities and in the field experiences of the author.

The immediate impetus to the construction of this theory was a growing dissatisfaction with the non-cumulative character of the field to which it purports to apply. Case study after case study of communities has appeared within the past few years, each contributing its part to a body of knowledge best characterized by the statement, "It is different here than elsewhere."[1] The author often inserts a particular comparison somewhere into his paper: Hunter's Regional City, Schulze's Cibola, Rossi's Mediana, and so forth. Each author owns his own town, defending it from the erroneous and somewhat heretical conceptualizations of others much the way a feudal lord defends the integrity of the local patron saint against the false counterclaims of nearby realms.

One firm generalization emerges from the literature: the power structure of local communities and the decision making processes to be found therein show a significant range of variation. This range can be only partly dependent on the differences in research technology employed by each researcher, for the same researchers have found different patterns in different communities. No firm generalizations emerge, however, concerning the sources of these variations.

There are two main reasons for the failure of generalizations of this sort to emerge. First, with few exceptions, comparative studies are rare. Most studies are concerned with establishing a pattern within one particular community, setting it off at best against one other community. Studies in which a large number of communities are systematically contrasted with comparable communities are the sources from which desired generalizations will emerge. The empirical relationships between power structures and other community social structures will provide the data.

The second main reason lies in the inadequacy of social theory. Despite the many community studies which have been undertaken since the classic Booth study of London, we are still lacking a conceptual scheme specifying with some degree of clarity what are the important elements in community structure. Indeed, the operational form that Hunter gave to the conception of community power structure will probably remain as his greatest contribution.[2] Before Hunter only

SOURCE: Reprinted from "Power and Community Structure," *Midwest Journal of Political Science*, 4 (Nov., 1960), pp. 390–401 by Peter H. Rossi, by permission of the Wayne State University Press. Copyright, 1960, by the Wayne State University Press. Original publication bore the following note: "A revised version of a paper delivered at the 1959 Annual Meeting of the American Sociological Association, Chicago, Illinois, September, 1959. Preparation of this paper and some of the author's research cited was supported by a grant from the Social Science Research Council, hereby gratefully acknowledged."

the Lynds[3] paid attention to this feature of social structure, and this interest of the Lynds did not start a tradition because they were unable to communicate the techniques by which they singled out the "X" family as the dominant center in Middletown. After Hunter laid out his quasi-sociometry, community studies experienced a revival, all centered around some modification of his device.

Of course without a conceptual scheme, comparative studies are difficult to plan and to achieve. What should the researcher and his team look for? He now knows that to define the powerful he can employ some modification of Hunter's balloting. The census and other published sources provide additional ways of classifying communities, but these provide at best only indirect indicators of social organization, and the researcher must still have a rationale for choosing among the possible indicators. Researchers are therefore forced to collect their own data. To do so obviously requires some *a priori* conceptions as to what is important. The vicious circle is closed: comparative community studies are one of the important sources of ideas concerning the structural concomitants of variations in power and decision making, but properly to conduct such studies requires some framework for the collection of such data.[4]

GAPS IN THE CONCEPTION OF COMMUNITY STRUCTURES

To characterize communities we need some sort of framework which can guide observations, alerting the researcher to the crucial elements in the structure of the community. What form should such a conceptual scheme take? Should we construct some grand scheme which would be the all around best way of characterizing communities or should we work piecemeal, building one scheme for one problem and another scheme for another? It is my conviction that the latter path will prove most fruitful: namely, the construction of schemes which are specific to the particular substantive problem at hand. Thus the best way of characterizing communities for the purpose of understanding fluoridation controversies in principle may be different from the best way for understanding some other community process.

Even if one were to grant the soundness of this notion of specific theories for specific purposes, there still remains a considerable problem in the construction of such theories. Although we have made much progress through the work of the human ecologists in classifying cities according to their economic functions and their relations to their environments, we have done little with the internal social organization of communities. In this last respect, perhaps the best known structural characteristic of communities is along stratification lines. A large enough body of research and thinking has gone into the definition of stratification both on the purely nominal level and on the operational level for the researcher to have a fairly clear idea of how to use this term, how to measure stratification systems, and how to locate the positions within such systems of particular individuals or groups. Similar amounts of thinking and effort have not been expended on invention of an appropriate methodology for studying other kinds of organized relationships among the members of a community. Although on the abstract level sociometric devices might seem useful tools in the study of large communities, on the empirical level they prove impractical.

The gap in the conception of community structure is most serious in the area of social organization. This paper is intended to fill in part of this conceptual hiatus by constructing a scheme for classifying the political structures of local communities. The scheme purports to be useful specifically for understanding variations in power structures. Hopefully it may also turn out to be of some utility in the study of closely related community characteristics.

A CONCEPTUAL SCHEME FOR THE POLITICAL STRUCTURE OF LOCAL COMMUNITIES

The purpose of the scheme to be described here is to account for the variations in power structures to be found among American local communities. It may also prove of some utility in other areas, for example, community conflicts. The general thesis underlying the scheme is a simple one: the pattern taken by the power structure of a community is a function of the kind of political life to be found therein. My reasons for postulating this relationship are also simple and somewhat obvious: the political institutions of a community are the ultimate locus of the decisions that are binding on the total community. Hence much of the power exercised is focused on the governmental institutions of the local community.

For our present purposes, it is useful to regard the political life of a community as occurring at two different levels, interrelated but to some degree independent. On the one hand, there is a set of governmental institutions manned by officials and employees with defined functions and spheres of authority and competence. On the other hand, there is the electorate, the body of citizens with voting rights, organized to some degree into political parties. We expect that phenomena appearing on each of these levels independently influence the forms taken by community power structures.

On the institutional level, there are several characteristics of local government that are of some consequence. First, communities vary according to the degree to which the roles of officials are *professionalized*. In many communities, mayors and city councilmen and often other officials are employed in their official capacities only part time and lack the opportunity to become fully engrossed in these roles. At the other extreme, some communities employ professionally trained officials—city managers, school superintendents, etc.—who are full time employees expecting to remain in their occupation—although not in any particular post—for long periods of time. In communities where local officials exercise their functions on a part time basis and where the qualifications for incumbency are not exacting, the incumbents are less likely to segregate their official roles from their other roles and hence extra-official considerations are more likely to play roles of some importance in their decisions. Thus the informal cabal which ran Springdale, as described by Vidich and Bensman,[5] hardly distinguish between their roles as city fathers and their roles as businessmen and professionals. At the other extreme are the professional politicians who run Chicago, whose independence is curbed very little.

A second important structural characteristic of local government refers to the rules by which officials are selected. Two aspects of electoral rules are significant. Electoral rules can either retard or facilitate the development of enduring political alignments in the community, and the latter are important determinants of the forms of decision making. In this respect, the crucial differences lie between communities which have non-partisan and communities which have partisan elections. Non-partisan electoral rules discourage the development of enduring political alignments by reducing the advantages to candidates of appearing on slates, whereas partisan elections facilitate cooperation among candidates and the drawing of clear lines between opposing slates of candidates. It should be noted in this connection that primaries are in effect non-partisan elections in communities which are predominantly Democratic or Republican.[6]

Another structural characteristic which tends to reduce the importance of political organizations is the rule concerning the number of officials elected by popular vote. Short ballots on which only a few candidates compete for the major offices tend to reduce organizational importance by lowering the benefits to candidates of cooperation with each other.

These structural characteristics of the governmental institutions of the local community underlie the ability of these institutions to develop an independence of their own and also indicate the extent to which conflicts within the community are manifested in the political realm or in some other fashion.

Moving now to the level of the electorate and its organization, there are two important dimensions to be considered. First, we must consider the political homogeneity of the electorate, roughly defined as the extent to which the community is divided equally or unequally among the contending political factions of the community. The more unequally the community is divided, the less likely are open political struggles to be the major expressions of clashes of interest and the more likely is decision making to be a prerogative of a "cozy few."

Borrowing from Gerhard Lenski, a second characteristic of the electorate might be called "political crystallization": the extent to which the lines of political cleavage within the community coincide with major social structural differentiations. In this connection the crucial modes of social structural differentiation are along class and status lines. The more political lines coincide with class and status lines, the more likely are community clashes to take a political form. These are important lines of differentiation within communities because they are likely to endure over time.[7] Political differences which coincide with class and status differences are for these reasons likely to be reinforced by the double factors of differential association and connection with important interests.

If we now consider the entire set of community characteristics distinguished here, we see that they may be conceived of as indicators of two more abstract attributes of communities: first, the institutional indicators express the degree of segregation of political institutions from other community institutions; second, the indicators relating to the electorate reflect the extent to which partisan politics is a crucial arena for the important decision making within the community.

It is important to note that these characteristics of communities can be easily translated into operational forms. The city charter can tell us how officials are elected and whether their jobs are full or part time. Election statistics and survey research can tell us the degree of political homogeneity and political crystallization.

Two broad hypotheses can be formulated at this point. (1) The more segregated are political roles from other roles played by incumbent officials, the more independent the governmental structure of a community from other institutional structures. (2) The more heterogeneous the electorate and the greater the degree of political crystallization, the more important the governmental institutions as loci for important decision making.

IMPLICATIONS FOR COMMUNITY POWER STRUCTURES

The studies of community power structures have universally found the upper levels of the occupational hierarchy to occupy prominent power positions. In no city—even heavily working class Stackton—have proprietors, managers, and professional men played insignificant parts. Often enough some members of these groups do not play as prominent a part as others, even though they are as wealthy and as important in the economic life of the city, but in all cities members of these groups were to be found in some kind of inner circle.

The disagreement among researchers concerns two important matters. First, there is disagreement over the pattern of power, with some researchers preferring the monolith as their model and others preferring polyliths or more complicated forms. Second, there is disagreement over the roles played by public officials and voluntary associations. Hardly anything could be written about Chicago, Stackton, or Philadelphia without reference to the mayor's office and other top level public officials. In contrast, in Regional City and some of the towns studied by C. P. Loomis and his research workers, public officials and often labor leaders appear as minor and insignificant personages. It should be noted that these two kinds of disagreements among researchers are related. A monolithic model for a power structure generally goes along with a very subordinate role for voluntary associations and public officials. Thus, in Hunter's Regional City public officials are explicitly viewed as the handmaidens of the elite group, and labor leaders are scarcely worth mentioning.

A polylithic power structure tends to mean a number of small monoliths each centering around a particular sort of activity. Thus in industrial Stackton, the civic associations and community service organizations were the preserves of the business community, whereas local government was safe in the hands of professional politicians resting on the mass base of the Democratic Party and its heavy support from among ethnic groups of relatively recent arrival from abroad. Indeed, respondents rarely reported that any one individual was powerful in all spheres of community life.

To some degree the disagreements among researchers on the forms taken by the power structures in communities and the place to be accorded public officials and associational leaders are functions of the different research techniques employed. Some approaches preclude the finding of polylithic power structures. However, in much larger part, the differences among researchers are functions of "reality," representing major ways in which communities *in fact* differ. My general thesis is that these differences are functions of the differences among communities in their political structures.

If we look carefully at the studies of community power structure we may discern the following types:

> (1) *Pyramidal.* Lines of power tend to have their ultimate source in one man or a very small number of men. Decision making tends to be highly centralized, with lower echelons mainly carrying out major policy decisions made by the small group at the apex.

Examples: Middletown, Regional City

> (2) *Caucus rule.* Lines of power tend to end in a relatively large group of men who make decisions through consensus. Decision making tends to be a matter of manufacturing consent among the "cozy few" who make up the caucus. Typical power structure in the small town or dormitory suburb.

Examples: Springdale, Mediana

(3) *Polylith.* Separate power structures definable for major spheres of community activity. Typically, local government in the hands of professional politicians backed by the solidary strength of voluntary associations, with the community service organizations in the hands of the business and professional subcommunity.

(4) *Amorphous.* No discernible enduring pattern of power. Logical residual category. No examples.

Note that the first two types of power structures are very similar, differing only in the number of decision makers who share power among themselves. The major differentiation is between the first two types wherein lines of power tend to converge and the last two types wherein lines of power tend to diverge.

The divergence of power lines has its source in the existence of the possibility for occupational groups other than business and professional to occupy positions of importance within major community institutions. This occurs typically when there is political crystallization in a community which is heterogeneous class wise or status wise. When the lower status or class levels have a political party representing them which has a chance to get into office, there is the possibility that public office can become one of the important sources of power.

The conditions under which the political parties have a vigorous life are defined by the structural features described earlier. Under partisan electoral laws, when officials are professionalized, when either the majority of the electorate favor the underdog party or when the parties are balanced in strength, then the political institutions and public officials assume a position of importance within the power structure of the community.

Another way of putting this thesis is to say that the leaders of the dominant economic institutions ordinarily wield power, but they are forced to take others into account when popular democratic rules allow the lower levels of the community an opportunity to place their representatives in public office. The elements of the community political structure we have distinguished here are those which facilitate the development of governmental independence from the business and professional community.

The general hypothesis may now be stated more precisely, as follows: *in communities with partisan electoral procedures, whose officials are full time functionaries, where party lines tend to coincide with class and status lines and where the party favored by the lower class and status groups has some good chance of getting elected to office, community power structures tend to be polylithic rather than monolithic.* Since these characteristics of community political structures are to some unknown degree independent of one another, different combinations of such characteristics can appear empirically. The patterns in such communities cannot be deduced from this hypothesis since we do not specify the weights to be assigned to each characteristic.

There are further expectations implied in the general hypothesis. Some examples follow:

(1) Homogeneous middle class communities, for example, dormitory suburbs and the like, will tend to have monolithic power structures, since the class basis for countervailing political power does not exist.

(2) In communities where the lower class party has a clear majority there will be moves on the part of the business and professional community to introduce structural changes in city government to undermine this majority, as for example, non-partisan elections, short ballot, and the like.

(3) In polylithic communities, city government and private community organizations try to limit the sphere of each other's operations by moving more and more functions into their own spheres of authority.

(4) In communities with monolithic power structures, conflicts tend to take on the character of mass revolts in which small incidents are magnified out of proportion because there are no regularized means for the expression of conflict.[8]

(5) Historically, the development of voluntary civic associations may be interpreted as a reaction to the loss of local political power by high status groups. Since these community organizations were not governed by the mass vote of the lower class groups, high status groups could keep control over them.

Additional similar propositions may be generated from the basic hypothesis set forth in this paper. Although I believe that such propositions will be upheld in general by empirical data, I am also sure that considerable modifications will be made in them.

CONCLUSIONS

To sum up, I have presented in this paper a conceptual scheme which provides a way of classifying the political structures of local communities. I have also tried to spell out how these political features may modify the power structures to be found in such communities. The utility of the scheme obviously requires for testing empirical data generated by comparative community studies. Though I have no doubt that the hypotheses presented here will at best suffer considerable modification when confronted with such data, I hope they will serve the purpose of providing some impetus for comparative community studies.

FOOTNOTES

[1] An early bibliographic review was published by the author as "Community Decision Making" in *The Administrative Science Quarterly*, I (March, 1957), 415-43. An incomplete list of more recent studies follows:
Warner Bloomberg, *The Structure of Power in Stackton* (Unpublished Ph.D. dissertation, University of Chicago, 1960). James S. Coleman, *Community Conflict* (Glencoe, Illinois: Free Press, 1957). William H. Form, "Organized Labor's Place in the Community Power Structure," *Industrial and Labor Relations Review*, XII (July, 1959), 526-39. William H. Form and William V. D'Antonio, "Integration and Cleavage Among Community Influentials in Two Border Cities," *American Sociological Review*, XXIV (December, 1959), 804-14. Orrin E. Klapp and Vincent L. Padgett, "Power Structure and Decision Making in a Mexican Border City," *American Journal of Sociology*, LXV (January, 1960), 400-406. Delbert C. Miller, "Decision Making Cliques in Community Power Structure," *American Journal of Sociology*, LXIV (November, 1958), 299-310. Delbert C. Miller, "Industry and Community Power Structures," *American Sociological Review*, XXIII (February, 1958), 9-15. Roland J. Pellegrin and Charles H. Coates, "Absentee Owned Corporations and Community Power Structure," *American Journal of Sociology*, LXI (March, 1956), 413-19. Nelson W. Polsby, "Three Problems in the Analysis of Community Power," *American Sociological Review*, XXIV (December, 1959), 796-803. Nelson W. Polsby, "The Sociology of Community Power: A Reassessment," *Social Forces*, XXXVII (March, 1959), 232-36. Edwin H. Rhyne, "Political Parties and Decision Making in Three Southern Counties," *American Political Science Review*, LII (December, 1958), 1091-1107. Peter H. Rossi, "Industry and Community," National Opinion Research Center, Report No. 64, October, 1957 (mimeo.). Peter H. Rossi and Phillips Cutright, "The Political Organization of an Industrial Community," in Morris Janowitz and Heinz Eulau (eds.), *Community Political Systems* (Glencoe, Illinois: Free Press, 1960, forthcoming). Peter H. Rossi and Robert A. Dentler, *The Politics of Urban Renewal* (Glencoe, Illinois: Free Press, 1960, forthcoming). Robert O. Schulze, "The Role of Economic Dominants in Community Power Structure," *American Sociological Review*, XXIII (February, 1958), 3-9. Arthur J. Vidich and Joe Bensman, *Small Town in Mass Society* (Princeton, New Jersey: Princeton University Press, 1959).
[2] Floyd A. Hunter, *Community Power Structure* (Chapel Hill, North Carolina: University of North Carolina Press, 1952).
[3] Robert S. and Helen M. Lynd, *Middletown in Transition* (New York: Harcourt Brace and Company, 1937).
[4] An important exception to this characterization is the studies undertaken at Michigan State University by C. P. Loomis, W. Form and others.
[5] Vidich and Bensman, *op. cit.*
[6] Non-partisan elections operate to the benefit of the highly organized political minority. Hence, usually, non-partisan elections operate to the benefit of the white collar groups in industrial communities and to the benefit of the Democratic Party in middle class suburbs.
[7] On a large space scale–i.e., for regions and nations–regional differences would also play important roles, but since the micro-regional differences in the American city tend to be wiped out quickly by residential mobility, they play only a minor role within communities.
[8] See Coleman, *op. cit.*

ABOUT THE AUTHOR–Peter H. Rossi is a sociologist widely known for his research and publications. Now Professor of Sociology at Johns Hopkins University, he was on the faculty of the University of Chicago from 1955 to 1967. Formerly, from 1951-55, he served as a member of the interdisciplinary Department of Social Relations at Harvard.

Rossi has been both Associate Editor of the *American Sociological Review* (1957-60) and Editor of the *American Journal of Sociology* (1957-58). For seven years, Rossi was Director of the University of Chicago-affiliated National Opinion Research Center, a survey organization which applies the skills and methodology of sociology to a variety of social and political problems. In 1966, under the aegis of this organization, Rossi was the co-author of *The Education of Catholic Americans*, and co-editor of *The New Media and Education; their Impact on Society*. Earlier publications include *The Politics of Urban Renewal* (1961) and *Why Families Move; A Study in the Social Psychology of Urban Residential Mobility* (1955).

Rossi received his B. S. from City College, and his doctorate in 1951 from Columbia. He has been a Research Associate for Columbia's Bureau of Applied Social Research and received Social Science Research Council awards in 1957 and 1958.

Libraries in Politics

The articles and research presented here are conducted within the frameworks suggested in the preceding section. They are concerned therefore with the library's external relationships. Among the library issues explored in this context are desirable political strategies for librarians in their quest for support, the role of the library board, censorship as a public issue. Only one piece examines the university library, yet the academic library may also be viewed in a political context and the same conceptual approaches applied to understanding the university library's external relationships. So while the literature presented treats largely of the public library situation, its lessons are directly translatable into the terms and requirements of every other library setting.

The Library's Political Potential

by Oliver Garceau

Here is a succinct identification of the public library's traditional position in politics. It has no natural enemies but neither has it natural political allies. Given these circumstances, the author explores the pros and cons of the various political strategies open to the library in its quest for financial support. This analysis raises many of the key issues which surround library development. Public librarians today might most heed Garceau's warning, that amidst a rapidly shifting political scene they may still be clinging tenaciously and dangerously to traditional group alliances and relationships.

As a tax supported institution the public library depends in the long run upon how much the voters will take from their pockets to pay for its services. In the past this has not been much. As has been said, the library record is one of an undercapitalized plant manned by an underpaid staff. This is not the result of public hostility; no library in our survey has to meet active opposition to what it is doing. No one opposes the library; almost everyone approves it. But with almost equal unanimity no one wants to pay much for it. What the librarians are working against is apathy within, as well as without the library. In a good many places they have attempted to break this down by tying their services to the going interests of their communities.

INVENTORY OF GROUP AFFILIATIONS

The library board has been thought of as a link between library and power groups in the community. As the previous chapter has explained, the typical library board is made up of elderly, lower-upper to upper-middle class persons, who speak for a limited range of a community's interests, and rarely from experience, for its reading needs. To avoid this, and following a legislative theory of board functions, some boards are broadened to represent racial, religious, economic groups, geographical areas, or voluntary associations. This has served to placate some restive minorities and appease the pride of some civic groups, but it has not served well as a means of mobilizing public opinion. The board does not really function as a legislature; its members do not think in terms of organizing the vote; and they do not speak for segments of the population whose library interests are essentially distinguishable.

In order to represent adequately the political power groups of even a small community, the board would have to be too large and unwieldy to perform its administrative functions. As it is now used in practice, the "representative board" sometimes copies the pattern of city politics rather than the realities of library politics. In several cities in the survey the city council representation was reflected in the membership of the library board, with the result that the librarian had to cope with representatives of nationality groups who as individuals were ignorant of and little interested in library services. What is more to the point, such representatives would not and could not mobilize political support to help put the library on a sound financial footing. Their appointment had political significance in the calculus of the mayor's office, but not in the political equation of the public library.

The outright attempts to recognize political realities in board membership cannot be considered successful. Board political influence follows another strategy, and when mobilized it can be impressive. Such mobilization, we found in our survey, is usually precipitated by a crisis when the library's welfare seems particularly endangered by official action, a new framework of government, or a ruinous cut in an appropriation, or it may be brought about by a library bond issue. Upon these specific occasions, with a real threat hanging over their heads or a definite objective in view, library boards in our sample have made speeches, button-holed their friends, swung their groups, clubs, and fraternities into action,

SOURCE: Reprinted from Oliver Garceau, *The Public Library in the Political Process: A Report of the Public Library Inquiry of the Social Science Research Council* (New York: Columbia University Press, 1949), Chap. 3, "The Library's Political Potential," pp. 111–151, by permission of the publisher and the author.

demanded official hearings, pounded the pavements and pushed doorbells in order to round up the necessary political strength. But such crises are extraordinary, demanding extraordinary exertion, when the political status of the library becomes so obvious as to command action. In the year-to-year pressure for funds, however, the typical library board in the sample does not carry much political power. Perhaps that is all the librarians can ask of a voluntary group of citizens who have a limited amount of time and energy.

It is the librarian, therefore, who is the political strategist in nearly all cases, and the board simply strengthens his hand. Board strength is partially measured in terms of the librarian's prestige and that of the people he knows. In places where society is conservative and inbred the librarian coming from the outside will find it difficult to break into the inner circles. A few library boards in our sample, made up of leading citizens or members of old families, have been of real service in introducing the librarians to the groups where political policy is made. We found that in old, stable, homogeneous societies library boards, with some justification, tend to favor homegrown librarians; for it is a great advantage to be a native, if not of the town, county, or state, at least of the section. This is particularly true of the South, where the necessity of recruiting trained personnel from the North presents a real problem in library and community relationship. In any community, however, the board can facilitate the librarian's access to power groups.

In a few of our cases, in which the retiring librarian has had an outstanding personality, the position of his successor is at first secure. He faces, however, the problem of continuing the narrative in his own style, a task that can sometimes be as difficult as beginning anew. If there is no great tradition to continue, the librarian, like many a minister and educator, has often felt obliged to become a joiner. About forty libraries in the sample are administered by executives whose membership in study groups, service clubs, civic associations, and fraternal orders cover the wide and ingeniously varied range of organizations in a nation of joiners. For the rest, only one or two librarians expressed a distaste for all organized groups, and quite a few more considered themselves too busy for outside activities.

For men librarians in the sample by far the more important, as well as numerous, contacts with the business and professional community are made through the service clubs, Rotary, Kiwanis, Chamber of Commerce, and Lions, with Rotary predominating, and other miscellaneous luncheon groups, such as Exchange Clubs, Advertising Clubs, Merchants Clubs, and so forth. Here the librarian meets and becomes friendly with people he never would otherwise see. One librarian, as president of Rotary, was a first-name acquaintance of seven out of his nine city councilmen, who are fellow Rotarians. This familiarity, not only encouraged but required by many such luncheon clubs, is considered by those librarians who practice it to be of real political benefit. From the experience of our survey, the influence of the service clubs in cities under 200,000 population would seem to be greater than has generally been recognized. The librarians have found them of great value in reaching that group of influential men who do not use the library, but are important in community opinion and political action. And many librarians who are not members of these clubs are guest speakers as often as they can elicit invitations.

As the world has a habit of being run by males, the woman librarian is handicapped in opportunities to penetrate the councils of political power. But too many able women with wide community influence appear in our sample for that handicap to be considered seriously crippling. The women librarians in the sample most often belong to the Women's Club or the Business and Professional Women's Club in order to obtain the same entrance into the women's world that the men have through the service clubs. The American Association of University Women and the League of Women Voters were almost universally considered strategically important affiliations. We found that women librarians are likely to be prominent in the Parent Teachers Association, which tends in many places to be a mothers' club. Women have, in general, an advantage in their direct contacts with the large library population of women and children.

Many public libraries in our survey still think of themselves to some degree in the nineteenth-century formula of social welfare institutions. Their librarians, men and women, take seriously their relationship to moral and civic reform, and their club affiliations follow suit. Many of them take an active interest in YMCA or YWCA work and in other organizations of similar outlook. Community Councils of Social Service Agencies and Adult Education Councils, where they exist, are the natural preserve for librarians seeking community relationships. Where such correlating agencies do not function, the alert librarian, by his many memberships and his interest in all civic activities, may become the central liaison and his library the clearing house for civic activities. It is likely, from our information, that he will participate in the Community Chest drives, Red Cross work, Boy or Girl Scout activities, guidance clinics, the Urban League, inter-racial forums, and associations such as those organized to fight tuberculosis, infantile paralysis, and cancer. Many librarians in the sample belong to clubs encouraging gardening, poetry, art, music, or the theater, but these are usually joined for personal, as well as political, motives. A few join historical associations, mostly local in character, and a fewer still join scientific societies. Aside from adult education affiliations, their ties with educational associations and teacher groups are few. We found that librarians have failed, by and large, to make the teachers of America feel that the library is an integral part of the community's educational system. Relatively few librarians in our survey have felt that their own active participation, or even membership, in teachers' groups and associations is part of the library's enlarged program.

The extended list of activities categorized as worth while and library-connected has left librarians little time for an active social life. Few in our survey belong to the elite clubs or the country-club set. This is of little political importance, but the fact that librarians tend to occupy the social position of a local civil servant, not that of a college president or even of the leading members of a college faculty, is important. Most librarians in the sample cannot command that kind of prestige. Their profession has not in fact become a learned one. We found that librarians have rarely joined forces with institutions of higher learning, made friends with college or university faculties, or taken advantage of the special skills and experience of faculties in such an important function as that of building a book collection. Graduate education in library schools has not yet broken down the barriers between public libraries and collegiate scholarship. Indeed, graduate education for librarians has so far reached only a few. Educationally speaking, with certain notable exceptions, the teaching level of the library curriculum and the promotional leadership of the librarian in our survey is similar to that of a broad vocational school. Librarians defend this level on the grounds that it reaches the masses and is politically profitable, but the political argument, as a long-range policy, is open to question, and the emphasis on easy reading for the masses begs the question of the library's purpose. The answer, that the public must be given what it wants, has been too readily accepted by librarians for them to command the public respect accorded to learning. In the equation of politics the policy chosen may well be a source of weakness, not of strength. Although this is one factor among many, the few libraries in our sample that have established alliance with higher learning seem to have profited by it politically as well as intellectually.

Like other institutions which carry on a permanent function presumably "above the battle," the library has traditionally been neutral in partisan politics. Librarians have in general scrupulously maintained that neutrality. The sample discovered only one overt exception, a librarian serving as a Republican county committeewoman, an activity which was part of a most unusual pattern of services and relationships conducted with outstanding imagination and vitality. There is, however, a growing political awareness on the part of state libraries that has led them to make use of the party system. One of the most active state libraries and state associations has felt justified in supporting the party that is most favorable to its program, following the developing strategy of organized labor and certain other pressure groups. We did not find this frank use of partisan means to obtain an impartial end employed to any extent in local politics, where party lines have been less meaningful and group organizations of greater significance.

The pattern of numerous community contacts that is growing among chief librarians is heavily stressed by the branch and county librarians we interviewed. Here the emphasis has shifted from a staff that knows books to one that knows people. Within large libraries this tends to mean persons who can speak well to group meetings; in rural work, persons who are neighborly. The objective is to humanize the booklist, a reading stimulant of uncertain effect. All but the smallest libraries in our sample maintain some personal relationships with traditionally library-minded groups, the Parent Teacher Association, the women's clubs, the American Association of University Women, and study forums, and try to supplement their printed matter with commentary. Individual reader guidance may be of the very greatest educational importance, but from our survey such personal, somewhat tutorial, relations cannot now reach a sufficient body of people to be of immediate political importance.

In library literature there is much emphasis upon neighborhood groups as the basis of branch community work. This looks well on paper, but in practice it is somewhat frustrated by the shifting of population. New York City, where the average length of residence in some neighborhoods was for many years as short as eighteen months, may serve as an exaggerated example of the situation in many of the larger cities. In one city in our sample a branch that was particularly active while the population around it was Jewish had to be closed and moved away for economy's sake when within a few years its books were left standing on the shelves by another ethnic group. In circumstances such as these the branch librarian can with difficulty find group affiliations that are stable enough to build into the library service. Not only the reading habits but also the communal clubs, lodges, and churches have changed so that a new problem has been spelled out, only to become illegible as the neighborhood again changed its dialect. The sociological currents have been carefully charted by analysts, both commercial and academic, and the findings have been incorporated in city plans. As a group librarians in the sample pay close attention to these studies; a few of them are serving directly on the planning commissions. But the library's poverty, the cumbrous machinery of public appropriations, and the traditions clustered around it as an institution make it inevitable that library building should lag behind the moving centers and shifting character of city populations. This puts a premium on elasticity of architecture and staff organization and of the policy followed for group services.

Some libraries have attempted to develop their own groups, known as the Friends of the Library. This does not appear to be a significant permanent development. Only five of the sample libraries had a "Friends" group organized or being developed, and they were of varying effectiveness and purpose. One highly developed group has a distinguished board of trustees of its own and has been organized into central and branch divisions. It has launched film forums, panel discussions, literary teas for regional authors, recreational programs for children, and training classes for volunteer storytellers. This is a group possessing a reputation for intellect and energy, actively interested in the library as a cultural institution. In one large city the Friends of the Library is incorporated; its membership is made up of the wealthy bibliophiles of the city organized for the express purpose of building up with gifts the research collections of the library. In the same city, however, a Friends organization of a branch was originally set up voluntarily by a local group to take proper advantage of their new building. With such wide variations in activities and purposes, few generalizations can be reasonably accurate, but the main difficulty in any Friends group will uniformly be to maintain a core of interest magnetic enough to hold it together. In general, therefore, the Friends of the Library tend to act effectively when an immediate issue is pressing, and then to atrophy or dissipate their energy in many directions.

The most satisfactory method of building up library strength through effective community service appears from our survey to be with groups already in existence. Almost all libraries in the survey, as we have said, have some relationships with women's clubs and leisure-time study groups, usually made up of women members. These groups are likely to come to the library, even if it makes no effort to come to them, so the most secluded librarians find themselves suggesting reading matter, if not drawing up book lists and annotating them. In some libraries in the survey, active guidance is given to program building; one library even conducted a Program Planners' Institute. Many, especially in the large cities, have close relations with the multitudinous organizations connected with American family life, with parents' groups, especially those of preschool children, and with veterans' wives associations.[1]

In general, libraries in the sample wait for adult groups to come to them for assistance, but many active librarians we interviewed find this passive role unsatisfactory and organize their own adult education agencies, usually together with other institutions such as museums, film forums, foreign policy associations, and recreational organizations. The existence of a meeting hall in the library building greatly facilitates such activity. In some cities in our survey the library has taken the lead in such delicate questions as race relations and American isolationism, endangering the library's reputation for political neutrality but taking seriously its mission as an educator. The most recent library-centered program to be tried is the Great Books Program, prompted by educational leaders at the University of Chicago, headed by Chancellor Hutchins. It is currently the most active and proliferating attempt to use the library directly as a center of serious adult education. As a technique of library participation and leadership through concentration on serious literature this program is somewhat of a new departure. As with all such programs, its span of life in its present form may prove to be limited. Voluntary leisure-time formulas have on the record been beset by an incurable faddism, particularly when set in so rigid a mold.

Libraries in the sample which are large enough to be departmentalized, have department heads who are often in close liaison with both lay and professional groups in their fields, that is, fine arts departments with music and sketching groups, literature with reading and writing groups. Our survey shows, however, that departments of philosophy and religion are not as successful in this as might be assumed. Many of our sample libraries serve church groups directly, and indirectly all take such a ubiquitous influence into consideration, but the church as an institution seems remote from the library world. This is especially true in large cities, but surprisingly evident also in small towns, where lay activities during the week run to church suppers and sewing bees. There are a few ministers on the library boards, and a few are reported to be heavy library borrowers and significant intellectual leaders. But strong church-library relationships, in the rare instances where they exist after the initial founding of the library, are usually library-inspired. At times the connection is unhappily the result of disagreement over books.

In the past the immigrant laborer of this country was often served with books in his native language, and his gratitude to the library was a real political asset. This service still exists in our sample, but it is dwindling in importance as the foreign-born shrink in proportion and in absolute numbers and as they become absorbed in the acculturation process. We have found no successor to this device for stimulating the workingman's interest in the library. Book lists and book collections are occasionally put into factories and department stores, but usually they have not proved popular. Of our sample not more than a half dozen libraries have made serious efforts to make the members of labor unions library users, and those that have are not encouraged by the results. Worker education, as such, in this country is not highly organized, and information upon union activities and policy, which is the reading matter most encouraged, comes from union headquarters. The average laborer does not read much, and when he does, does not get his books from the library. We found that his leaders do make use of the library for information on parliamentary procedure and how to run a labor meeting and as individuals for general reading, but this is not what is meant by "service to labor."

The middle-class character of the library may tend to repel the laborer; his ignorance, his grammar, even his clothes may be psychological barriers from his point of view. Probably in a very large majority of cases the librarians are uneasily aware of these barriers and anxious to overcome them. But the public library still looks and feels a little like a rich man's collection opened to the public. Despite their best intentions, there were librarians in the sample who retained a custodial attitude toward their books and preferred to have them go into homes where they would be respected and cared for. This attitude found overt expression in a half dozen cases, scattered across the country, where librarians and trustees strongly justified high fees for nonresident borrowers on the grounds that poor people in the outlying regions gave the books such dreadfully hard use. In a majority of our sample, librarians have not themselves seriously considered direct service to labor unions, though actively searching for direct links to organized groups. One large city library has allowed experiments with service to factories and unions to become confused institutionally and ideologically with the unionization of its own staff; and library board and chief librarian maintain a hands-off coolness to the project.

In several communities leaders of organized labor have frankly expressed appreciation for the good work being attempted by the librarian or certain members of the library staff, but are profoundly skeptical of the library boards. The conservative character of most library boards make librarians reluctant to open to labor groups the library assembly rooms so hospitably offered to women's clubs. Most librarians interviewed were unwilling to contemplate such a development. Some city libraries in the sample are developing bookmobile service to reach those who do not enter their buildings, but their light novels seem unlikely to replace the newsstand in labor's affections. This picture may change as labor becomes a more responsible power in the community, and as its leadership develops a more elaborate educational program. But at the present time in only a few cities do labor representatives defend library appropriations at the budget hearings.

In part, the apparent failure to build library collections specifically directed to labor's needs results from the fact that what is useful to businessmen is also useful to labor. They are both in the same economic system, using the same tools. The public libraries in our sample are developing their business departments with the informational needs of our industrial and commercial economy directly in view. Their special collections contain business directories, commercial atlases, statistical analyses, current information services, corporation reports, and government documents containing data valuable to the business world. They maintain a clipping service to make information available. They develop their own subject catalogues and train their own staff to know what is asked for and where to get it. In other words these are large information centers, gathering in one place and processing the written material for the whole city's economic interests.

The departments of science and technology are organized for a similar purpose. They are usually tied to the predominant industrial interests, although there are places where the department has given valuable reference aid to trade union research into matters such as general wage and price levels and standards of living. If the city is a great maker of glass, the collection of books on glass technology will be large; if the automobile industry is large, automotive engineering will be a key to library purchasing policy. This emphasis on a technical field is a direct service to that part of the city's economy which usually possesses great power. It runs the risk of narrowing the public utility of the library. The librarians point out, however, that business and technical services are so developed as to be of greater benefit to small businesses without the means to gather the information at their own expense than to large concerns that have special libraries of their own. The difficulty libraries face is in making small businessmen aware of the information they can get from the collection. There can be no doubt, from the testimony of department heads wherever consulted, that the presence of special libraries, privately owned and operated, increases the use of business and technological departments of public libraries. This follows from the greater familiarity with bibliographical resources and their benefits. It emphasizes the need for publicity. It also points up the advantages a department enjoys over the special isolated library, for the former can draw upon the wealth of the whole collection. As the wide extent of knowledge necessary to modern business practice becomes more and more evident, this advantage becomes more pronounced.

It has also become clear from our research, however, that if the library were to be used with the utmost efficiency by the business and industrial community, its resources in both books and skilled staff would be quickly overtaxed. Realizing this, one library in the sample is voluntarily given a fee by a large neighboring industry that uses it heavily.

Such an informal relationship is being formalized by another library. It is organizing for industry a bibliographical research service that will be supported by a yearly fee paid by the large, regular users, based upon a fraction of each company's over-all research spending, and by piece-rate charges for small, occasional users. The materials of the bibliographical research will be the property of the public library, but the research reports written up by the library's staff may be kept secret at the request of the purchaser. In this way it is hoped that the technical information necessary to industries can be made available at no increase in tax expense. It poses the question, however, of how much a public institution should organize its services for specialized private use. When another large public library submitted a similar plan to its business community, the Chamber of Commerce felt that the best solution lay in larger public appropriations and successfully helped bring the library's expanded budget through the year's tax hearings. Whatever method is used, the support given to libraries by satisfied business customers is a new political factor of importance, and librarians are nourishing it with much care.

In our sample the organized services to business and industry have in general been more effectively worked out than services to local government. Municipal reference libraries have been established in many large cities, located in or near city hall and adapted to official use, but they have rarely done the job of publicity and staff training that has been done in the field of library service to business. City government represents only a small number of people, it is true, but it is these very people who determine the public library's budget. The city departments are substantially competitors for limited public revenue, and the city council is the arena for reconciling these fiscal demands. Yet several municipal reference libraries visited were dusty and dead; one was in fact justified to us mainly as a useful listening post for city hall gossip. Small city and town public libraries have for the most part not yet explored the possibility of direct service to government. In sharp and revealing contrast is one state where the governor, who as a mayor had been well served by a municipal reference library, vigorously supported the establishment of the state library extension service, urged on, be it noted, by his former municipal reference librarian, now in the role of state library association lobbyist. Such a pat sequence of events is surely not always to be relied upon, but there is evidence in our sample to suggest that where the officers of government use the library it gains in political power. One part of the government that seems most universally unaware of the library aids available for its job is the city council. An alert city government will take advantage of the business and technology departments, but an alert librarian eases the politician's way to the library.

In rural library service the relationships are different. The need for technical information is met in large part by the county agents of the Department of Agriculture. What the farmer wants is up-to-the-minute market analyses and scientific information of immediate practical use; this the federal and state agricultural agencies are set up to give him. The farmer, in consequence, does not stand in need of the library for business purposes, but for broader informational reading, should he wish it, he is often greatly handicapped. The county agent's offices are lined with filing cabinets, not bookshelves. The natural division of information between the agricultural agency and the rural library should make the connection a close one, but such is not usually the case. County librarians in our survey, with few exceptions, have failed to establish close liaison with the agricultural and social service agencies around them. The most frequent co-operative effort found was between the county library and the Home Demonstration Agency, which merely continues the modest success the rural library service has had in reaching farm women, and has not made possible a substantial relation between library and farm in terms of vocational need. One state library is emphasizing rural sociological surveys, sponsored by many agencies, not wholly because of the new information disclosed, but also because such a common project discovers to these rural service workers the existence of each other. Serving a scattered population as the rural library does, it faces this basic problem, that there are few groups to work with and that individual or family service is expensive.

The most useful agency for county library service has been the rural school system. From their beginning and in their present activities the county libraries in our sample have a close and continuous relationship with the schools. It would be safe to say that by and large throughout the country supplementary reading for rural elementary school children comes from the public library. This is changing, as state aid for library books is encouraging schools to stock supplementary reading at no increase in local costs.

The urban elementary school picture is not very different, in spite of the greater urban emphasis on school libraries; for their development, with the whole weight of educational theory behind them, has none the less been slow. It is clear that the school library movement owes much to public library encouragement. Public libraries pioneered in children's service and have expanded it into school service. But the evidence of our survey seems unmistakable that as the educational administrators expand and elaborate their school library system, they will tend to take it into their own organization, divorcing it from the public library for administrative reasons, if for no other. There is only one instance in our sample in which the public library has developed an extensive school library system, in close co-operation with the school authorities. Elsewhere, as the usual situation, we find the public library filling in haphazardly with classroom collections where high school and junior high school libraries leave off.

The co-operation between schools and libraries varies from place to place, and in our sample there is no correlation with the institutional framework. There is no evidence to show that school district libraries, school board libraries, or libraries with *ex officio* school board members co-ordinate school and public library policies better than do independent systems. It is a safe generalization that closest relationships are established at the local level, informally and spontaneously, between branch and children's librarians of the public library and school librarians and teachers. Administrative common sense at local levels often brings about co-operation without even the knowledge of the senior administrative officers or boards concerned. In few cases is there a feeling shared by librarians and educators that they are working in a common cause. In some cases the schoolmen are happy to have the public library take over what library service the schools offer; in more cases the librarians are glad to give the schoolmen the administrative headaches and expense of their own libraries. Yet in only ten out of fifty libraries is no school service whatsoever given by the public library. The ties between the public library and the schools appear in most cases to be tenuous and uncertain.

Schools and libraries would seem to have much in common, but on the political scene the two institutions tend to go their own way and, directly or indirectly, compete for the tax dollar. In this competition the library is at a disadvantage, for it is clearly the junior partner in the local educational firm. The library board and the Friends of the Library are not equal in political power to the elective school board and the Parent Teacher Associations. Overshadowed as they are in any common program, librarians tend to seek their own little place in the sun apart from formal education, and the educators are often unaware of the institution in their shadow. The presence of school members on library boards, as has been said, does not seem to establish a working arrangement.

In some libraries volunteer groups are fitted successfully into the work of the library. In one, the Junior League sponsors radio programs and listening groups for story records and also puts on a weekly puppet show; the Council of Jewish Women provides volunteer story-tellers for children's hours and administers a service to shut-ins. Another library uses the Junior League for its service to hospitals, the library choosing the books, the Junior League buying and distributing them. Expensive service to needy cases seems to offer the greatest inducement for both financial and other voluntary aid. In one library the service to shut-ins is endowed; in another it has been financed in part by the Lions Club. Such voluntary participation not only saves the library money but also ties an influential philanthropic group into the library in a service relationship. The affiliation of active participation is the most durable means of encouraging voluntary leisure-time groups.

This relationship may extend far beyond the local library framework into the state and national picture, for such organizations as the Lions Club, the Federation of Women's Clubs, and the Red Cross are large and powerful politically. The American Library Association was able to get lobbyists from the General Federation of Women's Clubs, the National Grange, the National Congress of Parents and Teachers, the National Farmers' Union, and the Associated Women of the American Farm Bureau Federation to testify in 1947 for its Federal demonstration bill. What little force, besides lobbying routine, they put behind their action was the result of local library group affiliation. This minor ripple in the Washington stream of power may become quite a current in state politics, where women's clubs and farm organizations add voting strength to the library lobby. The research findings raise the question whether the technique of volunteer participation in library service could not be explored more widely. The example of hospitals is highly suggestive.

It is difficult, and therefore rare, for local public libraries to make contact with Federal agencies in such a way as to provide a national service. During the war libraries turned to organizing reading materials for war information agencies, defense plants, and the armed services. They did not repeat their World War I performance of providing libraries to the armed services; this was carried out directly by Federal agencies. But they did co-operate in every way they could devise with all activities that could be related to their resources and services.

Public libraries explored with great energy and enthusiasm the American Library Association's idea of becoming the central agency of morale and internal ideological defense, as well as the more direct service toward refurbishing skills, become rusty during the Great Depression. The library's impact on the community was deflected by the tremendous pace set by the industrial and military facts of modern total warfare. Perhaps the most successful integration of public library with war effort was achieved where the library building and staff became involved in the direct administration of civilian defense. Never put to the test of war at home, even this left the library pretty much on the periphery of the wartime lives of the community, and the liaison between public library and Federal Government remained tenuous. Since the war, libraries have placed great emphasis on vocational and educational guidance for the returning veteran, co-operating where possible with the Veterans' Administration. In all these activities, however, their affiliations with government departments really doing the job are sketchy and informal. In our survey this is especially evident in their aloofness from the field agencies of the Federal Government.

All these activities—group relationships, service to clubs, business and industrial departments, school affiliation, and liaisons with government agencies—would seem to add up to a widespread community influence resulting in considerable political power. But actually normal library influence amounts to little more than a surface chop running against the ground swell of public apathy. The opposition the library must face is not an active, directed campaign against it, but the general public unwillingness to tax itself for a service of which it makes limited use. Such organized opposition as there is, finds expression in taxpayers' associations, usually dominated by the large property owners, such as real estate interests; in an indirect way they can hold the fate of the library in their hands. They are not hostile to the library as such, but to taxes, and more especially to taxes, and directly to expenditures, that are not backed by a vigorous, organized vocal group.

Libraries usually depend upon the property tax.

They must attempt to gain by diplomacy what they have not the political power to gain by attack. Here library board affiliation with large property holders has sometimes softened the opposition. In one city library, where the state votes the property tax, the state legislature tends to vote any increase the city taxpayers' association is willing to impose on its members. The chairman of the library board, an influential businessman, had a prominent role in getting his friends to accept a tax rate increase this year. In some communities the Chamber of Commerce is approached as a taxpayers' association and placated as much as possible prior to tax hearings. In several cases we have found that the public library could successfully parry the thrusts of real estate lobbies by choosing a library trustee of high economic standing who was a large taxpayer of the community yet a warm supporter of library service. In one small town in a rural county the local manager of a very large absentee-owned corporation was able to play this role to perfection; for as observed by the librarian, it was not he, but the corporation, that paid the taxes, and he and his family enjoyed the books. But to match this case there are many in which the carefully chosen businessmen trustees have in practice thought in terms of taxes rather than in terms of public services rendered.

In one respect, and only one respect, public indifference is an advantage to the library: when people ignore what is on the bookshelves, they are not acutely concerned over book selection. Yet, historically there is inevitably tension and censorship of a kind established in every society that has put much faith in reading; witness the Puritans in this country. The business department of one library, hoping to be of service, approached the Small Business Men's Association with a description of its usefulness. After much prodding the association sent an envoy to the library to reconnoitre. He came back to report that he had uncovered a Communist outpost, bristling with radical, New Deal books, a threat to the American way of life. It was a small blast, and the library came through it unscathed, but it left the business librarian rather shaken about the value of stirring up the attention of his potential clientele, and he was completely confused about where to turn next. It is odd examples such as this, found occasionally in the sample, that indicate a deep-grained distrust of reading accompanying the apparent approval of it. This must be taken into account, as well as the open censorship attempted by church and patriotic groups.

Most librarians do, in fact, exercise constant vigilance in book selection. The censorship of library holdings does not often become a public issue, largely because it is an intramural activity. As a member himself of the white collar middle class that uses his library, the librarian has a green thumb for cultivating those books that will be popular and an equal knack for weeding out what will be considered dangerous. Most libraries effect a compromise between the extremes of removing entirely from the library books subject to criticism and on the other hand boldly displaying books which they believe are unjustly challenged. They do this by removing the questionable book from the open shelves, sometimes from the card catalogue, but retaining it on a private shelf in the librarian's office, to be handed out to the hardy customer who inquires for it, provided he is beyond the tender years of adolescence. Many librarians in our sample are ruthless in their own censorship, often unconsciously so, because they feel certain that they act as the library public would have them act. Book selection becomes inevitably a question of political judgment; it is not just a technical problem. In this most librarians, in following their own predispositions, are better politicians than they may realize.

One of the first research methods attempted in this study of the matrix of political forces within which the public library must operate was directed precisely at the issues of censorship. It was thought that, at the very least, book selection and censorship policies would give valuable leads to the interest groups in the community who were actively concerned, negatively and positively, with public library service. It soon became apparent, however, that while librarians were in general extremely insistent upon the stereotypes of democratic freedom of expression and diversity of opinion, they were inclined to count with close attention the political costs of asserting these democratic rights in their own institutions. There were very few cases of public criticism of library holdings and still fewer in which organized groups had gone on record with regard to books. It also became apparent that the reason lay in the caution of the librarian rather than in the tolerance of the community.

It is further important to note that librarians have reconciled democratic ideals with political practice by a general practice of minimizing to themselves the extent to which the issue arises and also by stressing that they are interpreting, as they properly must, the mandate of policy established by the library board. At least three librarians interviewed had so far suppressed the issue in their own conscious thinking that they could, with every evidence of honesty, assert that there was absolutely no censorship of any kind in their libraries, only for us to find that in fact the staff were following careful guide lines in book selection and, more important, had large bookcases full of books under lock and key that had been subject to public criticism. At the other extreme were those so constantly aware of the pressure of organized groups that they lived under very great emotional strain. One librarian had transferred the idea of limiting the overfrank book on sex to the much less relevant field of social reform, and would circulate "radical" books only to those who appeared substantially uninterested in radical change or who could be counted on to oppose "dangerous thoughts." A very few librarians interviewed regarded the issue with serious dread not untinged with hysteria, and in these cases there were circumstances that related their attitudes to particular situations on the board of trustees rather than to overt pressures from the community.

The research was unsuccessful, therefore, in its original objective of illuminating the group politics of library government by means of censorship issues. Politically significant uniformities did develop, however. The three great issues everywhere were sex, religion, and politico-economic change, the order of priority varying with the community, but moving up or down in intensity more or less together. Only the very largest libraries seriously attempted to resist all pressure and to select books on their merits alone. All libraries have inevitably political decisions to make in controlling the circulation of books subject to criticism. The psychological convenience of never facing squarely the conflict of abstract ideals and local reality has left under lock and key books whose sting has passed, of which the most commonly noted were *All Quiet on the Western Front* and *Grapes of Wrath*. The degree to which forgetfulness was encouraged to heal the irritations of past "mistakes" was strikingly revealed by the inability of librarians and staffs to recall what books were under lock and key, the inability to recall who in the community had ever objected to these books, and the genuine surprise with which librarians discovered what books had been sequestered. Undoubtedly many libraries need periodically to purge the purged and restore the shocking to the shelves of modern classics.

The politics of book selection is, therefore, a real enough part of library politics. But it is essentially a negative part, and confused by a good deal of rationalist idealism in conflict with practice. Yet there have been cases of courageous positive action. In the South our sample noted libraries prominently displaying a very full selection of social studies on race relations, books highly critical in their premises toward the prevailing social relations of Southern communities. There have been libraries that deliberately undertook through promotional devices to counteract prejudice and violent outbreaks of group conflict in their local communities. Evidence is not available to measure the political results in the long run of such library experiments with constructive education. It may be supposed that on the whole colleges and universities have strengthened their position, despite many temporary setbacks, through a firm policy of resisting the more narrow types of censorship. The libraries have on the whole stood out strongly for intellectual freedom as a principle, but in the group politics of their localities they have played safe with the safe groups.

THE STRATEGY OF GROUP RELATIONSHIPS

Although the library has no natural enemies, it suffers concurrently from the fact that it has no natural political allies. In a political system where governmental action follows the main stream of pressure from producer groups, as it does in the United States, the library, serving a minority of individual consumers, floats along helplessly. In this it is not different from many institutions representing consumers. Consumer groups as a usual thing benefit only incidentally and individually as rival producer groups struggle for political power. They are not organized economically, impelled emotionally, or united politically in such a way as to form a group that can join battle with the producers. Consumers must play balance-of-power politics, making temporary alliances with whatever forces are most favorable to their interests. Because producer groups are the great political rivals in our political system, the new alliance developing between libraries and big business research carries much significance. Here the library may have found an ally that can bring it real support. The dangers of such an alliance to a public institution, traditionally neutral in politics and nondiscriminating in its service, are too obvious to need description. Without some such alliances, however, the temperature of library politics and the nature of its support are likely to be low.

What the library does, the service it renders, does not build a persuasive political platform. This comes about, not from any failure on the part of the library, but because the character of its influence is imponderable; it cannot be made clear and incontrovertible. Its value to the community can only be measured by its effect upon the minds of individuals and the growth of their personalities. It is an article that can be sold on the political market only by the eloquence with which it can explain the inexplicable.

In order to get some tangible evidence to satisfy the public and their own consciences, librarians have developed certain standard statistical measures. They chart how many books are taken out; whether juvenile or adult; representing what category of reading. They tabulate the number of reference questions asked and answered and how many speeches to how many groups containing how many people. They compare the statistics month by month, year by year, and decade by decade. How much of this is needed to set administrative policy is not here to the point. As a device for showing the public what the library does, which is our present concern, these statistics are basically unreliable. Circulation figures cannot show how the library is influencing the minds of the public. Furthermore, the statistics are not always comparable; they can be increased by stocking cheap fiction and comic books; by lessening the borrowing period; by dissatisfied users who take out a lot of books, no one of which ever proves satisfactory; by the quick readers, the nervous types who must open and close a book a night; and by students who want to crib term papers from obscure sources. Reference figures are increased, often much against the librarian's wishes, by quiz programs, parlor games, and prize contests. These figures cannot take into account what happens to the reader for whom one book may have opened a new realm of experience, another for whom literary resources have opened up the possibility of an intellectual life. Yet in a profound sense this is what the library does; and it is out of an obscure belief in this serious contribution to an unmeasured number of people that the public gives support.

The evidence from library statistical studies has little political force. The old rationalist dream that all the people thirst for knowledge and, given the means, will educate themselves has been shattered by the facts now laid bare. In Berelson's *The Library's Public,* which analyzes existing studies of library use for the Public Library Inquiry, the character and size of the public library's actual clientele is made clear: few people read books; still fewer read much; and still fewer read for enlightenment. It has become evident that the major part of library service is given to a small portion of the population. The Likert survey, *The Public Library and the People,* also prepared for the Inquiry, indicates that of the 18 percent of the population who visited the library in the past year, "the 10 percent of the population who made the most visits account for 71 percent of all the visits that were made."[2] These figures are substantially corroborated by other surveys.[3] This is not a new discovery, but it has now been made so dramatic and convincing that the librarian can no longer defend his institution on the basis of active use of self-education facilities by the masses that are exposed to radio, newspapers, movies, and popular magazines. From a political point of view, however, it is significant that the public, although it may not use the library, believes it an important institution for others to use.[4] Three quarters of the population want it there, although many of them may never enter it. For what it is worth, this sort of left-handed approval is a library asset.

It is not, however, an asset upon which a library can build much of a constructive program. For that, our study indicates that the librarians are sound in their attempts to mobilize community support by library participation in group activities. By this method the temperature of library politics can be raised to the fusion point. One case history will have to suffice as an illustration of how this has been done. The Denver library serves a population of 322,412 persons. The librarian has shown great capacity for dynamic leadership, tying his library to a system that includes the library of the municipal university, a library school, a regional bibliographical center, and the Adult Education Council. He and his library provide the executive leadership in this system. He has become a man of importance in the city, serving, beyond his immediate interests, upon the executive committee of an opera association and as a director of the symphony society and a fine arts center. He is almost invariably called upon by the city to serve on committees connected with educational problems. His staff has followed his lead and affiliated with a much longer and more improbable list of clubs, committees, councils, centers, associations, commissions, leagues, campaigns, conferences, and fraternities.

These widespread personal affiliations are joined to a matured system of contacts with groups through library service, flexible and realistic in organization so that each staff member can perform the duties for which she is best fitted. To bring these contacts to a focus there is a co-ordinator of adult special services, who is also the person giving continuity to the work of the Adult Education Council, the offices of which are in the library. Her basic function is to co-ordinate all phases of library service and every department of library organization to serve the individual needs of community groups, which number more than two thousand in her card file. Under her is a field representative, who acts as the sales agent to groups, goes to their meetings, explains what the library can do, and reports back the needs to be filled by the various departments. Other members of the staff, quite regardless of their official title, have established contacts with groups in whose civic activity they have a personal interest and knowledge. This is the superstructure upon the usual framework of extension services. One of the more valuable features of it is the Adult Education Council, which is part of the library in fact and in the public mind. The key technique has been the freeing from intramural routines of about a half dozen staff members of unusual capacity for working in the field with people and groups.

When in 1947 the municipal institutions of Denver waged a campaign for building funds and it was finally agreed that each institution should use its own tactics, the library within five or six weeks mobilized a political following that voted in the bond issue for a new central building. This was done by having daily staff rallies to assign everyone to do leg work or make speeches. Mailing lists of key group leaders and library users were prepared. Publicity was written showing how the new building could better serve each large group and was sent separately to the Parent-Teachers Association, labor unions, clubs, and branch neighborhood organizations. Releases were given to the press, and one-minute radio spots were arranged through a regional radio council. The co-ordinator made forty speeches in five weeks, and the field representatives visited every AFL and CIO local in the city. The Adult Education Council suggested sixty volunteer speakers, who gave four hundred and fifty addresses. All of this carried the bond issue against a drift that defeated most of the other civic improvements.

When in the same year a proposed rewriting of the city charter threatened to modify the institutional relationships, particularly of the library board, the library spearheaded an attack against the charter by circularizing all library users, plus the huge mailing list prepared for the bond issue. In its circular the library was careful to give both sides of the case by including an official statement on the charter and the library by the president of the Charter Convention, who naturally favored what the library was opposing. A citizens' committee opposed to the charter was organized late in the campaign and undertook an intensive radio attack. The charter was defeated in almost every precinct. Although its defeat cannot be attributed solely to the merits of the library case, it is agreed that the library initiated the opposition which finally proved so effective. In both of these campaigns the basis of the library's political support was its group affiliations. It is clear that these can be so used as to mean real political power.

This one example does not prove the general political worth of group services. The figures and examples obtained by our survey are too fragmentary, and statistical norms for the measurement of library support are too unreliable, to attempt a correlation between wide community activities by the library and the strength of its public support. But it must be said in passing, and only for its suggestive worth, that the one library of the survey that is admittedly embarrassed by its riches from public taxation has as extensive a program of group services as the ingenuity of man can dream of. From these examples, and others less striking, but yet unequivocal, we may safely observe that services to groups are political weapons to be recognized by an institution so poorly armed as the library. It should be emphasized, however, that such a conclusion concerns the library as a political institution in a political situation. This is not to argue that group affiliations are necessarily the soundest approach to the educational objectives of the public library. Other considerations may limit the development of the use of such political ties.

THE LIBRARY FAITH IN PRACTICAL POLITICS

In political campaigns carried on by the library, the main armament is still supplied by the eighteenth-century rationalists. The traditional character of this pattern of values is not necessarily a handicap. The new realities, in all but a revolutionary or disintegrating society, are explained in the words, the ideas, the values, and the relationships of the past. The disparity between formal statement and current practice is not necessarily ruinous to an interest or to an idea. But the configuration of competing forces and the climate of opinion are in constant change. The particular interest, committed to a traditional body of thought, must exercise sustained political skill in reintegrating its own social myths in the total pattern of ideas. This is a never-ending imperative of political growth or even survival in our dynamic society.

The public librarians have shown energy and enthusiasm in this aspect of their political relationships and, drawing upon the historical resources reviewed above in chapter one, they have not lacked ideas or spokesmen. Recent international crisis and domestic tension have precipitated frequent restatement of the library faith. A broad and dramatic statement was given wide currency at the opening of the Second World War.

> We can either attempt to educate the people of this country—*all* the people of this country—to the value of the democratic tradition they have inherited, and so admit them to its enjoyment, or we can watch some of the people of this country destroy that tradition for the rest.... It is upon American libraries that the burden of this education must fall.... The libraries alone are capable of acting directly upon the present adult generation. The libraries alone are staffed by people whose disinterestedness is beyond suspicion.[5]

The American Library Association speaks in the same vein.

> To be great and remain free Americans must be educated. Books are the universal medium of education whether in school or outside—books to find the facts behind the newsreel or broadcast—books to fit us for a job, or to help us find it—books to explain the economic picture and the world changing before our eyes—books for our children—books to enjoy—books have become a necessity in an unstable world.[6]

Behind these statements can be felt the need for justification that the war made so universally pressing and the need to rephrase the old faiths in terms of the present demands of society. A resolution of the American Library Association Council, adopted December 29, 1940, is especially revealing.

> The American Library Association believes it is the privilege and duty of every library and library agency in North America to make its books and services contribute in all possible ways to the preservation and improvement of the democratic way of life.... Each one should make its services indispensable to its own community and to the country; and each member of every library board and staff must share the responsibility.

After demonstrating how the library can do this, it ends by saying:

> The diffusion of knowledge and understanding was never more important to the welfare of mankind. When, as now, it becomes necessary to mobilize all educational and cultural resources for defence and for the improvement of the American way of life, it must be deplored that millions of Americans do not have library service.[7]

The ancient saws and the modern instances are here combined to serve library needs. These quotations are representative in their focus upon the central themes of democracy as the ultimate value, education as the unquestioned program to achieve the desired society, the library as the inevitable device to implement value and program alike.

Although, when pressed, the library apologist reverts back to the eighteenth-century faith, he highlights it differently. The function is the same, but the method is changed. In the last century it was assumed that the reader in search of an education would come to the library; in this century it is assumed that the library must pursue the reader. In this pursuit the library faith has developed a second major strand, which may well be called "social utility."

> Instead of the library becoming a place of storage for certain traditional bodies of knowledge contained in books merely for their own sake, it becomes the warehouse and market exchange for all permanently important or temporarily useful information, in whatever form, that a given community may find to its advantage; in place of a remote temple of occasional and select learning, the enquirer finds a busy center of practical community affairs, attracting everyone by its convenient supply of some practical detail that he must have, and eventually holding him by its constant suggestion of the more significant knowledge that will extend his horizon.[8]

On this level the public library is seeking to establish itself in the pragmatic thinking of everyday political negotiation.

Recent statements of the library faith seek to unite the two levels of political discourse. The A.L.A. National Plan, 1947 model, says:

> The objectives of the public library are many and various. But in essence they are two to promote enlightened citizenship and to enrich personal life. They have to do with the twin pillars of the American way, the democratic process of group life and the sanctity of the individual person. The public library serves these objectives by the diffusion of information and ideas. By selecting and organizing materials, it makes an educational instrument out of a welter of records. By providing a staff able to interpret materials, it eliminates the gap between the seeker and the sources of enlightenment. When animated by a sense of purpose, reading skill, and community iden-

tification, the public library constitutes an important and unique service agency for the citizen. Lacking these attributes it is a passive badge of culture, tolerated by an indifferent populace.[9]

All interest groups must establish themselves in the Great Society by linking their group causes to abstract statements of moral purpose and a picture of the good society. To survive, any power system, small as well as great, must justify its being in terms of right. And every social group develops a body of discourse to establish the internal cohesion of its members. Yet it is also true that a social myth is most profoundly influential when it is so completely accepted as to be largely unarticulated. Endless restatements of what is already written in the group or the public mind, instead of engraving it deeper, may lead persons to seek evidences of the truth they had so easily accepted. Without vision, an institution languishes, but no human institution lives up to its high purposes or the promise of its beginnings. To use these purposes too often in affirming the institution's immediate social value may result in self-condemnation or stultify concrete political activity. The recent "great issues" strategy is a case in point.

Librarians suffer from the feeling that they are not acting up to their script and that the public does not convincingly play its assigned role. Realizing this, the American Library Association has attempted to rewrite the parts upon the following line of thought: since the public does not educate itself because of individual impulse, it should be aroused to do so by the great issues of the day. Within the last twenty-five years the profession has been exhorted to use successive enthusiasms in civic thinking to lure the public into the library. When adult education was the hope of the future, it was the mission of the library. When the Great Depression led people to think about their economic system, the library was to be their guide. When war challenged their whole way of life, the library was the symbol and the teacher of democracy's deeper meaning. The war was the perfect "great issue" and was seized upon with enthusiasm.

Since the war the issues have been individual and social reconversion. Prior to the 1948 change of top direction, the American Library Association had chosen inflation as the next great issue.

By exposing the library faith to constant repetition, by relating it, on an emotional as well as a concrete plane, with a rapidly changing succession of social conflicts and maladjustments, not only have librarians emphasized the disparity between ideal and performance, but the policy has also led the library to confuse its objectives and lower its standards of performance. This was pointed out by John Chancellor, the former American Library Association director of adult education, when he wrote, in 1942:

I do not believe that librarians will ever be able to make a strong case for the indispensability of their function to the war effort. Their primary function of diffusing knowledge is obviously important to social reconstruction. However, I feel certain that to the degree they neglect the latter job in order to pursue the more apparent and spectacular former course, they will lose in ultimate public respect and support.[10]

In the hasty pursuit of the great issues, the libraries have, as noted, depreciated the quality of their book collections and reduced the permanent value of the collection as a tool of serious adult education.

The appeal of the library as an information center seems at first glance to be on more secure political ground. In a world astonished by scientific miracles and in a country where so many values are measured by usefulness, the American library was surely destined to translate its faith into pragmatic terms. The concept that the library shall preserve all important information has therefore been extended to the concept that it shall contain all the information usable in its community. But this brings the library into competition with a political and economic system in which every felt need is served by a government operating and promoting agency or by a profit-seeking commercial enterprise. Such private enterprise, since its life depends upon doing so, will follow closely every wide popular demand. The newspaper, the movies, and the radio proverbially cultivate popular use with great care. The librarian, perhaps, is freer to take an unprofitable risk, but if he inaugurates a service for which the public has a great, unmet need, he will in time find his service duplicated and often displaced by a commercial venture. If the public demand is vital and closely connected with other traditional governmental departments, they will take over the means of distributing "practical information." Our example above was the Department of Agriculture. This has also happened in the legislative reference bureaus, which often have been transferred to the legislature after having been initiated by the library. Where the use is general and the need occasional, the library will find that neither private enterprise nor another government agency eager to do the job; but in such cases the public enthusiasm will be correspondingly low.

The library faith, real as it is, can only be an immeasurable, unseen force. When formulated, it is an intellectual abstraction, of moving eloquence, perhaps, to those who consciously articulate the norms of our culture, but not so binding upon the general public. Day-to-day local politics are immediately governed, not by such abstractions, but by the pulling and hauling of local interests. The librarians and their profession may need an occasional rededication to their mission, and they should constantly assess their activities in the terms of their true function. But they must also recognize that they do not live by poetry alone. In local politics the potential of libraries, like that of other public services, is measured chiefly in terms of consumer service. If the newer services of the library can increase the number of library consumers or the value received by them, by so much the library gains in political power.

The idealism of library literature and librarian oratory seems most unsatisfactory when an attempt is made to translate it directly into a program for action. From such a height of aspiration political realities take on too disheartening a character, and plans of action, especially the numerous national library plans of recent years, appear unrealistic to the earthbound practicing librarian. His reactions, as our survey has discovered, have sometimes hardened into apathy. From the perspective of political science, librarians appear to have suffered from taking their own social myth, not too seriously, but too literally. The emotional and political dilemma they encounter is another facet of the political scientist's own concern over the nonvoter and the politically apathetic in a democracy. Universal enlightenment is not a completely realizable ideal. Only a minority, probably a small minority, will really understand and participate actively and constructively in leading the enormously differentiated culture. Only a few will be really involved effectively and with sustained interest and activity in the democratic polity. It is now clear to librarians and political scientists that many who give gratifying superficial evidence of activity in the channels approved by the democratic and rationalist myth are more concerned with conforming to an orthodox pattern than with the substance of their activity. Dilettante participation for purposes of status is quite as far from the norm pictured in the library faith as are the much larger majority who remain wholly apathetic. Yet these same large elements in the democratic community may show highly sophisticated competence in manipulating the technical and complex factors in the culture which are their special vocations; and they may have an adequate reserve of common sense and intuitive judgment to hold the balance between competing power groups and to control the pace and general direction of social and political change. Disillusionment comes to librarians when they apply their library faith too exactly and more particularly when they use it as a measure for concrete library programs and apply it to particular political situations. That faith is essential in the strategy of their politics, but it must be used strategically and as a social myth, not as a measuring rod.

When the political forces of a community and the political moves open to the library are examined, the library faith, classical and modernized, retains a persistent validity. A few people use the library and feel that they benefit greatly; society assumes that they are important and that their intellectual enlightenment is socially valuable, for in some inscrutable way knowledge is virtue and information is power. More precisely, the democratic society believes that, few though they be, the minority who can use books and do want them should have access to library resources. This has proved to be a substantial reality of our socially mobile democratic life. That this reality has not brought wealth and prosperity to libraries is a basic circumstance of library politics. Unless the public changes its character, a possibility that seems highly improbable within any near future, or the library changes its function, a drastic remedy that even present fiscal stringency does not justify, the public library cannot expect more than a modest competence to live upon.

SUMMARY AND INTERPRETATION

Such realism is not a counsel of despair. There are certain political relations that the library can still exploit more fully than it has. The library faith itself has not been drained of all it can give. There will be no miracle of the loaves and fishes, but there is every evidence that the public library can make a satisfactory living and a continued contribution to society.

The potential of the board of trustees and the library staff as individuals in the community cannot, in many cases, be developed much farther. Some cases in our sample show a civic enterprise remarkable in its energy and scope. No one could be expected to do more, and few can do as much. There is a limit to what the library staff can contribute to community life, not only in time and effort but also in personal effectiveness. The librarian who is not a politician by nature can force his inclinations only so far, and his limits deserve respect. The board, which is busy and unpaid, obviously cannot be driven and probably should not be lured into doing much more than it is doing. The small number of librarians alone will prevent their blanketing the community with library relationships.

What librarians might do more effectively than they have done is to relate their community activities closely to political reality. They will profit by constantly reassessing the value of community groups in a rapidly changing and intensely competitive political scene. Many librarians in our sample are vaguely aware that their group ties are no longer the most effective, but they undervalue the importance of this or lack the political acumen to understand and rework the problem. On balance, this is perhaps the commonest political mistake we have noted. They have allowed a traditional framework to narrow their perspective, or a simplified version of human society to blunt their perception. The rare quality needed is imagination.

The new special service relation to groups is politically a most promising approach, because it keeps librarians aware that the parallelogram of political forces in a community is continually changing shape. This technique is open to any librarian, anywhere. Staff members should have special training for this varied work, a job which will require the nicest administrative understanding and skills.

The pattern of special service has been in general well worked out, but most libraries still have not developed an effective service to public administrators. This is a significant vacuum, for public policy is formed largely and probably increasingly at the administrative level. Every library can serve local, and some can serve state, officials. The research suggests the hypothesis that all librarians will find such service politically important.

A librarian cannot afford to neglect the issues of the day, for the use of his library depends upon how aware the public is of its resources, and publicity in terms of current issues can bring about such an awareness. Librarians will succeed in so far as they understand their communities, but not through an abstract concept of the citizen. The hortatory, however, can be overdone, as also the timely, to the neglect of library resources as tools for the serious reading adult, however rare he may be. Libraries would seem to weaken their position by overlooking their serious purpose and becoming trivial. They seem particularly vulnerable in their use of the ephemeral to induce nonthinkers to think "right." It is, after all, upon their contribution to the relatively few serious users that the public library will continue to depend. The political expediency of working with organized groups should not obscure the highly individual nature of library service.

These political tactics do not promise any great increase of income, to be sure. Our survey has, unfortunately, discovered no new sources of wealth which libraries can tap. It behooves librarians, therefore, to make as efficient use of their effort for clearly defined ends as is possible under their limited budgets. Such an objective raises the problems of the efficient unit of library service and the organization of an over-all library system and calls for an effective professional organization for leadership and for mobilized political power.

FOOTNOTES

[1] For the use of films in such group activities see Gloria Waldron, *The Information Film,* New York, Columbia University Press, 1949.
[2] Survey Research Center, "The Public Library and the People," Ann Arbor, Michigan, University of Michigan, 1949, p. 3, mimeographed.
[3] See Bernard Berelson, *The Library's Public,* New York, Columbia University Press, 1949, pp. 10, 99-101.
[4] *Ibid.,* pp. 85, 87.
[5] Archibald MacLeish, "Libraries in the Contemporary Crisis," *Library Journal,* LXIV (1939), pp. 879-82.
[6] ALA, *The Equal Chance,* Chicago, ALA, 1943, p. 3.
[7] *ALA Bulletin,* XXXV (Jan., 1941), 50.
[8] Learned, *The American Public Library and the Diffusion of Knowledge,* p. 53.
[9] Carleton B. Joeckel, Amy Winslow, and Lowell Martin, *National Plan for Public Library Service,* Chicago, ALA, 1948, p. 16.
[10] *ALA Bulletin,* XXXVI (Sept. 1, 1942), 555.

ABOUT THE AUTHOR—Oliver Garceau has been a pioneer in applying the concepts of political science to his empirical studies of professional organizations. His first major work, *The Political Life of the American Medical Association* (1941) was followed in 1949 by the very influential study of the library profession, *The Public Library in the Political Process.*

Born in Boston in 1911, Garceau has remained a New Englander. Both his undergraduate and graduate degrees were taken at Harvard University. In addition to receiving an M.A. and M.B.A., he was awarded a Ph.D. in political science in 1940. With the exception of the war years, when he was in military service, he was a member of the Harvard faculty from 1935 to 1946. He taught at Maine also, and spent the years from 1948 to 1958 as a Professor of Government at Bennington. In 1959–60 he was Research Professor of Government, Harvard University. During that time he also served as an executive associate and consultant for the Ford Foundation and on the Executive Board of the Inter University Core Program in Public Administration. His public library survey was written under the auspices of the Social Science Research Council. Since 1961 he has lived in Maine, and served as a consultant in political economy and political behavior research.

The Role of Interest Groups in the Formation of a Library

by Ruth Aronson

The writer was originally an active participant in this effort to get a tax supported library in a suburban community in upstate New York. Later she returned to study the situation, seeking in interest group theory an explanation of the actions of those who were involved and an understanding of the outcome. She found the real issue was not the formation of a library, but rather that the library issue had become the focus for a struggle for power between the older elements in the community and the newer residents. This same struggle could involve already established libraries in communities undergoing a considerable influx of new residents. Probably equally typical is the response she found on the part of local government. This is one of the very few explorations of the interests which identify with library issues. It points to the need and suggests the approach for more research if the profession is to develop its level of political sophistication.

This is a case study of a campaign by a League of Women Voters unit to organize community support for the formation of a public library in a growing suburban town in 1961. The purpose of the study is to expand our knowledge of the dynamics involved in terms of interest groups and their interactions.

It is the author's thesis that the resolution of a library issue which involves political action can be best understood in terms of interest groups which exert pressures and counter-pressures on one another and on the political body to be influenced. Library interest groups are successful to the extent that they are granted legitimacy by those in a position to make official decisions or can involve other interest groups so legitimated.

The outcome of any library community issue cannot be explained in a vacuum. Whether or not local government is favorable or unfavorable to a library issue may have very little to do with the merits of a proposal. In fact, the issue which is actually being decided may not be the library issue at all. What we may actually be observing are groups seeking to obtain or hold power. One of the major struggles in local government is between rural communities against urban encroachments. How these and other groups interacted was studied in one community. The political theories of Bentley, Truman and Ziegler provided the approach.

The social science approach is not new to librarianship. Writing in 1949, Bernard Berelson traced the changing interest of librarians from the *content* of the library, to a later preoccupation with its institutional procedures, to a present interest in the library's *function* as a communication agency. In this newer context, Berelson felt, the social scientist would contribute to library research by (a) clarifying the general context of the problem (b) defining the librarians problems (c) applying social science concepts and principles to the library and (d) providing the methodology for particular problems. (2)

Eleven years later, Ennis and Fryden reporting in the *Library Quarterly* on the kinds of changes which occurred in community use of a branch library confirmed Berelson's predictions, both by their use of social science methods and concepts and by their interpretation of the library's function as an institution of the community affected by the shifting, expansion, and contraction of community needs. (4)

A year later, Monypenny—using political theory as a base, was able to assign a more active role to

---

SOURCE: Reprinted from Ruth Aronson, "The Role of Interest Groups in the Formation of a Library," *Social and Political Aspects of Librarianship: Student Contributions to Library Science*, ed. Mary Lee Bundy and Ruth Aronson (Albany: School of Library Science, State University of New York at Albany, 1965), pp. 31-41, by permission of the publisher and the author.

the library in the community when he declared the library itself to be a pressure group with an obligation to participate in the government process. (8)

It is in this tradition of the social science approach that this paper is written. The library is viewed as an agency or institution in the total community setting affected by "... groups pressing one another, forming one another and pushing out new groups to mediate the adjustments." (1)

The method used in the present study is indebted to the concepts of community analysis developed by Blackwell (12), Taylor (6), Hunter (5), Thometz (10) and Miller (7). It differs from them in that it is tailored to the needs of a one person, three month project. This is a method which uses both objective and subjective data. As chairman of the County League of Women Voters Library Committee from 1960 to 1962, the author had access to primary sources of information which included organizational files, publications, newspaper clippings, correspondence and private notes. In addition to her role as objective fact gatherer, the author also served as a participant observer viewing directly "... who says and does what to whom in deciding what shall be done, how, and by whom." (10)

On the basis of the author's experience on the library project and as a result of preliminary discussions with some of the participants, a list of names active in four categories was chosen: Newspapers, LWV, Town, and Professional Consultants. In order to preserve privacy, each name received a number preceded with the initial of the category such as N-1, or LWV-5, or T-10, or P-5. Multiple affiliations are indicated by complex initials: e.g. LWV-T. An interview schedule to elicit information on the decision making process was administered to selected key persons.

THE LOCALE

Town is located in a central relationship to three major cities. Because of its strategic location and diversified transportation facilities, Town has proved to be one of the fastest growing municipalities in the state. With an exceptionally large land area of some 57.2 square miles, during the past 14 years (1950–1964) its population has doubled from 29,522 to a current estimate of 59,000. However the population explosion is projected to 130,000 by the turn of the century. There are two incorporated villages in Town: the Village of C and the Village of M, as well as several unincorporated, heavily populated areas. Additionally, new housing developments within these areas have organized local housing associations which have come to assume some of the characteristics of political pressure groups.

There is a supervisor and board form of government in Town which maintains a 27 man, paid police department. In addition there is a 1,000 man volunteer fire department made up of 13 fire companies. There are two centralized public school districts: North Town and South Town. Total school facilities include 16 elementary, five parochial elementary, four high schools and one university. There are 26 churches in the area and a number of service clubs. The volunteer fire departments and their auxiliaries, the PTA's, the church groups and the various service groups all represent possible pressure groups.

An analysis of population growth within Town reveals that not all areas developed at similar rates. The general direction of growth, however, was in line with national trends where most of the population increase took place in the suburbs.

Some indices reflecting the economic status for Town and its comparison with the city district in 1959–1960 indicate quite clearly that the Town population, on the average, enjoyed a superior economic status when compared with the general district population. Family income was $1,000 greater with a significantly higher proportion of the population in the middle and upper brackets. A large number owned their own homes which were more recently constructed and of significantly higher appraised value. It is important to note that almost 50 percent of the homes in Town were constructed between 1950–1960, a period which also saw the doubling of Town's population.

PREVIOUS ATTEMPTS

Business and Professional Women's Club. The first attempt to establish library service in Town was undertaken by the Business and Professional Women's Club in 1950. Activities of this group extended into 1956 and included public meetings, newspaper publicity, conferences with the town supervisor, bookmobile exhibits and (in 1955) an informal poll of Town organizations on their attitudes toward a Bookmobile service at an annual cost of $35,000 or about eighty-three cents per $1,000 assessed evaluation. The BPW Library Committee received responses from 24 organizations to its letter requesting a membership vote. Ten organizations voted in favor of the plan, twelve were against, one was evenly divided and one reported it would support a permanent library but not a bookmobile.

In 1957 the effort of the BPW movement was terminated but without success. A letter from the town supervisor dated February 4, 1957 to the chairman of the BPW Library Committee stated, "The town board decided not to include any item in the current budget for the establishment of (a county) library system (and that) . . . it would be established in the coming year."

Town Library Committee I. The second attempt took place in 1960, and it was initiated by Mr. N-T10, a reporter for a local paper and a resident of Town. This was called Town Library Committee. It was essentially a study group that met about six or seven times to listen to talks from professional consultants and reports on how other libraries had started. No action resulted from this. The group had planned to conduct an opinion survey which did not occur as a group project. Mr. N-T10, however, showed the author the results of a personal telephone survey he had made to several hundred residents in different geographical areas which indicated that approximately half of those surveyed approved of a library for Town and would be willing to support it.

LEAGUE OF WOMEN VOTERS

The League of Women Voters role began in May, 1959 when members attending the annual dinner voted to adopt the study of library facilities in the County. After careful study of minimum standards for evaluation of library adequacy, and regional library systems, it was felt that because of the area library federation's work with existing libraries, LWV should concentrate on the unserved areas which constituted 35 percent of the county population. Since Town was the largest of these areas, and since previous attempts at establishing a library had made Town residents aware of this situation it was decided to concentrate LWV efforts there.

An educational campaign called LACK (Libraries for County Knocking) was planned. This campaign was coordinated with the April 10th to 16th dates of the 1961 National Library Week. On April 10th to 14th, 31 members participated in a door to door distribution of 7,000 brochures. On April 17 and 21 a bookmobile toured Town, stopping at schools, housing developments, and shopping centers. Newspaper and television publicity covered this. The town supervisor in an interview with the LWV president and the library committee chairman was non-committal. An open hearing before the town board on April 27, 1961 was attended by LWV and representatives of several Town service clubs who presented the approval of their members to the town board. The board listened, thanked everyone, but made no commitments. During and after this period statements of endorsement were sent to the newspapers and town supervisor by the supervising principals of both central school districts, mayor of the village of C, the chairman of Independent Party of C-Village, some service clubs and a number of PTA's. Some of the PTA's endorsements were triggered by persons who were also LWV members. Both city newspapers editorialized support of the library movement.

AFTERMATH

The second town library committee came into being as a reaction to the town board inaction. Although not connected with LWV, its initiator, Mrs. LWV-7 was also a League member. Her husband, a lawyer, chairman of the C village independent party, and counsel to the C village board was also active in the minority party in Town. The Village of C had experienced a change in its administration when the Independent Party candidates were elected to the village governmental offices. This made the village a pocket of dissidence in the overwhelmingly Republican town with a strongly entrenched Republican supervisor and board. Nineteen sixty-one was an election year with elections for both village offices and town offices to take place in November and the library became an issue in the campaign when the Democrats added a plank to their platform in support of the library.

Despite a vigorous campaign and a constant stream of publicity TLC II failed. On September 16th, 1961 the committee together with Mr. P 15, director of the area library federation, who had acted as their consultant all through the summer, met with the town board to request support for a town library. A specific request for $51,374 was denied by the board. A September 25, 1961 meeting of the committee was poorly attended.

Others. In an effort to develop a more representative group, the chairman of the LWV library committee contacted the president of Kiwanis, who earlier had offered to co-sponsor a general meeting. A steering committee was formed consisting of the chairman of the LWV library committee, president of Kiwanis and chairman of

TLC II. On Novermber 2nd, 1962, a dessert and coffee meeting was held in a local restaurant. The purpose of this meeting was to elect a nominating committee to form a Friends of the Town Library. Fifty persons representing 33 organizations attended.

This meeting was very successful and aroused enthusiasm. A nominating committee was elected whose chairman was Mrs. LWV–T11. The committee also contained a member of Rotary, the president of the Town Exchange Club, T 13, and representatives of the South and North Town PTA's, Town Chamber of Commerce and the Village of C.

After several meetings the nominating committee decided to abandon the idea of a Friends of the Town Library and instead moved to form an association library with the eventual goal of affiliating with the area library federation. A board of trustees was named. The key man in this decision was Mr. T 13, a lawyer who had been in politics locally for a number of years and was reputed to have "connections" with the town board and particularly with the town supervisor.

INTERPRETATION

Keeping in mind that an interest group need not be a formal organization but may represent a force or direction of effort, that an interest group is meaningful only in relation to other groups and changing times and that it is not homogeneous, it is now appropriate to examine those groups that played a role in the process that finally led to an association library.

The role of the pertinent groups will be interpreted individually, and where appropriate, interview data will be used in the analysis.

Town Board–All group pressures were aimed at the town board since the requests were for a tax supported, town library. This was not an initiating board. In this respect, the board's behavior reflects Sokolow's finding that "In fact the rural power leadership may have a built in bias for *not* taking action and may discourage the raising of 'big' issues" (*9*). By failing to take any positive action over a number of years, the board succeeded in impairing the interest of other groups in their attempts to establish a Town library.

It was the feeling of a good many individuals within the community that the town board was dominated by the town supervisor. In his contact with library interest groups, the supervisor demonstrated a unique capacity for straddling the fence; never outrightly opposing libraries, but careful to avoid displeasing those opposed to increased service and spending.

The Community–For purposes of analysis, the community may be divided into the old community and the new community, remembering always that these are not strictly homogeneous groups and that many of the early leaders in the library interest groups were old community residents.

Although the old community town population was not a strictly rural group in the farming sense, nevertheless, it demonstrated many of the characteristics described by Bundy.

> These life-long residents, like the conservatives in any community are most likely to resist change, to be satisfied with things the way they are. They will resent projects which are not sponsored by their own leaders and organizations. They are least likely to have experienced modern library service such as a large city provides. Perhaps most important to them the library is not a public institution they are required to support through their taxes. People who want to use libraries pay a fee and get non-resident cards at nearby libraries. (*3*)

Mr. N-9 pointed out in his interview that ". . . the older residents were more for the status quo or patience while the newer residents were more pressing for action."

In contrast to this, the newer group represented an urban background, where, as Mr. N-9 stated "the library was there and accepted as part of the landscape." Mr. T-1 put it "There is a library on every corner in the city. If Town residents use the library in the city, the city would eventually discourage this use or if used it would make the city facility obsolete. The population movement is toward the suburbs. It isn't fair to rely on cities when you live in suburbs."

Another way in which the newcomers differed from the old residents was in the techniques and attitudes used in the approach to the town board. The newcomers were more demanding and less reluctant to use pressure. Mr. T-1, when asked how he would go about this if he were to do it over again, stated: "What I would do is start with the premise that public funds must be used–go about getting a maximum of community support through every publicity device there is–when you are sure you have the kind and the amount of real substantial support to make a political impact–then approach your politicians–not hat in hand–but with a nice big stick." In contrast to this, Mr. T-13 ". . . we felt that we would not again try to pressure the town board as the TLC 2 group had done. If we were to do it over, we would do the same thing we did—start an Association—impress upon the town board that the citizens want a town library and would not object to the use of public money."

In-Group and Out-Group—For the purpose of this paper, the Ins (In-Group) may be defined as the people who either had political power or had access to those in power and were in sympathy with them. The Ins are not to be thought of as an anti-library faction since, as will be seen later, some of their members were influential in turning the course of events to an association library. The Outs (Out-Group), primarily Democrats and for the most part concentrated in C Village (South Town) supported libraries both from conviction and as a form of political leverage against the Ins.

Speaking of this in retrospect, a Democrat, Mrs. LWV C-17 considered sponsorship to be of value in this sense "A minority may not win the election itself, but by influencing the majority to do something about the issue, it will have effect that way." Mr. C-13, a Republican, evaluated the Outs support of the library as a ". . . purely political situation for them. They thought that since the Republicans were in town offices and had done nothing about the library—their support of the library (would win them community support). Their whole attitude was 'look what we've got.' They want to start at the top." It would seem then, that the Outs acted as a pressure group on the Ins as well as a threat to the town board.

The Organizations—The history of the development of the several organizations was described in Section V. This section is concerned with the interactions of these groups and its effect on the community and town board which reacted to them. Here again it must be remembered that these are not separate entities but actually part of the community, and its members included the Ins and Outs in varying proportions.

Of the several groups involved in the library movement, the BPW was distinctive in the sense that its efforts and impact preceded by several years the activities of the more recent groups. The library issue was dormant for several years between the termination of BPW activity and the initiation of later action. In its pioneering effort, the BPW was thwarted by the controlling role of the old community and the eye to eye response of the town board which felt comfortable in its role of interpreter for the dominant old community. The BPW's contribution to succeeding groups was a heightened community awareness of the need for a library.

The role of CLC I was a brief one and its main contribution was to keep the issue alive before the community through newspaper publicity.

The LWV entered the picture in a changing environment. Unlike the isolated milieu the BPW found itself in, the area had developed a regional library system in the area library federation, whose director acted as a consultant to LWV. The rapid population increase in the Town added an additional significant factor: the increase of newcomers with their expanding demands.

> Where innovation does occur in rural politics, it generally is introduced from outside the local community. Professional persons with outside contact . . . provide one source of change. Proposed change is also brought into the community by an influx of new residents. In rural communities undergoing significant population increases, the major issues of government often become conflicts between 'old settlers' and 'new comers,' as the latter press representational and service demands on the boards dominated by the former. (9)

In addition to the changed environment, there were special characteristics of the LWV itself which were valuable in this situation. Of approximately 250 LWV members, 50 resided in Town and were active in local PTA's and other groups. They were thus able to influence the Town groups to endorse the idea of a town library. LWV also contributed leaders for later groups and interacted with other community groups. Of primary significance, however, is the League's history of studying significant government issues which gave them a design for approaching this particular problem. Its history included a method for action on issues. Once it had its data, machinery existed for making group decisions for action and implementing these decisions. The committee charged with the responsibility for action received the organized support of the entire local league.

The League was perceived by the community as providing information and "starting the ball rolling." Mrs. C-2 perceived LWV as "very active. Studied problem and gathered material." Mr. C-1 characterized LWV "As usual, a group of women voters banded together in an organization out to make trouble, can move mountains." Mr. C-13 remembered LWV "It sponsored the Kiwanis meeting." The Kiwanis meeting was of particular significance to Mr. C-13 because it gave him entry into the library group.

The action of LWV gave impetus to the formation of local groups. The first of these local groups was CLC II. While its membership contained a number of Ins, they were ineffectual in shaping its policy because its leadership was invested in the Outs.

In an effort to form a more broadly based and effective group, the chairman of CLC II, the chairman of the LWV library committee and the president of Kiwanis formed a steering committee to sponsor a joint Kiwanis-LWV meeting. This meeting was a turning point. The nominating committee elected at this meeting gave entrance to a number of the Ins. The key man in this was Mr. C-13, a lawyer who had "been in politics" locally for a number of years and was reputed to have "connections" with the Board and particularly with the town supervisor. He was described as a "controlling person." Describing the process which led to the appointment of a board of trustees of the association library, Mr. C-13 stated "A group of us at the Kiwanis meeting planned to meet to implement—do something concrete." This need for something concrete reflected a feeling among those active in the library interest groups. Fatigued with the experience of talk, meetings, and organizations they were willing to modify their original goals to see something "real" happen. Mr. C-1, a resident of the Village of C and a member of the Outs, but a member of the first board of trustees for one year stated: "I saw an association library as a middle point evolution toward a public library—but I never envisioned a permanently unendowed library as a permanent unit. An association library to get started. Meetings—we voted—they seemed like an interminable period."

CONCLUSION

In summary, the picture that presents itself is one in which all organizations at different times exerted pressure on both the town board and the community. The old community and town board at one time resisted. With a change in population and values the community supported library service but was blocked by the town board and the in-group which felt threatened. The in-group responded by taking the opportunity afforded by the formation of a new library group to turn the demands of the new community for library service into something less directly threatening to the board. This quieted the out-group which had no power to legislate and did not choose to bring the issue to a referendum.

The final outcome represents a compromise; namely the establishment of an association library in lieu of a tax supported town library. This compromise was necessary as a means of mediating between conflicting groups. The group dynamics involved could apply to any issue involving town government.

This study points to the importance of a broad orientation for the student of library science. Library administrators must be aware of community dynamics and interaction if they are to realize the full potential of the library as an institution in the community. Further studies might concern themselves with the extent to which the comparison of large numbers of case studies of library formation might show a definite pattern of stages in community decision-making. Could a definite prediction of success or failure be based on characteristics of the interest groups at certain stages? Are there any consistent patterns related to success or failure?

BIBLIOGRAPHY

1. Bentley, Arthur Fisher, *The Process of Government: A Study of Social Pressures*, Bloomington, Indiana: The Principia Press, Inc., 1908.
2. Berelson, Bernard, "The Role of the Social Scientist in Library Research," *Rural Sociology*, Sept. 14, 1949, pp. 244-249.
3. Bundy, Mary Lee, *An Analysis of Voter Reaction to a Proposal to Form a Library District in LaSalle and Bureau Counties, Illinois*, Springfield, Illinois State Library, 1960.
4. Ennis, Philip H. and Floyd N. Fryden, "The Library in the Community" *Library Quarterly*, Vol. 30, No. 4, pp. 253-265.
5. Hunter, Floyd, *Community Power Structure: A Study of Decision Makers*, Chapel Hill: Univ. of North Carolina Press, 1953.
6. Taylor, C. "Techniques of Community Study and Analysis as Applied to Modern Civilized Societies" in Linton, R. (ed.) *The Science of Man in the World Crisis*, Col. U. Press, N. Y., 1945, pp. 435-436.
7. Miller, Paul A., Community Health Action: *A Study of Community Contrast*, East Lansing: Michigan State College Press, 1953.
8. Monypenny, Philip, "The Public Library as a Pressure Group," *Illinois Libraries*, Dec., 1961, pp. 720-730.
9. Sokolow, Alvin D., *The Nature of Rural Politics in the United States:* A Bibliographic Essay, Michigan State University, unpublished monograph, 1964.
10. Thometz, Carol, *The Decision Makers: The Power Structure of Dallas*, Southern Methodist Univ. Press, 1963.

11. Truman, David Bickness, *The Governmental Process: Political Interests and Public Opinion*, N. Y. Alfred A. Knopf, 1958.
12. Young, Roland, ed., *Approaches to the Study of Politics*, Evanston, Ill., Northwestern Univ. Press, c 1958, 3rd pr., 1962.
13. Ziegler, Harman, *Interest Groups in American Society*, N. Y.: Prentice-Hall, 1964.

ABOUT THE AUTHOR—Ruth Aronson received her B.A. from Brooklyn College in 1945 and her M.L.S. from the State University of New York at Albany in 1966. She has worked as a social investigator for the Department of Welfare and as a probation officer for the Municipal Court of New York City. She has held the office of program vice-president of the Albany League of Woman Voters. Since 1966 she has been with the New York State Department of Mental Hygiene as an assistant research analyst and is at present bibliographer for the School of Social Welfare and the Department of Sociology-Anthropology at the State University where she also serves as president of the newly-formed Organization of SUNY Librarians. She is co-editor with Bundy and Aronson of *Social and Political Aspects of Librarianship* (1965). She participated as a part of the writing team of the Department of Mental Hygiene's publication: *Functional Program: Bronx State School* (1966). Mrs. Aronson is married to a clinical psychologist and is the mother of five children.

Book Selection and Censorship: The Encounter

by Marjorie Fiske

> *While a great deal has appeared in the literature exploring the ethic of intellectual freedom and in spite of an abundance of journalistic reporting of actual cases, there has been little research into censorship as a political issue. This selection from Marjorie Fiske serves to explore this issue in these terms. Here she deals with the type of complaint and the library's response, exploring censorship cases which became public issues. Perhaps the most interesting observation she makes is that librarians working in situations where civil liberties are threatened are more likely to feel responsible on such issues than librarians functioning in freer atmospheres.*

Public criticisms of libraries range from the trivial to the traumatic. Patrons, parents, individual crusaders, and organized groups either object to general library policy, or demand removal of (or addition to) material on the shelves. They make their complaints to a desk clerk, a reader's aide or reference librarian, head librarian, school principal, superintendent, school board or library board. The approach may be casual or formal. The person first hearing the complaint may take immediate action or pass it on to someone on another level of the institution. The initial objection is sometimes publicized in a letter to a newspaper, or at an open meeting of a board. More often, the issue does not become a matter of public knowledge at all. From objections that are publicized, partisan episodes occasionally develop. A few have aroused segments of the community not usually concerned with library matters, eventually erupting into community-wide conflicts which were settled only after public hearings, school board elections, or staff dismissals.

Any categorization of the various types of book controversies necessarily underplays their complex and dynamic character; and by presenting those reported by our respondents, we are further handicapped by incompleteness and by blurring of the data. Few of our respondents had direct experience with public episodes or conflicts, and many of the reported events took place some time ago. Despite these shortcomings, there is evidence that under some circumstances a complaint can disrupt a whole community, while under others it may be turned into an affirmation of the positive role of the library.

PATRON COMPLAINTS

The complaints of individual patrons have not changed markedly during the professional careers of our librarians either in respect to the types or numbers of persons making them, or in the nature of the material complained about. There are users of libraries who write critical letters to the head librarian or make critical remarks to the person at the desk about books or authors on moral, religious, ethnic, or political grounds. In school libraries it is more likely to be parents than students who complain about library holdings. Yet even in communities where conflicts over school library books have been highly publicized, no school librarian reported a noteworthy increase or change in parental complaints. Less than 20 per cent came from parents. Only 6 per cent came from students, and they were, for the most part, relaying parental complaints, although a few worried lest a book be harmful to fellow students (table 9). All other objections were from within the school systems—from board members, faculty, administrators, or librarians themselves.

In replying to complaints from patrons or parents, librarians are fairly free to apply their own standards. A few school systems and some of the more centralized public libraries have developed more formal methods; but even with clearly formulated regulations, librarians tend to exercise a large amount of personal discretion. Some schools require all visitors to check in at the principal's office; then he, rather than the school librarian, is likely to hear the complaint. More commonly, the principal does not know the librarian's procedure,

SOURCE: Reprinted from Marjorie Fiske, *Book Selection and Censorship: A Study of School and Public Libraries in California* (Berkeley: University of California Press, 1959), Chap. 4, "The Encounter," pp. 45–63, by permission of the publisher and the author.

TABLE 9

Objectors To Controversial Books In Public And
School Libraries

(Percentages)

OBJECTORS	SCHOOL LIBRARIES	PUBLIC LIBRARIES
Librarian	42	65
Administrative personnel	23	—
Parent	18	7
Teacher	8	2
Patron	6[1]	21
Other	3	5
Number of respondents	95	132

Note: Data above is based upon cumulative figures for the three years preceding the study's field work.

[1] Students.

and in some schools principal and librarian have developed disparate ways of dealing with complaints. Generally in both public and school libraries the librarian is presumed to have the professional training and experience necessary for meeting complaints.

As may be expected, the largest group of patron and parental complaints reported in this study (about 50 per cent) involved "morals" and profanity (table 10). Typical complaints came from a grandfather who demanded the removal of a book for fear "nice young girls" like his granddaughter would read it, and from middle-aged ladies who murmured about language or morality to assuage their guilt for having read a risqué book. Despite the late Senator Joseph McCarthy's campaign, the program against "un-American" books and authors conducted by the American Legion, the activities of the Tenney Committee and its successors, and the controversy over UNESCO and United Nations materials in Pasadena and Los Angeles, no increase in patron complaints on political grounds was noted. They account for only 22 per cent of the specific objections reported. It is a source of wonder to librarians that politically-oriented book banning campaigns generate so much heat when there seems to be no widespread public anxiety on this score.

Criticisms of library holdings also include requests for the addition of material. In comparison with demands for withdrawals, however, they are insignificant, and most of them lie outside the realm of the controversial. One public librarian did report complaints from members of right extremist organizations that their publications were not available in the library. Another reported pressure from a Communist for the inclusion of Communist literature. Both demands were rejected on grounds that the libraries concerned were not affluent enough to afford the materials necessary to "balance" such acquisitions. Larger systems sometimes accept gifts of political periodicals or pamphlets and, in the case of periodicals, put at least the latest issue on display. Most libraries identify such partisan materials with a gift stamp. One librarian matter-of-factly reported

TABLE 10

Grounds For Objections To Books In Public And
School Libraries

(Percentages)

GROUNDS FOR OBJECTIONS	SCHOOL LIBRARIES	PUBLIC LIBRARIES	TOTAL, PUBLIC AND SCHOOL LIBRARIES
Politics	29	16	22
Sex/obscenity	28	44	38
Profanity	10	12	11
Race, religion	7	8	8
"Controversial" or "unsuitable"	11	7	8
Literary merit	7	8	7
Other	8	5	6
Number of respondents	95	132	227

that she also finds the gift stamp a useful device for all controversial publications, donated or not.

Librarians with more generous budgets may accede to such requests. A branch head in a large county library system ruefully reported buying a scurrilously anti-Semitic book under pressure from a member of a Pro-America club. Since the person who demanded that the book be bought had reported keen interest in the volume among members of her club, the librarian anticipated high demand. Actually, it was never checked out. After a time it was taken off the open shelves and put behind the front desk. "At least," this librarian remarked, "if anybody complains that we are not giving all sides of the question, we can show that it's in the catalog."

No marked difference in the pattern of individual complaints is apparent among the various communities included in the study. Reports from librarians in cities which have had publicized book episodes differ in no significant way from those of their colleagues in cities where no such episodes have occurred. The existence of extremist groups or a press which campaigns against certain books or authors has a marked effect on the librarian's own attitudes toward controversial material, but has very little bearing on the kind or number of patron complaints. Nor is the pattern related to size or type of population, although two public librarians believe that their comparative freedom from complaints can be explained by the low educational level of their respective communities. "These people seem to be used to the earthy treatment," was the way one summed up the situation.

Librarians handle individual complaints in a variety of ways. One approach might be characterized as philosophical (or "long-suffering"). At the other extreme is the reactive and restrictive method epitomized by librarians who say, "I just put a book that is complained about away for a while" or, more rarely, "I just burn them." One of the respondents in this latter group went on, in a rather self-pitying way, to ask "Did you ever try to burn a book? It's *very* difficult."

We shall have more to say about the consequences of the various ways of meeting patron complaints, but in passing, a third orientation should be noted. This was one in which the respondent went out of his way to assure the interviewer that there were no public complaints about the holdings of his institution. Such reports were most often made by school administrators or school librarians. In nearly every instance the respondent (or someone else in the same institution) would also emphasize that, in effect, "We have no complaints because we see to it that there is nothing to complain about." Two-thirds of the school personnel reporting "no complaints" have restrictive attitudes toward book selection. No school official or librarian reported "many" complaints, whereas eleven public librarians believed that they did have "many." Concepts such as "many" or "few" are highly relative, of course, and this discrepancy may stem from differences in philosophy as well as from differences in objective situations. More public than school librarians spoke about complaints in the manner of one discussing the daily routine; and unlike school librarians, most public librarians who reported "no complaints" did not have restrictive attitudes toward book selection.

Sixteen patron complaints were recalled as having become matters of official discussion (or controversy) within the ninety-one circulating units covered in the study. Whoever received these complaints referred them to someone else in the institution and they were then taken under advisement, generally by more than one person. Typically the referrals were upward in the institutional hierarchy —a staff member discussing the matter with the head librarian or principal, or, even more frequently, a head librarian taking it up with the board. The majority of complaints thus referred were of a political nature, involving UNESCO, United Nations, other international-relations materials, or the political sympathies or affiliations of an author. Two developed from religious considerations, both of them centering around Paul Blanshard's book *American Freedom and Catholic Power,* but for opposite reasons. One patron borrowed all available copies, "lost," and then paid for them. Another patron accused the librarian of being a Communist because his request for thirty copies of the book, which he wished the librarian to distribute among certain of his friends and acquaintances, was not acted upon.

Ten of the sixteen complaints which reached the level of institutional discussion came from individuals who claimed, or were assumed, to represent organized groups. Eleven of the sixteen occurred in communities where the existence of extremist groups was noted by the respondents. In fact, only one community where extremist groups were reported did *not* have at least one complaint which had developed into an institutional problem. In only three communities where no extremist groups were reported had any patron complaints developed into institutional problems.

The same holds true of complaints originating with staff members within a school or library system: they are most likely to be elevated to the level of institutional discussion in communities where there are extremist groups. This is not to say that respondents assumed that these complaints were sparked by extremist organizations. On the contrary, only two were clearly linked with such groups; two others were suspected of a connection with "some fringe group." Apparently the mere presence of an extremist group in the community is conducive to the elevation of a complaint to institutional discussion.

COMMUNITY CONFLICTS AND PUBLIC EPISODES

During the field work of this study only one librarian or school administrator participating in it directly experienced a controversy over books. Judging from press and personal reports, very few of their colleagues elsewhere in the state were so involved during this half year. Two institutions, however, continued to be subjected to long standing and highly publicized pressures.

Book-centered controversies rarely fit neatly into a typology, but for discussion purposes it is convenient to divide them into two categories. *Community conflicts* involve major segments of the population and receive extensive publicity both within the community and outside it. *Public episodes* are generally known within the community but do not involve major segments of the population.

There have been two book-centered community conflicts in the state since the end of World War II. One took place in a city included in this study, the other did not. Both were so well publicized that to describe them anonymously would be a pointless fiction. The first of these received nationwide publicity. In 1952 the board of education and the school superintendent in the Los Angeles public system were replaced, after a heated battle, on the grounds that the schools' treatment of the United Nations, and of UNESCO in particular, was not education but indoctrination. The attack is assumed to have originated with right extremist groups, and eventually it acquired the support of a number of civic and business groups in the city as well as of the Los Angeles *Times* and other newspapers. The new board and superintendent saw to it that all UNESCO and much United Nations material was removed from the school libraries and dropped from the curriculum. The official resolution of the board (August 18, 1952) specified "permanent withdrawal" of one UNESCO publication only and excluded adherence to any "UNESCO program," although leaving teaching "about UNESCO" to the schools. Our Los Angeles respondents reported that the intentions and consequences of this ambiguous declaration were far more restrictive than the wording suggests. A subsequent board and administration not only continued to act on this mandate, but expanded it to cover all "un-American" materials, including some of Dorothy Canfield Fisher's books.

Since the material thus removed had to be replaced, and since (went the argument) Los Angeles schools are supported by local taxpayers, the natural substitution was Los Angeles history and its current industrial and commercial development.

The 150 professional librarians in the school library system found themselves in a state of confusion as one directive pertaining to policy or to particular books or authors succeeded another. These directives were often, and as a matter of principle, delivered orally. Some were formulated extemporaneously to a single librarian who had telephoned headquarters with a question, or to a group of librarians at a meeting. The result was that librarians in the various schools were never certain as to what was "permissible" at any given moment. What may have appeared to the public as a conflict settled within a few months became, for the school librarians in the Los Angeles system, a chronic episode which lasted for more than five years.[1]

The field work of this study coincided with the Los Angeles school board election campaign of 1957. Despite announcements and descriptions of the study's objectives in professional journals and bulletins, and formal clearance with the office of the superintendent, the interviewers were sometimes hard put to convince school administrators, and occasionally a school librarian, that the study was in no way connected with the campaign. The observation was made that the results would be "biased" because of the election's heat—meaning, presumably, that school personnel would feel more free to speak negatively about the board than they otherwise would. As a matter of fact, they did speak more freely. Some preliminary discussions had been held in the city many months before the election. At that time, restrictive book selection and distribution practices were described as measures designed to "protect the school board," and the interviewer was assured that a member of the system had the choice of going along or resigning. Some of these persons were interviewed again later, when there appeared at least a strong possibility that the two most restrictive incumbents of the board would be replaced. At this time they not only reported their disagreement with board policies in some detail, but described how they had attempted to oppose or circumvent them. The point of this observation is not that the respondents were hypocrites or opportunists, but rather that opposition to the board was being expressed, analyzed, and documented in open public discussion. This free debate in turn served as a releasing mechanism for persons within the system.

The second book-centered community conflict also developed from an attack on school libraries. It took place in 1954 in the Tamalpais Union High School District, Mill Valley. Unlike the rapidly growing and highly heterogeneous city of Los Angeles, this is a small, middle and upper-middle class area. Many writers, artists and musicians, wealthy retired persons, business men, and professional people live in this community. The controversy centered on fifteen allegedly obscene or subversive books, a list which bears a striking resemblance to one used by extremist groups in Texas and elsewhere. Eight of the fifteen books were listed in the 1947 or 1952 editions of the *Wilson High School Catalog,* a publication held in high repute by librarians and educators throughout the country. Of these, four were either "especially" or "doubly" recommended.

This campaign was apparently initiated by one woman, but the county grand jury, and several organized groups in the community quickly became involved, followed by extensive publicity both within and outside the state. A climax was reached during a public meeting of the school district's board of trustees. School librarians and others who were present reported that the tension was so great that the audience screamed when a door slammed in the rear of the room. Neither librarians nor school officials could predict the outcome of this meeting. While it was in progress many participants believed that the campaigner had lined up heavy support from voluntary organizations and community leaders. Actually, of the twenty-five persons who spoke from the floor at the open meeting, nineteen opposed banning the books in question. When one of the members of the board read a strong statement on the freedom to read, concluding with a decision to retain all of the books in question, the hall rang with applause.

Library or book-centered episodes which did not develop into serious community conflicts have been more numerous. Still, only eight were reported by the two hundred persons participating in the study. One of these took place in the early 1930's; six occurred between the end of World War II and 1954; and only one has developed since that time. Judging from the press and from reports made to the Intellectual Freedom Committee of the California Library Association, this pattern seems fairly typical for the state as a whole.

To describe the eight episodes in brief: five stemmed from political objections, two were mainly religious (Roman Catholic), and one was a combined attack against "subversion and pornography." Two county library systems had two each, one municipal library was involved in two, and two school systems each reported one incident. The two religious complaints which developed into episodes originated with library board members; three of those that were politically-centered seem also to have originated with board members, although possibly under pressure from organizations in the community. One, an attack against library sponsorship of an American Heritage Program, was initiated by a right extremist group. Two were instigated by people whose lists of authors and books and whose objectives bear a striking resemblance to those of the Minute Women. (One was the woman who initiated the Tamalpais High School conflict and later tried her wings in another community.) The controversy of the early 1930's, centered on John Steinbeck's *Grapes of Wrath,* is said to have been started by the county board of supervisors. In addition to these eight more or less clear-cut episodes, one other institution in the sample has been subjected to continual attack since World War II. This is the public library already mentioned on which pressure is exerted by a coalition of press, extremist organizations and a member of the board of trustees.

Only four of the more than two hundred persons interviewed in the study had first-hand experience with these episodes: the head of a county system, the head of a municipal system, a school administrator, and a director of libraries in a city school system. In the county system, other staff members were informed but did not participate. The attacks focused on adult education programs and the competence of the chief executive to have the final say in book selection. In the municipal system which became involved in an episode, staff members were informed but not drawn in. The librarian of one of the schools where a public episode was reported by the school administrator had not held the post at the time when it occurred. Librarians in the school system where the director of libraries encountered the neighboring crusader were neither particularly well-informed nor disturbed by the situation. The implication was that they would trust "the boss" to take care of these matters in the best possible way. Both exposure and involvement tended to be at the top.

Do the conflicts and episodes which were settled by the imposition of restrictive measures have anything in common? Are there differences between them which may help explain why one is played out in a low key while the other becomes a threat to community equilibrium?

The Los Angeles school board members and superintendent who were under attack are said to have been neither vigorous nor united in defense of their policies. Moreover, the more powerful newspapers of the area sided with the attackers. In this case the conflict resulted in a defeat for the administration and its policies. The Mill Valley board and administration, on the other hand, united in a vigorous affirmation of their policies. The San Francisco *Chronicle,* which is widely read in the district, supported their stand, and, according to many observers, both the concept of intellectual freedom and the position of those who support it were strengthened in the process. It would take more examples than this to draw firm conclusions, but one might venture the hypothesis that a combination of defensiveness on the part of those attacked and press opposition leads to capitulation to pressures, whereas affirmation of existing policy by those under attack, and press support of their policies, combine to defeat the attackers.

This hypothesis is supported by the example of the community which has not had one isolable episode but is subject to continual pressures for the removal of books or other restrictive measures. Here the public library administration under attack has maintained a forthright and undefensive stand in support of its policies. The local press is on the side of the would be censors. Civic leaders look upon this newspaper as "crackpot" or "extremist." Its statements and restatements of a restrictive point of view, however, may account for the fact that the issues are not settled, but continue to be renewed, first over one book and then another. Or, in terms of our hypothesis, the administration which is under attack for having policies that are too liberal cannot achieve a clear-cut victory because the press supports those who attack its policies.

Among the eight episodes which did not become community conflicts we find certain common factors which may have helped to control them. In all cases, the administrator whose library policies were under attack matter-of-factly supported them; in none of the eight did the press favor the attackers although, to be sure, they did not give aid or comfort to the administrators being attacked either. Five of these episodes were settled without alteration in policy or a change in personnel; in the other three, the boards advised the administrators to compromise.

Few of the eight episodes were known to librarians or school administrators outside of the community in which they took place. Some were not even known to persons in other institutions within the community. School system personnel in the community where the municipal librarian had recently been embroiled in a publicized controversy with his board, for example, seem to have paid little attention to it or to a similar occurrence a few years earlier. The county librarian, however, whose offices were in the same community, was well informed.

The situation was different in the two community conflicts. Despite the fact that one took place more than five years before this study was undertaken and the other well over three, the majority of respondents throughout the state not only knew of them but brought them into their discussions spontaneously. As we shall see, a number of both school and public libraries reacted to these conflicts with precautionary or restrictive measures. These actions, with very few exceptions, were initiated within the school or library system, without impetus from the local citizenry. Paradoxically the Mill Valley conflict, which was a victory for the freedom to read, was cited as a reason for restrictive practices throughout the state more than the Los Angeles conflict, which was a defeat for freedom in the schools. One explanation for Mill Valley's greater impact may be found in the image and activities of the woman who set it off.

THE CENSOR OVER THE SHOULDER

Undaunted by her defeat in Mill Valley, Mrs. X expanded her original list of books and began to campaign throughout the state. Her face was added to her lists as part of her public image when she appeared on Edward R. Murrow's television program. The purpose of this program was to illustrate the kinds of pressures being brought to bear upon the Los Angeles schools. Along with Mrs. X, Murrow interviewed several school librarians (silhouetted for anonymity), a deputy superintendent of the Los Angeles schools, and the Los

Angeles County Librarian. The many librarians who saw it felt that except for the remarks of the County Librarian the program did them little credit. The highly dramatized nervousness and anxiety of the librarians, in their opinion, made Mrs. X, by contrast, appear to be both more persuasive and more attractive.

Strengthened by this not too unfavorable publicity (which was certainly not the intent of the program), Mrs. X then went about laying the groundwork for the introduction into the state legislature of a bill which would have allowed almost any degree of censorship in school libraries that local school boards might wish to exercise. The bill, unnoticed by librarians, was unanimously passed by the senate. Later it was soundly defeated in the assembly, after several voluntary organizations and the leaders of the two state professional associations of libraries had become alerted. In the spring of 1957 it was reintroduced, along with several other censorship bills, with substantially the same wording and the same cast of characters. This time "Mrs. X's bill," watered down to the requirement that local school boards prescribe a procedure for the selection and review of all texts and library books, passed both houses but was pocket-vetoed by the Governor.[2]

Mrs. X is widely deprecated by librarians as an emotionally unstable publicity seeker. Yet her name comes quickly to the lips of school and public librarians alike, and her original list of books and authors is well known. One librarian recognized it in the hands of a stranger at the opposite end of a reading room. When plans for the present study were described at a meeting of librarians nearly two years after Mrs. X's initial crusade, one of the first remarks made in the discussion was, "You ought to psychoanalyze her." This was followed, from another part of the room, with, "And librarians, too." Both of these remarks evoked murmurs of agreement from the audience, and taken in juxtaposition they can be interpreted to mean: we fully recognize that there is something irrational in Mrs. X's behavior, and we are concerned because it evokes something irrational in us.

If one opens an inner ear to the undertones of the interviews, the conclusion is inescapable that Mrs. X represents an approach to book selection which librarians find not only distressing but frightening, and they sense that their distress and fright are sharply out of proportion to her "objective" influence. Why this woman, whose campaigns have been marked by failure, has had such an impact is a question that cannot be definitively answered here. But it is tempting to speculate.

The "situation," as Mrs. X presents it, looks like this: there is danger—immorality and subversion—in books. Something must be done about it. One of the places to begin is in the school libraries and she, an educated, devoted mother, is obviously the ideal kind of person to undertake the task. Librarians see her furthering this particular cause at the moment but capable of shifting readily to any other—United Nations, group dynamics, fluoridation, or report cards—which might appear more rewarding. Her campaign, ambiguous in itself, triggers ambiguities in those she is directly or indirectly attacking. One respondent summed it up simply: "It's pathetic, but just let somebody raise an American flag over an issue or call forth visions of protecting the American home, and people don't think straight about the heart of the issue."

Hypocritical or not, Mrs. X takes a stand; and the air of conviction with which she does so in itself evokes uncertainties. On the one hand, it is good to speak up for one's principles, as Mrs. X appears to do. On the other hand, unless one is directly attacked isn't it better to keep quiet? "Minor antagonisms may easily set off major disturbances today—like with that woman in Marin County. So it's best to let dead dogs lie." Like most other people, librarians find it easier to be passive than to be active. At the same time librarians are keenly aware of social issues and more idealistic than most about human progress. When they do not stand up to the Mrs. X's they may find themselves in a state of conflict. "It *is* hard to know what to do, you know. We have to serve the district. At the same time we have ideas of what goes into running a library properly, and we have to serve those ideas too."

Librarians also worry lest Mrs. X's apparent upper middle-class façade so impress her listeners that they fail to see through her. This worry may derive from the ambivalence many librarians have about their own professional, and possibly social, status. The strong pride of profession characteristic of most librarians is often matched by anxiety about public stereotypes. The men fear that they are not considered sufficiently virile. The woman ask why Bette Davis, in the motion picture, *Storm Center*, was a frustrated, dowdy and middle-aged librarian. Uneasiness about status resulting from the position of the profession of librarianship in relation to other professions enhances these more personal uncertainties. Professional prestige is in part a consequence of the status of the training institution. Schools of librarianship are generally ranked lower in the academic hierarchy and in social status than, for example, schools of medicine or law. No matter how much dignity or pride of profession may be native to or imbued in the librarian, he cannot avoid awareness of this state of affairs. Furthermore, since all librarians doing professional work are not graduates of library schools, there is much uncertainty as to how to define a "professional." Most library leaders believe that eventually all persons with professional functions will have professional training, but some nagging doubts remain about the status implications of the clerical details essential to running a library.

The ambiguities of the image of Mrs. X harbored by librarians may activate conflicts they have about their own image, in much the same way that the neurotic conflicts of two marriage partners nourish each other. The consequences for book selection policy may not be dire, but they are frequently very apparent. The conflict between conviction and doubt may encourage the librarian to turn the basically rational process of book selection into a mystique. The conflict between action and passivity can result in appeasement. Status conflicts may lead to gross overestimates of the amount of public support available for crusaders such as Mrs. X and to equally gross underestimates of the support available to those she wishes to victimize. In the words of one public librarian: ". . . irresponsible people are making all sorts of irresponsible attacks. And what's worse, presumably responsible people are doing the same sort of thing . . . by paying attention to such attacks . . ."

AN ATMOSPHERE OF CAUTION

It was not at all unusual, once the librarian had been briefed about the study, for him to jump at once into a discussion of his awareness of caution (his own or other people's) as though he had been waiting for an opportunity to unburden himself. Several felt that the study itself was a rather "courageous" enterprise (a few called it "dangerous") and asked whether there was not a possibility that "someone will clamp down." Some respondents, mainly persons on the staff level in large and highly bureaucratized school or public library systems, recalled that they had felt uneasy when they read about the study in their professional journal and hoped they would not be interviewed. In speculating about the reasons for their feelings of caution, a remark about "this day and age" was not at all infrequent, and some mention of Senator Joseph McCarthy occasionally followed, qualified by a hasty, "I know he has been discredited nationally, but around here . . ." The area "around here" was usually not clearly defined. An alternative explanation was "California has a lot of crackpots, you know." But the respondent's own community was invariably "a literate and broadminded town." There is acute awareness of the climate of opinion, but it is often sensed as something "out there," in some other part of the state.

It may indeed be true that "California has a lot of crackpots." The experiences reported by librarians who have also worked in other states suggest, however, that they are not unique to California. Every state has, or has had, its Mrs. X. The question is not the number of extremists or the nature of their campaigns, but what are the prevalent reactions to them. In this respect, Californians may react just like other people but perhaps more so, because the social changes experienced in other states to varying degrees are, in many areas of California, carried to an extreme which is scarcely conceivable to the mid-Westerner or the New Englander.

The twenty-six communities in which this study was conducted are as diverse in their social as in their geographical characteristics. There are conservative segments of "old" communities which have become more conservative in the struggle to preserve tradition against the influx of new populations. There are sizable cities—mere villages twenty years ago—with little tradition at all. There are towns long characterized by a constrictive triumvirate of press, politics and voluntary groups; and there are communities traditionally conspicuous for courageous newspapers, far-seeing public officials, and an enlightened citizenry.

If the general orientation of the press, city officials, and school and library board members on issues such as civil liberties and intellectual freedom is taken as a rough index of community climate, our sample may be separated into three groups of communities. One is restrictive; another is permissive. In between is a group which for a variety of reasons, not least being rapid economic and population change, is difficult to classify. A common-sense interpretation would suggest that the librarian living in a comparatively uninhibiting atmosphere would feel freer to select controversial materials than the librarian who lives in a constrained community. But this is not true. The

TABLE 11
Practices Regarding Controversial Material,
By Community Climate
(Percentages)

PRACTICES[1]	COMMUNITY CLIMATE		
	RESTRICTIVE	MIXED	PERMISSIVE
Habitually avoid	13	21	25[2]
Not a criterion	40	43	22
Number of respondents	62	38	55

[1] Excluding "sometimes" and "no opportunity"—see Table 14. Columns, therefore, do not total 100 per cent.
[2] Nearly all of these restrictive librarians living in permissive communities are accounted for by one city which has a centrally and firmly controlled school library system and a public library system directed by a restrictive, and for the most part non-professionally trained, headquarters staff.

most restrictive of our communities have proportionately nearly twice as many non-restrictive librarians as the most permissive (table 11). The community categories were arrived at on too impressionistic a basis to draw definite conclusions, but an analysis of the experiences and practices of librarians who live in an atmosphere charged with threats to civil liberties suggests that they are more likely to feel a sense of responsibility about such issues than are librarians in permissive communities.

More than one librarian was startled during the interviews to hear himself remark that "There's safety in numbers, you know," or "There's no better way to discourage complaints than to insist on having them in writing [in triplicate] and referring them to a committee [or series of committees]." Such statements often prompted the speaker to look at his book selection procedures in a new light. The head of a large public library asked himself whether his delegation of all book selection to a staff committee, justified on the grounds that current output demands more specialization, might not in fact have been motivated by increased circumspection. Others wondered whether the trend toward centralization was not, in fact, the result of an increase in caution rather than an administrative adjustment to growth in school or library systems.

As we have seen, neither librarians nor school administrators explained their feelings of caution by pointing to an increase of direct pressures on their institutions. What strikes them, as they look about in their communities, is not attacks on ideas but the avoidance of them. One librarian noticed that her own young son could find no answer, either in school or in the children's section of the public library, to his question, "What *is* Communism anyway?" Another believes that people feel intimidated by ideas and are, therefore, increasingly fearful of libraries. Events such as the recent last-minute change of a high school radio forum from "Communism and Capitalism in America" to "To Go Steady or Not To Go Steady," because some parents did not wish to have their children discuss the first topic in public, can be reported by nearly every observer of a local scene.

Such avoidance amounts to pressure. Most librarians deplored this state of affairs and recognized its consequences. One head of a municipal library publicly stated at a local meeting that "I thought it was not only proper but a very good thing to have books like that [a history of Russia] .... If we're going to fight communism successfully, we have to understand it." But after the meeting an acquaintance warned her to be more careful in her public utterances because one participant in the meeting had picked up the comment as an indication that the librarian was "pro-USSR." She at first shrugged off the warning and told the acquaintance, "you can make a Communist out of anybody from some comment or other," but she later observed that "the incident has made me a little more cautious." General caution, or rather, precaution, of this kind is not limited to a few persons or a few institutions. As the next chapter will show, two-thirds of the books mentioned in the interviews as controversial were initially questioned by librarians themselves (and, in school, by faculty members or administrators).

The hush which has fallen over ideological discussion is not restricted to any one political arena or subject field.[3] In talking about books or authors that have been restricted or removed from their collections, librarians had as much difficulty in remembering names and titles objected to from the right as from the left, and sometimes even references to *Little Black Sambo* and *Huckleberry Finn* were whispered. In extreme cases, librarians may live a nightmare that has strong paranoid undertones:

I have avoided buying [books about Communism] because I do not trust my own judgment. I have traveled a lot . . . I might seem dangerous to some people. They might object to what I bought . . . The public thinks they own their schools and should choose the books.

One committee of school librarians became interested in the question of restrictive pressures on their institutions at about the same time that the present study got under way. They planned a mail-questionnaire survey, and it seemed reasonable to seek some help on questionnaire construction from this study's research staff. After two consultations, the relationship was abruptly broken off, rather clearly to the dismay of the committee on orders from "higher up." The explanation offered to the committee was that, even though the study was being directed from a university, it was known to be supported by a grant from the Fund for the Republic, and "We cannot afford to get mixed up with that group."

Further evidence of how the avoidance of issues in the community at large affects the librarian's own orientation was found among a few respondents who refused to talk about the Los Angeles conflict ("I am a civil servant and might incriminate myself") and among persons who objected to note-taking in the interviews ("In this day and age you don't like people taking down what you say"). Several were reluctant to express their opinions about the Murrow program with Mrs. X and the blindfolded librarians or about *Storm Center* because they are "controversial." As a branch head in a municipal system expressed it: "You have to be careful what you say to people when you have a public job." Two other public librarians decided not to attend a public meeting addressed by Mrs. X. They thought it best not to let themselves be seen—and identified as librarians—by her.

SEMANTIC CONVENIENCES

In the 1930's new or alien political ideologies, including nazism and fascism as well as communism were identified, defined and discussed, not only by scholars but in the press, on the radio, and in schools and colleges. Those who opposed such ideologies could sometimes cite chapter and verse explaining why they considered them dangerous. Today nondemocratic ideologies evoke anxiety. There is worry about the fact that they exist, but no very concrete idea of what in particular makes them dangerous. Anything which seems potentially troublesome is simply dumped into the witches' brew labeled "controversial" or "un-American." A book or an author complained about by any person for any reason may, quite legitimately, be called controversial. The fact that this term can be applied to a work is often taken to mean that it is "bad." The pros and cons of controversy are forgotten in the stress on the *con* in controversial.

School is supposed to provide the basic equipment and information necessary for responsible citizenship . . . . I suppose it's probably heresy, but that's why I think it's important to teach about Communism and have books about Communism . . . . Maybe the reason people are so excitable today [about the threat of Communism] is because they don't have the [intellectual] equipment and information necessary for dispassionate, mature behavior . . .

The tendency toward blanket rather than specific criticism is reflected in the nature of public concern with library books, or at least that part of public concern which appears to be organized. Authors, rather than works, are indicted, and the indictment is often general and undocumented. "Usually there's really no proof . . . . Just being accused seems to be equated with guilt." Such imprecision is at times confounded by witting or unwitting obliqueness. Many complaints, for example, focus ostensibly on pornography or obscenity but may very well spring from motives or prejudices having little to do with either. Such tactics are particularly convenient when the real motives or prejudices of the objector might be interpreted as in themselves un-American (e.g., racial or religious prejudices). They sometimes result in a kind of shadowboxing between the alleged prejudices of the objector and the susceptibilities of the librarian. Librarians recognize that however well developed their critical sense may be in literary matters, their personal sensibilities are often near the surface where they can be tapped all too easily. Some have had to work particularly hard to overcome their personal distaste for the sexual material common to much contemporary writing, especially when it seems to be introduced more for sales appeal purposes than as an intrinsic part of what the author has to say. It is with a sense of irony that they realize that some would-be censors simply utilize sex passages as a pretext. Many books are ignored altogether which are fully as "erotic" or "pornographic" or "obscene" as those which are attacked, and an examination of the controversial books often shows that they have something other than sex in common, such as a sympathetic treatment of race relations.

Similar examples of displacement are apparent in attacks ostensibly made on political grounds. Many books, at least as sympathetic to Communist ideas as Pearl Buck's and Eslanda Robeson's *American Argument* is presumed to be, appear in the publications lists of the past fifteen years. But it is this one book, suggesting a working relationship between members of two races, which has been singled out for attack by library critics. Objections to UNESCO materials in school libraries may have similar origins. The stated complaint is that these materials are un-American because they are too sympathetic to Communist countries, or because they imply the necessity of surrendering some of America's sovereignty. A closer look reveals that they also present the lowering of racial barriers in a favorable light.

It is not only the word "controversial" which is laden with emotional affect. "To censor," in all of its variations, and the word "pressure" are disliked or avoided by many of our respondents. "Why," asked a county library department head, "do you keep referring to pressure groups? To the public librarian, all groups are pressure groups." Words deriving from "to censor" were avoided not only in connection with a given librarian's own practice of book selection (sometimes clearly censorial) but in more abstract discussions of library philosophy. Librarians "screen," "select," and "guide." As a librarian in a large municipal library put it, "We haven't been censoring but we have been 'conservative'. After all, this is a conservative community, and that is how parents here want it to be." But, ruminated a few, when we take actual or potential controversiality into account in the screening, selecting and guiding, are we not indeed censoring? Others do not ask; the word is avoided. Selection which by-passes the controversial is justified by use of the same terms of opprobrium used by would-be censors. In speaking of contemporary works of fiction, one municipal librarian reported her views as follows: "If they are out-and-out obscene they should not be in the library at all . . . [but] 'touchy' books . . . have a legitimate place in the public library . . . . [However] since some people do find them objectionable, they are kept on reserve." Or, as another public librarian said: "You have to screen the organizations that want to put on exhibits because you don't want any 'neo-Communists' in the library. You also have to make sure there is nothing in the exhibits that might be considered controversial."

Such remarks, which were by no means infrequent in the interviews, were often followed by some such observation as "this means that we now have a good deal of freedom, you see." What these librarians seem to mean is that institutions having "conservative" policies are not as likely to attract public attention. Public attention sometimes results in community controversy and community controversy sometimes results in restrictive measures. Then you *really* have restrictions. This is the same line of reasoning that led some of our respondents to accuse those who have been involved in public episodes of using the wrong language. If, say these critics, the administrator or the school librarian had said, "We've called those books in for review," rather than, "We've withdrawn them," the segment of the public which is opposed to restrictive practices would not have become aroused, the restrictors would have been pacified, and no episode would have developed.

Some librarians have adopted an even more positivistic semantic philosophy, much of which is formally sanctioned in library policy and training. There is little talk of avoiding the controversial, or even of being conservative; rather, library materials must be in "good taste," they must be "suitable" or they must be "appropriate." In school libraries or library systems, the equivalent is likely to be the irreproachable statement, "Our materials must supplement the curriculum." The less sanguine school librarian adds, "and everyone knows that the curriculum, after all the commotion about textbooks, is pure!"

FOOTNOTES

[1] The relationship between the school board and the office of the superintendent in library matters is summarized only briefly here—the full story would require a separate study of major proportions. It should be noted, however, that since the completion of the field work of this study, another school board election has been held and the two most restrictive members of the board have been replaced. Reports indicate that a major liberation of book selection policy is under way, and the possibility is not remote that the full history of this controversy will now be told. It was predicted, incidentally, both in Los Angeles and elsewhere, that the then incumbent school board would prevent the study from being conducted because "it does not like" the Ford Foundation, and, in particular, it does not like the Fund for the Republic; further-

more, it does not like to have any kind of outsider "interfere" with local affairs. (If the Board did take notice of the study, it was a well kept secret.)

[2] State law already requires school board "adoption" of texts and library books for the elementary level; a 1947 revision of the state education code also requires that district boards "adopt" school library books distributed under contract by the county library and bought out of funds dispensed by the county school superintendent.

[3] Nor is it by any means limited to California. To take just one example, Marya Mannes reports ("Theater: Fancy Fare and Good Home Cooking," *The Reporter,* December 12, 1957): "There was quite a ruckus, you may remember, when the New York Public Library withdrew its sponsorship of the program (reference is to *Faces of War,* written and produced on CBS Television by Harding Lemay—including readings from Euripides, Shakespeare, Cervantes and Twain) in a last-minute spasm of alarm at being involved in a 'sensitive area,' an argument for peace being not, as one trustee was quoted as saying, 'in the public interest.' It was public interest, in fact, that brought the library back to its fundamental senses: the board expressed regret at its withdrawal and indicated a new awareness of the powers of TV for good."

ABOUT THE AUTHOR—Marjorie Fiske (Lowenthal) is a research psychologist whose research efforts have encompassed a broad spectrum, and the environmental settings in which they were pursued cover an exceedingly wide range. She has been Director of Field Studies for the National Federation of Business and Professional Women's Clubs (1941–43), and a research director for Columbia's Bureau of Applied Social Research (1943–46). She has also been employed as a research psychologist for an advertising agency. From 1949–53 she was with the United States Department of State. From 1956–58 she was a lecturer and research director of the School of Librarianship, University of California at Berkeley. Since 1958 she has been Director of the Adult Development Research Program at the Langley Porter Neuropsychiatric Institute in San Francisco, and she is also a professor in residence, Department of Psychiatry, University of California, School of Medicine, San Francisco.

Born in Massachusetts, Mrs. Fiske (Lowenthal) received her B.A. from Mt. Holyoke and her M.A. in 1937 from Columbia. She also studied at Harvard and the New School for Social Research. Her diverse interests are illustrated in her published works, *Book Selection and Censorship* (1959) and *Lives in Distress* (1964); and as co-author of *The Focussed Interview* (1956), *Mass Persuasion* (1946), and *Aging and Mental Disorder in San Francisco* (1967); and many articles in professional journals. She is a Fellow of the American Psychological Association, the American Sociological Association, and the Gerontological Society.

The University of Massachusetts Case

These news items from Library Journal *present a case which shows the university library in political terms. The interests in the situation are the librarian, library staff, the faculty, the administration, its regents and eventually the courts and the professional library association. The case reveals several issues, among which are questions regarding the right of a university administration to, in effect, replace a head librarian, and faculty dissatisfaction with library services. It is the latter issue which may be most significant for librarians, for while the incident or the outcome at Massachusetts may be unusual, the very basic differences which divide a faculty and its library may be quite typical of the university today. Frequently when increased and different needs from clientele put pressures on the academic library, there is an incapacity to respond in terms satisfactory to clientele requirements. While the faculty can only reflect its frustration in the face of inadequacy, it is the academic librarian who must somehow fashion the response appropriate to contemporary needs. This calls for a basic confrontation with the role, the purpose and the mission of academic librarianship.*

LIBRARIAN FIGHTS DEMOTION MOVE IN UNIV. OF MASSACHUSETTS SHAKEUP

University Librarian Hugh Montgomery, who has directed the library of the University of Massachusetts since 1952, is taking the University to court to fight his demotion from chief administrative officer to an assignment which consists of working on research and planning projects assigned to him by the newly created Director of University Libraries, a post presently filled on an acting basis by David Clay, an assistant professor in the philosophy department.

On September 21, Montgomery reports, he was summoned to the office of Provost Oswald Tippo, and informed of the change. No specific charges were made against him or reasons given for his reassignment, but there were references made to several personnel problems which had allegedly existed in the library over a period of time. It was suggested that, since he had accumulated a considerable amount of annual leave, he take a vacation to think things over. He was also asked to provide the administration with a statement of the role he expected to take in the future in the library.

The report of a faculty senate library committee and a faculty library building committee evidently figured in the administration's decision. A not very clearly defined climate of hostility is indicated by Montgomery's statement to Lj that

"Members of the professional staff have for some months been concerned over the apparent willingness of the University Administration, and especially Provost Oswald Tippo, to press faculty demands and requirements beyond the limits of the present staffing."

Critical tensions between librarians and faculty are also evident in a document adopted by the Board of Trustees on October 22. Document 67-018, or "Library Reorganization Document," described the necessity for great expansion of the University's library programs, especially in view of the new medical school and the recently established Boston campus. Increases in graduate study and faculty research were also cited as conditions pressing for reorganization.

Doubts concerning the abilities of the present library staff seem clearly indicated in references to the need for a staff which can "command the respect" of the faculty; one suggestion made in the "Library Reorganization Document" is that members of the faculty be assigned part-time to book selection, "considering the scholarly qualities needed in a selection staff." Future staffing needs are seen as partially being fulfilled by recruiting graduates who would receive on the job training in library techniques and procedures "while engaged in advanced study in relevant academic disciplines such as foreign languages, history, and the sciences."

Following the initial announcement of Mont-

SOURCE: Reprinted from *Library Journal*, 91 (Dec. 1, 1966), pp. 5914–5916, 92 (Jan. 1, 1967), p. 42, (April 15, 1967), p. 1557, (July, 1967), p. 2496, and 93 (Jan. 15, 1968), p. 142. "Copyright ©R. R. Bowker Co."

gomery's reassignment, nine members of his staff had a hearing with the provost which lasted two hours, during which the nine presented their opinions, but received no satisfactory clarification. The nine then wrote to President John W. Lederle expressing their dissatisfaction with the provost's lack of response, especially in the area of "problems of personnel management." Three days later, the president received a letter from Morrison C. Haviland, associate librarian, and Robert M. Agard, assistant librarian, commenting on the suddenness of the directive relieving Montgomery of responsibility as "without advance warning to the University Librarian or opportunity for discussion or orderly process." The letter also noted that the new acting director of university libraries had not yet put in an appearance as scheduled. The letter alluded also to uncertainty ... "prejudicial to good morale among the administrative officers of the University Library."

Montgomery engaged legal counsel and met with Provost Tippo on September 27, but unsatisfied by what he characterized as "nothing but double talk," he proceeded to file a petition for a declaratory judgment to "establish my right to employment by the university and its officials of proper legal procedures when duties are to be removed, redefined, or otherwise altered."

Legal complications appear unavoidable, as the University bases its actions on legislation passed in 1956 and 1961 to give the Trustees broad powers of appointment and dismissal of employees; Montgomery, on the other hand, sees protection in a Massachusetts law which provides civil service protection to all veterans, whether they are formally under civil service or not. This protection extends to barring dismissal or reassignment of a veteran without establishing sufficient cause. And considering that in Massachusetts the civil service authorities are notably eager to extend their activities into new areas, and have a rather lopsided record in favor of employee complaints, this is potentially only the beginning of a very considerable legal struggle.

Library Journal, December 1, 1966, pp. 5914–5916.

MONTGOMERY DEMOTION CASE UNDER MASS. L.A. SCRUTINY

The Massachusetts Library Association has moved to investigate the sudden removal of University of Massachusetts librarian Hugh Montgomery from his position as library director (Lj, December 1, 1966, p. 5914–5916) and the handing over of his responsibilities to an assistant professor in the philosophy department. A committee of leading public and university librarians was appointed by MLA president Rita Steele, librarian of the Fairhaven Public Library, to make recommendations for possible action by the association.

The committee includes chairman Fr. Brendan Connolly, S. J., director of libraries at Boston College; Gustave A. Harrer, director of Boston University Libraries; Joseph S. Komidar, librarian of Tufts University; Richard W. Morin, college librarian of Dartmouth College (acting as liaison in this case for the New England Library Association); Lawrence Wikander, librarian of the Forbes Library, Northampton; and Philip J. McNiff, director of the Boston Public Library.

The committee has met, and agreed that the available facts pointed to an inexplicably precipitate action by the administrative officers of the University of Massachusetts. It was further agreed that MLA president Rita Steele be asked to notify the University of the Committee's charge and its intention to investigate the matter more fully.

Meanwhile, another informal group of librarians from the western Massachusetts area had visited Provost Oswald Tippo at the University. They reported that Tippo claimed the reorganization move had been under consideration for some time, that the University could not accept the right of any outside group to influence its policies, and that in any case, further comment was declined because of the lawsuit which Montgomery is attempting to bring against U. of Mass.

Governor John Volpe came into the picture when he received a letter signed by 55 percent of the professional staff and 75 percent of the nonprofessional staff, expressing support of their former chief and asking the governor's assistance. The letter, signed by 71 staff members, emphasized the deterioration of morale at all levels of the library staff as a result of the University's action.

At least one high-ranking member of the staff is actively searching for another position, and others have expressed anxiety about future arbitrary actions by the administration. The recruitment of library talent to man the university's expanding facilities is seen as being severely hampered by the unfavorable impression created by the whole conduct of the incident.

Montgomery's suit against the University was transferred from the local courts to Springfield to expedite a decision. On December 5, at a hearing in Springfield, lawyers for the University asked that the case be thrown out on two grounds: That the Trustees of the University are not accountable to anyone for their action; and that administrative recourse has not been exhausted.

The judge refused to throw out the case, and another hearing has been scheduled for early in January.

Library Journal, January 1, 1967, p. 42.

MONTGOMERY CASE GOES TO COURT

The suit of University Librarian Hugh Montgomery, against Oswald Tippo, Provost of the University of Massachusetts; David Clay, Acting Director of Libraries; and the Trustees of the University was heard on March 20, before Judge Donald E. MacCauley of the Massachusetts Superior Court, sitting in Northampton. Montgomery was seeking a declaratory judgment to the effect that he was illegally deprived of his position when the university created the new position of Director of Libraries, and reassigned him to duties of an archival and research nature.

As reported in *Library Journal* (December 1, 1966, p. 5914), Montgomery has been working since September 1966 to bring the university to court and force a reversal of its action. During that time, the Massachusetts Library Association appointed a committee to observe the proceedings and make recommendations to the association; members of the staff of the library have petioned the governor, and widespread interest has developed in the case, which is essentially hinged on the question of whether an institution can fire or transfer or in any way change the responsibilities of an administrator without establishing cause. Montgomery has tenure and claims that, as a veteran, Massachusetts law affords him civil service protection against arbitrary reassignment.

A reliable source has reported that the matter dates back to an earlier study made of the university library, at which time recommendations were made for changes in the administrative structure to strengthen it for the university library's next major period of growth. The recommendations of that study are thought to be the basis of the university's action against Montgomery, but they have not been made public to date, and were not brought forward by university officials at the March 20 hearing.

The arguments for the university's position were stated by Special Assistant to the Attorney General Joseph Bartlett, Jr. They were:

1) Title and salary are the essentials of a position. If these are not changed, one still has the same position.

2) The legislature, by the "autonomy" or "freedom bill," has given the trustees of the university complete control over professional employees, although clerical and custodial workers have certain protection. Veteran's protection does not apply under this ruling.

3) No one can have a vested interest in a public position. If it were necessary to have the employee's agreement for any change in duties, it would hamstring administration.

Attorney Raymond Cross, speaking for Montgomery, declared that if all the duties of a position were taken away, and entirely new ones of an inferior level were substituted, the employee had been in fact relieved of his position even if title and salary remained. He cited material to show that the legislature customarily protected veterans and that they were so protected at the University.

Attorney Bartlett, speaking for the university, requested then that the suit be dismissed, but the judge rejected the motion and said that there were appropriate grounds for a declaratory judgment and witnesses were called.

University Librarian Hugh Montgomery testified as to the nature of his present and previous duties; his remarks were confirmed by Morrison Haviland, associate librarian for administration. Record books of the trustees showed no indication that Montgomery had been notified in advance of his changed status, or that the matter had even come before the trustees before the action of Provost Tippo in reassigning Montgomery, the earliest official records having to do with library reorganization being dated October 5.

The court ordered that briefs be submitted by both parties to the suit, concerning the powers of the trustees under the statutes; Judge MacCauley will review the transcript of the case and the briefs and provide a ruling on the applicability of the hearing procedures for Montgomery. Final action is not expected for another six to eight weeks.

Library Journal, April 15, 1967, p. 1557.

MASS. UNIV. WINS COURT FIGHT AGAINST LIBRARIAN

University Librarian Hugh Montgomery of the University of Massachusetts lost his court fight on June 5 against the trustees of the University, Provost Oswald Tippo, and Professor David Clay, who had been appointed to the position of Acting Director of University Libraries and given responsibilities formerly exercised by Montgomery (LJ, December 1, 1966, p. 5914; April 15, 1967, p. 1557).

The decision was handed down in Northampton, Massachusetts on June 5 by Hampshire Superior Court Judge Donald M. MacCauley in a ruling that held the trustees to have acted within the powers conferred on them by Massachusetts law. According to the ruling, they were empowered by law to: reorganize the university's library system; create a new position and title of Director of University Libraries and establish the descriptive job specifications for the new position; change the duties of the University Librarian; and appoint an acting director for the new position, pending the search for a permanent director.

Montgomery had based his legal action on a Massachusetts law which assures job tenure to veterans in civil service, but the court held that since his salary and title remained unchanged, his tenure rights had not been violated.

Montgomery has indicated his intention to resign from the staff of the University of Massachusetts library to accept another position. There has been no statement to date from the Massachusetts Library Association, which had taken an interest in the case and had appointed a committee to investigate it.

Library Journal, July, 1967, p. 2496.

MASS. COMMITTEE RAPS UNIVERSITY

The University of Massachusetts is criticized in the report of a special committee of the Massachusetts Library Association for "administrative procedure which fails . . . to safeguard the dignity and professional reputation of librarians as members of an academic community" in a case involving the stripping of administrative responsibilities from University Librarian Hugh Montgomery late in 1966.

Noting that the stories of the university officials and Montgomery differed on the question of whether the university librarian had received any previous notice that "there was a very basic difference between the administration's desires and Mr. Montgomery's performance," the committee concluded that "the University was seriously remiss in not having given Mr. Montgomery unmistakable evidence of its dissatisfaction through notice in writing at least six months before they intended to make the administrative change."

The conflict between Montgomery and the university, which resulted in court proceedings, was reported by LJ (Dec. 1, 1966, p. 5914; January 1, 1967, p. 42; April 15, p. 1557; and July, p. 2496). The court upheld the university and Montgomery resigned to take a position in the library of Wentworth Institute in Boston.

The six-man committee, which conducted the investigation for the Massachusetts Library Association and released its report on December 7, included: Brendan Connolly, S. J. (chairman), director, Boston College Libraries; Gustave A. Harrer, director, Boston University Libraries; Joseph S. Komidar, librarian, Tufts University; Philip J. McNiff, director, Boston Public Library; Donald E. Vincent, librarian, University of New Hampshire, who also was a representative on the committee of the New England Library Association; and Lawrence E. Wikander, librarian, Forbes Library, Northampton.

Library Journal, January 15, 1968, p. 142.

VI
KEY ISSUES

The administration of libraries now and in the decade ahead will be conducted amidst pressures and stresses unparalleled in library history. The stakes are high: the issue is whether the conventional library will perpetuate itself at the center or on the fringes of the culture's information activity. The administrative competence required to manage and direct organizations during stable times may not only be insufficient but actually at odds with and a threat to libraries in a time demanding fundamental change.

In this section, the editors have singled out the components which seem most critical. These are the nature of library leadership, the organizational capacity of libraries to change, and the strength of professionalism. This section introduces the conceptual approaches, the issues and ideas basic to a consideration of these elements in libraries. As in the rest of the volume, the reader will find here not solutions to problems so much as useful ways of conceptualizing organizational roles, patterns and behavior of libraries, librarians and library administrators. For it is out of these ingredients that more viable approaches to the ultimate solution of library problems may most hopefully be anticipated.

Leadership

Leadership in many ways defies explanation. It is a compound of many ingredients and may be examined, if imperfectly, in several ways. That rare executive who is able to perceive, understand and articulate his role as administrator, offers invaluable insight. But he is a most uncommon breed. Study of the backgrounds, values and behavior of executives provides another method even if one may not always admire the object of such detached analysis. For such study inevitably raises unsettling questions not only about the values, but also about the ability of those, who by virtue of their positions, make decisions affecting the welfare of many.

Leadership can also be viewed in terms of followers; for ultimately human beings, even in bureaucracy, get the kind of leadership they seek. This may nowhere be more true than in the library profession where the leadership class so accurately reflects the prevailing attitudes and values of the majority of librarians. For one key to holding a leadership post, both within a single institution as well as in a national society, is the ability to satisfy the rank and file. Leadership can also be viewed profitably along the time continuum. That is, the leadership requirements for crisis situations, such as during a period of exponential growth or when a library faces stress through attack from without, undoubtedly differs fundamentally from periods of stability; the successful leader in one context may prove totally unsuccessful in the other.

To truly understand the nature of the leadership role, its costs, its frustrations, as well as its rewards, is an essential ingredient of the individual who aspires to higher responsibility. The object of the selections following is to further the process of self-assessment and self-evaluation by the reader against some of these bench marks. But it is equally relevant for those who perform in non-administrative roles, for to understand the potentials of leadership is to influence librarianship to demand more forcefully styles and patterns of leadership appropriate to a profession in a time of change.

The Administrator

by Robert M. Hutchins

> *If the library of the thoughtful administrator were reduced to only three or four items of highest significance, it is hard to conceive of such a book shelf not including the following selection. In characterizing and differentiating the administrator from the office holder, Hutchins adroitly strikes at the heart of the issue. The decision process is an arduous one, calling for choices against as well as for. To play the role of administrator and to enjoy the rewards and to strive for the incentives is a common characteristic. To function honestly and effectively as a true administrator is something else again. But to paraphrase Hutchins is foolhardy in the extreme and the following piece makes the case for administration versus office holding as brilliantly and incisively as anywhere in the literature.*

At the outset I must confess that these remarks will have less generality than I could wish. I agreed to lecture on the administrator. I find that I am about to lecture almost entirely on the university administrator. I have spent more than half my life in university administration, and none of it in any other kind. The longer a university administrator administers, the more he is impressed by the peculiarities of his calling. These peculiarities are such that the administrator of any other enterprise can learn little from the study of university administration; and the administrator of a university, for whom these peculiarities have a morbid fascination, has little to say about the administration of an enterprise which is without them.

The business executive, for example, has a degree of authority within the business which is denied the university administrator. It is true that signs are now appearing that business may eventually be organized like a university, with the staff claiming a kind of academic freedom, participating in the formation of policy, and enjoying permanent tenure. When that happens, the university administrators of America will derive a certain grim satisfaction from the struggles of those captains of industry who have had the habit of complaining about the mismanagement of universities. But I fear that this will not be soon.

The university administrator is more like a political leader than any other kind of administrator. But even here the differences are, perhaps, more important than the similarities. The principal instruments of the American political leader are his party and his patronage. We cannot imagine his functioning at all without them. Both these instruments are quite properly denied the university administrator.

In this lecture it will appear that the task of the administrator is to order means to ends. I shall hope first to display the administrator at work with the means and shall try to suggest the qualities that are required for the performance of his duties in regard to them, whether or not the end is clear, correct, or given. I shall then pass to the administrator at work with the end, the administrator who is seeking to define, clarify, or discover the aim of his institution. This is the highest function of the administrator. To perform it, he needs all the qualities that are required for the disposition of means and, in addition, certain special, and very rare, abilities. The peculiarities of university administration relate both to the means and to the end. But the most difficult and most important problems are those which concern the end. I shall attempt to show the extraordinary significance of these problems at this moment in history. It is vital to civilization that university administrators face and solve these problems now.

Before I state what the qualifications of an administrator are, I should like to say that the mere statement of them will show that I do not possess them. I have been an administrator so long that I can tell you, I think, what an administrator ought to be. And this I can do even though I have never succeeded in being a good one myself. I discovered the things I know too late for them to be

SOURCE: Reprinted from Robert M. Hutchins, "The Administrator," *The Works of the Mind,* ed. Robert B. Heywood (Chicago: University of Chicago Press, 1947), pp. 135-156, by permission of the University of Chicago Press. ©1947 by the University of Chicago Press.

of use to me. There was nobody to give me this lecture when I began to administer. Even if there had been, it might not have helped much; for, as Aristotle remarked, men do not become good by listening to lectures on moral philosophy.

But if I had known that I was going to be an administrator, and if I had fully understood what the qualifications for the post were, I might have got a different education and tried to develop a different set of habits from those which I possess. One purpose of this lecture is to indicate the education and the habits which the prospective administrators among you should seek to acquire, so that you may perhaps be spared the remorse to which I am condemned.

The minimum qualifications of an administrator in his dealings with the means are four. They are courage, fortitude, justice, and prudence or practical wisdom. I do not include patience, which, we are told, President Eliot came to look upon as the chief requirement of an administrator. For reasons which will appear later I regard patience as a delusion and a snare and think that administrators have far too much of it rather than too little.

I do not include temperance, which in the case of the administrator would be the habit of refraining from making decisions that should be made by his subordinates. This is a matter between administrators and should not be discussed before the uninitiated.

Nor do I include the theological virtues: faith, hope, and charity, though the administrator needs them more than most men. I omit them because they come through divine grace, and I am talking about what the administrator can accomplish by his own efforts. Since it is not within his power to obtain the theological virtues, I must leave him to work that he may deserve them and pray that he may receive them.

When I say that the administrator should have courage, fortitude, justice, and prudence, I am saying only that he should be a good man. If the administrator is to function at all, he must have prudence or practical wisdom, the habit of selecting the right means to the end. But the administrator's life reveals that, though the virtues may be separated for purposes of analysis, they are one in practice. The administrator cannot exercise prudence without courage, which is the habit of taking responsibility; fortitude, which is the habit of bearing the consequences; and justice, which is the habit of giving equal treatment to equals.

Habits are formed by action. The way to become a good administrator is to administer. But this is also the way to become a bad administrator; for vice is a habit, too. The minimum function of the administrator is to decide, and, since he has to make more decisions than most men, he has the chance to be either an especially good or an especially bad man.

But you will say that most of the administrators you have known have not been especially good or especially bad men. This is because there are three courses, rather than two, open to the man who holds an administrative position. He can practice the four virtues I have named, he can practice their opposites, or he can decline to make decisions. Since the third is by far the easiest course, it is the one most administrators follow. I have known university presidents who have performed the almost superhuman feat of making no recommendations to their boards of trustees. I knew one who publicly took the view that the trustees made the decisions; he did not.

The administrator is a man who *decides* upon the class of cases committed to his care. If he fails to decide, he may be an officeholder; he is not an administrator. The shifts and dodges and downright dishonesty to which administrators will resort in an effort to become officeholders are an element of low comedy in the high tragedy of university administration. Lord Acton has familiarized us with the notion that power corrupts. He might have added a word or two on the corruption wrought by the failure to exercise authority when it is your duty to exercise it.

The chairman of a department once told a university president that a member of the departmental staff was so inferior that he should leave the university, and two weeks later he recommended that the same man be placed on permanent tenure at a large increase in salary. The reason, of course, was that he knew the president would turn down the recommendation. The president would bear the onus of blighting the hopes of the man in question, and the chairman could avoid the practice of the virtues. This came close to practicing their opposites; for it was cowardly, pusillanimous, unjust, and unwise. But it is more charitable and more nearly describes the state of mind of this chairman to say that he merely decided that he did not want to administer. Administration was unpleasant, and he would leave it to the president.

Administration is unpleasant, as anything which requires the exercise of the virtues I have named must be. It is doubtful whether even these virtues can be exercised without divine aid.

And the happiness which they give is not, I fear, a happiness in this life. The pressure upon a university administrator to become an officeholder is enormous. But there is an easy way of avoiding these troubles, and that is not to take the job. No man of mature years who accepts an administrative position in a university can claim that he did not know what his troubles would be. If there is such a man, he still has a way out; he can resign.

An air of martyrdom is unbecoming to the administrator. If he stays in office, he has only himself to blame, and his failures will always be his own fault. They will result from his lack of moral stamina or mental capacity or from his neglect of Bismarck's dictum that politics is the art of the possible. What is possible in any given situation depends to some extent on the material resources at the administrator's disposal, but far more on the abilities and spirit of his constituency. The administrator may make the wrong appraisal of his material resources or of the abilities and spirit of his constituency. He may overestimate his power to enlarge his material resources or to enhance the abilities and spirit of his constituency. If he is mistaken in any of these particulars, he has attempted the impossible and deserves to fail. If he fails, he should resign. He should not become an officeholder.

The administrator who is willing to be an administrator and not merely an officeholder will find that the strain is chiefly upon his character rather than his mind. Administration is a work of the mind, because it is ordering the means to the end, and the principle of order is the intellect. Prudence or practical wisdom is a habit of the practical intellect. It involves knowledge of the available means and some rational notion of the effectiveness of the available means to promote the end in view. But such knowledge is not difficult to come by, and much of what passes for administrative knowledge is not knowledge at all. Knowledge is not information. The characteristic of knowledge is organization. There are few principles of administration, and they are simple and easy.

Prudence cannot be taught any more than courage, fortitude, or justice can be taught. You can be told what these things are. You can be shown examples of their exercise. But you develop courage, fortitude, and justice by practicing them, and so you develop prudence, too. I do not minimize the intellectual difficulties involved in reaching an important practical decision. I merely say that these difficulties are of such a nature that previous formal instruction will do little to assist in their solution and that, compared with the strain on the character which the administration of the means carries with it, the strain on the mind is insignificant.

The strain on the character is very great. The administrator who is afraid of anybody or anything is lost. The administrator who cannot stand criticism, including slander and libel, is lost. The administrator who cannot give equal treatment to equals is lost. In a university he must give equal treatment to equals no matter how much it would promote his plans or assuage his feelings not to do so. I would recommend to the young members of the faculty of any university, other than this one, that they attack the administration. Their advancement will then be assured; for the administration will have to lean over backward to show that these attacks did not prevent a fair appraisal of the professors' scholarly contributions.

The administrator has all these ways to lose, and he has no way to win. Almost every decision an administrator makes is a decision against somebody. This is true even of decisions that look as though they were *for* somebody, like a decision to raise a man's salary. The administrator quickly learns that such a decision is really a decision not to raise the salaries of other men in the same department. In a university the administrator must appeal for support to those whom he has alienated in the course of his duty. Some idea of his situation may be obtained by asking what sort of co-operation the President of the United States would get from Congress in his second term if he had had the duty, and had conscientiously performed it, of fixing the salary and rank of the members of that body for four years. If the administrator were a judge, he could expect the litigants to go away and leave him alone after he had reached his decision. As an administrator he must expect that those whom he has decided against will remain with him and view his labors as something less than inspired.

The natural course, then, is to become an officeholder. Your life will be much easier, and you may even become popular. To the administrator the university often seems like a gigantic conspiracy to turn him into an officeholder. The trustees have accepted membership on the board because it is an honor. They are interested and pleased as long as the institution is prosperous—and peaceful. An administrator who administers is bound to cause trouble. Administrative decisions affect the lives, the fortunes, and even the sacred honor of members of the faculty. An administrator who wants the support of the faculty will make as few decisions as he can. He will try to develop automatic rules covering all subjects to avoid the embarrassment which decisions on individual cases must cause him. In regard to new appointments he will seek to escape responsibility by appointing committees to advise him. He will resort to every undercover technique he can think of in order to have it appear that he did not make the decision, even when he did.

The chairman of the committee of the trustees to select a president for an important college on the Atlantic seaboard telephoned me the other day to inquire about one of my friends. He asked whether he was a good administrator. In my innocence, thinking he wanted a good administrator as president of his college, I entered upon a glowing description of my friend's administrative abilities. I found that my tribute was received without enthusiasm at the other end of the wire, and asked if I had minunderstood the question. "No," replied the trustee. "You understood the question, all right. But you are giving the wrong answer. You see, our retiring president was a very bad administrator. Our faculty likes that, and they are afraid of any successor who will be better."

There are few sins of omission in administration, at least in university administration. Since the administrator's salary, prestige, and perquisites are high, he will be criticized under any conditions. But he will seldom be seriously disliked if he does nothing. People will say that he is a weak man and that he does not give the institution the leadership it should have. But everybody secretly yearns for the days of Coolidge, and academic communities, whatever their protestations to the contrary, really prefer anarchy to any form of government.

The temptation, of course, is to bury yourself in routine. There is so much routine—so many reports, so many meetings, so many signatures, so many people to see—all of some value to the institution, that you can conscientiously take your salary and never administer at all. You can spend your entire time doing things which any thirty-dollar-a-week clerk could do better and go home at night exhausted to report to your wife that you have had a hard day wrestling with university problems. The administrator who is determined to administer will find that the strain on his character is very great.

The strain on his mind results not so much from the intellectual difficulty of his problems as from his inability to command the time, assuming the ability and the willingness, to think. A university administrator has at least five constituencies: the faculty, the trustees, the students, the alumni, and the public. He could profitably spend all his time with any one of the five. What he actually does, of course, is to spend just enough with each of the five to irritate the other four.

The administrator who wants to administer will find that he cannot put in his time to the best advantage. On the one side are those things which are inevitable and urgent. On the other are those things which are important. The administrator should be devoting himself to those things which are important. But by definition he must devote himself to those which are inevitable and urgent. The question whether an assistant professor should have an increase in salary of $250 is not important, at least in an institution which has a deficit of one million dollars, which every well-regulated university should have. A deficit of $1,000,250 does not differ significantly from one of $1,000,000. But this question must be settled, while more important questions are postponed, because an offer from another university must be accepted or declined, or because the budget must go to the trustees at a certain time. And it must be passed upon by the administrator ultimately responsible, because, though $250 is not important, the quality of the staff is.

The problem of time, at least in a university, is insoluble. The administrator should never do anything he does not have to do, because the things he will have to do are so numerous that he cannot possibly have time to do them. He should never do today what he can put off till tomorrow. He should never do anything he can get anybody to do for him. He should have the largest number of good associates he can find; for they may be able to substitute for him. But he should be under no illusions here. The better his associates are, the more things they will think of for him to do.

Such thinking as the administrator can do will derive its value, not so much from his extraordinary knowledge or intellectual capacity, but from his locus in the institution. Like the architect, his view encompasses the whole and the interrelations of the parts. He is so placed that he can see the enterprise as a whole. He is likely to take a more detached view of the whole and its parts than any of the staff. Though he will not have much time to think, he can devote the time he has to thinking as objectively as possible about the whole. He has the knowledge, the position, and the duty to do so.

He has this duty in relation to all the means at the disposal of the institution. In a university, for example, the curriculum is a means to the end. It is not ordinarily committed to the care of the administrator; he has not the authority to determine what the course of study shall be. But the curriculum is not a means; it is the chief means to the end of an educational enterprise. Nobody else has quite the opportunity which the administrator has to see the whole of the curriculum and the interrelations of the parts. The administrator fails in his duty, therefore, if he does not try to see from his point of vantage what the whole curriculum and its interrelations should be.

He must then try to induce those to whose care the curriculum has been committed to face the problems it raises as persistently, as seriously, and as impartially as possible. In this connection, too, the administrator must be a troublemaker; for every change in education is a change in the habits of some members of the faculty. Nevertheless, the administrator must insist on the participation of the faculty in the constant reconsideration of the means which it is using to attain the end of the university; for his duty is not merely to decide upon the class of cases committed to his care, but also to see to it that the other members of the community do not become officeholders in relation to the categories committed to theirs.

The task of the administrator in ordering the means is to keep the institution up to its own standards. These standards are a reflection of the end. The curse of universities is easy standards. For example, the relations among the members of the academic community are such that the failure to appoint or promote congenial men is bound to create much unpleasantness. The temptation to yield is very great; but, if the administrator yields in one instance, he must yield in more, and, before he knows it, a new and lower standard has been established, which is lowered in its turn by the same process. The commitments thus made by the administrator—and, whatever his virtues, he is bound to make some—gradually reduce his effectiveness and combine with the gradual alienation of his constituency to bring his usefulness to a close. The administrator has many ways to lose, and no way to win.

The remedy is a term, at the end of which the institution can decide once more whether it wishes to be managed by an administrator or ornamented by an officeholder. Failing some provision for the automatic termination of his services, the administrator must be in a perpetual mood of resignation, by which I do not mean mournful acceptance of the universe. I mean he must be perpetually prepared to get out. This solution is not ideal. Nobody will tell the administrator he should resign; this would be impolite, and finding a successor is very difficult. The administrator is usually the last person to know he should resign. He can always rationalize his salary, prestige, and perquisites into a burning conviction of his necessity to the institution. He is like a dub playing golf. He makes just enough good strokes to go on playing the game. But the chances are that the dub should give up golf and take to reading the Great Books.

How does the administrator or his constituency know whether his decisions are right or wrong? Since he is deciding upon the means to an end, his decisions are right or wrong depending on whether they help or hinder the institution in its effort to achieve the end. Where the end is simple and clear, the appraisal of the administrator is easy. If the end of an army is victory, a general who wins is good. If the end of a business is profit, an executive who makes money is good. But the measure of the statesman can be taken only in the light of some defensible conception of the end of the state, and the measure of a university administrator only in the light of some rational view of the end of the university.

The administrator cannot make the right decisions without some similar illumination. How can he decide on the means if he has no clear vision of the end? It is impossible for the administrator who understands the end to achieve it unless he has the character to select the right means, and impossible for him to select the right means unless he has the mind to understand the end. The difficulty of understanding the end of a university—or perhaps the lack of mind of university administrators—is suggested by the fact that the leading characteristic of educational institutions today is aimlessness.

The end of institutions gets lost as they mature. The enterprise goes on because it started and runs for the sake of running. If any other consideration than that of self-perpetuation is allowed to enter, it is usually that of prestige. Let us be famous for the sake of fame. We see a similar phenomenon in the case of states which have lost any conception of the end of political organization. They say, let us be powerful for the sake of power.

The fact that the purpose of universities is rapidly lost has led to the suggestion that they should be burned down every twenty-five years, or that the original faculty should consist of men forty years old, that no additions should be made, and that they should all retire at the age of sixty-five. These proposals seem drastic, but they are little more so than the facts demand. It is imperative to force the periodic reconsideration of the purpose of an institution.

The institution may have lost its usefulness at the end of twenty-five years. Its aim may have been accomplished. Or some other aim should, perhaps, be substituted for the original one. The University of Chicago, which I regard as the most useful institution in the world, is so because its original aim has been the subject of some reconsideration. The idea of the founders of this University was simply to establish a university in the Middle West, and one with Baptist overtones. Now there are many other universities in the region, and the Baptist overtones are almost inaudible.

The task of the administrator in a new enterprise is relatively easy, for there the purpose of the communal activity is clear and fresh in the minds of all the members of the community. Men are appointed to the staff because they are thought to be qualified for and interested in working toward the end. As the inevitable mistakes are made, as the vested interests harden, as the aim is changed to self-perpetuation, the difficulties of administration increase. The alteration takes place very rapidly. George Vincent, later president of the Rockefeller Foundation, who was a member of the first faculty of the University of Chicago, used to say that on the day the University opened the faculty and students gathered in front of Cobb Hall and sang "Old Varsity" before the paint was dry. President Harper designed a new university, but his administrative autobiography makes depressing reading, because it shows how quickly a new institution congeals.

If the end of the institution has got lost, if the institution has congealed, if it suffers from the disease of aimlessness, then all the administrator's moral difficulties are intensified, and his mind undergoes serious strain. Now, in addition to summoning up the character necessary to select the right means, he must try to command the intelligence to discover the end. He must become a philosopher.

Men who possess and practice the virtues are rare enough. Good men who are also good philosophers are rarer still. Good men who are good philosophers and who are willing to run the extraordinary occupational hazards, moral and mental, of university administration, are a race which appears to be extinct. Yet if I were asked what single thing American education needed most, I should reply that it needed such men; for the whole system of American education is losing itself in the wilderness for the lack of them. The academic administrators of America remind one of the French revolutionist who said, "The mob is in the street. I must find out where they are going, for I am their leader."

The president of a state university said recently that the object of his institution was to do whatever any important group in the state thought was useful. This amounts to saying that any important group in the state can determine the purpose of the university. The president in question took this view because it was easy, it was simple, and it would pay. He would not think himself; he established the fact that it was positively wrong for him to think; and the groups he was willing to have do his thinking for him would support the work which, they thought, it was the university's purpose to do.

This administrator merely stated explicitly what is implicit in the conduct of almost every American university. Almost every American university is managed in terms of the social pressures prevailing at a given time. Another state university president lately remarked that he was going to offer athletic scholarships because he could not get anything through the legislature with his present football team. Since the American university has been unable to formulate any idea of its function, its function is to do what any powerful group wants it to undertake. It has no standard by which to judge these requests, because it has no conception of the end. The modern university and the modern department store are therefore almost indistinguishable, except that, because of the momentary shortages, the university offers, momentarily, a wider variety of goods than the department store.

Anybody who has watched the development of the American university will have no difficulty in predicting that in the next twenty-five years it will greatly expand on the side of natural science, engineering, and the applied social sciences, such as business, industrial relations, and public administration. I have the greatest respect for all these subjects. Perhaps this is the direction in which the American universities should move. But I would point out that, if they do move in this direction, it is improbable that they will do so because they have considered the end and concluded that what civilization needs is more natural science, engineering, and applied social science. If they move in this direction, it is likely that they will do so because powerful pressures in society push them.

As it is easy and tempting to become an officeholder rather than an administrator, so it is easy and tempting not to think about the end. As everybody in the institution prefers an officeholder to an administrator, so everybody in the institution prefers not to be reminded that the university has, or should have, a purpose. The worst kind of troublemaker is the man who insists upon asking about first principles, and the first principle of any activity is the end. The last question that will be raised about a prospective academic administrator is whether he has any ideas. If it appears that he has, he is unlikely to be appointed, for he will rightly be regarded as a dangerous man. The situation in American education is much the same as that in American politics: the men who are needed most cannot be chosen; the qualifications to do the job disqualify the candidate for the post.

Yet somebody in the institution must think about the end; for otherwise the institution will get lost or fall to pieces. Our universities present an especially acute aspect of the general problem of the one and the many. A university should be one; but it is peculiarly a prey of centrifugal forces, which are always driving it apart. This is because no end has yet been discovered and accepted by the American university sufficiently clear to make sense of its activities, to establish a standard for criticizing them, and to unify those who are carrying them on. Even a mob will disintegrate if it does not know where it is going.

The administrator must accept a special responsibility for the discovery, clarification, definition, and proclamation of the end. But he does not own the institution. The administrator's responsibility is to get others to join him in the search for the end and to try to lead all his constituency to see and accept it when it has been found. He must conceive of himself as presiding over a continuous discussion of the mission and destiny of the institution. He must insist upon this discussion, and he must see to it that it never flags.

The difficulty is that the aim and destiny of an institution are not discovered by instinct or tradition; they must be arrived at by creative thought. For this the administrator has neither the time, the atmosphere, nor the education which it demands.

It is suggestive that since Francis Bacon, who was, after all, a bad administrator and a bad man, no administrator who carried major responsibilities has published anything of any significance. In our own time Hawthorne, Arnold, Trollope, and Mill have held administrative posts and done creative work. But Hawthorne was an officeholder rather than an administrator, and the other three did not carry major responsibilities. Nor did any of them do any important thinking about the end of their administrative activity. There is little published evidence that any administrative officer has done so since Marcus Aurelius.

The end is the most important matter the administrator can deal with, but its consideration can always be postponed; there is never any time for it. Though the administrator shares his lack of education with his contemporaries, associates, and fellow-citizens, they may be able to do something about their inadequacy in their leisure hours. The administrator's leisure hours are few, his administrative problems follow him home and plague his dreams, and his intellectual condition at the end of the day's work is such that he is barely able to cope with a detective story. The university administrator can force himself to do some reading and thinking by teaching; but this is bad for the students.

Yet Plato's answer to the question, "What kind of administrators do states—and universities—require?" is valid for us today, after almost twenty-five hundred years. He said: "Unless either philosophers become kings or those whom we now call our kings and rulers take to the pursuit of philosophy seriously and adequately, and there is a conjunction of these two things, political power and philosophic intelligence, there can be no cessation of troubles, dear Glaucon, for our states, nor, I fancy, for the human race either."

Plato also tells us what kind of education is needed to produce the administrator we are seeking. Until the age of thirty-five the candidate is to devote himself to his education, spending the last five years in the most profound metaphysical studies. Then for fifteen years he is to acquire practical experience in offices which Plato describes as those suitable to youth. The object is, of course, to develop the habit of practical wisdom but even more to develop the moral virtues. In Plato's words: "And in these offices, too, they are to be tested to see whether they will remain steadfast under diverse solicitations or whether they will flinch and swerve."

At the age of fifty those candidates who have survived all tests and shown themselves the best in every task and every form of knowledge are ready to become administrators. But each will serve only for a limited term. The philosopher-kings alternate between periods of philosophical study and administration, with the longer periods devoted to philosophy. When the turn comes for each, they toil in the service of the state, holding office for the city's sake, regarding the task not as a fine thing but as a necessity. As a reward for these sacrifices they depart eventually for the Islands of the Blest, and the state establishes public memorials and religious rites in their honor as though they were divinities, or at least divine and godlike men.

Plato was writing a utopia. Utopias are the products of desperate situations. They are constructed when everybody sees that nothing can be done, except perhaps to indicate the ideals toward which future generations should strive. We look to Plato not for the specifications of a practical program to be taken over intact but for guidance in the formation by our own efforts of a practical program for our own day.

The essential points are that the administrator should not want to administer but should be forced to do so for the public good; that he should have a long period of education, culminating in profound speculative study; that he should undergo a great variety of practical experience to form his character and develop the habit of practical wisdom; and that he should serve for a limited term, after which he should resume his studies, if he expects at some later time to have another. This is the kind of scheme which is called for if the administrator is to have the moral and intellectual qualities which the times demand.

You will say that even this reduced and denatured version of the Platonic program remains utopian still. It is a sufficient reply that our situation is so desperate that nothing not utopian is worth trying. We know that the world may at any moment burst into flames. We know that we can hope to save ourselves only by the most tremendous and well-directed efforts. Bewildered and tortured humanity should be able to look in this crisis to those institutions created to elevate the minds and hearts of men, to symbolize their highest powers and aspirations. To say of a university now that its object is to maintain itself or to preserve accepted values and institutions is to deny the responsibility imposed by the community on those privileged persons whom it has set apart to think in its behalf, to criticize its ways, and to raise it to its highest possible moral and intellectual level.

We can take one of two positions about education today. Either it aims to transform the minds and hearts of men, or it is completely irrelevant. Either it is almost our only hope, or it is literally child's play, a way of keeping the young occupied until they can enter the army, which may be blown to bits without notice, or go to work in an economic system which is rapidly dissolving, or become citizens of a country and members of a civilization which—so we should have to tell them if we spoke frankly—are in the greatest peril in their history. Professor Einstein's estimate that in the next war two-thirds of the populations involved will be killed seems conservative, and who will say that there will not be a next war and that it will not be soon?

We know that agreements to control uranium deposits, to permit inspection of atomic-power plants and factories, to disarm, and even the solemn agreement which is the charter of the United Nations itself can last only so long as each of the participating members wants them to last. We know that a world government can arise only if the peoples of the world want it, and can endure only as there is a world community to support it. The prospects of a world civil war are not attractive.

We must have international agreements. We must work toward world government. But the significance of these agreements and of all efforts to frame a world constitution and get it adopted lies largely in the fact that all discussion of world unification may promote the community upon which such unification must rest. Such unification ultimately rests on the transformation of the minds and hearts of men.

If we must abolish war or perish, and if war can be abolished only by this transformation, then the aim of educational institutions is to bring about this transformation. And the task is one of terrifying urgency—so urgent that the triviality and frivolity of American education and the petty and selfish concerns of its leaders seem blasphemous as well as suicidal.

You may say that there is a disproportion between the end that I propose and the means I have chosen. You may feel that there is little in the record of educational institutions in this country to suggest that, even if they devoted themselves wholeheartedly to the work, they could save civilization. If this is so, then we should take the enormous funds now devoted to the educational enterprise and use them to provide a few, pleasant final hours for our starving fellow-men in Europe and Asia. The plight of mankind is such that if we seriously conclude that our activity is irrelevant to it, we should give up the activity. The world cannot afford the luxury of so wasteful a monument to an abandoned dream.

As the minimum function of the administrator is ordering the means, so his highest function is discovering and clarifying and holding before his institution the vision of the end. As the qualifications for the administrator's minimum function are courage, fortitude, justice, and prudence, so the qualification for his highest function is philosophical wisdom. At this epoch in history we can demand nothing less of the administrator than this combination of practical and philosophical wisdom, with the moral qualities necessary to sustain it.

The reward of the administrator may not be public memorials, religious rites, and a pleasant journey to the Islands of the Blest. For these things he should care not at all. His satisfaction will come, even if he fails, from having seen and attempted one of the most difficult works of the mind and one of the most challenging human tasks.

ABOUT THE AUTHOR—Robert Maynard Hutchins' life has been spent in furthering his views on the proper function of education and the role of the educated man. Freedom, justice and democracy are the goals to be pursued by the society in Hutchins' view, and education prepares man for such pursuits. Throughout his career Robert Hutchins has been an articulate yet controversial spokesman for the broad goals of higher education and he has fought strenuously to limit the encroachments of vocationalism and narrow specialization.

Born in 1899 and educated at Oberlin and Yale, Hutchins became a public figure when he was made Dean of the Yale Law School in 1927. He had received a law degree from that institution a few years earlier. In 1929 he joined the University of Chicago as its President. The focus of attention upon his youth was shifted quickly to the innovations he introduced at Chicago, including the elimination of required course attendance and course credit in favor of broad examinations, and curricular modification to channel student concentration upon the thinking process with emphasis on metaphysics and classics. Hutchins' statesmanlike role in educational leadership brought in many offers from outside the field. He resisted them all until he left Chicago in 1951 to become Associate Director of the Ford Foundation. He left the Foundation in 1954 to head the Fund for the Republic and later its Center for the Study of Democratic Institutions.

Robert Hutchins has expressed his views on education extensively and colorfully. Two representative volumes are *The Higher Learning in America* (1936) and *Some Observations on American Education* (1956). He has been an active partisan committed to moral goals and public affairs and has served in many public and private capacities including directing the Commission on the Freedom of the Press and the initiation and the assumption of the Presidency of the Committee to Frame a World Constitution.

The Business Executive: The Psychodynamics of a Social Role

by William E. Henry

While the following selection is now dated and even though it relies upon a very limited sample of evidence based upon motivation analysis of business administrators, it is a classic assessment of the personality construct of the business administrator. Those drives and psychological characteristics which motivate the business executive may be at a variance from the attitudes and tendencies which characterize the library administrator, but the burden of evidence would suggest that this is not the case. One may hypothesize that those personality traits which influence one toward an administrative career will be shared regardless of organizational setting. While many in librarianship do not share such psychological and behavioral propensities, perhaps those who function in administrative roles attain such posts because they have in common with the business administrator like drives and motivations.

The business executive is a central figure in the economic and social life of the United States. His direction of business enterprise and his participation in informal social groupings give him a significant place in community life. In both its economic and its social aspects the role of the business executive is sociologically a highly visible one. It has clearly definable limits and characteristics known to the general public. These characteristics indicate the function of the business executive in the social structure, define the behavior expected of the individual executive, and serve as a guide to the selection of the novice.

Social pressure plus the constant demands of the business organization of which he is a part direct the behavior of the executive into the mold appropriate to the defined role. "Success" is the name applied to the wholehearted adoption of the role. The individual behaves in the manner dictated by the society, and society rewards the individual with "success" if his behavior conforms to the role. It would punish him with "failure" should he deviate from it.

Participation in this role, however, is not a thing apart from the personality of the individual. It is not a game that the person is playing; it is the way of behaving and thinking that he knows best, that he finds rewarding, and in which he believes. Thus the role as socially defined has its counterpart in personality structure. To some extent, too, the personality structure is reshaped to be in harmony with the social role. The extent to which such reshaping of the adult personality is possible, however, seems limited. An initial selection process occurs which reduces the amount of time involved in teaching the appropriate behavior. Persons whose personality structure is most readily adaptable to this particular role tend to be selected, whereas those whose personality is not already partially akin are rejected.

This paper describes the personality communalities of a group of successful business executives. The research upon which it is based explored the general importance of personality structure in the selection of executive personnel. Many aptitude tests have been employed in industry to decrease the risk involved in the hiring of untried personnel and to assist in their placement. These tests have been far less effective in the selection of high-level executive personnel than in the selection of clerical and other non-administrating persons. Many business executives have found that persons of unquestioned high intelligence often turn out to be ineffective when placed in positions of increased responsibility. The reasons for their failure lie in their social relationships. No really effective means has yet been found to clarify and predict this area

---

SOURCE: William E. Henry, "The Business Executive: The Psychodynamics of a Social Role," *American Journal of Sociology*, 54 (Jan., 1949). Reprinted from *American Journal of Sociology* by permission of the University of Chicago Press. © 1949 by the University of Chicago Press.

of executive functioning. It is to this problem that our research[1] was directed.

From the research it became clear that the "successful"[2] business executives studied had many personality characteristics in common. (It was equally clear that an absence of these characteristics was coincident with "failure" within the organization.) This personality constellation might be thought of as the minimal requirement for "success" within our present business system and as the psychodynamic motivation of persons in this occupation. Individual uniqueness in personality was clearly present; but, despite these unique aspects, all executives had in common this personality pattern.

ACHIEVEMENT DESIRES

Successful executives show high drive and achievement desire. They conceive of themselves as hard-working and achieving persons who must accomplish in order to be happy. The areas in which they do their work are clearly different, but each feels this drive for accomplishment. This should be distinguished from a type of pseudo-achievement drive in which the glory of the end product alone is stressed. The person with this latter type of drive, seldom found in the successful executives, looks to the future in terms of the glory it will provide him and of the projects that he will have completed—as opposed to the achievement drive of the successful executive, which looks more toward the sheer accomplishment of the work itself. The successful business leader gets much satisfaction from doing rather than from merely contemplating the completed product. To some extent this is the difference between the dreamer and the doer. It is not that the successful executives do not have an over-all goal in mind or that they do not derive satisfaction from the contemplation of future ease or that they do not gain pleasure from prestige. Far more real to them, however, is the continual stimulation that derives from the pleasure of immediate accomplishment.

MOBILITY DRIVE

All successful executives have strong mobility drives. They feel the necessity of moving continually upward and of accumulating the rewards of increased accomplishment. For some the sense of successful mobility comes through the achievement of competence on the job. These men struggle for increased responsibility and derive a strong feeling of satisfaction from the completion of a task. Finished work and newly gained competence provide them with their sense of continued mobility.

A second group relies more upon the social prestige of increased status in their home communities or within the organizational hierarchy. Competence in work is of value and at times crucial. But the satisfactions of the second group come from the social reputation, not from the personal feeling that necessary work has been well done. Both types of mobility drive are highly motivating. The zeal and energy put into the job is equal in both instances. The distinction appears in the kinds of work which the men find interesting. For the first group the primary factor is the nature of the work itself—is it challenging, is it necessary, is it interesting? For the second group the crucial factor is its relation to their goals of status mobility—is it a step in the direction of increased prestige, is it appropriate to their present position, what would other people think of them if they did it?

THE IDEA OF AUTHORITY

The successful executive posits authority as a controlling but helpful relationship to superiors. He looks to his superiors as persons of more advanced training and experience, whom he can consult on special problems and who issue to him certain guiding directives. He does not see the authorities in his environment as destructive or prohibiting forces.

Those executives who view authority as a prohibiting and destructive force have difficulty relating themselves to superiors and resent their authority over them. They are either unable to work smoothly with superiors or indirectly and unconsciously do things to obstruct the work of their bosses or to assert their independence unnecessarily.

It is of interest that to these men the dominant crystallization of attitudes about authority is toward superior and toward subordinates, rather than toward self. This implies that most crucial in their concept of authority is the view of being a part of a wider and more final authority system. In contrast, a few executives of the "self-made," driving-type characteristic of the past of business enterprise maintain a specific concept of authority with regard to self. They are the men who almost always forge their own frontiers, who are unable to operate within anyone else's framework, and to whom co-operation and team work are foreign concepts. To these men the ultimate authority is in themselves, and their image does not include the surrounding area of shared or delegated power.

ORGANIZATION AND ITS IMPLICATIONS

While executives who are successful vary considerably in their intelligence-test ratings, all of them have a high degree of ability to organize unstructured situations and to see the implications of their organization. This implies that they have the ability to take several seemingly isolated events or facts and to see relationships that exist between them. Further, they are interested in looking into the future and are concerned with predicting the outcome of their decisions and actions.

This ability to organize often results in a forced organization, however. Even though some situations arise with which they feel unfamiliar and are unable to cope, they still force an organization upon it. Thus they bring it into the sphere of familiarity. This tendency operates partially as a mold, as a pattern into which new or unfamiliar experiences are fit. This means, of course, that there is a strong tendency to rely upon techniques that they know will work and to resist situations which do not readily fit this mold.

DECISIVENESS

Decisiveness is a further trait of this group. This does not imply the popular idea of the executive making quick and final decisions in rapid-fire succession, although this seems to be true of some of the executives. More crucial, however, is an ability to come to a decision among several alternative courses of action—whether it be done on the spot or after detailed consideration. Very seldom does this ability fail. While less competent and well-organized individuals may become flustered and operate inefficiently in certain spots, most of these men force their way to a conclusion. Nothing is too difficult for them to tackle and at least try to solve. When poorly directed and not modified by proper judgment, this attitude may be more a handicap than a help. That is to say, this trait remains in operation and results in decision-making action regardless of the reasonableness of the decision or its reality in terms of related facts. The loss of this trait (usually found only in cases in which some more profound personality change has also occurred) is one of the most disastrous for the executive: his superiors become apprehensive about him. This suggests an interesting relationship to the total executive constellation. The role demands conviction and certainty. Whenever a junior executive loses this quality of decisiveness, he seems to pass out of the socially defined role. The weakening of other aspects of the ideal executive constellation can be readily reintegrated into the total constellation. The questioning of the individual's certainty and decisiveness, however, results in a weakening of the entire constellation and tends to be punished by superiors.

STRONG SELF-STRUCTURE

One way of differentiating between people is in the relative strength or weakness of their notions of self-identity, their self-structure. Some persons lack definiteness and are easily influenced by outside pressures. Some, such as these executives, are firm and well-defined in their sense of self-identity. They know what they are and what they want and have well-developed techniques for getting what they want. The things they want and the techniques for getting them are, of course, quite different for each individual, but this strength and firmness is a common and necessary characteristic. It is, of course, true that too great a sense of self-identity leads to rigidity and inflexibility; and, while some of these executives could genuinely be accused of this, in general they maintain considerable flexibility and adaptability within the framework of their desires and within the often rather narrow possibilities of their own business organization.

ACTIVITY AND AGGRESSION

The executive is essentially an active, striving, aggressive person. His underlying motivations are active and aggressive—not necessarily is he aggressive and hostile overtly in his dealings with other people. This activity and aggressiveness are always well channeled into work or struggles for status and prestige—which implies a constant need to keep moving, to do something, to be active. This does not mean that they are always in bodily movement and moving physically from place to place (though this is often true) but rather that they are mentally and emotionally alert and active. This constant motivator unfortunately cannot be shut off. It may be part of the reason why so many executives find themselves unable to take vacations at leisure or to stop worrying about already solved problems.

APPREHENSION AND THE FEAR OF FAILURE

If one is continually active and always trying to solve problems and arrive at decisions, any inability to do so successfully may well result in feelings of frustration. This seems to be true of the executives. In spite of their firmness of character and their drive to activity, they also harbor a rather pervasive feeling that they may not really succeed and be able to do the things they want to do. It is not implied that this sense of frustration comes only from their immediate business experience. It seems far more likely to be a feeling of long standing within them and to be only accentuated and reinforced by their present business experience.

This sense of the perpetually unattained is an integral part of this constellation and is part of its dilemma. It means that there is always some place to go, but no defined point at which to stop. The executive is "self-propelled" and needs to keep moving always and to see another goal ever ahead, which also suggests that cessation of mobility and of struggling for new achievements will be accompanied by an inversion of this constant energy. The person whose mobility is blocked, either by his own limitations or by those of the social system, finds this energy diverted into other channels. Psychosomatic symptoms, the enlargement of interpersonal dissatisfactions, and the development of rationalized compulsive and/or paranoid-like defenses may reflect the redirection of this potent energy demand.

STRONG REALITY ORIENTATION

Successful executives are strongly oriented to immediate realities and their implications. They are directly interested in the practical, the immediate, and the direct. This is, of course, generally good for the immediate business situation, though the executive with an overdeveloped sense of reality may cease to be a man of vision; for a man of vision must get above reality to plan and even dream about future possibilities. In addition, a too strong sense of reality, when the realities are not in tune with ambitions, may well lead to a conviction that reality is frustrating and unpleasant. This happens to many executives who find progress and promotion too slow for their drives. The result is often a restlessness rather than an activity, a fidgetiness rather than a well-channeled aggression, and a lack of ease that may well disrupt many of their usual interpersonal relations.

THE NATURE OF THEIR INTERPERSONAL RELATIONS

In general the mobile and successful executive looks to his superiors with a feeling of personal attachment and tends to identify himself with them. His superior represents for him a symbol of his own achievement and desires, and he tends to identify himself with these traits in those who have achieved more. He is very responsive to his superiors—the nature of this responsiveness, of course, depends on his other feelings, his idea of authority, and the extent to which he feels frustrated.

On the other hand, he looks to his subordinates in a detached and impersonal way, seeing them as "doers of work" rather than as people. He treats them impersonally, with no real feeling of being akin to them or of having deep interest in them as persons. It is as though he viewed his subordinates as representatives of things he has left behind, both factually and emotionally. Still uncertain of his next forward step, he cannot afford to become personally identified or emotionally involved with the past. The only direction of his emotional energy that is real to him is upward and toward the symbols of that upward interest, his superiors.

This does not mean that he is cold and that he treats all subordinates casually. In fact he tends to be generally sympathetic with many of them. This element of sympathy with subordinates is most apparent when the subordinate shows personality traits that are most like those of the superior. Thus the superior is able to take pride in certain successful young persons without at the same time feeling an equal interest in all subordinates.

THE ATTITUDE TOWARD HIS OWN PARENTS

In a sense the successful executive is a "man who has left home." He feels and acts as though he were on his own, as though his emotional ties and obligations to his parents were severed. It seems to be most crucial that he has not retained resentment of his parents, but has rather simply broken their emotional hold on him and been left psychologically free to make his own decisions. We have found those who have not broken this tie to be either too dependent upon their superiors in the work situation or to be resentful of their supervision (depending, of course, upon whether they are still bound to their parents or are still actively fighting against them).

In general we find the relationship to the mother to have been the most clearly broken tie. The tie to the father remains positive in the sense that he views the father as a helpful but not restraining figure. Those men who still feel a strong emotional tie to the mother have systematically had difficulty in the business situation. This residual emotional tie seems contradictory to the necessary attitude of activity, progress, and channeled aggression. The tie to the father, however, must remain positive—as the emotional counterpart of the admired and more successful male figure. Without this image, struggle for success seems difficult.

THE NATURE OF DEPENDENCY FEELINGS AND CONCENTRATION UPON SELF

A special problem in differentiating the type of generally successful executive is the nature of his dependency feelings. It was pointed out above that the dependency upon the mother-image must be eliminated. For those executives who work within the framework of a large organization in which co-operation and group-and-company loyalty are necessities, there must remain feelings of dependency upon the father-image and a need to operate within an established framework. This does not mean that the activity-aggression need cannot operate or that the individual is not decisive and self-directional. It means only that he is so within the framework of an already established set of over-all goals. For most executives this over-all framework provides a needed guidance and allows them to concentrate upon their achievement and work demands with only minimal concern for the policy-making of the entire organization. For those executives who prefer complete independence and who are unable to work within a framework established by somebody else, the element of narcissism is much higher and their feelings of loyalty are only to themselves rather than to a father-image or its impersonal counterpart in company policy. These feelings differentiate the executives who can co-operate with others and who can promote the over-all policy of a company from those who must be the whole show themselves. Clearly there are situations in which the person highly concentrated upon self and with little feeling of dependency loyalty is of great value. But he should be distinguished in advance and be placed in only situations in which these traits are useful.

The successful executive represents a crystallization of many of the attitudes and values generally accepted by middle-class American society. The value of accumulation and achievement, of self-directedness and independent thought and their rewards in prestige and status and property, are found in this group. But they also pay the price of holding these values and of profiting from them. Uncertainty, constant activity, the continual fear of losing ground, the inability to be introspectively leisurely, the ever present fear of failure, and the artificial limitations put upon their emotionalized interpersonal relations—these are some of the costs of this role.

FOOTNOTES

[1] The research undertaken will be described in its entirety in a subsequent report. In summary it involved the study of over one hundred business executives in various types of business houses. The techniques employed were the Thematic Appercception test, a short undirected interview, and a projective analysis of a number of traditional personality tests. The validity of our analyses, which were done "blind," rested upon the coincidence of identical conclusions from separately analyzed instruments, upon surveys of past job performance, and upon the anecdotal summary of present job behavior by the executive's superiors and associates. The writer wishes to express his thanks to these executives: to Dr. Burleigh Gardner, of Social Research, Inc., under whose auspices the study was made; and to Carson McGuire, Robert F. Peck, Norman Martin, and Harriett Bruce Moore, of the University of Chicago, for their assistance in the collection and analysis of data and the clarification of conclusions.

[2] Success and failure as here used refer to the combined societal and business definitions. All our "successful" executives have a history of continuous promotion, are thought to be still "promotable" within the organization, are now in positions of major administrative responsibility, and are earning salaries within the upper ranges of current business salaries. Men in lower supervisory positions, men who are considered "failures" in executive positions, and men in clerical and laboring jobs show clear deviations from this pattern. This suggests, of course, that this pattern is specific for the successful business executive and that it serves to differentiate him from other groupings in industry.

The majority of these executives come from distributive (rather than manufacturing) businesses of moderately loose organizational structure in which co-operation and team work are valued and in which relative independence of action is stressed within the framework of a clearly defined over-all company policy. In organizations in which far greater rigidity of structure is present or in which outstanding independence of action is required, it is possible that there will be significant variations from the personality pattern presented here. We are currently extending our data in these directions.

ABOUT THE AUTHOR—Since 1945, William E. Henry has been a member of the Committee on Human Development at the University of Chicago. The Committee includes various disciplines within the behavioral sciences, and adopts as its focus the study of normal people, their behavior in real life situations, and the interrelations of social, psychological and biological variables at different points in their life cycle. Henry studied under the Committee, and received his Ph.D. under their auspices in 1944. He was born in Massachusetts in 1917, and did his undergraduate work at the University of Utah. Henry's specializations include projective techniques, and the psychological characteristics of modern society. He is the author of *The Analysis of Fantasy* (1956) and co-author of *Growing Old* (1961). He collaborated in the psychological material of an earlier work, *Warriors Without Weapons,* a study of the Pine Ridge Sioux. Henry serves at present as Professor of Human Development and Psychology and as Chairman of the Committee on Human Development of Chicago.

Leadership in Administration

by Philip Selznick

Perhaps the contribution to the literature of administrative leadership which offers the keenest insight is the following essay. Here leadership is correlated with the characteristic of rising above the range of choice inherent in routine decision processes. Selznick reasons that to be a leader one must concentrate his energy upon questions relating to the basic mission and focal point of the organization, rather than with the technical means of accomplishing such goals. The identity of the organization is thus maintained only when its basic integrity as an organization in quest of certain attainments is kept constantly in view. The measure of the leader's capacity is seen in his success at achieving a strategic balance between opportunism at one end and utopianism at the other, with institutional drift viewed as the ultimate product of the inadequacy of the administrator's leadership capacity. Like Hutchins, Selznick pleads not for the office holder but for the creative leader, the statesman whose characteristic art is seen as the building of an institution which embodies new and enduring values.

The main task of this essay has been to explore the meaning of institutional leadership, in the hope of contributing to our understanding of large-scale organization. We have not offered recipes for the solution of immediate problems. Rather, we have sought to encourage reflection and self-knowledge, to provide some new guides to the diagnosis of administrative troubles, and to suggest that the posture of statesmanship may well be appropriate for many executives who now have a narrower view and a more limited aspiration.

This final chapter summarizes the main ideas developed above, with some added notes on responsibility and creativity in leadership.

BEYOND EFFICIENCY

It is easy to agree to the abstract proposition that the function of the executive is to find a happy joinder of means and ends. It is harder to take that idea seriously. There is a strong tendency not only in administrative life but in all social action to divorce means and ends by overemphasizing one or the other. The cult of efficiency in administrative theory and practice is a modern way of overstressing means and neglecting ends. This it does in two ways. First, by fixing attention on maintaining a smooth-running machine, it slights the more basic and more difficult problem of defining and safeguarding the ends of an enterprise.

Second, the cult of efficiency tends to stress techniques of organization that are essentially neutral, and therefore available for any goals, rather than methods peculiarly adapted to a distinctive type of organization or stage of development.

Efficiency as an operating ideal presumes that goals are settled and that the main resources and methods for achieving them are available. The problem is then one of joining available means to known ends. This order of decision-making we have called *routine*, distinguishing it from the realm of *critical* decision. The latter, because it involves choices that affect the basic character of the enterprise, is the true province of leadership as distinct from administrative management. Such choices are of course often made unconsciously, without awareness of their larger significance, but then the enterprise evolves more or less blindly. Leadership provides guidance to minimize this blindness.

In many situations, including those most important to the ultimate well-being of the enterprise, goals may not have been defined. Moreover, even when they are defined, the necessary means may have still to be created. Creating the means is, furthermore, not a narrow technical matter; it involves molding the social character of the organization. Leadership goes beyond efficiency (1) when it sets the basic mission of the organization and (2) when it creates a social organism capable

SOURCE: From pp. 134-154 LEADERSHIP IN ADMINISTRATION: A SOCIOLOGICAL INTERPRETATION by Philip Selznick. Copyright 1957, by Row, Peterson and Company. Reprinted by permission of Harper & Row, Publishers, Incorporated.

of fulfilling that mission. A company's decision to add a new product may be routine if the new is but an extension of the old. It is a critical decision, however, when it calls for a re-examination of the firm's mission and role, e.g., whether to remain primarily a producer of a raw commodity or to become a manufacturer of consumer goods. The latter choice will inevitably affect the outlook of management, the structure and control of the company, and the balance of forces in the industry.

Not only the setting of goals by top leadership but many other kinds of decisions at all administrative levels can be part of critical experience. Anything may enter the area of critical experience providing it affects the ability of the organization to uphold its distinctive aims and values. If an atmosphere congenial to creative research is required, the methods of assigning work, policing diligence, or judging output must be governed by that aim. This often produces tension between those executives most sensitive to the special needs of the enterprise and those who seek to apply more general and more neutral techniques of efficiency.

In going beyond efficiency, leadership also transcends "human engineering," at least as that is usually understood. Efficiency may require improved techniques of communication and supervision, but these techniques are largely indifferent to the aims they serve. The human relations specialist like his predecessor, the efficiency expert, is characteristically unmoved by program, by the content of what is to be done. His inspiration does not derive from the aim of creating a particular kind of auto firm or hospital or school. Rather his imagination is stirred by the processes of group interaction and the vision of a harmonious team, whatever its end may be.

This does not mean that communication and other forms of human interaction are unimportant to leadership. They do become vitally important when they are given content, when they serve the aim of fashioning a distinctive way of thinking or acting and thus help establish the human foundations for achieving a particular set of goals. Indeed, the *attainment* of efficiency, in the sense of transforming a basically inefficient organization into one that runs according to modern standards, may itself be a leadership goal. But here the task is a creative one, a matter of reshaping fundamental perspectives and relationships. It should not be confused with the routine administrative management of an organization already fully committed to the premises of rational accounting and discipline.

BEYOND ORGANIZATION

The design and maintenance of organizations is often a straightforward engineering proposition. When the goals of the organization are clear-cut, and when most choices can be made on the basis of known and objective technical criteria, the engineer rather than the leader is called for. His work may include human engineering in order to smooth personal relations, improve morale, or reduce absenteeism. But his problem remains one of adapting known quantities through known techniques to predetermined ends.

From the engineering perspective, the organization is made up of standardized building blocks. These elements, and the ways of putting them together, are the stock-in-trade of the organization engineer. His ultimate ideal is complete rationality, and this assumes that each member of the organization, and each constituent unit, can be made to adhere faithfully to an assigned, engineered role. Furthermore, the role assigned does not stem so much from the peculiar nature of *this* enterprise; rather, the roles are increasingly generalized and similar to parallel roles in other organizations. Only thus can the organization engineer take advantate of the growth of general knowledge concerning the conditions of efficient administrative management.

The limits of organization engineering become apparent when we must create a structure *uniquely adapted to the mission and role of the enterprise.* This adaptation goes beyond a tailored combination of uniform elements; it is an adaptation in depth, affecting the nature of the parts themselves. This is really a very familiar process, brought home to us most clearly when we recognize that certain firms or agencies are stamped by distinctive ways of making decisions or by peculiar commitments to aims, methods, or clienteles. In this way the organization as a technical instrument takes on values. As a vehicle of group integrity it becomes in some degree an end in itself. This process of becoming infused with value is part of what we mean by institutionalization. As this occurs, *organization management* becomes *institutional leadership.* The latter's main responsibility is not so much technical administrative management as the maintenance of institutional integrity.

The integrity of an enterprise goes beyond efficiency, beyond organization forms and procedures, even beyond group cohesion. Integrity combines organization and policy. It is the unity that emerges when a particular orientation becomes so firmly a part of group life that it colors and directs a wide variety of attitudes, decisions, and forms of organization, and does so at many levels of experience. The building of integrity is part of what we have called the "institutional embodiment of purpose" and its protection is a major function of leadership.

The protection of integrity is more than an aesthetic or expressive exercise, more than an attempt to preserve a comforting, familiar environment. It is a practical concern of the first importance because the defense of integrity is also a defense of the organization's *distinctive competence*. As institutionalization progresses the enterprise takes on a special character, and this means that it becomes peculiarly competent (or incompetent) to do a particular kind of work. This is especially important when much depends on the creation of an appropriate atmosphere, as in the case of efforts to hold tight transportation schedules or maintain high standards of quality. A considerable part of high-level salesmanship is an effort to show the firm's distinctive capability to produce a certain product or perform a special service. This is important in government too, where competing agencies having similar formal assignments work hard to develop and display their distinctive competencies.

The terms "institution," "organization character," and "distinctive competence" all refer to the same basic process—the transformation of an engineered, technical arrangement of building blocks into a social organism. This transition goes on unconsciously and inevitably wherever leeway for evolution and adaptation is allowed by the system of technical controls; and at least some such leeway exists in all but the most narrowly circumscribed organizations. Leadership has the job of guiding the transition from organization to institution so that the ultimate result effectively embodies desired aims and standards.

Occasionally we encounter a self-conscious attempt to create an institution. The history of the *New York Times*, for example, suggests such an effort. Ideals of objectivity and public instruction have deeply affected many aspects of the organization, including the nature of the staff, the pace of work, the relations to advertisers, and its role among other newspapers. Of course, it is relatively easy to see a newspaper as an institution because it so apparently touches familiar ideals. Whether it truly embodies those ideals is a question that appeals to all as relevant and sensible. But we have argued that the formation of institutions is a far more widespread phenomenon and is a process that must be understood if the critical experience of leadership is to be grasped.

Institutional analysis asks the question: What is the bearing of an existing or proposed procedure on the distinctive role and character of the enterprise? Very often, of course, organization practices are institutionally neutral, just as many body functions are independent of the personality structure. But the question must be put. Thus recent efforts to establish statistical and administrative control units for the judiciary look to improvements in the division of labor among judges, and to similar matters, for the achievement of a more "orderly flow of litigation." The proponents of greater efficiency reaffirm their adherence to the principle of judicial independence, and they believe this principle is not affected by improved administrative controls; they seek to "serve, not supervise." In this case it seems altogether likely that a wide measure of reform in judicial administration is possible without seriously undermining the judge's traditional image of his own role and sense of independence. Nevertheless, the experience of other institutions suggests that the managerial trend can have far-reaching effects, and the question of whether a set of proposed administrative reforms endangers the maintenance of desired values is always legitimate and necessary.

The lesson is this: Those who deal with the more obvious ideals—such as education, science, creativity, or freedom—should more fully recognize the dependence of these ideals on congenial though often mundane administrative arrangements. On the other hand, those who deal with more restricted values, such as the maintenance of a particular industrial competence, should be aware that these values too involve ideals of excellence, ideals that must be built into the social structure of the enterprise and become part of its basic character. In either case, a too ready acceptance of neutral techniques of efficiency, whatever their other merits, will contribute little to this institutional development and may even retard it.

The study of institutions is in some ways comparable to the clinical study of personality. It requires a genetic and developmental approach, an emphasis on historical origins and growth stages. There is a need to see the enterprise as a whole and to see how it is transformed as new ways of dealing with a changing environment evolve. As in the case of personality, effective diagnosis depends upon locating the special problems that go along with a particular character-structure; and we can understand character better when we see it as the product of self-preserving efforts to deal with inner impulses and external demands. In both personality and institutions "self-preservation" means more than bare organic or material survival. Self-preservation has to do with the maintenance of basic identity, with the integrity of a personal or institutional "self."

In approaching these problems, there is necessarily a close connection between clinical diagnosis of particular cases and the development of sound general knowledge. Our problem is to discover the characteristic ways in which *types* of institutions respond to *types* of circumstances. The significant classifications may well depart from common-sense distinctions among enterprises according to whether they perform economic, political, religious, or military functions. We may find that more general characteristics, such as professionalized managerial control, competence to make full use of creative talents, or dependence on volunteer personnel, are more helpful in classifying organizations and in understanding the types of problems they face and the solutions that may be available. Students of personality have had similar objectives and have made greater, although still very crude, efforts to get away from common-sense rubrics. Yet, despite theoretical difficulties, real progress has been made, and clinical success in diagnosis and therapy lends confidence to the larger scientific quest.

RESPONSIBLE LEADERSHIP

As the organization becomes an institution new problems are set for the men who run it. Among these is the need for institutional responsibility, which accounts for much of what we mean by statesmanship.

From a personal standpoint, responsible leadership is a blend of commitment, understanding, and determination. These elements bring together the selfhood of the leader and the identity of the institution. This is partly a matter of self-*conception*, for whatever his special background, and however important it may have been in the decision that gave him his office, the responsible leader in a mature institution must transcend his specialism. Self-*knowledge* becomes an understanding not only of the leader's own weaknesses and potentialities but of those qualities in the enterprise itself. And the assumption of command is a self-*summoning* process, yielding the will to know and the will to act in accordance with the requirements of institutional survival and fulfillment.

From a policy standpoint, and that is our primary concern, most of the characteristics of the responsible leader can be summarized under two headings: the avoidance of opportunism and the avoidance of utopianism.

Opportunism is the pursuit of immediate, short-run advantages in a way inadequately controlled by considerations of principle and ultimate consequence. To take advantage of opportunities is to show that one is alive, but institutions no less than persons must look to the long-run effects of present advantage. In speaking of the "long run" we have in mind not time as such but how change affects personal or institutional identity. Such effects are not usually immediately apparent, and therefore we emphasize the lapse of time. But changes in character or identity may occur quite rapidly.

Leadership is irresponsible when it fails to set goals and therefore lets the institution drift. The absence of controlling aims forces decisions to be made in response to immediate pressures. Of course, many large enterprises do drift, yet they survive. The penalties are not always swift, and very often bare survival is possible even though the fullest potentialities of the enterprise are not realized and significant changes in identity do occur.

The setting of institutional *goals* cannot be divorced from the enunciation of governing *principles*. Goal-setting, if it is institutionally meaningful, is framed in the language of character or identity, that is, it tells us what we should "do" in order to become what we want to "be." A decision to produce a new product or enter a new market, though it may set goals, is nevertheless irresponsible if it is not based on an understanding of the company's past and potential character. If the new venture, on analysis, requires a change in distinctive competence, then *that* becomes the new goal. Such a goal is bound up with principles because attaining and conserving a distinctive competence depends on an understanding of what standards are required and how to maintain them. If a grain processing firm moves into the chemical industry, it must learn how to build into its new division the competence to keep pace with rapid technological changes on pain of falling behind in the struggle against obsolescent products and techniques. Because the technique of attaining this is seldom based on explicitly formulated principles, it would be prudent to staff the new division, *especially* at the top, with men drawn from the chemical industry rather than with men drawn from the parent firm and representing its tradition and orientations.

When an enterprise is permitted to drift, making short-run, partial adaptations, the greatest danger lies in uncontrolled effects on organization character. If ultimately there is a complete change, with a new character emerging, those who formed and sustained the organization at the beginning may find that they no longer fit the organization. There is also the likelihood that character will not really be transformed: it will be *attenuated and confused*. Attenuation means that the sought-for distinctive competence becomes vague and abstract, unable to influence deeply the work of staff and operating divisions. This occurs when the formulation of institutional goals is an afterthought, a way of rationalizing activities actually resulting from opportunistic lines of decision. A confused organization character is marked by an unordered and disharmonious mixture of capabilities. The practical result is that the organization cannot perform any task effectively, and this weakens its ability to survive in the face of strong competition.

In addition to sheer drift stemming from the failure to set institutional goals, opportunism also reflects an excessive response to outside pressures. To be sure, leaders must take account of the environment, adapting to its limitations as well as to its opportunities, but we must beware of institutional surrender made in the mane of organizational survival. There is a difference between a university president who *takes account* of a state legislature or strong pressure groups and one who permits these forces to determine university policy. The leader's job is to *test* the environment to find out which demands can become truly effective threats, to *change* the environment by finding allies and other sources of external support, and to *gird* his organization by creating the means and the will to withstand attacks.

Here, too, we come back to the problem of maintaining institutional integrity. The ultimate cost of opportunistic adaptation goes beyond capitulation on specific issues. A more serious result is that outside elements may enter the organization and dominate parts of it. When this happens the organization is no longer truly independent, no longer making specific compromises as necessity dictates while retaining its unity and distinctive identity. Rather, it has given over a piece of itself to alien forces, making it possible for them to exercise broader influence on policy. The transformation of compromise or even defeat into partial organizational surrender can sometimes be a conscious measure of last resort, but it also occurs without full awareness on the part of the participants. In our study of the Tennessee Valley Authority, referred to above, just such a phenomenon was observed. A political compromise with local and national agricultural interests was implemented by permitting part of the TVA as an organization to be controlled by those forces, with extensive and unanticipated effects on the role and character of the agency. The avoidance of opportunism is not the avoidance of all compromise; it is the avoidance of compromise that undermines institutional integrity.

Opportunism also displays itself in a narrow self-centeredness, in an effort to exploit other groups for immediate, short-run advantages. If a firm offers a product or service to other firms, expectations of dependability are created, especially in the matter of continuing supply. If supplies are abruptly discontinued, activities that depended upon them will suffer. Hence a firm's reputation for dependability and concern for others becomes a matter of great importance wherever continuing relationships are envisioned. To act as if only a set of impersonal transactions were involved, with no responsibility beyond the strict terms of a contract, creates anxiety in the buyer, threatens to damage *his* reputation for dependability, and in the end weakens both parties.

The responsible leader recognizes the need for stable relations with the community of which his organization is a part, although he must test the environment to see how real that requirement is. A large and enduring enterprise will probably have to contribute to the maintenance of community stability, at least within its own field of action. In industry, this may take the form of participation in trade associations and other devices for self-regulation. The marginal firm, on the other hand, can afford to be irresponsible in dealing with the community because it is less dependent on stable relations with other firms or with a special clientele or labor force. Such firms have also less need of responsibility to themselves as institutions, for they have fewer hostages to fortune. Generally, responsibility to the enterprise and to the community go hand in hand, each increasing as the transition from organization to institution becomes more complete.

If opportunism goes too far in accepting the dictates of a "reality principle," utopianism hopes to avoid hard choices by a flight to abstractions.

This too results in irresponsibility, in escape from the true functions of leadership.

In Chapter Three we outlined some of the sources of utopianism. One of these is the *overgeneralization of purpose*. Thus "to make a profit" is widely accepted as a statement of business purpose, but this is too general to permit responsible decision-making. Here again, the more marginal the business, that is, the greater its reliance upon quick returns, easy liquidation, and highly flexible tactics, the less need there is for an institutionally responsible and more specific formulation of purpose. Indeed, the very generality of the purpose is congenial to the opportunism of these groups. But when institutional continuity and identity are at stake, a definition of mission is required that will take account of the organization's distinctive character, including present and prospective capabilities, as well as the requirements of playing a desired role in a particular industrial or commercial context.

Utopian wishful-thinking enters when men who purport to be insitutional leaders attempt to rely on overgeneralized purposes to guide their decisions. But when guides are unrealistic, yet decisions must be made, more realistic *but uncontrolled* criteria will somehow fill the gap. Immediate exigencies will dominate the actual choices that are made. In this way, the polarities of utopianism and opportunism involve each other.

Another manifestation of utopianism is the hope that the solution of technical problems will solve institutional problems. We have discussed the "retreat to technology" as a way of avoiding responsibility for the multiple ends that must be satisfied if the institution as a whole is to be successful. To be "just a soldier," "just an engineer," or even "just a businessman" is inconsistent with the demands of statesmanship. It is utopian and irresponsible to suppose that a narrow technical logic can be relied on by men who make decisions that, though they originate in technical problems, have larger consequences for the ultimate evolution of the enterprise and its position in the world.

This brand of utopianism is associated with adventurism, a willingness to commit the organization as a whole on the basis of a partial assessment of the situation derived from the particular technological perspective, such as that of the propagandist in foreign affairs or the engineer or designer in industry. Here again the utopian as technologist becomes the victim of opportunism.

Responsible leadership steers a course between utopianism and opportunism. Its responsibility consists in accepting the obligation of giving direction instead of merely ministering to organizational equilibrium; in adapting aspiration to the character of the organization, bearing in mind that what the organization has been will affect what it can be and do; and in transcending bare organizational survival by seeing that specialized decisions do not weaken or confuse the distinctive identity of the enterprise.

CREATIVE LEADERSHIP

To the essentially conservative posture of the responsible leader we must add a concern for change and reconstruction. This creative role has two aspects. First, there is what we have called the "institutional embodiment of purpose." Second, creativity is exercised by strategic and tactical planning, that is, analyzing the environment to determine how best to use the existing resources and capabilities of the organization. This essay has not treated the problem of externally oriented strategies. On the other hand, what can be done to establish policy internally depends upon the changing relation between the organization and its environment.

The inbuilding of purpose is a challenge to creativity because it involves transforming men and groups from neutral, technical units into participants who have a peculiar stamp, sensitivity, and commitment. This is ultimately an educational process. It has been well said that the effective leader must know the meaning and master the techniques of the educator. As in the larger community, education is more than narrow technical training; though it does not shrink from indoctrination, it also teaches men to think for themselves. The leader as educator requires an ability to interpret the role and character of the enterprise, to perceive and develop models for thought and behavior, and to find modes of communication that will inculcate general rather than merely partial perspectives.

The main practical import of this effort is that *policy will gain spontaneous and reasoned support*. Desired ends and means are sustained and furthered, not through continuous command, but as a free expression of truly accepted principles. This presumes that at least the core participants combine loyalty to the enterprise with a sensitive awareness of the principles by which it is guided. Loyalty by itself is not enough, just as blind patriotism is insufficient. There must also be an ability to sense when a course of action threatens institutional integrity.

To be sure, this ideal of rational, free-willed consent is virtually impossible to achieve in organizations that have narrow, practical aims and whose main problem is the disciplined harnessing of human energy to achieve those aims. But such organizations, just because of this narrowness, are but meagerly institutionalized and have correspondingly little need for executive statesmanship. The creativity we speak of here is particularly necessary —and peculiarly possible—where, as discussed earlier, the transition from organization to institution is in process or has occurred.

To create an institution we rely on many techniques for infusing day-to-day behavior with long-run meaning and purpose. One of the most important of these techniques is the elaboration of socially integrating myths. These are efforts to state, in the language of uplift and idealism, what is distinctive about the aims and methods of the enterprise. Successful institutions are usually able to fill in the formula, "What we are proud of around here is . . . ." Sometimes, a fairly explicit institutional philosophy is worked out; more often, a sense of mission is communicated in more indirect but no less significant ways. The assignment of high prestige to certain activities will itself help to create a myth, especially if buttressed by occasional explicit statements. The specific ways of projecting a myth are as various as communication itself. For creative leadership, it is not the communication of a myth that counts; rather, creativity depends on having the will and the insight to see the necessity of the myth, to discover a successful formulation, and above all to create the organizational conditions that will sustain the ideals expressed.

Successful myths are never merely cynical or manipulative, even though they may be put forward self-consciously to further the chances of stability or survival. If a state university develops a concept of "service to the community" as its central ideal, as against more remote academic aspirations, this may have its origins in a sense of insecurity, but it will not be innocent in application. To be effective, the projected myth cannot be restricted to holiday speeches or to testimony before legislative committees. It will inevitably color many aspects of university policy, affecting standards of admission, orientations of research, and the scope of the curriculum. The compulsion to embody the myth in practice has a dual source, reflecting inner needs and outer demands. Externally, those who can enforce demands upon the institution will not be content with empty verbal statements. They will expect conformity and the myth itself will provide a powerful lever to that end.

The executive acts out the myth for reasons of self-expression, but also for quite practical administrative reasons. He requires *some* integrating aid to the making of many diverse day-to-day decisions, and the myth helps to fulfill that need. Sharp discrepancies between theory and practice threaten his own authority in the eyes of subordinates; comformity to the myth will lessen "trouble" with outside groups. Not least important, he can hope that the myth will contribute to a unified sense of mission and thereby to the harmony of the whole. If the administrator is primarily dedicated to maintaining a smooth-running machine, and only weakly committed to substantive aims, these advantages will seem particularly appealing.

In the end, however, whatever their source, myths are institution builders. Making the myth effective willy-nilly entrenches particular objectives and capabilities, although these may not be the ones that initially inspired the sponsors of the enterprise. Myth-making may have roots in a sensed need to improve efficiency and morale; but its main office is to help create an integrated social organism.

The art of the creative leader is the art of institution-building, the reworking of human and technological materials to fashion an organism that embodies new and enduring values. The opportunity to do this depends on a considerable sensitivity to the politics of internal change. This is more than a struggle for power among contending groups and leaders. It is equally a matter of avoiding recalcitrance and releasing energies. Thus winning consent to new directions depends on how secure the participants feel. When many routine problems of technical and human organization remain to be solved, when the minimum conditions for holding the organization together are only precariously met, it is difficult to expend energy on long-range planning and even harder to risk experimental programs. When the organization is in good shape from an engineering standpoint it is easier to put ideals into practice. Old activities can be abandoned without excessive strain if, for example, the costs of relatively inefficient but morale-saving transfer and termination can be absorbed. Security is bartered for consent. Since this bargain is seldom sensed as truly urgent, a default of leadership is the more common experience.

On the same theme, security can be granted, thereby releasing energies for creative change, by examining established procedures to distinguish those important to a sense of security from those essential to the aims of the enterprise. Change should focus on the latter; stability can be assured to practices that do not really matter so far as objectives are concerned but which do satisfy the need to be free from threatening change. Many useless industrial conflicts have been fought to protect prerogative and deny security, with but little effect on the ultimate competence of the firm.

If one of the great functions of administration is the exertion of cohesive force in the direction of institutional security, another great function is the creation of conditions that will make possible in the future what is excluded in the present. This requires a strategy of change that looks to the attainment of new capabilities more nearly fulfilling the truly felt needs and aspirations of the institution. The executive becomes a statesman as he makes the transition from administrative management to institutional leadership.

ABOUT THE AUTHOR—The works of Philip Zelznick, a theorist and keen student of formal organizations, are of equal interest to sociologists as to political scientists. In two monographs, focussing on very different organizations, he has employed the study of a specific organization to serve as the springboard for the development of theory. *TVA and the Grass Roots* was published in 1949. *The Organization Weapon: A Study of Bolshevik Strategy and Tactics*, first published in 1952, was the outcome of Selznick's work for the Rand Corporation. Selznick is also the author of *Leadership in Administration* (1957), and co-author of *Old Age and Political Behavior* (1959), and a sociology text now in its fourth edition.

Selznick was born in Newark in 1919 and attended City College of New York. He received his M.A. and Ph. D. from Columbia. His academic career began at the University of Minnesota. In 1947 he joined the Sociology Department at the University of California at Los Angeles. In 1952 he moved to the Berkeley campus, and served as Chairman of the Sociology Department from 1963-1967. He is chairman of California's Center for the Study of Law and Society. During 1948-52 he was a research associate for the Rand Corporation. From 1957 to 1962 he was a Consultant for the Fund for the Republic's trade union project.

Innovation

This section deals not with what change libraries should make nor even very much with the need for change in libraries. Rather it is concerned with their capacity for change. Basic questions are raised regarding the organizational environment required for change and the attitudes and personality factors associated with a receptiveness or resistance to change.

This question is of increasing concern to social scientists who study organizations and this section includes only a small fragmentary introduction culled from a growing body of literature. The readings deal with those factors which indicate willingness to change, adapt and innovate, and less with the equally important aspect of change implementation.

Innovational and Authoritarian Personalities

by Everett E. Hagen

> *This selection explores the personality dimension of change. Here is insight into why the innovator—and his antithesis, the authoritarian, behave as they do. Hagen's thesis, that traditional cultures will not change without change in the personalities of those who form its culture, may be applied to libraries. The reader is left with the gnawing question of precisely how to influence the culture of librarianship in order to attract those with different propensities.*

The interrelationships between personality and social structure are such as to make it clear that social change will not occur without change in personalities. We can more readily analyze changes in the personality type that is typical in traditional societies, authoritarian personality, if we probe that personality type further. We may understand it better if we delineate a contrasting case.

In discussing social change, Riesman has described tradition-directed and autonomous individuals, and in exploring the problems of colonial control Mannoni has referred to personalities dominated by a dependency complex and an inferiority complex respectively.[1] In the discussion below, the reader familiar with Riesman and Mannoni will be reminded of both pairs of contrasts, but neither seems to me to delineate fully the contrasting personality types that are typical of traditional and creative societies respectively. Hence instead of using the terminology of either author, I shall refer to "authoritarian" and "innovational" personalities.

I am using the term "innovational personality" rather than "creative personality" since the latter seems less descriptive. It will be well to begin the discussion by making clear the relationship between creativity and innovation.

CREATIVITY AND INNOVATION

Innovation consists of organizing reality into relationships embodying new mental or aesthetic concepts, the new relationships serving the purpose of the innovator better than the old. Analytically, and also in time sequence, innovation involves two steps: arriving at a new mental conception, and converting it into action or into material form.[2]

In technological innovation the second step may involve only design or rearrangement of some items of physical equipment or it may involve the organization of a group of human beings into a going concern that carries out a new concept. In the latter case it is entrepreneurship; the concept of entrepreneurship seems always to include the management of other human beings.

In the limiting case the process consists of the first step alone; the individual may solve a problem mentally without any overt action. Perhaps the mathematician most closely approaches this limit, his only material craftsmanship being that of writing down his concepts. In technical innovation, however, putting flesh on the idea is of the essence of the process.

Arriving at the new conception may be termed the creative act, and sometimes the term "innovation" is reserved for the second step.[3] However, the implication that putting flesh on the concept is not creative is illusory, for a concept of new productive equipment or a new method of organization of human beings is hardly complete when it is only an idea in the mind. The purely mental concept probably virtually never anticipates correctly all the properties the human or physical material will exhibit when it is being reshaped. Creative adjustment and revision will be necessary as the idea is worked out overtly. Sometimes, of course, the further creativity required is very little. I have suggested that in the adaptation of Western technical methods to optimum use in underdeveloped economies it is great.

There is no such thing as innovation in the abstract. Innovation is always innovation in some specific field, involving some specific materials or concepts, or relationships of some sort to other

---

SOURCE: Reprinted by permission from Everett E. Hagen, *On the Theory of Social Change: How Economic Growth Begins* (Homewood, Ill.: The Dorsey Press), pp. 86–98.

persons. Some types of innovation will involve overcoming resistances by other persons; others will not. Some will involve managing a large organization; others, working in isolation. Some will involve experiencing smells or dirt; others will not. Some will have an aura of learned or sacred activity; others of practical work. And so on. An individual will enjoy one or another type of activity or relationship in the degree to which its various aspects satisfy his various attitudes. An individual will not innovate in a sphere in which, on balance, he finds dissatisfaction in working. Thus, in addition to creativity, attitudes favorable to working in one or another field are necessary for innovation in that field. In the present chapter I shall discuss the general characteristics of creativity at some length and pay only brief attention to the added characteristics of personality that cause creativity to be exercised in one field rather than another.

INNOVATIONAL PERSONALITY

The Quality of Creativity

When it is stated that innovation requires creativity, the reader should not assume that the term "creativity" refers to genius. Creativity exists in varying degrees; the man who conceives of an improvement in a can opener as well as the man who conceives of the theory of relativity is creative. Technological progress results from the actions of men characterized by varying degrees of creativity. The discussion of creativity refers, therefore, not merely to the limiting case of genius but to the quality of creativity in general, in whatever degree it may be found in a given individual.

The major qualities that constitute creativity are easy to list imprecisely: openness to experience, and, underlying this, a tendency to perceive phenomena, especially in an area of life that is of interest to the individual, as forming systems of interacting forces whose action is explainable; creative imagination, of which the central component is the ability to let one's unconscious processes work on one's behalf; confidence and content in one's own evaluations; satisfaction in facing and attacking problems and in resolving confusion or inconsistency; a sense that one has a duty or responsibility to achieve; intelligence; energy; and, often, related to several of these, a perception that the world is somewhat threatening and that one must strive perpetually if one is to be able to cope with it. The type of creative personality that is driven by a sense that the world is threatening sometimes seems to belong to a different category from the person characterized by some of the other qualities listed. I shall discuss first the ideal or pure type of unanxious creative person, and then indicate how the sense of living in a threatening world qualifies the characteristics described.

Poincaré has suggested the "capacity to be surprised" and Carl R. Rogers "openness to experience" as essential to creativity.[4] I would judge that the meaning of the two is almost identical. What is referred to is an unconscious alertness that leads the individual to note that some aspect of an everyday phenomenon differs from the expected and to appreciate the significance of the difference. This is the capacity that leads an individual to note that, contrary to the body of scientific authority in his time and the conclusions of common sense, bodies fall at the same rate regardless of their weight if air resistance is the same; to have his curiosity aroused by the fact that iron filings adhere to a coil of wire as an electrical current passes through it; to observe that some men with paralyzed limbs handle them in ways that suggest that the paralysis of function begins at a point at which there is no physiological reason for it to begin—to note such a thing and say to himself, "What an interesting force must have caused that! I wonder what its implications are."

Basic to this quality of observation is assurance in one's own evaluation of experience, freedom from a tendency to take a generally accepted evaluation for granted and overlook facts inconsistent with it. Basic to it also is a tendency to assume that one can understand experience. The creative individual has a sense, deeper than any rational acceptance of cause and effect, that the world is orderly; that every phenomenon of life or of some large area of experience is part of a system whose operation can be understood and explained; that if he approaches the sphere of life in which he is interested it will respond dependably, even though perhaps in a complex fashion, so that if he has enough information he will be able to understand the response. If the world were not orderly, or if the individual were not confident and content in his ability to understand its order, he would not be unconsciously alert to unexpected aspects of phenomena, for they would contain no lessons for him.

Openness to experience, then, refers to a capacity to note phenomena that are starting points for new analyses. Creative imagination refers to a tendency to leap far afield from a starting point, to note relationships where others had not thought to find them. In part it is the product simply of superior innate intelligence, of a mind which can hold many factors in simultaneous consideration and analysis. But it is more than this. It embraces two kinds of mental activity. One is the capacity to use an interesting or unsatisfactory situation as a springboard from which one's imagination roams, apparently uncontrolled and seemingly undirected, in varying associational bypaths, regressions, and far reaches, then returns to the matter at hand either with a workable conception for the reconstruction or transformation of the unsatisfactory situation or with a novel analytical model of the significance of the observed fact. Conscious movement from one step of analysis to the next is at a minimum; the individual does not ask consciously whether the wandering is pertinent to the problem.

The other is the capacity to let one's purely unconscious processes work for one without any conscious awareness or acknowledgement of the activity and to admit the results to consciousness. Unaware that his mind has been working on the problem, the individual finds that a solution, an appropriate ordering, an explanation has come to him. Visualization occurs as he wakes from sleep, when he has been daydreaming, on rare occasions in a dream while sleeping, or perhaps while he walks his dog. "It came to me," the scientist sometimes says, or, "As the problem returned to my mind, I saw how it could be done." Subsequently he demonstrates to himself the logic of the solution. The solution was presumably reached by a sequence of logical steps or chain or association of thoughts (how else could it have been reached?), but these were unconscious, or, sometimes, in more precise psychological terminology, preconscious.

Such creative imagination is often stressed as a part of literary or, more generally, aesthetic creativity. But there is ample evidence from biographies of scientists that it is important in their creative achievement also. [5] There is less evidence concerning strictly technological creativity, but it is reasonable to suppose that this is because of absence of documentation rather than because of a difference in the creative process.

These two aspects of creative imagination have two important elements in common: the unconscious processes of the individual are productive rather than distractive in nature, and the individual is unafraid or little afraid of them. The aspect of a problem that some individuals react unconsciously to is a sense of frustration at not having an answer at hand. As a defense against that sense of frustration, the individual, if he lets himself go, experiences fantasies of magic achievement, crushing victories over persons who have slighted him, sexual conquest, the attainment of position so high that all of his wishes are gratified, and the like. Even if he does not let himself go, such fantasies occur in his unconscious processes. The unconscious processes of some individuals, on the other hand, react to the substance of a problem or surprising phenomena at hand, and aid in logical and imaginative analysis of it. When the individual "floats," his mind rearranges elements of thought in bold ways but ways which, when he returns to the details of reality, are fruitful. Every individual responds in some degree in both ways. Creative individuals are those who primarily respond productively.

The individual who responds with unacceptable fantasies may shut them out from his conscious mind, but he senses dimly the emotional surges within him and fears what is going on in his unconscious. Finding impulses in himself which he regards as evil or foul or dangerous, he is afraid of letting his unconscious processes come to the surface for fear that dangerous or evil or vile urges will appear. Hence his unconscious processes are not only primarily unproductive; even insofar as they are productive, they are unavailable to him. The results do not appear in his conscious mind. The creative individual, on the other hand, is not afraid of his unconscious processes, and their results appear in his conscious mind. In the technical terms of psychoanalysis, he can "regress in the service of the ego."[6]

More than other individuals, he understands his unconscious motivations.[7] It is commonly recognized that ability to understand one's unconscious motivations is an important element in artistic and especially literary creativity; one understands others and can portray them only to the degree that one understands oneself. It is less well recognized that the same understanding of self may be conducive to understanding of the physical world as well. The man who understands something of his unconscious motivations understands his interaction with phenomena outside him as a system in which there is causality. He is self-conscious; he watches his own behavior as an observer. This understanding seems to be the model for the individual's perception of the external world as a system and subject to analysis, the perception which gives him openness to experience, which makes him wonder creatively why some everyday phenomenon is as it is.

Such an individual is somewhat detached from himself and from his society. To some degree all that goes on is something he watches from the outside. This detachment seems to be an integral part of creativity. It does not imply lack of interest in the world or of concern about it. In fact, it is often peculiarly associated with a sense of moral obligation, of responsibility for society and the world, to be discussed later.

This sense of detachment has often been observed in creative workers in science as well as in literature and art. It must also be associated with technological innovation. It is difficult to see how any person can manipulate the world about him, put its elements together in new ways to obtain new order, except as he sees it as a system outside himself, detached from himself. Even the tinkerer who merely improves a machine must see the machine as a system to be analyzed rather than simply taking it for granted as an instrument if he is to be free to conceive of changes in it. The business administrator, whose function is to manipulate other men, often gives little overt evidence of this detachment; yet his understanding of how other men function is evidence of such understanding of himself, which again is a symptom of this detachment.

Because the creative individual assumes that the world will respond dependably to his judicious initiative, he does not feel threatened by unresolved situations. He has no need to turn to the judgment of others for reassurance or relief from anxiety, for the facing of unresolved situations arouses little anxiety within him. He trusts his own evaluations of them. His "locus of evaluative judgment" is within himself.[8] This does not mean that he is always sure that he is right, but only that he does not have anxiety about his own observations and evaluations. Knowing that the comments of others may suggest new avenues of approach or added relationships in a complex problem which has no one solution, he may turn to them, but as instruments to help him, not for reassurance.

He feels satisfaction at the prospect of testing his capacities against a problem and is drawn toward the attempt. If the solution does not readily appear, and the problem is of relevance to his interests, it remains a matter on a shelf in his mind, and he will anticipate the possibility of realizing a solution later.

Because he is not afraid of problems or of the world, he has a tolerance for recognizing apparently contradictory or discrepant facts. He will not unconsciously and conveniently ignore one of them because the discrepancy alarms him. But, because he perceives the world as orderly, he assumes that two discrepant facts, both having been verified as true, are not really contradictory but are part of a higher order whose nature he does not yet realize. Their apparent inconsistency, like any problem, is therefore a challenge to him, and he feels satisfaction in seeking a higher order within which they will both rest comfortably. He feels a need to place them in a logical or pleasing relationship. Too simple order is uninteresting and somewhat unpleasant to him.[9] He may have some fondness for disorder and conflicting logic since they suggest to him that a higher order is available.

As his experience and confidence in his ability grow, he will lose interest in simpler problems and will seek to attack more and more difficult ones, or sometimes merely different ones. The former trend is manifested by a painter who as his career proceeds passes from simple symmetry to balance of colors and forms so complex that the picture is confusing to the novice but brings the greatest aesthetic pleasure to the individual whose comprehension has grown until he can appreciate it, and the latter in a painter who moves from simple realism to impressionsim to expressionsim toward abstraction, as Rembrandt did. It is also readily noticeable in the other arts and in literature. In business the process is one of moving up the ladder to positions which are more difficult as well as more responsible.

In mathematics the peak of creativity usually comes early; almost all of the great mathematicians made their most original contributions before the age of thirty, whereas in some other fields creative activity reaches its peak later in life. The difference seems to be associated with some degree of difference in the locus of the creative process. In mathematics the immediate creative act is more largely unconscious; the new concept presents itself to the conscious mind in largely finished form; whereas in many other fields a greater element of conscious judgment enters. Perhaps almost no one has within him more than one great new view of the world. In a field unrelated to the complex facts of life, one in which abstract logical relationships alone constitute the materials, one may encompass the known logic and realize his new view in his twenties. Then, his mind being drawn thereafter to the area which proved so satisfying, he spends the rest of his life tidying up and making minor advances here and there. However, in fields in which the complex details and relationships of real life are pertinent to the creative act, accumulation of knowledge by strengthening the basis for judgment provides increasing grist for one's unconscious (as well as conscious) processes to work on as the years pass, and creativity matures later in life.

The innovator not only feels pleasure in solving problems; he also feels a duty to achieve. The avowed goal of economic innovators, the purpose which they have felt it their duty to serve, has varied greatly among societies, but the sense of duty is a constant. Often this sense is religious in nature. The doctrine that the specific religious dogma of the Protestant Dissenters is peculiarly associated with innovational activity is obsolete,[10] but a number of scholars observing economic growth in various societies have noted that innovators in the early stages of growth seem to be characterized by a common ethic which is appropriately termed religious in nature, whatever their religious dogma. They feel a personal responsibility to transform the world that far transcends a profit motive.

To these qualities should be added intelligence and energy.[11] Intellectual capacity is in part inherited, and no doubt innate capacity is higher among innovators than among the population in general. In part, however, the intellectual capacity of innovators is due to the qualities described above. An individual with a given intellectual endowment will use it the more effectively the greater the degree to which he perceives the world as an orderly system, the greater his contentedness in his own judgment and reactions, the greater his satisfaction in attacking problems or in resolving inconsistencies, and the less the degree to which his energy has to be used to suppress unacceptable impulses within himself. The person with lack of these attitudes toward the world will be inhibited from attempting to use his capacities. But these attitudes are not simply the products of high innate intelligence; they derive primarily from conditions of the individual's environment as he grows up, and especially in childhood, that are quite independent of his innate capacities.

Much the same factors determine the individual's level of energy. No doubt there are innate or, more broadly, constitutional determinants of energy just as there are of intelligence. The individual who is constitutionally endowed with an ampler than average reserve of energy stands a better than average chance of accomplishing creative deeds. But to a large degree the ability to draw on a great store of energy seems to depend on an individual's freedom from doubt and mistrust of himself, on his sense that the world is orderly and will respond dependably and pleasingly to his initiative. It is as though, not having to use his energy in conflicts within himself, he has it available to direct toward the world outside him.

The creative individual is not necessarily a happy man who faces problems with pure pleasure. Rather, most creative individuals are driven to creative activity by an incessant anxiety; their perception of the world as a threatening place leaves them only while they are active, then returns to drive them on again. Yet in other individuals anxiety is associated with rage that provokes urges and fantasies which persist in the unconscious and cause an individual to seal over his unconscious processes for fear of what he will find in them. (The anxiety is also largely unconscious; if questioned, the individual would probably deny its existence.) The two types of personality must be distinguished.

An individual acquires persisting anxiety if in his early life he faces a sequence of situations important to him that he cannot resolve satisfactorily or can resolve satisfactorily only by repeated attempts and with great difficulty—hunger, pressure on him to walk, and so on. The anxiety-creating situations may, however, be of two types which convey to the child differing perceptions of the world. He may become anxious because persons important to him, for example, his mother, seem willing to hurt him. If so, combined with his anxiety will be rage directed at her and fantasies of revenge. However, he must suppress these from consciousness since his mother is so important to him that he dares not admit that he hates her. He then seals over his unconscious processes, and their inaccessibility to him prevents him from being creative, or greatly cripples his creativity.

Suppose, however, that his experiences of infancy and early childhood give him a firm and satisfying impression of the loving nurturance of his mother, but that repeatedly he is unable to achieve as she seems to wish him to. He may then feel that the fault must lie in him, and there may become built into him anxiety that he may not accomplish enough, anxiety that drives him all his life to achieve in order to regain fleetingly that temporary feeling of security conveyed by his mother's praise and caresses. In this case, little rage and hatred may be provoked in him, and his unconscious processes will remain accessible to him. Given the other necessary qualities, he becomes the anxious creative individual.

Of course the perceptions sketched here as arising from his relationship to his mother may arise also in relationships to other persons important to him in early life.

He may not be quite as open to experience as the unanxious creative individual because he is more fearful of experience. The accessibility of his unconscious processes to him may be somewhat less than to the unanxious individual, since the tensions of his childhood may have caused some reactions in him which were fearful or unacceptable and had to be repressed permanently. But these handicaps to creativity are compensated for by his incessant scanning of the horizon and by the great energy which he is incessantly driven to exert in defense against his anxieties.

Indeed, innovational activity is always a reaction to some degree of anxiety. The individual who is not in the least pushed toward creative activity as a relief from anxiety but is only drawn toward it by the great pleasure it gives him is an ideal case; he does not exist in life. Creativity does not require complete access to one's unconscious processes, complete confidence in one's own judgment, and so on. It requires only somewhat more of these qualities than characterizes the average person. Moreover, some types of innovation may require only a moderate degree of creativity combined with dogged determination or a high degree of motivation to dominate other men. Thus the characteristics of creativity described may not be high in some economic innovators. Often, however, they are greater than appears on the surface, especially since in business it is often desirable to keep one's inner life to oneself and to cast an image of oneself as a highly conventional extrovert.

The Determinants of the Innovational Field

The discussion to this point has referred only to creativity in general. However, an individual is never creative in general; he is creative in some specific activity or activities. His being attuned to one or another sort of activity is therefore an element in his creativity.

Perhaps we may think of the characteristics which channel and release creativity into one field or another as being of three types: one's values concerning activities, one's anxieties or satisfactions in relationships with other men, and the scale of activity or influence in which one feels content or secure.

Perhaps there is, first of all, a rather direct attachment to one activity or another. In some sense an individual may enjoy for its own sake tilling the soil or tinkering with machinery or contemplating mathematical relationships. Second, one may have one or another attitude toward relationships with other men. One may find satisfaction in competition with them; the act of inner or outer aggression may give one pleasure or temporarily relieve one's anxiety. Or one may find a sense of security in being able to influence other men by one's logic or persuasiveness or in gaining a position of control over them. Or on the contrary one may feel uneasy in any close competition or co-operation with other men and may turn toward working in isolation. In combination these characteristics plus the alternatives objectively open to him will determine the occupation in which a man chooses to work. Third, if one is characterized by a drive to influence or direct other men, he may be content to do so on a small scale or, on the other hand, he may feel that he has not sufficiently proved himself or made himself secure so long as there are wider groups against which he has not tested himself. One may therefore be content to work in his own pond—perhaps intellectually or technically or socially a very important pond—or one may be driven to seek national influence in his profession or in society as a whole and reform all society.

The choice of technology as a field in which to innovate of course requires one or another of certain combinations of these attitudes. It was noted in Chapter 4 that the sense of identity of a member of the elite classes in traditional society makes him unable to function effectively in work which he associates with the menial classes. In general, the authoritarian personality of traditional society is uncreative. If, however, a deviant individual of the elite classes became creative, he would nevertheless be unable to innovate in technology so long as he retained the elite antipathy to manual labor, work with tools and machinery, and interest in the physical world.[12]

In recapitulation, then, the creative individual is unconsciously alert to new aspects of phenomena; he assumes that the phenomena of the area of experience of interest to him form a system that he can understand and manage, and that therefore encountering unexpected aspects will lead him to new understanding, not to frustration. He responds imaginatively to the stimuli that new observations provide; his unconscious mental processes deal with the substance of the problem rather than reacting to a sense of frustration with angry or aggressive fantasies or fantasies of magic solutions. And since he does not fear the content of his unconscious processes, their results are available to his conscious mind. He observes with detachment his own interactions with the world outside him; his recognition that both the reactions of the world to him and his reactions to the world have understandable causes, that he himself is a system, is probably the basis of his assumption that the larger world is orderly and understandable. He trusts his evaluations of the world. The prospect of resolving a problem therefore attracts him; he approaches rather than evades it. Many effective innovators are oppressed by a pervasive anxiety concerning life. Their anxiety, however, is not the result of conflicting urges whose balance creates paralysis; rather, it is a gnawing feeling that they are not doing enough, or not well enough. Repeatedly, they escape from their anxiety temporarily by creative achievement. Effective innovators also typically feel a sense of duty to achieve.

AUTHORITARIAN PERSONALITY

Against the foil of this description of creative personality, it is possible to enrich the discussion of authoritarian personality presented in Chapter 4, for many characteristics of authoritarian personality are simply the negatives of characteristics of the creative individual. For that reason they may be outlined in a few paragraphs. Authoritarian personality is not the only type of uncreative personality; what is described here briefly is not uncreative personality in general but one specific type.

One gains an understanding of most of the facets of authoritarian personality if one assumes that as a child the authoritarian individual acquired no perception of the phenomena around him as elements in system whose operation is amenable to analysis and responsive to his judicious initiative. Instead he must have gained two other impressions of the world that were overwhelmingly important in disciplining his later behavior. One of these is a perception of the world as arbitrary, capricious, not amenable to analysis, as consisting of an agglomeration of phenomena not related by a cause-and-effect network. The other is that the caprice of the world is not accidental but the play of willful powers far greater than his which serve their own purposes and disregard his unless he submits his will to theirs. These perceptions, we must assume, because the experiences which gave rise to them were very painful, have been pressed down out of his conscious mind; but he retains them in his unconscious, and they guide his adult behavior.

These perceptions breed in him a fear of using his initiative, an uncertainty concerning the quality of his own judgment, a tendency to let someone else evaluate a situation in order to avoid frustration and anxiety. Out of these perceptions also grows uneasiness at facing unresolved situations. Rather than rely on his own analysis to solve problems of the physical world or his relations to other individuals, he avoids pain by falling back on traditional ways of behavior that his parents and other earlier authorities taught him, and by relying on the judgment or will of individuals superior to him in authority or power.

To an individual guided by such perceptions it would seem to serve no satisfying purpose to be open to experience. Since phenomena and the forces that control them seem arbitrary to him, there are no useful deductions to be drawn from them. Moreover, a novel phenomenon would be disturbing since if it posed a problem it would arouse the anxiety associated with prospective initiative on his part. Hence for both positive and negative reasons he wears blinders to the interesting details of the world. He finds it safer to rely on traditional rules or on the judgment of older, wiser, and superior persons.

The painful experiences which gave rise to these perceptions must have created hatreds in him which shocked those around him. We shall see in Chapter 6 that they also tend to arouse in him both doubt of his manliness and homosexual inclinations and desires. He presses these fears and unacceptable urges out of his conscious mind and seals over his unconscious processes as best he can because he is uneasy about what thoughts and fears they include. Hence his unconscious processes are inaccessible to him. In addition, they would not be useful if they were accessible, for instead of reactions to the phenomena he has currently observed they consist of the inadmissible impulses and desires which he has repressed and which are activated anew by the anxiety created by facing a problem.

But rage and pain, though repressed, are still within him. He dared not express his rage against the superior authorities who early in life directed him arbitrarily, but once he is an elder in the community, or a father, or even an older brother, he can somewhat satisfy his aggressiveness by his dominance over his inferiors. Moreover, as he moves to successive positions of authority at successive stages in his life the anxiety he feels in ambiguous situations causes him to insist that his own authority not be questioned, just as it earlier required that he submit his judgment to superior judgment and will. Thus each traditional adult individual in traditional society presents strong resistance to the questioning of authoritative decisions or traditional ways. That resistance is an important obstacle to change.

In sum, then, the member of a traditional society is uncreative for several reasons. He perceives the world as an arbitrary place rather than an orderly one amenable to analysis and responsive to his initiative. His unconscious processes are both inaccessible and uncreative. He resolves his relationships with his fellows primarily on the basis of ascriptive authority. He avoids the anxiety caused by facing unresolved situations in the physical world by reliance on the judgment of authority.

The analysis is incomplete in two respects. It is based on an assumption concerning the authoritarian individual's early perceptions of the nature of the world and on a further assumption that he remembers these perceptions unconsciously and generalizes from them in ways that guide all his later behavior. Unless these two assumptions can be justified, the sketch is only a possibly interesting speculation.

FOOTNOTES

[1] David Riesman, *The Lonely Crowd* (New Haven, Conn.: Yale University Press, 1950), and O. Mannoni, *Psychologie de la Colonisation* (Paris, Ed. du Seuil, 1950), translated into English by Pamela Powesland as *Prospero and Caliban: The Psychology of Colonization* (New York: Frederick A. Praeger, Inc., 1956).

[2] The concept can hardly be put into overt form until after it has been conceived. The act of conception may be unconscious, however, and the innovator may not know that he has arrived at a new concept until he has produced a new artifact or a new organization. Conceivably, also, the innovator may arrive at a new result by trial and errror, and only when he sees the results analyze the operation and realize the relationships responsible for the results. The statement in the text ignores this case.

[3] Either the first step or both may also be termed "problem-solving." Insofar as a problem has been solved previously and one merely repeats a known solution, one's activity is not problem solving. But any activity, mental or overt, that is not purely random is problem solving in some degree. Even walking down a familiar street involves some new elements. Innovation or creative activity, more strictly defined, is performing activity that involves problem solving in a high degree.

[4] Poincaré's phrase is quoted by Erich Fromm in Harold H. Anderson (ed.), *Creativity and Its Cultivation* (New York: Harper & Bros., 1959), p. 48. "Scientific genius," said Poincaré, "is the capacity to be surprised." Rogers' phrase is in *ibid.*, p. 75. Several essays in this interesting volume are pertinent to the present discussion.

[5] An interesting brief discussion of its presence in scientists is presented by Professor Donald W. MacKinnon of the Institute of Personality Assessment and Research of the University of California, in a paper delivered at a convention of the Western Branch, American Public Health Association, at San Francisco, June 2-5, 1959, which I have from him in mimeographed form.

[6] Ernst Kris, *Psychoanalytical Explorations in Art* (New York: International Universities Press, 1952).

[7] Which include passive, so-called "feminine" needs, needs to be dependent and to be nurtured, needs for aesthetic gratification. These needs are greater in him, as measured by psychological tests, than in the average person. Professor Donald W. MacKinnon, *op. cit.*, discussed relevant research at the Institute of Personality Assessment and Research.

[8] Carl R. Rogers, in *Creativity and Its Cultivation*, p. 76.

[9] This is indicated by studies at the Institute of Personality Assessment and Research of the University of California of individuals from the arts and sciences whose careers demonstrate a high degree of creativity. See Frank Barron, "The Psychology of Imagination," *Scientific American*, Vol. CXCIX (September, 1958), pp. 150-66.

[10] Perhaps it never was held by scholars. Max Weber in *The Protestant Ethic and the Spirit of Capitalism*, trans. Talcott Parsons (New York: Charles Scribner's Sons, 1956), at times seems to argue this thesis but then backs away from it.

[11] For an analysis of leading American business executives which stresses their energy, see Osborn Elliott, *Men at the Top* (New York: Harper & Bros., 1959).

[12] Of course the same forces in his immediate environment which caused him to become deviant in ways that made him creative would probably also impinge on some of these attitudes.

ABOUT THE AUTHOR—Everett E. Hagen has been a student of economics in its international as well as its American framework. Born in Minnesota in 1906, he is a graduate of St. Olaf College, and received his M.A. and Ph.D. from the University of Wisconsin, the latter in 1941. His first academic post was as an economics instructor at Michigan State College. From 1942 to 1948 he held various positions in the federal government, returning to academia as a Professor of Economics at the University of Illinois in 1948. During his years in Washington, he was employed by the National Resources Planning Board, the Federal Reserve Board, the Office of War Mobilization and Planning Board, and the Bureau of the Budget.

In his international service, Hagen was an economic adviser to the Government Union of Burma from 1951-53, a member of a technical mission to the Government of Japan in 1956, and a consultant to the United States Council of the International Chamber of Commerce in 1955. He has also made research trips to Colombia, Brazil, and Saudi Arabia. At Massachusetts Institute of Technology at present he is a Professor of Economics and Political Science and a member of the Center for International Studies. Hagen is author of numerous articles in scholarly journals, and his monograph publications, some with co-authors, have centered on international developmental themes: *The Economic Development of Burma* (1956); *The Emerging Nations* (1961); *On the Theory of Social Change* (1962); and the *Economics of Development* (1968).

Bureaucracy and Innovation

by Victor A. Thompson

> *Other writings in this volume reveal bureaucratic characteristics inhibiting of change, but in this article the author focuses directly on this question. Among the salient points especially relevant to libraries, Thompson points out that without conflict there will be no change. Another traditional organizational constraint is the accentuation of fear of failure. The article provides a model of the innovative organization which is essentially that of the professional organization.*

It has become a commonplace among behavioral scientists that the bureaucratic form of organization is characterized by high productive efficiency but low innovative capacity. There is a growing feeling that modern organizations, and particularly the large, bureaucratic business and government organizations, need to increase their capacity to innovate. This feeling stems in part from the obvious fact of the increased rate of change, especially technological change, but also from a rejection of the older process of innovation through the birth of new organizations and the death or failure of old ones. It seems difficult to contemplate the extinction of existing and well-known organizational giants, for too many interests become vested in their continued existence. Consequently, many behavioral scientists feel that innovation must increasingly occur within the bureaucratic organizations. Also technical innovation is becoming costlier, and financing it may be easier through healthy, existing, organizations than through newly created ones.

This paper considers the obstacles to innovation within the modern bureaucratic organization and makes some suggestions for changes that would facilitate innovation. No attempt is made to answer the question as to whether innovation is desirable or not. By innovation is meant the generation, acceptance, and implementation of new ideas, processes, products or services. Innovation therefore implies the capacity to change or adapt. An adaptive organization may not be innovative (because it does not generate many new ideas), but an innovative organization will be adaptive (because it is able to implement many new ideas).

For a group of people to act as an entity, an ideology is required. This ideology explains what the group is doing, what it ought to do, and legitimizes the coercion of the individual by the group. For the modern bureaucratic organization, this body of doctrine could be called a production ideology. The organization is conceived as having an owner who has a goal to be maximized by means of the organization.[1] The organization is a tool (or weapon) for reaching this objective. The various participants are given money in return for the use of their time and effort as means of achieving the owner's goal. As Henry Ford said, "All that we ask of the men is that they do the work which is set before them." Management consists of functions and processes for perfecting the tool for this purpose, that is controlling intraorganizational behaviors so that they become completely reliable and predictable, like any good tool. From the standpoint of this production ideology, innovative behavior would only be interpreted as unreliability.

The production ideology leads to rapid and detailed specification and commitment of resources. Of especial interest is the detailed specification of human resources. Adam Smith's advice to reduce the job of pin making to that of making a part of the pin has been generally followed. This response will be termed the "Smith's pins" effect. It has been said that the detailed specification of human resources reduces investment costs per unit of program execution.[2] The production ideology results in jobs which typically require only a small part of the worker's training or knowledge. Consequently, this detailed specification of resources will be called "overspecification" of resources, somewhat argumentatively, no doubt.

SOURCE: Reprinted from Victor A. Thompson, "Bureaucracy and Innovation," *Administrative Science Quarterly*, 10 (June, 1965), pp. 1–20, by permission of the publisher and the author.

MONOCRATIC SOCIAL STRUCTURE AND INNOVATION

Large, modern bureaucratic organizations dominated by production ideology are framed around a powerful organization stereotype, which following Max Weber, will be called the monocratic organization. This stereotype reflects conditions prevalent in the past, two being important because they no longer hold: (1) great inequality among organization members in social standing and abilities and a corresponding inequality in contributions and rewards; and (2) a technology simple enough to be within the grasp of an individual.

In this stereotype, the organization is a great hierarchy of superior-subordinate relations in which the person at the top, assumed to be omniscient, gives the general order that initiates all activity. His immediate subordinates make the order more specific for their subordinates; the latter do the same for theirs, etc., until specific individuals are carrying out specific commands. All authority and initiation are cascaded down in this way by successive delegations. There is complete discipline enforced from the top down to assure that these commands are faithfully obeyed. Responsibility is owed from the bottom up. To assure predictability and accountability, each position is narrowly defined as to duties and jurisdiction, without overlapping or duplication. Problems that fall outside the narrow limits of the job are referred upward until they come to a person with sufficient authority to make a decision. Each person is to receive orders from and be responsible to only one other person—his superior.

Such a system is monocratic because there is only *one* point or source of legitimacy. Conflict cannot be legitimate (although it may occur because of the weakness and immorality of human beings). Therefore, the organization does not need formal, legitimate, bargaining devices. Thus, although it might be considered empirically more fruitful to conceive of the organization as a coalition,[3] according to the monocratic stereotype, the organization as a moral or normative entity is the tool of an owner, not a coalition. Coalitional and other conflict-settling activities, therefore, take place in a penumbra of illegitimacy.

The inability to legitimize conflict depresses creativity. Conflict generates problems and uncertainties and diffuses ideas. Conflict implies pluralism and forces coping and search for solutions, whereas concentrated authority can simply ignore obstacles and objections. Conflict, therefore, encourages innovations. Other things being equal, the less bureaucratized (monocratic) the organization, the more conflict and uncertainty and the more innovation.[4]

The monocratic stereotype dictates centralized control over all resources. It can control only through extrinsic rewards such as money, power, and status, because it demands the undifferentiated time of its members in the interests of the owner's goals. Even as the organization is a tool, so are all of its participants. There can be no right to "joy in work." To admit such a right would be to admit an interest other than the owner's and to lose some control over the participants.

The necessity of relying upon such extrinsic rewards forces the organization to make its hierarchical positions rewards for compliance. Such a reward system depends upon the organization's ability to find enough people who are willing to exchange their time for a chance at a small group of status positions. It is doubtful that this would have been possible without help from other social institutions, including religious ones. The general belief that work is not supposed to be enjoyable has helped, as has the social definition of success as moving up a managerial hierarchy. The further belief that the good man is the successful one has closed the system.

With education as a criterion of social class, the blue-collar group and a large part of the lower white-collar group have been eliminated from the competition for these scarce, status prizes. Furthermore, highly educated people are increasingly seeking basic need satisfaction outside of the organization—in hobbies, community activities, their families.[5] Consequently, organizations have become sorely pressed to find rewards sufficient to induce the needed docility. Although the use of money alone has raised the price of goods, it does not seem to have been very successful in promoting production interests.[6]

With the enormous expansion of knowledge flooding the organization with specialists of all kinds and with the organization increasingly dependent upon them, this reward system is facing a crisis. With all his pre-entry training, the specialist finds that he can "succeed" only by giving up work for which he is trained and entering management—work for which he has had no training.[7]

The extrinsic reward system, administered by the hierarchy of authority, stimulates conformity rather than innovation. Creativity is promoted by an internal commitment, by intrinsic rewards for the most part. The extrinsic rewards of esteem by colleagues, and the benevolent competition through which it is distributed, are largely foreign to the monocratic, production-oriented organization. Hierarchical competition is highly individualistic and malevolent. It does not contribute to cooperation and group problem solving.

For those committed to this concept of success, the normal psychological state is one of more or less anxiety. This kind of success is dispensed by hierarchical superiors. Furthermore, the more success one attains, the higher he goes, the more vague and subjective become the standards by which he is judged. Eventually, the only safe posture is conformity. Innovation is not likely under these conditions. To gain the independence, freedom and security required for creativity, the normal individual has to reject this concept of success. But even those who have adopted a different life pattern and measure their personal worth in terms of professional growth and the esteem of professional peers must feel a great deal of insecurity within these monocratic structures, because the opportunity for growth is under the control of the organization, and especially the work they are asked to perform.

One further aspect of monocratic structure needs to be briefly described before we proceed to assess the implications of these structural variables for innovation within the organization. The hierarchy of authority is a procedure whereby organizationally directed proposals from within are affirmed or vetoed. It is a procedure which gives advantage to the veto, because monocratic systems do not provide for appeals. An appeal implies conflicting rights which must be adjudicated, but the superior's veto of a subordinate's proposal legitimately rejects the proposal. An approval must usually go higher, where it is again subject to a veto. Thus, even if the monocratic organization allows new ideas to be generated, it is very apt to veto them.

Because production interests lead to overspecification of human resources, organizations in the past were composed largely of unskilled or semiskilled employees who carried out more or less simple procedures devised within the particular organization without previous special preparation. The white-collar unskilled or semiskilled have been conveniently labeled the "desk classes."[8] The work of the desk classes, as distinguished from scientific and technical workers, is determined by the organization rather than by extensive pre-entry preparation. Deprived of intrinsic rewards related to the work or the rewards of growing esteem of professional peers, they become largely dependent upon the extrinsic rewards distributed by the hierarchy of authority, thereby greatly reinforcing that institution. Their dependence upon organizational programs and procedures for whatever function they acquire induces a conservative attitude with regard to these programs and procedures.

Except for the successful few, the morale of the desk classes is one of chronic, though not necessarily acute, dissatisfaction.[9] Overspecification plus dependence upon extrinsic rewards of promotion result in vast overrequirement of qualifications. The individual often becomes qualified for the minor incremental increase in difficulty of the next higher job years before it becomes available. The resulting, easily recognized, mental and emotional condition has been called the bureaucratic orientation.[10]

The bureaucratic orientation is conservative. Novel solutions, using resources in a new way, are likely to appear threatening. Those having a bureaucratic orientation are more concerned with the internal distribution of power and status than with organizational goal accomplishment. This converts the organization into a political system concerned with the distribution of these extrinsic rewards.[11] The first reaction to new ideas and suggested changes is most likely to be, "How does it affect us?" Some observations of the decision-making process in business organizations suggest that search in these organizations is largely an attempt by the groupings in this political system to find answers to that question— "how does it affect us?" They also suggest that the expectations of consequences upon which these organizations base their decisions are heavily biased by these same political interests.[12]

If new activities cannot be blocked entirely they can at least be segregated and eventually blocked from the communication system if necessary. Typically, the introduction of technical innovative activities into modern organizations is by means of segregated units, often called research and development units. Segregating such activities prevents them from affecting the *status quo* to any great extent. The organization does not have to change.[13]

We should add that it is not only the organizational political system which causes the segregation of new problems. There is often no place in the existing structure into which they can be fitted. When a new problem appears, the monocratic production-oriented organization is likely to find that the resources of authority, skills, and material needed to cope with it have already been fully specified and committed to other organization units. Since no existing unit has the uncommitted resources to deal with the new problem, a new organization unit is established.

An organization runs into a great deal of trouble trying to stimulate innovativeness within these segregated units. Since it cannot use the extrinsic reward system upon which the political system is based, it must fumble toward a reward system alien to the monocratic organization. It must establish conditions entirely foreign to the conditions of production upon which the monocratic organization is based. Two milieus, two sets of conditions, two systems of rewards, must be established, the one for innovation, the other for the rest of the organization's activities. This duality is divisive and upsetting to the existing distribution of satisfactions.

Beyond the political interests in the distribution of extrinsic rewards, there are other factors which strengthen tendencies toward parochialism. The organization seems to factor its activities into narrow, single-purpose, exclusive categories and to assign these to subunits composed of a superior and subordinates. Very often strong subunit and subgoal identifications arise from this pattern so that members of any unit know and care little about what other units are doing.[14] The organization tends to become a collection of small entities with boundaries and frontiers. When work is completed in one entity, it is handed over to another, and interest in it is dropped. Interest tends to be in protecting the records and protocols of the hand-over transaction so that blame can always be placed on another unit. Although the narrow-mission assignments are justified as needed "to pinpoint responsibility," they actually encourage irresponsibility as far as new problems are concerned because they facilitate dodging responsibility for them.[15]

The production-oriented overspecification and commitment of resources prevent the accumulation of free resources needed for innovative projects, including time, and deprives participants of the diversity of input so important in the generation of new ideas. Thus, even when people are hired to *innovate* they may be treated as though they were hired to *produce* and kept tied to their work. Diversity of input is also lost because of the tendency to assign each activity to a separate unit, which concentrates whatever diversity of input there is at one or a few local points. Thus, there may be stimulating ideas and information discussed within a planning unit or a research unit, but it does not extend to the rest of the organization. The research unit may be very creative, but the organization cannot innovate.

In monocratic responsibility, praise and blame attach to jurisdictions. People are to be punished for mistakes as well as wrong-doing, and they are to be punished for failures which occur within their jurisdictions whether due to their activities or not. ("He should have prevented it. It was his responsibility.")[16] Although this theory is not strictly applied any more, it is still feared. Thus, an individual may hesitate to advise an organization to take a particular action even though he has good reason to believe that the probabilities for a satisfactory outcome are good. Should the project fail in this instance, he may be a personal failure. It is difficult to apply the concept of probability to personal failure. One feels, rightly or wrongly, that he can only fail once. Therefore, what would be rational from the standpoint of the organization's goal may appear irrational from the standpoint of the individual's personal goals.[17]

New ideas are speculative and hence particularly dangerous to personal goals and especially the goals of power and status. Consequently, the monocratic organization, structured around such extrinsic goals and explicitly committed to this stringent theory of responsibility, is not likely to be highly innovative.

A monocratic variant which is highly innovative should be mentioned. New organizations are sometimes begun by highly creative individuals who attract like-minded people, maintain an atmosphere conducive to innovation, build up a powerful *esprit de corps* and achieve a very high level of organizational creativity. Often these are small engineering or research organizations started by an engineer or scientist assisted by a small group of able and personally loyal peers. The organization is new and small and not yet bureaucratized. Many able young people may be attracted to it because of the opportunity provided for professional growth. As these organizations grow larger and particularly after the charismatic originator is no longer there, the monocratic stereotype reasserts itself and they become bureaucratized. This phenomenon is an old one, discussed by Weber as the "institutionalization of charisma." It is seen in one form in the post-revolutionary bureaucratization of successful revolutionary organizations.

THE INNOVATIVE ORGANIZATION

In summarizing the scattered suggestions for an organization with a high capacity to innovate, first the qualities and conditions needed will be discussed, then the structures or structural changes that will facilitate or create the required qualities and conditions.

General Requirements

First are needed resources for innovation—uncommitted money, time, skills, and good will. In human resources this means upgraded work and workers, optimally a person who has developed himself thoroughly in some area, about to the limits of his capacities, so that he has that richness of experience and self-confidence upon which creativity thrives—a professional. Complex technology requires the administration of "technical generalists," or professionals. A technology is incorporated into an organization through individuals. To incorporate it through overspecification or task specialization requires enormous co-ordination. Furthermore, co-ordinating the elements of a technology is part of the technology itself, as the current technical emphasis on systems design, systems engineering, etc., testify. The technology deals not only with simple relationships, but with the relationships between relationships as well. Hence, co-ordination is not a different, nontechnical process, such as management, but part of the complex technology itself. Although production interests may be well served by employing a few technical professionals to co-ordinate the many overspecified workers, the innovative potential of the technology can hardly be realized in this way.

The innovative organization will allow that diversity of inputs needed for the creative generation of ideas. Long periods of pre-entry, professional training, and wide diffusion of ideas within the organization, including a wide diffusion of problems and suggested solutions, will provide the variety and richness of experience required. Included should be a wide diffusion of uncertainty so that the whole organization is stimulated to search, rather than just a few professional researchers. Involving larger parts of the organization in the search process also increases chances of acceptance and implementation. This wide diffusion, in turn, will depend upon ease and freedom of communication and a low level of parochialism.

Complete commitment to the organization will not promote innovation, as we have seen; neither will complete alienation from the organization. The relationship between personal and organizational goals, ideally, would seem to be where individuals perceive the organization as an avenue for professional growth. The interest in professional growth provides the rising aspiration level needed to stimulate search beyond the first-found satisfactory solution, and the perception of the organization as a vehicle for professional growth harnesses this powerful motivation to the interests of the organization in a partial fusion of goals, personal and organizational.[18]

Instead of the usual extrinsic organizational rewards of income, power, and status, satisfactions come from the search process, professional growth, and the esteem of knowledgeable peers—rewards most conducive to innovation. Benevolent intellectual competition rather than malevolent status and power competition is needed. For these reasons, creative work, the process of search and discovery, needs to be highly visible to respected peers. Dedication to creative work cannot be expected if positional status continues to be defined as the principal sign of personal worth. But reduction of status-striving is also important because it is inescapably associated with personal insecurity,[19] which is hardly compatible with creativity. What is needed is a certain level of problem insecurity and challenge, but a high level of personal security.

The creative atmosphere should be free from external pressure. A person is not likely to be creative if too much hangs on a successful outcome of his search activities, for he will have a strong tendency to accept the first satisfactory solution whether or not it seems novel or the best possible. Thus, he needs indulgence in time and resources, and particularly in organizational evaluations of his activities. He needs freedom to innovate. He also needs considerable, but not complete, autonomy and self-direction and a large voice in deciding at what he will work.[20]

In summary, the innovative organization will be much more professional than most existing ones. Work will be much less determined by production-oriented planners on the Smith's pins model and more determined by the extended periods of pre-entry training. The desk classes will decline in number and importance relative to professional, scientific, and technical workers.

There will be a great increase in interorganizational mobility and a corresponding decline in organizational chauvinism. The concept of organizations as organic entities with some claim to survive will tend to be replaced by the concept of organizations as opportunities for professional growth. In the innovative organization, professional orientations and loyalties will be stronger relative to organizational or bureaucratic ones. Esteem striving will tend to replace status striving. There will be less control by superiors and more by self and peers. Power and influence will be much more broadly dispersed.

The dispersal of power is important because concentrated power often prevents imaginative solutions of problems. When power meets power, problem solving is necessarily called into play. The power of unions has undoubtedly stimulated managerial innovations.[21] Dispersed power, paradoxically, can make resources more readily available to support innovative projects because it makes possible a larger number and variety of sub-coalitions. It expands the number and kinds of possible supporters and sponsors.

Structural Requirements

The innovative organization will be characterized by structural looseness generally, with less emphasis on narrow, nonduplicating, nonoverlapping definitions of duties and responsibilities. Job descriptions will be of the professional type rather than the duties type. Communications will be freer and legitimate in all directions. Assignment and resource decisions will be much more decentralized than is customary.

The innovative organization will not be as highly stratified as existing ones. This is implied in the freedom of communication, but the decline in the importance of the extrinsic rewards of positional status and the growth of interest in professional esteem would bring this about anyway. Salary scales will be adjusted accordingly and no longer reflect chiefly awesome status differences.

Group processes will be more, and more openly, used than at present. The freer communication system, the broader work assignments, the lack of preoccupation with overlap and duplication, the lessened emphasis upon authority will all work in the direction of a greater amount of interpersonal communication and multiple group membership. Multiple group membership will facilitate innovation by increasing the amount and diversity of input of ideas and stimulation, and by acting as a discipline of the hierarchical veto. When a new idea is known and supported by groupings beyond the authority grouping, it is not easy to veto it. Multiple-group membership helps to overcome the absence of a formal appeal by providing an informal appeal to a free constituency of peers.

In an atmosphere which encourages and legitimizes multiple-group membership, the malignant peer competition of the authority grouping (of fellow subordinates) will no longer exercise the powerful constraints against "showing-up" with new ideas.[22] The greater ease of acquiring group memberships and the greater legitimacy of groups will reduce the risk of innovation to the individual. Responsibility for new ideas can be shared as can the onus of promoting them. Wide participation in the generation process will greatly facilitate acceptance and implementation.

Present methods of departmentalization encourage parochialism with its great resistance to new ideas from outside. Often it is not goals that are assigned, actually, but jurisdictions. (For example, although ninety-eight percent of the farms are electrified, the Rural Electrification Administration has not been abolished.) It is not a group of interdependent skills brought together to carry out some project, but a conference of sovereignty. At the simple unit level (superior and subordinates), it is often, but not always, an aggregative grouping—a number of people with the same skills doing the same thing. Lacking the stimulation of different skills, views, and perspectives, and the rewards of project completion and success, such groupings are likely to seek extrinsic rewards and to seek them through the organizational political system.

Other simple units, even though not composed of aggregations of people doing the same thing, are very often composed of overspecified desk classes carrying out some continuing program—getting out the house organ, or managing the budget, or recruiting, or keeping stores. In such an integrative grouping there may be more interpersonal stimulation, but overspecification—the sheer subprofessional simplicity of the jobs—prevents the diversity and richness required for anything but very minor innovations.

The aggregative grouping has neither interdependence nor goal. Group innovation is therefore impossible. Individual innovation in the interest of the organization is hardly likely, unless the organization offers rewards for it. Sometimes organizations reward individual innovative suggestions through suggestion-box systems. Such systems are rarely successful. As far as aggregative units are concerned, the lack of input diversity prevents any important innovative insights. For integrative units, suggestion boxes are frequently disruptive because the true authorship of the suggestion is likely to be in dispute, and the group will often feel that the idea should have been presented to the group rather than individually presented for an award.[23]

In the innovative organization, departmentalization must be arranged so as to keep parochialism to a minimum. Some overlapping and duplication, some vagueness about jurisdictions, make a good deal of communication necessary. People have to define and redefine their responsibilities continually, case after case. They have to probe and seek for help. New problems can not with certainty be rejected as *ultra vires*.[24]

The simple unit should be an integrative grouping of various professionals and subprofessionals engaged upon an integrative task requiring a high degree of technical interdependence and group problem solving. Or else the simple unit should be merely a housekeeping unit. Project teams could be drawn from such housekeeping units. Ideally, individuals would have project rather than continuing assignments. If project organization is not feasible, individuals should be rotated occasionally. Even if continuing assignments, or jurisdictions, seem to be technically necessary, organization units can probably convert a large part of their activities into successive projects, or have a number of projects going on at the same time, so that individuals can be constantly renewing themselves in new and challenging problems and experiencing a maximum input of diverse stimulation and ideas. It might even be possible for individual and unit jurisdictions and responsibilities to be exchanged occasionally.

If formal structures could be sufficiently loosened, it might be possible for organizations and units to restructure themselves continually in the light of the problem at hand. Thus, for generating ideas, for planning and problem solving, the organization or unit would "unstructure" itself into a freely communicating body of equals. When it came time for implementation, requiring a higher degree of co-ordination of action (as opposed to stimulation of novel or correct ideas), the organization could then restructure itself into the more usual hierarchical form, tightening up its lines somewhat.

Empirical evidence that different kinds of structure are optimal for different kinds of problems is compelling.[25] Almost equally compelling is the evidence that leadership role assignments need to be changed as the situation changes.[26] Bureaucratic rigidity makes such rational structural alterations almost impossible. It is hard to escape the conclusion that current organization structures are *not* the most rational adaptations for *some* kinds of problem solving. Although experimental groups have been successfully restructured from bureaucratic to collegial by means of verbal redefinitions of roles along lines perceived to be more appropriate to the task at hand,[27] such restructuring is probably impossible in real-life "traditionated" organizations as presently constituted.

The abandonment of the use of hierarchical positions as prizes or rewards, however, and the decline in the importance of extrinsic rewards generally, would render organizational structure much more amenable to manipulation. The personal appropriation of administrative resources (such as position and authority), almost universal in modern bureaucratic organizations and reminiscent of primitive agrarian cultures, could decline considerably.[28] If it should prove impossible for organizations to become flexible enough to allow restructuring themselves in the light of the problem at hand, it would be preferable to retain a loose structure in the interest of generating new ideas and suffer from some fumbling in the attempt to co-ordinate action for the purpose of carrying them out. After all, thought and action cannot be sharply distinguished, and a good deal of problem solving occurs during implementation. The thinking is then tested and completed.

Integrative departmentalization, combined with freedom of communication, interunit projects, and lessened subunit chauvinism, will create extradepartmental professional ties and interests, resulting in an increase in the diversity and richness of inputs and in their diffusion, thereby stimulating creativity. Intellectual competition is more likely to be provided by this broader milieu. It is more likely to be the generating area than the smaller authority grouping or the larger organization.

We need to think in terms of innovative areas rather than formal departments, in terms of the conditions for generating new and good ideas rather than of jurisdiction. In the innovative organization, innovation will not be assigned to an isolated or segregated jurisdiction such as research and development. The innovative contributions of everyone, including the man at the machine, are needed. Characteristically, the innovative area will be larger than the formal unit and smaller than the organization. Resource control should be sufficiently decentralized so that appropriate resource accumulation through subcoalition would be possible within the innovative area. In effect, the formal distribution of jurisdictions should be just a skeleton to be used when an arbitrary decision was required.

In the physical aspect of organizations, the architecture and furnishings of today's bureaucratic organizations seem to be departing further and further from the needs of the innovative organization. The majestic, quiet halls and closed, windowless office doors are not designed to encourage communication. They fill a potential communicator with fear. "Will I be disturbing him?" he wonders. It is doubtful that deep blue rugs have anything to do with discovery and invention. We all remember where the first atomic chain reaction took place. Modern bureaucratic architecture and furnishings seem to reflect an increased concern with the extrinsic reward system. We seem to be in the midst of a new primitivism; the means of administration seem to be increasingly appropriated by the officials. This may reflect an attempt by the monocratic organization to attract innovative technical and scientific talent. With success available to only a few and the organization increasingly dependent upon large numbers of highly trained professionals and subprofessionals, it is hoped that richness of surroundings will do what an inappropriate reward system cannot do.

The purchase of motivation with extrinsic rewards is becoming more and more costly, and innovation cannot be purchased in this way at all. What is needed is both much less expensive and much more costly—the devaluation of authority and positional status and the recognized, official sharing of power and influence.

IMPLICATIONS FOR ADMINISTRATIVE PRACTICE

Associated with all of these structural changes there will need to be many changes in administrative practices. Only a few of the most obvious ones will be mentioned. The present common practice of annual performance ratings by superiors would probably have to be dropped. Many believe that this practice is hostile even to production interests. It is clearly inconsistent with increasing professionalism, since professional standing is not determined by a hierarchical superior. Rather than a single system of ranks, with corresponding salaries, there will be a multiple ranking system and multiple salary scales. The managerial or hierarchical ranking system will be only one among many. Presumably, it will not carry the highest ranks. The American public has for a long time ranked several occupations above management.[29]

Job descriptions and classifications will have to accommodate an increasing proportion of professionals. The duties and responsibilities approach to job descriptions was designed for a desk class age. It does not accommodate professional work easily.

Peer evaluations will become more important in recruitment and placement, and it is possible that a kind of election process will be used to fill authority positions. At any rate, the wishes of subordinates will probably be considered a good deal more than is present practice. One would expect considerable modification in procedures relating to secrecy and loyalty. The innovative organization will be more indulgent with regard to patents, publications, and so on. The relationship between visibility and professional growth will require this, and increased interorganizational mobility will enforce it. Present fringe benefit devices that tend to restrict mobility will have to be altered.

Administrative innovation requires the same conditions and structures as technical innovation. Professionalization in this area also requires the elimination of overspecified resources. The unskilled administrative worker should go along with his blue-collar counterpart. Many administrative technologies are poorly accredited and some are perhaps spurious—pseudo skills in handling some more or less complex procedure. If the procedure is changed, these "skills" will no longer be needed. It is doubtful that the rapid expansion of administrative overhead in recent years has contributed to productivity, suggesting that some of this expansion may not have been technically justified and that it represents organizational slack made possible by increased productivity resulting from other causes.[30]

Administrative activities should be dispersed and decentralized down to the level of the innovative area, allowing administrative personnel to become part of integrative problem-solving groups rather than resentful onlookers sharpshooting from the outside. The innovative organization is innovative throughout and the innovative insights of the engineer, the research scientist, the machine tender, the administrative expert are all needed. If responsibilities and jurisdictions are occasionally exchanged, as suggested above, administrative responsibilities should be included in such exchanges. To paraphrase a famous expression, administrative work is too important to be left entirely to administrators.

Resistance to suggestions of this kind will be especially strong in the monocratic organization oriented to production and control. The re-evaluation of the relative importance of managerial and nonmanagerial activities and the declining emphasis on extrinsic rewards, both implied in increasing professionalization of organizations, will reduce this resistance. The "need to control" is an almost inevitable psychological product of the structured field which the modern bureaucratic organization constitutes. Altering the field alters the product.

The emphasis on the need for free resources, time, indulgence with regard to controls, decentralization, and many more, all suggest on the surface that the innovative organization will be a costly one. Perhaps a high level of innovation is too costly, but the available knowledge is not adequate to reach a conclusion. We do not know the value of the novel ideas, processes, and products, which might be produced by the innovative organization, and we do not know that our present methods of costing and control are the best approach to achieving low-cost production. Likert's arguments that present methods of cost reduction are superficial and actually increase costs in the long run by impairing the health of the social organism are impressive.[31] It would seem that the overspecification of work would automatically create the need for a costly administrative overhead apparatus to plan, schedule, co-ordinate and control so that all the overspecified parts are kept fully meshed and fully occupied. The problem is like that of keeping inventory costs down when a very large number of items must be kept on inventory. We cannot say that the organizational structure outlined will be either more or less costly, more or less beneficial to society, but it will be more innovative. We also suspect that it may be a fair projection of the organization of the future.

FOOTNOTES

[1] See Richard M. Cyert and James G. March, *A Behavioral Theory of the Firm* (Englewood Cliffs, N. J.: Prentice-Hall, 1963), pp. 27–28.

[2] James G. March and Herbert A. Simon, *Organizations* (New York: John Wiley, 1958), p. 158; and Herbert A. Simon, *The New Science of Management Decision* (New York: Harper and Row, 1960), p. 7.

[3] Cyert and March, *op. cit.*

[4] See Tom Burns and G. M. Stalker, *The Management of Innovation* (London: Tavistock, 1959); and Gerald Gordon and Selwyn Becker, "Changes in Medical Practice Bring Shifts in the Patterns of Power," *The Modern Hospital*, 102 (Feb., 1964), 89.

[5] See Robert V. Presthus, *The Organizational Society* (New York: Knopf, 1962).

[6] Recent investigations of work motivation indicate quite strongly that a poorly administered wage and salary system can make for dissatisfaction, but that a well-administered one has little power to motivate to high performance. See Frederick Herzberg, Bernard Mausner, and Barbara Snyderman, *The Motivation to Work* (New York: John Wiley, 1959), and M. Scott Meyers' unpublished report on recent motivation research at the Texas Instrument Company, "The Management of Motivation to Work."

[7] See Lewis C. Mainzer, "The Scientist as Public Administrator," *Western Political Quarterly*, 16 (1963), 814–829. Of the Federal executives in grades GS-14 and above, only about one in forty-five has had college training in public administration (derived from Table 42B, p. 361, in W. Lloyd Warner, Paul P. Van Riper, Norman H. Martin, and Orvis F. Collins, *The American Federal Executive* [New Haven, Conn.: Yale University, 1963]).

[8] Nigel Walker, *Morale in the Civil Service: A Study of the Desk Worker* (Edinburgh: Edinburgh University, 1960).

[9] *Ibid.*

[10] The contrast between the professional and the bureaucratic orientation has been studied and discussed by many people. A few references are: Alvin W. Gouldner, "Cosmopolitans and Locals," *Administrative Science Quarterly*, 2 (1957-1958), 281-306, and 444-480; Leonard Reissman, "A Study of Role Conceptions in a Bureaucracy," *Social Forces*, 27 (1949), 305-310; and Harold L. Wilensky, *Intellectuals in Labor Unions* (Glencoe, Ill.: Free Press, 1956), pp. 129-144.

[11] Burns and Stalker, *op. cit.*, and Melville Dalton, "Conflict between Line and Staff Managerial Officers," *American Sociological Review*, 15 (1950), 342-351.

[12] See R. M. Cyert, W. R. Dill, and F. G. March, "The Role of Expectations in Business Decision-Making," *Administrative Science Quarterly*, 3 (1958), 307-340; and Cyert and March, *op. cit.*, ch. iv.

[13] Burns and Stalker, *op. cit.*

[14] See Eliot O. Chapple and Leonard R. Sayles, *The Measure of Management* (New York: Macmillan, 1961), pp. 18-40;

March and Simon, *op. cit.*, pp. 150-154; Victor A. Thompson, *The Regulatory Process in OPA Rationing* (New York: King's Crown Press, 1950), Pt. II; and James R. Bright, ed., *Technological Planning on the Corporate Level* (Boston: Harvard University Graduate School of Business Administration, 1962), *passim*.

[15] Burns and Stalker, *op. cit.*

[16] See Victor A. Thompson, *Modern Organization* (New York: Knopf, 1961), pp. 129-137.

[17] Derived from Kurt W. Back's discussion of nonrational choice. See "Decisions under Uncertainty," *American Behavioral Scientist*, 4 (1961), 14-19.

[18] See Peter M. Blau and W. Richard Scott, *Formal Organizations* (San Francisco: Chandler, 1962), pp. 60-74.

[19] Rollo May, *The Meaning of Anxiety* (New York: Ronald, 1950), especially pp. 181-189.

[20] A good part of the literature on individual creativity is summarized in Morris I. Stein and Shirley J. Heinze, *Creativity and the Individual* (Glencoe, Ill.: Free Press, 1960).

[21] See Eric Hoffer, *The Ordeal of Change* (New York: Harper and Row, 1964), pp. 81-82; and Seymour Melman, *Decision-making and Productivity* (Oxford: Oxford University, 1958).

[22] See William H. Whyte, Jr., *The Organization Man* (Garden City, N. Y.: Doubleday, 1957), chs. x and xvi.

[23] See Norman J. Powell, *Personnel Administration in Government* (Englewood Cliffs, N. J.: Prentice-Hall, 1956), pp. 438-444. Powell believes that suggestion-box systems are better than no communication with the rank and file at all. Because of disputed authorship of suggestions, the TVA decided to give only group (noncash) awards.

[24] Burns and Stalker, *op. cit.* See also B. Klein, "A Radical Proposal for R and D," *Fortune*, 57 (May, 1958), 112; B. Klein and W. Meckling, "Application of Operations Research to Development Decisions," *Operations Research*, 6 (1958), 352-363; Albert O. Hirshman, *The Strategy of Economic Development* (New Haven, Conn.: Yale University, 1958); Alber O. Hirshman and Charles E. Lindblom, "Economic Development, Research and Development, Policy Making: Some Converging Views," *Behavioral Science*, 7 (1962), 211-222; and David Braybrooke and Charles E. Lindblom, *A Strategy of Decision* (New York: Free Press, 1963).

[25] Some of this evidence is reviewed in Blau and Scott, *op. cit.*, ch. v.

[26] The evidence is reviewed in Cecil A. Gibb, "Leadership," in Gardner Lindzey, ed., *Handbook of Social Psychology* (Reading, Mass.: Addison-Wesley, 1954), Vol. II, pp. 877-917.

[27] André L. Delbecq, *Leadership in Business Decision Conferences* (unpublished Ph.D. dissertation, Indiana University, 1963).

[28] See Victor A. Thompson, "Bureaucracy in a Democracy," in Roscoe Martin, ed., *Public Administration and Democracy* (Syracuse, N. Y.: Syracuse University, forthcoming).

[29] Alex Inkeles and Peter H. Rossi, "National Comparisons of Occupational Prestige," in Seymour Martin Lipset and Neil J. Smelser, eds., *Sociology: The Progress of a Decade* (Englehead Cliffs, N. J.: Prentice-Hall, 1961), pp. 506-516.

[30] See Seymour Melman, "The Rise of Administrative Overhead in the Manufacturing Industries of the United States, 1899-1947," *Oxford Economic Papers*, 3 (1951), 62-93, and *Dynamic Factors in Industrial Productivity* (New York: John Wiley, 1956).

[31] Rensis Likert and Stanley E. Seashore, "Making Cost Control Work," *Harvard Business Review*, 41 (Nov.-Dec., 1963), 96-108.

ABOUT THE AUTHOR—Victor A. Thompson, see p. 113.

Automation as Innovation

by Mary Lee Bundy

Although other articles in this section have concentrated in more depth upon organizational and personality factors associated with the ability of organizations to change, this piece is still the only effort to discuss the issues specifically in terms of libraries. The analysis suggests that libraries may be going through a period of "automation conservatism." Essentially they are using the computer to perpetuate existing practices. The conventional library is not yet using the potential of the computer to find new solutions to problems nor for the assumption of more advanced and more mature information roles. Automation of existing procedures may be a first step along the way but the danger is that libraries will use the computer simply to reinforce the status quo at a time when much more radical change is required.

The concern of this paper is not with library automation per se but rather in automation as a form of innovation in libraries. The observations and speculations offered here stem from an interest in better understanding and encouraging major change in the conventional library. This concern prompted the writer this spring to engage her research methods class in conducting case studies of library automation as examples of change.

This presentation is based in part on the findings from these studies, on interviews with a number of librarians from libraries which have or are contemplating automation and from a delving into the literature of the social sciences for insights and understandings regarding the nature of the influences which encourage and discourage innovation in organizations. Its purpose is to open for discussion major issues and key factors which decide whether or not libraries do adapt, in what ways, and with what success. The writer hopes this analysis and probing will focus attention on the human and social as well as the technical aspects of automation.

THE NEED FOR CHANGE

Whether one likes to think of the profession or of libraries undergoing major change and whether the majority of librarians are so disposed or so committed there is really no other choice. We are in an era characterized by Max Ways as one of radical change.[1] All the institutions in the culture must adapt if they are to survive. Changing requirements are such that no longer is gradual change sufficient and at no foreseeable time will the requirements for change cease. Under these conditions, the paramount concern of any organization should be how to maintain a capability for continual change. As Warren Bennis has put it,[2]

> "The profit, the saving, the efficiency, and the morale of the moment become secondary to keeping the door open for rapid readjustment to changing conditions."

Libraries are no exception to these realities of organizational survival. Indeed, the problem for the conventional library may be even more serious. In a time of other alternatives to the book and to libraries, libraries may already be threatened with permanent relegation to a custodial function. Unlike the newer entrants into the information field, libraries attempting to expand their functions are handicapped by the traditional, largely passive role they have played for historical views and attitudes influence both those in the profession and those outside it. Given these professional and organizational imperatives for change, it becomes important to assess those factors acting to facilitate change in libraries and those impeding change.

ORGANIZATIONAL CONSTRAINTS

The villain role in stifling creativity and innovation is generally assigned to bureaucracy as a form

---

SOURCE: Reprinted from Mary Lee Bundy, "Automation as Innovation," *Drexel Library Quarterly*, 4 (Jan., 1968), p. 100, by permission of the Graduate School of Library Science, Drexel Institute of Technology. This paper was originally presented at the Drexel Institute of Technology, Graduate School of Library Science Seminar "Data Processing in University Libraries," Sept. 18-20, 1967.

of organization. In the interest of assuring rationality and efficiency, bureaucracy introduces a necessary consistency and regularity. But in the process it also acts to suppress new ideas and to discourage departures. Harold Guetzkow expressed it,[3]

> "One then manages organizations by reducing the uncertainties, by discouraging originalities, by ridding the organization of the unexpected. In the very process of becoming a surviving, thriving organization, the creative innovations of the members are inhibited."

Under these conditions there is a tendency for organizations to become increasingly dysfunctional. Rules and regulations continue long after their original point or purpose has been lost or changed, tending to become ends in themselves. To put it in the words of another writer, bureaucracy has all the survival value of the dinosaur.

Bureaucratic organizations of course do change through both planned and unplanned processes. But some are better able to adjust than others. One reason why libraries have been more than ordinarily change resistant is partly because of the more authoritarian nature of their internal relationships. In highly authoritarian organizations change can emanate from the top, but if the top administrator is not encouraging change it becomes difficult if not impossible for it to be initiated at lower levels of the organization. Authority structures of this nature evolve and tend to continue until professionalism becomes a stronger force in the organization. As we have discussed elsewhere, librarianship comes closer in its clientele, bureaucratic and professional relationships to being a semi-profession whose members do tolerate the requirement for submissiveness at the expense of professional goals.[4] What should be a major internal impetus for change has instead been a weak one.

One would expect the failure of existing procedures to keep pace with the growing volumes of materials to be handled and with the increasing numbers of users to be satisfied, to be a strong incentive for change. And certainly these inadequacies are. But one of the responses librarians may also have is defensiveness. They become increasingly belligerent toward any indication they are failing and toward suggestions for improvement. As anyone who has encountered it or has tried to accomplish something within it can attest, the defense system they erect can be a very effective barrier to change.

Innovating organizations tend to be characterized by a willingness to take a certain amount of risk. Perhaps the heavy maintenance commitment assumed by libraries coupled with low financial support, has precluded any substantial investment in new possibilities. This would explain why major information developments when they did come, tended to emanate from outside the library profession by groups and agencies not tied either physically or psychologically to collection building as their major purpose.

Organizations to some extent impose roles and behavior on the people who work in them. But people are free to leave a situation which is incongruent with their personality structure and needs. Why then do we find librarians tolerating, even supporting organizations which stifle creativity and discourage change? The answer may be that libraries have very naturally attracted more than their share of what Robert Merton describes as ritualists, people who overconform on the means of the organization, for whom indeed the means have become the ends.[5] Organizations need ritualists for they are good soldiers, content, even eager, to preserve and maintain the system. But they are not likely to propose major changes in it and in fact may resist even minor modifications. Traditional library school training may well have encouraged this form of behavior with its emphasis on training for existing systems and in traditional practices.

We should say we are talking mostly about catalogers. And that frankly we do not know when their objections represent a legitimate defense of professional standards and when they are merely a resistance to any kind of change. In either case they seem conditioned to talk and think in terms of the integrity of the system, not the users' requirements.

There are other or related reasons why people initially at least resist an innovation. As in other organizations, librarians fear job displacement and status or power loss. These are not ungrounded fears for experience in many industries shows that whole groups of workers are rendered obsolete and the introduction of the specialist can mean a transfer of power. When decisions require advanced expertise, the administrator is forced to relinquish a certain amount of decision making power to the individuals with the expertise regardless of their position in the organization. Automation in libraries seems generally to cross departmental lines and so we find departments as well as individuals tenaciously defending their territorial rights. Automation is a form of change which introduces fears and hesitancies when a staff does not have background and understanding in computer use.

Automation or other major change may well require additional financial support and the library's ability to secure it depends on the role it has traditionally played in its community. If the library has been largely a passive agency performing necessary but not vital functions, managements may well hesitate to commit any large sums to automation. While they may support newer information functions, they are quite likely not to place them within the library. If the larger institution itself is tradition-bound we cannot expect much receptivity to proposals to make major change in the library.

These, then, briefly presented, appear to be major internal and external factors which can and do act to inhibit major change in libraries in the face of what may be a clear-cut mandate for change. In a mutually reinforcing process internal and external elements act to give libraries a strong set in favor of the status quo. Under outside pressure the library may tend to rigidify itself. Yet despite what may seem to be strong tendencies and overwhelming constraints, increasingly we find libraries automating at least some portion of their processes and procedures. Why? What happens to shake a library loose from these very strong commitments?

IMPETUSES FOR CHANGE

In a new field much credit must go to the original pioneers. The conditions must also of course be ripe for change—some awareness and recognition of the problem, availability of financial support and of the technology. But this does not explain why under the same conditions some libraries early introduced automation while others did not.

Ritualism is only one response individuals and organizations make to requirements for change. Another is innovation, accomplished by individuals willing to make change in both established goals and procedures. Somehow our conformist society manages to produce a few innovative types and the library profession to have attracted a share of them.

What makes the innovator run? We do not know with any certainty. Some cynics point to those who have carved careers from their automation activities as having adroitly identified their own career advancement with the new technology. This may very well be true but whatever the personal motives and ambitions of individuals, they must also possess the quality of creativity. This is not a quality reserved for the artist or the genius. It is a first and necessary part of the innovative process.[6]

All library change situations should not be idealized. Increasingly automation is becoming the thing for the administrator wanting to be thought progressive. Some administrators have acquiesced to automation only to the extent that it does not seriously disturb the internal status quo. This can very well mean that very major and fundamental problems still go untended. Nor is it by accident that libraries are beginning by automating the procedures they are. From all we know about people and organizations, they are far more likely to make a procedural change—indeed they make them all the time—than they are to tolerate a more fundamental change in their goals and objectives. (And we might add that some people go to automation conferences simply to soothe and reassure themselves.)

Libraries lack the profit incentive but they must ultimately satisfy a clientele if they are to continue to receive adequate financial support. Certainly many library administrators are sensitive to this reality and there are many professionally committed librarians motivated to make change in order to better serve their users. These are desirable ways conditions in the external environment encourage internal change in libraries provided librarians are receptive.

What is probably also happening in the external environment of libraries is that managements are becoming increasingly favorable toward automation generally. When college and university administrators are faced with mounting costs to support the library or are beleaguered by dissatisfied and irate faculty, they may well look to automation as a way to effect library improvements. In some cases they may virtually have foisted the change on the library. In the government setting we found concern on the part of the librarian that if the library did not modernize and update itself, other agencies might take on pending information storage and retrieval activities. If competition for the information function is motivating university library administrators we did not detect it.

Automation efforts, then, seem to get started not because libraries are change-oriented but as a response to external pressure—not always a rational or reasoned response—and because of individuals. These are people who by virtue of their interests and drives and abilities—and from professional commitment and concern—are motivated to initiate change. Another interesting facet we shall not attempt to explore here is the process by which innovators succeed in securing the resources and consent necessary to undertake change. Both internally and in relations with external groups, timing and strategy and power and personal persuasiveness are all elements. And not every innovator succeeds.

THE IMPLEMENTATION OF CHANGE

As human and organizational factors determine the "readiness to change" of a library so do human factors do much to direct the course of change. Resistances and differences do not disappear simply because a decision has been made to automate and the automation process itself engenders other human problems. What we want to know is what happens when automation is introduced in a library. How do people go about the task of making the change and why? In particular, what are the lessons to be learned from the experience of others?

People who have studied automation in other settings, tell us that our cases revealed behavior very characteristic of groups getting into automation for the first time. We found libraries contemplating automation without, it would seem, any real search for alternative, perhaps less expensive, solutions. It would also seem that the less experience a group has with automation, the more unrealistic their expectations of it. Somehow it is to solve all the hitherto unsolvable problems.

It also seems characteristic to tell the library user the advantages of the new system in terms of the production of the system instead of its advantages to him. We wonder if it is typical of automation personnel as well as librarians to become more concerned with the system than with the user? We found, too, the non-librarians putting in an automated system were operating within quite set and quite traditional notions of the library's function. For instance, we found them very proud of getting a printout of books in circulation. But, speaking as a user, this is not the point. What the user would like is a system which would register his need, locate the desired item, obtain it and deliver it to him. This is dissappointing for we might have looked to them for fresh insights or a particular concern for the user group.

Our study confirms how closely interwoven are the human and the technological aspects of change. If the change-over process does not proceed as expected or if it encounters major problems, this in itself can raise resistance and be discouraging even demoralizing to a staff. We wonder how typical it is to set unrealistic time schedules for getting a system installed and what the pressures are to go operational before the system has been adequately tested. These two factors seem to be the most self defeating aspects of the automation process.

By comparing the case where automation had been most successfully implemented with one which has been far less successful we gain insight into desirable approaches and techniques. In the success case first of all the head librarian was strongly behind the change. Further, a full time person was added to the permanent staff to implement automation. By design, staff members were very actively involved in the planning stages and all the staff undertook a special training program prior to the system being installed.

In the less successful case these ingredients were largely absent. The project from beginning to end seems in effect to have been introduced and conducted as an all-out project by an outside group with external deadlines. Indeed, some staff not only felt it was done by an outside group. They characterized it as being done *to* them by outsiders. As one put it, "We were at their mercy." The library staff reports one undesirable episode after another in the history of the project and the end of two years of effort finds them looking for outside help to straighten out the situation.

These differences are significant in themselves but they also identify two very important basic ingredients for success in implementing change and these are communications and leadership. By communication we do not mean merely communicating decisions and reporting although these are important. During a time of change normal working relationships can be severely strained. Considerable personal uncertainty is experienced partly because study may reveal or appear to reveal personal inadequacies. When the automation crosses departmental lines, traditional barriers between departments must be overcome. These are all reasons why people during this period need to be adequately informed and why special attention must be devoted to maintaining or improving channels of communication.

A major communications failure occurs because of the quite different orientations and perspectives of computer personnel and librarians. If outside personnel are to adequately assesss the library's needs they must immerse themselves thoroughly in its operation. In turn if librarians are to contribute to planning and work with the system once installed they must learn the technical aspects. It therefore is essential that operating staff work closely with automation personnel at all stages. This does not need to be an insurmountable barrier and yet it was here we found major communications breakdowns. Illustrative of this problem are comments made by staff in one or another library situation:

> "They didn't tell us anything in advance. All of a sudden it was here."
>
> "We spent two weeks trying to communicate the library's philosophy to them but in my opinion they certainly failed to grasp it."
>
> "Nobody knows what the other person is doing."
>
> "Communications aren't good between the catalogers and . . . We don't speak the same language. He doesn't understand how poor the print-outs are."

Closely linked to communications is administration under change. From all we know a more participative form of administration is required for successful change. Yet in our studies we encountered staff wanting more leadership and direction, not less. This could be because librarians are more comfortable with more authoritarian forms of management. But certainly administration should not be so haphazard or so laissez-faire, as to increase rather than decrease the natural uncertainty associated with major change or as to interfere seriously with the efficient installation of a new system.

We also noted that many staffs did not really see the larger point and purpose of what was being done. To communicate purpose and direction is a central function of management under stable conditions. Under change it becomes critical. Not everyone might share an administrator's ambitions for the library but common purpose is nevertheless needed if a staff is to work together instead of being continually at odds with one another. Staffs will respond far better to the specifics of change if they can see the larger picture. If a library is just not thinking beyond one or another immediate change, we would expect its choices to be poor and its energies misplaced.

These aspects are important and deserve far fuller treatment than we have given them here. We cannot overemphasize how interwoven are the human and technical aspects of change. Failure in one arena can spell out failure in the other.

THE CHANGE OUTCOME

Libraries need to assess not only how successful the change has been in itself but also what effect, whether planned or unplanned, it has or will have on its organization and on the library's goals of service. Even in the best situations we examined, staff members told us that after several years the kinks were still not out of the system. We have heard but not confirmed that many libraries which got into automation early are now at the point of virtually starting over. Even if this means that library automation is in a still primitive state, we believe we still have sufficient evidence to establish why librarians will ultimately, despite their reservations, accept automation. The major contribution the computer can make is in efficiency and people do not like to work in situations where they are continually made to feel inadequate. This conclusion is borne out by our cases of successful implementation. Even the "die-hards" had become reconciled and some were outrightly enthusiastic.

We also have at this stage some glimpses into what may be the long range impact of computerization. They point to the need to begin to consider the key organizational issues which may be at stake. For one, automation may well demand a revision of the traditional organizational structure in libraries. Automated processes seem to cross departmental lines; activities are transferred to different points in the process. In the long run may not automation require broader divisions in libraries and fewer departments?

It also appears that automation is putting some so-called professional activities at lower levels in the organization. Could this mean that middle echelon staff in processing departments will ultimately not be required? As computerization moves into other areas of library activity as well, will there not be quite major shifts in the numbers and types of personnel in libraries? Coupled with national information developments, we can envisage quite drastic change in the professional roles. Yet recognition of what could be sweeping change does not seem to have permeated the library literature or yet made any appreciable impact on library school curriculum.

What relation will the computer have to the issue of centralization or decentralization of library services? We can see a real need in colleges and universities to make service more convenient for the user but also for librarians to identify much more closely with their clientele. Can automation be used to bring services closer to people or will it merely support the large anonymous and passive form of central library bureaucracy?

This issue leads us to one which is even more important and basic, and that is the impact of automation on the user. Compared to the time and energy spent automating library processes, what is the pay-off to the user? Our experience suggests it may be very little indeed. The conventional library is automating processes which are quite irrelevant to the user's requirements while major needs go untended. In several situations we examined we found the library itself to be irrelevant in the sense that it was only a minor source of information for its constituency. It really did not matter very much what the library undertook in the way of automation of procedures.

To elaborate on this point in one setting, for the faculty member engaged in research at a university, a conventional library, despite a wealth of resources, cannot respond adequately to his needs. It is not staffed nor organized to respond readily and quickly to his requests. It is not arranged around his time pressures. It does not know his needs and his interests so as to keep him currently informed and indeed it does not really try. It frequently does not even traffic in the resources important to him, certainly not in the non-print sources and even when it stores non-conventional materials it does not provide ready access to their contents. There are many justifications for this, but the fact remains that a research faculty member does not and cannot depend on a conventional library as a major source of information. Merely automating existing routines will not appreciably and certainly not dramatically affect this situation.

It may be a practical first step to automate existing routines but we found little indication that libraries were thinking much beyond this point. And just because something can be done faster or with fewer people does not mean it needs to be done. What libraries could very well be doing is to automate obsolete systems. If they are to avoid this danger, they need to concern themselves with not what can be automated but rather with what libraries ought to be doing. Not in the 70's, *now*. If libraries do not actively aspire to more active, more vital and more mature functions will they not despite their automation efforts have stood still?

Our look, then, at the automation of library procedures leads us back to where we began. The central problem confronting the conventional library is to take on point and purpose and relevancy in today's terms. We can then decide—if we are on the right track let's move forward imaginatively. If we are on the wrong track, let's get off.

But there is little likelihood of libraries making the major shifts in their goals we believe called for unless they can overcome the organizational constraints identified earlier. Somehow they must shift their organizational environments so that they truly reward ideas and initiative and welcome expertise. Most importantly of all, the single, overriding, even consuming motivating force should not be commitment to the system nor even to efficiency per se, but to the user—to his needs, his requirements and yes, even his convenience. Then, we can realize the potential of the computer in library service.

We have only introduced and yet have made strong statements about a range of issues and elements which are revealed when we turn attention along the human dimension of change. The writer has meant to question and to probe but not to disparage and wishes to acknowledge her indebtedness to the librarians and others who frankly and freely discussed their experiences. These are complex questions and issues which cannot easily be resolved, but they do demand discussion and concern and further study.

Partly because the writer is in library education, but also because she is presently involved in a manpower research project, her interest lies in the implications of the change era for education and research in the library profession. The concluding remarks here deal with these aspects.

IMPLICATIONS FOR TRAINING AND RESEARCH

Given the need for fundamental and continual change and those suggestions as to the aspects and issues central to the initiation and implementation of change, what should characterize the library administrator of the future? (Like most discussions of leadership requirements this may be largely a rhetorical question. The prized expertise is technical competence and it could well be that the computer and systems specialists will not be content to work in service or middle management positions but may rather seek the rewards at the top.)

We would agree that the top level administrator of the future should at least be comfortable with the technology. And, however suspect the interpreneurial type, libraries will have need of achievement oriented administrators, at home with uncertainty and strongly motivated to take risks. Whatever his personal drives, the administrator will need to be far more problem solving, research oriented as well.

A consideration of the ideal requirements for leadership should include the dimension of statesmanship. The library profession needs men—and women—who can conceive and successfully communicate an important role for the library in the intellectual life of its community. But the political role should not be minimized—the administrator who deals with the art of the possible, who by virtue of his political astuteness and ability is able to secure the support and consent for an expanded library role. By the politician we do not mean the office holder, the administrator who bends with the breezes, who easily becomes no more than an administrative functionary, content to take far too little in the way of financial support and who under stress is likely to cling to an internal status quo which is not threatening to him personally.

Every profession needs its myths and heroes in retrospect and there is a human tendency to want strong leadership. But perhaps as Warren Bennis suggests, we must say "farewell to the great men" for the strong will and single mindedness with which they built great organizations can come in time to be the very qualities which make them resist change and new ideas. Eventually they become not an asset but a liability. It may be part of our coming out of professional adolescence to place less faith in leaders and more in professional men, described by Bennis as,[7]

> "And these men can hardly be called 'organizational men.' They seemingly derive their rewards from inward standards of excellence, from their professional societies, and from the intrinsic satisfaction of their task. In fact, they are committed to the task, not the job; to their standards, not their boss. And because they have degrees, they travel. They are not good 'company men'; they are uncommitted except to the challenging environments where they can 'play with problems.'"

Under these terms creativity for the administrator lies not in what he personally accomplishes but rather in providing an environment in which other men can be creative and productive. This means a far more flexible, more democratic form of organization than most libraries now enjoy.

What do these requirements suggest in the way of training for leadership position in the library profession? Preparation for managerial position will certainly require more than ordinary sophistication with the computer and with the systems approach. But even beyond this, training should emphasize a research oriented approach. It will also require human relations skills and understandings. The administrator should at least be introduced to advanced organizational and political understandings. If he is not to be a value-neutral, he must become concerned with professional and broader societal values, with searching for the point and purpose of library service in contemporary times. Perhaps training for administrative posts in libraries should be especially designed to concentrate on the requirements for change.

Librarians, too, must have background in the technology and its application to the information function. Specialties are required which must go beyond the one year program and many will require quantitative skills on the part of those who undertake them. One specialty might lie in the management area. But the field would be making a mistake in our view, if it tries as did the field of education to train for all the skills and specialties needed to run the complicated library enterprises of the future. Rather library schools might look to forging links with such departments as computer science perhaps through having their majors take minors in library and information science. But the major point to be made about professional training in this field is, as we have suggested, that the professional role is likely to be quite drastically different in the future. Library schools may even now be preparing librarians to fill quite thoroughly outmoded roles and in so doing helping to perpetuate the status quo in librarianship—and the uncertainty and sense of inadequacy which does much to explain why librarians resist major change.

We have not in this paper presented automation and innovation in terms of the research issues and problems, but our delving into the social science literature and our own initial studies suggests there is a whole realm of interesting and significant questions for study. That this field has not yet devoted research attention to these questions may be because its members tend to be either technically or humanistically oriented and have not appreciated the contribution the social sciences can make.

In particular we would recommend research in this area to doctoral candidates in library science for as a field for study it meets the requirements for doctoral study—theoretical models available from several of the social science disciplines which means the research can qualify as basic, research precedents in a body of studies conducted in a number of settings, a variety of situations now available for depth study in the library field. Shortly, as well, there should be a sufficient number of automation cases to permit taking meaningful "industry-wide" looks as well.

If they would excercise a little creativity and imagination, doctoral candidates in this field can get in on one of the most exciting—and decisive—episodes in library history. In the process they can carve out research careers for themselves and quickly become authorities on whatever aspect they select. Automation and the broader aspect of change and innovation is one of the most promising of the research frontiers in the library field.

FOOTNOTES

[1] Max Ways, "The Era of Radical Change," *Fortune* (May, 1964), pp. 112-115.
[2] Warren Bennis, Changing Organizations (New York: McGraw-Hill Book Company, 1966), p. 19.
[3] Harold Guetzkow, "The Creative Person in Organizations," *The Creative Organization*, ed. Gary A. Steiner (Chicago: University of Chicago Press, 1965), p. 36.
[4] Mary Lee Bundy and Paul Wasserman, "Professionalism Reconsidered," *College & Research Libraries*, 29 (Jan., 1968), pp. 5-26.
[5] Robert Merton, *Social Theory and Social Structure* (Glencoe, Ill.: Free Press, 1957), pp. 141-153.
[6] For one description of the innovational personality, see Everett Hagen, *On the Theory of Social Change* (Homewood, Ill.: Dorsey Press, 1962), Chapter V, "Innovational and Authoritarian Personalities," pp. 86-98.
[7] Warren Bennis, *Changing Organizations* (New York: McGraw-Hill Book Company, 1966), p. 25.

ABOUT THE AUTHOR—Mary Lee Bundy, see p. 94.

Professionalism

Perhaps this is the most appropriate issue with which to conclude this volume. For to be professional, those who seek the rewards of professional status must accept the responsibility for the welfare and progress of libraries as theirs, rather than the administrators'. The task, as in other bureaucratized professions, is to fashion and attain an organizational culture compatible with achieving the goals of librarianship.

Professionalism Reconsidered

by Mary Lee Bundy and Paul Wasserman

Librarianship as a profession is viewed here through analysis of the working situation by observing the actual behavior of librarians. Among the questions asked: Can the nature of the services rendered by librarians be termed professional? Is the obligation of the professional to his client recognized by librarians? Is the librarian primarily "job" or "career" oriented? Does he understand the issues at stake and how does he respond? How supportive of professional goals and standards are the professional associations? What is the contribution of the library schools to the inculcation of service values and standards, and in the provision of professional expertise?

Librarians, like many in other marginal or maturing professions often spend considerable time being concerned about whether or not they are truly professional; much effort goes into reassuring themselves that they are indeed professional and that they should therefore enjoy the recognition and rewards of professional status. Such preoccupation manifests itself in a wide range of activities common to all such upward-mobile and self-conscious aspiring groups. They conduct public relations programs designed to create a favorable image of their craft. Being much concerned about status differences, they discuss endlessly means of differentiating the professional worker from the lesser educated.[1] They establish and seek vigorously to strengthen their occupational associations; they promulgate a code of ethics and establish internal means of controlling members who violate it. They frequently turn to legislation to control entry into practice. Concomitantly, there is a striving toward the identification of a philosophical and intellectual base for practice. Ultimately their educational efforts find a place in the universities where they come eventually to seek academic parity for their instructional programs by meeting university standards of scholarship.

Many early claims of professionalism and early activities to attain it tend to be suspect since they are often a mélange of the real and the fanciful, in which pious longings are often confused with reality. A field's recruitment publicity is thus often based upon ill-conceived sloganeering or myths which often turn out to be nearer to what the discipline and those who practice in it would like to be than what they really are. The ethic presented by the group can be so vague as to defy relation to the realities of practice.[2] The educational preparation, or training as it is more frequently termed, conducted by the professional school, is often offered by instructors who are displaced, or perhaps misplaced, from practice, and it tends heavily to the practical, the mechanical, and the ritual. Only very gradually and very subtly does the university influence manifest itself in reorienting course content, so that a grudging tolerance for conceptual and theoretical issues comes to find its place alongside the pragmatic.

Even within firmly established professions the ethic may be more pious hope than reality. Carlin's findings in a study of the legal profession suggest that a group may so frequently and flagrantly overlook malpractice that it in effect condones it.[3] The widespread abuses of the Hippocratic oath by the medical fraternity in such instances as fee splitting and the proprietorship of pharmacies and optometry houses, attest to its hypocritical abuse.[4] It is doubtless true that professions discourage their members from making public disclosures of undesirable practice, acting only after there has been a public scandal. Certainly, much of the effort of professional groups seems to stem more from self-interest than from a true regard for their responsibilities.[5] Many groups which claim to be professional have never had a sense of community responsibility. Intra-group rivalry goes on within professions, while at the same time fields strenuously resist encroachments from other occupational groups through the use of political and economic mechanisms, and they strive to reassign less glamorous tasks to others. Conditions of ac-

SOURCE: Reprinted from Mary Lee Bundy and Paul Wasserman, "Professionalism Reconsidered," *College and Research Libraries*, 29 (Jan., 1968), pp. 5–26, by permission of the Association of College and Research Libraries.

ual practice in virtually every profession depart in important measure from the professional ideal.

These disparities, however, do not mean that the professions do not have well-established traditions of service or commitments to standards, nor does it mean that they are not committed to the advancement of knowledge and the practical art of their fields. It is to these ends that the attempt to achieve professional status for librarianship appropriately addresses itself. All established professions have an awareness of the conditions of practice required for a professional to grow and develop. They have frequently struggled to protect practice from political or other influences which would corrupt or misuse or downgrade, and on balance they must be viewed as a force for orderly progress within the democratic tradition. The more advanced professions, although their practice may remain imperfect, provide traditions, ideals, models, and directions for emerging professions.

Librarianship appears to be in the midst of a serious shortage of personnel. In order to attract from the limited reservoir of talented people who are sought and competed for by each of the professions, it must be possible to offer potential recruits rewarding and satisfying careers. To do so implies a speed-up in the process of professionalization. In order to fulfill their original mandate of serving as guardian of society's information needs and in order to influence positively the forward motion of progressive information development in a time of competition with other emergent information-oriented disciplines, librarianship must more fully take on the responsibilities and substance as well as the forms of a profession. Without such commitment, librarians may ultimately find themselves left only with custodial tasks while the intellectual aspects, as well as the more active forms of information service, are yielded to other groups.

Some in library education place all their hope in the next generation of librarians. In effect, they would write off most of those now in practice as essentially and permanently semi-professional. This attitude is unrealistic. It ignores the fact that during the next two decades, which may well prove to be most critical for determining whither (or whether) librarianship, the major decisions influencing variations and adaptations in information services will be made by those who are already in practice. Furthermore, such a view tends to be over-sanguine about the real advances of present educational programs over those of the past.

Viewed in historical perspective, the library schools may be seen to have been a decisive influence in whatever degree of professionalization has been achieved thus far. They have succeeded in placing their programs, at least in a formal sense, at the graduate level. Nevertheless, one may remain skeptical of the capacity of library education, and of library educators (except for certain isolated institutions and, regretfully, isolated individuals) to be fully transformed along the drastically variant lines which contemporary technological, societal, and behavioral advances clearly require.

Many librarians are without doubt best suited, either by temperament or through the remorseless habituation of long experience, to performing superclerical tasks. In some instances they may even be hostile to or suspicious of efforts to upgrade the intellectual demands put upon them in their practice, but it is not necessarily because they are uninterested or opposed to intellectual effort. Frequently they are highly literate, intelligent people who remain satisfied with or resigned to spending major portions of their working lives performing at a nonintellectual level. It is simply that the acculturation process in library education or in practice, or both, have been so devoid of genuine intellectual content that they have come to identify their roles, and the role of librarianship generally, as pedestrian and uninspiring. For them, as for many similar types in other humdrum fields which do not call forth the breadth of their imagination or the finest quality of their minds, there is sublimation in the form of home pursuits, hobbies, and travel. For them the battle is over. Library work is a nine-to-five routine—the best comes only on long weekends, extended holidays, travel, and early retirement.

The field also has many competent and thoughtful people (mostly in the earlier years of service and not yet ground down by the weight of experience and bureaucratic indoctrination) who are deeply disturbed by the disparity between what they believe constitutes professional practice and what most librarians now do. Many were and remain deeply disgruntled about the calibre and content of their educational preparation and are strongly motivated to improve practice in the field. It is to this group, uneasy and unfulfilled by their present roles, to whom this article is primarily directed, in the hope that it may contribute somewhat to enlarged understanding of what professional practice in librarianship involves and what needs to be done to advance this field toward such a goal.

Professionalism will be viewed here not in abstract academic terms but rather in the real world in which librarians practice, through a comparison of the behavior of librarians with what is customarily considered to constitute professional behavior. The central thesis is that it is in terms of three major relationships—with clients, with the institution where he performs, and with the professional group—that the decision as to whether one is or is not a professional is decided.

THE LIBRARIAN-CLIENT RELATIONSHIP

The client relationship is the central role of any professional whether the client be an individual or, as is frequently the case in the practice of law, a company or other institution. It is his *raison d'être*, his justification for the claims he places on individual institutions and on the society generally, even though not every professional works directly with the client. For even with the increasing institutionalization and bureaucratization of professional activities and the consequent lessening in the degree and frequency of client relations, the ultimate purpose remains service to the client. In an ideal and unambiguous relationship, the client relies upon the professional for the expertise which his problem or situation requires. The professional, by virtue of his training, experience, and specialized knowledge, offers the client the counsel, service, or prescription which he views to be appropriate *whether or not* this is precisely what the client wants or thinks he wants. The professional's guidance may not always be followed, but the judgment and recommendation of the professional are not open to question or debate by the layman. The professional *knows*.

When cast in this context, how does the librarian-patron relationship measure up? Generalizations are always fraught with risk, particularly when they attempt to characterize a practice stretched across a continuum as wide as that of librarianship. Yet, in spite of the hazards, perhaps some broadly relevant observations can be advanced here. In general library situations, that which is requested by or offered to the patron is ordinarily just not complex enough to be considered a professional service. The service provided would not overtax the capacity of any reasonably intelligent college graduate after a minimum period of on-the-job training.

This is not necessarily because librarians do not wish to serve (although some do not and have developed a practiced *hauteur* which quickly suggests to all but the doggedly persevering client that they are thought to be intruders or ignoramuses). Yet, in spite of this element and despite allegations that the collecting function takes high precedence over the service function, American librarianship has for the most part enjoyed a proud tradition of service. Perhaps in the past however, and even into the present, library work has had a decidedly feminine cast. That is to say, librarians achieve intrinsic satisfaction from the very act of serving and are content to perform in minor and inconsequential capacities. This can also manifest itself in other ways. Like the doting mother shoveling spoonfuls of food into the mouth of the child and joyful at the sight of consumption, the librarian may be too frequently insensitive to the limits of the information user's appetite, to the preciseness of his need or to the particularity of his taste. The willingness to play an inexpert role may well have been reinforced by the fact that the librarian has had some little knowledge about many things but not very much genuine understanding of anything. This portrait is not drawn to suggest that it is only the very most complex problems with which a librarian must concern himself, nor, to use a medical analogy, that the general reference librarian is any less consequential than the general practitioner. It is to suggest only that the druggist should not be confused with the doctor.

An apparently related phenomenon is the essential timidity of practitioners, clearly reflected in the widespread, deep-seated, and trained incapacity or high degree of reluctance to assume responsibility for solving informational problems and providing unequivocal answers. The problem may be viewed at two levels of service, each interrelated. At the general level, it is reflected in the extinction of the reader's advisor, that breed of librarian who could, would, and did actively channel readers along rational and productive lines by making concrete recommendations and introducing taste and discrimination into such choices. The reluctance to be assertive may be as much a function of insecurity born out of fears engendered by the limits of the modern librarian's mind to cope with the complexities of an ever broadening spectrum of knowledge, or awe of the growing sophistication of middle class readers among whom higher educational preparation is now widely characteristic, or because of the confusion which attends a set of objectives for library service which tolerates light diversion with intellectual development as equally viable missions. It is the client then who always determines his wants, and it is only the most iconoclastic librarian who suggests alternatives either by making precise recommendations or by skewing client choices through close control of the content of collections to reflect excellence. Perhaps, in this sense, it is the children's librarians who are the most professional. Not only are they experts in their literature who share commitment and high purpose, but they also presume to advise and direct their clients readily and to influence the client's independent choices by maintaining careful quality control over the composition of their collections. (It is of course easier to assume this posture with the child than with the adult.)

This problem is also seen at the general level in the conduct of reference librarians who balk at offering judgments about the quality of material or, at times, even at making comments upon the relevancy of material to particular informational problems. Rather than straightforwardly and self-assuredly advising a patron which is the singular or which the most promising sources, reference librarians appear to be most comfortable when providing numerous works or voluminous bibliographies. Moreover, it seems characteristic of the librarian's psyche to recoil from giving out straight answers. Instead, it is invariably the printed source in which the information is to be found that is offered. What may have been an appropriate rationale for such an approach in an earlier period seems less relevant in 1967. Whether a service which relies solely upon a book stock as the only true source of information is congruent with contemporary realities (except for such isolated cases as law or medicine) is subject to serious doubt. In a time of abundant and oftentimes more realistic alternatives to searching on printed pages, it is anachronistic for librarianship to remain so heavily committed to and dependent upon published sources to the exclusion of other possibilities. Viewed in solely economic terms, hours spent searching the literature for potential data which may no longer be current seems far less rational than employing alternative approaches, as for example, telephoning and asking someone who knows, even if the knower is five hundred miles away. While training and temperament have geared librarians to fact finding from published sources, by setting such a limit on the approach they circumscribe their role, and in the process, their professional value.

For the most part librarians remain medium- rather than client-oriented. In clinging tenaciously to the information container of another age, and as they continue only to acquire and stock and shelve books, they resist the idea that the more fundamental commodity of modern times is information and that it takes myriad forms. They will meet the client's requirements if it can be done with a book and only with a book. For the clientele the vehicle is beside the point, the point is the information sought. By concentrating exclusively on the book and by resisting alternatives, the librarian remains comfortable and unpressured, while the client finds other avenues of access to information because of the librarian's default.

As part of this same syndrome, we find large-scale collection building seen as the expression of the librarian's expertise rather than rapid uncomplicated access to intelligence. Yet, the most effective client service may well be enhanced when the librarian concentrates his efforts upon careful discrimination in choice of acquisitions rather than in fiercely competitive and feverish collection building.[6] Ultimately, means become ends; libraries are measured in terms of the size of their collections while the more significant measure, the quality and nature of the service they render, is ignored.

Viewed from another angle, catalog conventions, codes, policies, and procedures are also divorced from their ultimate purpose—service to the client. Detachment from clientele permits cataloging personnel to remain dedicated exclusively to the book literature, while ignoring or avoiding less conventional forms and media. As a consequence, these remain outside the control of the library and the patron dismisses the library as a source for any but the traditional published forms. The full potential of a very powerful tool to support clientele service is unrealized.

At another level of service, the library and the librarian functioning within the framework of a specific subject discipline, many of these built-in constraints are absent. Librarians here are typically more prone to deal with and give specialized treatment to nonconventional sources, and they are prepared to go further in pursuing information requests. Where there is lack of assurance on the part of the librarian or limits on the reliance which the client places on his expertise, it will most frequently stem from the inadequacy of the librarian's educational preparation in the substantive field. To function in a science setting without the requisite orientation in the science disciplines or in a financial environment without understanding a balance sheet or the working of the financial markets serves only to reinforce the tenacity of the librarian to cling to card catalogs and book titles rather than to venture forth upon the precarious ground of substantive information; it reaffirms in the client's view the belief that the level of sophistication to be expected as an aid in problem-solving from library personnel is minimal. In either case, the effect is far from the most efficacious ideal for the professional-client relationship.

The remedy here may be to close the chapter on that phase of library history which tolerates, as one example, the well-meaning English major who gravitates into medical librarianship. Granted the need for organizational skill, the service ideal, and technical grounding in information handling, it will only be when the client can respect the subject competence of the librarian that he will accept him and respect him for his professional competence in the meaning employed here. Now this is not to say that the subject librarian need be a highly trained and advanced student of a narrow and specialized discipline to perform effectively, but rather that there must come to be a better match than has yet existed in typical cases between his preparation and his field of practice. Under such terms, someone without rudimentary grounding in the biological and chemical sciences would be discouraged from medical library service and someone without economics and financial study from business librarianship. Of course, this would call for a reorientation in recruitment patterns away from the more traditional and disproportionately heavy reliance upon those trained in the humanistic disciplines and toward the sciences and the social sciences. With the increasing role of the federal government in the support of graduate study, as reflected in such programs as those of the Office of Education and the National Library of Medicine, such a prospect is less remote than when there were no incentives to offer library students and at earlier stages when library work was less related to information services and more to a predominantly custodial function.

Two prototypes of this professional ideal suggest themselves. One is the subject-expert special librarian. He is epitomized in the law librarian with a law degree, the fine arts librarian trained in fine arts, or the music librarian with substantive preparation in music. In the university setting, some but not all departmental and college librarians fall into this category. More recently the subject bibliographer has come to be found increasingly in the universities. Such an individual plays the role of subject collection builder and librarian. Sometimes drawn from the particular field of scholarship, sometimes from librarianship, he enjoys the respect of his clientele for his subject competence. It may well be that the next stage in the educational preparation of librarians will call for a fundamental modification, to build into the educational preparation of librarians a planned and programed sequence of enhancing the subject competence of its students, for there can be little doubt that when the librarian is comfortable, both in the subject matter of the field in which he serves and in the substance of librarianship, he is far more strongly equipped and so more likely to achieve fuller acceptance as a professional in his role relations with clients.

Pushed one stage farther, under these terms the librarian can move from a fundamentally passive to a more aggressive role in information prescription. At home in the subject field, he will be less reliant upon published bibliographic sources, and he will far more readily generate for himself the bibliographic and reference aids for his clientele, for they will grow naturally and logically out of his work in a subject area in which he is not alien. Because bibliographic organization and imaginative informational approaches to subject matter in burgeoning fields are so much sought by clienteles, here is an obvious path to improved clientele esteem.

The responsibility for a lack of aggressive professional service in problem-solving terms must be laid at the door of professional education for librarianship. For the schools, with only rare exceptions, have failed to breed an appreciation for the subtleties or the potentialities of the professional role. Where individual librarians have assumed significant information responsibilities for their constituencies, it has resulted from a combination of their own inherent and intuitive perception of their clientele commitments with imaginative application of bibliographic expertise and subject competence.

What the schools have produced is several generations of librarians committed zealously to the pattern of general service. While the library school student may have been exposed to a smattering of philosophy, and berated with and perhaps inspired by librarianship's service commitments and yearnings, nowhere was this likely to have been translated beyond the bounds of a vague service concept and on into the terms which might correspond with truly professional practice. Reference instructors (typically generalists themselves who rely on the descriptive terms of bibliography, simplistic isolated fact-finding exercises, or vague problems of reference administration) might seek to rationalize their offerings by suggesting that general, mechanistic, totally book-slanted orientations are intended for only the beginning stages of practice. This indoctrination, however, appears to have conditioned most librarians to perform throughout their careers at no higher level of attainment than that of this beginning practice. In learning a set repertoire of responses to meet only narrowly defined client requirements, librarians have not been provoked to consider the alternative of undertaking more demanding or new and differing responsibilities for their clienteles.

It would be naive for any occupational group to believe it could establish its professional role independently, for the ability of any professional to perform and the capacities in which he functions are in many respects circumscribed and influenced by external factors. This may be particularly true for librarianship, which has been a relatively passive pursuit. Since this has been so, it is not surprising to find that the librarian's role has come to be influenced by the expectations of the library's clientele and community which, in many instances, correspond to the minimal attainment level which he has set for himself.

A professional certainly cannot assume a professional role with a client without the client's acceptance of him in the role of expert. Varying factors have tended to prohibit such acceptance of librarians. One has been the conditioning of clienteles to view the librarian in negative stereotyped terms with a consequent reluctance to enlist him as an active ally in the information seeking process. On non-literary matters, the average person simply does not expect—and his experience reinforces this view—that the librarian would be able to help him. The unlettered may hesitate to seek help for fear of revealing their presumed ignorance to someone who appears so all-knowing and bookish and who would tend only to reinforce their feelings of inadequacy in an alien environment. The research scholar, reluctant to relinquish to another the tasks which he has performed unaided (except in the university, to graduate assistants who function under his guidance, and who as a consequence have the subject background to understand fully the nature of the work upon which he is engaged), requests only minor assistance from librarians.

These barriers do not appear to present insurmountable obstacles to professional performance. If the librarian succeeds in developing skill and finesse in reducing the hesitancies of those not accustomed to use libraries, larger numbers who genuinely require information may be expected to turn to them.[7] And as career preparation for librarianship came to comprise substantive preparation beyond the solely bibliographic, so would the disposition of the client change to place heavier reliance upon him for assistance of a more professional calibre. No ultimate wresting of control from the client is involved, for as in every other instance in which a professional is employed, the choice of whether or not to use the service, and then to accept or reject its guidance if it is found to to be unreliable or inexpert, is retained by the client.

The immediate institution in which the librarian performs may also have decided and frequently dysfunctional influences upon the client relationship. These institutional constraints will occupy us in further detail hereafter. Just as the wider environment influences the library, it also determines to a considerable degree the professional role of the librarian. The clientele group, in the aggregate, exerts its influence, for libraries, like other service institutions, tend to accommodate to those who use them. And such external forces have characteristically tended to perpetuate traditional roles for the institution and in the process for the professional role. Several examples shall be cited.

At a time when the population composition has shifted radically in virtually every older core city, the public library essentially retains its cultural orientation to the middle class, and this results in an institutional role and a concept of client service which corresponds with the strivings, literary tastes, and values of a middle class clientele which often is no longer present. The community typically is indifferent to this incongruity. In a university during the period when it seeks to develop its graduate and research programs (and this is the present state of a large proportion of American institutions of higher learning), the undergraduate service requirements continue to preoccupy the library as the influence of a longer history of undergraduate programs continues to hold sway, while the graduate and faculty constituencies are neglected. This situation often persists until the research faculty succeeds in exerting its influence upon the university and upon the library's administration. Not only are the libraries inclined to be biased in favor of one consistuency over another, but in each instance the community expects only minimal forms of service. Public library patrons tend to settle for recreational fare. In the university a classroom appendage, the reserve reading room, is too often confusedly equated with the entire library by administrators who do not understand the nature of a library and by librarians who do not understand either.

In the school library, client service is often a victim of the conflict between the ideal of service to support the individual student's intellectual growth and development, and to the curricular requirements of the school. Moreover, many school libraries carry out functions which bear no relation to either objective, as reflected in such activities as librarians substituting for teachers, or in the use of the library as a study hall or for class disciplinary purposes. There may be some fundamental question and ambiguity about who the client really is—the school, the teacher, or the student—and this only further compounds the conflict inherent in the situation.

In each of these instances, accommodation is to requirements which are not reinforcing of professional-client relationships, but are rather the contrary. Where service expectations are minimal from the community, and as these are furthered through the institutional orientation of the library, whatever the aspirations of the librarian, he is restricted from enhancing his professional role. The point is that this role is of course, to a considerable extent, conditioned by the public image of the library and the function of the librarian which is in need of drastic modification, if the professional ideal is to be furthered.

The client relationship has been dealt with thus far as a primarily individual matter, but it seems relevant also to consider it in its community context and in comparison with other similar fields. To take two illustrations, let us consider public health and social welfare. Energetic clientele effort conceives of its role as embracing more than only the existing consumer, but also reaching out and functioning as a professional service in improving the community as regards such affairs. For public health, this would include preventive measures in a program designed to reduce the incidence of disease, and in social service, the organization of activities committed to a reduction in the frequency of need for welfare assistance. The counterpart for library service could be found only through commitment to constituencies not now viewed as the library's responsibility—for the public library, the marginally literate and other non-users of traditional services; for the academic library—the devising of new forms and methods of information service beyond the passive collection function; for the school-library—a commitment to building collections and services to influence the teacher in *his*

continuing education and *his* effectiveness to perform. Such a perspective of the revised professional commitments for library service is not in conflict with the views of progressive elements in the library profession. Yet, far more persistent and far more pervasive is the widely shared consensus that libraries basically are for those who use them and that it is no part of the library's or the librarian's responsibility to shift in the direction of those who do not. The implementation of far-reaching, innovative, or imaginative approaches to professional/clientele services seems only remotely possible, or likely to develop in only isolated instances, when viewed against the general level of current commitments and current practice.

INSTITUTIONAL RELATIONSHIPS

Client relationships are importantly conditioned by the bureaucratic setting within which librarians function. As is equally true of other types of professionals who practice in formal organizations, librarians are faced with conflicts inherent in the incongruence between professional commitments on the one hand, and employee requirements on the other. Professionals view the freedom to function independently, the exercise of discretion, and the formulation of independent judgments in client relations based upon their own standards and ethical views, as essential to professional performance. The professional resents institutional authority which attempts to influence his behavior and performance norms, preferring control by colleagues. These requirements for independence are met to varying degrees in the institutionalized professions, and in librarianship, scarcely at all.

Librarians do perform in their direct client relationship with remarkably limited review or supervision, and stated conversely, with perhaps equally limited direction or training. The reference librarian is typically free to set his own limits on how or whether to deal with patron inquiries. He will, in fact, often spend more time on those questions which interest him or upon which he feels confident. Or, he will perhaps determine the relevance of an inquirer's need based upon his assessment of the prestige, the authority, the personality, the appearance, or the presumed social, economic, or intellectual stratum which the patron represents. Despite the democratic ethic upon which library service is founded, the human tendency to choose to deal with individuals or situations which do not threaten, or to cater to those presumed to be most important, remains unbridled.

It is not so much that the institution tolerates

such personalized judgments of the relative merits of a quest by the reference librarian out of deference to his expertise or evaluative acumen, as much as that the encounter does not appear to be viewed as critical or crucial enough to warrant inspection (as compared, for example, with preparing cards for a catalog which can be assessed as a permanent record of the success or failure of performance). If administrative pressure is exerted, it will most typically be directed toward expediting or handling of more requests so that larger numbers of patrons can be accommodated. In some large systems there may even be a deliberate striving for anonymity, with new staff members cautioned against trying to build a personal following.

While the institution may not directly interfere in the client encounter, in addressing himself principally to satisfying immediate client needs the professional inevitably runs counter to the system which is designed not to maximize client service, but for the over-all good of the largest number, even if this is only a most modest good. And since rigid adherence to bureaucratic ritual (rules and regulations) permits of practices which may be efficient in terms of the organization's requirements, in any given instance professional service to clientele may be sacrificed.[8] Ultimately, the bureaucratic routine imposes procedures which may be in conflict with the very goals of the organization—the dialectic is complete, means have becomes ends, and the intellectual and professional design is sacrificed upon the altar of economic and efficient work procedures.

This is not to suggest that there is not a need for order and control in organizations which traffic as heavily in stock and records as do libraries. With the growth in size and scale of activity, the need for procedural consistency is accentuated. Nevertheless, such regularization means that perhaps ironically in the very largest libraries with the greatest resources and thus the greatest potential for professional service, the tolerance for individual needs will be most sharply curtailed, the client service minimized, and the professional values most seriously threatened. The role of the library, as Walton has so concisely put it, is to find that precise balance which introduces only enough routine to keep order and record-keeping integrity, but not so much as to impair the opportunity to afford clientele convenient and unhampered access to resources.[9] Finding this balance may be seen as the task of the creative administrator. It is clearly not to be found in imposing burdensome ritual which may serve to stultify the opportunity for professional behavior and practice.

It is for this reason and to act as a countervailing force to the pressures for economy which would reduce standards of service that it is essential for professionals in organizations to assume decision-making responsibilities in relation to goals and standards of service.[10] Yet, with only rare exceptions, libraries fall into that class of organizations in which goal decisions are tightly controlled by the administrative hierarchy. They are consequently at the mercy of other tendencies of bureaucracy which run counter to professional aspirations and responsibilities. While professional spirit and zeal thrive most in an atmosphere which tolerates, even furthers, freedom of inquiry and pronounced license for unrestricted thought and action, the hierarchical system by its nature protects and perpetuates itself through its demands for submission, obedience, and acceptance. Since the hierarchical structure is reinforced when it withstands any pressure for rapid change, it tends to be organized in such a way as to inhibit the stream of ideas within the organization which might ultimately culminate in variations in organizational arrangements or practices. One consequence is that libraries tend not to advance beyond the levels of minimal service, for the organizational structure strives to reinforce the status quo. While there may be tolerance for procedural improvement, particularly when there is a universal climate provoking such modification (automation of circulation procedures may be a case in point) resistance to any more fundamental change such as goal modification remains as staunch as ever.[11]

Compliance of professionals is achieved through a reward system which distributes benefits and higher incentives for loyalty to the institution. While the professional presumably addresses his fundamental loyalty to the societal responsibilities of his calling and therefore to the commitments and responsibilities to the clientele which this engenders, the institution recognizes only organizational loyalty. As the professional seeks institutional rewards, security, and status, he pays for them with compliance and conformity at the expense of his professional obligations. The professional who retains a fundamental identification with clientele commitment is inevitably forced into a position of conflict with organizational requirements.

Bureaucratic structure clearly imposes restraints, yet these tendencies which are contrary to professional requirements are not necessarily irreversible processes or insurmountable barriers. Even so, librarians continue to tolerate and perpetuate conditions of practice which fall short of the professional ideal. Perhaps this stems from the lack of understanding on the part of many librarians as well as administrators of what the issues are. In many library situations, a librarian viewing his primary commitment as essentially to client service, rather than to institution, would be considered disloyal, uncooperative, or otherwise suspect, even among his peer group—fellow librarians. May this not perhaps be the case of the new breed of subject bibliographer being spawned in the academic library, forced to choose between allegiance to library or to subject discipline, and gravitating away from the rigid bind of bureaucracy and toward the more free flowing current of his scholarly company? By many librarians he is seen as a prima donna, impatient with necessary work routines, unwilling to help out in emergencies, a waster of time spent in idle conversation with his clientele about their work—renegade and spoiled.

Administrators in other comparable fields (particularly when they are drawn from the professional ranks as is true of most library administrators), are sensitive to professional needs, values, and aspirations, and as a consequence, strive to bend the bureaucratic limitations in order to accommodate to the working requirements of professional and other specialists in their organizations. Library administrators frequently view operational constraints to be of such overbearing importance that they are exaggerated through their administration. Too often the administrator (not infrequently one who blows the horn of professionalism loudest), has not a minimum understanding of the proper climate within which professionalism is cultivated. He will view professional standards from the standpoint of internalized organizational standards, see the products of graduate study as so many replacements for the firing line without regard for their needs or their immediate or ultimate aspirations. Under these terms, librarians are treated like interchangeable parts serving where and when needed. Librarians man desks and meet schedule commitments, and in the process, deny and are denied the opportunity to care, to grow and to act professionally.

Nor is the library administrator always sensitive to the changing requirements of the external environment within which his organization functions. In the academic milieu, the storm warnings have long been out to alert the administrator to the fact that for important elements of his clientele their information requirements are simply not being met effectively and that only dramatic modification of the library's role will alter things. Where the problem is economic, and this will typically be only a minor symptom of a more fundamental disorder, the library administrator does both his library and the larger institution a disservice when he accepts only the crumbs from the organizational table. Indeed, library administrators sometimes make a virtue of such martyrdom when they might better recognize that there are times and issues for which one must stand up and be counted, even if this implies putting one's job on the line. In the public library, the central issue relates to the basic role of the library during a period when social needs, modern technology, and other dramatic factors should be influencing a re-evaluation of the conventional middle-class and book orientation which was seen as appropriate for another time and under different circumstances.

People and institutions ultimately get the form of administration which they seek. If so, why during a period of drastic personnel shortages, have librarians tolerated forms of administration which deny them the opportunity for full expression? As the administrators do not often understand the nature of professional commitment—or are short-sighted enough to sacrifice it—so librarians come to assume that professionalism may simply be a slogan, or that administration may be the only professional practice. Since there is no basic commitment to clientele, or awareness of what is being sacrificed, they succumb easily to an authoritarian structure. In doing so, they need no longer assume more responsibility or undertake differing tasks, carry the burden of professional commitment, or take risks which put them in conflict with the organizational status quo. In the process, their submissiveness lends further credence to the bureaucratic ethos which holds that people need to be led for they are not mature enough to lead themselves. It is not simply that some librarians do not resist bureaucratic entrapment, nor that library leadership sometimes diabolically exploits the very individuals who must be inspired to adapt and to innovate rather than to be smothered in stale ritual, but that the environment created by library administrators and closing in the practicing librarian is diametrically at odds with the independence of action and freedom from restriction which most characterizes truly professional service.

Part of the difficulty in libraries is undoubtedly related to improper utilization of personnel. In recent years, a greater number of individuals who carry out so-called professional library functions have benefited from formal academic preparation for librarianship. Yet it is undoubtedly true that libraries have not tended to analyze systematically their position structures and requirements, and as a consequence disproportionate numbers of librarians are employed in capacities which do not call for their full range of preparation and expertise. Too many librarians are under-utilized in roles which call for lesser skill or training, with the result that there is much zealous guarding of the few cherished intellectual tasks from those with less formal preparation, if equivalent competence to perform. It is true that if a professional were to continue to perform at a concentrated peak level of strenuous intellectual effort all through the day, the strain would be intolerable. This is one reason why professors do not lecture forty hours a week, or social workers spend a full work day in case interviews. But, the problem in librarianship appears rather one of a need to attempt to reach equilibrium closer to the other end of this scale.

At precisely the same time when administrators bewail an abundance of unfilled positions, accurate analysis of working environments for members of these very staffs would all too frequently identify the sharp limits on opportunities for the expression of imagination and creativity—the burdens and ritual of desk covering, the routine and menial tasks more economically delegated to lesser paid employees. Imbalance in the proportion of time spent by professionals on chores which may be tiring, energy sapping, but professionally shallow and devoid of importance, may be quite widespread in libraries. The dignity and respect which might be accorded to professional, rather than to administrative pursuits, is too often denied. Exuberant professional spirit, high ideals, zeal, and commitment to innovation and experimentation are so often suspect and misunderstood that enthusiasm is ultimately thwarted by the bureaucracy until even the idealists succumb to the nine-to-five mentality or find other outlets for their creative aspirations.

Librarians are alert to and much concerned with the need to re-allocate certain routine chores to others less qualified; this is laudatory. But they do not as often recognize the fact that time spent in administrative work is also time spent in non-professional practice. And in this they have much in common with those in other disciplines who look schizophrenically toward the twin goals of administrative aspirations and professional satisfaction. Perhaps because the utility of administrative accomplishment is more clearly understood, and is so often attributed a higher value in a bureaucracy and in the culture, and because the goals of professional practice in librarianship are so confused and ambiguous, librarians more readily assume such administrative responsibility without remorse. And it may be for this reason that the assumption of an administrative role is so often equated with success. It naturally follows that the highest professional performance is seen as administrative activity, and that service to clientele through direct or indirect performance, comes to be viewed merely as a way station on the high road to the assumption of administrative responsibility.

It would be misleading to convey the impression that problems would be solved if only work assignments were to be better distributed, or if more dignity and stature were accorded to professional performance in libraries. Given the organizational propensities of librarians, personnel reclassification might lead only to more tightly circumscribing the librarian's role, if albeit at a higher level. What appears to be required is a more fundamental administrative reorientation toward an institutional climate which advances the professional spirit and yields organizational responsibilities to the professional group. Nor is this to propose democratic administration or a human relations approach as an end in itself, but rather that the decisions about the future of libraries and of librarianship itself may well hinge upon the extent to which professionalization is furthered.

As long as professionalism remains so weak and so ill-understood, libraries will remain unable to solve not only their immediate and pressing problems, but they will be unprepared and so unable to make the radical adaptations necessary to meet the rapidly shifting and growing requirements put upon them. Under these conditions outside intervention will come to influence the changes required, either by direct action upon the library or by fashioning new alternative forms of information service.

This may be what has happened in a number of university libraries where top library administrators have been relieved of their responsibilities or where outside insistence has resulted in the addition of more expert personnel to the staffs of the libraries. Perhaps administrators have served as the whipping boy for the limited level of professional attainment, when all who would aspire to professional standing should stand in the dock together. It may be that as some administrators charge, the majority of librarians are simply unprepared to assume mature responsibilities, although perhaps this is more a consequence of the bankruptcy of administrative leadership than of inadequacies among librarians. Nevertheless, to the degree that administrators countenance, if not foster, a set of organizational conditions less than appropriate for even minimal professional practice, it is they who are in greatest jeopardy and it is they who must beware.

THE PROFESSIONAL GROUP

Why is the record for professionalism in individual libraries so weak, and why has librarianship failed to move more rapidly toward maturity as a profession? In order to answer this question and thus better to understand the nature of the professional commitment, it is necessary to consider the wider grouping of which the librarian is a part as well as the nature of his professional relationships. In these terms, the professional group—the associations and societies—as well as the less formal personal identifications and group affiliations, are seen to be relevant. Through these relations are derived many of the patterns of the librarian's behavior and his continued professional growth. The process of acculturation into the group is begun during the educational sequence when the initiate is not only inducted into the field and affairs and is introduced to its intellectual substance, but is also indoctrinated in its commitments, its value orientation, and the standards which ultimately guide his practice.

Although the library-school tie may be securely attached, and while the bond may grow stronger as the nostalgia of each passing year adds further romance to old associations, the indoctrination process of the schools in feeding fuel to professionalism has been remarkably weak. The mystique, the induction rites, the salute to service concepts, the glorification of its heroes, the reinforcement of the field's sense of its own importance and accomplishments, all these have been present as long as one remembers. But, the substantive content, the body of significant professional knowledge, the theory, the philosophy and the ethic, these have evaded the field's grasp except in rare and isolated instances. Why should this have been so?

Perhaps the answer may in part be found in the role which library education has assumed in orienting its program so markedly to the requirements of those who come either while heavily engaged, or during the brief respite from practice after a period of past involvement. Many such students view library education grudgingly, as only a necessary intrusion, to be managed dextrously and conveniently, and to be related as much and as directly as possible toward reinforcing the operational skills which they have already gained on the job. The schools, perhaps seeing their role in much the same manner, conscious of the need to placate their clients, and having no firm philosophical orientation and commitments either, have provided institutionalized accommodation to precisely such requirements.

What is more, because the professional schools have tended toward weakness and have followed the more active vanguard in the field of practice, they have allowed the special interest groups—public, school, special libraries—to influence them in orienting their course sequences toward the presumed needs of particular areas of practice.[12] In the course of pursuing such a fragmented approach, librarianship has been divided rather than unified around a common theme, philosophy, or professional commitment. By offering technical courses for specific types of libraries, it is as if to suggest that the process of administration or organization of materials or informational problem-solving is fundamentally variable by type of library. Cross-fertilization is thereby reduced; school librarians see themselves as something apart from public librarians, and academic from special librarians. To suggest only one serious dysfunction, the ultimate end of this process is to reinforce the institutional barriers to cooperative and imaginative planning, and seriously to impede the logical next step in the evolution of library service—the invention and organization of regional and interinstitutional information systems.

Perhaps the most searing indictment of all, however, is that while library education has evolved to the graduate level in the university, when its content is measured against the honest yardstick of its intellectual contribution there is room to doubt whether its claim to professionalism has not been a ploy by those in library education who simply seek to rationalize their own roles as professionals. For if library education is not truly professional education, what then is the self image of the field's educational and administrative leadership?[13] This is not to say that library education is incapable of advancing to the stage where it is more centrally concerned with ideas, issues, theory, concept, and less with routine, description, procedure, and method, more with *why* and less with *how*, more with *what for* and less *how to*. But, the transition from description and homily and routine has only grudgingly given way to scholarship. There are still hundreds of students in *graduate* library programs memorizing names of famous modern librarians, committing to memory large sections of classification schedules, cluttering their minds with details of whether certain books have an index and table of contents or not, and taking superficial cultural romps through the various fields of knowledge to learn such things as the fact that Margaret Mead is an anthropologist, instead of studying the reasons for contemporary trends in societal information developments, the logic of comparative systems of classification, the structure of bibliography and information agencies as resources for problem solving, or the personal, organizational, and social group determinants of information need. To the extent that the details have overshadowed the more fundamental issues, so has education been routinized and stripped of its potential for embodying a content that is intellectually viable.

Part of the problem is one of the certification of mediocrity. At a time when the accreditation process in library education (jealously and zealously guarded as the prerogative of one national organization) should be strengthening the fiber of the educational product, it is accrediting and re-accrediting programs of doubtful merit thereby giving its imprimatur to schools very distant from any ideal or even advanced attainment. A truer service to professionalism would be to submit each program to ever more critical test, to encourage experimentation. The perspective of other organizations might well be sought (representation from SLA and ADI as illustrations), if only to encourage library education programs to foster timeliness and consideration of alternatives to their conventional fare. Present accreditation of graduate library education is in danger of fostering a negative standard—like the way in which a hack writer is encouraged when he watches an inferior television program and is sure he can do *that* well himself. Of course, the prescription of an absolute standard would be absurd, but it is certainly time for graduate level programs to aim higher. In a period so crucial for librarianship's future, when excellent students present themselves in abundance, to tolerate and certificate mediocrity and worse is a disservice to professionalism and to the students who are being prepared.

The relatively painless acquisition of the association's seal of approval may, however, be only symptomatic of a more fundamental ailment. Education for librarianship has simply not succeeded in attracting to the scholarly dimension of librarianship the theorists and researchers competent to build the concepts and the knowledge base upon which to construct an intellectual basis for professional practice. Drawn predominantly from, and committed almost overwhelmingly to, humanistic disciplines (when not to educational methodology), faculties in librarianship have failed or refused to see in library service a scholarly pursuit. Analytic insight is uncommon. Descriptive and historical orientations abound. Doctoral study has remained predominantly an academic exercise, serving either as the springboard to administrative advance or as the terminal research effort, short on methodological rigor and long on detail and bibliography.

Like the practicing librarian who bemoans the overload of clerical demands and busily perpetuates a role which tolerates the condition, academics accede to excessive course loads, teaching commitments in subject matters alien to their background and preparation, and wistfully lament the lack of time for genuine research and scholarship. But, the fact of the matter may simply be that they have not had the imagination or the conceptual orientation, the scholarly and intellectual footing to do more than remain a lap or two behind practice in their classrooms. For they seem to have almost universally failed to identify the basic problems or even to ask the most interesting questions, and so ultimately what they have taught proves to be irrelevant to contemporary requirements.

Lacking a conceptual base, typically barren of the analytical skills of the social or hard sciences, what scholarly effort is carried on by library faculties tends most frequently to center upon historical study or the applied survey. Where research has been fostered it has remained largely irrelevant to the educational offering, and even doctoral study has been characterized by a sterility and detachment from the fundamental issues in a way that is remarkable for a field so much at the center of societal concern. The link-up first forged with the social sciences at Chicago in the 1930's and 1940's has slipped away, and now information science seems the only serious intellectual issue to be engaging the attention of more than a handful of library scholars. Yet, there is danger in this that the technological issues and applications will so overwhelm the scholarly company in librarianship that alternative issues, with all of their behavioral, political, and organizational ramifications, will be swept aside and once more pragmatic means rather than philosophical ends will engage the attention of the field's most inquiring minds.[14]

Just as the schools provide or fail to provide the basic intellectual orientation and the body of knowledge fundamental to the claims of professionalism, the wider professional grouping acts to support professionalism in practice purely because it is a vehicle for wider personal recognition and reward. Within the scholarly disciplines, the source of recognition and prestige tends to be the peer group of colleagues rather than the local institution. Success and the achievement of career satisfactions are most often accorded only following distinctive attainment among the scholarly fraternity, even while there may be some degree of ambiguity and conflict between local and cosmopolitan orientations.[15] In the professions, career advancement proceeds differently. Except for the relatively small number of individuals engaged in research, writing, or other scholarly pursuits, the path to wider recognition through the channel of publication tends to be closed.[16] Perhaps for this reason librarians sense that they must concentrate so energetically upon purely local demands and requirements, since without having achieved profession-wide visibility, the route to advancement locally or laterally into other organizations is equated with recognition within one's own organization of the effectiveness of his performance. But, in a time of almost unlimited opportunity, the truer barrier to advancement may be the restriction upon mobility which handicaps the individual. While it is uncertain whether career advancement within libraries is promoted by profession-wide contribution (except in the case of academic libraries where such recognition is more common), the process of professionalization might be furthered if this were to be the case more generally. This is not to suggest that the goals of librarianship would necessarily be enhanced by a spate of ill-conceived and poorly executed articles, but rather that an institutional tone which honors such external commitment becomes a stimulus to professionalism, just as the converse may be equally true.

Librarians can and frequently do achieve visibility. It is also clear that professional involvement is often prelude to career advancement. While it is unquestionably true that some few in librarianship have adroitly identified the political utility of organizational engagement as a device leading to career opportunity, it is equally true that for many, many more, professional affiliations and participation serve as the tool of improved practice. This may be best illustrated by the special librarian's reliance upon professional colleagues in other institutions to expand the scope of his expertise, for as he draws upon his fellow librarians as external access points to information, he in the process expands the confines of his limited collections. In so doing, he reinforces immeasurably the professional contribution which he can make to his own organization.

We suspect that a significant hallmark of the librarian who functions as a true professional is reflected in the nature of his relationships. The professional constantly expands upon his circle of contacts and reinforces and strengthens existing colleague relations, pursuing an active role by continuing his growth through self-study and associating himself with the local and regional and national activities in librarianship and in other special disciplines with which his work puts him in contact. For him, keeping up with professional trends and advances through the journals and monographs is a matter of fact. To lose touch with current affairs would make him feel as uncomfortable and ill-equipped professionally as to remain out of touch with broader societal affairs would render him uneasy as a generally aware person in his culture. This is in contrast to the librarian who confines his relationships to those which are merely comforting, reassuring, and reinforcing of his prejudices and limitations.

Nor is this to suggest that all so-called professional activity is desirable. Those who have participated in groups in which meetings consist of members explaining why they have failed to complete assignments or committees which deliberate weightily the means for perpetuating themselves instead of considering their purpose or program, or still others which consume hour after hour preoccupied with minutia, need no reminder of this. It is likely that many energetic and imaginative librarians have been repulsed and disenchanted from professional engagement by participating in precisely such exercises in frustration. The associational excesses of the ritual, the routine, and the social do not characterize only the local groups; as a consequence the participation of some of the most thoughtful and committed of librarians has been shunted off.

It is interesting to speculate whether identification with professional norms and values may be impeded, enhanced, or otherwise affected by practicing in large libraries, compared to the situation of the librarian in the special library or the school, where he is functioning apart, and associating more with a distinct clientele or discipline. In theory, professional ties should be reinforced through daily interaction with professional colleagues. Yet, close colleague associations with other librarians seem also to foster undesirable aspects of professionalism. Professional values may be more strongly reinforced through interaction and identification with clientele. This would clearly be the case in those instances where such undesirable or negative manifestations as a strong alliance in defense of the status quo or a tendency to band together in common disregard if not active resentment of the clientele, were to be found.[17] While librarians working in concert may be better able to impose their standards and values on the institution, frequently they tend rather to reinforce and tolerate minimal service expectation.

If recent events in New York City libraries are a harbinger, more militant group solidarity when it takes shape may more likely be found in efforts to organize as collective bargaining agents rather than as professionally goal-oriented groups. While proponents of unionization reason that unions are fully compatible with professional goals and objectives,[18] in view of the emphasis in organized labor on such matters as seniority rights and employee benefits it remains to be seen whether the effect may not be a reinforcement of the very rigid authority structure of libraries which serves now as an impediment to innovation and furtherance of service commitments.

There are certain issues which require of professionalism that their proponents stand up and be counted. While the library profession supports an ethic with regard to intellectual freedom that calls for librarians to resist censorship pressure, the Fiske study documents the ways in which many librarians practice forms of self-censorship.[19] It is equally true that librarians do not always resist or are not always successful in resisting external censorship pressures. Whether or not the practice varies from the ideal, the ethic is viable. More librarians will stand up for it than if it did not exist and unless it were to be so flagrantly disregarded as to become a mockery, society will ultimately come to know and respect it and the group which supports it.[20] But, censorship is the most dramatic issue, not necessarily the one most central to professionalism. Librarians need equally to be militantly vocal about meeting minimum standards of excellence in such terms as the conditions, the support for, and the resources necessary for them to perform by acceptable standards.

In theory, if a professional cannot win minimum conditions for practice, he leaves. In actuality, he usually does nothing of the sort, for a variety of reasons good and bad. Many librarians are married women and hence immobile. Librarians frequently rationalize that it is better to remain and so offer some level of service while seeking to influence change for the better, much in the same manner as the optimistic woman whose life mission is to reshape some undeserving and unsuspecting male. There is perennial hope that conditions will improve. In these matters, librarians do no worse than faculty members of academic programs in which all who seek admission enter and everyone who enters ultimately graduates. No pat formula is at hand to describe whether in a given situation at a given time the conditions are irremediable, or must remain intolerable. It is only to be hoped that decisions may come to be made more frequently in terms of the professional commitment and the zeal for improved conditions, rather than the naive wish or the longing, and that aggressive professionalism will become a more widespread standard than patience and hope.

It will never cease to be an embarrassment to those who aspire to professionalism to find library situations in which the fiercest partisans for improvement are not the librarians themselves, but rather some outside or community group such as faculty members or teachers who struggle tenaciously for improved resources and conditions of operation. It is precisely here, in the passiveness or aggression of its commitment to the ideals and goals of library service, that those who practice it are assessed. Librarianship has not yet reached the stage in its development where it exerts the type of influence over its members which requires them to stand up and be counted on important issues or to refuse to practice in situations where resources are inadequate to do a minimal job. It therefore continues to countenance forms and levels of service which fall short of adequate standards. It has been conditioned by a national and educational leadership attuned to the acceptance of the modest and unassuming prospects of the past when resources were scarce or unattainable. In these more affluent times, librarians have still not been aroused to demand the conditions for effective performance which are typically far more readily within their reach now if only they will aspire to them.

For much of the history of American librarianship, the professional associations remained forward of practice. But, in many ways the one primary national organization now no longer speaks with authority for all the elements in librarianship. Information activity under various names is shifting dramatically and incorporating new forms and new paths to entry into practice. Libraries as they have traditionally functioned must either respond to contemporary requirements, or lose to competitive agencies and technologies. While the principal national association has been influential in many ways, its primary focus has been and remains political rather than professional. It has identified predominantly with the public library, and in the process lost touch with many of the most significant developments which should be influencing the library profession. Through its overly modest position on accreditation standards for graduate education, its non-existing role in the accreditation or certification of libraries, and by concentrating its zeal most strenuously upon aggrandizing the scale of its size, its political influence, and its economic power, it has contributed little to professionalization and tended, by default, to perpetuate inadequacy.

Like the libraries which it reflects, the American Library Association is a bureaucracy with the same built-in vested interests. To the extent that its key posts are held by those in administrative positions in librarianship, and that power in the organization is wielded by a relatively small coterie, it is less a professional association than an administrative confederation. Like other oligarchical organizations of large size and wide geographical dispersion, it proves incapable of attracting younger, innovating elements into its higher councils. By concentrating its efforts on improving situations in librarianship, it has not been in the vanguard of new or imaginative directions for librarianship. By assuming unto itself a wide range of national, international, research, and societal responsibilities, for which it is less than ideally equipped, it purports to do more than attain the political ends at which it is most successful. Conventions and meetings which appear designed in greatest measure to reassure the rank and file that problems are under control by reinforcing outmoded traditional approaches, are of only limited service to a profession in a rapidly changing world posing new demands.

Viewed against the perspective of history, librarianship can be seen to have made only slow and gradual evolution as a profession and exists now as only a marginal entry in the competitive race for professional status. The conditions of modern times, however, are such that if librarianship does not move much more rapidly forward toward enhanced professionalism, the field will not only decline rapidly, but ultimately face obsolescence. Already, traditional and conventional libraries are being replaced as new agencies and new practitioners respond more appropriately to changing requirements for information and professional service.

Progress in librarianship is made by only a relatively small number. Innovation remains on trial when it should be encouraged. The field stands conservatively and deeply rooted in the past at a time when such a stance exposes it to danger. Fundamental to advancement is the need to forge a new professional identity founded upon some of the characteristic elements which have been treated here.

FOOTNOTES

[1] Hence the term "professional librarian." One might question parenthetically whether there could be such a thing as a nonprofessional librarian. And would it be comparable to such a thing as a nonprofessional lawyer, nonprofessional doctor, nonprofessional dentist, etc.?

[2] Or, as in the case of the library code of ethics, grows from a lack of understanding of what the nature of a professional ethic really is, emphasizing as it does the "employees" obligation.

[3] Jerome E. Carlin, *Lawyers on Their Own: A Study of Individual Practitioners in Chicago* (New Brunswick, New Jersey: Rutgers University Press, 1962).

[4] For recent documentation of such practice among ophthalmologists see the testimony of Dr. Marc Anthony, of Spokane, Washington, reported in the *New York Times*, February 1, 1967, p. 43.

[5] Adam Smith had some comments to make about the practices of merchant groups which may not be too tangential to be relevant here. "People of the same trade seldom meet together, even for merriment and diversion, but the conversation ends in a conspiracy against the public, or in some contrivance to raise prices. Though the law cannot hinder the people of the same trade from sometimes assembling together, it ought to do nothing to facilitate such assembling, much less render them necessary." From *The Wealth of Nations* (New York, Dutton, [1937]).

[6] This point is elaborated in Paul Wasserman, *The Librarian and the Machine* (Detroit: Gale Research Co., [1965]), p. 50 ff.

[7] Although, at least in the public library, a fundamental modification of objectives is required for this to be the case. The alternative is to have the information responsibility assumed by others. A recent monograph suggests the establishment of a national information system at the community level. See Alfred J. Kahn, et al. *Neighborhood Information Centers: A Study and Some Proposals* (New York: Columbia University School of Social Work, 1966).

[8] As for example, in following such a policy as that in a number of university libraries which specifies that a librarian will not carry out extensive literature searches for any faculty member since the library could not be expected to provide such service for all who sought it.

[9] John Walton, "The Administration of Libraries," *Johns Hopkins University Ex Libris*, November 1957.

[10] For a fuller consideration of authority structure in libraries as an influence upon decision processes, see Mary Lee Bundy, "Conflict in Libraries," *CRL* XXVII (September 1966), 253-62.

[11] In many instances concentration upon automation may be viewed as an administrative strategy for diverting attention from more basic problems and thereby forestalling the necessary fundamental reassessment of goals and services.

[12] One manifestation which illustrates such influence may be seen in the meeting on library education for special librarianship convened each year by the SLA Education Committee during the annual conference. While the subject matter of the discussion varies from year to year, the common theme is the attempt to arrange for a dialogue between special librarians and library educators about the educational requirements for practice in the special library. See for example, *Special Libraries*, LVII (January 1967), for a report of the Second Forum on Education for Special Librarianship.

[13] This issue is elaborated in Bernard Barber, "Some Problems in the Sociology of the Professions," *Daedalus*, American Academy of Arts and Sciences, XCII (1963).

[14] In a way that may be analogous to that of the weak library which concentrates its zeal on automating its processes rather than in building client services and timely information access.

[15] See, Alvin Gouldner, "Cosmopolitans and Locals: Toward an Analysis of Latent Social Roles, Part I," *Administrative Science Quarterly*, II (December 1957), 281-306.

[16] There is one important yet subtle difference between a professional society and a scholarly discipline in the way in which recognition and prestige are awarded to its membership. Prestige in the professional society typically comes from office holding and work for the organization, while in a scholarly discipline, prestige more usually follows upon academic productivity as reflected in the form of articles and monographs. This may relate very essentially to the difference between librarianship and some of the more scholarly disciplines with which it is sometimes compared.

[17] Whether such characteristics tend to be more pronounced in academic libraries because of their unique status problems when compared with other types of libraries, would serve as the basis for an interesting line of inquiry.

[18] ". . . It is true that a union of professional people, whether they are researchers in an industrial laboratory or college professors, will be substantially different from that which you would find in an industrial organization of plant workers. But, the fact that they have joined a union doesn't change the fact that they still have professional standing, professional competence," in "How to Negotiate with a Professor's Union" (an interview with Dr. John McConnell) in *College Management*, II (January 1967), 25.

[19] Marjorie Fiske, *Book Selection and Censorship; A Study of School and Public Libraries in California* (Berkeley: University of California Press, 1959).

[20] See for example, the "Freedom to Read" statement prepared by the Westchester Conference of the American Library Association and the American Book Council in 1953 *ALA Bulletin*, XLVII (November 1953), 481-83. It is important to recall that at this very time other prestigious national societies assumed a position of studied silence. This was the case of the American Political Science Association, to cite only one of a number of such bodies, which might be viewed as having an important concern with the issues of censorship and political freedom.

ABOUT THE AUTHORS—Mary Lee Bundy, see p. 94, and Paul Wasserman, see p. 40.

Libraries and Labor Unions

Library Journal

> This article is a round-up of union activity around the country. It was included because it focuses on what Karl Nyren of Library Journal has correctly assessed to be a key issue confronting the library profession. The situations described provide an introduction to how unionization comes about and the various responses to it on the part of library staffs, administrators and professional associations. The crucial question is whether more widespread unionization of librarians will serve in the long run to impede or enhance professionalism. The model of organized efforts among elementary and secondary school teachers may afford something of a preview of things to come in librarianship.

One of the most dramatic changes which has come about in the last year is the unexpected interest of librarians in union activity. Whether it is traceable to the general flurry of activity that libraries are experiencing as a result of federal funds, to the decision of a major union to reach out into the professional fields in a major campaign, or to a maturing of forces long at work in the field, is difficult to say. In fact, the phenomenon is so new that conjecture is surely premature, and this article is devoted to an attempt to describe what is actually happening, in the belief that what is most needed at this point is facts.

Even a year ago, the few feeble attempts at unionizing librarians appeared to have reached a stable plateau of effectiveness which saw membership in a major union as contributing little more to change than membership in the ordinary staff association. Today, there are vigorous activities going on in major urban libraries and academic libraries—with professional librarians, not just clerical workers, showing marked interest. At this writing, two state library associations are seriously considering acting as unions, or bargaining agents; several states have passed laws making it legal for public employees—teachers, firemen, and librarians, among others—to engage in collective bargaining with their employers; and library administrators are studying labor books while their lawyers confer with one another a bit frantically across the country.

It is perhaps not just coincidental that the profession is at the moment engaged in its most searching attempt to date to classify its personnel and get some structure into the rather muddled mess that has always characterized the library personnel picture. Or that librarians' salaries, the shortage of manpower, and the tendency of staffs to increase greatly with the systems movement have been highly visible and much discussed features of the last year or two.

THE SCHOOL SITUATION

Of all groups, the public school librarians are being assimilated into unions in the quietest way. Teachers have always had relatively vigorous associations, and with the new collective bargaining laws they are beginning to enforce their demands with strikes as well as the quieter techniques of persuasion. In this case, whichever way the teachers go, the school librarians will probably follow, enjoying the substantial backing of their fellow educators whenever a specifically library issue results in conflict.

In New York city recently, school librarians, backed by the United Federation of Teachers, have felt quite free to wrangle with school administrators over how to run a library. In this case, the problem arose when school administrators went ahead with planning ESEA library programs without consulting their librarians or bringing them in on planning. As a result, the librarians charged, the acquisition of new books was so badly handled that books sat in cartons for weeks and months without sufficient help to process them or shelves on which to display them. Librarians pointed out that the administrators

SOURCE: "Copyright © R. R. Bowker Co., 1967. Reprinted by permission of LIBRARY JOURNAL." (The article was initialled K. N., and written by Karl Nyren.)

who bypassed them didn't have the expertise even to know that the federal grant money could have paid for all the processing of the books and brought them to the libraries ready to circulate.

Through their union spokesman, the teachers demanded representation on the planning level—or else. Backed by the whole teaching staff, and with tough, skilled UFT representatives, the school librarians showed that they could climb right into the ring with the school administration and slug it out, with consequent newspaper coverage of the whole affair.

The school situation is thus a step or two ahead of the public and academic library picture, and of course it has built-in differences. But some elements of the pattern are bound to be seen in all the areas as things develop, since the practice and the techniques of collective bargaining, at least when carried on by labor professionals, follow certain predictable courses. Thus the school administrators are scurrying about rather unhappily trying to find out where they stand in all this and what they should be doing, as a few public library directors are already doing.

The school administrators' main quandary, at the moment, is whether they should side with their staffs, or with their school committees; or whether, as has been proposed, they should stay poised in the middle, making sure that the inevitable negotiations be entered into and carried through in the most orderly fashion possible. Superintendents are in many, if not most, cases not too far removed from the teaching role, and are understandably a little unhappy at breaking up what they like to consider a big, happy family. In many cases, of course, teachers themselves take a rather more jaundiced view of their administrators and prefer to see them on the other side of the battleground with the enemies.

Superintendents also feel that their responsibility to the community and their students, even more than to their school committees, is an overriding concern. They have seen already the disastrous results of negotiations which were improperly planned and carried out, leading to costly and morale-damaging strikes. An additional complication in some areas is the existence of two or more teachers' associations or unions battling for control over the membership, as well as for the not inconsiderable political power that accrues to a strong union—enough to elect or deny election to many a borderline candidate for the school board.

ACADEMIC LIBRARIES

Where public school librarians have by nature identified with teachers, academic librarians have for years been attempting to identify themselves with college faculty, in order to gain the quite considerable benefits that could come from faculty status—including short hours, time for independent research, grants for study programs, long vacations, and, most important, tenure rights, which alone give the security that allows freedom of expression and movement, as well as association with such prestigious groups as the American Association of University Professors. As faculty, also, librarians would come under the protection of the accrediting agencies, which can sink a school's reputation if it mistreats its faculty members.

This has proved to be a partially successful ambition in a few cases, where both library administrators and college administrators were in a permissive mood toward their librarians. In many cases it has not and may never work out that the library "staff" become "faculty." For one thing, the faculty is often not all that keen on having librarians live next door or marry their daughters, and so more and more academic librarians are thinking of going the union route.

The most developed case seems to be at the University of California at Berkeley where, in 1965, 30 librarians formed the library chapter of the Berkeley University Teachers Local No. 1474. The group immediately went into action and submitted its complaints to the library administration. These included: disparity between benefits for librarians at different campuses of the university; a demand for time off to perform civic duties; a disagreement with the administration's designation of just who was "administrative personnel" and therefore unable to participate in union action, and with the university's definition of "academic status" as applied to librarians. In its initial statements, this group could be seen visualizing a really far-reaching association of librarians which would serve the needs, not primarily of administrators and institutions—as the ALA has often been accused of doing—but the needs of the majority of working staff members. Their publication, *CU Voice*, promised to "attempt to supply some of the answers not supplied by the professional library press ... (and) deal with problems and issues not generally discussed in the professional publications; with individuals rather than administrative complexes.... It will act as a clearinghouse for information about the conditions of librarians throughout the nation...."

Writing to *Library Journal* about union activities at Berkeley, University Librarian Donald Coney has some approving things to say about unions, although recognizing the dangers of attempting to generalize about a volatile situation in which he is also involved. He says: "I believe that unions in libraries are a factor to be reckoned with now and in the future. They appear to be a more effective instrument for representing the interests of employees to management than are professional organizations. Consequently, (we) will see the kind of competition for employee allegiance and support between unions and library associations similar to that which has developed in the teaching profession."

Donald Coney goes on to describe some basic distinctions in the nature of library staffs and teaching faculty:

"A conspicuous element in the campus society is a fundamental difference in the organization patterns of the professoriate and the other activities of the campus carried on by other classes of employees. Professors act primarily as individuals, each dealing with ideas in class and seminar rooms.... The primary focus of other campus personnel is on services and material objects. Individuals are organized in groups whose mode of operation is by division of labor. Thus, on the professor's side we have a very simple structure of individuals loosely held together in the conventional teaching department ... surmounted by some kind of general body like a faculty ... senate. The other part of the campus society is characterized by a series of separate, often highly structured hierarchical organizations. This sharp dissimilarity in function and organization and the attractive aspects of the dominant group—prestige and perquisites—are important elements of the situation in which a university's library union must develop."

It is of interest that, among the issues which have most exercised the new union of librarians at Berkeley, has been the need for an improved grievance procedure. They are covered now by a "nonacademic appeals procedure" which is felt to be less satisfactory than the tenure and privilege committee which oversees this area for faculty members of the rank of associate professor and professor. A court case developed over the firing, from the University of California Medical Center Library, of Miss Chizuko Ishimatsu, who served as head of the Catalog Department from 1962 until her dismissal in January 1965. The court upheld the dismissal, on the grounds that the requirements of the university's nonacademic appeals procedure had been satisfied. The library union group felt that the result was highly unjust and showed standards of job security inferior to those observed in industry "for generations."

Besides grievance and appeals procedures, and attendant job security issues, the California group has indicated a strong desire for "educational opportunities," which include leave with pay to attend courses, institutes, and professional meetings; and, perhaps thorniest of all issues to administrators, a voice in the way the library is run.

Various expressions of this aim have indicated ramifications from having a voice in major policy decisions, to academic freedom, to details of departmental management. Librarian Donald Coney notes that this last area "requires extensive ventilation before a feasible mechanism can be developed. A problem in dealing with this issue in ... a campus society lies in the inherent disposition of the professoriate to recommend the application of mechanisms appropriate to their relatively unstructured organization. Other classes in the society are drawn toward the faculty mechanism partly because of its visibility and partly because of the prestige values residing in the dominant class. For library administrations, the problem is to encourage the adoption of a mechanism which will provide 'voice' for all professional staff without damaging the delegation-of-authority mechanism—the management hierarchy."

Coney summarizes his thoughts thus: "It is apparent that the introduction of unions into a university library stimulates the identification of areas of staff concern, and moves toward their precise expression as a basis for reaching acceptable conclusions. This process is also a polarizing one; it invites adversary situations, it formalizes the informal; and narrows the areas of exception and easy adjustment. Unions add new dimensions to library administration, and new obligations to staff in their self-determination of interest. Unions are, no doubt, a function of scale—small libraries may continue indefinitely without them, but what happens at Berkeley may happen in any large library."

Meanwhile, a group of library employees at the University of Pennsylvania has affiliated with the American Federation of Teachers as Local No. 1740. In Pennsylvania, in contrast to California, salaries are a major source of unhappiness. Staff members feel that the ready source of supply of part-time help from the Drexel Graduate School of Library Science has allowed the administration to take advantage and hold salaries down. They are also highly critical of the way the library is run, and would like a voice in this area. The Pennsylvania group contains both professionals and non-professionals—some of the former being department heads and other high-ranking professionals.

It seems plain that the desire of staff members to get into administrative decision-making is one that can arise easily in any kind of library, with all kinds of interesting results, including something like open rebellion and embarrassment of the administration, or even a sufficient mobilization of public opinion against a poor administration to lead to its censure or removal. This is a painful prospect to contemplate, but one which would undoubtedly prove healthy for many a dreadfully-administered library. It could also result in useful contributions of thought and energy from a concerned staff with a new stake in the library's destinies. It seems unlikely that there could be any threat to good administrators or to sound administration; bad administrators might well shiver in their boots at the thought of employees being allowed to criticize their shortcomings in public.

PUBLIC LIBRARY PATTERNS

The public library developments have tended to follow a different evolution in recent years, with librarians joining unions of municipal employees, and often making up a minority among nonprofessional, clerical, and maintenance workers. In this situation, it is understandable that they have carried little weight, but have been content to share in general percentage pay raises and fringe benefit improvements—as well as in established grievance procedures. This seems to have been the case in the Free Library of Philadelphia, where a small number of librarians, mostly of less responsible ranks, have been members of the union to which all other library employees belong.

Philadelphia's experience dates back to 1961, when an ordinance was adopted by the Council of the city of Philadelphia, authorizing the Mayor to enter into an agreement with the American Federation of State, County, and Municipal Employees as the exclusive bargaining agent for "certain civil service employees in the City."

The agreement stipulated three classes of employees: mandatory, voluntary, and prohibited. As the terms suggest, mandatory refers to those classes of employees required to maintain union membership as a condition of employment. In the library, this group is composed of blue collar workers and very low level clerical positions such as Library Assistant I and Clerk I. Although the creation of this mandatory group gives the union a substantial membership from the total civil service ranks of the city, it has little effect on the professional library staff.

Philadelphia's "voluntary" classification is open to membership from librarians who are not supervisory personnel—as the term implies, they may join or withdraw from membership at will, a situation which makes for weak union participation. According to Director Emerson Greenaway, few members of the professional staff have become union members under this arrangement.

Philadelphia's contract with the union does not permit strikes, and it effectively excludes from union membership those library employees who might be expected to acquire roles of leadership in union activities; consequently, it can be expected to have little significance on the professional concerns of librarians.

The Cleveland Public Library has had two employee organizations, both dating back to 1937; neither, obviously, has exclusive bargaining rights—a factor which is probably a necessity for any really strong union program. Here again, one of the groups is affiliated with the American Federation of State, County, and Municipal Employees, which among other things, is badly in need of a new name or an acronym if we are to keep on talking about it.

In Cleveland, the president of the library union is the chief telephone operator, while the president of the staff association is a branch children's librarian. Librarians can belong to either or both groups, and sometimes do. As might be expected, there is something less than complete harmony between the two organizations, with the staff association representing more of the older and more conservative librarians, and having rather more social concerns than the union-affiliated group. Some union members belong to the staff association, according to one spokesman, to please their supervisors. Union membership rolls are secret, with the exception of the union's officers and representatives.

The union group claims that about one-third of its members are professionals, and that its membership is growing, after having taken rather drastic losses at times in the past, when the passing of good salary scales has made active union membership seem less urgent. There have been attempts, or at least discussions, aimed at merging the two groups, but to date nothing has come of them—a certain amount of mutual suspicion being evident here.

Uniquely, in Cleveland, anyone, regardless of how high his rank, can belong to the union—a source of potential strength which is not traceable to state labor laws, but rather to a friendly administration and board of trustees. Representatives of the union and of the staff association sit in on all board meetings, and are consulted for their advice in development of budgets, especially as related to salaries.

In exchange for this, the union has been able to offer its extensive labor connections in the Cleveland area for the support of budgets and on the side of the library in legislative matters, such as the passage of bond issues. The library union has also acted as a channel of communication to the administration for labor groups concerned with such questions as the location of branch libraries and the hours of service at various facilities.

Here, of course, one approaches again the ticklish question of an employee group influencing or making policy. Union liaison officer Irving C. Portman, who is also head of the library's book repair department, disclaims any substantial role of the union in this area, saying: "We have a very enlightened board now which consults us and is very fair. Policy, we feel, should be left exclusively to the board of trustees and the administration. Of course, we are free to approach the board if we disapprove of some action or policy."

On the other hand, the union has shown an interest in influence at even higher levels. Some of its ideas and actions sound almost like what one might expect of a strong and really well-organized "Friends" group: they can help or hinder appointments to the board of trustees, which in Cleveland is appointed by the elected members of the board of education. They look forward to supporting legislative measures that would relieve the library of its dependence on the intangibles tax—which could drop library support drastically in the event of a recession.

Library unions in Ohio still lack strong state legislation on their behalf. Although a law passed two years ago allowing a dues check-off, the legislature has so far refused to allow government employees to have full collective bargaining rights. A bill, with bipartisan support, is now before the legislature to accomplish this, but there is no great confidence in its passage in the present session.

The general picture in Cleveland is an encouraging one, however: a well-administered library, with a sympathetic and liberal board of trustees, has seemed to be able to work constructively with a union—which the trustees could probably have refused to recognize—to the advantage of all concerned.

At the Boston Public Library, and indeed in the whole state of Massachusetts, there is something approaching total confusion at this writing. A state law, passed in 1965, created exceedingly permissive conditions under which government employees could organize for collective bargaining. According to this law, city councils and town meetings are evidently bound to provide financial support for any legitimate agreements reached in a bargaining process between individual groups of employees and municipal officials.

The first action came from the schools, and first in this area from the nonteaching staffs. But the Massachusetts Teachers Association then took the field and has guided most of the teacher organization in Massachusetts—with the exception of Boston, where another local association has won bargaining rights for teachers in the city. The MTA has, it should be noted, lost no time in indicating its interest in a broadly defined area called "conditions of work." That this quickly spills over into an interest in policy making can be seen from the teachers' feeling that they should have something to say about the size of classes and should be consulted on the establishment of new programs.

A little late, librarians in Massachusetts have realized that collective bargaining is something they have to make up their minds about. The Massachusetts Library Association took up the matter at its Midwinter meeting and decided to look into the possible role of the state association as either an advisor or a possible bargaining agent for the many independent library staffs of the state which would not have the resources to act on their own in this new area. For an association of librarians to even consider this is a little like taking up do-it-yourself brain surgery, but it may contain the seeds of a highly appropriate response to this new situation.

One problem, wherever the question of unions has arisen, is that librarians feel doubtful that they can even communicate with union people—and with some good reason. For librarians, the overriding concerns are not likely to be wages, hours of work, and fringe benefits; nor, in general, do they feel themselves natural enemies of their administrators, their library boards, or their clientele. Added to this in Massachusetts, as in many places, "union" is a word that is more likely to call up an image of Jimmy Hoffa than of a professional and highly developed set of techniques for the representation of the interests of a group of employees.

Left to their own, the union people are also likely to put their foot in their mouth with public statements that strike librarians as being in bad taste. A flier put out during the campaign for unionization of the Queens Borough Public Library in New York was a good case in point. It would have looked fine in a strike of iron puddlers in 1930, but it has an anachronistic appearance today, to say the least. One of the problems of librarians communicating with labor people lies in the somewhat anachronistic speechways of union men, who are proud of their tradition and—especially the older ones—are militantly evangelistic in a way that is likely to scare librarians away rather than inspire them.

Massachusetts librarians have been looking forward to quiet deliberation on the union question, envisioning an arrangement which might involve the state association and the large staff association of the Boston Public Library. But the rug has been pulled out from under them with an announcement by the Mayor of Boston that the city is recognizing a union to represent all the library employees except the professionals—who were reluctant to sign cards during a recent union drive for signatures indicating a desire of a majority of the employees for representation. The professionals find themselves suddenly alone and somewhat small in numbers.

The Boston Public Library has had a staff association of great longevity and of dubious worth, except for its facility in arranging teas for departing co-workers. Its members have no very clear notion of what they would like to achieve by unionization, but it is clear that what comes first to their minds is not wages and hours, but criticism of administrative policies. It is probably safe to say that, as in many a large city library, the staff tends to be predominantly composed of steady old civil-service types, who work their way up year by year, or decade by decade, often from the bottom, to eventual roles as supervisors. The bright young people from library school come—and go. But the ones who stay are generally very parochial in their outlook, thinking of themselves as Bostonians and BPLers rather than as members of the larger community of librarianship. As such, their concerns with administrative policy tend to be negative and critical rather than oriented toward innovations which are the concern of the profession.

To this quite substantial group, a union is likely to offer a way of opposing the administration of the library, and turning grousing into action. This is a danger which can arise, especially in the big public libraries such as Chicago, where a considerable amount of union sentiment has been directed against what older employees call the "library science people": those who have not come up through the ranks, but have stepped into positions of status directly from library school.

The rest of the librarians in Massachusetts exist in rather small groups, in which administrators and other staff members work rather closely in small families, dominated by boards of trustees which are themselves weak, having only advisory status when confronted with city and town administrators in matters of finance.

One community, however, has seen the union route as a means to alleviate this general lack of powerlessness. The Watertown Public Library board has declared itself to be the bargaining agent for any negotiations to be carried on with the library staff. If it should turn out that town meetings are powerless to overturn collective bargaining agreements, public library boards in Massachusetts may find that they have come into possession of a miraculous new weapon for compelling adequate library support—a weapon similar to the power that school boards now have—for it is illegal for a community to refuse to appropriate funds for any operational budget approved by a school board in Massachusetts.

This interesting possibility has not faced a legal test in Massachusetts yet, but it will be one eagerly awaited by librarians and trustees. A note of urgency has recently been added: in at least one community, where other employees of the town organized, these employees got raises. The library, which was backed by no union bargaining power, was refused any budgetary increases.

Librarians in Massachusetts face dilemmas whichever way they turn, yet they must move quickly or lose opportunities which may not arise again. They must decide whether to affiliate with other nonprofessional workers, whether to create some kind of statewide mechansim in their professional association, and whether to try to go it alone or call in the services of experienced labor organizers. All concerned are surely in for a Nantucket sleigh-ride behind the whale of collective bargaining.

The Chicago Public Library very nearly made library—and labor—history in March, when its employees agreed to strike the library in retaliation against the library board's refusal to allow an election leading to a collective bargaining agreement. There is as yet no legislation in Illinois requiring public agencies to enter into collective bargaining with their employees, although one bill is in the works and has received approval by a commission appointed by the Governor. It would not, of course, allow strikes.

The threatened strike against the Chicago Public Library was averted by Mayor Daley, who brought the union representatives and the library board across the table to talk to each other. Some concessions were made, and peace is restored while everyone waits to see what ground rules will come out of legislative action.

The Chicago Public Library is generally considered a disaster area of librarianship, and an illustration of the principle that if an organization is big enough, it can do practically everything wrong and still survive. Chicago has had a union presence for several years, with only about 200 staff members, including almost no professional staff, officially signed up and taking part in the dues check-off. Shortly after the cancellation of the strike threat, however, officials of the AFL-CIO Federation of State, County, and Municipal Employees claimed that a heavy majority of all library employees had signed cards indicating their wish to have the union represent them.

Chicago has hostility coming out of its ears on the union issue, with the union pegging City Librarian Gertrude Gscheidle as the "prime conspirator" against them, with Board President Anthony Mentone and Board Member O. O. Morris close behind. The union group makes no bones of its disapproval of how the library is run. One statement to that effect goes: "The library employees know the deficiencies in the present library system. To a large extent they know what action must be taken to correct these deficiencies and bring to the city a library system of which we can all be proud."

Library union officials have circulated even more bitter statements, such as these excerpts from a circular of March 6: "None of us take pride in being library employees. Those of us who are professionals perhaps feel a greater degree of embarrassment because we feel a greater degree of responsibility towards the failure of the library to provide the best possible service to the public. We know that many of the public's complaints are justified ... we have allowed a bad situation to get worse."

But further complications come into focus as the message continues, and the recently hired "library science people," who have not worked up from clerical jobs, are seen as a distinct menace. The message decries the library's decision to terminate progress through the ranks to professional status, and doubts the "sincerity of the administration" in its statements that it is trying to "attract a higher calibre of personnel." Chicago, it must be said, looks like a place where introduction of a union may do little more than escalate an already noxious situation, and possibly raise even further barriers to improvement of staff and library service.

The Milwaukee Public Library—since 1965, and the passage of what may be the most liberal legislation of its type—has beefed up a union operation that goes back 30 years to a staff association. There are at present 130 union members from a staff of 450, including all classes of library employees and with professionals represented in the leadership. The president of the library union, Irve Zink, is chief of the history and social sciences department. Librarians with a rating of Librarian V and higher cannot join; this includes most, but not all supervisory personnel.

In a letter to *Library Journal,* City Librarian Richard Krug described the union arrangements and commented that it is too early to assess the results of the relatively new exclusive bargaining agreement which now prevails. He adds, however, that because of the union, supervisors are probably more sensitive to staff attitudes. As to whether the union will contribute to or retard library development, he felt the question was at present unanswerable on the basis of such short experience. The union is about to embark on a joint project with the administration to establish work rules for the library, in accordance with the current contract terms.

President Irve Zink of the union, however, told *Library Journal* that he expected things to be a little sticky for a while, until the administration got out of the habit of making "unilateral decisions." He cited a current disagreement: City Librarian Krug made a request to the civil service authority to abolish the rank of Librarian I, enabling beginning professionals to be hired at the next level, to which they would normally accede after two years service and passage of an examination. The union, learning of the move, has opposed it, on the grounds that it made no provision for those librarians presently on the lowest level. They want all Librarian I's moved up automatically to the next level. In addition, the union expects to be consulted on all matters that have to do with personnel classification and salaries.

The union also takes a proprietary interest in the maintenance of standards of library service, and feels that it should have a say on anything affecting the welfare of the library or the quality of its service. This goes about as far along the line of participation in administration as any union group can go, and could call for a complete revaluation of the role of an administrator.

The union is also looking forward to the passage of legislation which would enable establishment of an "agency shop," in which all library employees, whether union members or not, would be required to pay dues, on the theory that they were enjoying benefits without contributing to the effort being made to win them. Such a bill passed both legislative houses once, but was vetoed by the Governor; another is in the works, expected to pass again, and possibly will get by the Governor this time. Such a bill would of course strengthen the union treasury greatly, and increase the union's potential for action.

THE STATE ASSOCIATIONS

The Michigan Library Association has taken the most forward steps toward the involvement of a state professional association in the collective bargaining process. Here, the passage of legislation allowing public employees to engage in collective bargaining was welcomed by a committee of the association late in 1966 as holding no problem of jeopardy of professional status (an immediate concern almost everywhere), and has recommended that full use be made of the terms of the Act. The committee also recommended that the MLA offer its services to any local group to assist implementation of the legislation, including representation as a bargaining agent. It recommended further that all public employees in libraries join in one organization.

Here we may have a hint of another unexpected by-product of similar acts being passed in a number of states: a possible rejuvenation of the state professional associations, giving them for the first time something like real power, and enabling them to perform for their members functions which the American Library Association has never considered appropriate to its role.

There are many forces working today for a strengthening of authority at the state level. These include proposals to turn back more federal tax revenues to the states and giving state agencies discretion over the spending of federal grants. Should collective bargaining infuse new life into state professional associations, at the same time that statewide networks of library service are aborning, and state level library agencies are being strengthened, something very much like a trend would seem to be establishing itself.

To sum up the union trends in the public library sector, where the most rapid growth is now occurring, big changes are in store, and possibly very startling ones. Level-headed administrators will see both trials and rewards ahead. Regressive action can well occur when an irresponsible staff is combined with an incompetent administration. How the matter is handled across the country will in any case be of immense significance for the future of library service and of librarianship.

LESSONS FROM ABROAD?

It is noteworthy that the United States has come late to the unionizing of librarians, as of other professional and semi-professional employees of government agencies. Great Britain, Sweden, and the rest of Europe all have considerable experience in this area, and with varying results which may or may not be applicable to the United States at this point in time.

Swedish librarians have a number of professional associations comparable to ALA and SLA, as well as two trade unions: the Svenska Folkbibliotekarieföreningen (Association of Swedish Public Librarians), and De Vetenskapliga Bibliotekens Tjänstemannaförening (Association of Swedish University and Research Librarians).

Both of these are affiliates of the Swedish Confederation of Professional Associations, an organization with about 75,000 members at present. Swedish unionism tends to be a rather highly structured affair—on both sides of the labor-management fence—with such arrangements as schools or courses to equip members of both sides with the expertise needed in conducting negotiations. The emphasis generally seems to be on the maintenance of peace and a fairly constant rate of rewards to any individual group in relation to other groups in the economy.

This would seem to characterize the situation in England also, where a stability has been reached that makes unions seem almost quasi-governmental devices devoted to keeping everyone's head above water rather than offering a mechanism for any group to substantially improve its position in relation to the rest of society.

Thus British public librarians, along with all other local government workers, belong to NALGO, the National Association of Local Government Officers. This union represents them and presents a framework within which librarians are given a graded rating for their various positions and responsibilities in relation to all other government workers. To improve their position in relation to other groups, librarians have two possible courses: their professional organization, the Library Association, can make representations to NALGO on behalf of the status of its members; and librarians can become politically active and influential by seeking office in local branches of NALGO. The former has only advisory force, and the latter seems not to have been pursued with enough vigor or success.

The other main feature of the "labor" landscape for government workers is the national negotiating machinery, composed of negotiating committees for employees and for employers. Four trade unions, of which NALGO is by far the dominant one, make up the representation for the employees. This negotiating machinery produces a scheme of ratings for all government positions, a scheme which has no legal force, but is considered to be a consensus of what fair pay for any position should be—taking into consideration variables such as location, population, etc.

One of the major efforts then of any local group of British librarians consists of making sure it gets what is coming to it according to its ratings by the negotiating machinery. Action at any level involves application of rather gentle pressures, with the exception of a tactic which has been used on the national level with some success in the past —the blacklisting of positions offered at below acceptable rates. This has been done by newspaper ads calling attention to the offending positions; the implied threat of future discrimination against the offenders by fellow librarians has been reportedly very effective, with defiers of the blacklist finding themselves quietly barred from professional advancement. This has depended, of course, on a relatively high degree of professional solidarity.

The major effect of unions for British librarians, then, has seemed to be to give them a survival factor and to enable them to move in orderly fashion with the general economic improvements of the postwar years—in step with all their other government fellow-workers. It seems to offer no hope for a profession which revitalizes itself to move effectively and rapidly to raise the relative status of all its members, as have teachers in the United States and as librarians here may well do in the next few years. British librarians, on the other hand, are effectively defended against the really appalling treatment which large numbers of American librarians, particularly in more rural areas, have to live with. And in Great Britain, communities are required by law to support public library service, as we are required to support public schools.

There has been considerable discontent among British librarians at the quality of union representation they receive from NALGO, and formation of a separate librarians' union has often been urged. Their counterparts in the United States, many of whom are entering into affiliation with the AFL-CIO Federation of State, County, and Municipal Employees, might well ponder the possibility that this large American union of government workers may become a stable mechanism with its major focus on "wage justice" and the maintenance of minimum standards—with a consequent devotion to status quo and an evolution into the role of a quasi-governmental mechanism for the smooth running of society.

The development of white collar unionism outside the United States has generally seemed to follow this trend, and to have settled down to rather polite elbowing among white collar workers for status among themselves rather than arming groups for change in status. It is notable that the widespread teacher union movement of recent years in this country has devoted itself to a mass assault on the status quo of education; one cannot help but see that, among the more vigorous young librarians entering the union movement, some such vision is a major motivation: not security or "wage justice" but a technique for the advancement of their profession.

In this light, it is time that librarians give serious thought to the future of association with a general union of government workers, and to the terms of association with such a union. It is also time to suggest that the American Library Association's role be reassessed. If it cannot move with intelligence and despatch when confronted with developments of such potential significance as the union movement, obviously it needs changing. The alternative might well be the emergence of really strong state associations, which would be quite capable in a few years of forming a new federation more closely adapted to the real needs of a majority of librarians.

The question of unions for librarians is before us, having waddled out of the nursery where we tucked it in a few years ago; it has suddenly grown up to giant size and its parents must handle it warily.